CULTURE
AND
HUMAN DEVELOPMENT

An Introduction

JAAN VALSINER

SAGE Publications

London • Thousand Oaks • New Delhi

SAGE Publications Ltd
6 Bonhill Street
London EC2A 4PU

SAGE Publications Inc
2455 Teller Road
Thousand Oaks, California 91320

SAGE Publications India Pvt Ltd
32, M-Block Market
Greater Kailash – I
New Delhi 110 048

British Library Cataloguing in Publication data

A catalogue record for this book is
available from the British Library

ISBN 0 7619 5683 2
ISBN 0 7619 5684 0 (pbk)

Library of Congress catalog card number 99-75645

Typeset by Keystroke, Jacaranda Lodge, Wolverhampton
Printed in Great Britain by The Alden Press, Oxford

CULTURE
AND
HUMAN DEVELOPMENT

CONTENTS

LIST OF FIGURES

LIST OF TABLES

PREFACE

Ten years have passed since the predecessor of this book – *Human Development and Culture* (Lexington, MA: D.C. Heath, 1989) – was published. It was an experiment then – a textbook which admittedly was not a textbook, at least in the sense contemporary US college textbook publishers view it. The reviewers of the manuscript were of diametrically opposite views at that time. One suggested retaining the theoretical and methodological part of the manuscript, while getting rid of the comparative-cultural evidence. The other recommended exactly the opposite – cutting the all too complicated philosophical and methodological chapters and keeping the comparative-cultural stories. The author of the book was detected to 'dislike his discipline and the time period he lives in'. I felt quite misunderstood by such feedback, but did not care about it.

Sometimes it is important not to listen to the good advice reviewers give. The publisher published the book in the form I wanted it – despite the reviews – and I have enjoyed teaching with its help over the past decade. The book went out of print by the mid-1990s, yet the need for it was growing. To my surprise, I found the book in use in a number of universities in different parts of the world. Not on a large scale – as the topic and its coverage would not be commensurate with massive use – but selectively and, as it seems to me, in intellectually thoughtful ways. This was very pleasing, and I contemplated proposing a new edition of it. Unfortunately, the original publisher had gone out of business by that time.

Fortunately, the book had been ahead of its time. The new direction within psychology that began increasingly to emerge in the 1990s – cultural psychology – was precisely the area for which the original book had been intended. The 1989 edition brought the nature of psychology of development home to readers as culture-bound. This led to a number of critical methodological issues: What is culture? How can one study development? These general issues have been targets of further investigation in the cultural psychology of this passing decade.

After establishing the journal *Culture & Psychology* (published by Sage), I found myself increasingly in the middle of such disputes, which sometimes looked to me to be all too political and superficial. From the vantage point of the know-how of psychology and anthropology of the past 100 years, many of the re-inventions of 'revolutions' in contemporary psychology – be these 'cognitive', 'ecological', or 'cultural' – are of limited generality. So maybe the reviewers were right about my chronic dissatisfaction with modernity (or post-modernity)! Nice stories about 'post-modern identity' are often told in the social sciences, and yet I fail to be enthused by those. At times I see such story-telling as a convenient excuse for intellectual laziness, and a readiness to accept as given the superficiality of thought that dominates the mass communication realm of our social discourse.

So when Sage became ready to add a basic book on cultural psychology to their publications list, I was ready to re-write the book I had used since 1989. The result is here. It is now even more directly oriented towards methodological issues of the developmental side of cultural psychology than was its predecessor. Yet its main focus remains – it is a sophisticated introduction to issues of cultural psychology, with a strict focus on human development.

The need for a new book emerged gradually. I was listening carefully to the voices of students – expressed in their exam results, rather than in their course evaluations. Specific weaknesses of the previous version of the book became evident. Hopefully, in this new book these have been overcome – and probably replaced by other problems.

Over the past decade, different colleagues and friends were helpful in making suggestions for changes in the previous book. Some of them, including my students at the University of North Carolina at Chapel Hill and (since 1997) at Clark University, have given me concrete feedback that was instrumental in the writing of this new book. I am particularly grateful to people who read various drafts of parts of the present manuscript: Emily Abbey, Angela Branco, Roger Bibace, Peter Bodor, Patrick Davis, Ingrid E. Josephs, Aaro Toomela, Rene van der Veer, and others. At Sage, the enthusiasm and careful understanding of the developing area of cultural psychology that Ziyad Marar always carries with him, and the careful encouragement by Naomi Meredith to finish the manuscript on time, are most gratefully acknowledged.

The book has benefited from permission to reproduce illustrations from many copyright holders. First, Professor Unni Wikan of University of Oslo generously allowed the reproduction of the Omani women wearing veils. Cambridge University Press and Professor Emiko Ohnuki-Tierney allowed me to reproduce two figures from *Illness in contemporary Japan* (Figures 8.6 and 8.7. in this book). The University of Chicago Press is acknowledged for the permissions to reproduce photographic materials from Thomas Gregor's books on the Xingu Indians, and Nancy E. Levine's book on Himalayan polyandry. Greenwood Publishing Group allowed me to reproduce the figure on mean age at marriage in polygyny as practised in the Lake Victoria region. Oxford University Press permitted the reprinting of Gilbert Gottlieb's theoretical scheme.

Jaan Valsiner
Worcester, MA

Introduction

HOW DO WE CREATE KNOWLEDGE ABOUT CULTURAL HUMAN DEVELOPMENT?

Two central themes dominate this book, framing the specific issues discussed. First is the claim that *human psychological functions* – once these emerge in development – *are cultural in their nature*. Secondly, the topic that *human psychological development is culturally guided and personally constructed* is central to this book. The latter idea is at times expressed by the label *co-construction*: personal development of psychological functions is at the same time a construction process by the person, and it is directed by the person's social world. In the latter, various other persons, social institutions, ideological systems etc. are setting up directions for the personal construction of psychological functions to take place. Yet the social world cannot determine how individual development takes place, it can only guide its direction. The actual course of personal development is constructed by the person in relation to that guidance. In this sense, human psychological development is jointly constructed by persons and their social worlds, or co-constructed by the two.

In a general sense, this book is about cultural development of personality, or self. In psychology – despite many efforts to make sense of the complex notion of self – little basic knowledge about this complex subject is present. This is due to the fact that in psychological literature, often the theoretical perspectives of the author constitute a mixture of mutually incompatible ideas. In order to avoid this, a careful elaboration of what is the perspective from which the given psychologist looks at the issues under investigation is necessary. Therefore, the first chapters

of this book bring to the reader a glimpse of the philosophical notions of what development is, and how it can be studied. Furthermore, no new knowledge in a science can be productively obtained without a knowledge of the history of the ideas that have guided that science. Developmental psychology is usually considered to be a sub-discipline of psychology (as it is usually part of psychology curriculae in university-level studies), yet the history of ideas on which developmental psychology is based emerges from the realm of biology. It is thinking about biological development in the nineteenth century that has provided a strong basis for developmental science in the twentieth century.

The focus on culture in human development stems from the realm of cultural psychologies. Cultural psychologies are new directions in the psychology of the 1990s that attempt to make sense of the ways in which culture assists the person in the construction of his or her psychological world. Despite being a new development in this past decade, cultural psychologies have a long history which even antedates that of the rest of psychology. If the usual rendering of the history of psychology (as distinct from philosophy) mentions 1879 (when the Psychological Laboratory was established in Leipzig by Wilhelm Wundt) as the beginning of the autonomous discipline, then the forerunner of cultural psychologies – 'folk psychology' (*Völkerpsychologie* in German) – can point to its formal recognition in Berne, Switzerland, in 1860, when a professorship in folk psychology was established for Moritz Lazarus, one of the nineteenth century initiators of cultural psychologies. However, establishment of a socio-institutional label 19 years before does not by itself prove the primacy of the cultural psychologies relative to the traditions of experimental psychology of

Wilhelm Wundt. More importantly, the traditions of folk psychology reach our cultural psychologies of the 1990s through the philosophical and linguistic thinking of Johann Gottfried Herder, Wilhelm von Humboldt and Wilhelm Wundt himself. Wundt developed both the experimental and folk psychological traditions in parallel (yet keeping them separate). It is by way of later selective focus by psychologists (who have tried hard to show that their science is a 'hard', that is, experimental one, rather than a 'soft', or interpretive study of complex subjective phenomena) that the unity of the experimental and folk psychological directions has been forgotten. That point proves the necessity of careful integration of the history of the given science into its contemporary search for new solutions. *History of science is an integral part of the contemporary progression of science*, rather than a 'museum' of stories of past glory (breakthroughs in ideas and new discoveries) or ignorance. History of any science is written (and re-written) from the perspective of a present time, hence creating necessary foci of knowledge and their parallels – ignorance – at the same time. Histories are written from some perspective, and it is important for the study of psychology to make sense from which perspective any particular reflection upon history is constructed.

A central issue of any science is its methodology. For the hybrid science that emerges at the instersection of developmental and cultural psychologies – *cultural developmental psychology* – the issue of methodology is crucial. As I point out in Chapter 5, developmental and cultural orientations require the view of methodology as a thought system that unifies philosophical, theoretical, and empirical methods in the service of making sense of the phenomena we select for investigation. This view on methodology is that of classical science – requiring consistency of thought from the most abstract level of reflection to the most concrete of encounters with the phenomena. Methodology is not a synonym for a 'toolbox' of established (often labelled 'standardized') methods that psychologists use, but a process of construction of knowledge that unifies the theoretical and empirical sides of scientific investigation. Often one can hear claims in psychology that it is 'empirical science' (in opposition to philosophy). Such claims are recurring remnants of the 'fight for autonomy' that psychology has been involved in since 1879 – a fight that psychology is constantly on the verge of losing. No science can be 'empirical' only (if it were, it would become equal to accounting). Instead, each science has its empirical part, the meaningfulness of which for knowledge depends upon the theoretical productivity of the given

science. Methodology is of crucial importance since it relates the empirical and theoretical sides of a science. How it does it determines whether the given science provides new understanding of the phenomena, or keeps constructing illusionary accounts.

A good example of the difficulties involved in methodology (as a process that connects the empirical and the theoretical) comes from the history of chemistry. The historical roots of chemistry were in the very practical everyday efforts of trying to produce precious metals (gold) out of other substances. This tradition of alchemy reigned until the eighteenth century, when the invention of formal abstract depictions of transformation of chemical forms made it possible for modern chemistry to emerge. Alchemy operated on the basis of external apparances (that is, empirical observable properties) of the substances. These could be immediately perceived by the alchemist in the course of an experiment, yet these could not be explained by the perceived properties themselves. For instance, to explain the notion of 'salt' by way of its perceivable property (taste of 'salty') did not solve chemistry's problem of making sense of salts (yet indeed allowed for classification of substances into the category of 'salts'). Only when the abstract *formulae* of depiction of the organizational core of chemical substances were invented, did chemistry acquire explanatory power. Nevertheless, at the level of observables in any experiment, the perceivable properties of substances remain relevant as external appearances of the underlying chemical composition. Thus, H_2O remains (in the chemist's mind) the same substance, irrespective of whether its external form is that of steam, ice, or liquid.

This example from the history of chemistry may help to illuminate the difficulties psychology has in the twentieth century in making sense of its object matter. In many ways – making an analogical comparison – contemporary psychology is struggling to overcome its own 'alchemy' practices and create a system of science that could approximate that of chemistry. In psychology, interpretations of the nature of the phenomena in terms of their external appearances are widespread. In ways similar to alchemy (see the example of 'salt' being 'salty', above), a child psychologist – observing one child hitting another in a peer group – may classify this as 'aggressive behaviour', and claim that this behaviour 'expresses the child's aggressive tendency'. In other terms, the notion that 'aggression is aggressive' becomes created – and consensually accepted as adequate explanation of the child's hitting of the other. Similarly, psychology has accepted the explanation of phenomena by way of methods used to study them. For instance, the usual – and accepted – 'definition' of 'intelligence' is by way of 'what intelligence tests measure'. Both these examples are reminiscent of Molière's ironic depiction of esteemed medical doctors (of his time), who tried to explain why opium puts people to sleep. In front of a prestigious panel of experts, the candidate to the role of medical doctor answered, 'because there is, in it, a dormitive principle (*virtus dormitiva*)'.

Much of psychology is creating explanatory principles that are very similar in their nature to this 'dormitive principle'. Many explanations for psychological outcomes are given through circular reasoning – 'intelligence' leads a person to do well on 'intelligence tests' or 'be intelligent', 'introversion' is a personality characteristic that is assumed to make a person not talkative in social contexts, and so on. Instead of inventing ever new versions of the 'dormitive principle', psychological science needs to transcend a particular cultural common-sense system,[1] and explain psychological outcomes through understanding of the process mechanisms that lead to such outcomes.

There is thus a great need for re-thinking of much of psychology's research enterprise. This is usually easier done when a new sub-field is invented. Cultural developmental psychology is one such effort. The orientation in this textbook is to introduce interested persons directly to basic issues of the science of cultural developmental psychology, trying to by-pass the social and political processes that govern psychology in the 1990s. One of the ways of achieving this goal is to take a comparative-cultural stance on the issues of human development, and to demonstrate how science needs to be capable of explaining a large variety of phenomena. In contemporary psychological accounts of children and their development, it is usual to accept a prototypical middle-class European or North American child as the norm for the human condition, and treat differences from that norm as either non-normal aberrations, or as explainable by reference to 'cultural differences'. The latter explanation is certainly insufficient (as it follows the above-mentioned scheme of explanation: a *described* difference of the child from another is *explained* by the notion of difference). Therefore, the focus in this book is on universalistic theoretical integration – differences between children from different societies, large as these may be at the level of described phenomena, need to be theoretically explainable by the same general theoretical viewpoint. This does not mean that I want to superimpose my own perspective onto

the emerging science of cultural developmental psychology (these personal scientific perspectives are elaborated elsewhere: Valsiner, 1987, 1997, 1998). Rather, my aim in this book is to outline general directions of how such universal explanatory systems might be created. There are – and can be – many ways of accomplishing the goal of creating them. What remains a universal given for the ideology embedded in this book, however, is that scientific knowlege needs to be universal, rather than particular. In this sense, my perspective in this book is clearly oriented towards overcoming the traditions of 'post-modernism' that have proclaimed the fragmentation of knowledge into locally valid (at best) constructions. The focus in this book is to promote the construction of 'grand theories' that would unify knowledge of particular (cultural-contextual) phenomena.

The book thus includes empirical examples of human development from various societies. Each of these is contextualized in the meaning system where it is embedded, yet the story these examples are meant to tell is general. Under no circumstances can the socially (and personally) desirable example of the European or North American middle-class child be the normal case of children all in all. Rather, it is an equal example to any other children in their natural and cultural habitats. Thus, a North American middle-class child who is furnished with piles of 'educational toys' is in principle not different from Sebei boys playing with stones, and assigning multiple roles to these stones, who are viewed as being involved in a similar process (of exploratory constructive action – or 'play') through which they construct their own psychological worlds. Or, likewise, negotiations between well-fed middle-class parents and their children at the meal table for the child to eat more of the 'good food' are in principle similar – in terms of underlying processes – to negotiations of getting access to very limited sources of food in conditions of chronic malnutrition of both parents and children in other societies. The problem of child psychology has been the lack of effort to understand such generic similarities – and thus not arriving at generalizable knowledge about development.

Chapters 8–13 (Parts Three to Five) provide numerous empirical examples of the cultural contexts for development of children. Some aspects of development in childhood that were insufficiently covered in the previous version of this textbook (Valsiner, 1989) – like these of middle childhood – are now elaborated.

It should be obvious that the coverage in this book is not that of *cross*-cultural psychology, but that of cultural psychologies. Although many examples are taken from research that follows cross-cultural psychology's traditions, the major difference between cross-cultural psychology and the present perspective is in the contrast between elementaristic and systemic approaches to psychological phenomena. Cross-cultural psychologists have usually carried the methods of non-developmental psychology to the realm of comparing samples of subjects from different societies. The resulting contrasts are useful first-step approximations of from where cultural psychological developmental psychology might start its knowledge construction. Yet cross-cultural psychology utilizes the same explanatory tactics as the ones described above, and has therefore failed to provide generalizable knowledge about human development. Reasons for that limitation will become obvious in this book, as the axiomatic basis of developmental science is not combinable with methods from non-developmental psychology (from where most of cross-cultural psychology originates).

Aside from the textbook role of this book, I hope that its coverage will be of interest also to people well outside of the teachng/learning situations of institutions of higher learning. I have attempted to structure each chapter in ways that could allow for independent learners to make sense of the issues. Review questions at the end of each chapter are expected to be useful for

that purpose. I hope that this book constitutes an invitation for curious readers to construct their own understanding of the issues covered, rather than providing a canonical exposition of cultural developmental psychology. A science remains progressive as long as its creators remain sceptical of any canonical expositions that the author presents as if these were 'the true' pictures of reality. Surely the emergence of cultural developmental psychology is a wide open field requiring intellectual efforts to understand, rather than a newly propagated set of 'truths' by any author of any book.

NOTE

1 Psychology as science has been firmly captured by what its common language backgrounds afford. Presently, with psychology's institutional power centred in English-speaking countries, a number of psychological phenomena (such as Japanese *amae*) are not in the focus of theoretical work. When (until the 1930s) psychology was dominated by Germany (and built upon the German language), numerous concepts used then could not be continued with the language dominance shift. On the other side, the English language psychology superimposes the use of some concepts (e.g. 'parenting') that cannot be translated to other languages as a focus of theoretical interest.

PART ONE

DEVELOPMENTAL THEORY AND METHODOLOGY

1

STABILITY AND FLOW IN HUMAN EXPERIENCE: PHILOSOPHICAL PRELIMINARIES

Strange how people are under the impression that making a bed is exactly the same thing as making a bed, that to shake hands is always the same as shaking hands, that opening a can of sardines is to open the same can of sardines *ad infinitum*.
                    Julio Cortazar (1967, p. 248)

All human life is constantly novel as long as it lasts. There is no repetition of the same experience – each new occasion of making a bed, shaking hands, or opening a can is a qualitatively new event – even if it is similar to some previous, analogical, event. Yet, at the same time, we all live a relatively stable life. We do not doubt our identity as the given person from one morning's waking up to the next. We take for granted that the ways we move, talk, write etc. are in principle understandable for others (and remain 'typically ours' over time). Thus, the constant novelty of our life experiences is paralleled by our psychological construction of stability at the same time.

This unity of stability and change has been the philosophical puzzle for human thought over its history. Philosophers have either emphasized the stability of the world (Plato, Aristotle) or the process of change (Heraclitus). The science of developmental psychology that emerged in the nineteenth century on the basis of embryology, has had to face the tension between the notions of sameness and never-sameness since its beginning. In the context of the present exposition, it is important to look at the basic philosophical oppositions that drive the thinking of psychologists about development.

GENERAL FOUNDATIONS FOR THE DISTINCTION BETWEEN DEVELOPMENTAL AND NON-DEVELOPMENTAL PERSPECTIVES

The distinction between developmental and non-developmental perspectives is based on a set of general philosophical assumptions. Such assumptions are relevant parts of scientific methodology (see below, Chapter 5). Such different perspectives are made possible by the positioning of the researcher in some relation to the phenomena under study. It is the goal orientation of the researcher that makes him or her assume a perspective, accepting some axiomatic presuppositions rather than others, and never considering further possible assumptions. For example, all scientists would reject axioms that underlie religious conceptual systems (existence of deities, their 'influence' on the world) – even if in their personal lives the scientists are religious themselves. *Within the domain of their sciences*, the religious 'fixed truths' do not apply. This does not mean that scientists refuse to create explanatory concepts of a general kind as an axiomatic basis for their work. In fact, many general concepts used widely in sciences – 'energy', 'evolution' – are in a general nature not different in level than the posited axiomatic 'causal movers' in the sphere of religions. A good example is the propagation of the energy concept as if it were a generic 'first mover' of the universe – largely through the efforts of Wilhelm Ostwald (see Hakfoort, 1992). It is by social convention that scientists rule in or out one or another axiomatic statement about the origins of the phenomena they look at. Consider some obvious examples:

- Axiom 1: 'Human *psyche* is created by God' (rejected by science).
- Axiom 2: 'Human *psyche* is created by evolution' (accepted by science).
- Axiom 3: 'Evolutionary processes are the creation of a God' (accepted by some scientists – who may accept Axiom 2 and reject Axiom 1; and vehemently rejected by others).
- Axiom 4: 'Evolution operates by Natural Selection' (accepted by those scientists who reject Axiom 3).
- Axiom 5: 'Natural Selection is created by the spirits of the ancestors of the scientists who believe in it' (vehemently rejected by all!).

This little exposition of axioms demonstrates the relevance of subjectively set boundaries (by scientists and laypersons, alike) on the general starting points for scientific investigation. The beginning of any research effort is the researcher's subjective position in philosophical issues. This is the basis for constructing a concrete research programme, which is oriented towards arrival at generalized knowledge. Generalization of knowledge in scientific domains entails work on highly abstract levels, and terminological construction that is in principle independent of empirical work. Yet these constructions become linked with empirical efforts (see discussion of methodology in Chapter 5).

Common sense and science

In order to outline the philosophical bases of the developmental perspective, and contrast it with its non-developmental counterpart, the following contrasts are relevant. In each of the pairs, the ordinary mental lives of persons – which could be called *common sense* – give preference to one over the other. Since all science depends upon persons who do it, all science is in one way or another situated within the common sense of the given society at the given time. Common sense is based on the fundamental information that human beings get through their vision, hearing, touch, taste, smell etc. about the specific context, as well as on the internalized beliefs about one or another aspect of such sensory experiences.

Common sense exists as a device for ordinary human beings to live their lives. Hence it is oriented towards coping with the uncertainty of life through creating moments of stability, and explaining them. This makes it an opponent for the developmental orientation in science – assumptions of the developmental perspective

are easily overrun by the common sense efforts to create a mental picture of a fixed universe. Hence, the developmental perspective transcends the common sense reflection upon the world. Making the assumptions accepted by common sense clear, and rejecting those in the building of a science, is a relevant practice for any science.

The matter of perspective: does the Earth circle the Sun, or vice versa?

Many other sciences have gone through this rejection of common sense in the past. For instance, astronomy made that break with common sense assumptions when the Copernican model of the planetary system (all planets, including the Earth, circulate around the Sun) became accepted, and as the Ptolemaic system (which made the Earth the centre around which the Sun, among others, circulates). The Ptolemaic system was built in accordance with the common sense. Thus, from the viewpoint of our common sense perception and reasoning about the Sun (which, as we say, 'rises in the morning' and 'sets in the evening', moving around us during the day), it is the Ptolemaic model that is in agreement with our everyday experiences. Yet, this common sense experience – immediate and undoubtable as it is for our perceptual and cognitive systems – is proven wrong by science, which goes beyond the immediately available information and creates a model that explains the planetary system as a whole (not merely the Sun's trajectories) in ways that set the Sun to be the centre of the system. Without doubt, this overcoming of the common sense view in science was ideologically complicated – for decades the power of the Catholic Church in Europe was used to persecute scientists who went against the socially accepted view of the 'rightness' of the Ptolemaic system.

In a similar vein, chemistry transcended understanding based on the common sense in its development in the seventeenth and eighteenth centuries, as it moved away from alchemy to become modern chemistry. The practices of alchemy were based on the immediately perceivable qualities of substances (for example, 'salts' being 'salty' etc.), combined with socially desirable practical goals for investigation (for example, turning other substances into gold). Different moments of magical beliefs (internalized common sense notions) were seen as participating in the alchemic transformation process.

Entification: turning processes into static entities

Both alchemists and developmental researchers have had to cope with a difficult problem of reflecting upon transforming phenomena – human language itself is oriented towards turning dynamic processes into static entities.

Hence using language to depict a process easily leads to *entification* – the turning of a process description into an implied causal entity.

Consider the example of explaining some accomplishment of an organism through the notion of 'learning'. At first, the process by which the organism reaches a new state can be described as trying, getting feedback, trying again in a new way etc. This is *description of the process* by which the organism moves towards that new state. Since repeated verbal description of the process is cumbersome, a generic label – *'learning'* – is attached to it. That label is at first merely descriptive; it is a short-hand reference to the process it stands for. Yet its use in discourse soon leads it to acquire a new (surplus) nuance – it becomes used as a causal entity (for example, 'the child acquires skill X by learning', or 'learning causes development'). The temporal-descriptive facet of the original use of the word 'learning' becomes lost, and 'learning' becomes one of the categories of attribution. As we will see throughout this book, turning dynamic processes of development into static use of language descriptors, followed by giving the latter some causal flavour, is a conceptual obstacle developmental science has had to face during all of its existence.

In order to transcend the stability-oriented meanings of common sense and common language, developmental orientation needs to consider the *basic assumptions* on which both the non-developmental and developmental orientations are built. These basic assumptions take the form of oppositions of general concepts, which can be clarified by looking at the implications that the one and the other provide for our general thinking.

Assumptions about time: unsavable resource, or irreversible flow?

The central basis for any understanding of the biological world is the notion of time. In human cultural history, two views on time have emerged. First, there is the treatment of time as an independent dimension within which objects are located (the fourth dimension, added to the three dimensions of space). Such a view of time allows the thinker to locate objects in time–space, without any assumption about the nature of the objects' own interdependence with the time. Time here is not an inherent feature of the object, but an external dimension within which the object can be located. A statement like 'I saw a pig swimming inside Fontana di Trevi yesterday from 1 to 3 p.m.' indicates this kind of use of time. The fact of the observation is recorded in ways similar to the three-dimensional features of the object (for example, 'the pig was 67 cm long, 23 cm wide, and 34 cm high'), only here mentioning the time (from–to). The role this 2-hour long period may have played in the life of the swimming pig is not assumed to be of any relevance here.

The second perspective on time is based on the inherent dependency of biological organisms with the time of their growth. This perspective entails the notion of *duration* (a concept of Henri Bergson, 1907) that moves from the infinite past towards the infinite future, and can be experienced only in the form of a person's relations with the world in the immediate present – an infinitely small time period that unites the past (which is vanishing) and future (which is approaching). This notion of time is that of *irreversible time* – no time moment ever repeats itself, and time cannot be 'forced' to 'turn back'. Measuring time in units (second, minute, hour etc.) here entails determination of non-comparable units (year 1 in a person's life is not the same as the year that follows). Developing organisms do not develop *in* time, but *with* time.

In this philosophical realm, development entails constructive linking of the past with the future in the present. In the development of the human species, this has resulted in various reflections upon time, all of which – necessarily – depict time in the form of stabilized, relatively static means. It would be impossible to depict irreversible time in ways similar to its actual flow – any depiction of that kind would be as fluid as time itself, and hence cannot be described! Yet there can be models that retain the irreversible nature of time in their depiction, or attempt to translate time into forms where irreversibility is eliminated, or at least lessened.

Ordinary ways of discourse about time

Common language uses reflect these transformations of time in ways that emphasize the non-developmental aspect of common sense. Thus, we talk about 'saving time' (in analogy with 'saving money' – yet the hour you 'save' today cannot be put into a 'time bank' to be used tomorrow, it would not gain interest, or disappear through inflation!), 'using time' (but time cannot be 'taken' from one period to be 'used' in another, you cannot 'use' the hour from 11–12 a.m. in your life at 5 p.m.!). *Time is inherently tied to the activities in which the person is involved*. Talk of 'allocating', 'saving', 'using' time is actually talk about decisions to be involved in one or another kind of activity.

Yet, human cultural inventions have come to provide stabilizing representations for time in the form of time-measurement devices. Cyclicity in physical and biological processes is often used to build measurements of time. The day/night cycle provides the measurement unit of 'day', church clocks and wristwatches divide that cycle into 24 hours, each hour into 60 minutes, each minute into 60 seconds. It is here that the 60-based measurement stops – counting of milliseconds is 100-based. At the macroscopic end, the 'year' is a vastly imprecise unit (requiring alteration of 365 to 366 days every 4 years), and the initial reference point for counting years varies by convention of the given society. The imagery about the 'reaching the new millenium' on 31 December 1999 would be completely different if it were discovered in the occidental world that Christ indeed existed as a person, and was born 10 years BC! The ways of 'measuring time' vary between different societies, and are in many ways linked with the cyclicity of nature and the needs of the social-institutional organization of activities in the given community.

Turning the irreversible time process into reversible units of time

The co-existence of different bases for time measurement in human cultural practices reflects the historical complexity of measuring time. Efforts have been made to turn time into reversible units, similar to measures of length, weight etc. These static depictions of time can be seen as examples of 'reversible time'. Surely such units are convenient cognitive illusions, yet they have their practical utility. Thanks to that, continuous events can be turned discrete (for example, there can be specifiable 'end points' to experiences such as sitting in a lecture hall; or feelings of guilt after waking up at noon, and finding the alarm clock – set for 8 a.m. – in a battered state on the floor). *By trying to measure time, the duration notion is lost and time becomes represented in ways similar to space.* Practical needs for social organization of life activities in societies guide the thinking of persons about time in the direction of overlooking the irreversibility of the duration.

In sum – time is irreversible as it flows, intricately linked with our experiencing our relations with our worlds. As a result of human cultural history, we have attempted to describe it in terms of stable units, which have served practical purposes. For the understanding of development, units of time that are used in science need to retain some features of irreversibility.

Assumptions of stability and change

Any phenomenon can be viewed as being either stable, or in a process of change. The former view – here labelled the *assumption of stability* – is usual for these sciences, which do not need to consider development of the phenomena. This includes almost all physical and chemical sciences (with the notable exception of thermodynamics), and social sciences where the objective is understanding of the phenomena as they exist in a stable form. That stable form can be conceptualized in two possible ways – as an 'object-like' static representation, or as a dynamic process that maintains stability (see Chapter 2).

Most of psychology is built on the nondevelopmental premises, utilizing representations of the 'object-like' kind. Such accepted explanatory terms as 'intelligence', 'libido', 'personality dimensions' or 'traits', 'cognitive capacity' etc. are examples of 'object-like' static explanations. The appropriateness of such explanations is taken axiomatically. Therefore, disputes in psychology about issues like 'does the concept of "intelligence" explain our cognitive functioning, or not?' are pointless. Either such an explanatory role is accepted, or rejected.

The assumption of stability of the psychological functions and their explanation in 'object-like' terms, if accepted axiomatically, leads to the construction of human psyche as a stable conglomerate of such characteristics which entail something immanent in the psychological system of a person, and can be investigated as such. From that perspective, issues of development are left out of focus, and purposefully so. At most, some growth of the 'presumed quantity' of the 'object-like' qualities may be implied (for example, 'processing capacity' of the cognitive kind is axiomatically presumed to increase over a child's age).

The second version of the assumption of stability is that of *dynamic stability*. A phenomenon may be assumed to *exist in a stable state, yet its stability may be the result of constant dynamic processes that maintain that stability*. So, we can *observe* a stable phenomenon, but its existence is due to dynamic processes that make this stability available. At times the stability may disappear, and re-appear in a (observably) new form.

Example: biological stability is dynamic All biological systems can be used as examples here. Our biological body in any state of human development – from conception to birth to adulthood, until death – is externally viewable as in a stable state. From one day to the next, we do recognize our bodies as if they are the same (that is, use the stability assumption prescribed by our common sense). Yet the only reason why the bodies remain 'the same' is the complex of all dynamic, cyclical physiological processes that maintain this state of our bodies. That we exist in our stable forms – thanks to respiration, energy transfer in metabolism etc. – is all made possible by fitting physical environments. The reality of our stable state is dynamic, yet it is undoubtedly possible to see ourselves 'being' the same from immediate past moment to the present. Not so if we diverge to look at childhood photographs – yet our effort even there may be to look for similarity to what we are like now, rather than be fascinated by the very different size of our body then and there.

In science, axioms are not theoretically or empirically provable, but just basic starting points that are either accepted or rejected, depending upon the position of the researcher. A developmental scientist necessarily rejects the 'object-like' construction of stability, yet remains open to the opposition between 'dynamic stability' and 'change'. Periods of dynamically viewed stability are *a special case of development*. Thus, the moment of dynamic stability is a part of change (this is the focus of developmental scientists) – in contrast with the treatment of change as an aberration of the 'object-like' status of the person (which would be the non-developmental axiomatic stance).

All biological, psychological and social systems can be considered to be in a permanent process of change. Some of such change maintains periods of relative stability, other feeds into transformation of the system into a novel state. Some of these novel states are relatively minor modifications of the system (see below: open systems create heterogeneous classes, which are characterized by their variability). The developmental perspective needs axiomatic acceptance of the assumption of change, and constructs its methodology accordingly (see Chapters 2 and 5).

Infinity: 'good' and 'bad'

Philosophically, events occur in time and space. In time, their occurrence runs towards an end state that cannot be specified – infinity. Infinity is an end without end: after each next event there will be another one, and so on.

The development of new forms (in contrast to the repetition of old ones) has been the subject matter of philosophical analysis within dialectical thought in the past. The nineteenth century German natural philosopher Friedrich Engels (see Engels, 1940), continuing the dialectical traditions of Hegel, considered two kinds of movement towards infinity – 'good' and 'bad'.

'Bad infinity' involves the eternal repetition of the same form This kind of infinity is assumed together with acceptance of the assumption of stability (entity-kind). It implies a stable, immutable world, free of any change and devoid of development. Yet such a world is characterized by full predictability of the future – if we were to

know all the events that can exist, the future could be fully predictable. This is a completely deterministic perspective, which is not possible in the case of living systems. Mass production of the same model of some product in a factory is an example of 'bad infinity' – each and every car (of the same model) is expected to be exactly like any other one, as they roll off the assembly line, one after another.

In case of the 'bad infinity', the *notion of error can be specified*. In the mass production of objects which are supposed to be exactly the same as any other, production faults may result in malfunctioning, deviant objects. Some cars are 'lemons', some new computers have hardware problems that were not detected by the manufacturers, or that occur under specific configurations of the software. The 'faulty' specimens produced by the process of 'bad infinity' can either be repaired, or are abandoned as useless. In other words – 'bad infinity' may produce errors which can be specified, corrected (or not), on the basis of the fixed repetitiveness of the production of the same. 'Surprises' in the case of 'bad infinity' are of normatively negative kind – if they occur they are 'errors', 'faults', and do not lead to any new line of development. Prediction of future unfolding of the 'bad infinity' is simple – either the future brings new specimens of the same objects, or defective ones.

'Good infinity' implies the constant production of novel forms in time The novel forms may still belong to the same category on the basis of their general similarity, yet each new form is unique. In the case of 'good infinity', prediction of the specifics of future events is not possible, other than at a generic level (of the established similarity category). Thus, each year every graduate from a given university would be categorized as 'alumnus of university X' and yet each and every one of these graduates is different from their peers. Given that the university keeps graduating students every year, one can predict that next year new alumni will be added to the pool of previous ones. In other words – a generic prediction of the category is possible. However, it is not possible to predict *the specific* characteristics of each of the persons who would graduate next year. Furthermore, the difference of every next specimen of the 'good infinity' case from their previous counterparts cannot be described as 'error', but rather as a 'different version'.

The meaning of 'error' The concept of 'error' is in principle indeterminable in the case of 'good infinity', without further specification of criteria for it. For example, in evolutionary theories the notion of 'good infinity' (production of variation of specimens within a species) is linked with the criterion of 'selection' as the determiner of 'error'. Those versions of the 'good infinity' productions that did not survive the adaptational demands are considered to have been 'errors', while others – the ones that survived – were not. The 'error' notion here requires an additional (external) criterion; it is not inherent in the process of 'good infinity' itself.

Without doubt, labelling the two kinds of infinities as 'good' and 'bad' is an act of evaluation on the part of Engels. This evaluation here springs from the consistent base of evaluating the potential for development – in nature, psychology, society – in positive ways. *Developmental perspectives in any science necessarily need to accept the axiom of 'good infinity' as a given, since only on the basis of that general philosophical view is it possible to consider issues of development.* However, this axiom creates interesting problems for the issue of *predictability* (see below).

Summary of the two 'infinities': homogeneous and heterogeneous classes

Human mental orientation towards categorization is a major way to create relative stability in the life-worlds of continuous flux. Construction of categories – or classes of objects – can be accomplished in two different ways. Categorization on the basis of 'bad infinity' leads to the creation of *homogeneous classes* of objects.

Homogeneous classes of objects are compilations in which each and every member of the class is considered to be exactly **the same in quality** *as each and every other member of the class.* Each specimen of the class is exactly the same as any 'prototype' of specimens in the class. Variability between the specimens in the class does not exist. In line with the example of mass-produced cars, each car of the same model (= quality) is expected to be exactly the same as any other car of that model; if it is not, it is a faulty one. This is the same issue as was described above in the case of 'bad infinity'.

Heterogeneous classes are compilations of objects in which at least one member of the class is different from one (or more) other members, while the whole class retains its general quality by way of a generic name given to the class. Members of the heterogeneous class are **similar** to one another – given the generic class name – but not the same (see Figure 1.1).

In the case of heterogeneous classes, *variability within the class is the norm*. Each human being is different from other human beings, yet all of them belong to the class 'humans' despite being small or big, young or old, of different hair or skin

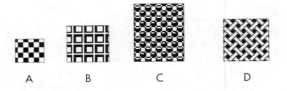

Explanation: Objects A . . . D are similar in their form (rectangles), but vary in size and internal texture. If referred to as 'rectangles' the class of objects becomes homogenized – the referrer overlooks the differences between the class members in texture and size

FIGURE 1.1 *A heterogeneous class of objects*

colour etc. The notion of homogeneous class considers all of its members as appropriate representatives of the class. The variability within the class is an important characteristic of the class – and not an 'error' (as it was in the case of homogeneous classes).

Heterogeneous classes can be viewed to 'form' over time (as a result of 'good infinity'). In this case, the heterogeneity of the class may reflect developmental outcomes. A developing organism necessarily generates outcomes of the developmental process that constitute a heterogeneous class. Consider as an instance the class of 'your own self'. Over your lifetime, this 'self' may be represented by recordings of its form – like pictures in your album. Surely 'you' were very different at different ages, while still being 'you' at all ages. The set of your childhood photographs is a heterogeneous set, in which 'you' on all photographs are different, while still keeping your identity as 'you'. The photographs in this heterogeneous set can be ordered so as to reflect your development from infancy to the present day, and thus they begin to reflect your development.

Parallels in set theory: 'crisp' and 'fuzzy' sets

The contrast between homogeneous and heterogeneous classes in mathematical set theory is reflected in terms of the difference between 'crisp' and 'fuzzy' sets (Zadeh, 1965). 'Crisp' sets are sets in which each member of the set either belongs to the set, or does not. There is no possibility that the membership of a specimen in a set includes partial (or doubtful) status. This 'either–or' way of making 'crisp' sets is contrasted with 'fuzzy' sets, in which each member of the set belongs to the given set to some extent (usually indicated by way of quantitative membership functions). 'Fuzzy' sets are examples of heterogeneous classes, while

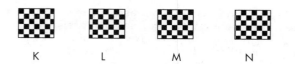

K   L   M   N

The set W {K, L, M, N} is a 'crisp' set – a homogeneous class. Each member of the set/class is similar to every other, each either belongs to the set (of 'rectangles') or not

A   B   C   D

The set Q {A, B, C, D} is a 'fuzzy' set. Each member A . . . D belongs to the set with some degree of 'belonging'. If Q = 'rectangles', then B and D are less central members of the set than A and C, yet B and D are also 'kind of rectangles'

FIGURE 1.2   'Crisp' and 'fuzzy' sets

'crisp' sets are examples of homogeneous classes (see Figure 1.2).

Homogeneous and heterogeneous classes in the minds of researchers

All biological, psychological and sociological classifications necessarily form heterogeneous classes. However, the thinking of researchers need not always adequately reflect this nature of reality. Historically, the sciences started from the use of the homogeneous class notion, superimposing it onto all phenomena studied by sciences. While it is possible to consider homogeneous class descriptions adequate for macrophysical phenomena, their use in the biological and social sciences has been an obstacle in the minds of scientists over the past two centuries. Thinking about heterogeneous classes as if they were homogeneous has made it difficult to appreciate the central feature of biological and social realities, namely their *variability of forms* which belong to the same general class.

There are social reasons why phenomena of high variability have been pushed to be (mis)-represented by categorization systems of the homogeneous class kind. For many *practical purposes* – usually those of *control over* persons or natural phenomena – forcing the phenomena into a homogeneous class fits the goals of social institutions. Thus, all soldiers in an army would be considered as the same, and treated as such (by way of uniforms, hair-shaving, uniformed

conduct); business executives are expected to be uniformed into wearing ties and driving expensive cars. Homogenization of classes in the case of social phenomena is a desired goal for social institutions, which control these classes by 'divide' (one class from another) and 'govern' principles. No surprise then that social sciences borrow the orientation towards representing variability of phenomena in terms of homogeneous classes, thus overlooking the variability as non-essential. Yet it is this oversight which may precisely deprive these sciences of an adequate look into their phenomena, and most certainly makes the study of development impossible.

A good example of how socio-institutional practices have guided psychologists' application of homogeneous classes in US psychology in the 1990s comes from the habit of reporting the age of (mid-childhood level) children in scientific discourse. While in most of the world (that is, those parts where age measurement is utilized) children's ages are reported in years from birth, psychologists in the United States in recent years have opted for a different measure. Regularly, when they have to report the age of children whom they studied, they report the *school grade level* from which the children were taken. Thus, a question 'How old were the children in your study?' may be answered 'They were 7th graders'. This move toward inexactness ('7th graders' in the United States can be of any age between 12 and 14 years, depending upon circumstances) indicates two socio-institutional assumptions, based on the US system of education:

1 that child researchers all over the world share the knowledge of age ranges in different grades in US schools; and
2 that for the given study, the social context of schooling *is of higher priority than* chronological age.

Usually, both these assumptions are unwarranted, and reflect the socio-institutional ethnocentrism of the given investigator. But beside that, *the act of describing the children as '7th graders' is one of homogenization of the heterogeneous class sample* (by chronological age, as well as by many other features of a personal kind) on the basis of their sharing the given institutionally organized ('7th grade') social environment. The assumption that school homogenizes the children into '7th graders' despite their individual schooling histories is already embedded in this way of reporting children's *age*. Of course there are practical reasons that are to be taken into account (for example, researchers' easier access to children within a given grade, in the school context) which may pave the way for this transformation of the meaning of 'age' into grade. Of course, a different kind of homogenization takes place if the meaning of age in terms of the precision of years is used. Thus, all children from age 12 years 0 days to 12 years 364 (or 365) days would belong to the homogenized age set of '12-year-olds', here based on the assumptions of biological prominence of chronological age-based growth. Last (but not least), the precision of age-based homogenization of children's age 'classes' depends upon the researchers' accepted notion of appropriateness of how wide a heterogeneous class becomes homogenized. Thus, infancy researchers make careful distinction of groups in terms of months and weeks (and even days), while researchers of second-year children may limit their homogenization to the age marking of months, and researchers of adulthood may speak of 'adults' as involving any person from 20 years of age to 65 years. All the reflection upon these classes is given as if the classes are homogeneous, while obviously each of those is heterogeneous, and hardly comparable to any other (for example, comparisons of 'adults' with '7th graders').

Social highlighting of contrasts and the homogenization of classes

What function for researchers is served by presenting heterogeneous classes as if they were homogeneous? Why is variability within classes sometimes completely overlooked, sometimes turned into a target of investigation (for example, in the case of the study of 'individual differences' in many areas of psychology)? This selectivity may be viewed as a result of *socio-institutional highlighting of some contrasts* that are prescribed to be *homogeneous for purposes of using the results of knowledge construction*. Psychology is filled with such prescribed contrasts – homogenization of gender groups (even if it is blatantly obvious that a sample of men has variation within it, similarly to a sample of women), or of social classes (for some reason, the 'middle class' is presented as a homogeneous class in making contrasts with 'lower class', similarly viewed as homogeneous). Some other possible classes that could be involved in these contrasts (for example, the class of 'androgynes' – men and women of high presentation of both gender features; or 'higher class' contrasted with 'middle class') are usually absent from these contrasts between supposedly homogeneous classes.

It could be argued that the comparisons are made with specific socio-institutional goals in mind (for example, proving by research that 'lower class' children need intervention, or – in an extreme opposite scenario – are dumb and do not

need any 'wasting of resources' on them). Social institutions can use the same empirical data for vastly opposite objectives ('helping' versus 'scientifically legitimized stigmatization'), and which way the research findings are used is beyond the control of the scientists. For the purposes of social application of the findings, evidence about the heterogeneity of classes is either unimportant, or usable only in the further division of the classes into sub-classes of homogeneous kinds. Consider the act of decision to divide the class 'adolescents' into sub-classes 'normal adolescents' and 'delinquent adolescents'. The result of such splitting of one homogeneously treated class is now two homogeneously treated classes. Each adolescent considered is assigned (on the basis of some 'diagnostic means') to one *or* the other class, with differential implications for 'treatment' by the social institutions. It is very unlikely that the class of 'normal adolescents' is of great interest for the social institutions. However, the class of 'delinquent adolescents' may be made the target of segregation ('delinquent adolescents' are designated to be interned in special rehabilitation centres), or educational intervention (efforts to re-educate them towards 'becoming normal') etc. The individual characteristics of each 'delinquent adolescent' are of no importance for the socio-institutional system. These may become very important for the persons (clinical or prison psychologists) who work with the particular cases (for example, asking questions like 'can THIS delinquent adolescent NOW be released from this hospital or prison, after our TREATMENT, in the hope of no recurrence of the delinquent act?'). The latter questions are relevant for the psychological praxis.

Assumptions about systems: *open* versus *closed*

The object of researchers' investigation in the case of complex phenomena is a system (consisting of parts and their relations, the joint functioning of which creates the quality of the whole). A system cannot be reduced to its constituents and treated as a mere aggregation (or sum) of these constituents – since the systemic quality depends upon the working relations between the parts, and not merely a summary of the different parts. A list of human body parts, however full it may be (anatomically), does not include the quality of the movement, actions of the total body. The latter action depends fully on the ways in which the actions of different body parts are coordinated.

The distinction between *open* and *closed* systems is central for any developmental perspective. *Open systems are systems that are involved in exchange relationships with their particular environments*. All biological, psychological and social systems are open systems. Of course, each of these three kinds of systems entails a different notion of *what kinds of exchange relations* are involved, what are the objects of such exchange. In the case of biological systems, such exchange relations may take the form of exchange of substances (for example, food intake, water supply, air supply). Physical open systems may be viewed as exchanging matter and/or energy with their environments. Socio-political systems may depend upon exchange of capital, or other economic means, with their environments. Sociological systems may be said to use 'symbolic capital' in their exchanges (Bourdieu, 1991).

In contrast, closed systems are systems that exist without exchange relationship with their environments. Such systems can never develop – they can only disintegrate and lose their systemic quality. Biological systems remain open systems as long as their life-supporting exchange relations continue to function; once these exchange relations are reduced to none, the systems turn from open to closed ones (and can only disintegrate).

Psychological systems as open systems

What could be the object of 'exchange relations' in the case of psychological systems? Obviously, different kinds of psychologies – assuming they attempt to build themselves along open-systemic lines – may have different answers to that question. A cognitive account may use the notion of 'information exchange' between the organism and the environment. I would narrow down the present account to that of cultural functioning of human personality, in which case *the exchange with the environment takes the form of* **constructed signs** *being* **communicated between** *the person and his/her environment*.

This claim is based on the notions of signs as constructed entities. It builds upon the semiotic perspectives of Charles Sanders Peirce. Semiotics is the science of signs. Signs are devices that *present and represent* some aspects of target realities. These signs are of varied forms and functions; they are jointly constructed by the person and his/her social worlds, yet as constructed, they become the medium for the *exchange relationship* between the person (as system) and the environment (social world).

What are signs?

Signs 'stand for' something else – *in generic terms, they* **present** *that* something to somebody in some capacity. Peirce emphasized three kinds of signs:

1 An *icon* is a sign that denotes its object on the basis of a similarity that exists between the sign and the object it represents. Thus, a sculpted human figure is an iconic representation of the person, since the sculpture represents the person.
2 An *index* is a sign that denotes its object by way of representing the results of the object's impact. For example, a footprint is an index of the foot that made it. The search for fingerprints by the police in the context of a crime is an effort to identify the person by his or her indexical sign.
3 A *symbol* is a sign that represents an object by way of associations and general ideas that operate in such ways that the symbol is interpreted as a representation of the object. The word *foot* (which, as a word, has nothing in common with the object foot, as it is neither the result of the action of a foot nor a physical replica of it) is a symbol of the object foot.

The construction and use of signs is *semiotic activity*. Human beings are constantly involved in constructing signs, and exchanging sign-encoded communicative messages with others, via the impact of these messages upon the environment (and the return role of such impacts upon the person). Thus, if your friend asks you 'How are you?', you, instead of delving into the complexities of the questions 'Who am I (his or her 'you')?' and 'What does HOW mean?', would utter a ritualistic answer, 'Fine, thank you'. Your friend as well as you can hear the response – you have externalized the uttered symbol – 'fine' – to your and of your friend's acoustic environment. *Both of you now perceive that symbol-encoded message*, which feeds further into your life experiences. The communicative exchange is simultaneously part of self-relation (you hear yourself saying that you are 'fine') and other-relation (your friend hears the same).

Signs connect experiences from past to future

The possibility for such presentation – let X 'stand in' for Y – can have three temporal orientations. First, the sign can *re-present* some facet of already lived-through experience. Secondly, the sign can *co-present* a present experience which is being 'lived through' by way of its concurrent construction. Finally, the sign can **pre**-*present* some possible future experience.

Consider an example: a person says 'Life is hard'. This statement reflects all three aspects of presentation – **re**-presentation (it is a synthesis of past-to-present experience), **co**-presentation (as it is stated here-and-now, as depiction of the person's generalization from the present) and **pre**-presentation (expecting the future to continue in these terms, or expect some oppositional reversal, like '. . . but tomorrow is another day'). All three co-exist in the utterance.

How can we depict open systems? View from co-genetic logic

The notion of exchange relationship entails directionality (of two kinds: from 'outside' to 'inside' of the system, and vice versa), and some medium of exchange (in the human case – signs). The exchange relationship is a *continuous process*, which makes it possible for the system to maintain itself and develop. In order to be able to study that process of relationship, the system, its environment and the medium of exchange need to be clearly differentiated. This is guaranteed by the formal system of *co-genetic logic* (Herbst, 1995). This logic is a formal system to analyse *interdependent emergence of forms and their contexts*.

The emergence of any system simultaneously brings with it the emergence of its environment. Thanks to this differentiation, it is possible to think about the relationships between the system and the environment (see Figure 1.3). When the system disappears, the differentiation of the 'inside', 'outside' and 'boundary' disappear simultaneously. In this sense, the logic of emergence and disappearance is **co**-genetic – all parts of the system and its environment (and their relation) are mutually defined via each other. The environment cannot be 'taken away' without the disappearance of the system, and vice versa.

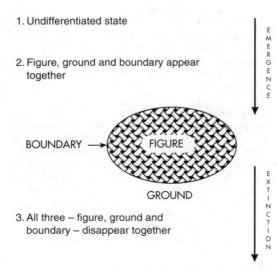

1. Undifferentiated state

2. Figure, ground and boundary appear together

BOUNDARY → FIGURE

GROUND

3. All three – figure, ground and boundary – disappear together

EMERGENCE

EXTINCTION

FIGURE 1.3 *Unity of emergence, existence and disappearance of the figure, ground and the boundary*

If we consider development to be a result of the open systemic nature of the organisms who develop, then our analysis of such development needs to concentrate on the constant interdependence between the organism and the environment. This is a basic question for methodology – how to study development in ways that give us knowledge about its general principles (see Chapter 5).

Multilinearity of development

The open systemic nature of development guarantees that the same developmental process can take place through more than one single route. There are multiple ways in which a developing organism can move from its initial state (X) to its new state (Y), as depicted in Figure 1.4.

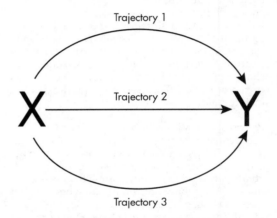

Trajectory 1

X   Trajectory 2   Y

Trajectory 3

FIGURE 1.4 *Multilinearity of development, and the phenomenon of equifinality*

Multilinearity entails the *principle of equifinality* – the same outcome can be reached through different routes (see Figure 1.4). Equifinality is thus characteristic of all living processes. Two persons may become candidates for the same job – and both would fit the job well. One of the candidates arrives at his or her present skills through diligent training, supported by parental models, based on his or her background potentials. The other may arrive at a similar level of performance through compensating his or her lack of background potentials, or support systems. Their developmental processes are completely different, yet the outcome is similar.

Assumptions about developing organisms: maximizers or satisficers?

The notion of *maximization* enters into the social sciences from economics. It entails a strategy of *maximizing one's benefits while minimizing one's costs.* This notion is surely applicable in cases of business decision-making, where all the information about costs and value gains is (a) available and (b) stable. But neither of these conditions can be assumed to be true for developing organisms. The latter are 'trading in futures' – making decisions now about possible benefits and costs in the future. Under such conditions, it is no longer possible to try to find solutions that are the very best, but rather those that are the safest that still satisfy the need.

That latter exemplifies the *principle of satisficing*. The notion of satisficing was brought into economic and psychological thought by Herbert Simon (1957). Business firms, as well as persons, accept 'good enough' solutions to problems which need to be solved here-and-now, and for which the very best solutions are unknowable. A person accepts 'good enough' solutions not because he or she prefers those, but because there is no other alternative. No one would settle for a 'merely good' solution if the very best were clearly reachable. From that point of view, *maximization is a special case of satisficing*, that is, the case in which the only sufficient solution is the single very best one.

Developmental processes are filled with uncertainties of the future, and with the unknowability of the precise linkages between the present actions and future outcomes. Hence, by their open systemic nature, all developing organisms are satisficers, rather than maximizers. As an example, consider a man (or woman) who is trying to make a decision whether to marry his or her current friend. Marrying is an act that takes place at the time, but the actual results of the marriage can be known only in the future. Furthermore, the partner who is being considered is an active human being who may prefer to act otherwise. Hence the decision-making person cannot utilize the 'cost/benefit' analysis that is characteristic for maximization solutions. There is no algorithm available for calculating the benefits and costs of marriage with this (or another) partner. In contrast, it is the satisficing strategy that can be utilized in the problem-solving. The question becomes 'Are our relations *good enough*

to get married?' and 'Do I trust them to be so in the future?'. If the conditions are deemed to be sufficient, the marriage proposal (or arrangement by others) may follow.

Human development entails the use of satisficing strategies as the norm, and maximization cases are an exception. While satisficing dominates actual development, efforts to capture the interests of the developing persons often try to superimpose a maximization orientation. Consider the variety of toy manufacturers who promote their toys to the parents of a child with the message that their particular toy is 'the best' available on the toy market for the intellectual development of their child. The toy-seller's interest is in creating an attitude of necessity in the parents. If the parents 'buy into' such a maximization framework, they may be further persuaded to buy the promoted toy. If, however, they stick to the satisficing strategy (for example, 'this toy may be very good for the child's intellectual development, but many other toys – including the ones he already has – are also sufficient'), they may escape from under the influence of advertising (and the toy-seller does not make the sale).

SUMMARY: PHILOSOPHICAL BASES FOR SCIENCE

All science is built upon philosophical underpinnings. Psychology has a history of complicated relations with philosophy – at times denying its importance, at other times emphasizing that importance beyond limits. In this chapter the main basic assumptions of a philosophical kind that are necessary for the study of human development and culture have been outlined. The irreversibility of time is an absolute given for the study of all living phenomena. Likewise, semiotic mediation – the appearance of signs in relations between human beings and the environment – constitutes the defining characteristic of cultural psychology. Hence, cultural developmental psychology can be considered a science of how human relations with the environment acquire new forms through on-going experience.

REVIEW QUESTIONS FOR CHAPTER 1

1   Explain similarities and differences between common sense and science.

2   What is *entification*? What kind of role does *entification* play in the thinking of scientists?

3   How is it possible to 'save time'?

4   Explain why all sciences that study development need to assume irreversibility of time?

5   Explain the notion of *dynamic stability*.

6   Explain the distinction between 'good' and 'bad' infinity.

7   Discuss the meaning of 'error' in the case of 'good' and 'bad' infinities.

8   Explain the difference between homogeneous and heterogeneous classes.

9   What are 'crisp' and 'fuzzy' sets?

10   Why do researchers turn heterogeneous classes into homogeneous ones?

11   Explain the distinction between *open* and *closed* systems. Why are only open systems applicable to cultural and developmental phenomena?

12   What are signs?

13   Explain the distinction between *icon*, *index* and *symbol* in C.S. Peirce's understanding of signs.

14   Explain how signs connect human experiences of the past with expectations for the future.

15   Explain the notion of *co-genetic logic* (Herbst). Demonstrate the inevitability of the co-existence of the figure, ground and the boundary between them.

16   What is *multilinearity* of development?

17   What is *equifinality*?

18   How are the strategies of *maximization* and *satisficing* related?

19   Why can development be considered a satisficing, but not maximizing process?

2

THE DEVELOPMENTAL APPROACH

The philosophical bases outlined in Chapter 1 set the stage for a look at the developmental perspective in science. This perspective is shared by developmental biology and psychology, and could be equally viable if disciplines like developmental cultural anthropology or developmental sociology existed. It is an interesting feature of the history of the social sciences that they do not – and probably the existence of developmental psychology within psychology is a coincidence. It is often the case that the term 'developmental' in psychology is used as a synonym for child psychology. Yet child psychology need not be developmental in its orientation. For example, the study of infants, or adolescents, can be devoted to their ways of being – their existing capacities, conduct patterns etc. – and not address issues of the development of these functions at all.

In the most general terms, *the developmental perspective in any science entails investigation of general laws of emergence of novelty in irreversible time*. This statement uses two notions that are complicated in scientific discourse – *novelty* and *general laws*.

What is novelty?

Novelty is detectable by comparing what has already emerged (past) with what is currently emerging – as the past becomes a new past (currently future). As could be seen in Chapter 1, the irreversible nature of time provides the person with no return to the previously lived-through experiences. Instead, we all rush ahead towards the future, constructing it at every present moment, on the basis of our *reconstructions* of what happened in the past. Such reconstructions are possible because of *similarities* (not sameness!) between present and past experiences (in accordance with 'good infinity' and heterogeneity of classes). A recognition of something in the present as familiar to something in the past is possible

thanks to the helical nature of development in irreversible time (see Figure 2.1).

In Figure 2.1, due to the spiral unfolding of irreversible life course experience, at each curve the person can find similarities with the closest previous curve lived through. On the basis of such similarities, the person constructs a class (A) based on similar experiences. The crucial question here is whether the class A is conceptualized as a heterogeneous, or as a homogeneous class (as was described in Chapter 1). Thus, our going to sleep routines every night may be similar to one another, despite the fact that each new night is certainly a new one – that of today occurs only today and will never repeat itself in the following days of my life.

Furthermore, in my effort to feel stable, I use the class of similar experiences (A', A'', A''') as the basis for my expectation that the next event of a similar kind, in the future, would proceed along roughly similar lines to the ones I reconstruct

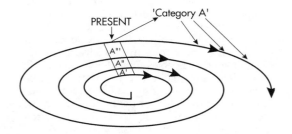

The person detects similarities between experiences A', A'', A''' while being in time moment PRESENT. This leads to formation of category A, which is then usable to detect further similar instances in the foreseeable future.

FIGURE 2.1 *How is it possible for a person to construct adaptive psychological stability on the basis of never-recurring life experiences?*

(in the present) to have occurred in the past. Human beings, precisely because their future is indeterminate, use psychological devices to create images of stability for the future. In that psychological construction process, they overlook the uniqueness of each lived-through experience, and try to construe one's life course events as predictable, recurrent and known. This is a *psychological, constructed illusion* that is based on the need for adaptation within a constantly changing environment. It is a very adaptive illusion – necessary for human psychological life. Yet it makes individuals 'blind' to exactly those aspects of their relations with their environments that make development possible – that is, novelties.

Novelty at two levels: personal and comparative-collective novelty

In actuality, the central role of novelty for the study of development should be no surprise (or novelty!) to anybody. If human personal lives proceed on their unique time course, by necessity (that is, by definition) every new moment in human experiencing is novel, independent whether a person detects it as such, or not. Thus, a schoolchild might think of every next lesson over the school day as 'the same old boring stuff', yet in reality the dramatic unfolding of each lesson is new. The child would not reflect upon that for reasons described above (illusion of sameness as adaptive device).

However, not every aspect of personal life's novelty is a construction that is novel at the level of the given species (that is, of *Homo sapiens*) or given society within the species. The first independent walking step that a particular infant takes is undoubtedly an example of personal novelty, but it is no novelty at the level of the species. For *Homo sapiens*, the early beginnings of bipedalism (walking on hind-limbs) are hidden very far in the past of biological evolution. Once the practice of bipedalism developed in the species, it became a collective novelty, in contrast to other species. Species-typical ontogenetic patterns of motor development are no longer novelty at the species level (no longer a collective novelty), but continue to be that at the level of individual life courses where each new generation goes through similar (not the same!) processes of development. The phylogenetic (species-level) history provides stable background for unfolding of individual novelty experiences *within a certain range of possibilities*. Thus, nobody can expect human children to develop locomotion patterns where the tail is utilized as important support (in fact, the idea of humans being born with a tail may evoke horror feelings), yet that is something clearly expected from each and every kangaroo.

A similar story occurs in respect to social organization of collective life. Specific collective rituals marking transition moments in human development (birth rituals, birthdays, communions, weddings, funerals) are collectively organized stable moments in the life of a society. They themselves are not viewed as producing novelty (yet novelties are embedded inside them – at every new instance, for new persons, weddings, baby-naming ceremonies, and funerals can take a different specific form). These relatively stable collective frames set up the stage for individual persons' unique experiences while being actors inside these frames – one bride at her wedding may be excessively bored by the need to be friendly to the horde of guests and avoid whisky being spilt on her uncomfortable wedding dress; another one would consider the role of the bride to be the highlight of her life – compared to the past – and it will always be remembered positively in the boring life with that husband in years to come.

Novelty as a conservative phenomenon

Given the linkages between the collective and personal kinds of novelty, it should be clear that all novelty is based on the previously established state of affairs (personal or collective). In this respect, it is conservative in its nature – it occurs in 'small steps' in relation to the previous state of affairs, rather than in 'huge jumps' in relation to that state. This 'small step' nature of novelty also makes it possible to ignore it in the creation of the psychologically adaptive illusion of time-free categories. Novelty is *constrained* by the conditions under which the given open system develops (see the notion of 'bounded indeterminacy' in Valsiner, 1997). Development is based on construction of novelty, but when constructed, that novelty becomes ordinary and becomes taken for granted as if it never were novel.

Laws as goals in science

Science is a framework for construction of knowledge about the world that is true independently of the ideological stances of scientists. Hence, in the history of science, efforts to keep ideologies out of the knowledge construction process have been notable. One way to arrive at such elimination of ideological impacts is to construct general laws – general rules by which the processes we look at function, in different historical times and under varied socio-ideological circumstances. Thus, laws of gravity would operate in any time and place on Earth, independent of the concrete objects, persons who use the objects, and climatic conditions.

General laws are expressed in abstract terms, and are formulated in ways that do not require immediate specification. The basic physical law of gravity is stated in generic terms, and is not expected to be in need of specification in the case of meteorites, bombs, feathers, or newspapers falling down. These general laws guide specific research efforts, yet do not compromise their generality.

However, the formulation of general laws in the social sciences is complicated by the embeddedness of these disciplines in the socio-institutional matrix of ideologies. Social sciences operate under a hidden or explicit orientation on behalf of institutions (which highlight which parts of the phenomena become objects for investigation) and implicit ideologies that suggest the ways in which to approach these (see Chapter 5 on frames of reference). Part of such orientation is the highlighting or masking of the goal of attaining general laws: an ideology may suggest that in the social sciences general laws are not attainable (as any generality would diminish the ideological guidance), or that these are not necessary since social sciences operate towards construction of local, context-bound knowledge.

In psychology, a number of efforts have been made to construct general laws. Gestalt psychology of the Berlin school (with Max Wertheimer and Wolfgang Köhler as the major originators of the direction, see Ash, 1995) was particularly eager to formulate general laws by which human conduct is organized.

The main Gestalt orientation implied that any psychological phenomenon (of perception, or action) strives towards a complete form. Thus, the 'law of *Prägnanz*' entailed that *any percept will strive towards the simplest and clearest structure possible under the given circumstances*. For example, consider four dots in Figure 2.2. In Figure 2.2*A*, the viewer probably experiences the tendency of viewing the dots as corners of an invisible square. The contours of the square are added by the viewer to the objectively available visual stimuli. Now, if some of the dots (of the same spatial location) are increased in size (as three of the four are in Figure 2.2*B*), the viewer may begin to see the configuration of a triangle and a separate dot.

Gestalt laws are dynamic (as they deal with the formation of the percept), but *not developmental*. The viewer complements the given stimuli by superimposing upon it a psychological organization. Yet the posited direction of the Gestalt laws is of the making of the incoming perceived stimuli, perceivable in terms of the simplest and clearest configuration. In case of development, just the contrary; such simplicity and clarity is constantly broken. General laws of development

A These four dots are likely to be perceived as a square

B These four dots are likely to be perceived as a triangle (of larger dots) and a single dot

FIGURE 2.2 *An illustration of the basic principle of Gestalt psychology*

can be formulated in ways that consider universality of the construction of novelty over time. Heinz Werner's and Bernard Kaplan's 'orthogenetic principle' (see below) is an example of a general law of development.

Efforts to reveal general laws in psychology have been hostages to the galloping empiricism that has taken over all of psychology in the past five decades. Instead of general laws, local and context-embedded knowledge is sought through researchers' incremental contributions to the 'empirical literature' in a given area. The possibility of general laws is even at times denied – under the influence of the undisciplined direction of thought-rhetoric which is loosely labelled 'post-modernist' philosophy.

Aside from historical fads and fashions in the social sciences that have reduced the focus on general principles, there exists an objective complication for arriving at general understanding of development. In contrast to non-developmental general orientations, where the range of phenomena is finite (even if variable), the phenomena of development are infinite. The focus on novelty within a general developmental perspective necessarily means that the whole set of phenomena of development is never fixed in a standard way. It is constantly changing, and any general law of development needs to account for this open-endedness of the developmental process.

CONTRASTS BETWEEN NON-DEVELOPMENTAL AND DEVELOPMENTAL APPROACHES

In most general terms, non-developmental and developmental perspectives are opposites that deal with the same phenomena. They can be contrasted, but not eclectically mixed. The study of transformation addresses issues that the study of 'things-as-they-are' finds super-fluous, unnecessary, or even 'error'. The non-developmental perspective is based on the *axiom of identity*:

$$X = [is] = X$$

Based on this axiom, it makes good sense to ask questions about 'What *is* personality?', 'What *is* intelligence?', 'What *is* memory?'. Questions of development are ruled out from that axiomatic basis – why ask a question of how x came to be x, *if we already know* that **X is X**.

The developmental perspective is based on the *axiom of becoming and dynamic self-maintenance*. It takes two forms:

$$X —[becomes]→ Y$$
$$X —[maintains itself as]→ X$$

Both becoming and remaining are *processes* that guarantee both relative stability and change in the case of development. A particular system that remains, for some time, in a relatively 'steady state' constitutes an example of temporarily stopped development (rather than a non-developing system). In the case of remaining, the particular system that is maintained in its general form depends upon constant innovation of the form by new parts. Biological organisms maintain themselves by the processes of new cell production and old cell death, while the form (the structure of the organism) in general remains the same.

Identity is not self-maintenance

Thus, the **axiom X —[remains]→ X** is not the same as the identity axiom of non-developmental perspectives, i.e. **X = [is] = X**. In the case of remaining, *process of maintaining innovation* is implied, whereas in the case of the identity axiom, no process (that makes the identity) is implied. The identity axiom is blind to the processes that make the identity possible. In a similar vein, non-developmental psychology is blind when questions of development are asked – and purposefully so, since its goals do not include making sense of laws of development.

Thus, the non-developmental and developmental perspectives differ axiomatically, and can be coordinated only in terms of one serving as a background system for the other. For instance, data about non-developmental aspects of children (for example, 'All the children in this sample were cognitively at the level of concrete operations à la Piaget') can be relevant as background knowledge to developmental questions (for example, 'How do these children become formal-operational in the course of the next year?').

This example leads us to an important clarification about the nature of stage accounts of human development (often called 'stage theories'). In developmental psychology such accounts abound – Jean Piaget's set of cognitive stages (sensorimotor, pre-operational, concrete operational, formal operational), Lawrence Kohlberg's system of six stages in moral development, Erik Erikson's different stages of life course etc. *An account of human development in terms of specifying a sequence of stages through which each person could proceed is not, in and by itself, a developmental account.* It is merely a setting up of similarity classes of given psychological phenomena, ordered by the species-based expectations for human life course. Each of the stages becomes viewed as a class (often treated as if it were homogeneous), which is followed by the person's arrival (via development) in the realm of the next class. This non-developmental account can serve as a background for asking developmental questions – which take the form of explanations of in which ways persons develop from one of these age-ordered classes to the others. In other words, 'stage accounts' do not explain development, but can be the basis for looking for developmental explanations. Piaget's 'stage theory' is not a developmental theory (since transition from one stage to the next remains unexplained), while his theory of 'progressing equilibration' is a developmental theory (since it attempts to make sense of how cognitive structures are transformed into a new form).

Which sciences utilize the developmental perspective?

The developmental perspective clearly exists in sciences such as developmental biology and developmental psychology. Developmental biology looks at the emergence of biological structures in all species of the plant and animal realms. Developmental psychology looks at the emergence of psychological phenomena of animals and humans over their life courses.

A developmental perspective is necessarily represented in modern medical sciences, especially in cases where the phenomena require an interest in variability, and the constant emergence of novelty (such as immunology). At the level of our biological functioning, there already exist necessities to cope with unexpected changes in the biological environment. The best example here is the organism's necessity to cope with ever-new mutants of ordinary viruses (for example, those of influenza) that are transmitted relatively quickly across large populations (and geographical distances). Given the mechanism of biological defences against viral infection (through micro-infection – due to immunization – protecting the organism against further instances by means of antibodies), the organism is constantly operating as a necessary detector of 'known' versus 'previously unknown' viruses. The latter (= novelty!) challenges the biological system to cope with it. The previously known strains of viruses no longer matter (as the organism has developed defences against them).

FORMAL BASES FOR DEVELOPMENTAL MODELS

Any science can make use of formal symbol systems, if such use provides for abstracted general knowledge which it is not possible to attain through the use of ordinary language. Efforts to provide mathematical models for developmental processes have taken a number of directions (summarized in Valsiner, 1997, Chapter 3), mostly outside of psychology (developmental biology: formal modelling of growth of multicellular organisms, or of forms of biological kind).

What is necessary for formal accounts of development, given the axioms of becoming and remaining (given above)? First, we need to specify the relations within a system, clearly accounting for possibilities of transformation of the system into a new form. Secondly, we need to specify relations between the system and the environment – which are the basis for any transformation of the system.

Complex systems can be viewed as hierarchically organized. Hierarchical organization is present if between any two parts of a system, a *uni-directional relation of dominance* (for example, **X** <>>> **Y** where >>> indicates the dominance) is defined. As a *relation*, the uni-directional relation of dominance necessarily includes the 'backward direction' (<) flowing from the sub-dominant to the dominant part. Equality of the parts is obtained when two mutually oriented uni-directional relations are combined (for example, **X** <->>> **Y** and **X** <<<->**Y** combine to give us **X** <<<->>> **Y**). In principle, it is possible to describe any system in terms of unidirectional and bi-directional relationships. The particular structure of these relations can provide a picture of the form of the system.

Transitive and intransitive hierarchies – linear and cyclical orders

Hierarchical organization of systems – starting from notions of classical logic – can take two forms: *transitive* and *intransitive*. The former kind is usually implied when we speak of hierarchies, as it gives us models of strict hierarchy (see Figure 2.3A). Such a hierarchy is based on the logical notion of transitivity:

If A > B and B > C then A > C

The use of > in this classical–logical scheme of transitivity is similar to the focus on uni-directional dominance relations, as mentioned above. Hence strict hierarchies are called *transitive hierarchies*. In Figure 2.3B, the notion of transitive hierarchy of the *branching* kind is given. It involves three levels ({A}, {B, C}, {D, E, F, G}), and the transitivity applies between levels:

$$\textbf{A} > \{\textbf{B, C}\} \text{ and } \{\textbf{B, C}\} > \{\textbf{D, E, F, G}\},$$
$$\rightarrow \textbf{A} > \{\textbf{D, E, F, G}\}$$

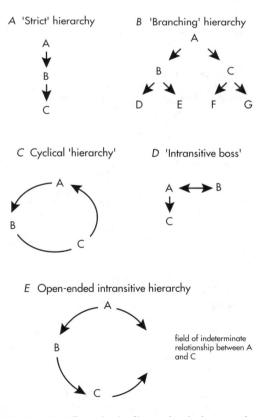

FIGURE 2.3 *Different kinds of hierarchical relations within a system*

Transitive hierarchies (of both linear and branching kind) are not open to further development. It is not specified within the structure of the hierarchy how it might become transferred into another state, and there is only one possibility for how the hierarchy might disappear – by being demolished 'from above'. If a transitive hierarchy is in place, it can change by 'mutation' of its most dominant part (for example, A becomes suddenly replaced by W), which may lead to automatic changes at the lower levels. Nevertheless, *how* such change of the hierarchy could proceed is not formally given *in the hierarchy itself*.

Transitive hierarchies are therefore possible models for *outcomes* of development (which are treated as non-developmental 'givens'), but not for the developmental process itself. That is within the class of *intransitive hierarchies*. Such hierarchies are based on logical intransitivity relation, which is:

If $A > B$ and $B > C$ then *it is not true* that $A > C$

rather

it can be that $A < C$, $A = C$, or the relation of A and C is indeterminate

Here we can see that *intransitivity guarantees 'open ends' in the hierarchical structure*. There is no strict rule that links C to A, but there are a few (strictly defined set) possibilities. Each of those gives us a different picture:

- The case $A < C$: This creates a cyclical structure where the *lowest* part of the hierarchy is *actually the highest* (see Figure 2.3C). From the viewpoint of classical logic, this is an impossibility. However, it is not an impossibility in the drawings of M. Escher, where falling water may land in the position from where it falls.
- The case $A = C$: This is a case of branching (see Figure 2.3D) where A is not directly related to C at all. It simply links with C without B having anything to do with it. Both of these cases are not open to reconstruction of the system, although both can be seen as producing variability (either by constant reverberation or the 'lowest' being in control over the 'highest' – in the previous case). The only developmentally open option is the following one.
- The case where the relation A to C is indeterminate: The relation may be in the process of emergence (=not yet determined, Figure 2.3E). How it becomes established determines the formation of the structure as either a linear hierarchy, or as a cycle.

The rule of cyclicity of systems in nature

A general rule can be stated: *most biological control systems are of cyclical nature, involving circular transformation of biological substances so as to re-create the control system itself, and provide some necessary outcomes for other processes.* Cyclical control systems are examples of intransitive hierarchies. A relevant example of such a control system is Krebs' cycle – the basic biochemical cycle in the human body which turns incoming nutrients into energy, while reproducing itself at the same time (see Figure 2.4).

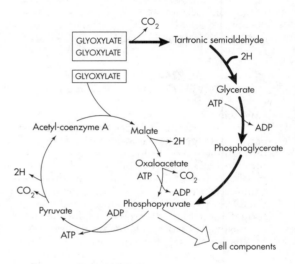

FIGURE 2.4 *The Krebs' Cycle*

The crucial nature of cyclical control mechanisms (such as Krebs' cycle) is their unity of stability and change in their regulation of the biological system. On the one hand, the cyclical nature of the biochemical reaction sequences *makes it possible for the control mechanism to reproduce its functional structure* (within which all the relevant chemical substances are constantly recreated – the substances are new, but their chemical form, their formulae, remain the same within the cycle). The cycle that reproduces itself maintains itself in a regime of dynamic stability, thus making it possible for its 'by-products' (for example, chemically coded energy resources) to be utilized for transformation of other parts of the organism. Thus, while the relevant cyclical control mechanism (such as Krebs' cycle) reproduces itself throughout the organism's life course, *its by-products make it possible for the organism to transform into a new structural form* (within which the control cycle becomes integrated). On the other hand, the dynamic stability of one cyclical control mechanism provides for the open-endedness of development of other parts of the organism. Within the same system, some parts (of the cyclically closed kind) support development in other (open) domains. Schematically, it could be depicted as in Figure 2.5.

In Figure 2.5 we can see a cyclical self-reproducing open system A–B–C, which reproduces itself only due to the regular supply of environmental input (External Impact X in the Figure). It produces, by way of by-products at each link (A→B, B→C, C→A), some regular results which exit from the system. In the case of the 'by-product W', the basis for novelty construction is created. Note that W in and by itself does not create that novelty, but only *potential* for its emergence. The actual basis for the emergence of novelty – within the same organism, but in a different location – would be some non-systematic External Impact Y that operates upon the domain where novelty can emerge (which is prepared by W).

This example will fit well with the notion of systemic causality (see Chapter 5). Here it is brought in as an example of how self-maintaining cyclical processes can open the system for specific novelty emergence, conjointly by its action and external impact. The openness for novelty emer-gence depends upon the stability of a working self-maintenance system.

Relevance of unstructured fields for development
Many psychological phenomena exist in a state of relative unstructuredness (see the 'domain for novelty' in Figure 2.5). The realm of human feelings 'is *kind of* known' to the feeler – but not immediately well-structured. The person solving a new problem operates in a field of '*kind of knowing*' how one could try to solve a problem – yet the ways to solve it are not fully known.

The fact of incompleteness of psychological phenomena is crucial for any developmental perspective. If there were no uncertainties within the phenomena, development (of novelty) would be impossible. These domains of uncertainty can be called unstructured fields which are open for further development.

EFFORTS TO DEFINE PSYCHOLOGICAL DEVELOPMENT

Defining development has not been an easy task for developmental psychologists. In the history of the discipline, it is Heinz Werner and Bernard Kaplan's 'orthogenetic principle' that

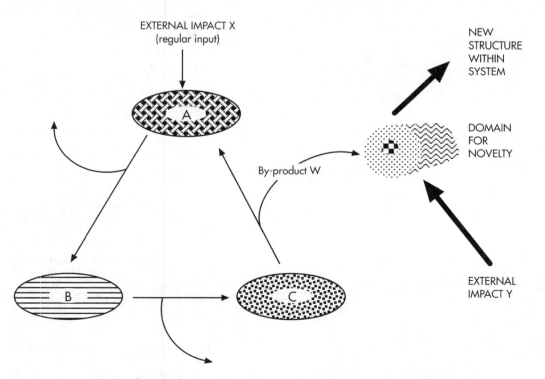

FIGURE 2.5 *An example of a cyclical system that produces novel growth*

can be taken as a general law of psychological development. It carries over ideas from the roots of developmental psychology in embryology (von Baer, 1828), yet it is formulated in reference to psychological development. In its original form, it reads:

> Developmental psychology postulates one regulative principle of development; it is an orthogenetic principle which states that *wherever development occurs it proceeds from a state of relative globality and lack of differentiation to a state of increasing **differentiation, articulation, and hierarchical integration***. (Werner, 1957, p. 126; added emphasis)

Werner's definition of development is classic. The three terms used to elaborate his point – differentiation, articulation and hierarchical integration – require clear understanding (see Figure 2.6).

Differentiation is the *process of emergence of structure within a previously unstructured field*. In a similar vein, it is a process of re-structuring of the previously structured field (see Figure 2.6 parts *A* and *B*, respectively). While differentiating, the emerging (or re-structuring) parts of the whole become *articulated* (take specific forms). Differentiation and articulation proceed together. Opposite processes to these are de-differentiation and disarticulation – which entail the disappearance of the structure and the emergence of an unstructured field.

Development entails *hierarchical integration* – the emergence of relationships between articulated parts of the structure in which generic dominance relations exist. From an articulated field of {A,B,C}, one of the elements becomes dominant over the others: {A} > {B,C}. Hierarchical integration means that developmental phenomena are multi-level emerged constructs, where some levels regulate others. As a result of Werner's definition of development, developmental science orients its interest on the emergence and functioning of regulatory systems that organize psychological phenomena. Hierarchically superior parts of the system regulate their inferior-status counterparts.

Werner's developmental theorizing included the definition of five genetic (that is, developmental) *levels of mentality* (Werner, 1948, p. 53). I here emphasize these levels as examples of the unity of opposites.

1 The syncretic/discrete opposition.
2 The diffuse/articulated opposition.
3 The indefinite/definite opposition.
4 The rigid/flexible opposition.
5 The labile/stable opposition.

Development is directional. All these conceptual opposites imply the existence of *direction of development*. Development is a process oriented between two anchor points – the point of origin, and the point of future orientation. In contemporary uses of dynamic systems notions for modelling development this Wernerian feature is encoded into the notion of *attractor point* (see Van Geert, 1994a) – a reference point in the future towards which the current formal model assumes that the developmental process strives.

The *syncretic* nature of psychological phenomena refers to their contents (or functional) state without differentiation. A dream image can contain several meanings which are maintained as separate in our waking lives. The fused meanings in the dream are an example of syncretic phenomena, while the waking-time distinction of the meanings refers to a differentiated (*discrete*) picture. The unstructured fields of phenomena (described above) are syncretic. We will return to the issues of syncretism in Chapter 12, describing how the social institutional canalization efforts in schooling operate upon the tendency towards differentiation – at times supporting it, at others maintaining the developing system at the level of syncretic organization.

The opposition *diffuse/articulated* was devised by Werner to refer to the *formal structure* of psychological phenomena, such as the forms of musical patterns, speech flow etc. For example, a moan 'oohhhhgrrrohwow' emitted by a human being is diffuse in its form, and becomes articulated if it is transformed into an utterance 'Oh! Wow!'.

A

B

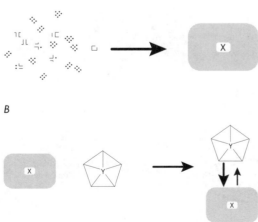

FIGURE 2.6 *Graphic depiction of Heinz Werner's notions of articulation (**A**) and hierarchical integration* **(B)**

The content/form distinction in the case of the first two oppositions allows for distinguishing of phenomena of syncretic meaning but distinct form (e.g., the word 'love' is distinct in its form, but syncretic in its meaning). Discrete meanings encoded in diffuse forms can be thought of in a similar vein (for example, the gender self-identity 'I am a man' can become encoded into diffuse forms of man-like style in actions of a mundane kind. The other two pairs – syncretic content and diffuse form, and discrete content and articulated form – are easily understandable within the general orthogenetic scheme (Figure 2.6).

Development entails hierarchization and subordination. The *rigid/flexible* opposition applies to this process – hierarchical organization is the basis for flexible (rather than rigid) behaviour. Flexibility guarantees plasticity. It also leads to stability (rather than to a labile state).

Probabilistic epigenesis as the basic developmental perspective

Werner and Kaplan's 'orthogenetic principle' is a general law of development. It is a developmental parallel – in its conceptual functions – to the basic non-developmental Gestalt laws.

As a general law, it does not provide any specificity to the question of *how the different levels of the hierarchy of the developing system relate* one to another. Different solutions can be offered – based on rigid causal linkages (for example, the higher levels of organization rigidly determine the events at lower levels) or on notions of interaction or transaction between the levels. Rigid causal subordination would not fit for any developmental system (as it rules out open-endedness of the production of novelty). In contrast, labels like 'interaction' or 'transaction' do not have explanatory value; they are too vague to lead to further enquiries.

Gilbert Gottlieb (1976, 1992, 1997) has developed a model of probabilistic epigenesis as a solution to the problem of relationships between levels of hierarch. His work has mostly been concerned with phylogenetic and ontogenetic issues of development, and he based his decades-long work on the early development of ducklings (described in detail in Gottlieb, 1997). In the theoretical domain, Gottlieb emphasizes the flexibility of the developmental processes by positing the existence of *bi-directional influences* between all the levels (see Figure 2.7).

The four levels of hierarchical integration – **environment**, **behaviour**, **neural activity** and **genetic activity** – are bi-directionally linked through probabilistic processes. Both the lower levels of the hierarchy (genetic activity, neural

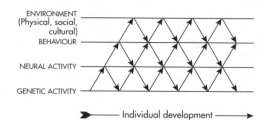

FIGURE 2.7 *Gilbert Gottlieb's general model of probabilistic epigenesis (from Gottlieb, 1992, p. 186. Reprinted by permission of Oxford University Press)*

activity) set up *possibilities* for the upper levels (behaviour, environmental impacts), and vice versa. The specific course of an organism's life course will be worked out through the probabilistic encounters between the different levels. Each of these encounters includes a starting state of *a field of variability*, from which new developmental forms emerge.

Central role of variability in developmental models

It follows – from the focus on novelty as central to development – that developmental perspectives treat variability of the phenomena as the centrally relevant starting data for their enquiries. Even in its minimal form – of two events, one growing out of the other, such as **a →A** (or **a becomes A**) – a direct comparison of **A** with **a** results in the detection of variability. Development can be described (in its outcomes) as constant increase of the variability over time. This claim, of course, is wrong: it assumes that the previously emerged forms remain actual over time (rather than disappear), which would entail a reverse process of reduction of variability – simultaneously with its growth through novelty. A more adequate claim would be that development entails constant modification of the range of variability of the phenomena that the developing organism can display at any next moment – inventing new versions of conduct and 'dropping off' others.

Curiously, the centrality of variability has not been widely recognized in developmental psychology. Under the influence of non-developmental theoretical orientations, child psychologists, instead of retaining a consistently developmental focus (with concentration on variability), have found ways to get rid of variability (see Fischer and Bidell, 1997; Valsiner, 1984 for further analysis of treatment of variability).

However, when consistently developmental questions – about emergence processes – are asked, the focus on variability returns to psychological research. This has been observed in cognitive (Fischer and Bidell, 1997; Siegler, 1996) as well as sociocultural domains of psychology (Valsiner, 1997). The focus on variability leads to new methodological elaborations (which will be described in Chapter 5).

Unity in multiplicity of developmental trajectories
In Chapter 1, the notion of multilinearity of development was charted out. Yet in this chapter it is the universality of general laws of development that has been emphasized. How would these two orientations – towards universal laws and multiplicity of trajectories of development – fit together? Clearly the 'orthogenetic principle' and Gottlieb's law of probabilistic epigenesis are examples of universal linear tendencies that are expected to be true for each and every developing organism. Yet it is obvious that actual courses of development are variable – in fact, unique for every individual organism.

The unilinearity of general laws of development and multilinearity of actual individual courses of development are not contradictions. The general laws are *abstract principles* that are precisely ready to cater for a multiplicity of particular courses of development. For example, the 'orthogenetic principle' posited the general course of development (towards growth of hierarchical organization). Within that general direction each and every individual organism – as long as it develops – produces its own unique trajectory of development. Yet all these unique trajectories observe the general law of development.

Contemporary possibilities of computer modelling allow researchers to chart out families of individual developmental trajectories that fulfil the general laws of development, while they need not be observed in empirical practice. This opens up possibilities for experimental theoretical psychology (Van Geert, 1994a), formulating precise (mathematical) models of development in their abstract forms, and then using computer-simulated production of all possible developmental trajectories as the data to evaluate the adequacy of such generalizations. Paul Van Geert has demonstrated that a variable set of developmental trajectories – depending upon the particular input parameters – can be generated on the basis of the same abstract algorithm of unfolding development (Van Geert, 1994b).

SUMMARY

The contrasts between developmental and non-developmental perspectives in psychology need to be charted out in general, and with intellectual precision. This was the aim of this chapter. Study of organisms in their periods of intense development – such as study of infants or adolescents – is not necessarily developmental simply because the targets of the research effort – the children – are undergoing development. Instead, it is the researchers' ways of creating their basic research questions that make a study of any target organism, be this a child, adult, or animal, developmental (or not).

Despite the relative rarity of developmental perspectives in contemporary psychology, that general perspective has had a prominent intellectual past in the history of psychology and related sciences. In Chapter 3, some key historically relevant thought systems will be analysed. For the present coverage I select from among the many some who worked at the intersection of developmental and cultural psychologies. Their work is recognized in contemporary developmental psychology – but only partially. A re-analysis of the ideas of the 'giants' of the past, on whose shoulders we all seem comfortably to ride, may lead us towards generating gigantic breakthroughs in our own times.

REVIEW QUESTIONS FOR CHAPTER 2

1 Explain the notion of novelty. How can one detect novelty?

2 What are the differences between two levels of novelty: personal and comparative–collective?

3 Why is novelty a 'conservative phenomenon'?

4 Why are general laws important for a science?

5 Explain the *axiom of identity*. Why is the identity axiom at the centre of non-developmental perspectives?

6 Explain the axiom of *becoming and dynamic self-maintenance*.

7 What is the difference between identity and self-maintenance?

8 Explain the meaning of transitive and intransitive hierarchies.

9 Describe Krebs' cycle, and explain its theoretical relevance.

10 Why are unstructured fields relevant for development?

11 Describe Werner and Kaplan's *orthogenetic principle* and explain its component terms: *differentiation, articulation* and *hierarchical integration*.

12 Explain the *syncretic < > discrete* opposition as relevant for development.

13 Describe Gottlieb's model of *probabilistic epigenesis*.

14 Why is a focus on variability of relevance to developmental perspectives?

15 How do you understand the notion of general abstract unity within the diversity of developmental trajectories?

3

THEORETICAL BASES OF DEVELOPMENTAL AND CULTURAL PSYCHOLOGY

Theories are the central focus of any science. Most of the theories may be proved wrong, or abandoned, in the course of time, yet during their use they give direction to the empirical research efforts of scientists. As was clear in the previous chapter, the developmental perspective is rooted in embryology – the science of development of the embryo. It was begun by Karl Ernst von Baer in 1828. Embryology is a central part of developmental biology. The generic 'orthogenetic principle' of Heinz Werner and Bernard Kaplan (presented in Chapter 2) is a twentieth century synthesis of the embryological thought of the nineteenth century.

A number of seminal thinkers have played a role in the history of developmental and cultural psychologies. Researchers from both Europe and North America were equally prominent in setting up the new perspective. Science knows no national boundaries; it entails a worldwide community of scholars who try to solve the same problems. The Americans James Mark Baldwin and George Herbert Mead, the German sociologist Georg Simmel, and the Russian scholars – Lev Vygotsky and Mikhail Bakhtin were the forerunners of our contemporary interest in cultural psychology. Many of their ideas are nowadays found to be 'well ahead their time', as in our contemporary psychology we are only beginning to re-discover them. This of course indicates that psychology – like any other science – develops in a non-linear fashion. It is not automatic that progress in every new decade – for example, the 1990s as compared to 1980s, or 1970s – is of the kind that surpasses that of previous decades. Sciences – much like people – can enter into investigation directions that turn out to be 'dead-end streets'. Yet research in these directions can continue for a long time, and defend itself against being considered as an unproductive development.

Profound development in any science depends upon the invention of basic (core) new ideas, and their productive use in empirical practices. This makes theoretical innovation the core of any science. Yet invention of new theoretical constructs is not sufficient – the new ideas need to translate into new empirical practices. How that is done in cultural psychology will be discussed in Chapter 5. In this chapter, I will overview the basic contributions of selected thinkers of the past. This selection is not meant to single them out at the expense of many others whose thinking has contributed to the intellectual basis for contemporary cultural psychology.

THE ROLE OF JAMES MARK BALDWIN

James Mark Baldwin (1861–1934) was one of the crucial contributors to both the developmental science and socio-cultural perspective in psychology. Besides, his impact was profound in biology – he was a co-inventor of the 'theory of organic selection' in 1896 (together with Henry Osborn and C. Lloyd Morgan). The ideas on which that theory is based originated in his observations on developmental issues – his daughters' motor development in infancy. This is one of the rare occasions where intellectual productivity in the domain of psychology has proved crucial for other sciences. It is usually the case that ideas from other sciences are taken over in psychology, often in ways that resemble 'cargo cults' of traditional societies.[1]

Like many American men of the 1880s who later became psychologists, Baldwin at one time was not far away from ending up with a career as a clergyman. Serious study of psychology in those days entailed an education in Germany (and in German), where psychology had established itself as a science separate from philosophy and physiology. Yet that separation did not to create a large divide between psychology and philosophy; from the time of the first professorship dedicated to questions of psychology in 1860 until the 1920s, psychologists in Germany were expected to be competent in teaching both philosophy and psychology. This guaranteed that the new discipline of psychology addressed issues of basic psychological processes – of human behaviour, perceiving, thinking, memorizing, language, religiosity etc. – rather than becoming decimated in the service of applied concerns. Psychology could develop in the context of basic science concerns. In no science can successful applications drive scientific discoveries, and psychology is no exception.

Baldwin spent the years 1884–5 at three different universities in Germany. He returned to the United States in 1886, and held a sequence of university positions in the USA and Canada. After being forced out from US academia, he spent a few years in Mexico City where he led the establishment of a psychology department at the Universidad Autonoma de Mexico. Baldwin then emigrated to France, where he remained intellectually and socially active until the end of his life (1934). Yet his contributions to psychology ended with the First World War – after 1915 he did not publish any new work on psychology.

Baldwin's theoretical ideas

All of Baldwin's ideas were oriented towards understanding the process of development. The task was huge, and Baldwin was ambitious. Aside from that, he was intelligent – a property that rarely fails to arouse jealousies among other academics. His efforts to build a comprehensive system of 'logic of development' (he called it 'genetic logic') has been found hard-going by psychologists in the decades that followed, and this work has largely been overlooked. Baldwin was in the habit of inventing new terminology, which was not a favoured step with his readers.

Basic mechanism: circular reaction

For Baldwin, the crucial mechanism of development was *circular reaction*. This is a reaction by the organism to some environmental input which introduces a novel moment into the world. In our contemporary terminology, circular *re*-action is simultaneously *pro*-action – the organism acts in response to some stimulus not to adapt to that stimulus, but with anticipation of the immediate next possible events. This action changes the environment, which then provides the organism with an altered stimulus, to which the organism provides another new way of acting. The circular reaction process produces novel forms of action (see Figure 3.1).

The circular reaction results in overproduction of a variety of novel forms of action – yet *within the range of nearness* to the previously used ones. Some of these innovations survive, others disappear. The organism is constantly creating novel versions of conduct. In a way, Baldwin believed in the constant creativity of biological organisms.

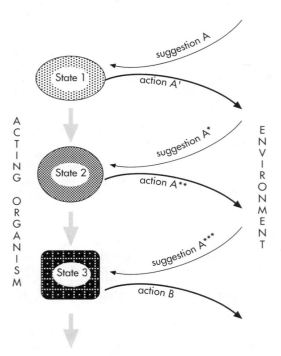

FIGURE 3.1 *The notion of circular reaction in Baldwin's theory*

Forms of imitation

The organism's world provides many examples that can be used for action. The notion of circular reaction implies that mere direct copying of externally given models would be a very impoverished notion of imitation. Baldwin distinguished two kinds of imitation: the first of which ('imitative suggestion') could be subsumed under the common language notion of 'imitation', whereas the other ('persistent imitation') is actually a form of constructive experimentation (through the use of circular reaction).

Imitative suggestion is the process through which the organism, from one trial to the next, moves towards the increasingly model-like nature of imitations of a given model. For example, the child attempts to imitate a word, and step by step these imitation efforts approach similarity with the model. Yet imitative suggestion is a constructive – not replication – process. At times, the previous result of imitation becomes the model: for example, a child imitates a word, gets it wrong, but continues to imitate the wrong model (now resulting from the child's own imitation). In any case, the imitative suggestion can result, at its maximum effect, in the creation of an exact replica of the model. Imitation at most leads to faithful replication of the model; and at least to incomplete imitation. Going beyond the model is not possible within the framework of imitative suggestion.

Persistent imitation is the process of constant creation of novelty in the process of imitating a model. Here the imitation is actually re-construction of the model in new ways (hence, it can be called 'imitation beyond 100 per cent of the model'). The encounter with a suggested model triggers the process of circular reaction, which leads to constant creation of novel versions of the model by the imitating person. The results are not 'copies' of the model, but creative reconstructions. They are – in terms of art or music – variations on the theme given by the model.

Both imitative suggestion and persistent imitation exist in human development. They are most evident in the process of play. In human life, there are situations in which precise copying of the models is crucial, and others in which the models need to be creatively transcended.

Play as crucial process

The notion of play is one of such general meaning that people use it in various ways. The usual common language use of this word contrasts it with 'work' and sets these two up as irreconcilable opposites ('play' is not 'work' and 'work' is not 'play'). Baldwin's writing about play does *not* follow this generalized meaning. Instead, 'play' in his understanding is the general process of creating novelty – and thus is part and parcel of persistent imitation.

Consistent with the rest of Baldwin's viewpoint, the person is capable of the intra-personal selection of ideas by way of playful – creative – application of knowledge to new experiential contexts that are characterized by uncertainty (and heterogeneity). Hence,

> The instrumental meaning is always and everywhere *a re-reading imaginatively, purposefully, personally of an actual or truthful meaning*, and the truthful reading is always and everywhere *a re-reading as common, stereotyped, actual of an imaginative personal construction . . . We make-believe in order that we may believe!* (Baldwin, 1908, pp. 183–184; original emphasis)

Here is the crucial developmental moment in Baldwin's psychology of play: the playing child operates in the 'make-believe' world, and through operating in it, turns it into the next step of reality in his or her development. It is through play that the person 'rises above' his or her current capacities, and constructs novel ones. This very idea was the cornerstone for Lev Vygotsky's focus on the *zone of proximal development* (see below). For Baldwin, the constant process of 'make-believe' carries the function of developing the new state of the developing person (who begins to 'believe'). The person creates his or her desired – not yet existing – image of what they want to happen, and then creates the conditions that lead it to become reality. Even if the latter happens in a form different from the imagined hope, it is nevertheless based on the original move of 'make-believe'.

Baldwin saw important parallels between play and art – both, in their own ways, would operate to maintain and develop the psychological system of the person. That system is constantly in movement – it distances the person from some domains of life, brings him or her closer to others, creates new personal constructions (including those of pathological extremes). The psychological system of a person is an open system in its constant creation of novelty.

Baldwin's empirical examples were obtained from his daughters' make-believe play, like the following:

> On May, 2 I was sitting on the porch alone with the children . . . aged respectively four and a half and two and a half years. Helen, the elder, told Elizabeth that she was her little baby; that is, Helen became 'mama' and Elizabeth 'baby.' The younger responded by calling her sister 'mama,' and the play began.
>
> "You have been asleep, baby. Now it is time to get up," said mama. Baby rose from the floor, – first falling down in order to raise, – was seized upon by "mama," taken to the railing to an imaginary washstand, and her face washed by rubbing. Her articles of clothing were then named in imagination, and put on, one by one, in the most detailed and interesting fashion. During all this "mama" kept up a stream of baby talk to her infant: "Now your stockings, my darling; now your skirt, sweetness – or, no – not yet – your shoes first," etc. etc. Baby acceded to all the details with more than the docility which real infants usually show. When this was done, "Now we must go tell papa good-morning, dearie," said mama. "Yes, mama," came the reply; and hand in hand they started to find papa. I, the spectator, carefully read my newspaper, thinking, however, that the reality of papa, seeing that he was so much in evidence, would break upon the imagined situation. But not so.

Mama led her baby directly past me to the end of the piazza, to a column in the corner. "There's papa," said mama; "now tell him good-morning." – "Good-morning, papa; I am very well," said baby, bowing low to the column. "That's good," said mama in a *gruff, low voice*, which caused in the real papa a thrill of amused self-consciousness most difficult to contain. "Now you must have your breakfast," said mama. The seat of a chair was made a breakfast-table, the baby's feigned bib put on, and her porridge carefully administered, with all the manner of the nurse who usually directs their breakfast. "Now" (after the meal, which suddenly became dinner instead of breakfast) "you must take your nap," said mama. "No, mama; I don't want to," said baby. "But you must." – "No; you be baby, and take the nap." – "But all the other children have gone to sleep, dearest, *and the doctor says you must*," said mama. This convinced baby, and she lay down on the floor. "But I haven't undressed you." So then came all the detail of undressing; and mama carefully covered her up on the floor with a light shawl, saying, "Spring is coming now; that'll be enough. Now shut your eyes, and go to sleep." – "But you haven't kissed me, mama," said the little one. "Oh, of course, my darling!" – so a long siege of kissing. Then the baby closed her eyes very tight, while mama went on tip-toe away to the end of the porch. "Don't go away, mama," said baby. "No; mama wouldn't leave her darling," came the reply. (Baldwin, 1895, pp. 362–363; original emphasis)

Being ignored – even by one's own children – is a creative challenge to a psychologist. The open-endedness of human constructive play provides the basis for resilience in adaptation to very difficult life circumstances, precisely when it is important to overcome previous fixed social role relations. Play unifies what is, and what is desired to be. In children's role-play the 'inner' (memory-based) experiences are brought together with the present external situation. The constructive nature of imitation takes the form of a trans-formation of immediately available objects into functionally different ones (even against the odds of availability of the real ones; for example, making the column into 'papa', instead of making use of the readily available real specimen).

Furthermore, the roles in play can be changed at every moment. This freedom of reconstruction guarantees the developing person flexibility for further development, under unpredictable circumstances. Yet, there exist limits to the con-structive nature of play: some aspects of the 'outer' reality can be made into insurmountable obstacles for functional re-definition (for example, one of Baldwin's daughters saying to the other 'You cannot be an earthworm, you have too many legs', Baldwin, 1906, p. 114).

The psychologist's contribution to evolutionary theory

Usually, it is the case that psychology imports ideas from other sciences, rather than provides these other sciences with fruitful ideas. Baldwin's notion of construction and overproduction of novel behavioural forms, with subsequent selec-tion process of some of these forms to be main-tained, was Baldwin's contribution to evolutionary theory (his notion of 'organic selection').

The question at stake is that of the raw material for selection. The Darwinian evolutionary idea emphasizes the notion of selection, but does not elaborate about how whatever ends up being selected emerges in the first place. Hence the Darwinian idea can explain the results of devel-opment only after these results have emerged. Selection explains how what already has emerged could have come into being. It cannot explain future development, because in order to be selected among others, more than one version of new forms has to emerge. The Darwinian evolu-tionary perspective is built on the explanation of *past* → *present* transitions, treating the present versions of phenomena as proven success ('best fit') of the selection process.

In contrast, an explanatory perspective that emphasizes *present* → *future* transitions is neces-sary. Baldwin's solution was to devise a future-oriented (feed-forward) model of construction of novelty on the basis of the environmental input. Baldwin focused on the process of construction of novel forms (through the notion of circular reaction), which serve as bases for selection. Through the circular reaction, the organism constantly creates new forms of acting, on the basis of the previous feedback about previous actions. The feed-forward notion is necessary for the recognition that organisms adapt not to the given conditions as those exist at the moment, but *anticipate future changes*. They pre-adapt to the expected changes in the environment by attempting to bring about some desired changes themselves.

Heterogeneity of experiences

Baldwin was one of the first developmental scientists to understand the theoretical dangers of viewing the organism's environment in terms of its static features. The world of the developing person is variable. That variability takes realistic forms – which are due to social interaction. As Baldwin noticed:

the child begins to learn in addition the fact that persons are in a measure individual in their treatment of him, and hence that individuality has elements of uncertainty or *irregularity* about it. This growing sense is very clear to one who watches an infant in its second half-year. Sometimes the mother gives a biscuit, but sometimes she does not. Sometimes the father smiles and tosses the child; sometimes he does not. And the child looks for signs of these varying moods and methods of treatment. Its new pains of disappointment arise directly on the basis of that former sense of regular personal presence upon which its expectancy went forth. (Baldwin, 1894b, p. 277)

From such heterogeneity of the person's social environment follows the need for selective treatment of that heterogeneity by the person. The person – in order to handle the heterogeneity – creates a static template (a 'schema') that is expected to inform him or her about expected future events. The previously established 'schema' allows the person to become selective as to the variety of actual present environmental inputs.

According to Baldwin, the person makes use of the social experiences and creates his or her own self:

The individual becomes a law unto himself, exercises his private judgment, fights his own battles for truth, shows the virtue of independence and the vice of obstinacy. But he has learned to do it by the selective control of his social environment, *and in this judgment he has just a sense of this social outcome.* (Baldwin, 1898, pp. 19–20; original emphasis)

The social control, previously executed by other persons, gradually becomes reconstructed by the person oneself. This personal autonomy – the person is the agent, the instigator, of his or her own action – is a result of the social process of development (Baldwin, above: '*in this judgment he has just a sense of this social outcome*').

It is obvious that the social nature of a person is expressed in his or her personal individuality. That individuality becomes differentiated from its social roots, and acquires relative autonomy. Mere slavish mirroring of the social world is rendered impossible already because of the heterogeneity of the latter. To cope with it, there is the need for 'systematic determination' of the new knowledge by way of *internalized* selection mechanisms that operate within mental processes – or within cognitive schemata. For Baldwin, there was no need to insist upon the separate domains of 'cognition' and 'sociality' (as we often see in the 1990s). He saw both of these as part of the process of the feedback/feed-forward loop in the relation of person and environment. The heterogeneity of the socially mediated environmental input leads to the establishment of 'cognitive schemas', which in their turn guide the person's acting upon the environment towards more variability, through novel action.

The latter again feeds back to the person. Both the environment and the person become increasingly unique.

When viewed within the inter-individual frame of reference, the world of persons is that of a heterogeneous collection of unique personal adaptations to the heterogeneous environment. Human individuality and uniqueness are the logical outcomes from Baldwin's developmental model of person < > environment relations (refer back to the notion of bi-directional culture transfer in Chapter 2).

Particularization and generalization
But how can anything general be said about phenomena that not only are highly variable, but are involved in constant construction of further variability? It is precisely such proliferation of particulars that creates the necessity for the emergence of means of psychological organization. It can be argued that the semiotic capacities of human beings must have emerged as a necessity to cope with the ever-increasing unpredictability of the environment – including here the social environment of peers.

Baldwin saw the person < > society relationships as a process of *particularization* of general meanings by persons in specific contexts on the one hand, and *generalization* (of persons' thought variations by society) on the other. Society is thus a complex of various particularizations of general meanings by concrete individuals, and institutionalized generalizations of some of the ideas of some individuals. A person who uses general ideas accepted in a given society (for example, 'fairness') would situate the general idea in a particular context (for example, '*It is not fair that* X [where X = 'I got a B in my exam', 'I am so fat', 'my mother does not understand me' etc.]). Each of these particularizations works (simultaneously) in the direction of generalization, by modifying the generalized meaning (of the notion 'fair' etc.).

Sembling (empathy)
The topic of empathy has been of some use in contemporary psychology – yet its historical roots are usually underemphasized. Baldwin played a central role in the translation of the German concept (*Einfühlung*, mostly theorized by Theodor Lipps) into the English-language psychological literature. Baldwin translated it as *sembling* – in line with his own ideas of persistent imitation (Baldwin, 1906, p. 122: 'to semble' = to make like by imitation). In later decades the competing translation (suggested by E.B. Titchener and J. Ward) of that concept – *empathy* – has become accepted in psychology. Yet the term has been imprecisely used.

For Baldwin, the process of *sembling*

consists in the *reading-into the object of a sort of psychic life of its own*, in such a way that the movement, act, or character by which it is interpreted *is thought of as springing from its own inner life*. (Baldwin, 1906, p. 124; added emphasis)

Sembling thus entails projection upon one another of the oppositions that persist within one's own 'inner' < > 'outer' relationships, as those are construed within the mind's 'inner imitation'. It was claimed to be present in both play and art. Thus, the self *'sembles itself'* – a person is constantly projecting into him/herself some characteristics which subsequently develop in him/herself. Again, we can observe Baldwin's scheme of 'circular reaction' in place – in the process of self-sembling. In their development, the child takes on new roles, attaches their personal understanding to their external demands, and that leads to further development of the self.

Sembling is based on imagination, which is oriented towards possible future events and is viewed by Baldwin in his characteristic prospective way, emphasizing directedness towards ideal goals:

the sort of meaning known as ideal, due to an imaginative *feeling-forward*, has an essential place in the development of the affective life. The entire movement of cognition and feeling alike has not only the interest and intent to conserve its data and preserve its habits, but also the interest and intent to achieve, to learn, to adapt, to acquire, to *feel-forward*. (Baldwin, 1911, p. 125; original emphasis)

Baldwin's 'genetic logic'
Psychology has been in a methodological crisis ever since its establishment as a separate social institution. It is particularly the study of development, that is, the investigation of real (but yet – at the given time – ephemeral) emerging phenomena, that brings to the attention of developmental scientists the full extent of that crisis. It was clear to Baldwin that developmental science (or, as he termed it, 'genetic science') could not develop using the inferential tools of non-developmental sciences. He understood the futility of the acceptance of quantitative methodology in psychology. This perspective – if viewed from the standard accepted position in the 1990s – seems a complete heresy in science. Yet, Baldwin explained it by pointing to the specific nature of developmental phenomena:

The . . . quantitative method, brought over into psychology from the exact sciences, physics and chemistry, must be discarded; *for its ideal consisted in*

reducing the more complex to the more simple, the whole into its parts, the later-evolved to the earlier-existent, thus denying or eliminating just the factor which constituted or revealed what was truly genetic. Newer modes of manifestation cannot be stated in atomic terms without doing violence to the more synthetic modes which observation reveals. (Baldwin, 1930, p. 7; added emphasis)

As can be seen, Baldwin's rejection of quantification in psychology is based on the recognition that (a) psychological phenomena have multi-level intra-systemic organization, and (b) these complex phenomena give rise to new ones. In such a case, any effort to classify parts of the complex phenomena (or even the whole phenomenon) and subject the resulting classification to quantitative data accumulation would amount to missing the point of scientific analysis.

Baldwin's postulates of method
On the positive side, Baldwin specified two 'postulates of method'. The first (or 'negative') postulate emphasized the irreversibility of time in development:

the logic of development is *not* expressed in convertible propositions. (Baldwin, 1906, p. 21)

A convertible proposition is of the form

$$\{A <relates with> B\} = \{B <relates with> A\}$$

In contrast, Baldwin's notion implies that development cannot be expressed in such terms, because the inclusion of irreversible time renders such convertibility impossible:

$$\{A < relates with> B\} \textbf{ is not equal to}$$
$$\{B < relates with> A\}$$

In developmental analysis, the *'relates with'* is replaced by *'becomes'*:

$$\{A < becomes> B\} \textbf{ is not equal to}$$
$$\{B < becomes> A\}$$

Baldwin's first postulate specifies the realm of possible relations that are allowable among the formulae of 'genetic logic'. Each proposition includes a temporal directionality vector. Thus, the reversal B becoming A is *not* implied by the notion of A becoming B.

This notion is of revolutionary implication for developmental sciences. It *undermines the notion of reversibility*. In the case of developmental processes (see Chapter 1) that take place within irreversible time, reversals are not possible. Furthermore, categorization of observable objects without consideration of their time 'location' is not possible. For example, our usual tendency is to divide a time series:

$$A \rightarrow B \rightarrow C \rightarrow D$$

into categories A, B, C, D, and assume that these categories of detected items are *independent of one another*. Baldwin's developmental logic undermines that latter assumption, as it indicates that B is an 'outgrowth' from A, C from B, and D from C. There is no independence possible – instead, we have an organic series of transformations which needs investigation.

How could such analysis proceed? Baldwin located the place for such analysis in *the looking at the prospective progression*, rather than in prediction or *post factum* explanation. Thus, his second (so-called 'positive') postulate claimed:

> that series of events is truly genetic which cannot be constructed before it has happened, and which cannot be exhausted backwards, after it has happened. (Baldwin, 1906, p. 21)

The 'positive' nature of this postulate is in its focusing of the study of development on the *unfolding novel processes*, rather than their prediction, or retrospective explanation. The phenomena of *emergence*, *becoming* and *transformation* become the objects of investigation. Such investigation would entail *preserving the irreversible time sequence* in the data.

Pancalism (aesthetic synthesis)

Baldwin's final synthetic solution to the problem of the social nature of human psychological functions took the form of an aesthetic synthesis. He labelled this focus 'pancalism', or 'constructive affectivism', as it was claimed to unite aesthetic feeling with a distanced view of the object. Aesthetic synthesis entails retaining the object–subject differentiation (that is, the subject does not 'fuse' themself with the object), yet it simultaneously entails the emergence of a novel feeling that overwhelms the subject. In Baldwin's terms:

> What we are justified in taking the real to be is that with which the free and full aesthetic and artistic consciousness finds itself satisfied. *We realize the real in achieving and enjoying the beautiful.* (Baldwin, 1915, pp. 276–277; original emphasis)

In aesthetic experience, *the singular event* – a person's encounter with a particular art object in a here-and-now situation – *becomes generalized by the person to represent something at the level of great abstraction*. The aesthetically operating person relates to the object in terms that are generic, even

as the actual encounter is not different from a mundane one. For example, an external observer watching a person who faces a well-known painting with admiration, and another observer who enjoys to look at a mountain forest turned yellow in the autumn; or a couple enjoying making love – are all involved in a generalized aesthetic experience. Their deep feelings are arriving at a synthesis of lived-through beauty, which would be of importance for them in their further construction of life course. The results of such aesthetic synthesis become internalized sources of motivation. Baldwin arrived at the idea of aesthetic synthesis by the end of his career. Some years later, the young Lev Vygotsky started his interest in psychology from the question of aesthetic feelings.

GEORG SIMMEL'S SOCIOLOGY OF TENSION WITHIN THE SYSTEM

The irony of intellectual history in sciences is that most creative scientists are not recognized as such in their lifetime and in their own country. Georg Simmel is certainly a good case. Recognized in our time as one of the classic sociologists of the turn of the century, and well known in American sociology at that time, he was little known (or appreciated) in his native Germany. He lived in Berlin for most of his life (1858–1918) and could not gain academic recognition for his perceptive sociological essays.

Simmel worked on many sociological issues, of which some are relevant for the history of cultural psychology. First, his *subjective* versus *objective culture* distinction (Simmel, 1908; in English, Simmel, 1971) is a forerunner of the personal versus collective culture notions exemplified in this book. Furthermore, Simmel demonstrated the unity of conflict and non-conflict in human social lives, and the relevance of secrecy in social and personal psychological phenomena.

Subjective and objective culture

In the developmental opposition of nature and culture, the nature 'signifies a particular phase in the development of a subject – namely the phase in which it enfolds its own potential and which ends as soon as a more intelligent and purposive will takes over these forces and thereby brings the subject to a condition which it could not reach by itself' (Simmel, 1971, p. 228).

The act of cultural changing of nature – the unfolding of the natural developmental potential – is that of *cultivation* (see also Chapter 4 – Figure 4.1). For Simmel, 'cultivation is not merely the development of a being beyond the morphological state attainable through nature alone, but development in the direction of an original inner core, a fulfillment of this being according to the law of its own meaning, its deepest disposition' (Simmel, 1971, p. 229).

This unity of outer and inner development resonates with the ideas of George H. Mead (see below). Culture exists only if a person – as a human being – draws into their development something that is external to them. This possibility requires recognition of the distinction between the internal and the external, and the treatment of the other (that is, of the external by the internal, and of the internal by the external) as an object of goal-oriented actions.

Culture is created by human beings through the use of purposefully constructed objects. This entails teleological – goal-directed and intentional – interweaving of the subject and the object. From here comes the distinction of the subjective and objective cultures:

The term 'objective culture' can be used to designate things in that state of elaboration, development, and perfection which leads the psyche to its own fulfillment or indicates the path to be traversed by individuals or collectivities on the way to a heightened existence. By subjective culture I mean the measure of development thus attained. (Simmel, 1971, p. 233)

This general explanation of two cultures can be simplified if one considers the similar concepts of collective and personal cultures (Chapter 2). The person's 'socialized being' is partly determined by its opposite – the 'non-socialized being' (Simmel, 1910, pp. 381–382). The person develops through constant opposition and unity of the subjective and objective cultures – the person is constantly *at some generalized psychological distance* from the social other, striving to diminish the distance simultaneously with the tendency to increase the distance. Simmel's views are close to George H. Mead's later development of the notion of 'the generalized other'.

The cultural relevance of secrecy

From his duality of cultures' – objective and subjective – perspective, Simmel could appreciate the role of *purposefully maintained social and psychological distance* between persons. In everyday language, this takes the form of secrecy – persons hiding from others some aspects of their personal (or institutional) information. The history of human societies is filled with the establishment of secret societies; human interpersonal relationships are similarly filled with efforts to make secrets, keep secrets, persuade others about a secret not to be revealed (so that the others would do precisely that!), and so

on. The social and psychological phenomena of secrecy are profound, highly variable, and recurrent. Secrecy is not a phenomenon of an 'abnormal' kind – practised by persons who have accomplished something socially or morally deplorable – but a perfectly normal inter- and intra-personal psychological phenomenon. In fact, its absence can be viewed as pathological. It could indicate lack of structuring of human personality – the personality would lack the super-ordinate structure of flexible self-presentation dependent upon the needs of the given context. Only fools (and some presidents) are expected to reveal 'the truth' all of the time!

From Simmel's perspective, the invention of the act of making and keeping secrets is 'one of the greatest accomplishments of humanity', since

Secrecy secures . . . the possibility of a second world alongside of the obvious world, and the latter is most strenuously affected by the former. Every relationship between two individuals or two groups will be characterized by the ratio of secrecy that is involved in it. Even when one of the parties does not notice the secret factor, yet the attitude of the concealer, and consequently the whole relationship, will be modified by it. (Simmel, 1906, p. 462)

Secrecy is a universal sociological form, which has nothing to do with the moral valuation of its contents. Personal secrecy is of central relevance in adolescence (see Chapter 13). Maintaining secrecy about different issues in gender relations (see Chapter 7) or adults–children relations is a major way of creating both social distinctions and pathways for overcoming these distinctions. Secret organizations exist in many societies, but by way of some persons becoming members of such societies, the secrecy becomes selectively unveiled. Those who are initiated into the secrets of the 'secret society' become its members who know the secrets, and are expected to uphold the secrecy. Yet these very same persons are in a position of power in that they can reveal the secrets. Secrets cannot exist without keepers/revealers – that is, without persons who can dismantle the secrets by revealing them.

The proof of the dynamics of keeping and revealing secrets is the activity of flirtation, and in the cultural history of clothing human bodies. The basic need for clothing (thermoregulation of the body) has been turned into the cultural process of *hiding and revealing the body simultaneously* (see Chapter 7 for more elaborate discussion). Simmel pointed to this duality of unified opposites:

By ornamenting ourselves or part of ourselves, we conceal what is adorned. And by concealing it, we draw attention to it and its attractions. This could be called an optical necessity which incorporates the simultaneity of consent and refusal – the formula of all flirtation – into the first stage of clothing as well. (Simmel, 1984, p. 137)

The simultaneous functioning of opposite processes within the same whole is the core of Simmel's theoretical construction. The dynamics of hiding and revealing – in clothing, in flirtatious behaviour, in the relations of the public and private domains of human activities – are all built upon the assumption of intermediate distance between the self and the other. The self is always removed (distanced) from oneself in the direction of relating to the other, yet the other – from that intermediate distance – is not the self. The other directs the self to look back at oneself from that intermediate position (see Figure 3.2).

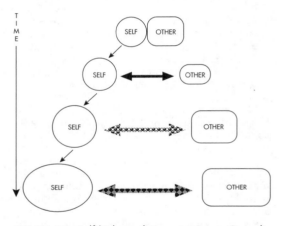

FIGURE 3.2 *Self/Other relations in Georg Simmel's theoretical system*

The person constantly distances oneself from the self as it is, in some direction of the other. The other can become a valued goal in itself – orientation towards money can be the maximum distancing direction constructed by human beings (Simmel, 1990). Yet the process of such distancing is always ambivalent – with united opposites in conflict, creating ambivalent patterns of temporary dominance of one over the other, reversals of such dominance, and the feeling of 'generalized distancing'.

The relevance of conflict

In line with the notion of the unity of opposites, Simmel's treatment of conflict allows for new insights into social and psychological regulation. The usually valued state of human being – that of stable harmony – is actually a state of dynamic

stability based on the work of mutually opposite processes. Contradiction and strife are present at any moment of life – thus behind any stable state of 'harmony' is actually a balance of intertwined contradictory processes. Thus, at every time period of peace in a society, processes that make wars possible are co-present with those that maintain the peace (Simmel, 1904, p. 799). Likewise, in times of war, social processes that can produce peace are functioning in a sub-dominant way. Hence societies can move between war and peace with remarkable ease. In Simmel's terms,

The end of peace is . . . not distinguished by a special sociological situation, but rather out of some sort of real relationships within a peaceful condition antagonism is developed immediately, if not at once in its most visible and energetic form. The case is different, however, in the reverse direction. Peace does not attach itself so immediately to struggle. The termination of strife is a special undertaking . . .

The particular motive which in most cases corresponds with the transition from war to peace is the simple longing for peace. With the emergence of this factor there comes into being . . . peace itself, at first in the form of the wish immediately parallel with the struggle itself, and it may without special transitional form displace struggle. (Simmel, 1904, p. 800)

Simmel's analysis of transitions from peace to war, and from war to peace, are examples of his general scheme of the person (or a society) always being different from itself in relation to its opposite partner, the other (Figure 3.2, above). In the state of war, or conflict, the other is the state of peace; the warring sides become oriented towards the peace while the war continues.

The crucial point for Simmel was the unity of opposites within the same whole. Simmel's perspective is *systemic* and *dynamic*. It was influential in the beginning decades of sociology in the United States, and was largely forgotten in Germany.

GEORGE HERBERT MEAD'S UNITY OF THE PERSONAL AND THE SOCIAL

George Mead was born in 1863 in Massachusetts, into the family of a Puritan minister. His father's academic activities (at Oberlin Theological Seminary) meant George's home was filled with classics of literature, philosophy and theology, George himself was able to observe his parents engaged in intellectual debates. Both parents provided George with an environment that was conducive to religious academic growth, both at home and associated with the life of the college.

George entered Oberlin College in 1879, taking an interest in philosophy, but he found himself at odds with the ways in which philosophy was taught. The young Mead was exposed to a selection of English psychology and Scottish philosophy. The social context of Oberlin was aimed at the appropriation of Puritan theological views; questioning of basic values was discouraged, and 'the right ways' were expected to be well internalized. Yet these 'right ways' were not necessarily those of the main tendencies within American society of that time; the Oberlin intellectual atmosphere bred a remarkable degree of religious dissent.

It was during his college years at Oberlin that George Mead was working through his complex relations with religious dogmatism. Dislike of dogmatism was to be the main feature of all his intellectual creativity. After graduating in 1883, Mead became a schoolteacher, in an effort both to earn a living and to contribute to society. However, the realities of teaching in a high school soon brought him to despair. US high schools have a long history of conflict between the power of the principals and the intellectual humanism of some (often younger) teachers. As in most social systems, the former invariably wins over the latter, and in George Mead's case this led him to quit his teacher's job and move further into the 'real world'. In April 1884 he joined the crew of a land surveying team in Minnesota. The social context of such work – being associated with an engineer and axeman who 'smoke, drink, and swear like troopers' – did not encourage the young man of 21 to concentrate on the study of philosophy.

By January 1885 Mead finished with this 'healthy outdoor activity' and settled down in Minneapolis, working as a private tutor. He set his sights on furthering his own education, and in early September 1887 he left the Midwest to study philosophy at Harvard, continuing his private tutoring in order to make ends meet. After a brief stay at Harvard, he followed the route travelled by most US academics at the end of the nineteenth century – to Germany. From the autumn of 1888 to that of 1891 Mead studied first in Leipzig and subsequently in Berlin.

In Leipzig, he joined the many who wanted to learn the latest about psychology from Wilhelm Wundt. He considered specialization in 'physiological psychology', a subject within psychology that Wundt had made scientifically reputable. Mead became enthusiastic about the European kind of socialism, and speculated eagerly on its possible use in the United States. He tried to accomplish that later – in the context of Chicago, where he was a practical mediator between employers and workers.

Mead's own insights about his native country are worth consideration. He saw the new US society moving towards a new form of self-government, which was an exaggerated (liberated from social class constraints, one might say) and generalized version of the centrality of community. The new citizens of the United States, according to Mead

> had changed the character of the state which gave the former colonists their political consciousness. When they recognized themselves as citizens it was no longer as members of the English social hierarchy. For this they had substituted a political national structure which was a logical development of the town meeting. The state has never impressed itself upon the American citizen. It is nothing but the extension in representative form of the political habits of the town meeting . . .
>
> The habit of self-government in local affairs was an inherited English method, but the creation of a national state out of these habits was purely American. (Mead, 1930, pp. 212–213)

Mead's theoretical ideas

Mead was committed to the 'specifically American' social dominance of community-centred thinking in both his theoretical ideas and practical efforts to mediate in the process of social reforms in the context of Chicago. Hence the relevance of the community in his thinking about the self, which is present in all of his work. Mead was making a slow but productive effort to make sense of the mechanisms of such relations between persons and their community. He was a good speaker (his lectures at the University of Chicago were special for many students – although it must be said some liked them, while others hated them), but a very poor writer. Mead basically wrote short journal articles (often book reviews), and by the time of his death in 1931 he had finished only one book manuscript. The books attributed to Mead – including his 'classic' *Mind, Self and Society* (Mead, 1934) – were compiled after his death from the lecture notes of his students.

Internalization, dramatization and autonomy

In ontogeny, language develops from the 'outer' towards the 'inner' direction. *It is the person's inner speech that creates the autonomy of the self*, through the capacity for imagination. Notice here the parallel with Baldwin's similar ideas (above).

The development of inner speech was viewed by Mead as passing through a state of *self-oriented dramatization* of conduct. It is in that conduct that the two parallel processes of communication – with oneself and with the other – participate in intra-personal growth:

The young child talks to himself, i.e., uses the elements of articulate speech in response to the sounds *he hears himself make, more continuously* and persistently than he does in response to the sounds he hears from those about him, and he displays greater interest in the sounds he himself makes than in those of others. We know also that this fascination of one's own vocal gestures continues even after the child has learned to talk with others, and that the child will converse for hours with himself, *even constructing imaginary companions, who function in the child's growing self-consciousness as the processes of inner speech – of thought and imagination – function in the consciousness of the adult*. (Mead, 1912, p. 403; added emphasis)

This quote is a rich (intensely compressed) expression of the basic processes that Mead posits to take place in human social development. The curious phenomenon of children's 'play with language' and lengthy monologues were phenomena Mead noticed. Yet, at the same time, the developing person is the target of the speech of many other persons. So, simultaneously the child hears others, and him- or herself, speaking. In general, the production of speech comes under the child's own control, whereas the speech input from others is never controllable by the person themself. This can explain Mead's remark that the child pays 'greater interest in the sounds he himself makes than in those of others'. In fact, Mead may have picked up the process of establishing control over one's own speaking. In the process of communication, it is equally important to stay silent at some times – as it is to talk at others. A child experimenting with his or her own monological speech may be developing self-control strategies.

Mead also emphasized the *double input* into the child's developing communication possibilities. When the child speaks within a social context (that is, with an addressee, who will respond to the speech), the child experiences input into their conduct in two ways: immediately (by way of hearing what he/she is saying), and through the other (by way of the addressee's response). This creates a necessary duality (self/other differentiation), that serves as the basis for further construction of one's role as *the person who is speaking*. In that role, there are multiple options. First, the immediate self-feedback from one's speaking can be overlooked; the child thus becomes involved in the immediate *external dialogue* with the other person. Here the speaking acquires the nature of mutual responding. The child is fully immersed in interacting with the other person.

Secondly, it is possible that the interaction (based on mutuality of speaking) and intra-action (feedback from one's own speech) become

coordinated in some ways. This involves the child's dialogue between what he/she said (and what he/she heard) and the responding by the other person. The child can here work out ways of distancing between what is said by him/her, and by the other. Here is similarity with Simmel's focus (see above).

Thirdly, the child can 'block' the speech input of the other person in the setting, and develop routines with an *invented social partner*. The constructive nature of play makes such construction easily available. Detecting such 'imaginary companions' (by others) leads to the simple labelling of the event as 'pretend play'. Yet – as Mead indicated – the 'pretence' here is an indication of a construction of a counterpart interlocutor who is fully under the control of the child themself. Through generalizing from these 'imaginary others' over childhood, the developing person arrives at the intra-psychological consciousness (where thought and imagination play the same, de-personalized, role). The person creates their 'social other' – first as a concrete, yet imaginary, companion, and later as an abstracted and de-personalized 'generalized other'. It is in relation to that 'other' that further development, through assuming social roles, takes place.

The self's movement through social roles plays a central part in the coordination of the social and the personal in development (Mead, 1925, pp. 271–273). We could summarize Mead's model to entail *a double* (that is, intra- and extra-personal) *feedback loop of constructive relations* (see Figure 3.3).

In Figure 3.3, the social action upon the environment (the extra-personal loop) constructs novelty in the social world. Having changed the social world – through assuming social roles and carrying out actions appropriate within such roles – the altered social world feeds back as 'input' to the internalization system of the person. This feedback leads to the construction of novelty

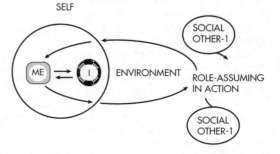

FIGURE 3.3 *Self/Other relations in George H. Mead's theoretical system*

in the intra-subjective domain. That reconstruction has double input – from the external world (modified through the person's actions within a social role), and from the 'hidden intra-psychological' domain which is not accessible to anybody. Mead labelled the latter the 'I'. The 'I' is never accessible directly – neither by the person themself, nor by any other person. It has active impact upon the main intra-psychological units of the self-system – the 'ME's. The 'I' can only be known from the results of its action – the modification of the 'ME's. The modified 'ME's act further in two directions towards externalization (into the world of the social environment) and towards modification of the 'I'. However, it is only through the action in the external world that one can learn about the modified 'ME's' system.

Double differentiation of person and society
In an effort to overcome both the separation of the person and society, as well as the intellectual fusion of these in pragmatist talk, Mead suggested a double-feedback loop model of differentiation of *both* the person (in terms of different 'ME's, as well as that of the 'generalized other'), and the social world (social institutions). A person acting within an environment changes it, and feedback from this process and outcome leads to the intra-psychological reconstruction of the self. The latter, in its turn, feeds into further actions upon the environment, with a resulting change etc. The process of differentiation of the subject and object maintains the dynamic relation between them, yet the process is constantly undergoing change. As Mead explained:

> response to the social conduct of the self may be in the rule of another – we present his arguments in imagination and do it with his intonations and gestures and even perhaps with his facial expression. In this way we play the rules of all our group; indeed, it is only so far as we do this that they become part of our social environment – to be aware of another self as a self implies that we have played his rule or that of another with whose type we identify for purposes of intercourse. The inner response to our reaction to others is therefore as varied as is our social environment. . . . (Mead, 1913, p. 377)

The inner and outer worlds of acting persons thus become differentiated in coordination, and transformation in one leads to some transformation in the other. This idea is very close to that of Georg Simmel (see above).

The social and the physical realms: a basic difference
Hegelian dialectical notions are present in Mead's conceptualization of the self. The need to address the dialectics of the self emerges from the distinction of the physical and social worlds that Mead clearly drew:

> The other selves stand upon different basis from that of physical objects. Physical objects are merely objects of perception, *while the other selves are perceiving subjects as well as perceived objects.* (Mead, 1905, p. 403; added emphasis)

In essence, probably any conceptualization of the self that includes the notion of development has to confront the question of *qualitative structural transformation*. That latter issue can, in principle, be resolved by either some notion of inherent harmonious 'growth' (to another form of complexity), or by some indeterministic notion that entails a reference to a chaotic or fuzzy 'intermediate state', from which qualitatively novel structures may emerge via some 'leap'.

Dialectical models of any kind are a version of the latter, as they specify that (a) some contradictions exist between parts of the previous system (hence, the system may produce a chaotic-looking outcome for a while), and (b) the contradiction leads to a 'break' with the past in the form of the emergence of a qualitatively novel form of the system. Mead tried to make sense of the dialectics of the human self by viewing the internalization process in inherently dialectical terms.

Dramatized autonomy of the self
It is through the movement into, through and out of the roles of other selves that construction of inner autonomy becomes possible:

> . . . the child can think about his conduct as good or bad *only as he reacts to his own acts in the remembered words of the parents. Until* this process has been developed *into the abstract process of thought,* self-consciousness *remains dramatic,* and the self which is a fusion of the remembered actor and this accompanying chorus is somewhat loosely organized and very clearly social. Later the inner stage *changes into the forum and workshop of thought.* The features and intonations of the dramatis personae fade out and the emphasis falls upon the meaning of the inner speech, the imagery becomes merely the barely necessary cues. But the *mechanism remains social,* and *at any moment the process may become personal.* (Mead, 1913, pp. 377–378; added emphasis)

The roles are constantly being constructed as they are being assumed by the person – the self-processes construct both the external bases for social dramas, and the internal models of assuming such constructed roles. Mead provides a way to look at the construction of genetic dramatisms.

The dialectic opposition exists in the relationship between the 'outer' and 'inner', and takes the form of internalization. This notion of internalization (interiorization) was also used by Lev Vygotsky, who tried to make sense of human beings' social nature.

LEV VYGOTSKY'S DIALECTICAL SYNTHESIS

Lev Vygotsky (1896–1934) has become a guru figure in contemporary cultural psychology. Part of such fame is deserved: his ideas produced a creative synthesis of many of the basic notions of his time. Yet many of the contemporary heroic accounts of Vygotsky are merely rhetorical, and do not serve to develop his ideas further.

Vygotsky's life and work has been analysed elsewhere (Van der Veer and Valsiner, 1991). The important feature of his professional role in psychology was his lack of formal psychological education. He was rather a literary scholar who became a psychologist through a series of co-incidences, in the early 1920s. All of his work in psychology was done within one decade (from 1924 to 1934), and in the midst of a period of tumult in the Soviet Union.

The core of Vygotsky's work was the demonstration of the presence of construction of novelty in the process of living through experiences. Development, from his viewpoint, entailed differentiation of psychological functions (from 'lower' to 'higher' kinds). This distinction was emphasized by the 'Würzburg School' of psychology (Narciss Ach, Oswald Külpe, Karl Bühler), who attempted to study the higher psychological functions through experimental methods. Vygotsky added to their distinctions the centrality of semiotic mediation – the higher psychological functions became distinguished by the *use of signs* as underlying the volitional processes. The use of signs allows human beings to synthesize new meanings – both in the reflexive (generalization of word meanings) and the immediate affective domains. The issue of *developmental synthesis* through *cultural (semiotic) means* was the distinctive feature of Vygotsky's psychological system.

Vygotsky's theoretical contributions

Vygotsky's main contribution was in his consistent application of the basic socio-genetic principle (borrowed from Pierre Janet) to issues of human development. The *'Janet–Vygotsky' Law* (as it could be appropriately labelled) *of human development* is a claim that

. . . every function in the cultural development of the child comes onto the stage twice – first in the social relations between people, and then within the person's intra-psychological self-organization system.

The focus in this law is on explaining the origins of higher psychological functions – those that involve wilful regulation by the person of oneself and of others. The law is not meant to cover all psychological functions – the lower psychological functions (which do not involve cultural organization) emerge in their species-specific, biologically set up, ways. The higher functions, once those establish themselves, begin to regulate the lower ones.

The process of transfer of the psychological processes from the sphere of social relations to that of self-organization is internalization. For Vygotsky, the concept of internalization was important, as the locus of functioning of all (higher and lower) psychological processes is in the person. True, the person is social, in terms of belonging to some social group, community, and being involved in interchange using signs. The person's social nature is the basis for his or her individuality.

Bi-directional process of internalization (interiorization)

Vygotsky clearly assumed a standpoint that used the bi-directional culture transfer model (elaborated in Chapter 4) in his account of internalization. Internalization is a constructive process – the person reconstructs the psychological functions that originally take place between him or her and others into their own self-regulating processes in forms that are not simple replicas of the former. The self-organization system resembles the processes observable in the social relations, but is not the same. Notice the similarity of this idea with that of James Mark Baldwin ('circular reaction').

Vygotsky built his notion of interiorization on the shoulders of the intellectual giant of psychology of the early twentieth century, Wilhelm Wundt. Wundt had used (in his *Völkerpsychologie*) the example – or better, a story – about how the developing child moves from efforts to reach an object to the indicative gesture, through social interpretations of the child's effort. The same example from Wundt's work was also used by George Herbert Mead. Vygotsky rendered that example in his own way. The adult – seeing the second-year child's efforts to reach an object – interprets these efforts as if the child 'wants the object' and that the child 'orients me towards the object he wants' (in the understanding of the adult). Feedback to the child leads to 'fine-tuning' of the orienting movement – into the *indicating gesture* (pointing). The child can point to different objects at a distance, and the adult follows the lead of the pointing. As a result, the child masters the possibility of directing the adult's attention by way of pointing. As Vygotsky claimed,

> The functions of the movement itself have undergone a change . . . from a movement directed toward an object it has become a movement directed toward another human being. The grasping is converted into an indication. Thanks to this, the movement is reduced and abbreviated, and the form of the indicatory gesture is elaborated. *We can now say that it is a gesture for oneself.* (Vygotsky, 1960, p. 196; added emphasis)

The infant's efforts to grasp objects succeed at close distance, and fail in relation to objects out of reach. As the infant is a participant in the social world, the efforts (which fail), through their interpretation (as expressions of 'wanting', projected into the child by others), lead to the change of function of the new behavioural form. The gesture – of pointing – emerges from the realm of the infant's actions and becomes a tool for interaction. The toddler points to many objects, catching the adult's attention, not wanting to have those, but just for the sake of pointing to them. This catches the attention of others, as well as keeping the child's attention also. In this sense, the social context has guided the child to establish a gesture that the child can use in regulating his or her own action.

The final step in the development of the pointing gesture is its interiorization. On the basis of pointing to themselves (externally), the child works towards the construction of intra-psychological tactics of 'mental pointing'. The intra-psychological domain of human beings needs to establish psychological tactics to direct one's attention to a particular issue (of thought, or feeling), maintain that attention on the selected target (that is, attention concentration), and distance oneself from other (undesired) intra-mental phenomena (for example, in the case of adults, overcoming floating thoughts, fears, worries, or the pervasive 'singing' in the mind of some TV commercial). This requires intra-mental control over one's own mind. Vygotsky (following Wundt) hypothesized that the internalization of the pointing gesture, from toddlerhood onwards, is the process through which these higher mental regulation devices are established.

Of course, these devices (of 'pointing in one's mind') cannot be expected to maintain the same form as was the case of the toddler's pointing gesture. There is no index finger 'in the mind'

which would, in the literal sense, do the 'pointing'. Instead, the *function of pointing* is carried by some other substance – of a subjective, only introspectively available, kind. The intra-mental life is available to us through speech. The use of speech was also viewed by Vygotsky as undergoing interiorization.

From social to internal speech

For Vygotsky, speaking was the preferred medium for making sense of the world. He himself was well known as a good speaker, and he could make sense of visual scenes through speaking.[2] In his efforts to understand the functioning of human mind, Vygotsky emphasized the mutual process relations of three domains:

Spoken words < > Inner speech < > Thought

The relation between these three domains was constructive. Speaking of a word would lead to 'speaking for oneself' in abbreviated forms, and eventually can lead to the reconstruction in terms of 'pure thought'. The reverse direction also entails reconstruction – according to Vygotsky, the thought *is not expressed* in word, but *completed in* it.

The recognition of specificity of different levels of psychological phenomena by Vygotsky was part of his acceptance of the principle of hierarchical organization (integration) of psychological systems. He accepted the distinction of psychological functions into lower (*involuntary, unmediated*) and higher (*voluntary, mediated*) classes. The latter were results of development – human higher psychological functions emerged on the basis of lower ones, through synthesis.

Centrality of psychological synthesis in development

The question of whole/part relations was crucial for Vygotsky. However, he, differently from many of his contemporaries, gave it a developmental focus of psychological synthesis through the use of signs.

The question of how complex phenomena of a psychological kind are created from simpler components was a crucial issue in psychology at the beginning of the twentieth century. The development of different holistic research directions – of Gestalt psychology (of Max Wertheimer, Wolfgang Köhler and Kurt Koffka),[3] of *Ganzheitspsychologie* (of Felix Krueger, Friedrich Sander and Hans Volkelt),[4] of the efforts to study complex mental processes experimentally (Oswald Külpe, and the 'Würzburg School'), and of the phenomenological approach (Edmund Husserl, after Franz Brentano) – constituted the field of knowledge at the time.

A crucial role in Vygotsky's reasoning was played by Buridan's ass. This animal – a donkey – was supposedly discussed by the medieval philosopher Buridan. The donkey supposedly died of hunger, when put in a choice situation facing two equal stacks of hay placed at exactly equal distance, as shown in Figure 3.4. The donkey is unable to imbalance a balanced decision situation. In contrast, human beings actively introduce changes into the situation, which imbalance it, and thus make it possible to act. Instead of the fate of hunger–death (depicted in Figure 3.4*A*) of the donkey, human beings invent a tool or sign (or import it/them from their repertoire of previous achievements), and proceed to solve the problem (Figure 3.4*B*; see also Chapter 5 on Vygotsky's 'method of double stimulation').

The imbalancing of the 'Buridan's ass' situation is possible only in the case of an active organism (who can move from the present stalemate situation to a new setting definition). This can lead to the construction of new solutions to the problem, which are embedded in new affect. Vygotsky was interested in phenomena of *emergence of generalized feelings* first in the realm of human emotions. Being an avid reader and theatre-goer, he constantly came across the phenomenon of a feeling generated by a small phrase in a short story, or theatre performance, leading to a generalized feeling about the world at large. He was interested in how a writer, by inserting a minimal phrase in a text, could create in the reader such emotional generalizations.

Behaviour can be understood only through the study of the history of behaviour

This developmental idea was central to Vygotsky. He was not the originator of the idea (indeed, this nice saying is attributable to his contemporary, Pavel Blonsky). Vygotsky's consistent focus on development made him one of the earliest users of the *axiom of historicity* (see Chapter 4 for its formulation).

How does the 'history of psychological phenomena' (rather than 'behaviour') function in development? In the course of development, different psychological functions come into existence in ontogeny, aided by support from the culturally organized environment. The fate of these functions varies: some disappear after they perform their function, others become automatized and are integrated into larger units of action. It is the latter that become kinds of 'psychological fossils' – abbreviated versions of once extensive behavioural forms.

For example, in adult psychological functioning, most of the basic ways of gaining knowledge

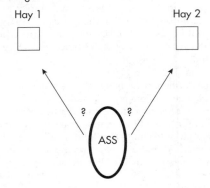

A A donkey situated between two piles of hay dies of hunger

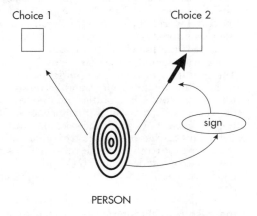

B A human being between two equal choices creates a technique for turning what is equal into an unequal choice

FIGURE 3.4 *Buridan's ass and human cultural action*

(for example, proof of classic theorems in geometry) that were once mastered in school contexts, are lost from the realm of cognitive operations of an adult. Yet the theorems themselves may remain as basic knowledge, accepted in immediately trusted ways. For example, a triangle is a geometric figure for which it may be retained that the internal angles of it add up to 180 degrees. The particular path to prove this (as a theorem) has been lost after its acquisition, while the result becomes self-evident truth. Yet when necessary for further advancement of some idea, the pathways of proof may be re-constructed in a novel way. The power of formal education is in the fossilization of the pathways to knowledge – which could be re-activated in a constructive way under new circumstances.

These fossilized psychological phenomena play

a crucial role in defining the potential of human psychological adaptation to new conditions. In any contemporary state of the person, these reflect the past history of development, and future potential for development. Yet, at the present, these fossilized phenomena are not utilized.

The 'Zone of Proximal Development' (ZPD)

In our contemporary psychology, Vygotsky gets credit for creating this concept, which is viewed as a success in problem-solving in education. That concept became popular among many educators, primarily in the United States, in the 1980s. Yet its scientific texture includes aspects that are mind-boggling for most empirical investigators.

The history of Vygotsky's formulation of the concept is given elsewhere (Van der Veer and Valsiner, 1991; see also Chapter 13), as it emerged in his dialogue with educators in the Soviet Union in the early 1930s. The concept provides a way to unite two issues of a general, abstract kind, which are usually overlooked by psychologists.

The first of these two is the time-relation between the present and the future. The Zone of *Proximal* Development is a concept that draws our attention to the immediate potential developmental pathways which exist in some under-developed form in the present. The focus of researchers who use the ZPD notion is on the *construction of the immediately novel state* of the psychological functions.

Who constructs that novel state, and how? All psychological functions are necessarily intimately personal – so all development of psychological functions is confined to the psychological system of the person themself. Yet that personal construction process can (and is) socially assisted and directed. At times, it is socially repressed. So, the open-systemic nature of psychological systems guarantees *both* the personal uniqueness of developing psychological functions (for example, what develops in childhood is not just 'will' but 'Mary's will to do X'), and its interdependence with the world of other human beings (for example, Mary's mother who tries to direct, 'cultivate', or 'educate' the purely individual phenomenon – 'Mary's will to do X'). Now, some of these functions at a given time have already become formed, others are in the process of formation, and still others are beyond access to the developing person at the given time.

Vygotsky's thinking about the phenomena of the ZPD emphasized precisely that unity, and located the domain ('zone') where development takes place. The person's development is being constructed in that 'zone' (or realm of psychological functions that at the present time are in the process of formation, but which are not yet established). These 'half-ready' functions are both the targets for the person's own efforts at their full formation, as well as those for any kind of social intervention efforts. Thus, for Vygotsky, the ZPD (Zone of Proximal Development) included

. . . those processes in the further development of these same functions which, as they are not mature today, still are on their way already, are already growing through and already tomorrow will bear fruit; already tomorrow transfer to the level of actual development. (Vygotsky, 1935, p. 120)

The finalization of the development of the emerging psychological functions can be accomplished in two ways: by *individual activity* (play in childhood, fantasy in adolescence and adulthood), and by *social guidance*. Obviously, it is the former – characterized by Baldwin's persistent imitation notion – that is obligatory; the role of social guidance is secondary to the persistent imitation. As Vygotsky pointed out in one of his lectures in 1933:

In play the child is always higher than his average age, higher than his usual everyday behavior; he is in play as if a head above himself. The play contains, in a condensed way, as if in the focus of a magnifying glass, all tendencies of development; it is as if the child in play tries to accomplish a jump above the level of his ordinary behavior.

The relationship of play to development should be compared with that of teaching–learning [*obuchenie*] to development. Changes of needs and consciousness of a more general kind lie behind the play. Play is the resource of development and it creates the zone of nearest development. Action in the imaginary field, in the imagined situation, construction of voluntary intention, the formation of the life-plan, will motives – this all emerges in play . . . (Vygotsky, 1966, pp. 74–75)

The notion of teaching–learning (*obuchenie*) entails both the active construction efforts by the learner (the individual component) and efforts by others to guide those in some direction (the teaching component). The relationship between those two features is described in Figure 3.5.

At any present moment of time, the developing organism is facing the future. This happens on the basis of the previously formed, and semi-formed psychological functions – all of which belong to the Zone of Actual Development. The fully established psychological functions provide support for the emergence of new ones. It is the newly emerging – but not yet formed – functions (in Figure 3.5 these are depicted as A and B) that

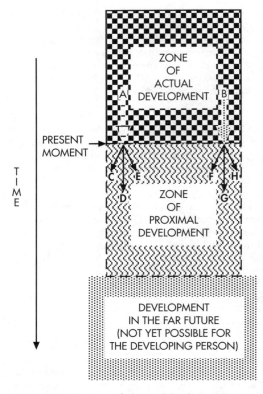

FIGURE 3.5 *The zone of proximal development*

are crucial for making the future into the present. Each of the not yet formed (but developing) functions include principled uncertainty of their future advancement. For instance, A can turn into states C, D, or E; B into F, G, or H. Which of these directions will actually be taken would depend upon the coordination of circumstances – the decision by the developing person, the guidance of 'social others'. It is here where social suggestions play their guiding role.

The role of crises periods

In ontogenesis there exist different age periods of openness for development. After periods of well-differentiated states of development there are suddenly periods of 'turmoil' – previously established patterns of psychological functions seem to disintegrate, and new functions emerge slowly from such states:

> The progressive development of a child's personality, the continuous building of the new that was so clearly expressed in all stable age periods, seems to fade away or stop during crises periods. The extinction and contraction, disintegration and decomposition of the previously formed processes that characterized

the child of the given age move to the frontal plane. *The child during the critical periods does not so much acquire, but loses what was attained before.* (Vygotsky, 1984, p. 251; added emphasis)

Development thus can be described by over-production and loss. This idea continues the line of thought introduced by James Mark Baldwin on the unity of evolution and involution. Vygotsky gave this notion a concrete application to childhood development. The involution process dominates over that of evolution during the age periods of 'crises'. However, each 'crisis' has its own 'culmination point' [*kulminatsionnaia tochka*] that is, the locus at which the dialectical synthesis is accomplished. Thus, development takes place in uneven ways. Rather than being an example of monotonic progression (see Figure 3.6*A*), it can better be described as a time-sequence of non-monotonic 'jumps', following periods of turmoil and regression (Figure 3.6*B*).

The non-linear model of development – through periods of crises – depicted in Figure 3.6*B*, fits well with the open-systemic nature of development, and with the recognition of the cyclical nature of causality (see Chapters 2, 4 and 5). Vygotsky viewed *temporary regressive periods* as constructive for development. These regressive phases are not 'fallbacks' to a previous state of existence (regression to childhood), but indicators of the psychological system's current de-differentiation – which is expected to be followed by a new re-organization and a 'leap' to a qualitatively new level.

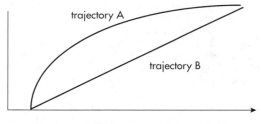

A Development as a case of monotonic progression

trajectory A

trajectory B

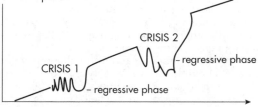

B Development as a case of progression through crisis periods

CRISIS 2

– regressive phase

CRISIS 1

– regressive phase

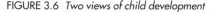

FIGURE 3.6 *Two views of child development*

MIKHAIL BAKHTIN: SOCIAL LANGUAGES AND CARNIVALIZATION

Bakhtin's intellectual heritage can be located in Continental European thought of the beginning of the twentieth century. His 'dialogue of cultures' notion was borrowed from the philosophy of Oswald Spengler. Like most of his contemporaries in the 1920s, Bakhtin relied on the works of Theodor Lipps, Wilhelm Wundt, Hermann Cohen and others. In the years after the 1930s until his death, Bakhtin's ideas were moving in lines parallel to the development of German hermeneutics of Hans-Georg Gadamer. All in all, Bakhtin was a very well educated scholar who synthesized various philosophical, literary and psychological traditions of European cultural history. Yet he remained interested in his main discipline – world literature – all through his life (Konkin and Konkina, 1993). Uses of Bakhtinian thinking in psychology are extensions from his literary scholarship.

Bakhtin carried over to the notion of culture the systemic, holistic focus that has characterized German philosophical views on personality. Thus, culture for him was analogous to a living organism, heterogeneous and contradictory within itself. Bakhtin's view of culture was holistic, and systemic. Bakhtin's target of investigation was literature (the novel, in particular – his main work was on François Rabelais), and not human psychological functioning in its everyday contexts. It could be said that his object of investigation – the novel (rather than the functioning person) – focussed him on the study of the multi-voicedness of discourse. In the novel, the reader can have access to all of the depicted story in the course of reading, discovering ever-new nuances of the text. In contrast, the immediate interaction of human beings would not easily allow for such backward-referencing.

While analysing novels, Bakhtin turned to wider issues of the role of language in social life. It is that generalization that has made it possible to take some of Bakhtin's ideas over into psychology.

Making social discourse one's own
Like other thinkers about the role of language, Bakhtin tried to make sense of the evasive nature of language. Precisely because human beings are users of a language, it can be said to inherently belong to them. Yet, at the same time, language is shared between different human beings. All speakers of English – while uttering their specific phrases – do share the English language. They can understand one another on the basis of such sharing. So language has existence beyond the particular language user. Yet it depends upon these users.

How can language function both individually and socially? Bakhtin's solution was to posit a process of persons' 'taking over' the language for their personal uses, modifying the language use through personal inclinations. Bakhtin saw 'the word' (or discourse) as a 'boundary phenomenon' that exists between the active person and the social world. From that standpoint,

> The word language – is a half alien [*chuzoye* – not belonging to me, unknown, in Russian] word. It becomes 'one's own' when the speaker inhabits it with his intention, his accent, masters the word, brings it to bear upon his meaningful and expressive strivings. Until that moment of appropriation [*prisvoenie*] the word is not existing in neutral and faceless language (the speaker does not take the word from a dictionary!), but [it exists] on the lips of others, in alien contexts, in service of others' intentions: from here it has to be taken and made into one's own. (Bakhtin, 1934/1975, p. 106).

Bakhtin's explicit emphasis on the active role of the person – who is the agent who makes the alien word to be one's own – restores the focus on duality to the study of persons' relations with their languages. The latter are not uniform (not taken from a dictionary), but represent *intentional, goal-oriented uses* of language for their own *personal* purposes. The use of the term *prisvoenie* guarantees the personally active, yet bi-directional, nature of the described processes.

Multi-voicedness (heteroglossia) expressed in dialogue between social languages
Speaking of the novel, Bakhtin attributed multi-voicedness due to different social languages as woven into the text by the author. Thus,

> The internal multi-layeredness of the unified national language into social dialects, group styles, professional jargons, languages of genre, languages of generations and age cohorts, languages of [ideological] directions, languages of experts, languages of groups of people and passing fashions, languages of social-political days and even hours (every day has its own slogan, its own lexicon, and accents) – this internal multi-layeredness of each language at each moment of its historical existence is the necessary assumption of the genre of the novel. (Bakhtin, 1934/1975, p. 76)

What characterizes novels may also fit society at large. The heterogeneity of the collective culture can be viewed as a dynamic hierarchy of social languages. Within this heterogeneous whole, opposite forces – tending towards unification of the whole and towards its fragmentation – are assumed to be operating. Such centripetal and centrifugal tendencies (see Bakhtin, 1934/1975, p. 85) lead to individualized heteroglossic speech. Hence in speech we have 'internal dialogicity' – different 'voices' of different languages of the whole are in a dialogue with one another. Furthermore, this dialogicality entails movement towards the future in irreversible time. In each dialogue,

> While fitting in the atmosphere of what is already said, the word at the same time is defined by what is not yet said, but what is already implied and already expected by the word of response. (Bakhtin, 1934/1975, p. 93)

By focusing on what might be about to be said, Bakhtin makes his view of dialogue open for further developments. The actual meaning of an utterance is generated on the background of language, through the encounter of a myriad of experiences of the person. *The person actively encounters the word of the others, and creates his or her own personal understandings.* Understanding is created in the process of responding in a dialogue.

Carnivalization

In the texture of social life, role relations can undergo temporary transformations. This has been observed in the case of rituals, some of which can be subsumed under the label of carnival. Carnivals entail temporary reversals of power relations between social roles – during a carnival, the owner can play the role of a slave, and a slave that of owner. Bakhtin saw carnivals in social life as major places where tensions that have occurred in social power relations can be 'ventilated out'. The crucial aspect of carnival is its rule-governed nature – the social *role* relations may be reversed, but the social *rule* system for how to act in the reverse social roles remains in place.

SUMMARY: THE 'GIANTS' AND THEIR SHOULDERS

Aside from the five thinkers of the past covered here, there were obviously many others who contributed to the history of contemporary cultural psychology (see Valsiner and Van der Veer, 2000, for a thorough overview). Here I have emphasized only the few whose role in cultural psychological discourse comes up as a background for many contemporary applications. Thus, the role of Lev Vygotsky has been emphasized widely in the international social sciences of the 1970s

and 1980s, while the popularity of the uses of Bakhtin's ideas seems to pick up in the 1990s. George Herbert Mead has been well known in the areas of sociology and 'symbolic interactionism' ever since the 1930s, yet in psychology his ideas have been left to bear upon relatively few issues. At the same time, the work of James Mark Baldwin and Georg Simmel has been only occasionally used, even though these two scholars have been central in promoting the focus on development in psychology, and sociology.

It is often claimed that our contemporary social sciences benefit from riding on the 'shoulders of the [intellectual] giants' of the past. Undoubtedly there exist many claims to be following the 'teachings' of many of the thinkers covered here – there are 'Vygotskyians', 'Bakhtinians' and 'Meadians', and even a handful of 'Simmelians', who are involved in the social sciences disputes of our times. Yet these tribes may be involved in the phenomenon known in anthropology as 'cargo cult', – believing that goods brought in from prestigious places have magical qualities that will solve the problems of the cult followers. When it comes to the history of the social sciences, such beliefs are unfounded. Followers of any theorist of the past cannot have an easy ride on the 'shoulders of the giants', but need to become giants themselves, if they truly want to solve their problems.

NOTES

1 The notion of 'cargo cult' refers to the assignment of magical properties by the recipients to cargo brought from far-away places (European objects brought by ship to Polynesia), beyond their pragmatic utility. Psychology seems to attach such magical properties to many borrowings from other sciences – genetics (belief in genetic determination of complex psychological functions), applied mathematics (granting statistics the role of 'the scientific method'), neurophysiological technology (the fashion of utilizing magnetic resonance techniques to map brain activity for psychological tasks). As has been the case in those societies which have been vulnerable to 'cargo cults', their own invention of appropriate technologies has remained underdeveloped.

2 He himself explained that he could not make sense of a painting before starting to speak about it – only through the act of speaking did the meaning of the visual forms emerge. Vygotsky could lecture for 6 hours in a row, without notes.

3 The Gestalt School of psychology emerged in

Frankfurt-am-Main and Berlin from 1912 onwards, and flourished in German psychology until the mid-1930s. It was built on the foundations laid by Carl Stumpf, and entailed primarily a focus on cognitive phenomena (thinking), visual and acoustic perception. Wolfgang Köhler is known for his experiments on problem-solving among chimpanzees and hens, Max Wertheimer was one of the forerunners of modern cognitive psychology. Developmental interests in the Gestalt School were represented by Kurt Koffka.

4 This school was in direct opposition to the Berlin Gestalt tradition (even though in their ideas there was much similarity). Differently from the Berliners, the 'Second Leipzig School' (which was located in Leipzig, and followed from the 'First Leipzig School' of Wilhem Wundt) was oriented towards the phenomena of development, and took interest in complex unformed – yet important – phenomena such as feelings.

REVIEW QUESTIONS FOR CHAPTER 3

1 Explain Baldwin's notion of *circular reaction*.

2 What is *imitative suggestion* in Baldwin's theory?

3 Explain the notion of *persistent imitation*.

4 Why is play relevant for development?

5 Analyse the heterogeneity of human experiences. How would you connect this heterogeneity with the relevance of persistent imitation?

6 How do you understand the claim that a person is social because he or she is individually unique (as a person)?

7 Explain *particularization* and *generalization* in Baldwin's terms.

8 Explain Baldwin's coverage of *sembling*.

9 Why did Baldwin dismiss the uncritical application of the quantitative method in psychology?

10 Explain Baldwin's first ('negative') postulate of method.

11 Explain Baldwin's second ('positive') postulate of method.

12 What is *pancalism* in Baldwin's theory?

13 Explain Simmel's distinction of the subjective and objective cultures.

14 What is *cultivation* in Simmel's understanding?

15 Explain the relevance of secrecy – for persons, and for social systems.

16 What is the relevance of conflict in human lives in society?

17 Explain Mead's notion of self-oriented dramatization.

18 Explain Mead's I < > ME < > social environment dynamic relations.

19 What is the 'Janet–Vygotsky Law'? Describe and explain its meaning for human development.

20 Describe Vygotsky's explanation of the emergence of the indicative gesture.

21 Explain Vygotsky's understanding of external speech, inner speech, and thought.

22 Explain the relevance of Buridan's ass for cultural psychology.

23 Explain the notion of the 'Zone of Proximal Development' (ZPD).

24 From the perspective of the ZPD, where would be the location of adequate social intervention into a person's development?

25 What are 'crises in development' and what is their function for development?

26 In Bakhtin's thinking, to whom does the word belong?

27 Explain the notion of *heteroglossia* and provide your own examples.

28 What is carnivalization?

4

CULTURE AND DEVELOPMENT

Human psychological development is cultural in its nature. When claims like this are made, the need to be explicit about the meaning of the word 'culture' becomes crucial. 'Culture' is used in so many ways in contemporary society at large (for example, talk about 'multiculturalism' in the United States) and in the social sciences that it is on the verge of losing its meaning. Of course, this happens most often when a particular concept becomes a target for symbolic power re-negotiation between different institutions.

There is a certain irony in too wide a use of scientific terms – these become used so widely that they lose their value. If all human conduct is repeatedly declared to be cultural (which it undoubtedly is), it is of no scientific value when it does not lead to new insights. Re-labelling tricks in science are unproductive, since they divert the constructive efforts of scientists from making sense of their objects towards defending and attacking different denotations superimposed on the object. The term 'culture' is too easy to use as a label, which creates the conceptual difficulty for its use.

CULTURE AS USED IN PSYCHOLOGY

Culture has been used as a term in psychology in two main directions. First, it has been used to designate some group of people who 'belong together' by virtue of some shared features. This is the tradition of *cross*-cultural psychology, where different ethnic groups (labelled 'cultures') are compared with one another (for example, 'the American culture', represented by a sample of college undergraduates, might be compared with 'the Italian culture', represented by a sample of university students from Rome). It is obvious that such use of the term culture is limited to being a label (of the country), and has no substantive explanatory value. If used as causal explanation, it is an example of the invention of 'dormitive

principles' – posited causes that are consensually held to provide sufficient answers to enquiry (see Introduction). For example, the '*Italian-ness*' of Italian subjects explains their behaviour, in contrast to the '*American-ness*' of the American subjects. The construction of explanations like this is circular – Italians are found to be Italian because they are from Italy, and Americans to be American because they are from America. Furthermore, the use of *culture* as a label of the country creates an illusory homogeneous class of the people so designated (refer back to Chapter 1). Without doubt, this use of culture is not accepted in this book. I use the notions of *society, ethnic group*, or *tribe* to designate groups of persons who can be classified together by some kinds of cultural artefacts. These are terms that refer to a collective unit of persons who belong together through shared history of living in the given environment, making their community, speaking their language – all over generations. Yet such unity is not culture as such; it is the social basis for culture to be constructed.

Culture as semiotic mediation

I use the second designation of *culture* in this book – that of semiotic (sign) mediation that is part of the system of organized psychological functions. These functions can be intra-personal (that is, the functioning of a person's intra-psychological processes while being involved in experiencing the world: feeling, thinking, memorizing, forgetting, planning, etc.). They can also be inter-personal: different persons are involved in chatting, fighting, persuading each other, avoiding (one another, or some domains of experiencing). Last, but not least, culture, seen as semiotic mediation, is a tool in the goals-oriented actions by social institutions, which try to regulate both the inter-personal and intra-personal psychological functions. As will be shown in the latter chapters, most human life course transitions are organized by social institutions so as to assist the persons involved and (simultaneously) maintain their acting within their social roles.

CULTURE AS USED IN ANTHROPOLOGY

Anthropology has borrowed from psychology when it comes to viewing cultural transmission. The latter has been an analogue to psychologists' discourse about learning. Thus culture has been defined as a 'mass' of '. . . learned and transmitted motor reactions, habits, techniques, ideas, and values – and the behavior they induce' (Kroeber, 1948, p. 8). This definition was obviously created under the influence of the behaviouristic psychology that has dominated psychology in the US over the current century.

The holistic focus on phenomena is likewise not lost in anthropology – culture has been defined as an integrated whole in which systemic interconnections between physiological drives and their transformations through social institutions were the core of the concept. Within that perspective,

> Culture is an integral composed of partly autonomous, partly coordinated institutions. It is integrated on a series of principles such as the community of blood through procreation; the contiguity in space related to cooperation; the specialization in activities; and last but not least, the use of power in political organization. Each culture owes its completeness and self-sufficiency to the fact that it satisfies the whole range of basic, instrumental and integrative needs. (Malinowski, 1944, p. 40)

The concept of culture has become a target of ambivalent attitudes in contemporary anthropology. Its static connotations lead anthropologists to reject it, yet all of cultural anthropology is based on privileging the *ontological* view of culture. Cultures exist, they 'are', in some stable form (which can be described by participant observations, and through interviewing informants). It is not surprising that anthropologists have been mostly describing such observable patterns of cultural life in other societies (than theirs) – rituals, social rules, meanings *as those exist*. It is rarely that anthropologists look at phenomena that come into existence, or at rituals in terms of their failure (e.g., Freeman, 1981).

Homogenization of culture

The consensual beliefs of previous decades that culture is a relatively homogeneous and stable entity (shared by all of its 'members', that is, persons), is being eroded by a number of critical tendencies in the social sciences (Strauss, 1992). In contemporary anthropology there exist three major kinds of views on 'culture' in anthropology (see D'Andrade, 1984, pp. 115–116):

1 *Culture is seen as knowledge*: it is the accumulation of information (irrespective of the extent to which that information is shared between 'members of the culture').
2 *Culture is seen as consisting of core conceptual structures that provide a basis for an intersubjectively shared representation of the world in which the persons live*. This perspective does not emphasize the moment of accumulation (of information), but is rather a set of rules that makes it possible for persons to arrive at shared understandings.
3 *Culture is a construction of conceptual structures by activities of persons*.

Undoubtedly these explanations of culture indicate appropriation of concepts brought to anthropologists' social discourse by the popularity of the 'cognitive revolution' in psychology and related disciplines. The centrality of the person, who experiences his or her life and gives rise to all psychological – cognitive and affective – phenomena, is under-emphasized in cognitive anthropology.

If we carefully examine all three cognitive views on culture, we can reach an understanding that much of anthropology tries to study culture *through persons* (individual members of the culture) without taking the persons *as persons* into account. In this respect, anthropology seems to be under the influence of the 'cognitive revolution' in psychology (and other disciplines). This modern state of affairs seems to repeat other episodes in anthropology's history, where psychoanalytic or behaviouristic ideas were appropriated from psychology. Yet the conceptual problem – how can personal culturally constructed knowledge be 'shared' inter-personally – remains unclear.

'CULTURE' IN CULTURAL PSYCHOLOGY: A PSYCHOLOGICAL DISTANCING DEVICE

It is precisely the capacity and propensity to make and use semiotic devices that allows human beings to become distanced in relation to their immediate life contexts. The person becomes simultaneously an actor, who is immersed in the given 'situated activity context', and a reflexive agent who is distanced from the very setting in which he or she is immersed. This duality is relevant for transcending the adaptational demands of the here-and-now context, and guides the development towards increasing autonomy. Yet any autonomy is a result of the immediate dependence upon the here-and-now context (as the open-systemic nature of any developing system, be it biological, psychological, or social, entails).

Psychological distancing always includes the context within which the person is, and in relation to which the distancing takes place. It takes the form of *I reflect upon this context in which I am a part*. This reflection – which is cognitive and affective at the same time – allows the psychological system to consider contexts of the past, imagine contexts of the future, and take perspectives of other persons (in the form of empathy). Without distancing, no considerations by a person of contexts other than the given here-and-now would be possible.

The distancing notion has been central in the history of aesthetic thought. In an effort to make sense of aesthetic experience, Bullough remarked:

> Distance does not imply an impersonal, purely intellectually interested relation . . . On the contrary, it describes a *personal* relation, often highly emotionally coloured, but *of a peculiar character*. Its peculiarity lies in that the personal character of the relation has been, so to speak, filtered. It has been cleared of the practical, concrete nature of its appeal, without, however, thereby losing its original constitution. (Bullough, 1912, p. 91)

Distancing is possible thanks to the construction of hierarchically organized self- (and other-) regulation mechanisms – through meanings. Any labelling of an object or situation entails distancing: the person who makes the statement 'THIS IS X' actually performs the operation 'I (from my position) IN RELATION TO THIS (object that is indicated) CREATE THE MEANING OF THAT OBJECT, WHICH I CLAIM IS X'. Two moments of distancing are involved here: first the SUBJECT (I) is distanced from the OBJECT ('this object out there'); then, secondly, the OBJECT *is distanced from itself* by way of the meaning (X). Yet the subject, object and the designated meaning remain within the realm of the given setting. Meaning-making distances the subject, object and the meaning in a context-inclusive way.

The process of distancing through meaning-making can escalate in the direction of increased abstractness. Increasingly more general meanings can be utilized to replace the first act of designing meaning for something. Semiotic mediation allows for flexible construction of meaning hierarchies – as well as their subsequent destruction. Consider, for example, the following case of quick escalatory construction of distancing through abstractive processes of meaning-making:

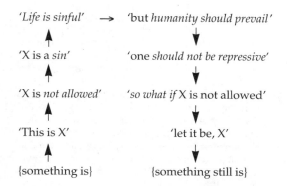

The example shows how through a semiotic move from X to a generalized and abstracted meaning-making process a person can distance themself from the given setting, create an opposition with it (yet remaining part of the setting), and through an autodialogic process (see Josephs and Valsiner, 1998) return from the distanced personal-cultural deliberation to the acceptance of whatever the given context entails. The person is constantly constructing, demolishing, and reconstructing hierarchies[1] of meanings that regulate the person's position in relation to the here-and-now context.

One of the results of such hierarchical construction of levels of abstracted meanings is the emergence of novel abstracted qualities, such as aesthetic experience. The latter unites the immediacy and distance of the object of such experience into a new affective whole, which can be viewed destroying the hierarchy and turning it into a field in which abstract notions and concrete events are merged into one holistic feeling. This process of aesthetic synthesis is the cultural-psychological phenomenon that Lev Vygotsky (see Chapter 3) tried to explain.

Interpersonal differences in distancing through meaning-making

Different persons in the same context necessarily construct their personal (and discrepant from one another) meaningfulness of the context, using semiotic means of different levels of generalization. Consider different perspectives on the same life event – experiencing fog at sea:

> . . . for most people it is an experience of acute unpleasantness. Apart from the physical annoyance and remoter forms of discomfort such as delays, it is apt to produce feelings of peculiar anxiety, fears of invisible dangers, strains of watching and listening for distant and unlocalized signals. The listless movements of the ship and her warning calls soon tell upon the nerves of the passengers; and that

special, expectant, tacit anxiety, and nervousness, always associated with this experience, make a fog the dreaded terror of the sea (all the more terrifying because of its very silence and gentleness) for the expert seafarer no less than for the ignorant landsman.

Nevertheless, a fog at sea can be a source of intense relish and enjoyment. Abstract from the experience of the sea fog, for the moment, its danger and practical unpleasantness, just as every one in the enjoyment of a mountain-climb disregards its physical labour and its danger (though, it is not denied, that these may incidentally enter into the enjoyment and enhance it); direct the attention to the features 'objectively' constituting the phenomenon – the veil surrounding you with an opaqueness as of transparent milk, blurring the outline of things and distorting their shapes into weird grotesqueness . . . note the curious creamy smoothness of the water, hypocritically denying as it were any suggestion of danger; and, above all, the strange solitude and remoteness from the world, as it can be found only on the highest mountain tops: and the experience may acquire, in its uncanny mingling of repose and terror, a flavour of such concentrated poignancy and delight as to contrast sharply with the blind and distempered anxiety of its other aspects. This contrast, often emerging with startling suddenness, is like a momentary switching on of some new current, or of the passing ray of a brighter light, illuminating the outlook upon perhaps the most ordinary and familiar objects . . . (Bullough, 1912, pp. 88–89)

Bullough's introspective example of the transformation of the immediate (that is, dangers involved in the immediate action context) personal sense of a person on a ship deck in a fog (or climbing a mountain) into an overwhelming feeling of aesthetic pleasure reflects the role of affective-semiotic processes in their constructive action. Yet the emergence (or lack of it) depends upon the *social role positioning* of the meaning-maker in the given context. The captain of the ship does not have the luxury of either enjoying or being fearful of the fog (which is possible for the passengers). Soldiers in war zones do not have the luxury of contemplating about the unfairness of the war and the need for peace (this luxury is with those who may see the war scenes on television while sitting comfortably in their living rooms).

In developmental psychology, a distancing model has been worked out over three decades by Irving Sigel (1970, 1993), following the theoretical traditions of Karl Bühler and Heinz Werner (Sigel, 1998). Distancing is indicated when the person (actor) establishes a SUBJECT < > OBJECT relationship with the immediate setting. Thus, any goal-oriented action in a here-and-now

setting (with objectives oriented towards an outcome in the future) entails distancing.

In the human species, it is the semiotic constructivity that advances forms of distancing, turning those into very complex forms. The use of signs makes human beings free to transcend the here-and-now situation of behavioural adaptation needs. Persons can reflect upon their current actions – and thus distance themselves from what they are currently doing.

Moving beyond the natural: Lévi-Strauss's contrasts of Fresh/Decayed and Raw/Cooked

From the systemic perspective on which the present approach is based, culture is the means for breaking the immediate (natural) relationship between the person and the immediate (here-and-now) setting through the construction of semiotic mediators (signs). Lévi-Strauss in his analysis of South American Indian myths emphasized the presence of two lines (axis) of transformations human beings consider in their reflection about the world (Lévi-Strauss, 1983, p. 142).

First, the contrast is between the *fresh* and the *decayed*. This is the axis that characterizes nature. Organisms die or are killed by predators – and turn into fresh food for somebody. Yet if the food is not consumed, it decays. Objects (for example, plant or animal foods) gathered or captured from nature are fresh at the outset (the time of becoming the human possession), but with time they decay and become the opposites of the fresh. In the history of human societies, the possible source of food known as scavenging (obtaining meat of animals killed, and abandoned, by other animals) must have set up the FRESH < > DECAYED opposition as crucial for survival. The developing hominids had to create knowledge about edibility of meats discovered at intermediate levels of decay (if such meat was found on their way). In our contemporary world, this uncertainty is diminished through the socio-institutional establishment of until what date/time a given food product is culturally considered as 'consumable'. The proto-hominids of some two million years ago did not have this benefit of encountering a dead beast in the jungle with a label 'consume before 22 November'.

The second axis is that of cultural modification of the food – the contrast between the *raw* and the *cooked*. Here the human beings actively alter the natural object by way of some planful transformation, using either heating (to cook) or cooling (to preserve the 'raw' or 'fresh' state) of the 'natural product'. The history of human cooking parallels the history of human societies as different from animal species. It is based on the control of heat-production processes. In our contemporary world, we take the technologies such as ovens, stoves, microwaves, freezers, refrigerators for granted. Such luxury of control over the heating and cooling of foods was not available to the developing human species. For them, every next step in cooling/heating technologies was a major cultural accomplishment.

Together with the heating/cooling technologies must have come the meaningful importance of such manipulations in general, beyond the act of food preparation or conservation. As will be seen in Chapter 7, the whole cultural functioning of the human body in the course of reproduction is built around the images of feeding, and those of heating and cooling (of one's blood). Many of the indigenous medical remedies utilize the notions of cooling the excessive heat of sick bodies.

Moving beyond the natural: cultivation

The third contrast (not emphasized by Lévi-Strauss, who was merely trying to make sense of mythology) that operates in parallel with the RAW < > COOKED oppositions is that of *natural* versus *cultivated*. The latter is possible only for living objects of human manipulation of nature. The plants from the 'natural' world (forest), or wild animals, can be appropriated by human beings and turned into cultivated plants (in their gardens, ploughed fields) and domesticated animals. Both cultivated plants and domesticated animals are further divided into foods (in which case they are killed, and turn into raw food which enters the opposition with the cooked), and into companions (domesticated animals functioning as pets, or as work-animals; plants cultivated and maintained for their aesthetic or symbolic value).

The three oppositions of culture and nature are shown in coordinated fashion in Figure 4.1. Here we see how at different phases of the development of the biological object (plant, animal, human) the oppositions NATURAL < > CULTIVATED and RAW < > COOKED can become applicable.

In Figure 4.1, two main oppositions of culture – CULTIVATED < > NATURAL (Georg Simmel's focus) and RAW < > COOKED (Lévi-Strauss's central opposition) – are set up side by side, on the timeline of life and death. Up to the time moment of 'loss of life quality', the issue of culture pertains to the efforts to purposefully change the natural growth of the organism into a different mould. The growing organism – be this a domestic animal, or human child – was to be cultivated in order to make the organism cultural. The same focus was used in colonial history of the past and early anthropology – to cultivate the 'primitive' people into the mores of the 'cultured' ones (that is, the colonizers) operated on the basis of the NATURAL < > CULTIVATED opposition.

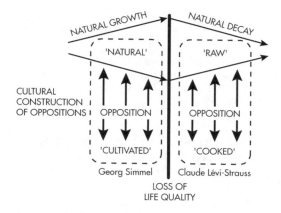

FIGURE 4.1 *Entrance of culture in to the opposition construction between the person and the world*

Lévi-Strauss's opposition of RAW < > COOKED enters onto the scene of culture when the developing organism has lost its life quality, and becomes an object of consumption. The development of human culinary arts is a testimony of the mastery of turning the raw food into one or another kind of cooked meal. Even the processes of natural decay are at times utilized in the process of food preparation.

Two complicated cases of cultural construction of transition from the Simmelian cultivation emphasis to the Lévi-Straussian cooking focus are the killing of domestic animals, and ritualistic cannibalism. In the first case, domestic animals are carefully fed to cultivate them to the desired level of weight and fatness (or lack of it). The goal is to cultivate the animals in order to turn them into food that is culturally treated by cooking. In the second case, the indigenous practices of cannibalism in human tribal warfare have often been based on the symbolic power that the eating of one's relative's or powerful enemy's meat was believed to provide. In both cases, the cultivated 'social other' becomes a cooked symbolic power source.

To summarize – culture (in the sense of semiotic mediation of the relations of the person with him- or herself, and with the external world) operates on the basis of functional oppositions. These oppositions give rise to a vast variety of outcomes – forms of conduct that members of a given society accept as legitimate. As we see later in this book (Chapter 9), such seemingly opposite events as infanticide and care for the survival of infants are the result of basically the same cultural processes, which under different conditions generate opposite outcomes.

The first basic question – following our systemic localization of culture within a human psychological system – is that of communication. How is it possible to transfer one's created cultural system from one person to another? In a more profound case, how is it possible to transfer the constructed cultural mediating devices from the parents to their offspring? Such inter-generational transfer is extremely important for continuity of society.

CONTINUITY ACROSS GENERATIONS: UNI- AND BI-DIRECTIONAL CULTURE TRANSFER

Aside from being open systems, developing persons are subjected to efforts by others to direct their development in one or another way. Thus, the open-systemic functioning of the persons of one generation (for example, parents' external-ization of their desires for their children, in the process of child rearing) provides a structure of directed relations of the members of the other generation (children) for their interchanges with their environments. We can refer to this as *canalization process* – where desired directions are indicated by the adults to the children, but the latter have open possibilities to re-negotiate the suggested direction. Such canalization process includes knowledge transfer. It occurs jointly in the parents and the offspring. There are two main models of knowledge transfer that have been the basis for thinking about human development.

The uni-directional culture transfer model
The uni-directional notion considers the develop-ing person – the recipient of the cultural trans-mission or socialization endeavours – to be *passive in his or her acceptance (or failure of it – a 'miss' or an 'error' of the 'transmission') of the cultural messages.* The recipients' role is merely either to accept the messages aimed at them, or perhaps fail to do so; but in any case, the recipients are not assumed to reorganize the received message. The messages are *de facto* viewed as fixed entities. They are either accepted by the recipients as givens, or (in case of their incomplete acceptance) with an 'error of transmission'. The most widespread concrete application of such a uni-directional model is in technical systems – Claude Shannon's mathemati-cal information theory (Shannon and Weaver, 1949) is built on the assumptions of such trans-mission. The role of the recipients of these messages is that of mere acceptors of all the 'influ-ences', rather than that of constructive (albeit limited) modifiers of those.

The uni-directional model is deeply rooted in our common-sense fits with the nature of technological systems, where the information to be transmitted is fixed, closed to development, and where the exact copy-like nature of trans-mission of the given message is a desired goal. Surely nobody is happy about modifications in computer files or poor quality xerox copies. In both cases, the desired transmission quality is 100 per cent replication of the original, and anything less than that may be a serious fault or error. But of course we are not expecting xerox copies *to develop*, in relation to the original, any new properties!

The focus on unilinearity of transfer is at times hailed as a new frontier of science. Thus, in genetic engineering the possibility of cloning an organism is both viewed as a new way for 'technical repair' of the present genotype (thus a positive result), and as a danger for emergence of unpredicted 'cloned monsters' (which would entail the fear of uncontrollable outcomes of genetic engineering). Yet in the sphere of social transfer of knowledge (called education), the emergence of 'uncontrollable psychological monsters' has been accepted as an inevitable part of the misery of the adults (parents who are in trouble with their adolescents).

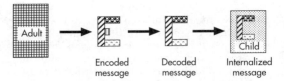

Encoded message   Decoded message   Internalized message

FIGURE 4.2 *The uni-directional model of transfer of culture from one generation to the next (transmission without novelty)*

The uni-directional model of transmission is widespread – it permeates our common language meanings. Likewise, it has its counterpart in the language of psychology and education. Thus, it is often considered that children's psychological functions are 'shaped' or 'moulded' by their parents, teachers, or peers. Knowledge is viewed as something given – which is to be 'learned' (as opposed to re-created). Discourse in traditional education, anthropology and child psychology has habitually accepted the implications of the uni-directional transfer view. This has been made possible by the lack of understanding of basic processes of development.

The bi-directional transfer model: active co-construction
Development of any kind and level (biological, psychological, sociological) is an open-systemic phenomenon in which novelty is *constantly in the process of being created* (see Chapter 1). Hence the

uni-directional transfer model cannot fit any of the open-systemic processes. It is the second model – the *bi-directional transfer model* – which can fit the nature of open systems. The bi-directional model is based on the premise that all participants in the cultural transfer of knowledge are actively transforming the cultural messages. In fact, it might be more adequately called the multi-directional transfer model – since the active role of all participants leads to multiple courses of reconstruction of messages.

The 'older' generation – parents, teachers, older peers, mass media etc. actively assemble messages of a certain unique form, which are meant to canalize the development of the younger persons. Yet these younger persons – equally actively – analyse the messages, and re-assemble the 'incoming cultural information' in personally novel forms. Thus, their analysis/synthesis of these messages is the process of exchange relations with their cultural environments that developmental sciences would study. Novelty is expected to result from the syntheses some of the time, in forms that are personally unique (even if they resemble socially known phenomena: for example, a child's first synthesis of a word meaning is new for that child, while the word may be well defined in the given language), as well as in forms that are unique in general (for example, new inventions in technology, arts, or sciences).

This view of cultural transmission entails construction of novelty *both* during encoding and decoding of the cultural messages. In some sense, the 'message' as such never exists in any 'given' form, as it is reconstructed by the encoder (who may start with a certain goal in mind, but shift it while creating the message), and by the decoder in a similar manner. As the roles of the encoder and decoder are constantly being changed into each other, cultural transmission involves transformation of culture in real time, by participants in the social discourse.

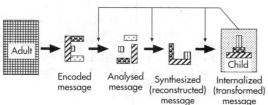

FIGURE 4.3 *The bi-directional model of transfer of culture from one generation to the next (the transmission process leads to novelty through personal reconstruction at internalization)*

HUMAN PSYCHE ORGANIZED BY CULTURE: PERSONAL AND COLLECTIVE

As is emphasized repeatedly in this book, cultural developmental psychology is process-focused. It treats human psychological phenomena (labelled here *psyche* in their full complex) not as entities, but as processes. These processes include culture – in the form of functioning semiotic mediators, signs – in specific locations in the processes.

Personal and collective cultures: their relations

Psychologically, the developing person and the surrounding world are cultural phenomena – in their reliance upon construction and reconstruction of signs in the course of development. It is possible to make a distinction between '*personal* culture' and '*collective* culture'. This distinction is merely a heuristic device to remind ourselves that the person, in their personal uniqueness, is always related with the cultural meaningful world through the process of constant internalization and externalization.

The notion of 'personal culture' refers not only to the internalized subjective phenomena (intra-mental processes), but to the immediate (person-centred) externalizations of those processes. The latter make personal culture publicly visible, as every aspect of personal reconstruction of one's immediate life-world reflects that externalization. Thus, the personal system of created meanings becomes projected to the world through personal arrangement of things that are important for the given person. This is reflected in the personal construction of publicly visible symbolic domains: body decorations, clothing, social display of personal objects, etc. It is also visible publicly in personally relevant inter-personal interaction rituals.

As is usually the case, heuristically valuable conceptual distinctions are re-constructed in the history of science in different versions. An effort to bring the term culture to function within the subjective personal sphere can be found in Georg Simmel's work at the turn of the nineteenth century (the distinction between the 'subjective' and the 'objective' cultures – see Chapter 3).

The subjective and objective cultures are mutually linked – there can be no subjective culture without its objective counterpart. However, the objective culture is a more autonomous entity, relative to particular subjective cultures. This parallels the relation of personal and collective cultures here. Simmel's objective culture is similar to the notion of collective culture. The reason for the label 'collective' (rather than 'objective') is in the personally constructed externalization nature of the collective culture. *The collective culture is composed of externalizations of personal meaning systems of always limited groups of persons.* The resulting collective culture is a relatively stable entity of collective origin. So, my collective culture may consist of all of my experience of other persons – friends, acquaintances, passers-by, beggars at church steps, policemen in the street, TV personages, old paintings created by artists years ago, and so on. These other persons have externalized their personal-cultural systems in specific ways. I, living my own life, encounter the results of these externalizations and use those as input into my own construction of my personal culture. I externalize the results of that construction, and thus become one of the participants in the collective culture of somebody else.

The developing person is constantly surrounded by social suggestions from the collective culture, either directly – by way of externalized cultural messages from specific 'social others' – or indirectly (by way of collective-cultural encoding of activity settings). The forms into which these messages are encoded are highly heterogeneous, ranging from the usual 'airwave' transmission of acoustic and visual information to external forms and colours of objects, haptic and tactile, or olfactory experiences of the child, and to specific emotiogenic episodes in which the child is a participant observer (Rogoff, 1990).

The emergence of collective cultures has been demonstrated by classic studies of social norm construction (Sherif, 1936). Human beings, when jointly experiencing a situation, create a joint understanding of the situation which becomes consensually validated and begins to function as a social norm. In the classic social psychology experiment on the 'autokinetic movement', Sherif demonstrated how such norm construction operated in the case of minimal perceptual stimuli.

The autokinetic movement occurs if, in a completely dark room, a single point of light, fixed at some distance from the viewers, is perceptually seen as moving, since it lacks any background framework relative to which its location can be fixed subjectively. If a person *is asked to report the extent of the movement,* he or she establishes subjectively a range and a point (in the dark), relative to which the stationary point is subjectively seen as moving (due to the viewer's own eye movements). When different persons view the same light point, their personally constructed norms for evaluating the movement differ. Yet if they are requested to report their estimates in publicly accessible ways, or discuss them in a group, their subjective norm system becomes collectively coordinated. A *group* norm for how to

see the stationary point 'moving' becomes established. Sherif's experiments with autokinetic movement (Sherif, 1937) demonstrated clearly how human beings create mental evaluation norms (for illusory perceptual experiences – such as the perceived movement of a non-moving light point), how they homogenize these norms inter-personally to create group norms. Furthermore, once such group norms are established, the members of the group can turn those into their internal standards of evaluation. Group consensus can create social illusions (based on perceptual ones) which come to regulate the person's own psychological system, as well as his or her expectations for others. In Chapter 10, we will encounter specific examples of how the family of a handicapped child collectively constructs the norm that the child is very intelligent – despite evidence to the contrary.

The social construction of group norms, and the resiliency of these norms, is constantly evidenced by various kinds of religious sects that establish their own standards for how to live themselves, and how to evaluate others' living their lives. A classic description of such a cult is given by Festinger, Riecken and Schachter (1956). A group of people becomes united around the calling by the cult leader to be 'prepared for the end of the world'. The expected event – the collapse of the whole world – is fortified by the 'miracle of God's revelation' to the group leader. It constituted the 'symbolic version' of the stationary light (viewed as moving) in Sherif's autokinetic experiment. An event expected in the future, but prepared for today, is indeterminate – and therefore open for the construction of group norms by people oriented towards that outcome. The goal-oriented group establishes its internal norms, ingroup/outgroup distinction ('we the special people versus "the others"'). The only difficulty may arise if the known doomsday passes without the event. Under conditions of rationality, this should falsify the system of group norms and beliefs. Yet, under the circumstances of sect-like groups, the disconfirmation can fortify the norms.

Collective cultural phenomena are particularly observable in the case of small groups oriented towards common goals (such as religious sects, adolescent gangs, football teams, small firms etc.). This is because their internal meaning systems have developed in directions that are detectable by the outsiders (among which researchers are included). These small groups and collectives also often establish ritualistic performances, which are observable by outsiders. All this provides a usable 'anchor point' for researchers – yet this may prove to be in itself an illusion (similarly to Sherif's autokinetic phenomenon). The easily observable phenomena of group, gang, or collective kind are outcomes of some collective-cultural processes that remain in a flux.

Collective culture as dynamic process

Collective culture is constantly constructed and reconstructed by various persons who are organized into a hierarchical structure of the given society (with constant migration within the hierarchy). *Collective culture is created via communicative interchanges between persons who construct it.* Thus, the collective culture is always present in a variety of parallel forms (constructed, in parallel, by different persons participating in different social groups).

It is not possible to continue along the tradition of labelling cultures (which is widespread in cross-cultural psychology) and describe collective cultures by way of country or ethnic group labels (for example, 'American collective culture', or 'Russian collective culture'). Such labelling would eliminate the heuristic value of the term, translating it back to the homogeneous notion of 'culture' that has plagued theorizing in cross-cultural psychology and anthropology.

Instead, the notion of collective culture is meant to assume heterogeneity (which could be seen as inconsistency from other vantage points) within its organization of the persons' social worlds, and in terms of semiotic systems is close to Mikhail Bakhtin's notion of hierarchy of social languages (see description of Bakhtin in Chapter 3). Different persons mutually linked within the same social unit – be it family, work-group, crowd, or a society as a whole – externalize their personal cultures in their unique ways. This creates the multi-voicedness of the social discourse within the given social unit. Within such multi-voicedness, different dominance relationships between these externalization results can be seen. There can be *consensus creation* (out of different externalized meanings). The created consensus subsequently begins to operate as a dominant 'voice' in inter-personal interaction, reducing the heterogeneity. Consensus creation leads to hierarchies of social languages that can be re-vamped – unless these become fixed by socio-institutional power by way of linking it with some general value (or action of a deity or spirit). Likewise, the dominance hierarchy of social languages can emerge by a top-down process – of superimposition of a general meaning (and its ideological implications) upon specific events. For instance, a declaration 'this is a *sin*' links a particular indicated object with the ill-defined general notion of 'sin', with its prescriptive ramifications (be these repentance, purification, or execution).

In the process of creation of social language hierarchies, care is taken to isolate and eliminate some of them from further discourse. Thus, for example, in the collective-cultural organization of the language hierarchies of science, the discourse using mythical explanatory material is rejected as non-scientific. Among different appropriate scientific languages, some (for example, the language of physics, or physiology, or biology) may become set up as hierarchical superiors to others (for example, the language of psychology, sociology, or history). Under such hierarchical conditions, a particular science may aim at adopting the social language that has become constructed to be superior to its current accepted language use. Psychology is a particularly good example – it is constantly attempting to emulate other sciences, be these physics, genetics, physiology – depending upon the particular historical period. In some societies, the dominance of some social language is set in place by institutional power – and as a result one can observe psychology in the former USSR being made 'pavlovian' in the 1950s, or in the US 'behaviouristic' (by creeping consensus) after 1913. The constant reorganization of the hierarchies of social languages indicates a basic social-historical process of discourse wars, rather than scientific breakthrough in our knowledge. Our contemporary fascination with a scientist declaring that she or he has found the 'gene for intelligence' is not different from similar statements by phrenologists of the nineteenth century (who could find a specific part of one's skull indicative of the same).

Developmental sciences as historical sciences

History is a science of basic processes of transformation of systems. As such, it belongs to basic sciences (like physics, chemistry etc.), only with a very different object of investigation. *History deals with the laws of development of open systems.*

The history of the notion of history itself has had its unfortunate transformations. Being first linked with the depiction of changes in societies – as written by chronicle-writers – it acquired the consensual meaning of ideological dependency upon the history writer, and was thus denigrated to the status of 'non-science' (or to that of social science). It is only in the second half of the twentieth century that the basic scientific nature of history becomes seen in its universal sense. This change is due to the introduction of the notion of history in physical chemistry (by Ilya Prigogine), and dependent upon the acceptance of the notion of irreversibility of time. Chemical reactions can result in irreversible transformations of matter, and hence chemistry can become a historical science.

In most general terms, there exists the basic axiom of historicity:

AXIOM OF HISTORICITY:

the study of *the time course of the formation* of selected phenomena

can

explain the present state of these phenomena.

This axiom indicates the unity of all developmental sciences, from chemical to biological to social. It has major implications for research methodology (see Chapter 5) since it requires time-based registration and analysis of the processes of becoming.

In accordance with this axiom, the notion 'the study of the time course of the formation' is not a question of simple empirical description. It directs the researcher to construct general models of time-inclusive processes, test these models on empirical historical data, and modify the general models. The axiom states that an adequate model of the process of formation can explain its outcomes (but not vice versa).

In developmental psychology, the axiom of historicity is slowly being put into research practice. The pioneers in this were James Mark Baldwin, Lev Vygotsky and Pavel Blonsky (refer back to Chapter 3). Blonsky's maxim 'behaviour can only be studied as history of behaviour' is a concrete elucidation of the axiom of historicity. In contemporary developmental psychology, computer modelling of time-based processes opens new doors for developmental science. This new direction is carried forward by the Flemish developmental psychologist Paul van Geert (see Chapter 2). Van Geert's development of new experimental theoretical developmental psychology – where theoretical models are experimentally generated, and then tested in their full range of generated versions against the full realm of phenomena – is a major fresh direction in contemporary developmental methodology (Van Geert, 1998).

Genetic dramatism

The notion of genetic dramatism was introduced by Bernard Kaplan. According to him, it 'is a critical and self-critical method for making us aware not only of the remarkable range of "worlds" we inhabit, but also of the symbolic ways in which we constitute such "worlds" and ourselves within those worlds' (Kaplan, 1983, p. 67).

Personal psychological phenomena in their socio-cultural contexts are captured by the notion of 'dramatism' – *the idealization of the actual* together with the *actualization of the ideal*.

By considering symbolic action constructive and creative, all episodes of dramatism are unfolding in time. For example, consider re-dramatizing the affective reaction of a boy – Milton Erickson's 3-year-old son – having sutures after suffering bleeding from a split lip and displaced tooth:

> After verbally reflecting his son's pain and the desire for the suffering to stop, Erickson turned to his wife to comment on the large quantity of blood on the pavement, and asked her to check whether it was "good, red, strong blood." They agreed that it seemed to be, but that this could be better determined against the white background of a sink. Once there, they and the no longer sobbing boy could observe that his blood "mixed properly with water," and gave it "proper pink color." Further inspection showed the boy's mouth to be "bleeding right" and "swelling right." Having satisfied himself aloud of his son's "essential and pleasing soundness in every way," Erickson told the boy that although he would have stitches in his lip, it was doubtful that he could have as many as he could count up to; he might not even have ten, though he could count to twenty. It was too bad that he could not have seventeen like his sister Betty Alice, or twelve, like his brother, Allan; but he could have more than Bert, or Lance, or Carol. The boy counted stitches as they were taken, and expressed disappointment when only seven were required. (Cirillo and Kaplan, 1983, pp. 237–238)

This insightful example into the process of co-construction of a genetic dramatism oriented towards helping the child to cope with the accident includes the use of specific collective-culturally accepted meanings. First, the checking of the 'proper' quality of blood, and of the (altered body state) 'being right' and 'swelling right' creates the supportive construction for the boy in the altered context (and under pain). These cultural organizers assist the child to restore a relatively calm reflection upon the traumatic event. The further introduction of competitiveness with siblings and peers, linked with the boy's capability to count, turned the procedure of getting the stitches from a medically traumatic event (which would endanger the boy's self/body) into a competitive accomplishment, thus diminishing the painfulness of the procedure by inserting a different meaning into the situation.

In general, every human life situation can be the birth-ground for construction of a genetic dramatism. Its universality is guaranteed by the readiness of human beings to play, fantasize and become involved in risky (yet thrilling) activities. Persons themselves create such dramatisms – and their 'social others': expect these to happen. Many of such constructions are expected by the collective-cultural orientation of the persons towards such constructions. The period of pregnancy, childbirth and the rest of childhood are filled with many dramatized occasions. In different societies the specific topics and periods of creating such dramatisms differ. Through dramatization, the semiotic capacities of distancing and reflecting upon the situation in new ways are made possible.

SUMMARY: FROM CULTURAL PSYCHOLOGY TO THE STUDY OF DEVELOPMENT OF HUMAN BEINGS

Culture is a part of the systemic organization of human psychological functions. It takes the form of constructing and using signs to transform the here-and-now setting of the human being. Human beings can distance themselves from any current setting through such cultural (semiotic) means. Yet they remain parts of the setting. Hence, *human cultural relating to the world entails simultaneous closeness to, and distancing from, the actual situation* the person is in.

This dynamic and constructionist view on culture creates the bridge between cultural and developmental psychologies. The former investigates the process of sign construction, use, and its results. These results involve novelty – the emergence of psychological phenomena that did not exist prior to the creation of new understanding, here-and-now, by way of a sign. Cultural psychology looks at the micro-settings of construction of the new. In this, its focus overlaps with that side of developmental psychology which takes interest in the *microgenesis* of psychological phenomena. Microgenesis is the process of emergence of novel forms in real time.

Of course, developmental psychology is not exclusively oriented towards microgenesis. It also

makes sense of ontogenesis, and phylogenesis, of developing biological systems. Developmental and cultural psychologies share the axiom of historicity (described above), while remaining only partly overlapping in their scopes of investigation. Developmental psychology is a sub-part of developmental biology – and it is the biological side of its scope that would not overlap with cultural psychology.

The overlap between the two sciences provides us with a hybrid – *cultural developmental psychology*. It borrows from general cultural psychology the notion of *semiotic regulation* of personal and collective cultures, and from developmental psychology – the focus on the *emergence of novelty*. This hybrid requires a fresh look at how knowledge about development can be obtained – which is the realm of methodology. Methodology, as will be seen in the next chapter, is a way to unify theory, methods and phenomena into one scheme of knowledge construction.

NOTE

1 The notion of hierarchy has been very limited in psychology's discourse. Usually by it is meant *linear hierarchy* which operates according to the *transitivity* rule (e.g., if A is dominant over B, and B dominant over C, then A is also dominant over C). However, there can be hierarchies that follow the *intransitivity* rule (if A dominates over B and B over C, it is not to be that A dominates over C; see also coverage in Chapter 2). One version of hierarchies that are intransitive is cyclical dominance relation, where A dominates over B, B over C, and C over A. In these latter versions, simple determination of dominance is not determinable, as can be seen, A both dominates over C (through the intermediary of B), *yet is simultanously dominated by C.*

REVIEW QUESTIONS FOR CHAPTER 4

1 Explain how the term *culture* has been used in psychology.

2 Explain the notion of *culture* as semiotic mediation.

3 How has the notion of *culture* been used in anthropology?

4 Analyse the process structure of psychological distancing.

5 Explain the contrast RAW < > COOKED.

6 Explain the contrast NATURAL < > CULTIVATED.

7   Describe the uni-directional culture transfer model.

8   Describe the bi-directional culture transfer model.

9   What is *personal culture* and how can one study it?

10 Explain the notion of collective culture. How is it related to the personal culture?

11 Describe and explain the *axiom of historicity*.

12 What is genetic dramatism?

5

DEVELOPMENTAL METHODOLOGY IN CULTURAL DEVELOPMENTAL PSYCHOLOGY

25 years ago when I became involved in the training of American students in experimental psychology, I got rather apprehensive at finding that students were frequently taught that there was only one acceptable way of conduct in the laboratory; there has to be set up rigidly a hypothesis, or a set of hypotheses, and the main job of the experimenter was to prove or disprove the hypothesis. What is missed here is the function of the scientist as a discoverer and explorer of unknown lands rather than only as a deductive methodologist. Hypotheses, to be sure, are essential intellectual elements of inquiry, but they are so, not as rigid propositions, but as flexible parts of the process of searching; by the same token, conclusions drawn from the results, again, are as much an end as a beginning.

Werner (1959, p. 64)

Any science is oriented towards construction of general knowledge. In this respect, each scientist is a discoverer of new lands, trying to make sense of the unfamiliar in terms of the familiar. It is here where the question of the rigidity of pre-conceived general notions – mentioned by Werner – makes a difference between a scientist and an ideologist. The latter tries to superimpose on the unfamiliar some strictly held general notion. That general notion may be shared by some – or many – persons who adhere to it. The ideologist claims to gain support from social consensus – even if the general notion may be limited or inappropriate to reality. The more inappropriate, the more can the ideologist adhere to the comfort of social consensus.

In contrast, the scientist uses previously created general ideas as beginning guidelines for further enquiry, which is expected to lead to the change of the general ideas into a more appropriate form.

The scientist may also follow a particular general idea with full conviction – yet together with such conviction the possibilities for doubt are entertained. If some specific evidence contradicts the general idea, the latter would be changed, or abandoned.

There is always a tension between the general and the specific in science. All the concrete efforts of scientific research are targeting specific objects in their specific contexts. Yet the reasons for such enquiry are general and abstract. Hence the question of how to arrive at general knowledge has been at the centre of any science's concern. This finds its expression in scientists' discourse about methodology, which is a topic fiercely ideological in contemporary psychology. From the very beginning of their studies, psychology students are persuaded that *the* only 'scientific method' in psychology is '*the* statistical method' (and that the only kind of 'scientific knowledge' is based on quantified data). Such ideological claims are profoundly unscientific – since they replace the focus of researchers on the complex process of knowledge creation by a scenario where science is supposed to be created by way of following a pre-given standard protocol for data collection. Such modern reliance on the 'standardized methods' is akin to medieval scholasticism (with inquisition-like testing of the 'solidity of scientific character' through examination of whether 'the right' methods are used by the scientists). Nothing can be more productive for stopping active and open enquiry into the nature of phenomena of any science. In this respect, psychology risks the loss of its scientific status by way of insisting upon the use of a fixed set of methods. Ironically, it is precisely that scientific status that the insistence on the rigid application of such methods is supposed to defend.

DIFFERENT WAYS OF LOOKING AT METHODOLOGY: 'TOOLBOX OF METHODS' VS STRATEGY FOR GENERALIZATION

What methodology means for a given science depends upon the history of that science, its relations with other sciences, and with the socio-political realms of the given society. The latter connection is particularly eminent in the social sciences, which are interwoven with social ideologies. It is less prominent in the physical sciences – even if the conflict with the Catholic church about the models of planetary system (Earth-centred, versus Sun-centred) that led a number of scientists to be politically persecuted is evidence to the contrary.

In our contemporary psychology, methodology is often viewed as a collection of ready-made methods – a ready 'tool-box' – that can be applied to any research question a psychologist may be interested in. Likewise, it is often claimed that psychology's methodology includes necessary quantification of the data, and that only quantified data have the solidity of objectivity. This stance fits well with the notion of psychology as 'empirical science' – an ideological invention that is tautological in its substance, and which leads to a practical focus on accumulation of disconnected 'pieces' of empirical evidence.

The notion of 'empirical science' is tautological because any science entails a link between general theoretical constructions and some part of empirical reality. An expression like that is akin to claims such as 'sweet sugar' or 'rainy rain'. Of course, in the history of psychology the emphasis on it as 'empirical science' has been used to defend the discipline against different excesses of social theories entering into the field with strong presuppositions. Psychology's ideologies-linked nature has led to efforts to defend itself as science against ideologies.

Psychology is 'empirical science' because it is constantly under the influence of social ideologies that originally needed to separate the discipline from general religious-moral ideologies. This was accomplished by setting up the opposition SPECULATION < > DATA-BASED SCIENCE. In contrast to religious and philosophical treatises of human psychological issues, psychology as science attempted to be near to phenomena of the real kind. Early psychology's concerns with perception and introspection maintained a close link between the phenomena and the data. The value of research was determined by how well the data represented the phenomena about which they were to give new knowledge – and not on the basis of the use of 'right' methods.

However, the content matter of psychology is never sociopolitically neutral. The need to control the conduct of human beings is a task for numerous social institutions in any society, which – especially around the time of the First World War – integrated psychology into their social role schemes and practices. Psychology *became a discipline of value for application in a society* – and hence part of the social ideologies of application. It is not surprising that the first successes of psychology in practical application were linked with testing of intelligence (and selection of personnel – especially in the 1920s). As a result, the focus on the 'rightness of methods' (for example, 'standardized' methods became considered as 'right' ones) emerged as an ideological notion. It took over psychology through the concerted efforts – inherently contradictory ones (Gigerenzer et al., 1989) – to turn statistical thinking into the norm for 'correct inference'. Interestingly, psychology thus moved a full circle, from the fight for liberation (from socio-religious political dogmatism) to establishing its own domain of basic knowledge, which became overtaken by the political interests of institutions that wanted to appropriate that knowledge for their practical goals. The result was a new form of subordination – but now no longer to religious-philosophical but social-administrative dogmas.

'Theories and systems'

The history of psychology is indicative of such a move into new dependence. The defence against ideological interventions has led psychology to be wary of any kind of theorizing – except for general frameworks (or 'systems') that are usually implied. Yet these latter frameworks are treated not as heterogeneous systems of ideas, but as homogeneous 'party lines' which are opposed to others of the kind. This is exemplified in the presentation of different ideas under the classificatory ethos of 'theories and systems' of psychology. In such presentations, labels like 'Vygotskian' or 'Piagetian' research are often used as common labels that are supposed to *socially legitimize a topic of research* (for example, social support for mental action, or the child's construction of knowledge). The relationship between these 'psychological systems-parties' follows the lines of the political power-renegotiations in the given society. In one decade of psychology in the United States the 'cognitive science' is turned into the dominant direction for research, and local discourse between psychologists (and in the lay press) pays homage to the 'new scientific frontier'. A decade later, the previous orientation goes out of dominance, and is replaced by some other.

The treatment of theoretical frameworks as 'systems' (read: 'parties') is the basis for the *introduction of discontinuity between the general thought and empirical practice.* The 'theory parties' are not connected with the specific methods the researcher uses. Instead, the party line-following researchers are assumed to choose freely between different available methods in the 'toolbox'.

For example, a researcher may use factor analysis of correlational data based on a sample of children and their teachers' actions, claiming affinity to a 'Vygotskian' approach. There is a major intellectual discrepancy between the claimed 'theory/party' cover, and the empirical application of methods. The application of the 'Vygotskian' label violates the following assumptions inherent in Vygotsky's theorizing: (a) psychological synthesis is not available in the 'measures' that are correlated and factor-analysed; (b) the definitive data source is the single case in its context, not a sample. These violations – either of them, or both together – are sufficient to eliminate the value of the empirical data from any 'Vygotskian perspective' that is claimed by the researcher. The notion of methodology as a 'toolbox of methods' allows for proliferation of construction of empirical data, but not for construction of general knowledge.

Socially guarded rigidity of reasoning

Methodology in psychology is an object of fierce discussions and socio-political power clashes capable of making otherwise reasonable human beings into quasi-fundamentalist zealots. Viewed from a cultural-psychological perspective, this results from the negotiation of the role of the given brand of scientists within the wider social system of societies. As scientists are negotiating their roles as any other social group does, it depends upon the given society how the usual social processes. Ingroup/outgroup distinctions are being made, with stigmatization of the outgroup (if the latter is less powerful, yet dangerous), or idealization of an outgroup (with take-over intentions) also taking place. Last – but not least – such negotiation of the role of scientists in the given field can include recurrent construction of fights with 'straw men' (for example, 'post-modern' psychologists beating upon the supposed 'behaviourists' or 'positivists' for all the ills of the contemporary psychology), or wholesale banishing of some perspectives from the sacred realm of 'science' (see Parker, 1998 for an analysis of the role of post-modernism in psychology).

Of course, different sciences differ in the ways they use these basic social processes. Psychology (and other social sciences) may give more examples of such rhetoric battles than many natural sciences. Yet this may be an illusion – psychology's major rhetoric battles are easily visible to outsiders due to the overlap of the meanings of scientific and everyday concepts. So, if Psychologist A accuses Psychologist B for the latter's 'non-objective' study of 'intelligence', the topic can be perceived as understandable and valuable ('intelligence' of course must be studied 'objectively'!), whereas when similar claims are made in relation to 'cold fusion' in physics the knowledge domain is foreign to laypersons' minds.

Scientists are basically not different from any other layperson when they deal with meta-scientific rhetoric issues of the social group. As Kurt Lewin remarked,

> Like social taboos, a scientific taboo is kept not so much by a rational argument as by a common attitude among scientists: any member of the scientific guild who does not strictly adhere to the taboo is looked upon as queer; he is suspected of not adhering to the scientific standards of critical thinking. (Lewin, 1949, p. 279)

In contemporary psychology, this remark can be seen to reflect the frequently privileged social discourse about 'the method'. This seems to be aggravated in the fight between the proponents of 'quantitative' and 'qualitative' methods. Yet the fight itself is immaterial, as methods cannot be extracted from the major methodological circle.

Methodology as a cycle

If construction of general knowledge is the focus of methodology (as in any science), then methodology cannot be seen as a 'toolbox' of different ready-made methods. Rather, it needs to be viewed as a process of human mental construction of generalizations. It entails mutually linked components of general assumptions about the world at large (axioms), specific constructed theories of the given target area, understanding of pertinent phenomena, and – finally – ways of constructing specific methods to transform some aspects of the phenomena into purposefully derived data. *Data are always constructed*, or – better – *derived from phenomena*, on the basis of the investigator's reasoning. The data are not collected as pre-given – on the basis of the richness of phenomena on the one hand, and in accordance with the researcher's construction of axiomatic and theoretical kinds on the other. A look at methodology as a process cycle is given in Figure 5.1, which shows the present author's general model of methodology as a cyclical research process. The components in the process are depicted as existing at different levels of generality – the axiomatic views of the

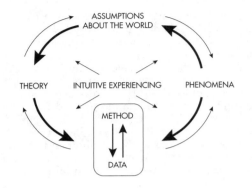

EXPLANATION: Methodology is depicted as a circle (or cycle) that unites all sides of research, as well as the subjective world of the researcher (who intuitively experiences all of the sides). The relative strength of the oppositely directed arrows at each connection indicates the dominance of the role of one direction of inferential 'movement' over its opposite counterpart

FIGURE 5.1 *The methodology cycle that unites the empirical and non-empirical sides of the research process (from Branco & Valsiner, 1997)*

world are more general than theories or intuitive reflections about phenomena; and the latter more general than the methods that generate data. An explicit emphasis is reserved for the subjectivity of the researcher – who intuitively experiences phenomena in connection with his or her axioms, and constructs theories from their own personal standpoint. Scientists are not feelingless robots, but subjective, personally involved human beings who have their subjective preferences, and positions from which they look at the targets of their research.

The methods and the data are constructed by the researcher on the basis of the specific structure of the process cycle. Methodology here is equal to the cyclical process of general knowledge construction, where different parts of the cycle feed differentially into other parts. Different researchers set up these dynamic relations differently, given their credo of how science creates knowledge.

Figure 5.1 represents the methodology cycle that the author's work is based upon. This version of the cycle could be considered *bi-modally deductively driven*. The contrast of 'fat' and 'lean' arrows in the cycle indicates the particular direction of the dominance of one part of this scheme over the other. Thus, construction of the METHODS ⇆ DATA relation is dominated – in the ideal case – by its joint basis in both the theory and the phenomena. Relatively moderate (yet existing!) corrective feedback can exist in the

direction from the METHODS ⇆ DATA loop towards reconstruction of the theory. Science is theory-driven in general, but theories can be modified on the basis of empirical evidence in some of their structural parts. Theories rarely change in their entirety, on the basis of empirical input. Yet, when found to be built on untenable basic assumptions, they can be re-done in major ways.

The practice of data derivation may introduce some changes into the phenomena as well. For instance, a researcher who has interviewed the subject on a topic about which the subject had not previously thought, may start an avalanche of personal and social reconstruction efforts of the phenomena. An interviewer may ask questions of an interviewee about how her father provided tactile contact when she was a child, linking that information *by implication* with the general notion of 'parental abuse' (given the contemporary popularity of social discourse about 'child abuse'). After the interview, the interviewee may construct the personal conviction that her father's tender touch in her childhood was really a case of 'abuse', and may hate her father accordingly. The next time the interviewer approaches the interviewee for further questions, the phenomena will have changed on the basis of the research process.

The description given in Figure 5.1 is not meant to be normative, except for the *cyclical linking of the parts of the methodology process*. The components and the notion of cycle are normative givens, while the exact build-up of the arrows of relationships may vary from one investigator to another. For instance, Figure 5.2*A* shows *a completely inductive model* of the methodology cycle.

In Figure 5.2, it is presumed that the empirical data are the basis for all other aspects of the methodology cycle construction. Given the METHODS ⇆ DATA relation, the researcher's theory becomes created, and his or her notion of phenomena becomes changed. Both the constructed theory and changed view of the phenomena lead to reorganization of the researcher's axioms about the world at large. This version of the methodology cycle exemplifies the maximum case of belief in the 'blind empiricism' – the case where the data are seen as the most powerful and unquestionable guarantee for scientific knowledge.

By reversing the direction of arrows in Figure 5.2*A* (as is done in Figure 5.2*B*), we get an example of *a completely deductive model* of the methodology cycle. Here the basic general views of the world (axioms) completely determine all other parts of the methodology cycle. Both the completely inductive and completely deductive models are

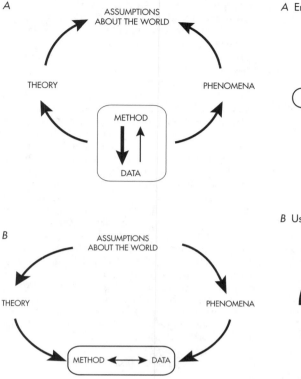

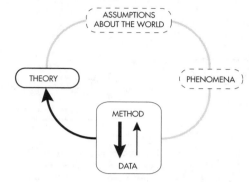

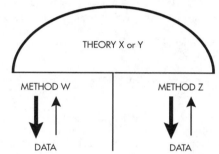

FIGURE 5.2 *Two versions of the methodology cycle: inductively (A) and deductively (B) determined*

FIGURE 5.3 *Two contemporary transformations of the methodology cycle*

examples of orthodox-religious solutions to the issue of methodology, since no corrective feedback possibilities are included in either case (*A* and *B*). The fact that the completely inductive model is 'data-driven' (whereas its deductive counterpart is 'dogma-driven') makes it no less rigid – the 'religion of the data' is no different from the dominance of the dogmas of deductive kinds.

Existing received methodological practices in psychology certainly do not make full use of either of these opposite extreme models, but translate the methodology cycle into its limited partial versions (see Figure 5.3). In Figure 5.3*A*, we see how the axiomatic and phenomenological parts of the methodology cycle have become overlooked in specific research practices, which retain only the METHODS ⇆ DATA and THEORIES linkages. Furthermore, THEORIES become used as general 'umbrellas' for empirical work that subordinates DATA to the selection of 'correct', 'objective', or 'powerful' METHODS (depicted in Figure 5.3*B*). The latter case is illustrative of the notion of 'psychology as empirical science' that was described above.

The role of the researcher in knowledge construction

As was obvious from Figure 5.1, *the constructor of any scientific knowledge is a living human being –* and not a pre-programmed robot or computer program. The scientist, like the layperson, operates on the basis of the person's subjective intuitions in creating his or her particular version of the 'methodology cycle'. Yet in that process the scientist can (and does) build on unproductive meanings that guide one's intuitions. It is particularly in the case of social sciences that the scientist's personal-cultural intuitions are collective-culturally canalized.

The actual process of knowledge construction entails integration of two inductions (as described by C. Lloyd Morgan, 1894) in a scientific thinking process which emphasizes synthesis of new understanding of reality (see Figure 5.4).

The scientist is constantly operating on the basis of the person's intra-mental understanding ('first induction', A–B) of what it is that is being

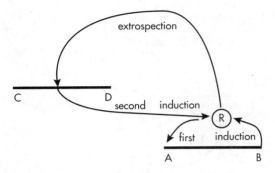

EXPLANATION: R is the researcher, who examines the intra-psychological realm (AB) for understanding about the phenomena (which are located in the external world, as CD). As a result of such examination ('first induction'), R creates guidelines for observing the phenomena extrospectively. Results of that external observation feed into R's further understanding of the phenomena ('second induction'). The two inductions are mutually linked in a systemic loop where R's knowledge is contstantly innovated by both.

FIGURE 5.4 *C. Lloyd Morgan's 'two inductions'*

studied, how to study it, and what to expect. Yet, differently from philosophers, the scientist moves from such intra-psychological reflection into an effort to gain knowledge about the object of investigation through observing the others (through extrospection). The results of such observation lead to the 'second induction', (C–D). The 'second induction' is the process of relying on the empirical evidence that is constantly emphasized in psychology. Yet without the 'first induction', the 'second induction' is unable to make sense of the data. There is a frequent saying used by empirical psychologists – 'let your data speak for themselves' (this slogan emphasizes Morgan's 'second induction'). However, the crucial question about that slogan remains, 'which language do the data speak?' and 'how have the data learned to speak at all?'. These questions emphasize the role of the 'first induction'.

Morgan's effort was to demonstrate that the unity of both inductions is necessary for scientific inference. The process by which new knowledge emerges from that unity of inductive processes is *abduction*. Abduction is a process of creative synthesis – a qualitative 'leap' of our understanding – into a new general state. In psychology, phenomena of abduction have been described as 'insight' – sudden arrival at problem solutions by humans (Bühler, 1907) and animals (Köhler, 1925). Only through abductive inference can scientific knowledge progress. It is the break-

throughs in our basic understanding of both nature and society that science provides through overcoming the confines of lay thought and value constructions.

A scientist can thus project into the phenomena his or her particularly strong beliefs and values, which then lead him or her actually to see the phenomenon *as if its inherent nature confirms* one's hypotheses. Hence it is a rather ambivalent and at times questionable practice that is widespread practice in psychology, where hypotheses are required to be stated and then proven to be correct. In reality, such a practice defeats itself (see Smedslund, 1995) as it eliminates the possibility to learn about the phenomena precisely by proving one's initial idea to be wrong (disconfirmation of initial hypothesis). If we prove what we thought was the case, then we knew it before the effort of the study. Hence confirmation is less productive for knowledge innovation than disconfirmation – in the latter case, the empirical research introduces relevant corrections to the initial view. Empirical research is important in breaking up the scientist's previous culturally canalized interpretation. Yet without such previous interpretations there would be no place in which to situate one's empirical evidence.

Social privileging of methods in different psychologies

We can provide an example of how two different methodological perspectives differentially privilege different operations in the derivation of the data from the phenomena. In Figure 5.5, an effort is made to contrast the contemporary 'received view' of data derivation in psychology, with that of the emerging direction in cultural psychologies. Admittedly, these two pictures are somewhat general composites – each particular tradition in psychology at large, and among different versions of cultural psychology, would differ in the specific patterns of such privileging. In all cases, implicit cultural canalization of scientists can prevail if it acquires collective-culturally consensual validation in the community of researchers. For example, the dominant direction of researchers towards use of 'standardized methods' is a result of social consensus. It has no basis in the methodology cycle (as described above). The discouragement of the research directions that retain the holistic nature of the phenomena (left half of Figure 5.5A) – except for the study of problem-solving – is equally a result of a social ingroup/outgroup formation process.

As is obvious in Figure 5.5B, cultural psychology's research effort specifies the direction of the researcher's cultural canalization while in the 'traditional' direction this issue remains out of

A Contemporary psychology's existing and social organization of researchers' orientations

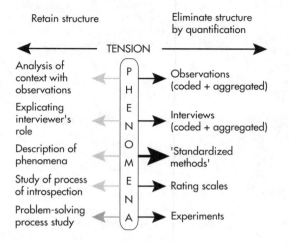

B Cultural psychology's orientation

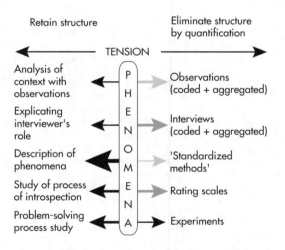

FIGURE 5.5 *Privileging and disprivileging different research orientations*

focus (yet it exists). Analysis of the contexts of the phenomena, and of the researcher's role in the research process, become emphasized under the social privileging of the holistic research orientation. If viewed historically, the holistic orientation in contemporary cultural psychology recreates the version of privileging that existed in psychology at the beginning of the twentieth century.

METHODOLOGY IN CULTURAL DEVELOPMENTAL PSYCHOLOGY

Methodology is a relation between basic assumptions, theories, phenomena, methods and data. Both the 'religious' versions of the methodology cycle (Figure 5.2) and 'empiricistic' versions (Figure 5.3) are not applicable in the case of science. The specific content focus of a science sets up the kinds of axioms that the methodology cycle needs to include. These axioms are organized by general knowledge-constructing orientations of the researchers, which are here called *frames of reference*.

Frames of reference in researchers' perspectives

Frames of reference are *general conceptual positioning devices in the minds of researchers*, who set up their research questions and construct methods in ways that unify different levels of the methodology cycle. The same phenomenon can be studied very differently – from the different perspectives specified by the different reference frames. Frames of reference are thus constructed restrictions upon the ways in which METHODS are constructed, in ways that fit the constructed THEORY which is based on the general visions. Frames of reference thus narrow down the focus of empirical research efforts in ways that should maintain the consistency of the methodology cycle.

How can this happen? If a research question is based on axioms (general visions of the world) that are formulated within one frame of reference, then the corresponding theory built on the basis of these axioms needs to remain within the given frame, and the particular methods that are created must also be within the same frame. Or, if there exist changes between reference frames in the move from AXIOMS to THEORY to METHOD, such changes need to be substantiated. Let us consider an example:

AXIOM: human personality is GENDERED (= features of personality, whichever way thought of, are linked with the gender of the person, male or female).

THEORY: the GENDERED nature of personality features operates as an INTENSIFIER of those features of the personality that are STRONGLY (as opposed to WEAKLY) GENDERED, and as a DE-INTENSIFIER of those features that are WEAKLY GENDERED. Here the notion of quantity of the strength of gender is posited, and assumed to be determinable in the case of each personality feature.

SCENARIOS FOR CONSTRUCTING METHODS. All methods to be constructed would take the form of persons' SELF-REPORT, yet the specific ways of constructing these methods would vary.

Scenario 1:

1 Each person answers 'true' of 'false' to each item of his/her personality trait/feature 'checklist', the general format of each item being 'I am [personality feature term]'.
2 Each term in the list is labelled (by the researcher) as either being 'masculine' or 'feminine'.
3 The sum total of a person's 'true' answers to 'feminine' items is compared with the sum total of the same person's 'masculine' items.
4 Samples of men and women are subsequently compared with one another, finding out that women have endorsed a statistically significantly greater number of 'feminine' items (on the average) than men, and that men (on the average) have endorsed more of the 'masculine' items than women.
5 A conclusion is made that the women's STRONGLY GENDERED personality features are related to their being women, and correspondingly the discounting of opposite-gendered features (weak for them) indicates the truthfulness of the posited theory (and reverse proof from men).

EVALUATION of Scenario 1: The theoretical question was set up within the intra-individual frame (see below), and the method constructed continued to be within that frame. Yet the method does not allow derivation of data that would be directly pertinent to the theory (which posited determinability of GENDEREDNESS of *each* personality feature and its further role). Instead, the empirical endeavour is moved into a summative accumulation of data (step 3) and further into the inter-individual reference frame (step 4). The conclusion (step 5) does not pertain to the theory that was set up, because the reference frame has been changed. The theory would have required direct analysis of GENDEREDNESS of each item in the checklist, and evaluation of the centrality of the given feature within the personality structure of the given person (individual subject). Instead, the researchers provide a group comparison of pre-determinatedly gendered items, summed over each person's response sheet and across persons who belong to the same gender group. The empirical evidence in this scenario does not illuminate the proposed theory.

Scenario 2:

1 Each person answers 'true' of 'false' to each item of his/her personality trait/feature 'checklist', the general format of each item being 'I am [personality feature term]'.
2 Immediately next to each item are two rating scales:

how
FEMININE
is this feature?
{minimum} 0 —— 1 —— 2 —— 3 —— 4 {maximum}

how
MASCULINE
is this feature?
{minimum} 0 ——1 —— 2 —— 3 —— 4 {maximum}

3 *All 'true' answers* of *rating of at least 3* on *either* 'feminine' or 'masculine' scale are selected for further analysis. These constitute the STRONGLY GENDERED FEATURES category. Similarly, *all 'true' answers* of ratings 0 or 1 on *either* 'feminine' or 'masculine' scale are selected for further analysis. These constitute the category of WEAKLY GENDERED FEATURES.
4 Each of the features in the two categories, written on a separate card, is given to the same person in the form of a pile of cards. The person is asked to divide the cards into three piles: 'important for my personality', 'unimportant for my personality', and 'can't judge'.
5 The resulting classifications of 'important' versus 'unimportant' are tested for any inclusion of STRONGLY GENDERED items in the category of 'unimportant', and, conversely, for any inclusion of WEAKLY GENDERED items in the class of 'important'. This comparison is carried out within each research participant – the theory is tested on each individual case. The theory gains empirical support if all STRONGLY GENDERED items are found to be 'important', and all WEAKLY GENDERED ones in the class of 'unimportant'. In case of overlaps, simple non-parametric statistical devices (chi-square) can be used to evaluate the extent of overlap.

EVALUATION of Scenario 2: In this hypothetical project, the frame of reference is maintained to be that of the intra-individual kind, at the transition from theory to method. In full accordance with the theoretically posited quantified nature of strength of genderedness, the method probes it directly (albeit on the basis of self-evaluation, which is appropriate here) for each personality feature (step 2). Note that it is not posited in the theory whether the strength of 'genderedness' has to be of the same kind as the gender of the respondent. That is why (at step 3) the STRENGTH of either the 'masculinity' or 'femininity' rating is used as a selection feature. The theoretically posited notion of 'intensification versus de-intensification' is translated (step 4) into a card-sorting task, applied within the same person. It is only here that the process notion (implied in intensification/de-intensification) becomes method-wise translated into a decision of a static kind (important/unimportant), the adequacy of which may be questioned. However, otherwise the study maintains consistency between the levels of generality of the methodology cycle, through the consistent use of the intra-individual frame of reference.

Thus, consistency of methodology is based on a clear decision about which frame of reference is adequate for which research question. Four different frames of reference can be outlined: the first two (intra-individual and inter-individual) are fit for non-developmental perspectives in psychology, and the remaining two (individual ecological and individual socio-ecological) fit the needs for consistently developmental methodology.

The intra-individual *(intra-systemic)* reference frame

The intra-individual frame of reference treats all issues of an individual system's organization (for example, a person's, or society's, or that of a small social group) as if it is fully determined by relationships within the system. The use of Scenario 2 above for the study of intrinsic organization of human (self-reported) personality structure is an example of how this frame of reference can be used in psychology. In more familiar terms, consider Freud's construction of generic personality structure as involving the notions of id, ego and superego. These three components are located – by researchers' designation – within each person, and their particular set of relationships gives rise to the immense variety of psychological phenomena of personality-in-contexts. The intra-individual frame of reference, when applied to personality, decontextualizes the personality system from its environment. Instead, it *focuses upon the specific ways in which complexity of the intra-systemic kind is organized.*

There are various ways in which such systemic organization can be posited. First, there is the possibility for projecting into the system one single causal agent. For example, in psycholo-

gists' discourse we may hear statements like 'Johnny behaves badly *because* HE **IS** HYPER-ACTIVE', or 'Susan cannot succeed in her studies *because* SHE **IS** LEARNING-DISABLED.' Both of these statements are tautological (for example, 'learning disability' is a term based on detection of a child's difficulties with study, or 'hyper-activity' detected on the basis of behaviour which falls out of the 'good' kind, in the evaluator's mind). They entail a PROJECTION INTO THE PERSON (Johnny or Susan) of specific psychological characteristics, and THEN consider those characteristics to be causes of the person's ways of being. The explanatory terms thus projected are unitary (an example of the *elementaristic direct causality* model, see below). If a number of parallel causal explanatory terms is projected into the system in a similar way, the intra-individual frame still unifies the projected multiple causality.

It is possible to construct *systemic direct causality* model (see below) projections into the person, as is the case of linking the projected explanatory terms with one another in some system. Thus, Johnny's 'misbehaviour' can be explained by a particular relation (within his personality) of the feature of HYPERACTVITY with Johnny's INTERNALIZED NORMS FOR 'GOOD BEHAVIOUR' (see Figure 5.6).

It is easy to see how the two kinds of projections of causal explanatory entities into the system are the same. Projection of general labels into the system (for example, 'Mary succeeds in her studies because of learning') are merely a short-

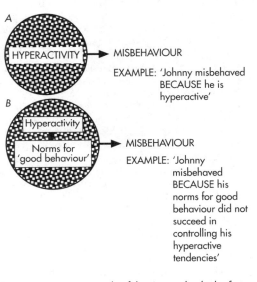

FIGURE 5.6 *An example of the intra-individual reference frame*

hand reference to a complex system by which the 'learning' takes place. It is possible to de-compose such unitary labels into complex systemic causal networks, yet in both cases the projection of causality to the realm within the given system eliminates the focus on the relations of the system with its environment. As was pointed out in Chapter 1, such relations are central for the study of development. Therefore, the intra-individual frame of reference is not adequate for the study of development.

The inter-individual *(inter-systemic)* reference frame

This frame involves comparison of features that are projected into the systems, on the basis of external features of the projected characteristics that differ between the systems. In contrast with the intra-systemic frame, the focus here is removed from the projection itself (which is taken for granted) to the differences in the 'expressions' of the projected characteristics from one system to another.

This reference frame is most widely used in non-developmental psychology. It involves comparisons of individuals ('Mary does better than Susie on test X'), or samples of subjects (for example, the gender comparison in Scenario 1, above). In the application of this reference frame, somebody is always 'doing better' than somebody else, supposedly because he or she 'has' some characteristics inherent in the person *in different quantity* than others. The inter-individual frame of reference is widely popular in psychology as that discipline has idealized quantitative tactics of data construction, which makes comparisons between 'more' and 'less' cases 'having X' an appealing and easy empirical research goal.

The inter-individual frame of reference relies on the human propensity for evaluative competitive comparisons. Not only is a finding 'Johnny *does better* than Jimmy in arithmetic' a statement about differences between the two children, but it simultaneously reflects the sayer's evaluative preference. Why is it assumed that having a higher score in an arithmetic test is 'better' than having a lower score? This value is encoded into our collective-cultural meaning system of seeing educational achievement as valuable. Compare it with 'Johnny does better than Jimmy on tests of hyperactivity.' Here the value-added meaning is unclear: is Johnny's hyperactivity greater than Jimmy's, or lower (see Figure 5.7).

Most of the inter-systemic frame uses are supported by inherent values which the researchers,

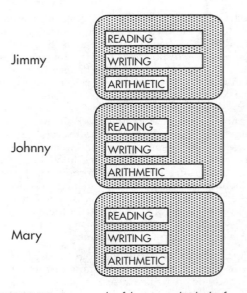

FIGURE 5.7 *An example of the inter-individual reference frame*

as well as consumers of scientific data, project into the data. This may explain why, in most of non-developmental psychology, the inter-systemic reference frame is the overwhelmingly dominant one. It is an almost automatic move on behalf of researchers that a new research problem becomes framed within the inter-systemic reference frame (see Scenario 1, above).

However, from the perspective of developmental methodology, both the intra-systemic and inter-systemic reference frames are inadequate. If development is defined as an open-systemic phenomenon (refer back to Chapter 1) which is possible only thanks to the system's constant exchange relationship with the environment, then both the intra-systemic and inter-systemic reference frames purposefully overlook that exchange relation. This may be sufficient for the research goals of non-developmental psychology, but is clearly inappropriate for a consistently developmental science. For the latter, two other reference frames are appropriate.

The individual-ecological reference frame

The individual-ecological frame of reference considers a system (person, social group, community) which is the focus of attention of the investigator as that system acts upon its environment, and as the results of such action participate in the transformation of the system. This is generally depicted in Figure 5.8.

The Figure depicts researchers' interest in the process of the developing person's actions upon the environment, and the feedback from these actions that leads the development of the person (from time 1 to time 2 to time 3 etc.). This reference frame involves mutual consideration of the person and the environment, and focusing upon their relationships. It allows a glimpse into the goal-oriented actions of the person – who acts upon the environment with some future-oriented purpose (for example, solving a problem). The action results in feedback from the changed environment upon the person. That feedback participates in the change of the person into a new state.

Human development through problem-solving activities, over the whole life span, is a realistic phenomenon that can be studied through the use of the individual-ecological frame. Each problem for our actions is given by some problem situation in a here-and-now setting. We set up a goal (desired solution) and try to act towards reaching that goal. The process of trying will lead our modification of ourselves: we transform due to the exchange-relation with the problem situation. The goal-oriented problem-solving effort is the context for development of the problem-solver. It is not necessary to compare the problem-solver with others of the kind (this was the focus of the

inter-systemic reference frame), but the *process of unfolding of solutions and construction of novel ones* is the focus area of the individual-ecological frame.

Many classic developmental scientists have used the individual-ecological frame of reference. Jean Piaget's studies of children's knowledge construction, using his 'clinical method', is the best example. The knowledge-constructing child in Piaget's problem-solving tasks is confronted with a field of knowledge he or she does not yet understand. By way of acting upon objects within that field, knowledge becomes constructed by the child. In non-developmental psychology, the classic studies of problem-solving by Max Wertheimer, Karl Duncker, Herbert Simon and others use this frame (Duncker, 1945; Simon, 1957; Wertheimer, 1945/1982).

The developing person depicted through the lens of the individual-ecological reference frame faces the surrounding environment alone. This may be adequate for looking at development in many animal species, but not in the case of human beings. Humans not only face their environment, they do so together with other humans who provide social suggestions for the ways in which to deal with the environment. The human environment is culturally organized – it includes man-made objects, and many persons who act

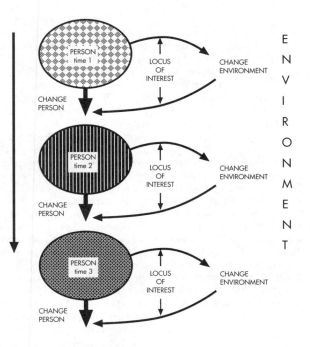

FIGURE 5.8 *The individual-ecological frame of reference*

upon a particular person's action towards an environmental setting.

Consider the 'problem' I as a lonely tourist may encounter in a city square, entering a tall building with a clock-tower, built in the Middle Ages. The architecture of that building suggests to me that I am entering into a *church* (rather than McDonalds), and my actions in relation to any aspect of the environment in that church are guided by my constructed meaning of that building as *church*. I may stay silent while in that building, even though *nobody has explicitly told me to be silent in that particular building*. I carry the meaning of *church* with me from my past personal history, and activate it when I see the building. A researcher – using the individual-ecological frame of reference – who tries to ana-lyse my conduct, would not pay attention to my meaningful reconstruction of the building as church. That researcher may adequately detect that my exchange-relations with the interior of the building lead me to being silent, but explanation of that emergent conduct is not available.

An alternative course of events of a similar kind entails explicit information about a particular environment that is encoded in ways of cultural marking. For instance, I exit from the church and need to find a bathroom (or 'rest room', lavatory, WC, or toilet). In the city square there is an establishment of such a kind, with two entrance doors of exactly similar nature. One of them is marked by letter 'M', the other by letter 'W.' The first one, however, also has a sign 'out of order' on it. Given my physiological needs and the openness of the other door, I could enter the door marked 'W'. Yet I would not, and even the idea of that entrance fills me with embarrassment. Instead, I will run around in the town, looking for another establishment clearly marked by 'M' (assuming the use of English here).

From the perspective of the individual-ecological reference frame, my relation with the environment remains unexplainable. The func-tions of the semiotic marking of the doors are not parts of the environment as such, but cultural regulators designating the gender segregation of public toilets. As a culturally structured person, I interpret these markers and link the interpretation with my conduct. A person who has no under-standing of such markers would not be con-strained by them. Given the cultural organization of human psychological development, a frame of reference that considers *both* the immediate exchange with the environment *and* the role of various (direct or indirect) social suggestions, is necessary.

The individual-*socio*ecological reference frame

The individual-socioecological reference frame is an extension of the individual-ecological one. It includes *both the focus on system < > environment and the role of others' social regulation of that relationship*. The developing person faces their environment, acts upon it, and transforms them-self. However, the environment is largely pre-prepared by another person (for example, parents set up 'appropriate environments' for children), and the person's acting within an environment is socially guided in explicit and implicit ways. The individual-socioecological reference frame thus includes (a) person, (b) environment, (c) person's acting towards the environment [so far the features of the frame are the same as those of the individual-ecological one], (d) the guiding role of the acting by some SOCIAL OTHER and (e) the transformation of the person as a result of this socially guided action by the person. Schematically, the frame is depicted in Figure 5.9.

The schematic depiction here is a modification of the one already present in Figure 5.8. The role of the SOCIAL OTHER as added leads the investigator to focus on the field here designated as FIELD OF CANALIZATION OF DEVELOP-MENT. This field is the arena for encounters of the developing person, the environment (which in itself is not a purposeful agent), and the 'social other' who attempts – in a goals-oriented way – to guide the person towards some desirable ways of encountering the here-and-now environment, as well as the future developmental transition of the person.

The researcher who adopts the individual-socioecological reference frame would study the same phenomenon that a user of the individual-ecological frame might study, yet do it differently. In the case of the individual-socioecological frame, the researcher needs to analyse the struc-ture of social suggestions that exists in the par-ticular episode of encounter between the person and the environment. Some of these suggestions are encoded into the environment itself, others are produced by the other persons who are active in the same environment, regulating the person's conduct in it. Let us look at how two researchers – one from the perspective of the individual-ecological, the other from the perspective of the individual-socioecological reference frame – would analyse the same sequence of problem-solving. Our example comes from Robert Siegler's work on children's arithmetic problem-solving. A particular girl, Whitney (5 years of age), is challenged by an addition task, and the following example unfolded:

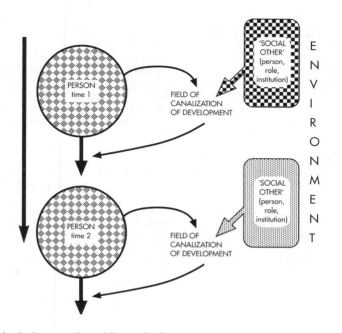

FIGURE 5.9 *The individual-socioecological frame of reference*

[1] *E:* How much is 4 + 3?
[2] *W:* 5,6,7, I think it's 7.
[3] *E:* 7, OK, *how* did you *know* that?
[4] *W:* Because *I am smart* and *I just knew it.*
[5] *E:* You can tell me., *I heard you counting. I heard you.* Tell me how you counted.
[6] *W:* I just – *I didn't count anything* – [long pause] *I just added numbers onto it.*
[7] *E:* Can you tell me how you added numbers?
[8] *W:* No.
[9] *E:* *Come on, Whitney – come on, **we have to do this**,* OK?
[10] *W:* OK [in a bored voice]. 3, add one makes 4, add one makes 5, add one makes 6, add one makes 7, add one makes 8.
[11] *E:* *Wait,* but how did you know what 4 + 3 was?
[12] *W:* 'Cause *I did what I just showed you.* I *just used my mouth* to figure it out.
(Siegler & Crowley, 1991, p. 613)

The authors (Siegler and Crowley) utilized this kind of problem-solving situation using the individual-ecological frame of reference. For them, the goal was to find out in which ways Whitney handles the addition task – ending with a 'diagnosis' of her cognitive strategy. This focus is sufficient for the authors' purposes, yet it is blind to the side of social regulation of the child's encounter with the task. The latter becomes available when the same transaction episode is viewed from the individual-socioecological reference frame.

The use of the individual-socioecological frame in this case needs to begin from the *analysis of the background*. In the given school (where the experiment is conducted), there can exist specific social suggestions in the classroom about what ways of solving arithmetic problems are adequate, and which not. For instance, the teacher in the classroom may introduce the rule that while adding numbers, children should *not count.* This constitutes a set-up background social suggestion that becomes visible in the experiment itself only when challenged (see line [5] – Experimenter puts Whitney into a situation of being 'caught' counting, which is vehemently denied by Whitney who clamed that she 'just added numbers' – line [6]). Whitney's explanations of how she arrived at the solution indicate further carry-over from social suggestions of others ('because I am smart' and 'I just knew it' [4]), or personal invention of action description ('just used my mouth' [12]).

The *immediate social guidance* of the child's relation with the adding problem is likewise visible here. The Experimenter refuses to accept Whitney's denial of counting, and confronts the child's refusal to explicate her strategy by begging her ('come on, **we have to do this**, OK?' [9]). He then misperceives the child's demonstration of the *way* of solving the problem as if it were a mistaken solution [10–11]. Whitney agreed to demonstrate how she added numbers, and was no longer trying to solve the previous addition problem, while the Experimenter assumed she was repeating the solution. He was trying to keep Whitney 'on task' even after he himself had moved the goal to the demonstration of the method of solution.

It should be clear that the use of the two reference frames here provided very different information about the development of the specific addition strategy (in the given trial). The individual-ecological frame made it possible to find out how the child solved the problem, but not how the solution of the problem was culturally organized. The latter entailed negotiation of the problem-solving child with the 'social others' of immediate (the Experimenter) and back-ground (the school rules) kinds. These two kinds of information are relevant for different research purposes. The information based on the individual-ecological reference frame is sufficient for investigation of cognitive development *per se*. However, for cultural developmental psychology, this frame is insufficient. Instead, the same phenomena can be analysed with the help of the individual-socioecological frame in ways that open empirical access to cultural organization of development.

FRAMES OF REFERENCE AND MODELS OF CAUSALITY

The use of different reference frames is co-ordinated with scientific models of causality that can be applied in psychological research. For the purposes of clarification of these models, let us use a simple 2×2 table as depicted in Figure

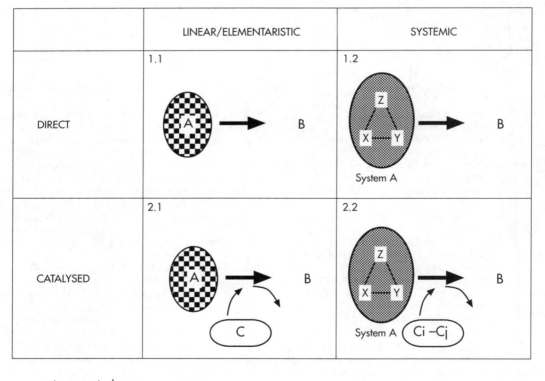

A = single cause
B = outcome
X,Y,Z = parts of casual system A
C = catalysing conditions
Ci–Cj = catalysing system (either Ci or Cj separately do not catalyse the system A –> B causal link, but in mutual relation they do)

FIGURE 5.10 *Four models of causality*

5.10. The two parameters that make up the table are the contrast between *linear/elementaristic* or *systemic*, and *direct* or *catalysed* versions of causality.

Linear causality

This contrast of models of causality entails the question of *the nature of the cause*. In the case of the linear/elementaristic model, the cause is given as a unitary entity that leads necessarily and unconditionally to the given outcome (cause A → outcome B). This linear/elementaristic causality model can include *multiple parallel* causes that all lead to the same outcome (A → B, H → B, Q → B). These multiple parallel causes remain elementaristic, as long as it is not posited that they are involved in mutual relations.

For the assumption of the entity-version of stability to be succesful, psychology would need also to assume that the connection of the assumed causal entities and their consequences is unitary (one-to-one, or constitutes a case of complete isomorphism). This is illustrated by the following:

Causal entity	Its consequence
A	a
B	b
C	c

This is an example of three linear causal linkages working in parallel. Each cause leads to its own consequence. There are no multiple consequences assumed (such as A leading to a and c), nor is it assumed that multiple causal entities would lead to the same consequence (A and B → b, for example).

Systemic causality

In the case of systemic causality, the given outcome (B) is *a result of mutually interdependent relations of the parts of the causal system* (for example, system A {Z< > X < > Y} in Figure 5.10). None of the parts (Z, X, Y) taken separately causes B, but *their systemic interaction leads* to B.

The model of linear causality is most often used in conjunction with the intra-individual or inter-individual reference frames. Statements like 'Johnny's good results at school are caused by his intelligence' (intra-individual reference frame) or 'Girls do better than boys in housecleaning because of their gender' (inter-individual reference frame) serve as examples here. Thus, non-developmental psychology largely relies upon these two models of causality. In contrast, developmental explanations cannot take the form of direct (linear or systemic) causal statements, because the developmental processes are context-bound. Hence, causal models that emphasize context need to be used.

Catalysed causality

Since developmental models cannot be context-free, notions of direct causality are not sufficient for the study of development. Let us call context-bound causality models examples of *catalysed causality*. *Catalysed* here is a term to refer to conditions that need to be present for a particular causal linkage to occur, and the absence of which does not allow the causal process to lead to an outcome. Both elementaristic and systemic models of causality can be catalysed. The catalysing agents can be unitary, or form a system of their own (see cell 2.2 in Figure 5.10).

Evaluation of the types of causality

The notion of catalysed causality retains the relevant context-dependency of developmental phenomena. Actual causality that leads to new developmental phenomena is made possible by sets of circumstances (catalysing agents). The latter can block the given causal connection, or enable it. Actual development is thus *contextually opportunistic*, which allows for multilinearity of development, as well as its redundant nature.

Models of catalysed causality are usable in sciences that deal with living systems. Thus, cancer researchers talk about *carcinogens* (agents that cause tumour) and *co-carcinogens* (agents that need to be present for carcinogens to cause tumour; without their presence the tumour is not caused and co-carcinogens by themselves do not cause tumour). In the psychology of learning, experimenters who condition animals assume that the success of their conditioning efforts depends upon certain 'incentive conditions' – circumstances of the setting and the state of the animal – without which the conditioning cannot succeed (for example, the hungry state of the animal).

It is clear that catalysed causality models fit the use of individual-ecological and especially individual-socioecological reference frames. Development can be explained by the action of basic mechanisms which are brought into action (or kept from it) by different conditions. Kurt Lewin (1927) propagated the *conditional-genetic* ['genetic' means *developmental* here!] *analysis* in psychological investigations. This is in line with the use of catalysed causality models. The researcher's goal is to find out which developmental new form emerges if a set of particular conditions is present (in comparison to the case of absence of these conditions).

No matter which frame of reference is used by researchers, science operates on the basis of comparisons. The issue is only which comparisons are being made, for what purposes, in the given frame of reference. The comparisons involved in the four reference frames were:

- **Intra-systemic** frame: comparison of the posited causal system *in* the organism, with its outcome (expression).
- **inter-systemic** frame: comparison of different systems on the basis of outcomes (expressions).
- **individual-ecological** frame: comparison of the person's action with the task conditions for that action.
- **individual-socioecological** frame: comparison of the person's actions with the social suggestions regulating these actions *and* with the task conditions for that action.

Comparisons can be made in different ways – qualitative (A differs from B), quantitative (A is bigger than B; A differs from B by X units of measurement etc.); evaluative (B is 'lagging behind' A), and many others (for example, normative B differs from A by 'being abnormal'). Science involves constant comparison of states of affairs of the phenomena, and their conditions, and construction of generalized knowledge based on these comparisons.

TWO WAYS OF GENERALIZATION OF KNOWLEDGE

Psychology includes a focus on arriving at general knowledge from specific empirical evidence. How is that possible? In the most general case, it happens through a move from some specific observation (or observations) to a general abstract model, which is then subsequently tested again on further observations. These new observations lead to the re-formulation of the initial model in its abstract form, which in its turn leads to testing it under novel circumstances (see Figure 5.11.)

As is obvious, the reconstruction of abstract models goes on constantly. Each new empirical observation can lead to modification or re-doing of the abstract model, and each modification of the model leads to researcher's search for new observations. This shows how Morgan's 'two inductions' work together in the construction of new knowledge.

The scheme depicted in Figure 5.11 fits equally the two research tactics that have been used in psychology, and which have often been conceptualized as if they are opponents (or even irreconcilable opposites) – the *sample-based study* and the *individual-case-study*. Most of contemporary psychology has assumed the normative stance of the sample-based study tactic.

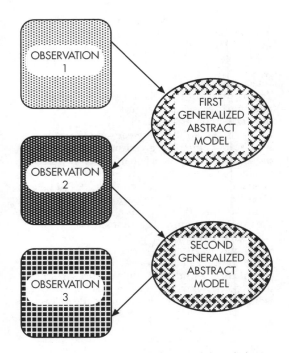

FIGURE 5.11 *Construction of general knowledge in psychology*

What is a sample?

A sample is a selection of individual cases, treated as elementary units in a composite labelled 'population'. That selection can be performed in many ways – with the notion of 'random sampling' maintaining a socially normative status in psychology. It is assumed that random selection of individuals from a population to create a sample guarantees that the sample represents the population. If it does, then results obtained in the study of a sample can be generalized to the population.

This normative notion of generalization – from samples to populations – has two problems: First, *the population as a full set of specimens of a given kind cannot be considered to be finite* (except for those cases where it equals the sample, that is, all specimens of the given kind are sampled). The population is not a homogeneous class, but a heterogeneous one. For example, the population of 'Americans' is in principle infinite – each new immigrant changes the population; each child born (or old person who dies) changes it as well. To get a random sample that adequately represents a changing population would be equivalent to considering a photograph of a runner to represent the running process in full.

This problem of a sample being a static representation of a dynamically changing population is an obstacle for all developmental sciences, not only of developmental psychology. A further complication with the notion of a population is the assumption of *mutual independence* of all specimens in a population. This assumption is necessary for any notion of random sampling, and yet accepting this assumption overlooks the reality of unknown linkages between specimens in a population. The 'population of Americans' (from which researchers may attempt to create a 'random sample') includes persons who are members of the same family or kinship group, of the same community, or belong to the same ethnic or racial sub-group. Each of these social organizational frameworks create interdependencies between persons. Such interdependencies undermine the notion of 'randomness of selection' of the sample from the population. The researcher who performs the operation of 'random sampling' operates with the assumption that the externally determined criteria (for example, demographic, etc.) of the sample match those of the population. Yet the researcher has no information about the inherent interdependencies between the sampled persons – some of which may be results of parallel indentifications.[1] In sum, the notion of 'random samples' cannot be specified by inherent criteria, which may be specific for a sub-part of the population. Such internal structuring of sub-parts of the population would not be known to the researcher.

Secondly, psychologists in general, and developmental psychologists in particular, are not interested in populations in themselves. They use populations as a basis for making statements about individuals. Both in the abstract, and in practice, psychologists' goal is to study persons (not populations consisting of persons). Practical psychologists need to make decisions about concrete persons, whereas sample-based data do not allow direct use of the abstracted evidence in concrete cases. The reason for such limitation is the homogenization of the sample – and, on its basis, of the population – through uses of the average or prototypical cases of the sample as if those represent the typical case of the population as a whole (see Lewin, 1931; Valsiner, 1986). In the course of such homogenization, the original variability of a population is turned into abstracted uniformity of the individual in general. This is followed by applying that homogenized abstraction to a real person (see Figure 5.12), which constitutes psychology's *central systematic error* in its knowledge construction.

This central systematic error of treating aggregated data – generalized to an assumed population – as if applicable to individuals from that population takes place at the move from inductive generalization (from samples to popu-

lation) to deductive application of the generalized results under new circumstances. The inter-individual variability (that is, the heterogeneous class status of individuals within a sample) becomes eliminated in the process of data aggregation within the sample, and in the generalization of the aggregate to the whole population. The individuals are becoming treated as a homogeneous class. This change of class status (from heterogeneous to homogeneous) allows the researcher to treat new individuals (W,X,Z,L in Figure 5.12) *as if* they are represented by the population averages (or prototypes) that have emerged in the phase of inductive generalization.

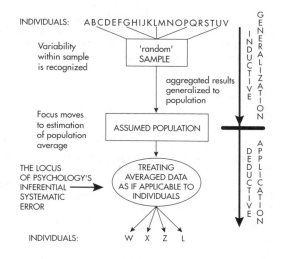

FIGURE 5.12 *Psychologists' consensually accepted error of transfer of knowledge from populations to individuals*

An alternative look at generalization: 'Unity in diversity'

The idea that the diversity of individual forms gives us evidence of general lawfulness is present in psychology from the very beginnings of differential psychology. William Stern launched the study of psychological variability – the target of differential psychology – in 1911 as a study of unity in generality (Stern, 1911). The general principles are organizers behind each and every person's specific organization of psychological functions. No individual in a sample or population represents the general principles (as a 'typical case'), but these principles are present in the case of each and every individual.

Stern's generalization process entails a move from single case empirical studies, to a generic model of the systemic nature of the phenomena, which is then tested on another single case (this process was depicted in Figure 5.11). The number of subjects needed for this kind of generalizing stance is relatively small (since each of them is analysed as individual systemic cases). The sampling of these cases from the available part of the 'population' pointedly avoids any notion of 'random sampling'. Instead, populational information about variability of individual cases allows planning of the sample to include at least three cases from the whole range (assuming it is known, and the individuals participate in the study) – from both extremes of a distribution, and from its middle. Only the latter case may come from the region near to the sample average (in the sense of the sample-to-population generalization strategy). By discovering the ways in which the extreme cases in the sample function similarly to the near-average case, it becomes possible to create a generic systemic model that is applicable to each and every individual. In the latter part of this book, examples are given how two extremes of a cultural-psychological phenomenon (for example, twin infanticide and twin glorification) are organized by the same general mechanism.

GENERAL STRUCTURE OF THE METHOD: DEVELOPMENT STUDIED AS IT UNFOLDS

It should be obvious from the coverage above that developmental cultural psychology requires methods that fit the appropriate reference frame (that is, the individual-socioecological frame) in the context of actual empirical research practices. It is the microgenetic method (Sander, 1927; Werner, 1927) that is appropriate for developmental analysis. In the case of cultural psychology, the materials used in microgenetic studies need to be specified as to their meanings.

The microgenetic orientation can be defined as any empirical strategy that triggers, records and analyses the immediate process of emergence of new phenomena. It entails three specifiable components:

INITIAL ⟶ INTERMEDIATE ⟶ FINAL
STATE   FORMS
                 (new forms   (newly
                 in making)   emerged
                                     forms)

CONDITIONS
that trigger
emergence

The crucial feature of the microgenetic orientation – absent from other methods-constructive focus in psychology – is the concentration on the unfolding of the INTERMEDIATE FORMS. These intermediate forms can be variable – some are 'preliminary states' of the final forms, others are forms that emerge, but do not develop into a final state. They disappear without arriving in the final form state, yet their importance in the emergence of novelty may be profound.

The microgenetic orientation has had its relevance in developmental psychology, in the psychology of perception, and in personality psychology. One version of this orientation is known to our cultural developmental psychology – Lev Vygotsky's 'method of double stimulation'.

Vygotsky's 'method of double stimulation'

Vygotsky was consistent in his emphasis – along the lines of James Mark Baldwin – on the study of *actual processes of development*. It was necessary to re-think existing methods of psychology to allow for the study of the differentiation process. Hence his 'method of double stimulation' entails the analysis of the process by which the subject constructs further differentiation of the stimulus field, given the goal-orientation of a task.

The main reason for constructing such methodology was for Vygotsky the need to discover the moments where a person arrives at a *dialectical synthesis – both* within the line of actions (similarly to Wolfgang Köhler's 'insight'-based problem-solving by apes, see Köhler, 1925; Vygotsky and Luria, 1993) *and* between the lines of action and semiotic reflection. In the latter case, the current problem-solving situation can be re-structured in terms of its meaning, which guides the person's relations with that situation. Human capacity to move from acting to speaking to contemplating, and to generalization of the meaning to general states of the psyche (for example, the states of 'depression' or 'happiness') constitutes a process of psychological differentiation where higher mental functions become integrated into the structure of all functions in a control role (see Chapter 11).

The method of double stimulation is a developmental quasi-natural experimental setting in which the subject who participates in research is provided with a richly structured environment, which can be re-organized in a goal-oriented way (see Figure 5.13).

In Figure 5.13 the subject faces a pre-structured field of stimuli. This is the whole experimental setting into which the person enters, and where the given experiment takes place. The researcher may have structured the stimulus field for the subject – or may have used an already existing setting (the so-called 'natural setting') to put the

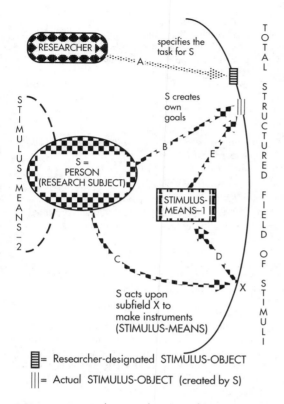

= Researcher-designated STIMULUS-OBJECT

||| = Actual STIMULUS-OBJECT (created by S)

FIGURE 5.13 *A schematic depiction of Lev Vygotsky's 'Method of double stimulation'*

subject into a position where the phenomena of research interest may become observable.

Making of the goal (Stimulus-Object)

The researcher suggests to the subject a particular task – an action upon some part of the stimulus field structure (arrow A in Figure 5.13). The subject may follow that suggestion (cooperative subjects usually do), or not. In the latter case, the subject may make another part of the stimulus field into one's target (arrow B), and act upon it in a goal-directed way. This is very often the case when experimenting with children is attempted – the children may find another object than the experimenter's suggested goal-object to be worthy of acting upon.

A most interesting scenario of a psychological experiment emerges when the subject accepts the researcher's suggested goal (task), but proceeds to act upon it with their own personal interpretations of the nature of the task, the reasons for acting upon the given part of the stimulus field, and the characteristics of the action. For example, the researcher instructs the subject in an experiment to act 'as quickly *as you can*', yet the

specification 'as you can' indicates the person's current motivation for action. So, instead of the researcher's expectation that the subject will act with maximum speed, the subject may decide that 'as you can' is equal to 'as you please', and instead of maximum speed might act slowly.

Following the specification of the goal region – Stimulus-Object (or StObj) in Vygotsky's terms – the subject is now led to *construct his or her means* to reach the end goal. Vygotsky's method brings into the researchers' focus *the process of differentiation of the goals and means to reach those goals*, and the process of creation of appropriate instruments to reach those goals. The notion of 'double stimulation' entails two differentiations: first, that of 'Stimulus-Object' and 'Stimulus-Means', and secondly between two kinds of means that can be used to organize the subject's conduct in the experimental field.

Two kinds of instruments: action tools and signs

The subject (in Figure 5.13) proceeds to turn to some sub-field (X) of the stimulus field in order to use parts of it to make an action instrument to reach the goal (StObj). The action means are created in the situation (unless the person carries appropriate objects with them) – hence their construction is directly observable, as the task triggers their making. This is depicted by arrows C and D in Figure 5.13 (making of Stimulus-Means-1 (StM-1): action tools). The constructed stimulus-means is then applied in action towards Stimulus-Object (arrow E).

The second kind of Stimulus-Means (StM-2) are semiotically encoded personal-cultural experiences that an individual subject carries with them into any new experimental situation. The personal understanding of the given situation, its role in social life (as well as for the subject him- or herself) is constructed instantly by the person, when entering into the field. It is based on all previously lived-through experiences.

This interpretation activity of the subject is not controllable by the experimenter, and it cannot be eliminated. Vygotsky's methodological idea was *to turn that inevitably uncontrollable moment of human interpretation into the target of investigation*. This is an orientation which fits the basic assumptions of developmental methodology. It leads to re-thinking of the usual focus on 'independent' and 'dependent' variables.

The functional equivalent of the 'dependent variable' in the case of Vygotsky's method is the microgenetic process – made explicit by the sequence of subject's actions and speaking efforts – by which the subject attempts to reach the goal. As was clear from above, the functional equivalent of the 'independent variable' is the whole structured stimulus field. Or, in other terms, the usual non-developmental discourse in psychology about 'independent' and 'dependent' variables is circumvented by Vygotsky (and by other Gestalt psychologists).[2]

Instead, the method of double stimulation allows the researcher to probe into the intermediate state of development (after the previous state has become imbalanced by experimental intervention, but the final state has not yet emerged – see the microgenetic scheme above). It fits James Mark Baldwin's claim that development can be studied when it is actually taking place (rather than predicted before, or explained after). It also exemplifies the notion of historicity of developmental research.

Example of the method of double stimulation in research practice

Let us use the work of Vygotsky's co-worker R. Levina (1968) as an example of how the method of double stimulation (in one version) has been applied. A child is faced with a problem-solving task – getting a candy down from the top of a cupboard. This Stimulus-Object is accepted by the child. In the room there are various objects that could be utilized for getting the candy down (a stick is hanging on the wall). The following sequence makes the child's efforts explicit:

Anya T. (3 years, 7 months of age)

Action	Interpretation
(1) Reaches silently	
(2) COMMENTS: 'It is very high'	Use of StM-2 as commenting on action
(3) Climbs onto a couch, reaches	
(4) COMMENTS: 'I should call Lyuba so that she'll get it' (reaches)	StM-2 (summoning help)
(5) COMMENTS: 'Can't get it, too high'	
(6) *Grasps the stick*, leans on it but does not use it	Bringing StM-1 into the action field
(7) COMMENTS: 'No way to get it, very high' (holds the stick in one hand, reaches towards the candy with the other)	Attempts to move with StM-1
(8) COMMENTS 'The hand is tired . . . . . . Can't get it. We also have a high cupboard, papa put things on it and I couldn't get them' (Reaches)	Brings in background life experience -StM-2
(9) COMMENTS: 'No, I can't reach it. I am still little.' (Reaches, stands on chair, swings the stick, aims at the candy) 'Pah-pah'	StM-2 – self-categorization ('little') Unites stick and knowledge of shooting into *one structure* (StM-1 and StM-2 united)
(10) Laughs, moves the stick forward. *Looks quickly at the candy, smiling. Gets it with the help of stick*	PROBLEM SOLUTION
(11) COMMENTS: 'See, I got it with the stick. I'll hang it up at home, and my cat will be reaching for it'	StM-2: new projected use of the task

From Levina, 1968, pp. 107–108

This little glimpse of the efforts of a young child who solves the problem of getting a candy down from a high place is indicative of the focus of Vygotsky's interests. That focus was very closely linked with the traditions in Gestalt psychology of looking at the processes that lead to solutions to complex problems. Chimpanzees in Köhler's experiments would also demonstrate the phenomena of quick breakthroughs in problem-solving – usually known as *insight*. Insight can be observed in Anya's conduct in steps 9 and 10. After failure – explained concurrently in speech ('I am still little'), Anya moves to create a synthesis of a 'shooting game' (aiming with the stick and 'pah-pah') followed by sudden arrival of the solution.

Vygotsky's cultural-historical orientation led his method of double stimulation to proceed beyond the Gestalt-psychological focus on insight in the problem-solving process. His method allows the researcher to observe how the reflection by the subject – both about the task and about themselves – is linked with the problem-solving process. This is why the Stimulus-Means-2 (words, utterances, etc. – signs in general) and Stimulus-Means-1 (action tools) enter into structured relationships with one another for the sake of solving the problem. Human beings solve problems through *integrating signs and action tools into one structure of the goal-directed effort*. Setting up tasks for such efforts, and observing the process by which a particular subject builds that integration of means into one means–end structure in real time is the focus of Vygotsky's method.

Relevance of Vygotsky's 'method of double stimulation' for developmental psychology

The 'method of double stimulation' entails a number of radical ideas in reconstructing developmental psychology's experimental method. It is in effect a method that brings out the meaning construction (or re-construction) process of human beings, involved in an ongoing activity of a goals-oriented kind. There are a number of ways in which Vygotsky's method revolutionizes contemporary psychology.

First, it is explicitly structuralist – as the subject is viewed as encountering the *whole field* of the experimental setting (and not merely the elements of it that are purposefully varied – 'independent variables'). The reality of the structured nature of psychological phenomena has been often lost in the automatic quantification that is involved in the construction of data from the phenomena (see Figure 5.3 above). Vygotsky, following Jean Piaget's version of clinical method, as well as the experimental rigor of Gestalt psychology, created a situation of experiment where the dynamic structural complexity could be brought out through the combination of the task and the structured stimulus environment.

Secondly, the subject is considered as *the active agent* who reconstructs that field – by introducing into it the goal sub-fields ('Stimulus-Objects', in Vygotsky's terminology), and means to reach those goals ('Stimulus-Means'). This functional differentiation of the experimental structured stimulus field into two kinds of relevant parts (goals and means), while leaving the rest of the field to constitute the background, is *guided* by the experimenter, *but cannot be determined* by him or her. The experimenter gives the subject a task embedded within the field, but the subject can refuse to perform that task, and turn it into another one. In other terms, the *psychological experiment is only partially controllable* by the experimenter.

Vygotsky did not eliminate the major generic scheme of experimentation – that of Stimulus → Response – from his version of the developmental look at the experiment. The basic scheme

STIMULUS → [PROCESSING ORGANISM = PARTICIPANT] → RESPONSE

remained intact. Instead, Vygotsky modified the focus of experimental research: instead of merely recording formal correspondences between the change of the stimulus and the alteration of the response, Vygotsky suggested the careful analysis of the microgenetic process that goes on in the construction of the response by the subject.

Vygotsky's method of double stimulation is of central relevance for the methodology of cultural developmental psychology. It allows one to look at the emergence of meaning together with the provision of solutions. It is explicitly focused on the study of the processes (rather than outcomes) of a psychological kind. It fits the general individual-socioecological reference frame (see above).

SUMMARY: SOME FINAL POINTS

This chapter has given an introduction to the scientific methodology of cultural developmental psychology. Science cannot be reduced to the 'right use' of the pre-given, fixed and consensually validated methods. Instead, researchers are active thinkers who create their own methods in accordance with their general assumptions, intuitions about the phenomena, theoretical constructions and focused interests. It is not the case that sciences develop in a progressive fashion: for example, claims that psychology in the 1990s is more developed than that of a hundred years before are most often self-serving rhetoric-blinders of intellectually lazy researchers (of the 'normal kind' *in the terms of* Thomas Kuhn).

Cultural developmental psychology unites two crucial but methodologically complicated *foci* within psychology – that of *culture* and that of *development*. Both these foci have been alien for the intellectual tradition that has – by way of historical coincidences (see Danziger, 1990) – become consensually designated as 'the mainstream' of psychology. It is not surprising that cultural developmental psychology builds ties with the two neighbour disciplines, of anthropology (on the side of the focus on culture), and of developmental biology (on the side of the developmental focus). The latter has recently – still within the discipline of psychology – been integrated into developmental science (Cairns et al., 1996). Yet for any developmental science to be productive, its whole methodological orientation requires reorganization in accordance with the general methodology cycle (Figure 5.1). Most of the methodological traditions of non-developmental and non-cultural psychology would not fit into either developmental science or into cultural developmental psychology.

We saw the main directions in which methodological decisions about research in developmental cultural psychology need to proceed. First, *it is the individual-socioecological frame of reference that is adequate for research*. Other reference frames may be combinable with it, yet the centrally normative focus needs to retain the interdependence of person, environment and its collective-cultural guidance. A concrete elaboration of this general idea was found in Vygotsky's method of double stimulation. Secondly, *the forms of causality that are adequate for researchers' thinking are of a systemic kind*, and possibly emphasizing the conditional (catalytic) nature of the causal linkages. Uses of widely recognized summative causal models (based on the assumptions of analysis of variance) are not applicable in cultural developmental psychology.

Thirdly, cultural developmental psychology is built on the primacy of the study of processes of emergence which are collective-culturally guided and personally semiotically reconstructed. This makes the *microgenetic class of methods privileged* over the methods meant to study only outcomes of processes.

Fourthly, and finally, there is no value-discrimination involved in cultural developmental psychology about the distinction between quantitative and qualitative tactics of data construction (from the phenomena). Which of these tactics is preferred in a concrete case depends upon the nature of the phenomena, the basic assumptions of researchers, and on the theoretical constructions (see Figure 5.1). Neither quantitative nor qualitative methods *per se* can be labelled 'objective' (or 'scientific'), their status in these valued roles is determined only through their fit with the rest of the methodology cycle. In other words – resonating with the reflection by Heinz Werner at the beginning of the chapter – rigidity of thought has no place in science, and especially in a developing science.

NOTES

1 Consider a study of adolescents in the United States. A researcher may sample the adolescents 'randomly' by way of external parameters – age, sex, school performance etc. Yet if some of the sampled adolescents are fans of a particular Hollywoood actor, they are mutually linked by their parallel identification, and their presence in the sample would bias the use of the sample as representing US adolescents as a population.

2 The rhetoric of 'variables' became dominant in psychology after Vygotsky's death – since the 1950s. It has led to *indexicalization* of psychological know-how; the notion of 'variables' as some parameters that can be varied has been replaced by accepting differences between different index conditions (such as 'male' versus 'female' in the talk about 'gender' as an 'independent variable'. Strictly speaking, that talk would fit reality only if psychologists were to produce gender change of their subjects as their varying of the independent variable . . . of course this does not happen.) Most of psychology's 'independent variables' are actually indexes of some generic kind (age, sex, socioeconomic status), not different in their nature from any other signs.

REVIEW QUESTIONS FOR CHAPTER 5

1 Discuss the notion 'empirical science'. In which ways is it impossible for any science to be solely empirical, or non-empirical?

2 Present the 'methodology cycle' and explain how it works.

3 In what sense are the data *derived* (*constructed*)?

4 How does a *completely inductive* version of the methodology cycle work?

5 How does a *completely deductive* version of the methodology cycle work?

6 What is insight, and what role does it play in science?

7 What is a *frame of reference*?

8 Describe the *intra-individual* (intra-systemic) reference frame.

9 Describe the *inter-individual* (inter-systemic) reference frame.

10 Describe the *individual-ecological* reference frame.

11 Describe the *individual-**socio**ecological* reference frame.

12 What is linear causality?

13 What is systemic causality?

14 What is catalysed (linear or systemic) causality?

15 Explain the two ways of creating general knowledge.

16 How do you understand the notion of 'unity in diversity'?

17 Describe the microgenetic orientation to the construction of research methods.

18 Explain Vygotsky's 'method of double stimulation', explicitly describing the notions of Stimulus-Object and two kinds of Stimulus-Means.

19 In which ways does Vygotsky's 'method of double stimulation' revolutionize psychology's notions of experimental research?

PART TWO

ANALYSIS OF ENVIRONMENTS FOR HUMAN DEVELOPMENT

As I outlined in Part One, developmental cultural psychology is a clearly theoretically and philosophically based scientific discipline. It deals with complex, dynamic phenomena of human construction. These complex phenomena exist due to their relations with their contexts. The rest of our book will include elaborations of human development in relations with cultural contexts.

The core of our coverage is the understanding that both persons and contexts are *culturally constituted*. They are interdependent with each other: persons can exist as they always live within their contexts; and contexts exist because they are constructed by persons. The cultural nature of human psychology specifies the meaningful nature of both persons-in-contexts and contexts-as-created by persons. In this respect, the life of humans as species differs dramatically from other biological species, even when rudiments of cultural organization of life can be found, as among higher primates.

Part Two includes two chapters that describe the social organization of the life world of a person (Chapter 6), as well as the issue of cultural organization of physical environments. Human development is taking place under conditions that allow for *increasing distance* from the 'natural world'. In parallel with such distancing, *the very same cultural tools allow human beings to merge* with their socially constituted environments. The focus of cultural psychology is precisely on the study of the ways in which human beings can distance (and de-distance) their lives – both external activities and intra-psychological functions – in relation with their 'natural' states. Human beings can reach a state of unity with a social activity (for example, a trance achieved in the context of a ritual) as well as separate themselves from most of the social world (for example, the hermitic tradition). These opposite psychological states are not available without semiotic mediation.

All human psychological phenomena exist within their settings. The settings are meaningful (as persons create these, by attributing them to the environment), structured, and dynamically modifiable. The immediate developmental environment is that of the *cultural-ecological niche*. Issues of the organization of environments are covered in Chapter 7.

6

STRUCTURE AND DYNAMICS OF FAMILY/KINSHIP GROUPS, AND MARRIAGE FORMS

Human development is always embedded in some social group context. This ranges from the minimal (mother and child) to the maximum case of collective institutions of infinite membership (for example, 'society'). Between these two extremes is a great variety of social groups that differ from one society to another. These groups take different forms within the same society at different historical periods – largely mediated by changing economic conditions. A person may be simultaneously a member of various groups. These groups are in between the person and 'society as a whole'. They mediate the person's relationship with the otherwise indeterminate abstraction 'the society'.

There is nothing extraordinary about these mediating groups. As any social group, the mediating groups form their distinctions of 'insiders' and 'outsiders', create mythologies about the groups, use these to defend the boundaries of the groups for various reasons, and reproduce not only in the biological but also in the social sense. A child is born into a group setting, and even if that initial setting may change, the person is embedded in some form of mediating group throughout life. That constantly changing group guarantees sufficient conditions for the development of all human beings who are involved in social relations with one another.

When we discuss issues of 'family', we touch upon the primary mediating group in its fullness. Usually, psychologists' focus is on the caregiving of children – the 'vertical' axis of family life where older adults dominate over the young. Yet this is but one of the many functional relations within the family structure. For example, caregiving for ageing parents is an equally relevant issue in most of the family systems. Here the younger adults give care to the older ones. Furthermore, the issue of care for spouses (so to speak, a 'horizontal' – in

age and social power roles – relationship) is also catered for by the primary social group. The family functions as a social group that provides for the needs of its members to cope with very many life conditions. Therefore, here we concentrate on the dynamic and functional side of the family.

THE FAMILY: A MULTIPLY-BOUNDED SOCIAL GROUP

One of the most central myths about human social life organization is that of the centrality of the nuclear family. Despite many claims in different societies about the crucial role of the family as the cornerstone of society, it has proved impossible to define what family means. As we will see below, this definitional difficulty is due to the ideological social values that are involved when social discourse about family takes place.

The word family in the sense of residential and biological unit is a historically recent invention. Before the eighteenth century, there was no term in European languages to refer to a mother–father–children grouping as a social unit. The Latin *familia* was a term linked with the physical location (house) in which the social group (which in Roman times included servants, and slaves) lived (Gies and Gies, 1987, p. 4). Hence the difficulties to define family in the social sciences are antedated by the wide uses of the notion long before social sciences emerged themselves. The immediate reality of the primary social group may make it deceptively simple to view family as the social group – based on marriage relation – who live together in a given household. From the viewpoint of contemporary European or North American middle classes, this seems clear. This view is supported by the strict and clear separation of households. Looking at an

American suburban neighbourhood there is no difficulty distinguishing the home territories of the Smiths and the Joneses, and (even without ever entering the clearly separate houses) presume that each family includes at least one parent and one or more children. However, if one tries a similar observation in a small Italian town, or in an African rural village, one meets with far less success. Even if a particular house in the Italian case includes parents and children, then what about the grandparents who may live in the same town in a separate house, where the parents and children visit and hang out every weekend, and from where the grandmother visits the parents' house daily to maintain order in the house and do the childminding. Are we here talking of *two* families (which could be the case if the single main criterion were shared household), or of *one* family (which is simply distributed over two households)? Furthermore, the members of both households may claim that their family has been intact in the town for centuries, and that most of the members of the family are (by now) buried in the local cemetery.

The role of *the lineage of ancestors* in defining a family – by the primary social group itself – creates a major difference between functional (that is, the view from the inside of a family) and demographic efforts to define the family. Surely the ancestors are not included in any population counts of the living, yet their psychological role in the family may be substantial. It is clear that the multi-faceted nature of life-organization of the primary social groups is a basic challenge for social scientists.

Troubled definition efforts

An example of a definition of the family may help here to see both the confusion and set of parameters used in the definition effort:

> I will define family as a social arrangement *based on the marriage* and the *marriage contract*, including *recognition of the rights and duties* of parenthood, *common residence for husband, wife, and children*, and *reciprocal economic obligations between husband and wife*. (Stephens, 1963, p. 8; added emphasis)

This definition is a good example of the challenges that social scientists face. It is clearly ethnocentric – fitting the European-type societies. It fits the contemporary European and North American contexts where there is explicit focus on *rights* and *duties* of persons who enter into a *contract* (marriage contract), and where the patterns of life organization prescribe *neolocality* (that is, newly married establish their own household, separate from that of either's parents).

They can economically afford such arrangement. Furthermore, their mutual relationship entails *economic obligations* in the horizontal (wife ↔ husband) axis, but not on the 'vertical' one (for example, children ↔ parents axis). In the latter, the economic obligation – if mentioned – may entail parents' obligation to provide for children's life needs, but not for children (before adulthood) to provide for parents' economic needs. This does not fit with the realities of many societies where children are integrated into productive economic activities from early age onwards.

Types of family

When human beings fail to define a concept, they switch to classifying the issues subsumed under it. Despite the difficulties of defining family as a key concept, social sciences have had no difficulty in inventing different ways to classify families. In parallel, multiple criteria can be used. No single criterion is sufficient. First, if the sharing of a household were to be the single criterion for a family, then any students sharing the same house or apartment would be considered a family. Or if only recurrent sexual relationships were sufficient, many young people's intimacies would become labelled as family, despite their lack of common home territory. If marriage were to be the only criterion, then any marriage partner – including cases of theogamy – would result in a family. Thus, a devout medieval girl in a convent may consider herself 'married to Jesus', yet this does not mean that her family now would include her and Jesus (who may well be unaware of his marital status). No single criterion is thus used exclusively, and combining of different criteria gives us possibilities to create typologies of families.

Combining a shared household (and its locality) with marriage as a social bond

This combination of criteria provides the typology of families by way of their establishment of household. The fact of marriage is the basis for the use of the hosehold-sharing criterion. In the *neolocal family*, the married group (couple, or polygamic group, see below) establishes a new household which becomes shared for all activities – economic, reproductive etc. In the *patrilocal family*, the married unit joins the household of the husband (or husbands – as in the case of polyandry). In the *matrilocal family*, the married establish their household with the wife's natal home.

Obviously, the latter two forms overlap with the criterion of sharing household with kinship group members. The matri- and patrilocal families are also *extended* families, families where members of different generations (parents of the married adults) share the household. The parents of the husband (or wife) share the home territories of the patrilocal and matrilocal cases (respectively), and maintain a power role within these home territories. The young married persons enter their home territory and establish their lives there, guided by the parental generation.

In many cases, families include sets of relatives of the same generation (brothers, sisters etc.) who share the same household. Such *joint families* are prominent in the context of India. They can partly overlap with the notion of extended family (if the parents share the same household). Here the criteria of kinship and sharing of household are combined to specify family types.

Family as an organized small group

Efforts to define family – or classify family types – may have overlooked the functional side of any family, that it is *some version of a functioning social group of different-aged members who are related to one another through some kinship and joint living relationship*. In this respect, family operates as any pre-structured social group.

Contemporary social psychology has accumulated empirical evidence about the functioning of social groups which are mostly occasional, lack pre-structuring, and are not meant to work together for substantial goal attainment (see Petrovski, 1984, for a critical analysis of social psychology in the realm of small group research). Most real-life small groups operate with specifiable goal orientations, and can be characterized by their history of internal social relationships. Family certainly belongs to the realm of such groups. Social psychology of small groups that is based largely on a-historical selection of college undergraduates into small group experiments on life-wise irrelevant tasks is not an adequate model for family.

Thus, most evidence in social psychology cannot be directly used for making sense of the family. The social psychological processes that are involved in the coordination of a family are constrained by the history of the relations between persons within the family. All participants in the family system develop interdependently over their particular life courses: children become adolescents and adults while their parents move through their adult age into old age, and their grandparents from their old age to the realm of ancestors. The latter – cultural construction by the presently living family members of the history of the family – can constrain present actions. For example, members of European royal families are restricted by their family histories in the choice of marriage partners. Similar restrictions do not apply in the families of middle or lower classes in the same societies. The latter families do not build their current identity upon specific exclusionary family history.

Family as a goal-oriented small group
The central psychological issue in the functioning of a family is the *coordination of goals-oriented actions* of the family members. This involves strategic action towards one's goals, taking into account the goal orientations of other family members. Thus, a 15-year-old girl may set herself the goal of becoming a school dropout in order to enter a glorious film career in Hollywood, only to find out that her parents have different goals for their accomplishment of bringing out their daughter. The latter might entail academic excellence at school, then at college, and then a remarkable career in a less fancy occupation like lawyer or medical doctor.

The range of expected goal orientations *is pre-arranged by the social roles the family members assume*. The very fact that parents construct their notion of responsibility (as parents) for giving their children 'the best' narrows down their range of goal orientations – both in respect of their children, and their own development as adults. Children, merely because they are children of the parents, are not expected to create similar goal orientations relative to the parents. Grandparents, again simply because of their kinship role, can create goal orientations in relation with their grandchildren that differ from these of the parents.

Different family structures can provide varied social role relationship hierarchies as the starting point for the social group. The role of the father can be prominent in European Christianity-dominated families, while that of the mother-in-law can play a similar role in Hindu joint/ extended family.

It also includes *processes of coalition formation* between different family members. In order to reach some goals, children may make coalition with other siblings, or with grandparents, to re-organize the parents' existing goal orientations. Parents may try to create coalitions with grandparents in order to have a 'united front' facing the children. The mother and father may have different goal orientations for the child – and the child can make coalition with one of the parents, attempting to neutralize or overcome the goal orientations of the other. Much of the intra-familial communication is strategic and future-oriented. As an example, let us consider a description of a complex family context – Hindu joint family.

Psychological functioning of Hindu joint family context

Hindu joint family involves the sharing of the same household territory by the parallel kin and their offspring (brothers or sisters, their spouses, and their children). Two lines of dominance – male and female – are mutually intertwined, both honouring the age of the participants. It also can involve the extended nature of the family – where the parents of the married adults are not only present in the household, but are the symbolically established leaders of the household (given the relevance of age). Under the traditional pattern of authority, the eldest male member of the joint family was considered the head of the whole family. He had authority over others – yet not unlimited authority. He could not use the power arbitrarily, without collectively coordinating his decisions. In the second generation the eldest son used to hold a superior position among the other male members of the family, yet had a position subordinate to the head and the elder women. Thus, decisions within a joint family relied on making of coalitions between less and more powerful members of the family. The age-respecting dominance system allowed the older members of the family – particularly the older women – remarkable power.

The public and private domains of the joint family differed in their gender-distribution of control spheres. Within the family, the mother-in-law was in full control over the life of the whole family, with the daughter-in-law doing most of the practical work (Raina, 1988). The mother-in-law would take care of the daughter-in-law's basic needs, control and regulate her conduct, and protect her against any offences by other family members. She would decide how frequently the daughter-in-law could visit her natal household. The daughter-in-law had to be fully obedient and demonstrate that in everyday action: massage the mother-in-law's body, show respect by ritualistic imitation of drinking the water in which the mother-in-law's feet had been washed, and remain subservient generally.

The latter particularly is the case of female members of the joint/extended family, where the crucial role in the running of the family is in the hands of the mother-in-law. The particular system of social relations within Hindu joint family created a collective-cultural meaning system of attributing high value to becoming mother-in-law (see Menon and Shweder, 1998). Becoming mother-in-law meant takeover of the running of the whole joint family system in the sphere of home life. Becoming mother-in-law obviously required passing through the phase of being

daughter-in-law in the joint family of one's husband. Despite the heavy workload involved in that phase, women in the daughter-in-law phase of their lives internalize the value and positive expectations for their 'promotion' to the upcoming role of mother-in-law which is the state of 'mature adulthood' in the Hindu life course. Agewise, this period could extend from around 30 years to about 50 (Menon and Shweder, 1998); and it follows the active role of daughters-in-law in bearing children (with preference for male children, with the eldest son eventually bringing in a daughter-in-law by marriage). For the mother-in-law, such life course transition amounts to guaranteeing sufficient life conditions at the time of being old (when her daughter-in-law, in her turn, has become mother-in-law to her son's new wife). The Hindu joint family system is an organizational framework that guaranteed lifetime 'social security' within the system of kinship network. Like in any other society in the history of humankind, it was (and is) the kinship network that acts as a 'buffer' against possible economic and natural disasters. Modern governments' social institutions that have attempted to take that function over have usually failed. The reason is very simple – political parties, governments, presidents and political dictators come and go, but the specific position of a person in a kinship network remains.

In this respect, the workload of daughter-in-law in the Hindu joint family is meaningfully overdetermined. In addition, it is work that just needs to be done, and the role of the daughter-in-law in getting it done is unquestioningly accepted by all members of the traditional Hindu joint family. For example, a young married Oriya woman (a daughter-in-law) described her daily routine:

As soon as I get up, I sweep out the house and then I go to the bathroom. I clean my teeth, have a bath, and then I start the breakfast. Once the breakfast is done, people come in one by one to eat. I serve each of them breakfast. Once that is done, we have our breakfast together. *Bou* [husband's mother] and I eat together. And then I start preparing lunch – what we'll be eating at two in the afternoon. Once that is done, again people come in one by one to eat. By three, we would also have eaten and I would have washed up after lunch. Then, I come and sleep in the afternoon. I sleep for an hour. I get up at four. I again sweep out the house and go down to start making something to eat with tea. I knead the *atta* [wheat flour] and make *parathas* or *rotis* [different kinds of bread]. Again, people come one by one to eat. I serve them and then it would be sundown by now and I offer *sandhya* [evening worship] before I start cooking the night meal. I am usually cooking till nine in the night. Then I go and watch the serial on TV. After that, at about 9:30, everyone will come to eat and I serve them. And then we eat. After finishing eating, we go to bed. The dishes are left as they are till morning. I just keep them till the morning when I wash them. In the morning, the first thing I do is take out and wash the *ointha* [polluted by leftovers] dishes, then I leave them out in the sun to dry, while I sweep out the kitchen, wash it out, and then take the vessels back in again. (Menon and Shweder, 1998, p. 154)

This self-description of the daughter-in-law's daily activities is revealing as to how practical (cooking and cleaning) and symbolic (handling of 'impure' substances) are coordinated. Furthermore, it indicates a special (but in dominance unequal) relationship with the mother-in-law.

Both the actual household work and symbolic systems of actions (*puja*) support the cultural organization of the existing social roles within the joint family. One of the symbolic acts that has left outsiders baffled is the Hindu daily custom for the daughter-in-law to drink the water in which the mother-in-law's feet have been washed. The daughter-in-law in the above example mentioned *puja* in a minimal way. When she was asked explicitly, she indicated that most of the symbolic rituals are performed by her mother-in-law, except for the feet-washing ceremony:

All I do is wash the feet of our *burhi ma* [husband's father's mother] and drink the water after my bath and before I go to make breakfast. I used to do it for *bou* and *nona* [husband's mother and father] in the beginning **but they stopped me from doing it**. They said it was enough to do it for *burhi ma* and **get her blessings**. (Menon and Shweder, 1998, pp. 154–155; added emphasis)

This explanation points to the symbolic role of the feetwashing and waterdrinking ceremony in the family context. The importance of the act itself is twofold – the daughter-in-law demonstrates her subservience in action, and gets the *blessing* of the older woman. Not surprisingly, it is the *eldest* woman in the family towards whom the ritual here was directed.

The intricacies of the Hindu joint family network also provide a new insight into the usual (Western) perception of arranged marriages in the Indian context. The perspective from which such arranging of marriages for daughters and sons is viewed is usually ethnocentric (for example, 'How awful, the young people do not have opportunities to marry whom they want!'). In the actual joint family context, the arranging of marriages for the children is a realistic consequence of the close social group nature of the whole family system. This is especially central

for the integration of the daughter-in-law (wife of a son) to the mother-in-law's (and husband's natal) household. Marrying in this context is a part of intergenerational continuity of the family system, and not an act of personally constructed dyadic love relations. Marriage was historically a social duty of persons towards the family and the community, rather than being primarily of personal interest.

Given the historical transformations within Indian society over the twentieth century, both the ways of organizing joint family patterns and deciding upon marriage choices have changed. The Hindu joint family system is itself an adaptation to the history of mostly rural ways of living, where multiple generations maintain joint agricultural production capacities. Contemporary industrialization and migration of young people to cities introduces substantial changes into the social organization of family. Nuclearization of the family is a result. It brings with it change in traditional social role relations in the family (Raina, 1988).

Similar changes can be seen in the arrangement of marriages. Educated Hindus have started to delay marrying off their daughters as soon as possible (after puberty), sending them to gain higher education. Under education, and mass communication bringing down barriers between societies, new generations of young people in India are reconstructing the previously normative family and marriage arrangements in new ways. Yet the historical gender-norm tendencies prevail. For example, in a sociological study of 1500 rural youth from seven villages in Karnataka (Uplaonkar, 1995), opinions as to who makes decisions about marriage differed dramatically for young men and women (see Table 6.1).

For all women, the stated acceptable decision for marriage was with the parents, whereas for men 42 per cent indicated that the choice should be that of the man, with or without parents' involvement. Surely data from urban environments could provide a different picture, and the picture would change over time. The important information in Table 6.1 is about the sociological patterns of joint family life. Changes (and resistance to them) in the family patterns are mediated by the personal cultures of the persons involved. It is the 98 per cent of young women in Table 6.1 (who were of lower educational levels) who have internalized and reproduced in the reported opinion survey the notion of acceptability of parents' choice for marriage. This social norm may become an obstacle in the personal lives of the respondents at some time, yet its internalization maintains the relative stability of the society and slows down the possibilities for rapid change. It is particularly important to point

TABLE 6.1 *Attitudes towards freedom of choice of marriage partners in a rural sample of youth (16–30 years of age) in Karnataka, India*

Specific form of attitude	Respondents		Total % (n)	
	Men %	Women %		
1 Parents' choice WITHOUT the consent of self	19	98	57	(859)
2 Parents' choice WITH the consent of self	39	2	21	(314)
3 Self-choice WITH the consent of parents	41	0	22	(325)
4 Self-choice WITHOUT the consent of parents	1	0	0.1	(2)
Total	100 (n = 770)	100 (n = 730)	100 (n = 1500)	

Source: Uplaonkar, 1995, p. 420

out that it is young women's 'conservatism' (in contrast with young men) that is evident in these data. As Hindu joint family matters are primarily under the control of the mother-in-law, and daughters-in-law have their female gender-role goal orientations towards achievement of such status, it is no surprise that an existing social order attempts to maintain itself through the consensual convictions of women. This leads to a rather multi-faceted view on the role of social discourse about gender relations – so widespread in contemporary European and North American feminist circles. Stories about 'exploitation', 'slavery' etc. of women and children may refer to some aspects of social realities, yet be told with goal orientations of different kinds.

Family intrinsically defined

We can now try to give a wider definition for family, based on the notions of marriage – its organization and symbols, ancestorship, and social relations within a kinship group. Family is a sub-group of the kinship network, which defines its membership by a social norm of ingroup/outgroup distinction. This is an *intrinsic* definition of family – in effect, it leaves it up to a particular group (or even one individual) to specify what part of the kinship network belongs to the family (OUR family, MY family), and what not. As will be seen from Figure 6.1, there are very many possibilities for such intrinsic definition of the family. Hence, family ceases to be a productive scientific term. As it is seen as *intrinsically* definable, it is no surprise that efforts to arrive at *extrinsic* definition either fail (if they try to capture the family in all of its versions), or force the use of particular criteria (e.g., household, marriage type, ancestry etc.).

The intrinsic definition effort would not be useful for epidemiological study of the family, since it is centred on a person's immediate feeling of who is considered to belong to the family. The participants in the same marriage group may have different feelings about one or another member of the group belonging (or not) to the family. Thus, use of family as a scientific concept is probably unproductive. What is visible behind family as a specifiable structure is that of marriage. But then, why is family a topic of so many discussions?

Why talk? Social control over primary social group

Family – as we saw above – is a poorly defined term. Yet it is a term we encounter very frequently in the processes of social communication, in chats at dinner parties, journalists' discussions on 'the fate of the contemporary family' on TV-screens, and in preachers' attacks on anybody who tries to undermine the purity of 'family values'.[1]

Social talk about some target object (such as the family) is not about what that object is actually like, but an effort to propagate some ideal of that object, as it could – or should – be. Different social institutions attempt to orient the activities of the primary caregiving group – the family – in directions that are relevant for them, and only tangentially in the interests of the family. Thus, discussion about the 'modern family' in terms of its progress or decline, 'problems' in it etc., is discussion that utilizes family as the battleground for social fights between different ideologies of institutions. The family as the actually functioning primary social group functions anyway – without any need to become involved in any discussion of its own functioning. Once such

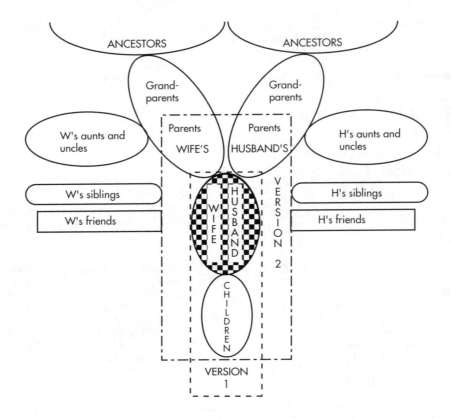

VERSION 1: nuclear family (husband + wife + children)

VERSION 2: extended family (husband + wife + children + grandparents)

FIGURE 6.1 *Family definition possibilities*

discussions surface in the social discourse field of a given society, their function is to organize the social world at large through the alteration (or preservation) of the family. In other words, declared 'problems' of 'the family' are actually problems of the given society exemplified on the basis of the discourse about family.

This focus gives a fresh look at why people – laypersons, journalists, politicians, psychologists – talk about family. Consider, for instance, frequent discussions of child-rearing which often emphasize the centrality of the family in this role. Our focus makes issues of child-rearing into a topic of communication between the persons who actually do it (older siblings, parents, grandparents) and those who *attempt to direct it*. The latter are ideologically guided, their efforts to communicate about child-rearing are guided by specific set goals. The latter need not be oriented toward the manifest 'target' of the messages (for example, the well-being of the child in devel-

opment), but rather use these 'manifest objects' as means to attempt other kinds of social objectives. For instance, there was an intense effort in eighteenth century Europe to persuade parents about the health dangers of giving the baby cow's (rather than mother's) milk (see Chapter 10). Ostensibly such discourse was about children's health – yet its social function was to attempt to regulate mothers' conduct by letting them persuade themselves that they should breast-feed their babies. Similarly, the health care discourse in the history of Europe was filled with myth stories claiming that masturbation leads to physical decline (in the eighteenth century), or to insanity in the nineteenth century (Hare, 1962). Here the focus of the communication effort was not to describe the actual functions of autoerotic practices, but to fight for repression of the notion of pleasure in sexual activities by stern messages about dangers to healthy persons. The intense discourse was a goal-directed canalization effort

– to eliminate the 'solitary vice' (of masturbation) in favour of the 'healthy and legitimate' goal of heterosexual child-bearing (Laqueur, 1990, p. 229). Social construction of anxieties about masturbation included massive direction of parents to be on the lookout for early 'tendencies' and to stop those in the beginning. It was presented publicly as an act of 'impurity', and even wax models were used to display the 'dreadful consequences' (Hall, 1992). The goal of repression of personal sexuality was mandated by the desire to control the activities of human beings by social and religious institutions. Likewise, our twentieth century focus on the relevance of attachment formation in the first year of life, and our concern about the dangers of AIDS, are examples of social guidance of the conduct of those persons whose feelings of responsibility are targeted for intervention.

Talking about women

Perhaps the clearest example of the goal-orientedness of human communicative efforts is the talk about women. In different societies, social discourse about women can take place with different talk-goals. The simplest one is *ontological* – simple reflection of the 'true state of affairs'. In this case, the statement 'women are inferior to men' does not carry any performative or evaluative role, there are no goal-orientations involved. This is different if the same statement is made in another mode – *prescriptive*. Here the ontological statement is supplemented by the hidden agenda of some prescription for action, for instance:

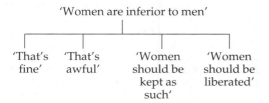

Very often, social scientists utilize phenomena from other societies yet have in mind goals of changing their own. Much of anthropological or cross-cultural psychological research is of such kind. Margaret Mead's descriptions of the 'permissive sexual attitudes' of Samoa adolescents were a commentary upon the US society at the time. In our present days, many efforts to demonstrate women's 'inferior status' in non-Western societies is linked with the missionary efforts of our times. Thus, women in non-Western societies are perceived to be 'enslaved' by some exotic practice (such as wearing a veil, or restrictions on occupying public space, in Islamic societies), and calls for social change are made on

that basis. Yet such interpretation may turn out to be nothing more than the researchers' projection of their own cultural meanings onto the phenomena of another society. For example, concerning female roles in Christian and Islamic contexts, Fatima Mernissi remarks:

> In Western culture, sexual inequality is based on the belief in women's biological inferiority. This explains some aspects of Western women's liberation movements, such that they are almost always led by women, that their effect is often very superficial, and that they have not yet succeeded in significantly changing the male–female dynamics in that culture. In Islam there is no such belief in female inferiority. On the contrary, the whole system is based on the assumption that women are powerful and dangerous beings. All sexual institutions (polygamy, repudiation, sexual segregation, etc.) can be perceived as a strategy for containing their power. (Mernissi, 1987, p. 19)

A major task for basic knowledge in cultural developmental psychology is to recognize such 'implicit agendas' in lay talk. The issue of men's and women's roles in the contexts of marriage are often talked about from some prescriptive perspective. Here my goal is to emphasize the ontological interpretation of the marriage issues.

STRUCTURAL BASES FOR THE FAMILY: MARRIAGE FORMS

The foregoing discussion of the complexity in defining a family seems to return consistently to the centrality of one criterion for the family – the social role relation of marriage. Family is based on the establishment of marriage ties. However, marriage is a relationship that takes many forms, if it is viewed cross-culturally and historically.

Marriage can be defined to be

> . . . a *socially approved relationship* between one or more persons and one or more women, involving sexual union as well as *rights and duties* which vary from society to society; any children born within the relationship are recognized *as legitimate offspring of the spouses*. (Raha, 1996, p. 2; original emphasis)

Marriage as organizer of role relationships

At the level of human societies, marriage is a framework to organize economic and social role relationships between persons who assume marital roles. Depending upon its set-up, the children are considered either legitimate (in which case they are 'born in marriage'), or illegitimate (born 'out of wedlock' or marriage). Ownership of property is regulated through marriage.

Inheritance rights differ from society to society as to the inclusion or exclusion of offspring born outside of the marriage. There are many stories of persons trying to get married to gain access to and control of the spouse's wealth. Furthermore, economic arrangements around marriage ('bride-price') are one of the widely described topics in cultural anthropology. In sum – marriage provides a locally socially legitimate form for economic and procreational activities of human beings. Different societies provide us with many different marriage forms (see below), each of which is adequate for the given society at the given historical *time as it has been made socially legitimate and personally acceptable* in the collective-cultural construction process. Aside from the acceptance of a particular marriage form in the given society, persons within that society would need to internalize their own understandings of the form to make it personally feasible to live in the given arrangement.

Marriage as a symbolic act

At the level of personal cultures, marriage can take many forms, which transcend the realm of human social relations. Such forms need some collective-cultural support, yet depend upon the personal-cultural construction of the person him- or herself.

The symbolic nature of marriage becomes most dramatically evident in the case of *theogamy* – marriage of a person to a deity. This entails collective-cultural acceptance (and promotion) of the adequacy of such marriage, and personal-cultural internalization of the marriage bond. At times this kind of symbolic marriage becomes established through real-world human substitutes (for example, a woman marries a man she considers her deity – symbolically she marries the deity, while in practice, a man). Theogamy can take other forms, especially in religious communities (see moments of theogamy in the Oneida Community, described below).

For example, the Gopastri religious community (in South Canara, India) included about 120 families grouped together in one quarter of the town (Prince Peter, 1963, p. 90). The women in this community considered themselves married to the god Krishna as polygynous spouses. Men were viewed as incarnations of Krishna – and treated as husbands. Children born from these unions remain with the mother, and are considered offspring of Krishna. They (and their mothers) are maintained by the livelihood produced by the temporary husbands. The community follows matrilineal descent (girls carry on the mothers' position). Examples of such cases of theogamy are historically to be found in the social group of Hindu temple dancers (the *devadasi*, see Valsiner,

1996, 1998 Chapter 7). Theogamy is a good example of harmonization of the everyday reality with an appealing and unfalsifiable meaning system.

Psychological constructions of the ambivalence of sexuality among young persons entering marriages have been utilized by social institutions to bond the persons with them. In the early days of Christianity, the social fight about chastity (avoidance of marriage, or re-marriage, or entering into 'virgin marriages') was a topic for the new religious system to appropriate resources through the personal-cultural belief systems of rich women who had converted into the new religion (Drijvers, 1987). Propagation of ascetism by St Jerome to Roman women included the turn away from healthy, body-fulfilling everyday activities, to physical and mental self-torture (including sexual abstinence).

Religious systems have captured the selves of young persons precisely during, or around, the issue of entering marriage. In the medieval context, the Catholic Church propagated virginity inside marriage, leading to the devotion by the married couple to the Church. For example, the saint Cecilia

> . . . was forced to marry the youth Valerian, whom she proceeded to convert on their wedding night by telling him that there was an angel who would kill him if he made any sexual advances toward her. When Valerian asks how he too may see the angel, she sends him to Pope Urban, who baptizes him. On his return home, not only does he see the angel, but he and Cecilia are crowned with two wreaths in token of their commitment to chastity. (Elliott, 1993, p. 64)

Christianity managed to re-direct the meanings of sexuality as signs of health into that of a pro-creational tool, which is ambivalent ideologically. A central notion in the Catholic Church has been the acceptance of the image of the Virgin Mary with a focus on the dual themes of virginity and motherhood – both positively valued, yet in inevitable tension between themselves.

Semiotic organization of marriage: internalization/externalization

Society provides the frame (roles, ritual of entrance, rituals of progression), persons internalize their own versions of such rituals, make the roles their own. *Wedding rituals* are common in all societies. As such, these rituals operate to demand from all participants (bride, groom, relatives of both sides) the performance of a sequence of symbolic actions, which are meant to guide the internalization of the value of the newly established roles (of husband and wife) and of the whole set of social role expectations that come with it.

Economic supports for marriage

In the history of human societies, the establishment of marital relations has usually been related with some form of economic exchange between the bride and groom sides of the newly established relation. The question of material wealth that the family clans would exchange when their children marry has been the central issue around marriage as a social form.

In the history of Africa, the phenomenon of 'brideprice' has been a recurrent topic for discourse – first among missionaries and colonial administrators, later among anthropologists and social scientists. The phenomenon of 'brideprice' entails *provision by the side of the groom specified economic value to the background family of the bride, as a condition for becoming married to the bride.* The interpretive ambiguity of this practice (on behalf of European – especially English) colonizers is obvious, as the language use here implies the activity of *purchasing* a wife (and paying for her). This interpretation was not that of the indigenous population, among whom, the institution of brideprice – especially on behalf of the bride – was seen as a kind of 'marriage insurance' protecting the married woman against possible ill-treatment by the new marital context. For grooms, the brideprice was a way to symbolically mark the right to exercise genitorial rights for the children the wife would bear. The activities around paying the brideprice were parts of the lengthy getting-married rituals.

The nature of the kind of brideprice that has been used in Africa has changed together with the history of the socioeconomic context. Thus, in Gikuyuland (in Kenya) over the twentieth century, the brideprice has constantly become transformed to increase monetary liquidity, as can be seen from Table 6.2. It is clear that the historically traditional value-object involved in Gikuyu brideprice payments – cattle – had been almost completely replaced by cash payments by the 1970s. In parallel, the costs involved in brideprice have increased together with the education of women. Fathers of educated girls would often include the schooling costs into the expected brideprice (Ferraro, 1976, p. 107), thus creating economic stress for the traditional system which has been crumbling under increasing migratory urbanization. In the past the Gikuyu father could distribute the brideprice paid in cattle between his own and other relatives' households. This increased the agricultural productivity of the whole kinship system. Under the new tradition of payments in cash the liquidity of the monetary instrument leads to its investment outside of the kin network system. As a result, the brideprice can become dysfunctional in terms of consolidating social ties.

The economic differentiation of costs covered by the sides of the bride and the groom is not absent in any society where marriages take place. The two sides of family clans take care of different aspects of contemporary wedding rituals. Marriage forms are the specific social organization framework that sets up the structure of the family.

Forms of marriage

There exist four major forms of marriage:

1 *monogamy* (marriage of one man – husband – with one woman – wife);
2 *polygyny* (marriage of one man – husband – with more than one woman – co-wives);
3 *polyandry* (marriage of more than one man – co-husbands – with one woman);
4 *polygynandry* or group marriage (marriage of more than one man with more than one woman).

Of the four types, polygyny and monogamy have been the two more widespread marriage forms over the history of humankind. By one estimate (Stephens, 1963, p. 33), 80 per cent of the societies

TABLE 6.2 *Historical changes in the kinds of brideprice payments in the Gikuyuland in Kenya*

Historical period when marriage was contracted	Percentage all in cattle	Percentage mixed	Percentage all in cash
Prior to 1935	46	8	46
1935–45	38	0	62
1946–55	32	5	63
1956–65	13	7	80
1966–70	6	0	94

Source: after Ferraro, 1976

all over the world (and throughout recorded history) have allowed polygyny and practised it, in one way or another. In contrast, polyandry and polygynandry have been historically rare – yet viable in the conditions where these are practised (Levine, 1988).

Each of the forms of marriage has emerged under socioeconomic circumstances where it could be a viable option for fulfilling the basic functions of the marriage bond – creating the core of the family, and the socially legitimate reproductive unit. Many of the forms have co-existed in the same society at the same time – if ideologically accepted. Thus, monogamy exists in many societies in parallel with the other (plural) marital forms – if the latter are *legally allowed, accepted by cultural meaning systems* and *economically feasible*. If all the latter conditions are not concurrently present, plural marriage forms will not be observable in a society.

A process view of marriage

Marriage is a process of being in a marital relation. In this, the process involves its history – marriages are established, develop, and end. The existing four major forms of marriage – monogamy, polygyny, polyandry and polygynandry – can be viewed as potentially transferable into one another, *if the social rule system of the given society allows such transformation*. Very often it does not. The general pattern of transformations is depicted in Figure 6.2.

Figure 6.2 illustrates an unrestricted case of transformations between the four marriage forms. What is involved is simple addition or loss of spouses to transform one form into another. Thus, by getting from monogamy to polygyny, a wife is added to the monogamic arrangement. To revert to monogamy, a wife is eliminated. In a similar vein, monogamy becomes polyandry by

adding a husband to a monogamic state, and reverts to monogamy by eliminating a husband. In a similar way, both polygyny and polyandry can become polygynandry, and revert back either into themselves, or into monogamy (in case of the breakdown of the polygynandrous group).

In terms of social group as an adaptational buffer that guarantees human functioning, it is the polygynandry that is the most versatile marriage form, followed by polygyny, polyandry and – finally – monogamy. In polygynandry, the chances for reproductive success of all co-husbands – through the reproductive success of the co-wives – is of enhanced flexibility. For instance, issues of male infertility, if these occur, are masked by the group-based treatment of the child-bearing and child-rearing issues. Such masking is not possible in monogamy or – especially – polygyny (where male infertility is publicly visible through absence of children from co-wives). In balance, the intra-group social psychological processes in case of polygynandry may reduce some of this versatility in reality, and make it a fragile marriage form that may break down into any of the other three forms.

If the criterion of adaptability is used to evaluate the marriage forms, then monogamy is the least versatile way of organizing marital relations. It is vulnerable to mishaps – ranging from no reproduction (male or female infertility) to threats due to the premature deaths of either the wife or the husband, if there are children. Not surprisingly, then, societies that emphasize (or selectively sanction) monogamy build other 'safety frameworks' either informally (through the monogamic marriages being parts of wider kinship networks that would compensate in case of need), or formally (for example, different social programmes for families 'in trouble', set up by religious or government institutions).

The general scheme of transformations in Figure 6.1 is meant to view the dynamics of the marriage forms in an abstract sense. Different societies – due to specific cultural constructions that have emerged over their histories – have set up different restrictions upon the acceptable and promoted transitions between the marriage forms.

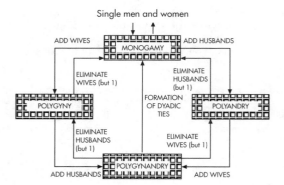

FIGURE 6.2 *Transformations between the four forms of marriage (theoretically possible transformations – no restrictions)*

HOW DO DIFFERENT MARRIAGES FUNCTION?

As was emphasized above, different marriage forms – as bases for family arrangements – are human culturally constructed means for coping with all the needs of human lives, rather than static states of 'correct' or 'incorrect' relations between men and women. In this section, we will try to analyse how different marriage forms can function in three respects: economic, social and psychological.

The analysis level of *economic function* of each of the marriage forms pertains to elaboration of how the basic livelihood of the given family is possible, under the given marriage form. It considers marriage partners as economic actors – both in the home and outside of it. All the aspects of everyday life that need to be coordinated – management of household tasks (cooking, cleaning, laundry, social relations) combined with management of childcare, children's informal or/and formal education, work outside home for hire or for guaranteeing food and water resources – all these functions are filtered through the given marriage forms.

The level of *social relationships* within each marriage form covers the *social role expectations* that exist within that form, as well as social rituals through which the family group proceeds. Individuals in practice certainly differ from the role expectations, reconstruct these, and through that change their family life (which may involve transitions between marriage forms).

Finally, the level of *psychological organization* of different marriage forms entails our reconstruction of the affective and cognitive reflections of the role bearers in different life situations within a marriage form. Here we can expect high inter-personal variability in the personal-cultural reconstructions of one's role in the given marriage form.

All three levels of analysis are interdependent. The most general (economic) level sets up the stage for the social relationships level, yet the latter is constructed through the personal-cultural processes of internalization and externalization of the expected social roles. In the following elaborations, let us look at each of the marriage forms through the lens of these three levels.

The polygynic marriage

The polygynic form of marriage is historically the most prominent form worldwide (see Clignet, 1970). Such prominence has been based on the asymmetry between genders in their biological functions: women can bear children, men cannot. Thus, in socioeconomic contexts where it was deemed necessary to enhance the reproductive success of men (via women's reproductive functions) in contexts of economic value of children (as economic assets), polygyny could easily be set into practice (see below, the case of Mormon polygyny).

Distribution, economic basis

Polygyny has been described to exist all over the world, at different times and in different socio-economic circumstances. Different religious frameworks (in our time we usually think of Islam as an example, yet it has existed under other religious frameworks as easily) have made use of it. Ancient civilizations of India and China permitted polygyny, and signs of it can be seen reflected in the Old Testament. The pre-Christian tribes in Europe practised it. It was the emergence of Christianity in European contexts from the third Century AD that started to limit it as a viable marriage form. Slowly it succeeded – aided by economic changes and through monopolization of the collective-cultural meaning system.

Economically, polygyny provides an increasing number of participants in both household management and economic subsistence. The co-wives are simultaneously childbearers and co-workers whose labour guarantees the livelihood of the whole marriage group and of the wider kinship network.

Social organization

Polygyny can exist in a number of basic forms, each of which sets up different conditions for the social roles of the participants, and – consequently – for the psychological mechanisms of its maintenance. The first distinction of the forms of polygyny is the contrast between *sororal* and *non-sororal* types.

In the case of sororal polygyny, the co-wives are sisters (obviously of different ages). As sisters, they bring to the marriage their pre-established pattern of sibling relations. These include (a) age-based dominance hierarchy (elder sisters – who probably are first to marry the husband – have had roles of taking care of their younger sisters as they grew up together). The female side of the sororally polygynous marriage is thus based on the long history of relations between siblings who are turned into co-wives. Such social role basis makes sororal polygyny better protected against possible psychological problems (for example, jealousies) than a non-sororal polygynic arrangement might be. It is estimated that about 50 per cent of known polygynous societies practise sororal polygyny (Van den Berghe, 1979, p. 67).

The second basis for distinguishing forms of polygyny is the *residence pattern*. The co-wives may either reside in the *same home compound*, or in locations *removed geographically from one another*. The social role relations in the case of these two types are necessarily different. In the case of a shared home compound, the co-wives are in constant contact with one another in household management matters. They may cooperate in agricultural work, and in childrearing issues. In this framework, the power of running the household is in the hands of *co-wives as a small social group*, with its own structure. The latter is determined by their seniority status (earlier wives dominating over later married – or younger – ones). The role of the husband is limited here, to the final arbiter of co-wives' possible relationships problems, and to the publicly presentable figure-head of the household.

In contrast, when co-wives live in separate households, there is no (or minimal) mutuality of relations between them. They are united through the husband (who visits each household at some times), yet each co-wife fully controls her own household in ways similar to single women (of our contemporary society)[2]. In this case there is no need to coordinate the actions in one's household with any co-wife, and not even with the husband (whose temporary presence also equals lack of control or relevance in the running of the household). Possible friction between co-wives here is likely on the basis of real or imagined dangers to the property sharing of the husband, but not on the basis of immediate, face-to-face, relationship issues (as in the case of co-wives inhabiting the same home compound).

As an illustration, let us consider the case of a Gusii (a tribe in Kenya) woman named Jane (described in LeVine and Pfeifer, 1982, pp. 71–72). Jane had married her husband, Ongaro at 18. Ongaro already had one wife, who was sick and requested that Ongaro marry a second wife so that there would be help with the farm and with the household. It is important to note here that the first wife herself suggested to the husband the move from a monogamic into a polygynic state.

At first, Jane's marriage was of the separate households kind. Ongaro moved with her from Kenya to Tanzania (where he was involved in some trade). However, when they returned from the stay in Tanzania, Jane had to share the home compound with the ailing senior co-wife. Because of the co-wife's ill health, Jane had to take on the major share of household work. When the co-wife died, the marriage entered again into a mono-gamic phase – yet Jane had to continue with the full load of the household and farm work.

Aside from the economic role, Jane had to be reproductively successful. Ongaro *did not pay the brideprice for her before she had demonstrated such success* (by bearing him two sons). She then had seven years without childbirths, followed by years when she gave birth to seven more children.

In the 1970s Ongaro married a new wife – and the marriage again entered into a polygynic state. The new co-wife lived in town where she took care of a bar that Ongaro owned there. The marriage here was again that of separate households. The friction that emerged on Jane's side was based on economic uncertainty – she was afraid that Ongaro might give half of his land to the co-wife. The life course of Jane served against such danger – in 1974 her eldest son married and became employed. As the mother of an adult son who was both married and employed, Jane felt secure about her economic dominance in Ongaro's family. Despite tensions with Ongaro, she considered her home life very satisfactory, since she was economically safe and enjoyed rewarding relations with her children.

The co-wife in town failed to bring children to Ongaro, and he divorced her. He then married another woman – for whom he purchased land near town – with whom he had two children. This purchase was an addition to the whole family resources, and did not constitute a threat to Jane. Again, the polygynic marriage here was of separate households type.

In this example, we can see how a polygynic marriage can move between the shared house-hold and separate households conditions. The role of the co-wives in these two is different, as are their economic concerns. Sexual functions did not enter into the decisions about marriage, or frictions in the marriage – sexuality was important for procreation (for example, barren-ness of a co-wife was sufficient for divorce), but did not constitute a basis for friction. In contrast, potential danger to Jane's own property (within the marriage) was viewed as a serious challenge.

Aside from economic and childbearing func-tions, polygyny is to guarantee the continuity of the once-established household. Since the major threat for a household has historically been that of the death of the wives (in childbirth, or from any health complication), polygyny functions as a social buffer against dramatic upsets in the organization of the household. The Sebei (in Kenya) have a saying: 'A man but with one wife is a friend to the bachelor' (Goldschmidt, 1976, p. 231). If a man has no second co-wife who could immediately compensate for the functions of the household care should the first co-wife become incapacitated, he would have to import a female relative from some other part of his kinship network. This new 'import' might not enter the caregiver's role as simply as an existing co-wife.

Age structure of polygynic marriages

As a rule, polygynic marriage begins as a mono-gamic one, and after some time may become extended to polygyny. Hence, structurally, the cases of underdeveloped polygyny are not separable from monogamy. This has led some analysts to point out that in societies where polygyny is practised, it does not dominate in terms of demographic majority. This is understandable, since expansion from the monogamic to polygynic phase of marriage is a difficult and expensive step. Since marriages are usually economic exchange events (between clans), the man who wants to add a second wife to his marriage needs to be affluent enough to pay the brideprice for the second time. This is possible if the accumulation of wealth (largely through the work of the first wife) makes such expansion possible. Naturally, there is some time period (ranging from four to 10 or more years) between the first and subsequent marriages. As a rule, the husband is already older than the first wife at their marriage; adding every new wife is likely to add to such age difference.

In Figure 6.3, data on the age structure of polygynic marriages of the Luo (in Kenya, from Ruisinga Island in Lake Victoria Basin) are presented. In the Luo case, the husband (on average) is about 10 years older than the first wife (28 years vs 18 years). The second wife (also aged under 20) is added about the time the husband is 38 years old, which means a 20-year age difference between him and the second wife. The third wife may be added another 10 years later, bringing the age difference to 30 (women marry as co-wives when they are teenagers). By the time the third wife appears in the Luo household, the first wife's children may be almost of the same age as the third wife. The graph in Figure 6.3 reaches a plateau in the ages of

husbands and senior wives by the times of arrival of the fourth and fifth wives, possibly because the averaged data are limited by mortality in the 40s/50s age range.

The wide gap between marriage partners creates a large number of young widows – who in the Luo society need to be integrated into some social group through re-marriage. As is evident from Table 6.3, in the Luo case the widows become mostly re-married to the deceased husband's brother. This is a widespread social rule in African contexts. Yet the man who marries a widow must marry another woman as well (Ssennyonga, 1997, p. 271). Very few widows remain unmarried – partly as a result of their religious background (conversion to Christianity).

There are, however, important restrictions on re-marriage. If a Luo widow loses a child before her re-marriage (but after her husband's death), none of the husband's relatives may remarry her. Instead, a man of inferior status is induced to remarry the widow. The collective-cultural social network for the support of the widow is not non-evaluative as to the woman's reproductive life.

Practices of levirate

The example above indicates the role of the kinship group in organization of continued marital relation of the widow(er). The assigned member of the kinship group to marry the widow is called a *levir*, and the resulting marital tie a *levirate*. The practice of levirate guarantees the continuing social and material support for the widow (by the kinship group), as well as maintaining the control over economic resources of the widow's household by the kin group at large.

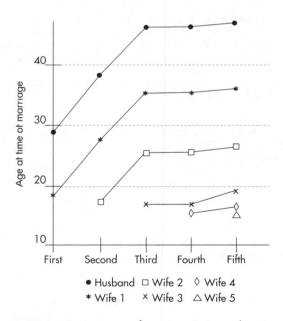

FIGURE 6.3 *Mean age of marriage in Luo polygynic marriages (from Ssennyonga, 1997, p. 270, reprinted by permission of Greenwood Publishing Group)*

TABLE 6.3 *Relationships between deceased and current husbands of remarried widows among the Luo, Ruisinga Island*

Relationship with the deceased husband	Number	%
Widow is remarried to the husband's		
Brother	34	63.0
Cousin	6	11.1
Son	1[a]	1.8
No relation	2	3.7
Widow is not remarried	11	20.4
Total 54		

[a] This case indicates remarriage to the son of the husband and another co-wife, a result of the polygynous marital context.

Source: Ssennyonga, 1997, p. 271

As in the case of any marriage, partners' opinions as to why they enter into levirate varies. A sample of expressed opinions by Maragoli women (in Western Kenya) is given in Table 6.4. Most of the stated explanations refer to concrete everyday life rationales (tradition, resources etc.), with very few (3 per cent) of the women mentioning particular psychological ties with the partner (companionship). The centrality of widows' immediate life needs, and the primary tie being that of a woman with her children (rather than with her husband) supports this orientation. Furthermore, levirate becomes a natural extension of the polygynic marriage form – marrying the widow as an additional wife (who remains living in her previously established household, taking care of it) is fitted with the multiple marriage system.

Of course not all levirate relations turn out harmonious. If the relations deteriorate, the next male partner for the widow need not be from the deceased husband's kin group. Hence the levirate relation can become a transition of the widow from the husband's kin group support system to other social relations.

Spatial development of a joint home compound

The polygynic marriage with a shared home compound includes both unity and differentiation in the structure of the household patterning. Different members of the marriage group set up their separate house units within a compound in ways that mark their status difference, together with their belonging to the same marriage group. Figure 6.4 describes the growth of a Luo polygynic shared home compound. In the first (monogamic) phase of the marriage, the first wife gets her own house directly facing the gate into the home compound (Figure 6.4A). In the past, the husband used to build his house in the middle of the compound; currently this is turned into a daytime resting (and meeting visitors) location. The back gates to the gardens are right behind the wife's house. When co-wives become added to the compound, they likewise get houses at the back of the compound (relative to the front gates) (see Figure 6.4B). The quality of the house of the senior wife is expected to be better than that of subsequent co-wives. When sons grow up, they establish their own houses near the front gate, but facing the centre of the home compound (with rear door towards the front gate, see Figure 6.4C). If the husband's brother shares the compound, he has a house in-between the sons and co-wives.

Psychological organization

The psychological mechanisms that make polygynic relations possible include (a) maintenance of equality of the persons in their social roles through a differentiated structure of inequality; and (b) joint goals in subsistence.

Maintenance of equality through inequality This claim at first glance seems internally contradictory, as it unites two opposites (equality and inequality) which are usually viewed as mutually exclusive. Yet there exists no social group that involves equal participants in all possible senses. Rather, even when equality of members is claimed to be the case, the realities of existence of the group demonstrate inequalities. Thus, the presentation of a group (to outsiders, and to group members themselves) may emphasize the *meaning* of equality that sets the psychological basis for acceptance of inequalities in the ongoing life of the group.

In the polygynic marriage system, the use of the meaning of equality is symbolically presented

TABLE 6.4 *Maragoli (Western Kenya) widows' stated reasons for consenting to levirate relationships*

Reasons	Frequency of mentioning	%
Our tradition	38	16.3
To access productive resources	36	15.4
To benefit from deceased husband's estate	35	15.0
For children to benefit from education fund	33	14.2
To get financial support	30	12.9
To have a son	25	10.7
Childless – to have children	16	6.9
Not to be implicated in husband's death	9	3.9
Needed a companion	7	3.0
Levir to build house for me	4	1.7
Total	233	100.0

Source: Gwaku, 1998, p. 182

A The monogamic phase

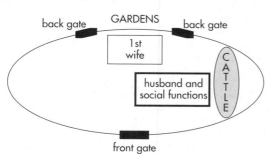

B Move to co-wives sharing home compound

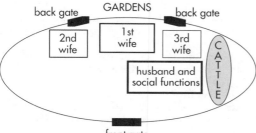

C Sons establish their houses on the compound

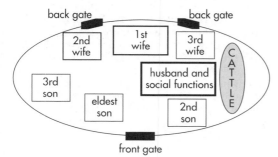

FIGURE 6.4 *The development of the structure of a Luo home compound with developing polygynic marriage (after Ssennyonga, 1997)*

by the social norm *that the husband must treat all co-wives equally*. This norm is particularly set into practice in the ritualistic functions within the life of the polygynic marriage group. The husband – when making gifts to his wives – must give each of them a gift equal in value. Deviations (by the husband) from that norm are carefully monitored (by the co-wives, first of all), and may lead to friction within the group. Yet, at the same time, the co-wives are – already in their social roles – not equal at all. They function in accordance

with a prescribed dominance by seniority; they are of very different ages, physical capabilities, they are in different stages of their reproductive careers. Some have more children (which is a value marker for women) than others. If any of them is barren, this may be a basis for serious social stigmatization (within the group) and may lead to loss of the marital status for the woman (divorce). The reality of the relations between co-wives in a polygynic setting is filled with inequalities from the very moment of the women's entrance into their social roles. Yet semiotically these inequalities are organized through the social norm of equality (through constructing an ingroup through 'we'-feeling), which leads to the acceptance of intra-group differentiation. The example from the Oneida community (see description below) indicates this well – the community members presented themselves to others and one another as parts of a 'we'-feeling group, yet that semiotic unity was dependent upon John Noyes's central personal role within the 'we'-group. Once his role crumbled (as he aged), the 'we'-community dissipated.

The polygynic marriage group is also united by the wider web of ties between the kinship groups of all its participants, fortified ritualistically by any social gathering, and economically by the exchanges of resources that take place around marriage (brideprice etc.).

Joint goals in subsistence If the polygynic marriage is of the shared home compound kind, it is the coordination of everyday subsistence (farming, feeding children etc.) tasks that unifies the group. The mechanism of creating group unity through shared tasks is a classic fact in social psychology (for example, see the 'Robbers' Cave' experiment; Sherif et al., 1961). Joint actions by co-wives, on a daily basis, particularly under conditions of economic uncertainty (such as loss of crop due to drought) and the need to maintain the household, create the *activity basis* for the psychological well-being of the group. This joint activity basis can be enhanced by the history of the co-wives' relationship (as in the case of sororal polygyny).

The usual ('Western') problem of sexual jealousy is largely out of place in the case of non-monogamic marriage forms. Sexuality is a normal part of lives of all participants, male and female. It is regulated for procreational purposes (as the value of it is in having children). It is not expected to be linked with co-wives' feelings towards the husband (who is psychologically distant from the wives anyway – 'love marriages' in the Western sense of recent centuries are not the norm in polygynic cases).

A case example: the introduction of polygyny in US history

Interestingly, under special sociohistorical conditions, Christianity-dominated social units have re-structured the strict limits set upon the transformation of the marriage forms (that is, the general picture of Figure 6.1). It is uniquely in the course of history of the United States (rather than Europe) that such experiments have taken place. The United States is a country with a very specific history: on a relatively large territory, different religious and political groups who had escaped from Europe could establish a relatively well-balanced system of co-existence. The denominational nature of religion in the United States, together with religious freedom, has allowed different small religious groups to establish their particular forms of communal living. Such forms, at times, have explicitly transcended the privileged nature of monogamy, in favour of polygynandry or polygyny. Notably, such transcendence has been related with efforts to build new forms of society, usually on the grounds of strong religious orientation.

The history of the State of Utah is remarkable in that it provides a good example of a case – and one extending to a whole state of the Union – where an experiment in re-setting the limits upon transformation of marriage forms has taken place. The Mormon context emphasized reproductive success (rather than sexual pleasure) as evidence of religious devotion. Yet the history of the adoption of the polygynic form of marriage antedates the Mormon exodus to Utah in 1846.

The history of adoption of the polygynic marriage form by the Church of Jesus Christ of the Latter-day Saints (Mormons) on the basis of an interpretation of the Christian history is informative in two ways. First, it demonstrates how a new – previously completely alien – form of social organization of everyday life can be put into practice if completely (redundantly) set up by a social institution. Secondly, the history of Mormon polygyny entails a story of sociopolitical power struggle between the Mormon-dominated State of Utah and the US Federal Government, in the second half of the nineteenth century. That fight brings out the questions of freedom of belief, construction of images of social stigmatization, and socialization of children under conditions of constant danger.

The Mormon Church was founded in 1830, with the notion of monogamy as the only acceptable marriage form firmly in place. From 1823, the 17-year-old Joseph Smith – who was to become the founding figure of the Mormon Church – began to have visions of the basic wrongness of other religions, together with his own feeling of the mission to create an alternative. The new religion was based on ideas from the Old Testament, which included notions of plural marriage. Yet the prevailing ideas of the persons who converted to the Mormon Church were in opposition to such practices. Nevertheless, on 12 July 1843, Joseph Smith reported the divine revelation that polygyny would be the religiously idealized form of marriage for the Mormons. It was explicitly linked with the need for social power within the communities of the members of the new religion (Foster, 1984, p. 136). If the Mormon Church were to gain independent control of its own social system, it had to be in a position of control over all the major life course decisions of its members – of marriage, childbearing and divorce. According to Joseph Smith, God had instructed the taking of plural wives: if taking one wife, approved by the Church, was a commendable act, then in the case of moral purity and success in work the man could deserve – again as sanctioned by the Church – the addition of a second wife. The result – increase in fertility of the man – was of high value and a religiously cherished notion. Furthermore, marriage in the case of Mormons (like in other cases) is primarily a symbolic, and secondarily a legal act. Joseph Smith himself married a number of women,[3] yet this seemingly extensive set of heterosexual relations is probably better viewed as a symbolic creation of cohesion of the religious community. By marrying, the Prophet could bind a small group of devotees to his religion – the spiritual commitment prevailed over the procreative role of the marriage. While Joseph Smith proposed different women to marry him, the ones who agreed went through a phenomenon similar to religious conversion. In almost all cases – of Mormon plural marriage in general – the initial suggestion to marry plurally produced horror, shock, or confusion. Yet,

> Those who eventually accepted the principle almost invariably *went through a period of inner turmoil lasting from several days to several months*. During this period, they may go without adequate sleep, food, or normal social contacts, fervently praying that God would reveal the truth of the new beliefs to them. Those who eventually accepted plural marriage almost invariably *had a compelling personal experience revealing the truth of the new standards*. (Foster, 1984, p. 153; added emphasis)

This description verifies the internalization process that was socially triggered through the Church leaders' suggestions for entering into plural marriage. For those who personally reconstructed the suggestion – through their own religious revelation – the actual marrying became supported both by external social suggestion and approval (on the one side), and by their own intra-psychological reconstruction of their acceptance of it (on the other). Thus, through the procedure of creating marriages of plural kind, the strength of those (which did take place) was guided redundantly – *both* by the relevant others surrounding the person (who were united in the community) *and* by intra-personal psychological 'breakthrough'. Furthermore, plural marriage was often considered to benefit the woman's spiritual status within a belief system that emphasized the continuity of life in afterlife. Last, but not least, plural marriage provided the women with sharing of economic resources, and operated as a form of social security.[4]

Conversion can of course occur under many circumstances, yet situating it in the context of accepting an alien form for one's own marriage was the powerful test that cemented the success of Joseph Smith's activity. Yet the practice of living under conditions of plural marriage, while being persecuted and in hiding, was not necessarily an easy task for Smith. It ended with Smith being murdered in 1844.

The establishment of the Mormon Church in Utah was the result of the activities of Brigham Young (1801–1877). The move in 1847 from Illinois to Utah was necessary because of the 'state of civil war' that attacks by anti-Mormon local inhabitants displayed. The 'Wild West' of North America was indeed a land of opportunities –

including among those the possibility of living peacefully and in accordance with one's own religious beliefs. The fear of anti-Mormon pogroms was a good reason to move the whole community of the Mormon Church to a new location. After establishing themselves in Utah, the declaration of polygyny as the respected doctrine of marriage within the Church was made in Salt Lake City in 1852.

Schematically, the Mormon transformation is depicted in Figure 6.5. Polygyny was culturally reconstructed not only to be allowed, but also as a religiously sanctioned form of marriage, possible only to the most pious followers of the religion. Hence the transformation from monogamy to polygyny (by adding wives) was socially controlled; return from the highly desired status was blocked. While polygyny became selectively positively valued, other plural marriage forms remained as strictly blocked from possible use as those are in the case of monogamy (see below).

The Mormon polygyny is an example of both religious control over the lives of the persons in marriage, and of enablement of their individual potentials. This is particularly well seen in the social relevance of women in public life (Foster, 1979). Utah was the first state in the US where women had equal voting rights (1870). The religious context of the Mormon polygyny guaranteed that the enhancement of women in spirit (by way of Church-sanctioned marrying) led to symbolically enhanced public roles.

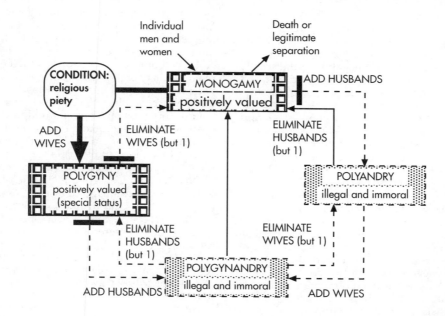

FIGURE 6.5 *Transformation of marriage forms with re-arranged restrictions (an example of Mormon polygyny)*

The crusade against the Mormon religious freedom of organizing the lives of the communities in Utah was relatively slow. In 1857 Utah was invaded by Federal troops. Yet their presence did not change the local context for another 20 years – possibly because of the concentration of the political processes of the US on the Civil War in the East. In the 1870s and 1880s, the pressure of the US Federal Government against the Mormon Church intensified. The raids on 'polygamists', their imprisonment and the efforts by the Mormon communities to counteract by peaceful means such acts of intervention make the history of Utah of the second half of the nineteenth century a parallel phenomenon to the totalitarian social systems of the twentieth century. It was the US Federal Government who, demonstrating the outer boundaries of the notion of democracy, sent special agents to Utah to take control over local life, and to eradicate the 'vice' of polygamy. The acts of the Government were certainly based on the consensual denouncement of Mormon polygamy (see Sheldon, 1976). Such public outcry against it flourished already in the 1830s and 1840s in Illinois and other states where Mormons lived prior to the exodus to Utah. It was a projection of Puritan dissatisfactions with their own religion upon another religious denomination (Cannon, 1974). The anti-Mormon popular literature in the 1870s and 1880s (in New York) presented the Mormons in Utah as complete 'sexual perverts', their detractors projecting into them a 'vicious sexual lust' of their own. Such social stigmatization surely had a 'grass roots' base, and was not instigated by the Federal Government. The Mormon experiment in reconstituting the privileged marriage form went precisely against the propagation of the strictly monogamic, non-hedonic and moralistic patterns of female social roles in US society in the first half of the nineteenth century. The social representation of 'true womanhood' emphasized four cardinal virtues of women – *piety* (of the mother), *purity* (of the daughter), *submissiveness* (of the sister) and *domesticity* (of the wife) (see Welter, 1966, p. 152). All these virtues were shared by the Mormon social system – yet in ways that encoded them differently in the polygynic marriage system. The social representation of 'true womanhood' in the Mormon case meant a far greater independence (in the sphere of domestic life) than was assumed to be appropriate for the rest of women – those who did not share the Mormon religious background – in the United States at the time. Mormon women played an active role in building up the polygynic marriage form, with a basic (in our contemporary terms, it could be labelled 'conservative') emphasis on procreation.

... a husband should remain apart from his wife at certain seasons, which, in the very constitution of the female are untimely. Or, in other words. Indulgence should not be merely for pleasure, or wanton desires, but mainly for the purpose of procreation. The morality of nature would teach the mother, that, during nature's process in the formation and growth of embryo man, her heart should be pure, her thoughts and actions chaste, her mind calm, her passions without excitement; while her body should be invigorated with every exercise conducive to health and vigor; but by no means subjected to anything calculated to disturb, irritate, weary, or exhaust any of its functions. (From a letter from one sister to another, dated 1853: Whittaker, 1984, p. 55)

This letter was later made into a part of an official Mormon pamphlet propagating the social role of women. Its content pertains to the organization of pregnancy (see further treatment of this issue in Chapter 8). Here it indicates the focus on the central role of women in procreation, and relative distancing of the husband from that domain (while recognizing the husband's leadership role in other spheres of social life). Thus, the Mormon conceptualization of 'true womanhood' was characterized by *pious interdependence with the male patriarch role* in the service of the religious calling. The latter was best demonstrated by success in childbearing, child-raising, and productivity in agricultural production.

Differences in crucial practices are always a simple basis for social stigmatization – the wider US population had no difficulty stigmatizing the Mormon system as if it were non-pure in its morality, *solely on the basis* of knowledge that non-monogamic marriage was considered *possible*. Nobody bothered to enquire into the actual religious piety of the Mormons, as soon as it was known that plural marriage was considered morally acceptable, or even ideal for religious values. This whole example is an empirical test of the unity of ideological tolerance in the history of the United States at local community levels. The issues of tolerance and intolerance are mutually linked as parts of the same whole (refer back to Chapter 3 on Georg Simmel). The Mormons were stigmatized and forced to leave for the West because of the local dislike for their differing practices. Of course, the political aspect of control over resources entered into the picture. As the Mormon Church took over the political power in Utah, it became an issue of political control over resources that was played out on the grounds of a 'moral crusade' against Mormon polygynic practices.

The power of the Federal Government finally prevailed: in 1890 the Mormon Church was forced to publicly declare that it would not sanction any more plural marriages. Yet it was precisely acts of such power that had already undermined the marriage system in Utah. Being under siege, polygynic families needed to hide their status (for example, by one of the co-wives being merely a 'maid' in the given household). Wives were ordered by the Federal legal system to testify against their husbands, and could be imprisoned themselves if they refused to do so. As a result of wives' imprisonment, the household and care of the children were in jeopardy. Children had to be taught to distrust unfamiliar persons who asked questions about 'who is your father?', and misinform anybody who might be an informer for the Federal Government (Bradley, 1983). The local communities in Utah developed a healthy distrust towards outsiders, and questions about who is whose father became inappropriate even in the public discourse of Mormons themselves. The children experienced this kind of siege as they would experience any similar dramatic contrast between home and public domains under other social conditions.[5] These experiences were social outcomes of the community's conflict with the larger administrative power, and not inherent in the polygynic marriage form itself. Before the external threat became exaggerated (for example, in the 1860s), reports of ordinary family life in Utah households provide evidence of ordinary social relationships between marriage partners, and childhood experiences like in any family (Hartley, 1983).

The mundane nature of Mormon polygyny continues in its contemporary practices, which have survived and re-gained prominence (at least in those aspects of social life arrangements that adhere to the religious calling in a most devoted way). The cultural-psychological intricacies of contemporary Mormon polygyny are studied in detail by Irwin Altman and Joseph Ginat (Altman and Ginat, 1996). While documenting a whole range of ways in which modern polygynous marriages in the Mormon areas function – including successes and failures – the pattern of coordination of dyadic and communal arrangements in the everyday lives of the marriages becomes evident. The dyadic (husband–wife) psychological relations can be extended to include superordinate (social group) structure, in which all co-wives and the husband establish their roles in the midst of making sure that all everyday life arrangements (work, childcare, education, religious activities) are guaranteed. The success in the establishment of the social group framework depends upon the establishment of relations between co-wives, aided (or hindered) by their particular living arrangements. In the contemporary Mormon case, these arrangements are more complex than in the cases of African polygyny

(for example, the contrast between 'shared home compound' and 'separate homes for each co-wife'). The fitting of multi-wife and many-children polygynic Mormon families into regular US architectural practice of planning one-(monogamic)-family housing has been a creative effort. Furthermore, the collective memories of previous religious persecution have not disappeared, and the possibility of their re-surfacing is a factor to be considered. On the other side, the internalization of the religious value of communal marriage – in parallel with practical solutions such living affords (sharing of housing, co-wives helping one another with issues of childcare) – maintain polygyny as a viable form of marriage in those areas of the United States where a collective-cultural religious framework provides background support for it.

Altman and Ginat demonstrate how the set of everyday objects and activities mediates the social relations in – and psychological construction of – the persons' roles in polygynic marriages. The core of such marriage is complementarity of the husband's *patriarch-role* (head of the family), and the roles of the individual co-wives as *women-mothers*. The latter role of women entails home-centred control over space, cultural marking of the space and organization of activities (cooking, childcare, laundry). The co-wives jointly control communal space, and individually their own personal territories. The smoothness of the co-wife relations depends upon their individual control over their personal space, and objects within these spaces. The space/object domain is both the arena for establishing and maintaining co-wives' relations, as well as an indicator of their state. Thus,

> Sally, Harvey's first wife, said that the way she, Harvey, and Molly managed and decorated their homes mirrored the gradual deterioration of the marriage and their relationships. When Molly first joined the family she and Sally shared everything. They *wore each other's clothes* and *cooperated in decorating the home*. They discussed cooperatively how to furnish the living room, where to put furniture, what to hang on the walls, how to arrange objects. But over time things began to deteriorate, Sally claimed, because Molly became selfish and Harvey began to prefer Molly. In successive moves, Sally always kept her very personal things – books, desk, cedar chest, photographs, silverware. But she stopped caring about other things in the home, to some extent because Harvey began giving Sally's furniture to Molly without discussing it with her . . . Sally finally divorced Harvey for many reasons, but his violation of her attachment to places and things mirrored other problems in the family. (Altman and Ginat, 1996, p. 234; added emphasis)

The closeness between persons is built (and indicated) by their unconditional sharing of personal objects (and activities). Wearing each other's clothing would indicate an effort at inter-personal closeness. The effort carries within it ambivalence – as the previous state of the relation was not that of closeness. If the closeness is not established through the effort, the division of the objects (into personal versus communal) can indicate change in the relationship. Thus, the polygynic marriage form (of shared households) sets the stage for *potential* establishment of close inter-co-wife ties through the sharing of joint, similarly goal-oriented tasks. Whether this actually happens depends upon the specific persons involved, and the dynamics of their actual establishment of their relations. That latter process is not determinable by any social set-up of conditions; the relations may work out to be good, but also to become negative. Precisely this uncertainty is taken into account by the redundant compensatory mechanism – each of the co-wives establishes their own personalized object environment (room etc.) which serves for each of them as *her own* place. It may be dyadically shared with the visiting (common) husband, but not with other co-wives (except if the relations are indeed of the kind that makes such sharing possible). The co-wives have their individual places, and on the basis of those can establish close relations with one another.

The making of the home place for the husband is a very different matter in contemporary Mormon households. Given the history of stigmatization (which resulted in the need to hide the polygynic lifestyle from the public), and distribution of the homes of the husband's wives, the strict visiting schedule (which is described by anthropologists looking at polygyny in Africa) has been both impractical and undesirable. It has given rise to a flexible scheduling of the husband's movement patterns between households. At times the husband himself (in his patriarch's role) decides where he goes for the given night; at other times this scheduling is completely in the collective hands of the co-wives; or is determined by particular needs of the given household. In any case, it is the husband who may lack personal territory of his own in any of the homes.[6] In each, the particular co-wife has full control over the organization of the home. Since the husband regularly visits all of the homes, his own pertinent personal objects (clothing) are distributed between the homes (as an object-based marker of the husband's psychological presence in each, and in an equitable way). For example,

Howard distributes his clothing among the homes of his four wives, Constance, Valerie, Barbara, and Rose,

all of whom live in separate dwellings. He keeps some of his clothing in his own drawer in a bureau in each wife's bedroom. They, too, have adopted a system that emphasizes his communal relationship to homes and wives.

They also told of the amusing confusion that arises in managing Howard's clothing. He sometimes ends up having to wear bizarre combinations of colors because he does not know where things are, sometimes all of his socks end up in one wife's home, or he is missing a key piece of clothing for a particular outfit, and so on. With great amusement, the wives said Howard bangs into walls and furniture in the middle of the night, not sure where he is, and is always looking in the wrong drawer for his clothing. (Altman and Ginat, 1996, pp. 266–267)

The amusing telling of the story of their shared husband's confusions fortifies the indication that each of the co-wives is in control over their respective home grounds, while they collectively appreciate the husband in the role of the head of the family, and (each personally) have their particular emotional relationship with him (which is dyadic, irrespective of whether the relations between co-wives are positive, ambivalent, or negative). Full control over the home ground as the core role for the wives is encoded into the Mormon religious teaching, which separates the home as the unquestionable dominance domain of the women from the public domain as the (equally unquestionable) dominance domain of the men. This distinction is similar to gender role distinctions between public and private (family) domains in many other societies, especially those in which polygyny is a socially privileged form of marriage. In respect of all of these societies, it is not possible to make simple statements about one or the other gender being 'dominant'. The dominance is clearly specific to the particular kind of place (home versus work), and the polygynic marriage form guides women to be necessarily dominant in the home domains.

Children's experiences in polygynic marriage contexts

As the history of polygyny in Utah shows, children's experiences of plural marriages depend heavily upon the valuation of the context of the given marriage. If that valuation is positive – polygyny is a socially accepted and valued (yet not necessarily practised) – form – the experiences of those who grow up in these unions would differ from the contexts where the valuation is either ambivalent (for example, the Utah case where polygyny was valued by the Mormon Church, and derogated by the US Government and its public propaganda system). As one of the results of this history, children in late nineteenth century Utah were necessarily guided to hide their family membership from external enquirers. For example, a daughter of a Utah polygamist described her experiences in childhood thus:

I had a very happy childhood, except for the years of the Underground [note: this was the period of Federal persecution of Utah Mormon families in their home context]. That was terrible. The officers sometimes came at three in the morning to search the house. At night if we opened the door, people would go scurrying – people who had been looking in the windows to see if father was there . . . We never knew where father was so if the officers asked us, we couldn't tell them. (Dredge, 1976, p. 136)

The whole family was under stress at times of such persecution, and the reported horror of such experiences in childhood had nothing to do with the polygynic nature of the child's home. Anne Frank, hiding from Nazi persecution with her family in the attic of an Amsterdam house could describe her childhood in similar ways. For a more adequate description of the childhood experience, one needs to consider the emotional and informal-educational sides of childhood. The presence of co-wives – from the children's perspective – entailed access to different kinds of skills (for example, one of the co-wives could teach the child to knit, another to read). Further-more, where there were positive relations within the family the different co-wives would be relevant emotional support resources for the children. In one account,

We [children] went from one home to the other [implying here: two co-wives, each having a home next door] and were always welcomed by the mother [of that particular home]. There were quarrels between us children, but no different than those between other brothers and sisters. This was largely due to the justice of our father. He was so absolutely just in his treatment of our mothers and their children, there was never a tinge of jealousy in the family. (Goodson, 1976, p. 103)

These examples have been drawn from the Mormon experience. There must surely be others, including cases of jealousy both in co-wives' and their children's relations. Yet such phenomena are constructed under different social conditions – the plural marriage forms merely set up the context for those differences.

In general, the experiences of children in poly-gynic marriages vary greatly, as the particular forms of these marriages are variable. Kilbride and Kilbride (1990) have provided an elaborate account of the impressions of Ugandan children who have grown up under polygynic marriage

conditions. As expected, personal experiences cover the whole range of psychological condi-tions, from reporting high levels of group cohesion and cooperation, to cases of jealousy and stigmatization of children (by other children, and by co-wives).

First, 'Marjorie' (a daughter of a wealthy Ugandan agricultural official, who has 25 children from four wives) narrated her memories of childhood:

I remember seeing my father bringing a new wife. When she came my mother was taken by my father to my home district where my father built a shamba, and she stayed there while the new wife was staying with my father in the place where he was working. The place where my mother was now staying was near the school where my sisters were boarding, so they could come home during the weekends. They could come to see my mother.

When I passed to Class 6, I went to study where my father was working. By then he had two more wives. All these women had children. *We were all going to school together, staying in the same house. We were doing everything as sisters.* I like my stepmothers; they were good. *I never know who my father loves best, whether my mother or the others.* But I *knew he gave 'respect' to my mother, being the first wife.* This was according to the traditional way. *The wives gave respect according to how one comes*, first come, second come, and so on. *These women gave so much respect to my mother. Myself and the stepsisters, we don't say, 'who is your mother?' We are all like sisters and brothers.*

My father's wives had many gardens. They could plant six acres of cotton for the wives. There was no famine in my family. It was a large family. I used to go to the garden with my stepmother. *I could tell them a lot of stories, and they laughed so much.* I went back to my mother's house for holidays where I stayed with my two sisters. My mother was so strict with me! It was my future. She had to teach me cooking, responsibilities like doing dishes, all as woman's duties. My favorite relative was my mother's elder sister. She gave us a lot to eat so we liked her so much. She had only one son, but mother had ten of us. (Kilbride and Kilbride, 1990, pp. 206–207; added emphasis)

This personal story includes a number of points that demonstrate how a polygynic marriage could work as a social system. The success of the childhood family environment depended upon the father's treatment of the co-wives equitably – both in the sense of respecting each of them, and respecting their seniority rank. The co-wives can be traced here to set up a unifying social context for all of the co-sibs (for example, *children* would not ask the question of who is whose mother, as it is unimportant). Different co-wives obviously differed in how they treated the children in different practical tasks. Marjorie here was not particularly complimentary about her own mother (mentioning that the mother 'never liked us so much': Kilbride and Kilbride, 1990, p. 207). Of course, it need not be forgotten that the mother had 10 children, which necessarily means shortening of attention to each single one. The flexible environment of the household of the other co-wives was thus contrastive (or reconstructive) for Marjorie and those of her needs that were not fully granted by her own mother.

Cooperation and non-possessiveness in the kinship group of the co-wives

The role of female relatives (Marjorie's mother's elder sister) is important here. It is coordinated with the role of the father, and set the stage for non-problematic growth of the child, leading to this positive retrospective account.

In contrast, 'Robert' tells a different story of his experiences. His father had four wives, his mother being the second in rank. Robert reported asking questions about his 'real mother', and being stigmatized and mistreated by the children of the other co-wives at school. He was negatively treated by the fourth co-wife (while living on her home grounds, to attend school from there). Among his memories of childhood, the question of organization of eating in the shared home compound is of relevance:

> Some of the things that I have experienced basically on the side of eating are that when eating we do not assemble at one particular place, each mommy with her children. This results in jealousy because the wives cook different types of food. And also one may be eating only one type of food, such as *Ugali*, without changing. So it results in admiring the food of the other mommies. (Kilbride and Kilbride, 1990, p. 209)

The specific social-psychological organization of food-related activities is of central importance for regulating social relations (see Chapter 8). The possibility for open comparison of foods made by other co-wives created the basis for inter-child competitiveness on the basis of inter-mother comparisons.

Summarizing his growing-up experiences, 'Robert' remarked:

> The advantages which I have experienced under polygyny are that with work like planting, co-operation works, and when one of the family is sick, contributions occur in great number. Biblically, *that is a time for showing love, peace, and unity* as the commandment says to love your neighbor. Another advantage is that *barrenness cannot occur*. African

tribes, particularly the Bunyala, believe that immortality is recaptured in one's issue (offspring). They believe that the more wives one gets, the more children he expects, and the more chances of purportedly capturing immortality. If robbers have appeared at the compound, the polygamous family can react seriously *to defend whatever is to happen*. Also, no money is wasted, employing some people to defend the home. And some believe that polygyny is a sign of wealth.

> Some of the disadvantages that I have experienced in a polygynous family are so many. When my mother is given something by father such as money for buying new clothes that is the time when rough words come from the first, third, and fourth wives that their children also need clothes or whatever she has gotten. Who to educate becomes also a problem because of financial difficulties in obtaining school fees. Feeding the family becomes impossible, hence stealing other people's properties results sometimes . . . *Jealousy generates among such a family*. For instance, maybe one of the sons of the second or third wife is employed somewhere. The rest of the wives complain that what he gets is only to feed his 'really' mother . . . (Kilbride and Kilbride, 1990, pp. 208–209; added emphasis)

The psychological mechanisms of the problematic functioning of Robert's home context are obvious here. Once jealousy has appeared in the relations (through promoted competitiveness), it can become the basis for constant evaluation of what happens with economic provisions – whether these come to the mothers from their husband, or from their sons.

This example verifies once more that the crucial issue around which the polygynic family can go astray is the handling of economic resources, rather than issues of sexuality. Surely it is easier to maintain the polygynic household under conditions of affluence (Marjorie's case) than when the whole family is under economic strain (Robert's case).

The polyandrous marriage

In contrast to polygyny, polyandry is a rare form of marriage. It has been documented mostly in the Himalayan mountain regions and in different parts of the Indian subcontinent. Even when it has been described in contemporary times, its existence is closely tied to the economic conditions of life in the given society.

The economic basis of polyandry

Polyandry sets up cultural limits on the reproductive proliferation of the men, through limiting their procreating capacities to the joint wife.

This is necessary under strict economic demand conditions. For instance, Himalayan polyandry exists largely on the basis of the economic need not to partition the land between sons from generation to generation, as that would hinder agricultural productivity. Polyandry in the Himalayas is further supported by the combination of economic activities – working the fields (which requires male labour) and going on trading trips (also a male activity) facilitates the economic well-being of the polyandrous household.

Economic concerns can be related with collective-cultural norms. If (as was the case in the history of Southern India) it was the norm that a *household must always include a male member* while (at the same time) *males were recruited into military campaigns* at different times (and with uncertainties of survival), then most clearly polyandrous arrangements are functional to maintain normal conditions of life for the families. Yet when the conditions change, the marriage form can transform. Thus the marriage form is not an outcome, but a means to social ends, and it protects itself against its downfall. As Aiyappan remarked (in 1937):

> Whenever modern European culture has penetrated and modified indigenous culture, polyandry is giving way to monandry, but on the other hand, in rural areas remote from foreign influences, polyandrous families are still numerous and are surprisingly free from jealousy and discord. The suppression, therefore, of sexual jealousy between the brothers who are the common husbands of a single wife is a function of their culture. The chief cultural forces that lead to the suppression of the emotion in the men are (1) the ritual of marriage . . . by which they are made joint husbands; (2) the economic motive to prevent the disintegration of the family property by limiting the number of heirs; (3) the influence of parents who, during the earlier years of marital partnership, supervise and regulate the sexual life of the co-husbands by assigning each of them a particular night to be with the wife; and (4) public opinion which applauds successful polyandry. Under conditions of culture change all these forces have weakened and in every family in which economic and other ties have been modified, bickerings are heard that have their root in sexual jealousy, growing individualism and rebellion against the authority of elders in sexual matters. (Aiyappan, 1937, No. 130)

Social organization

Polyandry exists in different forms. First, there is the form of *fraternal polyandry* – a set of brothers marrying the same woman (the Aiyappan quote above refers to this form). Here marriage to the same wife entails literally the younger co-husbands' 'growing into' the marriage. So, for instance, if the oldest brother (of four) is 17 at the time of the marriage (and perhaps the bride 15), then the other brothers could be 13, 10 and 7 at the time of their joint marriage (assuming 3-year birth interval between brothers). The oldest brother may have become psycho-sexually ready to marry, while his younger brothers are still developing through their middle childhood and adolescence. This creates continuity from childhood relationships between brothers and their joint marriage. This continuity supports the creation of the *'collective husband'* status of the set of brothers. The co-husbands (brothers) function in a united way as a well-integrated social group – persons become parts of the whole 'collective husband'.

Early marriage of brothers as a collective husband can also lead to later marital problems (see Levine, 1988, for description). The 'coming of age' of the younger brothers at times leads to demands to add other wives to the marriage (thus turning it into polygynandry) or requiring separate wives for themselves (turning polyandry into monogamy).

Polyandry also occurs in the form of *matriarchal polyandry* (for instance, in the Indian region of Malabar). In matriarchal polyandry, the husbands of a woman are not necessarily related to one another by kinship or consanguity ties (Majumdar, 1960). Matriarchal polyandry is either *matrilocal* (that is, different husbands come to share the wife's household, either simultaneously or in succession), or *patrilocal* (a husband and wife couple, inhabiting the husband's home territory, invites another husband to join them in marriage). The reasons for adding a new husband to an existing marriage vary, but usually relate to infertility or economic needs.

An example of such transition comes from the description of Tibetan polyandry by Prince Peter (1963, p. 370), who has been one of the most notable Western researchers interested in polyandry. Ishe Palkid (a woman) was married to Rigzin at her age of 21, and almost immediately gave birth to a stillborn child. Efforts to become pregnant again during the following five years failed. Rigzin was alone cultivating the fields, and needed further help. He suggested to her to invite another man (Paldan) to join them in marriage, and she agreed. Paldan joined the household and shared the agricultural work, yet Ishe Palkid did not become pregnant during the following seven years. The need for an heir was high, so the polyandrous group decided to adopt a boy from another family.

Psychological organization

The crucial point in polyandrous relationships is the reverse of that of polygyny. In polyandry, the wife has to treat all co-husbands (who also vary by age, and seniority) equally. The issue of specific paternity of children is de-emphasized at the level of public presentation, even if it may be recognized in private. In any case, the having of a child by the whole marriage group is valued positively, de-focusing from the question of concrete paternity.

For most couples, the problem of sexual equity is handled by having the wife spend an entire night with one husband at a time and with all husbands in a more or less equal measure. Because men often are away on trading trips, a strict rota is not feasible, and the scheduling tends to be flexible. A general rule is that a husband who has been away has the first rights to spend the night with the wife. Otherwise the goal is rough balance, and when all things are equal, the senior brother, the brother who took the principal role in bringing about the marriage, or the brother currently closest to the wife may take precedence (Levine, 1988, p. 164). Jealousy is a rare phenomenon – everything in the everyday relationships is done so as to not let it emerge, or – if it does emerge – to re-direct it:

> Jealousy and sexual rivalry between brothers are the exception. The *problem more commonly is one of greater and lesser compatability between specific husbands and the wife*. A wife may prefer one of the husbands and let her preference be known. Relationships change over time, so the neglected husband can hope for the future – while complaining that women are fickle; and preferences are tolerated so long as no one is excluded. Most women initially like the eldest husband more, for the two often are close in age; and it is the eldest with whom most establish the first sexual relationship. In later years a woman is apt to turn to younger husbands with whom she may have a more equal relationship, *whose upbringing she may have supervised*, and who likely are seen as more sexually attractive. Temporarily neglected husbands are more free to pursue extra-marital affairs, while women attempt to control the actions of their favorites. (Levine, 1988, p. 165; added emphasis)

The phenomenon of supervising the growth of the husband is intricate in itself. Polyandry (in its fraternal form) provides the condition for the wife to have the secure company of a multi-aged small group of husbands. The youngest of the co-husbands may indeed assume a role of both a young husband and an adopted male child (that is, one whose childhood and adolescent growth was supervised by the wife). Such a double role can fortify the psychological stability of the marriage on the side of the wife – as long as the older co-husbands do not create problems on the grounds of their being treated unequally.

The conjoint (polygynandrous) marriage

This marriage form is rarest of all of the four forms. It entails marriage of more than one husband with more than one wife. The crucial distinction of this form from co-habitation of monogamic marriages within the same household is the absence of symbolic 'ownership' of a particular partner (which is the case in monogamic marriages).

Distribution, economic basis
Polygynandry is found usually in societies that practise polyandry. It cannot be found in strictly polygynous societies. Its economic basis is similar to that of polyandry.

Social organization
Polygynandry is in effect a combination of polygyny and polyandry. Social roles of the partners thus entail unity (of the marriage group) and differentiation (between different aged co-wives and co-husbands). Hence polygynandry occurs often in parallel with polyandry, and easily moves between different marriage forms. Thus, in the case of Jaunsar-Bawar (a tribe in Uttar Pradesh, India, practising all forms of plural marriages, and studied consistently), under the conditions of hill economy,

> Several brothers must work together, and the wife or wives, share the responsibilities of running the house, with a group of husbands. Most wives prefer to have co-wives to help them and sometimes a clever woman is found who is fond of one the husbands, and pleads for a co-wife, to release herself from the obligation of sharing the bed with other brothers. The new wife acts as a safety valve for domestic tension. Theoretically, the wife is the monopoly of the eldest brother, normally she caters to the sexual need of all the brothers, but she can time her intimacy, and show preference to any of the husbands, meeting the protests of the aggrieved husbands, by excuses and even demanding a co-wife. Sexual relations need not necessarily be confined within the household group, and under the prevailing conditions of hill economy and the double standard of morality that the society recognizes, sex is not an overpowering factor in the life of the people, neither is inhibition considered a virtue. Food and personal decoration cause more anxiety. (Majumdar, 1954/55, p. 92)

It is important to emphasize here (as well as in other plural marriage forms) that the role of sexuality in marriage can be culturally constructed in different ways. In the plural marriage forms, it is not highlighted as *the* basis for marriage. The basis is elsewhere – for example, in economic relations between family clans (exemplified by brideprice). Sexuality is undoubtedly important, but it is not *the* central issue in marriage. It leads to more important aspects of persons' cultural movement through life courses (such as having children, and grandchildren). In a day-to-day life context, other issues – who cooks for whom? what? who gives whom presents? – are by far more important. This may be combined with intolerance for the extra-marital sexual affairs of the spouses – yet sexuality here is a *cultural object* for social treatment.

Psychological organization

The same principles for curbing potential jealousies (eliminating them before they emerge) apply here as apply in polygynic and polyandrous marriages. The participants need to construct for themselves a superordinate unifying meaning – religious or secular (for example, based on 'rights', 'respect', 'progress', 'humanity' etc.) – of a general kind. It becomes translated, by individuals, into their everyday life practices by guiding them away from emotional reactions to specific forms of sexual, procreational and resource distribution practices.

The Oneida Community experiment

The creation of the Oneida Community was the life work of John Humphrey Noyes, who grew up in Vermont, graduated from Dartmouth College at age 19 (in 1830), and became converted into the 'free church' of Perfectionism. At the time, the social world of the North-East United States was filled with various kinds of 'free churches' emerging in opposition to the orthodoxies of the established denominations. Perfectionism rejected the Calvinist doctrine of the depravity of human beings and their inability to do good except through God's intervention. Instead, perfectionism was close to the Wesleyan doctrine that accepted the possibility that human beings could attain a state of perfect love between oneself and God. Noyes's version of perfectionism was quite explicit (and extreme): as a 23-year-old seminarian he declared that not only can a man be perfect, but that he himself actually was. For such clarity about himself, he was dismissed from Yale Divinity School. Yet he began to collect followers to his ideology, including his wife Harriet Holton (whom he married in 1838, emphasizing in his proposal that marriage should not monopolize or enslave 'each other's heart', and expressing his wish that his wife would love all men and women: Carden, 1971, p. 9). He conceptualized the abolition of monogamous marriage as an ideal heavenly condition. Moving back to Vermont, Noyes established (by 1846) his first polygynandrous marriage-based community, involving four

monogamous couples. In the community it was construed as 'God's will' for the participating persons to feel together not only in their religion, but also in their sexual relations.

Noyes's experiment was explicitly autocratic: he was the dominant organizer of the marriage system, and (as he was perfect, by self-admission), was chosen for that role. His 'theocratic governance' of the first experiment (which was put under stress by the local community accusing the Noyes household of adultery and immorality) carried over to the construction of the Oneida Community. Noyes selected his followers, and autocratically set up the social rules within the community.

The Oneida Community of Noyes lasted for 30 years, from 1849 (when Noyes became its leader) to the end of the 1870s (when it broke down through an internal rift). In its hey-day, it was economically self-supporting. In its religiousness, it was an example of very strictly internalized religious beliefs which did not need many external rituals for support. There were no regular religious meetings or prayers, Christmas was scarcely recognized (but Noyes's conversion date – 20 February – was celebrated). Yet in evening meetings of the community, both work tasks and social relationship issues were discussed. Noyes paid maximum attention to eradication of the exclusive dyadic relations that tended to emerge from the sharing of co-spouses.

Schematically, the marriage form Noyes set up for his community is depicted in Figure 6.6. Here, due to the communal nature of life, *'having wives'* (or husbands) was ideologically reproachable – as no human being should *possess* another in a perfect Christian community. Hence the move from either monogamy or polygynandry to polygyny or polyandry was strictly blocked. Given Noyes's orientation, monogamy could (on joining the community) only be transformed into polygynandry (which was the case for Noyes, his wife, and other followers), while the reverse movement was blocked. Individuals could join the community by-passing monogamy, but could not – at least within the community – move further into a monogamous relation.

Based on this organization of marriage, Noyes established a social organization that generated support for the form itself. The 'tyrannical nature' of monogamy was overcome by way of a number of tools. First, the involvement of all community members in the economically productive activities (and active participation in decision-making) created a moment of sharing. Secondly, the meaning of sexual relations was changed – in accordance with perfectionism – from being sinful to being the way to attain perfection. The feelings of shame were targets of Noyes's preaching:

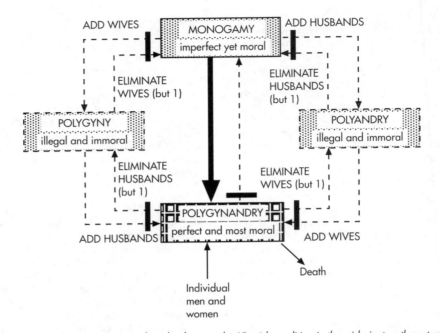

FIGURE 6.6 *Transformation into privileged polygynandry (Oneida tradition in the mid-nineteenth century)*

To be ashamed of the sexual organs, is to be ashamed of God's workmanship . . . of the most perfect instruments of love and unity . . . of the agencies which gave us existence . . . is to be ashamed of the image of the glory of God – the physical symbol of life dwelling in life, which is the mystery of the gospel. (cited via Carden, 1971, p. 56)

If this message were to be taken literally, one could have imagined the Oneida Community to be a nudist colony. Nothing was further from reality – in fact all who visited the community noticed the members' perfect moral demeanour. The message was really not for organization of public life, but input for internalization by individuals. That internalization succeeded – by way of intertwining religious devotion and personal pleasure. In a diary of one of the female members of the community, the following description (which was published by the Community as an example for appropriate ways of feeling) entails clear fusion of the God and the particular partner:

[The Lord] stirs up my heart from time to time to an appreciation of his mercies, which is as enlivening and satisfying as the reception of new mercies.

In view of his goodness to me and of his desire that I should let him fill me with himself, I yield and offer myself, to be penetrated by his spirit, and desire that love and gratitude may inspire my heart so that I shall

sympathize with his pleasure in the thing, before my personal pleasure begins; knowing that it will increase my capability for happiness. (Mary Cragin's Journal, Carden, 1971, pp. 56–57)

The propagation of the personal pleasure of sexual relations as an indicator of pleasing the God was not unique in the Oneida Community as a religious group. Other religious movements in other parts of the world (such as devotional *bhakti* sects in Southern India, see Hardy, 1983) have reconstructed the pleasurable nature of sexual intercourse in ways that connect it with religious servitude.

In Noyes's context, however, it led to two practical problems. First, the birth rate of the Oneida complex family needed to be curtailed. In tribute to Noyes's economic realism, the Oneida Community was always oriented towards economic self-sufficiency, and a sudden upsurge of reproductive success could have been detrimental. This problem was solved by social suggestion to male members of the Community to practise continence. Noyes instructed his followers to concentrate on the sexual expression of love (as it was that of 'its most natural and beautiful form') in the form of mutual enjoyment of the process of intercourse, without male ejaculation. Here we can observe an effort to make the male partner responsible for birth control by way of regulating his sexual behaviour (see similar cultural re-definition in the Gikuyu *ngweko* system, Chapter 13). Judging by the actual number of childbirths in the Oneida Community, this method of birth control worked sufficiently well.

The second problem entailed the regulation of choices of love partners that members could select, in ways that would enhance the religious ideology, rather than undermine it. Here Noyes developed the rule of an ascending scale of perfectionism as a characteristic measurement system for community members. By that rule, the community members must select sexual partners who are above them on the scale of perfectionism (with Noyes himself, of course, occupying the highest position in this perfectionism scale). By inventing such a scale, Noyes created a system where any selection of a sexual partner was directly linked with evaluation of one's own (and desired partner's) perfectionism. Sexual relations in this way were both results and vehicles for local 'upward mobility' – where the criterion was the person's internalization and externalization of community values. The core of decisions about selection of partners was based on Noyes's ideology, followed by a similar link to the actual act of sexual intercourse. *Noyes's social experiment had completely appropriated human sexuality for the build-up and maintenance of his religious community*, while reversing the notion of repression of sexuality by turning it into a centrally recognized positive human need.

The Oneida Community had its own 'life course' – one which overlapped with that of its theocratic leader, John Noyes. As Noyes himself grew older, there was no person fitting to take over his pivotal role. Furthermore, the generation of young members of the community differed from their parents. Their parents had entered the communal lifestyle based on their religious conviction (and among the ones who claimed such conviction, Noyes carefully selected the most appropriate group members). In contrast, children born within the community were members of the community by virtue of kinship ties, not through conviction. Furthermore, the community emphasized children's education, and critical orientation (in general, not in respect to the perfectionist belief system). About one-third of children who grew up in the Oneida Community got some education outside of the community. Thus, as would be expected on the basis of the bi-directional culture transfer model (as was described in Chapter 2), the second generation of a community like Oneida would demonstrate a wider variability of forms of internalization of collective values.

John Humphrey Noyes stayed as the leader of the Oneida Community until 1877, after which

he created a committee (with his son Theodore as its head) to lead the community. Noyes's son was himself a non-follower of perfectionism, and was reluctant to lead the community. Internal dissent within the community grew, but this dissent was first and foremost about power roles within the community (with Noyes's departure from leadership, no heir to his throne was strong enough to take over). The complex marriage form started to break down as a result of the political infighting, resulting (by 1880) in a tendency to begin to establish monogamic relations (and issue monogamic marriage licences). In 1881, the Oneida Community was transformed into a joint stock company. Another of the many efforts at creating a communal living arrangement that would be harmonious had ended.[7]

A closer analysis of the Oneida Community reveals its intricate internal structure. It was a community that set up polygynandry as its core marriage form. Yet within the polygynandrous system, one could see moments of theogamy (if one considers the ideological linkage of plural marriage relations to belong to all participants being bonded with the God *through their plural relations*). Theogamy here is monogamous (as only one God, rather than a plurality of deities, is worshipped). Furthermore, Noyes's 'ascending scale' of perfectionism created a shade of polygyny (of Noyes as the 'perfect' husband being the partner for many community women – and for the women growing up in the community their very first partner).[8] From the viewpoint of female community members (who could decide whom to select as their partners) the system included a shade of polyandry. While it is a definitional given for *polygyn*andry that it includes moments from every other marriage form, Noyes managed to create a social system through his particular structuring of that form that fitted the socio-economic needs of the community (of his creation).

The monogamous marriage

In the history of biological species, monogamy has been rare in the animal world (see Kleiman, 1984). As was observed above, its presence in humans is a result of cultural restrictions upon transitions in the system of marriage forms. Yet, in the context of the modern industrialized world, it has become a normative and sufficiently well-functioning marriage form. It fits the needs of limiting the inheritance of property (across generations) and constitutes a mutual relationship based on the notion of property ownership (exemplified by language: 'my wife', 'my husband').

Distribution, economic basis

Monogamy has been canonized in those societies that have taken up different forms of Christianity as their religious belief system (that is, from the third and fourth Century AD onwards).

Since most of the science of psychology has emerged in occidental societies that share the Judaeo-Christian religious history, let us look at the restrictions that the religious system of Christianity, since its rise to relevance in the fourth century AD – has set upon the general scheme. This strictly restricted scheme is presented in Figure 6.7.

As can be seen, societies that have been built on the basis of Christianity have strictly restricted any transformation of marriage out of the prescribed monogamic form. Adding husbands (or wives) to an existing monogamic marriage is strictly blocked, and all other three marriage forms are made to be not only illegal but also immoral. This redundant control – blocking transformation and stigmatizing the other possible forms – guarantees that all marriage-related issues are immediately viewed as necessarily those of monogamy.

Christianity created a two-trajectory social role expectation for women – either marry, or remain chaste and dedicate oneself to religious service. As a developing religious cult in the Roman Empire (where it moved into a majority position by around 350 AD), it emphasized body-related symbolic marking of the religious commitment. Thus, sexuality became appropriated as a basis for religious commitment (remaining chaste for religion, or faithful to husband). Christianity was viewed as particularly successful among women (Stark, 1996, pp. 99–100). Similarly, it is the women who have been designated the role of 'socio-moral guardianship' of the monogamic marriage. Last (but not least), the monogamic practice divides the resources (husband candidates) in ways that give the given husband-bearer full role in the marital system. This fullness of the role may be constrained by external rules upon women's conduct. A Fulani (in Mali) perspective (from a standpoint of polygyny) upon European monogamy is revealing in this sense. When the researcher – Paul Riesman – explained that in Europe bigamy is outlawed,

... the women would say with a dreamy and envious air, 'What a good law you have!' Every woman, if she does not yet have a co-wife, lives under the constant threat of the arrival of one, and it is a threat against which she can offer no legal resistance. Thus the man may attenuate his wife's hold not only over her own children and her cattle but also over himself, the husband, in sharing himself between two, three, or four wives ... A wife may ask for a divorce in such a case, but since the husband's action is not considered to be wrong, the wife must return to the husband [all the valuables] which he had brought into the marriage ... since it is the husband who keeps the children in any case of separation, to ask for a divorce would be, for the wife, to abandon her children. (Riesman, 1977, p. 92)

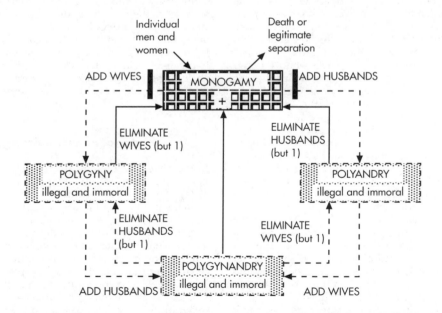

FIGURE 6.7 *Transformation with strict restrictions (monogamy in the Christian tradition since the fourth century AD)*

Again, we can see the centrality of control over resources (including here issue of 'ownership' of children at divorce), above other concerns. Probably the Fulani fascination with European monogamy would look different if the husband in monogamy were to keep the children.

In the spirit of missionary efforts, political dominance gained by European countries at times of colonial expansion (sixteenth to twentieth centuries) resulted in superimposing upon other societies the monogamy-privileging marriage forms. Other forms of marriage of the 'natives' were to be transformed to strict monogamy. Such colonial efforts resulted in superficial masking of the accepted marriage forms by superficial acceptance of monogamy.[9]

Social organization

The social roles of the wife and the husband are defined in monogamy by strict prescriptions and boundary maintenance against a move to any other form of marriage. Over the past 17 centuries, the organization of monogamic marriages has moved from a social role basis to that of internalization of exclusive interpersonal relations (in terms of use of the meaning of 'love' as the basis for establishment and maintenance of the relation). This historical development has been linked with the development of the capitalist economic system out of its feudal predecessors. It has differentially proliferated through different strata of Western societies, especially among its middle range (for example, the European aristocracy in the twentieth century, like in previous ones, cannot build marital relations on the basis of love, but has to consider the social history of the potential marriage partners).

Psychological organization

In contrast to other marriage forms (which function to eradicate feelings of jealousy), monogamy is largely built upon the personal-cultural construction of jealousies. Often jealousy is equated with the organizing concept of *love*. Love is a basically ill-defined concept, which nevertheless governs the feelings of human beings in their personal cultures in very powerful ways. As love may be linked with the notion of belonging (of one marital partner to the other), the linkage to a monogamic relation as 'mutual ownership' of the other is easily made. The basis for building such affective limits on the borders of monogamy is the symbolic 'ownership' of the other (by the husband of the wife, and by the wife of the husband). Such ownership is cultivated through the collective-cultural myth systems of a society (for example, a belief that *if* the spouse is *not* jealous, the spouse 'does not really love' the partner). In dyadic marital relations, testing of the fullness of the 'ownership' of the other can occur constantly from the beginning (as well as from times before) the marriage. For example, the bride or wife may indulge in genetic dramatisms of jealousy over the husband's real or imaginary female friends, thus both testing the 'love tie' of the relationship and trying to channel the husband's interests (see Brusco, 1995, pp. 115–116 for a description of marital relations in Colombian marriages). The needs of the traditionally economically more insecure partners – the women – are guaranteed by their implicit power control over the marital tie through the inevitable embeddedness of the husband in the wife-controlled negotiations of the family with its needs of everyday life.

Structures of ending

Further restrictions upon monogamy can be seen in different conditions of possible *ending* of a monogamous relation. These range from the absolute impossibility of legal divorce, to the case (practised in contemporary societies) of allowing divorce in relatively relaxed conditions. The former extreme ruled out change of marriage partners (that is, the only possibility of new marriage partnership was re-marriage after a spouse had died); the latter transformed the monogamic marriage form into a case of *serial monogamy*.

Serial monogamy can be seen as a version of polygyny without polygyny, that is, a way of marrying many partners without plurality of these partners at the same time (Clignet, 1970). It is monogamic because at any time only one husband and one wife are involved in it. Its development into full polygyny is arrested by legal and moral boundaries. As such, it constitutes a solution to human life course organization which entails multiple partners without allowing such multiplicity to occur at the same time.

Serial monogamy can be found in the sequence where partners separate, and re-marry. The crucial – and critical – condition is the abandonment of the previous spouse in favour of a new one. This condition differentiates serial monogamy from either polygyny or polyandry, in which new spouses are added to the marriage *without* the abandonment of the previous ones. Psychologically, this difference entails a cultural construction of an opposite nature. The reasons for abandonment have to be constructed in the personal-cultural domain. Serial monogamy is necessarily linked with conflicts of denigration of the previous marital partner for any collective-culturally appropriate reason (be it witchcraft accusation or 'he does not love me any more').

Furthermore, the form of serial monogamy creates multiple households for children born in different phases of the serial monogamic relations of particular parents.

Episodic attacks on monogamy

The centrality of the marriage form for any political ideology of a society is demonstrated by the turning of the issue of marriage into an ideological topic during periods of social change. Thus, one of the immediate efforts of the Russian communists coming to power in 1917 was to demand the elimination of the notion of 'women in marriage' as 'property' of their husbands. In their characteristically enthusiastic way, and in the context of the provincial town of Vladimir, they attempted to 'nationalize women' together with the nationalization of any other economic resource. The text of the decree includes notably revolutionary overtones:

> From the age of eighteen, every young girl is declared State property.
>   Every young girl who has reached the age of eighteen and who is not married, is obliged, under pain of prosecution and severe punishment, to be registered at a bureau of free love.
>   Once they have been registered, young girls have the right to choose a spouse between the ages of nineteen and fifty.
>   Men likewise have the right to choose a young girl who has reached the age of eighteen, if they are in possession of a certificate confirming that they belong to the proletariat. (Stern and Stern, 1981, p. 26)

The function of such 'nationalization' is the shift of allegiance of the loyalties of persons from inter-individual attachment bonds to those mediated through a social institution ('free love bureau') which set selective criteria for admission (for men, who needed to prove their social class origin). The 'bourgeois marriage' was a potential obstacle for the new social system, and hence came under attack.

Such attacks on monogamy were inevitably short-lived, since in monogamic marriage it was not necessarily the men who exclusively 'possessed' the women (as it might seem from the outside), but rather the women possessed the men in the intimacy of their monogamic households. A similarly failed experiment of altering marriage patterns occurred in the hippie movements in Europe and North America around 1968, when the proponents of the 'sexual revolution' chastised the 'bourgeois' habits of monogamic marriage. The life histories of many of the young revolutionaries of the time, however, demonstrate a return to monogamic marriages of their own a

while later. The collective-cultural general social representations (which the four different marriage forms can be seen to be), redundantly supported by personal-cultural feelings of 'psychological closeness', 'love', 'parenthood' etc., prevail within societies in a remarkably conservative way.

SUMMARY: ADAPTIVE FLEXIBILITY OF HETEROSEXUAL ARRANGEMENTS

The question of marriage forms is central for cultural-psychological understanding of the contexts in which the bi-directional cultural transfer over generations takes place. Each of the basic forms of marriage creates a different meaning for the notion of family. Each of the forms of marriage (and family) are cultural means for organization of human lives.

None of the forms has higher inherent value than any other, despite the fact that participants in each find ways to privilege their own preference. That is done by accentuating their existing conditions in contrast (and opposition) to others' ways. Thus, statements of horror by monogamists about the possibility of life in plural unions – or similar horror of polygynists at the idea of living under the 'impoverished' conditions of monogamy – are semiotic ways to create boundaries between the 'ingroup' and 'outgroup' ('WE are right, THEY are wrong'). Similarly, by creating wild imaginations about the other ways of living (for example, fascination by bored monogamists with the assumed pleasures of polygynic or polyandrous marriages), that boundary becomes maintained ('WE are insufficient, THEY really are better'). Such personal externalized valuations are parts of the personal cultures of their authors, rather than definitive statements about the psychological, social, or economic conditions of the described marriage forms.

Each of the marriage forms constitutes the temporal structure for marriage. Each requires different ways of handling the social role relationships between the participants. The flexibility of the cultural-psychological system of creating meanings helps here. In cases where jealousies are imminent dangers for the functioning of a marriage form, a specific set of cultural means is used so that the emergence of jealousies is made either impossible, or at least highly improbable. The very same personal feeling (jealousy) can be collective-culturally promoted to maintain the boundaries of another marriage form (monogamy). In *both* cases – of attenuation and amplification – of jealousies as psychological, internalized boundary control mechanisms, we can see the personal-cultural system functioning in the service of the given life space organization.

Aside from the personal-cultural constructions of human life course within the matrix of marriage forms, *these forms also play an important role in cultural mediation of persons' relations with the social groups in which they are parts.* The cultural forms of marriage and family guarantee sufficient maintenance of the whole texture of social life in a given society. It is therefore not surprising that the issues of family and marriage are recurrent targets for different social institutions in their power relations and goal-oriented actions within a society. As our example of the Mormon re-organization of married lives, as well as that of the Oneida Community indicated, it was the religious institutions which made use of re-formulation of marriage forms (and their collective cultural valuation) to bond persons in these marriages further to their specific goals.

NOTES

1 This phenomenon of preaching on the topic of 'family values' is prominent in the contemporary United States, yet it is not unknown in most other countries.

2 Note that in societies where polygyny was practised historically, the status of 'independent single woman' would not exist. All women would be in some form of marital relation.

3 Different accounts of numbers of Smith's wives vary, ranging from 27 to 84 (Foster, 1984, p. 151).

4 This is a general function of plural marriage forms in societies where the social status of being a 'single woman' was highly negatively valued, and socially stigmatized.

5 For example, the need of Iranian families in the 1980s – who would be involved in the forbidden practice of watching videos and non-allowed TV at home – to make sure that revelation by children about that would not take place at school.

6 In addition, the husband's role entails social overstimulation – in his rotation between different households (each filled by a multitude of his own children), he has no possibility to be alone. However, being alone is a basic need for the human mature personality. Contemporary Mormon husbands adjust their lives by creating privacy in their workplace, or even – in some extreme cases – spending some nights alone in motels (Altman and Ginat, 1996, p. 258).

7 There were many efforts in US society of the nineteenth century to build small communes that would follow teachings of different forms of social equality, some secular, others deeply religious. The United States has been a continuous testing ground for experiments in creating small-scale socially harmonious communities – all of which have failed after shorter or longer times.

8 Until the 1870s, when Noyes grew old, it was consensually accepted that he would be the first to initiate girls in the community who were coming of age, into adulthood.

9 For example, British enforcement of monogamy in (what is now) Ghana led to superficial declaration (by polygynously married persons) of the first (senior) co-wife as the monogamic spouse, while retaining other co-wives as if these were 'mistresses' in the sense of the colonialist powers.

REVIEW QUESTIONS FOR CHAPTER 6

1 How can one try to define family?

2 Explain the notions of joint and extended families.

3 What are: *patrilocal, matrilocal* and *neolocal* families?

4 Analyse the ways in which Hindu joint family functions.

5 Why is talking about family pervasive in the social sciences?

6 Discuss marriage as an economic transaction.

7 Explain how the four major forms of marriage are mutually interlinked.

8 Explain the economic and social organization of *polygynic* marriages.

9 Describe the age structure of *polygynic* marriages.

10 What is *levirate*?

11 Explain the psychological organization of *polygynic* marriages.

12 Analyse the psychological functioning of polygyny among the Mormons in the United States.

13 Explain what kinds of experiences can be expected for children from polygynic marriages.

14 Explain the economic and social organization of polyandrous marriages.

15 Explain the psychological organization of *polyandrous* marriages.

16 What is the role of 'collective husband' in *polyandrous* marriages?

17 Explain the economic and social organization of *polygynandrous* marriages.

18 Describe the marital organization in the Oneida Community.

19 Explain the economic and social organization of *monogamous* marriages.

20 Explain the psychological organization of *monogamous* marriages.

21 In what ways is *serial monogamy* similar to, and different from, the plural marriage forms?

7

CULTURAL ORGANIZATION OF HUMAN LIFE ENVIRONMENTS

Human development is taking place under conditions that are *increasingly distanced* from the 'natural world'. What does that mean in terms of ordinary human thinking? A person wanders around in a street and sees a cat in a similar activity. The person not only perceives the presence, and movements, of that animal, but immediately begins to make sense of the event in terms of their own personal culture. The animal becomes referred to as 'this is a cat', which may become linked with personal affective tone of liking the cat ('what a kitty!'), or hating it ('that stray cat in the street!'). By personally relating to the cat, the meaning-making person simultaneously distances themself (by way of the use of language within their mind) from the cat. The cat becomes an *object towards which the person can assume different agent positions* (for example, trying to approach the cat and stroke it; or threaten it from a distance so that it would run away). The semiotic reflexivity about the object allows for a wide range of such distant positions. The meaning constructed of the four-legged and be-whiskered miauwing being creates a multitude of scenarios for possible action. Human action results from taking one or another of such positions.

The focus of cultural psychology is precisely on the study of the ways in which human beings can distance their lives – both external activities and intra-psychological functions – from their 'natural' states. Increasing distancing from the natural world entails construction of cultural artefacts that mediate between the persons and their environments. *Cultural psychology deals with the analysis of forms and functions of such mediated distancing.*

Similarly to the cat example, human beings relate to any physical setting in which they are located, by way of **simultaneously** *being part of the setting **and** distancing themselves from it*. This is

the core of the function of culture within the human mind. One can claim that the tension between participation and non-participation in a here-and-now setting is a uniquely human cultural phenomenon. It makes aesthetic relation to the environment possible – human beings can reflect upon the world in terms of art, music and literature as aesthetic objects, rather than in terms of treating these as mere consumer objects.

THE SETTING AS A MEDIATED PLACE

Each human life context is organized culturally. This applies to any environment – including remote natural spots – where human beings happen to be. Even settings in the jungle, rainforest or desert – as long as there is at least one human being who experiences those – are cultural. The experiencing person reconstructs the natural setting in terms of their personal-cultural experience. In nature, there exist no 'nice meadows' or 'mysterious forests', such designations are results of the externalization of human personal cultures. Such externalization produces the action valences for the producer – the 'dangerous-looking forest' is a semiotic mediator for its producer not to enter the setting, or do it with care. Likewise, the diurnal or seasonal changes of light of a setting becomes meaningful. The night can be viewed as 'dangerous' or 'erotic', the winter as 'dull', etc. Man-made neighbourhoods can become felt like 'safe' or 'dangerous' – without any basis for such designations other than the personal culture of the meaning-maker.

All architectural constructions are cultural distancing artefacts – from the simplest construction of a hut in a jungle, to skyscrapers in modern cities. Architectural places entail one or another form of making a distinction between the human and the natural worlds. Floors (in contrast to ground), walls (in contrast to bush), windows, roofs etc. demarcate the human constructed space from the rest – the natural or 'other' cultural spaces. Layouts of towns create the urban/rural distinction. Within urban spaces, one can distinguish different settings by their meaningful functions. Thus, bars, restaurants, cafes, health clubs, churches, temples, cinemas, theatres, brothels, etc. are all constructed with some meaningful function intended on behalf of their planners. These functions are marked by specific signs embedded in the architectural design, and in interior and exterior temporary markers of its function. Such architectual spaces are holistic structures for living, within which specific cultural meanings are already pre-encoded.

A comparative-cultural example: what is a home?
Human beings arrange their home habitats under many climatic and symbolic conditions. In Figure 7.1 we can see a variety of such examples.

In Figure 7.1*A* we can see a rather ordinary free-standing US middle-class home. It stands at a relative distance from its neighbours, and is assumed to guarantee the privacy of the owners relative to the neighbours. Yet it (at the same time) belongs to some 'neighbourhood community'. The separation of the home of the family from others is granted by the way the house is built, the unity with others is granted through creating concatenations of the homes as 'community'.

In Figure 7.1*B* we can see a rather large family house in England, which is inhabited by one owner (Mrs Windsor), her husband, and all the service people. It is both private (the grounds surrounding the house are heavily guarded against intruders), yet on special public occasions townspeople, tourists, and other hangers-around locate themselves in front of the house, trying to get a gratifying glimpse of its owners. At scheduled times, the owners may display themselves on the balcony, thus gratifying the public need. Yet the owners are very disappointed because highly technological photojournalists can penetrate the privacy of their home grounds at moments not designated by the owners. Again, the separation from others, and unification with them, are two parts of the same whole.

In Figure 7.1*C* we see a tree-house (*khaim*) of the Korowai of Irian Jaya (the Western part of the Island of New Guinea, incorporated into Indonesia). The tree-houses – built on traditional ancestral territories – can be up to 35 metres in height, regularly ranging between 8 and 12 metres from the ground. Both the stairs (ladder) and the beam of the entrance into the tree-house are smeared with animal fat to ensure its continuous welfare. The interior of the house is divided into a male and female part, with the fireplace as the centrally important centre place. The people sleep around the fire, which is used for cooking. Smaller domestic animals are

FIGURE 7.1 Examples of homes. A, *an American suburban house*

B, *a British family home (Buckingham Palace) (photograph by Chris Gilbert)*

C, *a tree-house (khaim) of the Korowai of Irian Jaya (photograph by Johannes Veldhuizen 1986, reprinted by permission from Van Enk & De Vries, 1997, p. 21)*

brought up to the tree-house to share the quarters – thus being safe from the predators of the rainforest. The Korowai live mostly on lowlands (around 1090 metres above sea level). Their material technology is mostly concentrated on production of weaponry (shields, bows, arrows, knives. spears), fishing and hunting technology, methods of raising pigs, and techniques of sago production. Since the 1980s, Korowai village settlements are also seen with houses – still built on poles, but only 1.5 metres high – where different ancestral families are forced to live at close quarters.

The nomadic lifestyle sets up demands upon the way home dwellings are constructed. In Figure 7.1D we have a typical nomadic home construction that proliferates all over Central Asia – a round tent, which can be moved from one location to another. The tent depicted here is typical of the Tibetan highlands.

Figure 7.1E shows a sedentary village in the Himalayan mountains. The people who inhabit the village practise polyandry (see Chapter 6). The house in the foreground has two entrances, which indicates that a polyandrous marriage located in it has ended in a divorce.

As we can see, what constitutes the home as a dwelling place for human beings varies immensely in its specific forms, yet the basic function of separation and unification of the

D, *Tibetan tents (from Jones, 1996, p. 101, photograph by Lis Jones, reproduced by permission)*

E, *houses in a village in the Himalayas (from Levine, 1988, reproduced by permission of the University of Chicago Press)*

persons and the natural (for example, tree-house) or sub-urban (US and UK family houses) are similar. Furthermore, such reconstruction of the environment goes beyond the case of the home: all man-made environment is semiotically mediated.

Human cultural construction of 'natural environments'
Sometimes such constructions imitate features of the natural environments. Carefully planned parks in cities are cultural artefacts that resemble their natural counterpart (forest), yet are not

those. Similarly, fancy hotels may include as recreational areas architecturally re-constructed natural-looking waterfalls and pools – yet these are cultural reconstructions that operate as semiotic devices, rather than 'real' or 'natural' places. Human beings strive for 'naturalness' in their lives from a position of already being separated from it by culture. Each case of regaining 'naturalness' is itself a cultural construction.

Even human *uses* of purely natural – unaltered – environments turn the latter into culturally organized ones. A person wandering through a jungle turns it into a personal-culturally meaningful setting, by interpreting the perceived trees and bushes as 'beautiful' and the tropical heat as 'tolerable'. The person remains culturally guided even when alone, and even if in the middle of a natural environment where no other person has traversed before. Cultural mediators allow human beings to *modulate* their psychological distance from the natural world, by turning the latter into a cultural one.

BASES FOR CULTURE IN PERSON–ENVIRONMENT RELATIONS

The non-cultural encounter of the organisms with their environments is based on immediate (non-modulated) relations between the environmental possibilities and the organism's actions. This is captured by James J. Gibson's concept of affordance, introduced by him in the 1960s and 1970s. Gibson, a student of Kurt Koffka, built his ideas upon his mentor, as well as on the work of Kurt Lewin, who both represented the Gestalt orientation in psychology.

The affordance concept
Gibson was not interested in issues of development, but in the question of how organisms pick up information from their immediate environments. He launched a campaign in favour of immediate perception, and rejected the notion of psychological (cognitive) construction. In this respect, the notion of distancing used in the present context would have been completely foreign and unacceptable for Gibson. Yet his elaboration of the notion of affordance can serve as a starting point for cultural constructionist psychology.

Gibson explained the notion of affordance in the following way:

> Affordances are not simply phenomenal qualities of subjective experience . . . they are not simply the physical properties of things . . . Instead, they are ecological, in the sense that they are properties of the environment relative to an animal. (Reed and Jones, 1982, p. 404)

Gibson proceeded to elaborate different kinds of affordances. As he was not interested in issues of development, it was easy for him to concentrate upon the focus on how environmental textures relate with the species-specific action possibilities of a given species. Thus, automatized behavioural processes (for example, locomotion, catching a ball, swimming, flying and landing an airplane) could be linked with the affordances of the environmental conditions (surfaces on which locomotion takes place, properties of the liquid in which the organism swims, or of the air through which airplanes fly). The *organism here was assumed to be the adult, skilled organism* of the given species. The question of *how that organism came to be* in this adult form was of no relevance for Gibson's use of the affordance concept. The organism would pick up information from the environment about what the latter affords, and act in a matching way. The organism is not trying to construct new ways of action, or trying to change the affordances of the environment.

It is clear that this perspective is not in line with cultural psychology of human development, where it is assumed that

(a) organisms actively reconstruct their environments (that is, change the affordances) as they develop; and
(b) that reconstruction is assisted by cultural (semiotic and instrumental) mediation.

Gibson's focus on affordances pertains to the non-cultural and un-mediated encounters between the organisms and their species-specific environments. It can be viewed as *a basis for cultural construction* of mediated relations between human beings and their environments. Gibson himself was an opponent of constructionist perspectives in psychology, yet his ideas can serve as a fertile ground precisely for such perspectives.

INSTITUTIONAL ORGANIZATION OF HUMAN ENVIRONMENTS

Many of the ways in which children of different ages are represented in psychology are part of a cultural framing of child development issues by social institutions. Different social institutions – governments, religious groups, local village communities etc. – have their goal-oriented ways of dealing with issues of human development.

Environmental organization
Social institutions can prescribe how specific environmental settings for human beings are to be set up. As we will see (in Chapter 13), the location of flagpoles and their relative height in front

of US school buildings indicates institutional marking of the boundary between the local community and generalized values that the school-building carries with its functions. Likewise, building environmental settings that emphasize distinction of the activities within the setting from those around them entails obligatory marking of the difference semiotically. Medieval cathedrals are oriented upwards towards the presumed living quarters of the deity, Hindu temples follow careful floor-plans and location with regard to symbolically appropriate directions.

Social discourse organization

Social institutions can prescribe how persons are expected to talk about different issues of human development. Depending upon those, a particular aspect of human development (for example, expectations for infants' 'toilet-training', or adolescents' 'rebelliousness') can be highlighted within the collective-cultural domain. Others may be made into 'taboo topics' for communication in public. As a result, the whole know-how about human development is selectively directed by collective-cultural meanings.

Institutions *give direction and evaluative flavour* to social discourse about some target object. This can be done in a number of ways. First, and most obviously, social discourse can be guided towards the *guidance of action* in some direction. For example, consider discourse about AIDS or street children in the First World societies. That discourse may lead to provision of funds for the needy, and to concrete action.

The second way of guiding social discourse is to create domains of the unspeakable, or *inhibit social discourse in some domains*. This could lead to de-focusing of the person's attention from the issue, which will thus escape from possible action upon it. For instance, the Western medical establishment would cover with silence discourse about fatal results due to medical mistakes. However, such purposeful silencing may result in a particular semiotic power of the unmentionable (see Ohnuki-Tierney, 1994). The notion of *zero signifiers* – signs based on absence of some (otherwise expected) semiotic material in the communicative message – is a vehicle for inhibiting explicit social discourse. Public talking about issues, topics and powerful personages (especially spirits of potentially dangerous kinds) can be de-emphasized through silence, changes of topics, 'hushing up' the less culturally skilful partner (for example, '. . . shh . . . HE could hear us'). Inhibition of social discourse can also operate at the level of how not to talk publicly about some issues of life. As will be seen in Chapter 9, the US and Thai collective-cultural guidance of how one *should* talk about newborns (Thai: not praise the baby, lest evil spirits get it; US: praise the dubious beauty of the newborn) exclude as unmentionable the opposite way (for Thai, the beauty of the newborn; for the US, his or her ugliness).

The third direction is most interesting – social discourse can be institutionally canalized so that some previously 'taboo' topics are not only turned into ones that can be spoken of, *but which must be* (potentially endlessly) *spoken about*. The crucial criterion here is elimination of connection between the hyperactive talking and acting – people actively talk 'empty' about issues considered relevant (for example, TV talk-shows), exhaust oneself by talking, and fail to plan any action. This latter method of social regulation of discourse is widely utilized in 'open societies' – which, by showing off openness to the public talk about sensitive matters, actually close these matters from the domain of action. Bureaucracies that govern social institutions are habitual generators of such foci of hypertalk.[1]

Social institutions promote texts – myths, TV commercials, moralistic and educational stories – with a specific goal orientation in mind. The presentation of different aspects of human development is not merely re-presentational (this is how X *is*) but rather prescriptive-presentational (this is how X *should be*). This is particularly evident in advice given to parents for raising children, or to medical patients on different kinds of possible treatment.

Semiotic demand settings (SDSs)

Human psychological development proceeds through negotiation between the perception and action through the use of affordances, and the suggestions for feeling, thinking and acting that are proliferated through the collective culture. For human beings, the world of objects is available immediately under limits upon action (for example, the need to act under time pressure etc.), yet otherwise the environment is mediated through meanings.

We can talk about demands that the meaningful nature of a particular structured environment sets up for persons' feeling, thinking and acting. Let us call these settings *semiotic demand settings* (SDSs): human-made structures of everyday life settings where the properties of the objects are co-determined by perceptual-actional and cultural-meanings based possibilities and expectations (see Figure 7.2).

Any domain of human personal experience can become culturally guided by some socio-institutional focusing of the person's attention in one part of it. The suggested focus (see Figure 7.2A) can operate in two ways. First, it guides the person to reflect upon the focused experience in socially legitimized ways (Discourse Ways 1 and

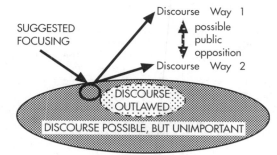

FIGURE 7.2 *The Semiotic Demand Setting*
(above) *a general model of a semiotic demand setting;*
(below) *an example of a semiotic demand setting: a recycling centre*

2). Note that there can be more than one legitimate discourse way (that is, different, at times oppositional, meaning systems can be used to make sense of the same focal experience). If these different legitimate discourse ways are utilized by different persons in communication, heated and potentially endless disputes may result.

Secondly, the suggested focusing upon one part of the experiential field can entail outlawing a focus of interest on the adjacent part. Different areas of experience are made culturally unavailable for human reflection. This may happen in order to avoid addressing issues that are too complex or believed to be 'dangerous' (culturally directed voluntary forgetting), or (more likely) is just a way of culturally directed oversight or involuntary forgetting. In both cases – voluntary or involuntary – this oversight or forgetting is of psychological value.

An example: from garbage 'dump' to 'recycling centre'

Figure 7.2*B* represents an example of a semiotic demand setting. In this photograph of standard US containers for garbage, we can observe the dramatic role socially suggested legitimization of discourse entails. These garbage containers are presented as a 'recycling centre' (rather than a mere garbage dump, which it functionally is for persons who bring their throw-aways to the place). The presentation of the containers as a 'recycling centre' has two demand implications. First, it requires the persons to act – by sorting their garbage into appropriate categories (of cardboard, white glass, green glass, brown glass, plastic, newspapers etc.). Secondly, it guides persons towards talking about such acting in terms of the value of the process of getting rid of the garbage in this newly meaningful way: the garbage will no longer be seen to contaminate some landfill somewhere, but will be 'put back to productive use' by the recycling plants (= social institutions which acquire the symbolic status of hero, fighting against humankind being overwhelmed by the garbage it produces). The persons who diligently sort their rubbish into prescribed cultural categories can (and are expected to) feel good about their participation in the shared institutional effort of 'saving nature'.

This legitimization of one way of talking, feeling and thinking about 'recycling' curiously outlaws some other aspects of the same issue (that is, the domain covered by 'discourse outlawed' in Figure 7.2*A*). The participants in the 'recycling effort' are *not allowed* to think about the fact that they actually give away their property (for example, old plastic containers, glass bottles, etc. still are the property of the owners who once bought these) to some recycling institution which, after recycling the materials, will earn profit from re-selling those. To talk of giving away one's garbage to the recycling system as an act of *donation of valuable property* (for example, similarly to fund-raising campaigns asking people to donate money for valuable causes) is outlawed. By cultural definition, 'garbage' has no value, and is to be thrown away (from the home grounds of the persons). Building upon that complex of meanings, the social institutions that set up 'recycling centres' create a semiotically re-focused way to look at the activity of recycling as a communally benevolent act.

At the personal-cultural level, the internalized models of how one acts with garbage are all around us. Any moment when we decide where to dispose of some no longer necessary object – a cigarette leftover, a used bus ticket, or wrappings of a just consumed delicious hamburger – we face our personal-cultural focusing (suggested by one or other social institution over our whole lifetime) upon our experiential field, guided by legitimate ways of feeling about 'dirt' in our environments. Dog owners may carry newspapers with them while walking their dogs in a public park, so as to clean up what the dog produces and throw it into an appropriately designated (by city authorities) garbage container. Or we carry a piece of garbage with us for a considerable distance in search of a bin for it and ignore the fact that on our way we encounter numerous objects of similar kind, just thrown out on the street.

The issue of conflict between internalized personal-cultural constructions of one's relations to garbage emerges particularly vividly when persons from one society are transposed to the context of another. Tourism (as a case of temporary migration of an inherently ambivalent kind, see below) provides nice examples of such tensions. Thus, an account by a Belgian female tourist travelling in China reveals a serious affective turbulence:

> The garbage [created by the traveling tourists] is gathered together and put in a plastic bag that hangs on Emilie's backpack. Today she is the garbage woman. Until now we have always carefully carried the inflammable [sic] waste, mainly tins, to a following city. Paper, plastic, sanitary towels, and the like are burnt. Miriam describes the horrible waste problem that Nepal causes. A large number of hikers traverse through the country on foot or by bike. On their way they mostly bury their garbage. This damages the subsoil in great degree and on a large scale. The Chinese are not conscious about the environment either in the disposal of waste. I have never understood the indifference with which *they dump waste in tourist places or in the middle of nature*. Probably that has to do with something in me that comes from my scout upbringing. When I traveled for the first time through China by train, I mindfully kept my litter the whole day. Fellow-travelers just thoughtlessly threw everything on the ground. I felt extremely indignant. When the team of cleaners of the train came to clean up, I proudly handed over to them my plastic bag of garbage. *No reaction. Shortly after, I saw them push open a window and throw everything outside.* (Shi-xu, 1995, p. 326; original emphasis).

This example complements the socio-institutionally suggested focus on garbage (and its disposal). The women depicted travelling as a Western tourist group are involved in chatting about the 'deplorable practices' of the others, and acting in ways so as to feel good about themselves as defenders of their internalized standards of 'care for the environment'. The institutionally suggested narratives of how to handle 'the garbage' become transformed into personal-cultural action, talking, feeling and thinking directions.

How can persons survive in a pointedly suggested social universe?

The co-constructional nature of human development creates a buffer against the various social suggestions. Furthermore, the heterogeneity of institutional goal orientations within the 'nested systems' (in Bronfenbrenner's terms, see below) does not allow any one single 'voice' to gain full dominance. Certainly there is an effort by social institutions to overtake the heterogeneity and monopolize the suggestions.

The difference of the personal culture from the socially suggested demands of the collective-cultural world allows for personal psychological survival under intense suggestions. Persons can counteract, reject, or neutralize incoming social suggestions. They can ignore the given semiotic demand setting. Or they can feel outside of its influence, while formally fulfilling the expectations. It is the heterogeneity of the multiple contexts that allows for such flexibility.

Urie Bronfenbrenner's systemic model

How is the multiplicity of contexts for human development organized? Urie Bronfenbrenner (1979) has introduced a multi-level system of description of how persons relate with their social contexts. His 'nested systems' model includes four mutually inclusive systems: *micro-*, *meso-*, *exo-* and *macrosystems*

Microsystem

A microsystem is a pattern of activities, roles and interpersonal relations experienced by the developing person in a given setting with particular physical and material characteristics. (Bronfenbrenner, 1979, p. 22). The crucial point here is the focus on experiencing – the person experiences his or her particular immediate life context in personal terms. If that context is that of home and the person is at peace with his or her home context, that experiencing can attain a positive, trustful feeling tone. But it can also take the form of a 'war landscape' (to paraphrase Kurt Lewin's initial point of his field theory), in which case the feeling tone of the experiencing person in the home context can be insecure, ambivalent, or outrightly negative. The external specifics of the environment may be the same – exactly the same physical home environment and interactive rituals with other family members can acquire feeling tones for the experiencing child that range from one extreme to another. The developing child may feel (in his or her terms) 'mother's control' – or 'mother's care' – perceived in the mother's suggestions to dress warmer while going out. The experiencing person makes their developmental way through life in the middle of microsystems.

The same microsystem can be of different cultural-developmental relevance for children at different age/competence levels. In the clinical description by Lev Vygotsky, we can observe how three children experience the same microsystemic conditions – in a family – differently:

The essential circumstances were very straightforward. The mother drinks and, as a result, apparently suffers from several nervous and psychological disorders. The children find themselves in a very difficult situation. When drunk, and during these breakdowns, the mother had once attempted to throw one of the children out of the window and she regularly beat them or threw them to the floor. In a word, the children are living in conditions of dread and fear due to these circumstances.

The three children are brought to our clinic, but each of them presents a completely different picture of disrupted development, caused by the same situation. The same circumstances result in an entirely different picture for the three children.

As far as the youngest . . . is concerned . . . he reacts to the situation by developing a number of neurotic symptoms, i.e. symptoms of a defensive nature. He is simply overwhelmed by the horror of what is happening to him. As a result, he develops attacks of terror, enuresis and he develops a stammer, sometimes being unable to speak at all as he loses his voice. In other words, the child's reaction amounts to a state of complete depression and helplessness in the face of this situation.

The second child is developing an extremely agonizing condition, what is called a state of inner conflict, which is a condition frequently found in certain cases when contrasting emotional attitudes towards the mother make their appearance . . . On the one hand, from the child's point of view, the mother is an object of painful attachment, and on the other, she represents a source of all kinds of terrors and terrible emotional experiences for the child. . . .

Finally . . . the third and the eldest child presented us with a completely unexpected picture. The child had a limited mental ability but, at the same time, showed signs of some precocious maturity, seriousness and solicitude. He already understood the situation. He understood that their mother was ill and pitied her. He could see that the younger children found themselves in danger when their mother was in one of her states of frenzy. And he had a special role. He must calm his mother down, make certain that she is prevented from harming the little ones and comfort them. Quite simply, he has become the senior member of the family, the only one whose duty it was to look after everyone else. As a result of this, the entire course of his development underwent a striking change. This was not a lively child with

normal, lively, simple interests, appropriate to his age and exhibiting a lively level of activity. (Vygotsky, 1935/1994, pp. 340–341)

In Vygotsky's example, we can see two time perspectives intertwined with each other. First, there is the cyclical occurrence of the life events at home (the mother's episodes of drinking, interspersed with 'calm' periods). Secondly, there is the fact that the three children are in their ontogenetic time/life courses at different levels of understanding of their immediate microsystem. That understanding defines the part of experience – its personal-cultural reconstruction – that the developing child co-constructs. Microsystems are created with the participation of the developing child.

Mesosystem

A mesosystem comprises *the interrelations among two or more settings* in which the developing person actively participates (such as the relations between home, school and neighbourhood peer group, for the child) (Bronfenbrenner, 1979, p. 25).

A mesosystem is a system composed of microsystems, and their relations. It is formed, or extended, any time when the person changes his or her settings. Human migration in its different forms (described below) guides the reorganization of mesosystems. The child who daily migrates between home and school, acting differently in each, co-constructs his or her own mesosystem. A particular developmental issue for psychology here is the emergence of the capacities for switching between different microsystems (that is, creating a mesosystem).

Exosystem

An exosystem refers to one or more *settings that* **do not** *involve the developing person as an active participant*, but in which events occur that affect, or are affected by, what happens in the setting containing the developing person (Bronfenbrenner, 1979, p. 25).

The exosystem for a developing child may include the working context of the parents (where the child need not participate). Yet changes in that context are of direct relevance for the child's life. For example, if the father – working outside home – loses his job (= an event not controlled by the child), it has immediate implications for the child. Or the decision by a local school board to ban some classics of world literature from the school library may lead the child either to be ignorant about such literature, or, by an alternative co-constructive pathway, hypercompetent, working *against* the social norms that are set up by the exosystem (Poddiakov, 1998).

Macrosystem

The macrosystem refers to consistencies, in the form and content of lower-order systems (micro, meso- and exo-) that exist (or could exist) at the level of some parts of the given society or in the given society as a whole, along with any belief systems or ideology underlying such consistencies (Bronfenbrenner, 1979, p. 26).

Bronfenbrenner emphasized consistency within a hierarchical system (macrosystem) that unifies the other three, along the lines of shared cultural organizing concepts. Thus, schools in France, different from one another as they are, are still 'French' in their nature, and contrasted with similarly variable schools in the United States, which are considered 'American'. Macrosystem includes the potential forms of organization of human development that need not be put into practice, but could be. Hideo Kojima's notion of an *ethnopsychological pool of ideas* of parents (Kojima, 1996) can be seen as a set of such ideological organizers, ready for use by social institutions.

Bronfenbrenner's nested system view allows us to see the connections between various levels of organization of person–environment relations. It is the most general – macrosystemic – level at which efforts by social institutions are made to guide the operation of other levels. Ideological, religious, commercial and power interests lead the top-down reorganization of the socio-ecological hierarchy.

COVERING AND UNCOVERING THE BODY: CULTURAL CONSTRUCTION OF HUMAN BEINGS

All interaction between individuals of a given species is coordinated by their bodies – and carries different functions. In the world of non-human species, such functions of interaction include establishment and maintenance of social relations, aside from cooperation or competition in food acquisition. Different interactive body-coordination rituals – such as grooming (in many primate species), copulating, food-sharing, tending to the offspring etc., are widespread in non-human species.

Human beings are the only species who have developed an elaborate system of meanings for such coordination of bodily functions. On the basis of grooming, massaging and dressing the hair have developed. Bodily closeness is carefully regulated by collective-cultural rules (see Chapter 13 for *ngweko*). Forms of abbreviated body contact – such as embracing (and its abbreviated form, the handshake; see Gurevitch, 1990) – have become markers for social and personal regulation of distancing between persons.

In a similar vein, human beings are the only species that has created the cultural necessity to cover (and uncover) different parts of their bodies on different occasions, and who have created special cultural devices – body painting, tattooing, clothing etc. – for it. Furthermore, in the case of humans we see the emergence of elaborate cultural norms of dressing up in different stylistic ways (for rituals, ranging from body painting for hunting or war rituals, to wedding rituals), as well as dressing 'down' and becoming naked in other stylistic ways (as in the case of striptease, modelling nude for artists, or encountering sun on the beaches).

Many of these cultural practices are constructed without coordination with the climatic conditions of an event, as many a sweating but overdressed participant in rituals taking place in hot climates knows very well. From the initial function of thermoregulation, clothing one's body has moved to be a marker of social class, and a vehicle for inter-personal interaction. As Perrot has pointed out,

> Because clothing oneself is an act of differentiation, it is essentially an act of signification. It manifests through symbols or convention, together or separately, essence, seniority, tradition, prerogative, heritage, caste, lineage, ethnic group, generation, religion, geographical origin, marital status, social position, economic role, political belief, and ideological affiliation. Sign or symbol, clothing affirms and reveals cleavages, hierarchies, and solidarities according to a code guaranteed and perpetuated by society and its institutions. (Perrot, 1994, p. 8)

Non-human primates obviously have no worry about how to dress up for some social occasion – such as showing themselves off to the human audience of a zoo. The same is not true of humans who put themselves on show in some way, who dedicate much of their effort to planning how they would be seen by their watching public. Even if the decision is to be seen naked (or quasi-naked), such nakedness is a result of cultural construction of one's appearance. A woman who decides to pose nude to an artist is doing that through the cultural meaning construction of 'modelling' – her naked body is dressed in that meaning.

Differentiation of cultural reconstruction of the human body

In the history of humankind, we can observe gradual movement from the unmediated to the culturally mediated presentation of the body, to others and to oneself. Intentional modification of the surface of the body must have been the first step towards its enculturation. Body painting for different ceremonial occasions – both the multitude of exotic-looking versions in the 'traditional' societies, and their counterparts in our contemporary fashions of use of cosmetics – has been the core of cultural organization of the body.

From the basis of such a core, it is possible to view two directions of further differentiation. First, there exists a culturally universal *tendency towards making body marks permanent through enforcing them into the skin.* Body scarification traditions in many societies, and the more elaborate practices of tattooing, are examples of this direction. Here the body surface itself becomes modified – in contrast to the removable body paintings. The collective-cultural system provided a socially shared meaningful basis for such permanent transformations of the body. Scarification of the body became viewed as granting beauty to the body, and tattooing has been widely known as a form of marking a person's social status in a society (for example, tattooing practices in the Pacific region; Gell, 1993).

Different ritualistic body modification practices – such as male and female circumcision, ear-piercing, wearing braces to direct the growth of teeth, or reconstructive surgery on the body (see Haiken, 1997) – can be viewed as extensions of this direction of differentiation of the body as a cultural object. Here the actual modification of the body may take place inside of the body (for example, gold fillings in teeth, silicon implants to the breasts, or penis prostheses). Although some of the outcomes of such modifications may be visible externally (such as, a modified breast, or chin, or nose, following cosmetic surgery), it is a personal-cultural role that such modifications play for the person who has had these modifications performed. A woman may feel good about having gold fillings in her back teeth, even if no one but her dentist would ever see them.

The second direction in differentiation *creates the body as cultural object through non-bodily objects that become attached to the body.* Here is the joint starting point of various kinds of body markers, and clothing. From that perspective, objects that we usually classify as body decorations (rings, anklets, ear-rings, beads, wigs etc.), and others that we classify as clothes, are of a similar kind. The cultural history of clothing is a field where the role of culture in human psychological functioning is revealed in colourful and very heterogeneous ways.

Human cultural construction of clothing starts from the first objects that are used to cover genitals (see Figure 7.3). Both the objects of 'minimal clothing' shown demonstrate the un-differentiated state between the body decoration and body-covering objects. The penis sheath (Figure 7.3A) is a widespread male cultural object in many societies (especially in New Guinea). The *uluri* belt (depicted in Figure 7.3B) is the regular item of women's clothing among the different ethnic groups of the Xingu group (in the Amazon region in Brazil). The *uluri* consists of a band of twine worn around the hips. Attached to the band is a piece of bark that covers the pubis tightly, creating an image of the woman's external genitalia. A long thin cord leads from this bark through the labia of the vagina, through the buttocks, and appears as a kind of tail at the rear.

Wearing the *uluri* belt is a sign of mature womanhood among the Xingu. Girls prior to puberty do not wear it; they become able to wear it after passing through their adolescent ritual of becoming women. In fact, the women in the photograph in Figure 7.3B are Mehinaku women who are taking part in the ceremony of giving the rights to wear *uluri* belts to just initiated girls (Gregor, 1977, p. 163). Women after the end of their reporoductive years (when their vagina is said to have 'closed up') are not to wear the *uluri* belt. In different settings of public or private kinds, the *uluri* belt can be worn differently. The Xingu woman wearing the *uluri* belt feels dressed, taking it off in contexts where she feels uncomfortable means for her to become naked. This indicates how relative are cultural constructions of nudity and feelings about being nude. Contemporary women wearing two-piece bikinis on a beach may feel fully clothed, and a suggestion of a simple removal of the upper part of the bikini – for more suntan – may be perceived similarly in terms of the horror of becoming naked. In contrast, Omani women taking off their veil (*barqa*, see below) may feel similarly 'naked', even if their body is completely clothed.

The *uluri* belt is a general object of clothing for Xingu women. In general, among the Xingu, it is the men who outperform women in the extensiveness of body decoration. For women, aside from the *uluri* belt, two other clothing objects are ordinary. First, the kneebands (which are meant to acccentuate the calves, giving them a 'bottle-like' beauty),[2] and the waist belt. The latter is a communicative ground for expressing the woman's age, ritual status, or mood. If the woman is sad, ashamed, or in mourning for a deceased husband or lover, she removes strands from her waist belt.

Clothes as markers of social distinction

Clothes have marked social class throughout the history of Europe. It is thanks to the French Revolution of 1789 that strict class-marking of clothing was abolished, with everybody gaining the freedom to dress as they pleased. Yet very soon (in 1800) prohibition against women wearing

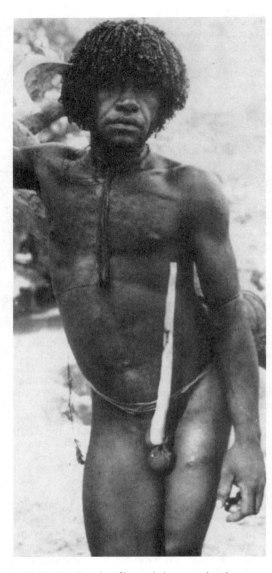

FIGURE 7.3 *Examples of basic clothing as cultural covering of body*

A (above left) *male clothing: penis sheath (from Glynn, 1982, p. 62, reproduced by permission)*

B (above right) *Mehinaku women wearing* uluri *belts (from Gregor, 1977, p. 98 and p. 163, reproduced by permission of the University of Chicago Press)*

trousers was introduced in Paris. Cultural coding of social class through clothing entailed also the disfunctionality of many clothes – fitting with the social roles. 'Society women' in European history were not expected to walk (but were carried), and

their clothing styles were poorly fitted for anything but moving around slowly (Perrot, 1994, p. 95). Surely our contemporary high-fashion designers continue to appeal to their audiences with similar marking of 'high style' (of their brand names) by way of blatant non-functionality of their creations. At the same time, and in line with the globalization of the fashion industry, they sell their names to be put as labels on ordinary and functional objects, in a price range available to the majority of buyers.

The differentiation of clothing as appropriate to social context in European history reflects the changes in relationships with human bodies as symbolic objects. This is particularly evident in the case of the history of special clothing for major night-time activities (that is, sleeping). According to Perrot,

> from the eleventh to the sixteenth century, people in the West either kept their clothes on or slept 'naked to naked' . . . This ingenious nakedness and absent modesty, accompanied by a very strong sociability in and around the bed, disappeared during the sixteenth century, allowing the 'nightshirt' to re-appear during the seventeenth and to last for more than three hundred years. This nightime garment reflected new sensibility about what touched the body . . . it indicated a change in the boundaries of modesty . . . and privatized activities such as sleep. (Perrot, 1994, p. 165)

While in the seventeenth and eighteenth centuries people could be found to be in their nightshirts in other rooms of the house than the bedroom, by the nineteenth century the wearing of nocturnal garments in middle-class Europe became confined to the bedroom only.

Configuring the body: corsets and bust-holders

Women's bodies have been targets for cultural regulation of human lives throughout the centuries. Given the powers of women – in reproduction and in basic home organization – it is through the modulation of the public availability of the perception of women's bodies that human social relations, between genders, social classes and between women themselves, have been negotiated. While different aspects of upper-body modifications (hairdos, hats, face-painting of the traditional or modern 'cosmetics' kind) and lower-body modifications (changing women's feet as in ancient China, or selecting shoes) are of cultural importance, it is the presentation of mid-body that has been the target of much cultural modification.

The human mid-body can be culturally modified by direct intervention actions. In our contemporary case, this happens through efforts to 'watch the weight' and go to health clubs (in case of affluent social classes) to trim off the ever-growing fatty substances from the waistline. This is accompanied by socially acceptable talking about it (whereas talking about body-painting, such as cosmetics, is not encouraged). In the history of human mid-body presentation (which has been important for the affluent social strata, in accordance with their culturally constructed values), the solution was external – both men and women confined their bodies into special devices, corsets, that would force the real body to look socially appropriate (see Figure 7.4).

Figure 7.4A shows an example of a corset from 1851. It is functionally an external garment. It provides the body with the vertical desired form (waistline) by whalebone (later elastic) inserts that would force the body to conform to the prescribed pattern. It was tightened by lacing in the back. The example shown (for women) did not include shoulder straps (which were at times present), but it emphasizes the breasts (possibly further fortified by 'bosom inserts' to modulate the visible breast size) as well as the hips. As a garment worn over the underclothes, the corset could be decorated for external presentation of affluence and aesthetic beauty.

By the end of the nineteenth century and the beginning of the twentieth, cultural attention to mid-body sculpting became differentiated into sculpting of the breasts and (separately) of the hips (in contrast to the mid-nineteenth century corset which did both tasks). With the appearance of a 'breasts-holder' into the realm of women's underwear – the brassière (Busthalter) in 1916 (Cunnington and Cunnington, 1992, p. 229), the possibilities of exaggerating the body parts that, for the Western world, were linked with sex appeal (rather than remaining neutral as

A

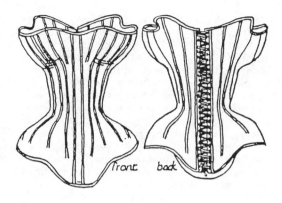

B

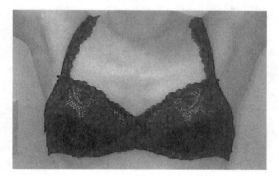

C

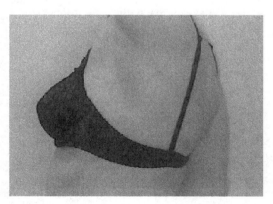

FIGURE 7.4 *Body sculpting devices:*
A, A corset – from year 1851 (from Cunnington and Cunnington, 1992, p. 149, reproduced by permission)
B, A contemporary bra (front view)
C, A contemporary bra (side view)

offspring-feeding devices) became flexible. The bra was an extension of previous 'bust bodices' (which were worn *over* the corset, to accentuate the breast size and to decorate the breast area). With the disappearance of the corset from fashion and the appearance of transparent fabrics in women's dress-making, a new version of cultural focusing on the breasts appears as an undergarment.[3] As such, it brings the social presentation function (previously located on the exterior of the overclothes) into the interior of the layers of clothing. The brassière was a synthesis of the overgarment ('bust bodice') and undergarment (camisole). It emerged in the re-construction of the multi-layer system of clothing, in ways that are parallel to other ways of breast presentation. (for example, through implants to increase breast size). The issue of modulation of breast size (enlarging or diminishing) is an issue encountered in adolescence at puberty (see Chapter 13).

The brassière – known in English as a 'bra' since 1937 (see Figure 7.4B and 7.4C) – has the cultural potential of sculpting the woman's body in two ways. First, it can purposefully increase or decrease the visibility of the breasts. Much of the history of women's fashion in European societies has moved from one (showing off as large breasts as possible) to the other ('flattening' of the breasts). Secondly, it creates the 'insider' ('feeling well' in this bra) and 'outsider' (letting others see the decorations on my bra, or bra in general) distinction. It is not surprising that many bras are made with elaborate externally displayable designs (to be visible – or barely so – through the semi-transparent overgarment), while others look 'plain' from outside. As it is limited to the breasts area, it is a special sculpting device for that part of the body. The continuity with its preceding sculpting device – that of the overgarment corset – can be seen in the maintenance of the fastening of the bra – at the back (the most uncomfortable location), similarly to the lacing of the corset.

The decorative functions of the bra are substantial. In Figure 7.4B we can observe how carefully the makers of the bra have played with the partial stripping and covering of the breasts. The laced upper part of the bra cups are quasi-transparent, while the lower parts are solid in their visual hiding of the breasts. The place of the nipples is particularly carefully turned into an area of ambiguity – it is not transparent but at the boundary of being so. The shoulder straps in the front continue the lacing of the cups, while on the back they turn into minimal framing devices of the woman's back (see Figure 7.4C).

An additional cultural-psychological issue that becomes notable in Figures 7.4B and 7.4C is the care with which the woman in the photograph has eliminated the hair that naturally grows in the armpit. In different societies (and differently at different historical times) the armpit hair has become either culturally positively, or negatively, valued.

Cultural construction of layering of body covers

The cultural construction of human underwear is one of the best examples of historical change in the *pre-bodiment*[4] of collective-cultural meanings. As a concept, underwear is ambiguous – it refers to something worn *under* something else. It creates an additional cultural boundary between the human body and its socially presentable appearance. For example, wearing a T-shirt on our bodies does not involve any distinction of overwear versus underwear. Yet wearing the same T-shirt under another garment (say, a sweater) may create such distinction. Yet it may be culturally non-obligatory to maintain this distinction – when feeling hot, the sweater can be removed and there remain no ambiguous feelings in remaining dressed merely in the T-shirt. However, if the particular T-shirt becomes remodelled and *designated to be worn as underwear* by collective-cultural suggestions, such feelings (for example, of embarrassment in revealing the underwear-shirt in public) come into being. Furthermore, by its cultural designation as underwear, the given object of clothing can become associated with the cultural role of the part of the body with which it is in contact. Hence in Western societies of socially promoted repression of sexuality, and designation of the female breasts as sexual objects, the underwear worn over the area (bra, shirts) can acquire a semiotic role and come to function as a sign of sexuality in the act of object fetishism. In contrast, in other societies there need not be any collective-cultural focusing on the breasts of women in place. Under these circumstances, there are no ambivalent feelings about public display of the breasts on behalf of the women, and no social regulation demanding that women's breasts be covered. *Collective culture creates its areas of negotiating social issues through focusing on selected parts of the human body.* On such selected 'working fields' of the collective culture, using both interventionist (implants, scarifications, cosmetic surgery) and covering (by layers of clothes – under- and overgarments), personal-cultural development takes place through the everyday socially regulated pre-bodiment practices.

The differentiation of under- and overgarments led to specific constructed rules about their mentionability in communication. Language use in reference to undergarments has been carefully normed. Furthermore, the social rules for public display of the underwear are carefully worked out for the given social class in the given society.

In seventeenth to eighteenth century upper-class English society it was proper to speak publicly about those parts of women's undergarments that were publicly visible (= made visible by the wearer), but not about the hidden parts. Similar rules can be observed in twentieth century middle-class social talk – reference to one's underwear in public is an unlikely topic of such talk, while (of course) gossip about what might happen in the private quarters of public figures (such as presidents or film stars) is a socially accepted and even promoted pastime.

Creating distance and observational control – the veil

One of the most prominent Western projections (see Mernissi, 1987) into the social world of Islamic countries is the assumption of women's enforced subordination – in the form of segregating them to home spheres, eliminating them from public domains, and 'forcing' them to hide their faces. Such pointed discourse – of the Western societies – is a good example of socio-institutional guidance of understanding away from the complex reality.

In most Arab societies in the Orient different kinds of veils (*burqas*) have been designed and used (see Figure 7.5).

Burqa is first and foremost a form of face-dress – an overgarment not different from clothes used to cover knees, ankles, heads (= hats), breasts, abdomen etc. As Unni Wikan compared Sohari (in Oman, Arabian Penninsula) women's wearing of *burqa* with that of Western women's wearing of clothes, no grand exotic picture emerges:

FIGURE 7.5 *Omani women wearing facial veils (burqa) (from Wikan, 1972, pp. 90 and 91, reproduced by permission from Unni Wikan)*
A (above) Burqa *with partial face coverage*
B (below) *Full facial coverage*

> To feel decent and honorable, a Western woman covers much of her body when she goes out in public. The Sohari woman covers body and face. Changing social conventions specify for each the manner and style appropriate for different settings and situations. At the present time, a Western woman need not feel shy to show herself naked before her husband; a Sohari woman need not feel shy to uncover her face in his presence. Yet the Western woman often chooses to go about dressed, as the Sohari woman would have chosen to keep her *burqa* on, had she in fact had the option. The Western woman may, without offense to public morality, discard her bathing suit in a group of all-female bathers. The Sohari woman may discard her *burqa* in [an] all-female gathering. Yet both of them may voluntarily choose to remain covered. Naked, they may feel shy, exposed, vulnerable and even ugly; clothed, they feel protected, proper, and perhaps pretty. (Wikan, 1982, p. 99)

The personal-cultural reconstruction of a clothing object is remarkable here – by personalizing the *burqa*, a woman makes the face-covering

device part of her personal-cultural construction. As such, it becomes a part of the extended self – extending from herself to the garment, rather than a mere acceptance of an externally super-imposed rule that women should wear face masks. Face masks also create for women a particular power position in those settings where they have no explicit power – the public settings. While wearing veils in such settings, they can see what happens in the public sphere without their own reactions to that, and their identity, being revealed. The Arab veil is not a method of 'female oppression', but merely a distinguishing object of clothing (in the collective-cultural sense) which can become a personally meaningful extension of the person.

Veils are not necessarily parts of merely women's attire. Under some collective-cultural conditions, men wear the veil (and women need not). In the Tuareg societies (in the Saharan desert in Africa) men are the ones who wear face veils that cover their mouth region, leaving just the eyes visible in social settings. This is done largely in defence against evil sprits, as well as against the sun and sand in a desert nomadic lifestyle. The veil can be worn by both men and women, but most certainly by men, and, among men, by the men of higher social class (the nobles). The Tuareg noblemen are perceived by outsiders to be

. . . notable for their haughty and arrogant demeanour. They walk with a long swagger and hold their heads high with dignity and aloofness; even when atop a camel they hardly deign to incline their heads to a pedestrian. The veils promote this atmosphere of mystery and apartness . . . That the cold, long look

FIGURE 7.6 *Tuareg men in veils (from Johannes and Ida Nicolaisen, 1997, p. 126, reprinted by permission)*

through a slit of cloth impresses the foreigner is indisputable and is used to this end, but it is exactly when in the presence of the outsider with whom he is on familar terms that the Tuareg is most relaxed in his veiling. (Murphy, 1964, p. 1266)

Outsiders' views of the insiders are thus almost certainly limited by what – and how – the insiders want to present. The veil, for men and women, is a cultural tool for modulating psychological distance. While the Arab women cover their faces, the Tuareg women cover their hair – and not necessarily their face. The Tuareg women have had a very central power role in their societies, which historically were of matrilineal descent. The regulation of psychological distance through face coverage and exposure was little emphasized for them.

In contrast, the Tuareg men of noble kind find it shameful to expose their mouths in social contexts, particularly those involving close kin (Figure 7.6). This cultural regulator of 'shame' (*tekeraki*) and 'respect' (*isimrarak*) need not apply to lower social classes (slaves), among whom men can be seen in public with uncovered mouths.

The Tuaregs have an appropriate saying – 'the veil and trousers are brothers' (Rasmussen, 1991, p. 757). The veil for the Tuareg noblemen is a symbolic protection against others' envy (or 'evil eye', *tehot*) as well as against others' 'evil mouth' (gossip, or *awal*). In terms of general cultural concept, the male veil indicates respect (which defends the person against pollution).

The veil for the Tuaregs is essential for the modesty of the noblemen – similarly to its functions for women in Islamic societies. In accordance with the hypothesis of Robert Murphy (1964), the veil functions as a cultural tool that allows the person to generate *generalized psychological distance* between themselves and others. It can be worn by different persons (who turn its wearing into a symbol of a social, or gender, class), in different ways (rigorous versus 'sloppy') on different social occasions. It can be taken off in front of some 'social others' (but not in front of others). It can be decorated by colour, texture of the textiles used, and by attachments to it. All the properties of clothing – simultaneous potential for covering and exposure – are applicable to the veil. The same properties are there in the application of cosmetics to the face in our contemporary world (see Chapter 15). If for the Tuaregs the veil is compared with trousers, then modern women making up their faces can be seen as creating a veil on the surface of the skin.

Clothing: how produced and for whom?
Clothing is a peculiar cultural construction of objects because it is vulnerable to two processes that increase its variability. First, obviously, there are the processes of fashion that move as waves through collective-cultural meaning systems in a society. The remarkably avid success of such waves in internalization into personal cultures guides constant innovation of persons' self-presentation.

Secondly, there is the variability of clothing created by the anthropomorphic variability of human bodies. Each object of clothing needs some tailoring for the particular person who might wear it. The social class background of the role of tailors is remarkable in European history – one of the central resistance points of the higher social strata was the insistence upon the superior value of tailor-made (as opposed to factory-produced) clothes. Furthermore, the introduction of the sewing machine in 1830–60 in Europe guaranteed the proliferation of industrial clothes-making skills beyond the tailors themselves, leading to women's employment in the garment-making industry (Coffin, 1996).

By the end of the twentieth century, the making of clothing and suggestion of its meanings is completely overtaken by mass production. As a result, the person who makes clothes their own does not start from the question of the clothing fitting their body, but their body fitting into the clothing. Once selected, and obtained, the object of clothing is turned into one's personal-cultural artefact. Focus on personal individuality comes from selection, not construction.

The covered body: cultural organization of the body in movement
Human social life entails constant constraining on one's own and each other's conduct. It is not only the ways in which the human body is covered (or uncovered) in one or another setting, but how that (clothed, semi-clothed, or unclothed) body moves in the given activity setting. The patterns of human movement are culturally organized. This can entail amplification of the movement in special cases, such as making music and dancing, or attenuation of the movement on other occasions (for example, children forced to sit still in school lessons, or during rituals; promotion of the non-moving body as being culturally desirable etc.).

Patterns of human movement are most directly under the control of social others in specific settings. Social institutions often craft rituals of conjoint and coordinated movement of decorated bodies (for example, military parades of persons dressed up in parade uniforms). Angry crowds of people can become uncontrollable through their heterogeneity of movement. Ceremonies of calamity, such as funerals, entail prescriptions for slow movement of the participants. Fashion models are specifically prepared for moving their bodies on the catwalk. Children can be instructed not to move their bodies in one or another way so as not to appear 'improper' – it is precisely some of these ways in which striptease artists may be instructed to move in order to appear 'proper' in their profession.

In the history of human societies, human movement patterns have been targets of ideological controversies. The Catholic Church (as well as the forces of the Protestant Reformation) fought a war against the movement of bodies in contexts of dancing, resulting in downplaying the flexibility of hip and leg movements in dance (see Wagner, 1997). That restriction did not work in the context of Latin and South America. In Christian churches in Africa (and in Afro-American churches in the USA), the basic dance rhythms of the history of the societies have become the rhythmic carriers of the religious services. Human body movement is an interface between the personal-cultural body and the activities that the person undertakes in the given setting.

MIGRATION AND CULTURAL CONTEXT FOR DEVELOPMENT

Human beings move around during their life course. In the history of the species, moving around in one's habitat has transformed into many forms. The hunter–gatherer societies needed to be constantly on the move to gather or hunt the relevant food resources. When human beings took up land and cattle cultivation, their migratory patterns became reduced. It is in the case of farming and cattle breeding as major economic activities that one can observe most stability of the familiar joint activities, over time and generations. The need to take care of the fields, or of the cattle, day after day, and year after year, leads towards minimization of movement of the life space of persons over geographic territories. In contrast, trading activities may entail the necessity to undertake long trips, with or without the whole family. Other economic activities (for example, peripatetic entertainers, like the Qalandar in Pakistan – Berland, 1982; or nomadic pastoralists – Hobbs, 1989) can entail constant nomadic lifestyles.

So, all in all, human beings are on the move – but in different ways, extents, and for a variety of reasons. In this respect, migration of some kind is a central part of human life. However, there are different forms of migration that can be considered in different ways.

1 Permanent migration   Persons, or family groups, move from previous home territory to a new one, without return. Pilgrims who came to North America from Europe to colonize it, or the convicts which the British Crown sent off to Australia, constitute examples of such permanent migration. The history of the world is filled with examples of permanent migration, due to escaping from horrors of wars or famine, or in search of golden opportunities for affluence and happiness.

2 Quasi-permanent migration   Persons (or family groups) leave their home grounds and establish new home grounds elsewhere, while retaining the original grounds, and move between the original and new home grounds with some periodicity. The new home territory may be considered the main home place, yet the previous one is episodically re-visited and re-inhabited. Most rural to urban migration (at least in the case of the first generation of urban dwellers) is of this kind – the new urban dwellers benefit from the new home environment while retaining ties with their rural kinship-governed territories. Family gatherings in the villages can serve as the occasion for maintaining social ties (which are most likely also kinship ties). The other homestead serves as a potential 'back-up' home territory for cases of emergencies. Thus, in the case of crises (economic or military) in the urban settings, the new urbanites may return to their rural home grounds. Likewise, in case of crisis in the rural areas, intensive movement to urban contexts can be observed as a way for survival.

3 Temporary migration   Under some circumstances, persons (or family groups) move between different locations for limited periods of time. In the case of human history, such temporary migration entails *child migration* – families sending children from one location to another for specific economic or educational purposes.

Child migration has existed in many versions, depending upon the needs of both the children and their natal families. The practices of 'baby farming' (see Chapter 9) – sending nursing infants from urban environments to villages to be nursed by wet nurses – in the history of France constitute a case of infant migration undertaken for the sake of the health of the child. In societies with informal education systems, sending a child to be an apprentice to a relative of substantial special skills (shaman, medicine man, blacksmith) served the purpose of offering the child the opportunity to acquire a possible future vocation, in return for the child's economic help in the household where he or she was sent. In historical times when formal education became important, sending children to school outside of the home territory (boarding schools, convents, monasteries etc.) served the same function.

Child migration can be linked with adult migration, as seen in the following example from Africa:

> Mende women often leave their marital households to bear their children and remain away for the first year or so while they are nursing their infants. . . . The expectant mother often takes some of her other small children, especially girls, with her to the birthing household, which is preferably her own mother's or sister's residence. . . . When the new mother returns to her marital household after a year or so, she may leave behind her weanling as well as some of the slightly older children who accompanied her to the weanling's birthplace, which was likely to have been these siblings' birthplace as well. (Isaac and Conrad, 1982, p. 250)

Thus, migration of both adults and children between households is an indicator of the dynamic use of wider kinship networks both to gain help (for example, childbirth taking place in a woman's natal home, leaving the baby in the care of a grandmother or aunt) and to give assistance (leaving older children in the household to help with subsistence tasks).

4 Constant migration A very special case of temporary migration is that of *constant migration*. It entails inhabiting two different environments in rapid succession. Both of the environments are prominent for the person who constantly moves from one into the other, and vice versa.

Much of human life is spent in constant migration. Adults migrate between their workplaces and homes, children commute between school and home on a daily basis. Although it is not usual to consider schoolchildren migrants, they can be seen as experiencing two social worlds of formal and informal education. Perhaps their migratory experience is so intense that it seems not to entail separation of the two worlds – yet the child can be only in one place at one time, and every transition between the places plays a psychological role. Our outsiders' look at people may underestimate the migratory experience. Thus, we may talk about 'schoolchildren' (who of course are at the same time 'homechildren', unless they are in a boarding school), or 'streetchildren'. Our reference to these children carries usually an affective ideological flavour: 'schoolchildren' are viewed positively (as they are learning at school), and 'streetchildren' evoke feelings of pity, or of criticism of the society in which they can be found. Yet, as the case of Huck Finn indicates, from a child's personal cultural perspective

this evaluation may be reversed. Furthermore, contemporary societies provide for new versions of children inhabiting public places – 'mall-children' (= children hanging out in shopping malls), 'school bus children' (a special US case where children are taken to/from school by school buses), or 'net children' (= children who escape their home psychologically, through 'surfing' on the internet) can be seen as modern versions of streetchildren.

The special case of streetchildren

First World journalistic accounts have created a rhetoric of calamity about streetchildren – who are mostly discovered in Third World countries, fighting not only their own poverty but that of their parents. The calamitous rhetoric that is usually constructed presents the streetchildren as victims of the social system, and good targets for missionary fights for their souls, saving them from their (seemingly) psychologically vulnerable life environments.

Social institutions that make streetchildren into targets of their social actions are likely to use similar rhetoric in defining the issues. A 'streetchild' is in this light viewed to be a homeless or neglected child who lives chiefly in the streets. Yet such definition is obscure (what does 'chiefly' mean?). UNICEF includes among 'streetchildren' those under-age persons who spend a major part of their waking life wandering in urban streets (with the age limit removed, that would include tourists, and adolescents in any country).

Such dramatized accounts of streetchildren are psychologically naive. The reality of children's lives in the streets entails a multi-faceted picture of both strengths and vulnerabilities (see the thorough review of existing issues and research literature in Aptekar and Stöcklin, 1997). Different sets of strengths and vulnerabilities can be found for any other children – 'schoolchildren', 'homechildren' etc.

The overwhelming majority (estimated at 90 per cent or more) of children whose main activities take place in the streets have homes (to which they may return from time to time), they work (and support their parents) and, despite (or possibly because of) the additional risks of inhabiting the streets (violence against streetchildren is a real phenomenon), develop psychological strategies of resilience. As children in the streets participate in the economic process of the society (see Pandey, 1991), their presence on the streets (that is, in the public domain of access) is ultimately based upon the economic possibilities of their survival. The question of streetchildren is not a question of where these children are to be found (in the streets, obviously), but what do they do there. The latter issue is actually that of children's participation in economic subsistence (see below).

In this respect, streetchildren at the end of the twentieth century may be functionally equivalent (in economic terns) to children working in textile mills, other factories and mines a century earlier. Yet there is a major psychological difference: factory/mine work would force upon children a behavioural routine (determined by the production process), while the activities in the streets require much personal initiative, flexible adaptability. Streetchildren can often be seen as in need of independence – a fact recognized by social institutions that create shelters for them (Áptekar, 1988).

Thus, most of the streetchildren are similar to school-attending children – they usually migrate between the street as their main place of life activity (rather than school) to their home conditions, and back. Very few streetchildren have been found to live completely in the streets; most have some kind of home territory to which they episodically return. A similar situation occurs with children from marriages of a serial monogamic kind (in Western societies, see Chapter 6): they may migrate weekly between the mother's and father's re-constituted family environments.

The linkage of the sociopsychological and economic situation in the child's background family and the child's gradually moving to become a streetchild obviously varies immensely across individual cases (for example, Borel and Silva, 1987), from the child's escaping from the psychological horrors of the home (and finding life in the streets much more adequate), to parents systematically sending the child to the streets to gain economic resources. Moving into the streets can result from rapid loss of economic standing, as the example of Musenda (narrating in 1994, at the age of 17), a son of a well-to-do Zambian politician who died when the son was 11, indicates:

> I went to school with children who came from well-to-do families when my father was still alive. To school, I was driven in a Benz and never thought of walking in my life. The thought of being a street child never even crossed my mind. It was my belief that the kind of life I was leading was going to last forever.
>
> When my father died in 1988, to my dismay, his relatives shared all his and our belongings and left us with nothing. Life became so rough and unbearable for us. Because of this, my mother decided that we go and live in the village with her parents. I had never lived in a village and village life was very unfamiliar to me. As a result when we got there I failed to adapt and decided to run away. I stole 50 kg of my grandfather's maize to raise transport money to get to Lusaka. It was my intention to look for work upon arrival although I had not completed my secondary education.
>
> Upon arrival in Lusaka, things did not turn out the way I had planned. Because I could not go to any of my father's relatives I had to survive by living at the Lusaka Inter-Terminus Bus Station with other boys I made friends with upon arrival. To earn our living we had to do some piece work. We never used to steal. At night, we slept under the shades of the bus terminus and covered ourselves with meal sacks. It never mattered. What was important to do was to survive each and every passing day.
>
> But to our surprise, policemen pounced on us for no reason at all. The only crime we committed was that of looking scruffy and dirty. But of course it was difficult to look clean when there was no money to buy 'extras' from the little money we got from the piece work and hand-outs. (Sampa, 1997, p. 17)

Musenda's story points to the issue of rural-to-urban migration, in the search for subsistence, as a process that leads to proliferation of the observable outcome of not-so-clean children inhabiting the public territory in towns, doing odd jobs and sleeping in public places. Such migration is not limited to children – it can involve adults, or whole families. The migration in Brazil from the North East regions to the capital Brasilia, or to the South, is largely migration in search for better living conditions.

Adult migration

As we see, adult migration also has its temporary forms. In the history of human societies, women have often left their marital households when ready to give birth to a child, and move into their natal household for the time of delivery and post-partum care of the baby. They may move back to their marital households as the infants grow into their second year of life.

Most importantly, adult migration is linked with economic opportunities. Once such migration takes place, the patterns of reliance on kinship networks may be maintained (see Holmes-Eber, 1997, on women's networks in urban Tunis). The specific gender roles set up the patterns of perception of such migration. Thus, migration of men from rural to urban areas is usually viewed in a society differently from that of women. For example, the social representation of female migrants to urban areas in Uganda as if they were necessarily earning their living through prostitution has been the basis for institutional crack-down on female migrants (see Ogden, 1996). In reality, the women who migrated to Kampala found different ways for earning subsistence, ways that included prostitution, but were not limited to it.

The examples given here indicate migration

of adults for solving a basic problem of existence – finding subsistence. Migration is a vehicle of adaptation, it is an inevitable, and often not desired, event. Yet in the world of the rich – in contrast to that of the poor – migration can be turned into a socially constructed need.

A special modern form of adult temporary migration is *tourism*. It could be claimed that tourism is a contemporary (secularized) version of the pilgrimages that preceded it in centuries past. As Muslims look upon a trip to Mecca as a religious duty and contribution, or Christians go to Rome to see the Pope blessing the crowds, modern tourists experience a sense of glory in visiting culturally meaningful (famous) sites. Tourists leave their home grounds temporarily for experiences not available at home, but with the clear goal (and security) of returning to the home environment. The architectural places created for tourists cater for such ambivalent needs – the swimming pools of luxury hotels in exotic geographical locations can be constructed in ways similar to those in the tourist's own town thousands of miles away, and yet that comforting (known) object is in the middle of a completely foreign (titillating, yet suspicious) macroenvironment that may begin at the very boundary of the hotel.

The developmental role of child migration

Migration of children from one household to another entails two components. First, it includes *provision of new experiences* (which are not available in the original household). As such, sending one's child to live for some years in the household of a relative who can teach the child special skills (so that the child can become a medicine man, blacksmith, or shaman) is not different from US parents' desire, in our times, to send their children away to college, medical or law school. In the former case the benefit is obtained through informal education by a relative (the apprenticeship model), in the latter, by migration to places of formal education.

In parallel with provision of relevant experiences for the child goes the *child's role in the subsistence in the receiving household*. As a household member, the child is expected to take on appropriate assisting roles, and perform tasks that are relevant for the whole of the household. The child sent to inhabit a relative's household for purposes of apprenticeship may also take care of the elderly members of the household, or mind younger children.

There are clearly many reasons why the sending of children to foster parents occurs. In Table 7.1 a summary of these reasons based on the social environment in Mali, Africa, is given. The intricacies of the child fostering system in the Mali social system go beyond the apprenticeship/ economic helper main axis. The fostering practice provides cultural compensation for biological insufficiencies (childlessness of a woman who gets a foster child), or gratitude (repay previous foster mother – point (4) of 'pull factors'). Fostering can help to deal with social insufficiencies (illegitimate child fostered out to another household; children of divorce).

TABLE 7.1 *Why do children migrate? 'Push' and 'pull' factors in child fosterage in Mali*

'Pull' factors (child is actively requested by the foster mother; purposive transfer of the child by the real mother)	'Push factors (child is fostered out by circumstances, or some crisis in the natal household or with the real mother)
1 Foster mother is childless	1 Biological mother migrated (seasonally or permanently)
2 Foster mother's children (especially her daughters) have all grown up and left home	2 Biological mother sick
3 Socialization of next generation with family values and traditions (especially boys)	3 Biological mother pregnant again – child sent to live elsewhere to avoid 'heat' from her stomach
4 Foster mother had previous foster child who has now grown up and married and repaid her former foster mother with one of her own children	4 Biological mother separated, divorced, or widowed (weaned boys usually left with their father's family)
5 Foster mother is child's name-sake (*tokora*) and decides to raise her	5 Child illegitimate
	6 Child being weaned – resulting in either temporary intra-household or semi-permanent fostering

Source: after Castle, 1995

Migration (of any form, and for any reason) entails both the tension of leaving behind the previous place, and the benefits of the experiential opportunities the new environment affords. In Table 7.2 data on the ages of children and the kinship relation of the households they have migrated to is given for the Upper Bambara Chiefdom in Sierra Leone , Africa. The data here come from a study conducted in 1966–8. Two aspects are noteworthy in this table. First, the *age range of children most often found living in households different from that of their parents is 5–9 years* (or, middle childhood). This is precisely the age range when children (in African history) have been both entrusted with relevant subsistence tasks, and (in any context) are introduced to educational opportunities. Secondly, the *overwhelming majority of the children* (over 80 per cent in each of the three age groups) lived in the *household of a kin-group member*. The migration of children of the Mende (in the Upper Bambara Chiefdom) was organized by the wider kinship network.

If one considers the place of residence of children of different households in the same Upper Bambara children (see Table 7.3), it becomes clear that by the age range 10–14 years, over half of the children are living in households which are neither their natal or near-natal (mother's natal) households. The increase in this percentage over child's age demonstrates how the mother/young child migration to the mother's natal household (child age 1–4 years) becomes substituted by the sending of children of later ages to other households.

The latter tendency leads to the question of children's role as participants in the economic activities of households. In summary, children's migration on a temporary or quasi-permanent basis is one of the ways in which both the survival of households (related through blood ties) and children's informal education takes place in pre-industrialized societies. The 'ownership' by parents of children, which is taken for granted in the twentieth century European and North American middle and upper social strata, does

TABLE 7.2 *Place of residence of children of Upper Bambara Chiefdom*

Residence	Ages 1–4 years		Ages 5–9 years		Ages 10–14 years	
	Frequency	%	Frequency	%	Frequency	%
With parents:						
father's household	127	67.5	170	64.2	50	45.0
with mother, in household other than father's	37	19.7	13	4.9	2	1.8
Elsewhere	24	12.8	82	30.9	57	53.2
Total	188	100	265	100	109	100

Source: after Isaac and Conrad, 1982, p. 245

TABLE 7.3 *Place of residence of Upper Bambara children (in 1966–68) who lived away from parents' homes*

Relationship	Ages 1–4 years		Ages 5–9 years		Ages 10–14 years	
	Frequency	%	Frequency	%	Frequency	%
Members of kinship groups:						
Mother's sister	11	26.8	21	13.5	15	17.9
Mother's brother	2	4.9	20	12.9	17	20.2
Mother's parent	13	31.7	24	15.4	3	3.6
Father's sister	4	9.8	15	9.7	5	6.0
Father's brother	1	2.4	16	10.3	9	10.7
Other	4		32		21	
Non-kin	6	14.6	27	17.4	14	16.7
Total	41		155		84	

Source: after Isaac and Conrad, 1982, p. 250

not prescribe jealous and defensive insistence of 'my child' being 'raised by myself only'. Instead, under different circumstances, the parent having the child can transfer the child to be raised by others – yet within the kinship network. The kinship network is the only functional social support network in human societies, and hence moving children to (and through) different positions within that network is of greater psychological relevance than 'strict ownership' of the children by parents themselves.

THE ECONOMIC ROLES OF CHILDREN, AND THEIR HISTORICAL CHANGE

As in most European and North American societies relatively strict laws outlawing children's labour were introduced at the beginning of the twentieth century, child psychologists have largely followed the social demand of their own (Western) social backgrounds to treat children's participation in economic production as a case of (at worst) 'exploitation' or (a less moralistic interpretation) an example of 'unfortunate childhoods of no play'. Similarly, children who work are viewed to be unfortunate as they lose chances of an educational kind – yet the economic costs of education may make it necessary for children to participate in paying for their education. At the same time, ethnographic accounts of children's lives in everyday life contexts (for example, Rogoff, 1990) indicate clearly that guided participation by children in the whole life of their family is the main context for social development.

From asset to liability
The social history of childhood over the past two centuries includes a major transformation in the role of children. *While children used to be economic assets* in societies where their participation in labour (taking care of fields and cattle, minding other children) was important, in contemporary industrialized, urbanized societies (which protect children against being employed), *children have become economic liabilities*. No surprise that under such conditions the number of children (of educated and urbanized parents) tends to go down. In parallel with the decline in reproduction, one can observe projection of the psychological (in contrast with economic) needs of the parents into the offspring. For instance, if in a rural African family of the nineteenth century the birth of many children was a way for the household to survive (half of the children born died in their infancy, the rest became economic helpers for the whole household), then the birth of a single child in a contemporary urban, educated middle-class setting brings with it the need to invest economic

resources in the education and vocational career of the child, on behalf of the parents.

History of human societies includes increasing dependence upon child labour during periods of European industrialization. The nineteenth century in Europe was a period during which children became involved in manufacturing tasks, and were turned into lesser-paid (than adults) factory workers.

The use of child labour in nineteenth century England and the United States was not only economically profitable, but also supported by religious beliefs. The Puritan belief in the virtue of industry and the sin of idleness would support the demand to engage children in activities (Abbott, 1908). Yet which kind of activities are implied remains open – work in the fields (or factories) is one option, activities in educational institutions quite another.

Segregating children and labour: saving childhoods for education
The introduction of legal regulation for the employment of children at the beginning of the twentieth century was an act of social re-canalization of child labour to children labouring in the factories of education (schools).

The social pressures on factory owners in the nineteenth century led to the opening of schools at factories. Yet, not surprisingly, the children were reported not to study much in such schools after a long (10–12 hour) working day. The social controversies about 'factory schools' (schools at factories, which were expected to give the children education aside from their regular factory work) led to the removal of children from the workforce. This entailed a takeover of control of children's activities by the educational institutions, and occupying the majority of children's time with school-work rather than with work on income-generating tasks. In their actual everyday lives children may become involved in economic activities in their 'spare time', but the educational system wins the control over their time.

Nevertheless children's participation in economic tasks remains central for their development, as children are necessary participants in the life of the family. Anne Solberg (1997) noticed children participating in different phases of fish processing in a northern Norwegian coast town. Children both took over accessible (but relevant) parts of the tasks (such as fish cleaning), and also became involved in their own profitable manufacturing of parts of the fish for their own sale to local households.

Children's independent work initiatives entail their mastery of relevant technology (from knives to machines), all of which pose dangers – yet they also promote accomplishment of the tasks. Again, the socio-institutional discourse 'wars' about childhood safety can be accentuated here. It is the adults of different belief backgrounds who argue about whether 'children are ready' (or not) for the difficulties and dangers involved. Very often, such disputes are a matter of comfortable liberal politics in affluent countries, while the life realities in the actual life contexts of the children do not spare them from dangerous and even excessively traumatic – yet survivable – experiences (see Aptekar and Stöcklin, 1997).

SUMMARY: CULTURAL STRUCTURING OF ENVIRONMENTS FOR DEVELOPMENT

My aim in this chapter was to show how human environments are culturally constituted. They are based on the *simultaneous* semiotic *distancing and relating* of the person with the given environmental setting. The human being makes sense of a given setting, and through that creates psychological distance between themself and the setting. Yet such distancing is always paralleled by being within the setting. In general, the person is under tension between *being in* and *being out*, in relation to the setting.

The notion of semiotic demand setting (SDS) was offered as the locus for cultural-psychological processes that take place at the intersection of a setting and a person. The setting carries with it a pre-organized set of meaningful demands. Such demands guide the person's feeling, thinking and acting within a given setting. The person may act and feel in unison with the SDS orientation, or contrary to it. Yet in both cases the person's psychological functions are culturally guided.

Social institutions 'fight' for the set-up of SDSs. They guide people to pay attention to specific issues in ways fitting the ideology of the institution, and away from unwanted targets of interest and ways of presenting those. They can also hyper-emphasize social discourse about some topics in some ways – creating an autonomous sphere of social talk which is segregated from any possibility for actions. Thus, the presence of multiplicity of opinions, disputes between these opinions, and a grand display of these (on TV, in the mass media in general) are substitutes for enhancing knowledge or for solving problems. Society is not a homogeneous social system, but entails many institutional goal-orientations that are encoded into social talk.

Human environmental settings *are cultural in their physical organization*. This applies both to the physical settings within which persons move (external environment: houses, streets etc.) and those which persons move along with themselves (clothing, body decorations etc.).

A crucial aspect of human cultural development is migration. Migration occurs for any age group, or gender group, depending upon specific circumstances. Migratory experiences differ by their permanence or temporariness, and, in the latter case, in the tempo of change of the settings. History of human societies indicates that the migration of children from natal homes to the homes of relatives, schools etc. has played a relevant role in their cultural development.

NOTES

1 For example, the United States Reduction of Paperwork Act (in 1980) requires all government agencies to indicate on each form the average amount of time people take to fill in the form. This constitutes a symbolic attention pointing to an irrelevant detail, and is actually a case of increasing of paperwork, rather than its rhetorically claimed reduction (Herzfeld, 1992, p. 121).

2 The focus on the beauty of the calves has surfaced in the history of body presentation in Europe – only among men (of affluent social strata). In the eighteenth century, when men wore stockings as overgarments for the legs, it was usual to emphasize the shape of the calves by special 'calf-pads' – inserts onto the calves inside of the stockings (see Cunnington and Cunnington, 1992, pp. 80–81).

3 The brassière appeared in the context where it was said 'gowns of utmost softness and *semi-transparency* have made a bust support essential' (Cunnington and Cunnington, 1992, p. 229). What was previously accomplished by an *over*garment (on top of the non-transparent corset, which itself did most of the job in presenting the breasts) now becomes a selectively displayable (through semi-transparency of the overgarments) *under*garment, in direct contact with the body.

4 I invent this term here as a corollary to embodiment. Pre-bodiment is the cultural manipulation of the body for social purposes, including both self-needs (embodiment) and communication with others.

REVIEW QUESTIONS FOR CHAPTER 7

1   Explain the notion of mediated distancing.

2   How are human life settings mediated places?

3   Compare your understanding of everyday life in Korowai tree-houses with those of Tibetan tents.

4   Explain the notion of *affordance*.

5   How do institutions guide social discourse about environments?

6   What is a *semiotic demand setting*?

7   Analyse the psychological issues of different forms of garbage disposal.

8   What is a *microsystem* (in Bronfenbrenner's theoretical system)?

9   What is a *mesosystem* (in Bronfenbrenner's theoretical system)?

10   What is an *exosystem* (in Bronfenbrenner's theoretical system)?

11   Explain the notion of an *ethnopsychological pool of ideas* (Kojima).

12   Explain how human interaction overcomes distance – compare handshake and embrace.

13   Explain the psychological function of body modifications.

14   How do clothes make social distiction?

15   Explain the cultural-psychological functions of the veil – compare Arabic women's and Tuareg men's use of the veil.

16   Describe different types of migration, and their psychological sides.

17   Explain the status of streetchildren in cultural-psychological terms.

18   Explain the role of child migration in child development.

19   How have the economic roles of children changed over human history?

PART THREE

CULTURAL ORGANIZATION OF PREGNANCY AND INFANCY

Cultural development of human beings in ontogeny begins long before the baby is born. All the psychological transformation of the adults (who are in the process of becoming parents of the child to be born) is collective-culturally guided. Such guidance is embedded in the texture of most ordinary everyday activities in which the persons involved participate. Belief orientations – encoded in signs – are linked with some of the parts of these mundane processes, and masked as necessities for the activities themselves. In this respect, the cultural nature of life course transitions is inherent in these transitions. Pregnancy is a good example: in its course, the cultural orientation of the adults becomes masked as a case of joint concern for the baby, who might be born well – if the cultural suggestions are accepted. The conditions for development in infancy are likewise organized through inserting cultural meanings into the mundane care of the offspring. It is not only the offspring whose development is culturally directed this way, but equally so that of the caring others.

Yet this cultural guidance process is necessarily multi-faceted. It includes semiotic support for getting pregnant *under appropriate social circumstances* – together with discouragement (or even prohibition) of it under others. During pregnancy, the collective-cultural meaning system is maintained through suggested following of taboos, prescriptions and rituals. Yet at the same time it has to deal with issues of termination of pregnancy – wanted or unwanted by the person. Not only are the pregnant woman's actions culturally overdetermined, but all other members of the household and of the kin network relate in specific ways to the woman approaching childbirth. This applies also to social institutions that have taken over the function of catering for childbirth in modern societies.

Once the baby is born, he or she enters into a pre-prepared cultural niche of development. Childbirth involves a ritualistic seclusion from the social world, followed by re-integration of the mother (and the baby) into the social world. This process is also filled with ambiguities. The social world surrounding the new mother and baby is the main support system for them in good times and bad. The mother and the baby belong to that system – especially to the kinship network. Yet, at the same time, public exposure of the newborn entails symbolic risks. The 'social others' around the mother and the baby are not necessarily benevolent. They may carry symbolic dangers – direct ('evil eye' by the person) or indirect (exposing the baby to negative forces simply by talking about it or mentioning it).

Cultural organization of childbirth and early infancy thus entails transformation of the psychological functions of the adults (the mother, the father, other members of the household or community) first, and of babies second. In some ways, the topic of pregnancy and infancy belongs to the realm of adult life stage development. It is our (Western) orientation on the development of fetuses and infants that has guided developmental psychology towards overlooking the simple fact that becoming, and being, pregnant, and giving birth to children, *are primarily* (psychologically) phenomena of *adult development*. The conceptual blinder here is beautifully hypocritical: our (adult) personal-cultural construction of the need for, and meaning of, children is being projected into the developing fetus and infant as if it were merely concern for the well-being of the offspring. In reality, which includes both abortions and fights against abortions, infanticide and support to handicapped infants etc., these issues are dealt with in ways that suit the needs of the adults first, and only secondarily those of the babies. Psychologically, the offspring are for the parents – while the prevailing collective-culturally suggested masking condition demands (from the parents) that they act and feel as if they are dedicated to the children.

The latter cultural mask – of parents existing for the children (rather than the other way round, or at least accepting mutuality in this linkage) – may be a result of European historical construction. Surely in many societies where people live under difficult nutritional, climatic and health conditions this mask is not always applied. It is not a simple matter to culturally expect a parent's dedication to the infant in a society where the infant mortality rate may be 50 per cent, and where children are needed precisely as economic assets for the family, rather than treated as objects of idle adoration. In the following two chapters, I intend to peep behind the cultural mask of the ideologies of child-orientedness, and try to restore a balance in looking at how the emergence of offspring in the human case exists between the needs of the children and the needs of the adults in the given society. We will see how collective-cultural meanings which are meant to regulate the operation of the society operate. Pregnant women and their offspring are used by the society to structure itself – hence the ideological nature of most of the issues that surround pregnancy, childbirth and early child development.

8

CULTURAL NATURE OF PARENT–OFFSPRING DIFFERENTIATION DURING PREGNANCY

It is obvious that becoming pregnant is a result of sexual intercourse (or at least of some manipulation in a test tube). Sex is of interest to males and females of many species, including humans. Yet, contrary to claims by people from the ambience of Freud's couch in affluent Viennese environments – sexuality is not the only, nor even the major, domain of human activities that are culturally regulated for the purposes of societal control over human conduct. Food-related activities are as important (or possibly even more so: as will be seen below, human sexual functions can be subsumed under nutritional ones, but it is unlikely that the reverse is true), and power issues stemming from property ownership, inheriting and production of exchange value are probably central to human psychological organization of dealing with getting and raising offspring.

BASICS OF SOCIAL ORGANIZATION: NORMS AND COUNTER-NORMS

Human conduct is always regulated by social norms of two kinds. First there are collective-culturally functioning *positively sanctioned social norms* that regulate sexual relations. In many ways these norms are set up to support the social order – of marriage (see Chapter 6).

In parallel with the positively sanctioned social norms, each social unit works out a set of *legitimate negatively valued counter-norms*. These are norms to make sense of how not to behave – a target of avoidance for social suggestion efforts. Yet at the same time as they act to repel the 'normal course' of persons in their development, these counter-norms create possibilities for alternative ways of conduct.

There exist numerous counter-norms for human sexual activities. The latter may be marked by negative connotational meanings, yet be cultur-ally acceptable alongside the privileged main social forms. Once persons actualize such forms in their actions, they may become socially stigmatized, or even persecuted – yet in this activity of singling out cases of counter-norm following, the society at large gains an opportunity to dramatize publicly the norms, and further the social suggestions for their acceptance. The history of burning witches in public places which can be found all over medieval Europe indicates the social relevance of people who have adhered to the counter-norms. If there were no such people, they would have to be invented.[1] In the realm of human sexual conduct, norms and counter-norms are dramatically charted out, and counter-positioned. The latter is most evident in the counter-norm status that homosexuality has for long occupied in different societies of the West – in contrast to being utilized at times as a normative part of human development in Papua New Guinea (see Herdt, 1997; see also Chapter 13).

Sex, relationships and social stigmatization

Sex is a subject matter that varies as to its public presentability immensely across societies and historical time. Together with other physiological processes of the necessary kind (eating, sleeping), it has been a playground for various cultural constructions. In all societies, acting within the domains of these activities is socially regulated by collective-cultural meanings. In some societies, like ours in Europe or North America, that regulation has taken a form of evaluative suppression, or repression.

The development of repression of sexuality has much to do with the Christian religious history of Europe, where the notion of inherent sinfulness of sexual activities has been promoted over 16 centuries. In contrast, in Islamic religious history one can observe efforts to regulate sexual conduct of women without the notion of sex being degrading (Mernissi, 1987). Under conditions of well-developed restrictions upon public conduct of women, the power of female sexuality and its adequacy has been recognized without promotion of guilt feelings for women. In a similar way, Hindu religious history has regulated female sexuality without repression. The sexual power of women is creative power, which has been made to be of crucial significance for the religious system (for example, the role of the *devadasi* or 'heavenly courtesans' in Hindu temples: Kersenboom, 1984). That power can be feared – as is evident in the Kali myth (see Menon and Shweder, 1994) – and efforts may be made to protect the world from the rage of a female deity. Such efforts can entail symbolic prevention – appeasing the feared agent in women (by adoration, gifts to the deity), creating protective omens against their vile power (see Chapter 9 on ways to prevent 'evil eye').

Of course, the powerful other can also be neutralized by turning it from the powerful to the powerless, and promoting the internalization of the latter role in the form of an inferiority complex. This has been the route to cope with female power in the European cultural history. The myth of women's inferiority and repression of sexuality in women – from St Jerome in the 4th century AD to Freud in the twentieth – can be viewed as a pre-emptive control strategy. Stigmatization paired with internalization (by the target of stigmatization) of the meanings on which stigmatization works is a powerful social control means. In numerous societies the opposite – explicit focus on sexual activities in- and out of marital ties (for example, the Xingu Indians in the Amazon region, see Gregor, 1985) – is accepted without repression. The recognition of the pleasurable nature of sexual encounters can even be made into a regulator of marriage, as in the case of the Dusun of Borneo (see below).

Sex and relationships

In different societies we can observe the collective-cultural regulation of acceptable sexual relationships to include different constraints.

The strictest case of limitations is in societies where sex is repressed, and accepted for the task of procreation only. It is assumed to take place in the husband and wife dyad, and only for purposes of getting children. The woman may have internalized embarrassment of sex, and thus controls it, bringing it to a minimum. The possibility of sexual relations with oneself (= masturbation) are likely to be ruled out. Homosexual relations are also ruled out. Like-

wise, extra-marital sexual relations would be ruled out. As a result, sexuality is repressed while being sufficiently available for procreation purposes.

A different pattern emerges from Mehinaku (Xingu, in the Amazon region in South America) social organization of sexuality and relations (Gregor, 1977, 1985). Here the procreational role of sex is recognized, yet made dependent upon the role of spirit action (see below). The spousal relations are fortified through cultural construction of jealousy feelings (and dramatic enactment of jealousy scenes). Hence there is clear social regulation of sexual relations, linked with marriage choices. At the same time, the pleasurable side of sexual encounters is collective-culturally accepted. Extra-marital discreet sexual relationships are an accepted practice, which become publicly dramatized when revealed. So the issue of sexuality is not repressed, but rather enhanced as an ordinary everyday life activity. It has positive emotional flavour, yet can turn into a negative one if it becomes linked with violence. In the Mehinaku social world, women are not supposed to see some of the male sacred activities. If – by coincidence or being nosy – this happens, men are expected to retaliate through gang rape of the woman who transgressed. Women live in fear of gang rape, while positively valuing their extra-marital relations in discreet locations outside the village. The Mehinaku case indicates that sexual relations between persons can be turned simultaneously into positively accepted and sought-for events, and into negatively feared ones (gang rape). The latter of course indicates violence against the person (played out in rape) and does not constitute a sexual relation other than by its physical side.

The contrast between these examples indicates the distinction between cultural *repression* of sexuality and that of cultural *regulation*. The former is an extreme version of the latter. Repression entails personal-cultural blocking of moments of sexual relations at the level of personal feelings; while regulation entails differentiation of acceptable and unacceptable settings for the experience of sexual pleasure.

Cultural regulation of sexuality can lead to the establishment of the role of sexuality as the basis for social order. Thus, the Oneida Community experiment (described in Chapter 6) turned human sexual needs into a vehicle through which the social roles within the small community were constructed. Likewise, the collective-cultural *prescriptions* for *enjoyment* of sexual relations (that is, inevitably a personal-cultural phenomenon) among the Dusun of Borneo (see below), and within the devotional religious (*bhakti*) movements in the history of India, indicate that cultural regulation can take complex forms, going far beyond the simple 'allow/disallow' dichotomy. Even in the history of Christianity-dominated Europe, the Catholic social institutions (in the sixteenth century, see Flandrin, 1985) accommodated to the realities of human sexual feelings and attempted to turn those into a means to secure religious following. The boundaries of the meaning of 'sin' were adjusted to allow for legitimate sexual pleasure in socially legitimate relationships (that is, in marriage), while ruling it out as 'mortal sin' outside.

Identification with the particular religious, ideological, or community norm and belief system can be built by setting up fusion of meanings in contexts of personally pleasurable experience (such as sex can be). A social system, instead of viewing the person's capacity for sensual pleasure (in sex, or otherwise) as a competitor to its collective-cultural system (in which case efforts of repression may be used, as in the history of European Christian traditions), *can view this orientation to pleasure as a potential ally* in accomplishing its goals. In that latter case, the social system may take over the personal pleasure in the service of its social goals. The picture is similar to the operation in the business world – companies may fight with one another to eliminate the other, or, if that proves unproductive, take over the competitor and get it to work for their own goals.

The social appropriation of sexuality takes the form of linking pleasure with specifiable social role or relationship conditions. Personal pleasure – it can be promoted – can be obtained only (or at best) within sexual relations of a particular kind: for example, in relations with the representative of the believed-in deity who may happen to be leader of the given religious group; or with one's husband or wife; or only when efforts are made to conceive a child. The act of pleasure may be viewed as of supernatural origin – thus fortifying the notion of the fusion of the here-and-now pleasurable event (for example, sexual intercourse) with collective-cultural social values and goals. When the partners in sexual intercourse believe that they serve their gods by way of maximally enjoying the process of such intercourse, the very private feelings of persons are appropriated by the social system through the new meaning given to a behavioural act (copulation) of a basic biological kind. Note that the cultural regulation in this case forms a mutual feedback loop – the pleasure in sex is viewed (by the believers) as given by the deities, and it pleases the deities further. What is at stake under these conditions is the persons' relationships with the supernatural world, rather than their 'satisfaction of primary needs'.

CULTURAL FRAMING OF CONCEPTION

Socio-institutional regulation of human sexuality is the basis for any cultural framing of conception. It creates the differences in the ways in which conceiving a baby can take place. Thus, in a case of a society with repression of sexuality, the goal of conception may be the only one that legitimizes sexual intercourse. In the case of a society where (as described below) the pleasurable nature of sexual intercourse is believed to lead to conception, sexuality within marriage (or within desired relationships) can be enhanced, with the goal of conception in mind.

Dusun beliefs about conception and pregnancy

The Dusun (on Borneo, Indonesia) believe that conception is possible in the 'hot state' of the male and female substances. They explain conception through reference to the observable phenomenon of sexual partners' mutually growing excitement in the process of intercourse. On the basis of this knowledge, the Dusun assume that this excitement leads to the 'heating up' of the blood of the partners in their sexual organs. Semen is considered to be a special case of 'hot blood'. The woman during intercourse is believed to have her blood concentrate in her abdomen, where it becomes hotter and hotter until a point is reached when it begins to 'boil' and turns into 'steam'. At this point, which is believed to be female orgasm, the baby is assumed to be conceived. The mother's 'steam-like drops of blood' (sexual fluids) and the father's semen jointly create the baby (Williams, 1969, p. 34).

The Dusun explanation of conception has all the bases in common life realities. Aside from its ordinariness, such belief has a number of properties that operate as regulators of male/female gender role relations. First, female orgasm becomes not only a desired, but a culturally necessary goal, in the marital intercourse. Orientation towards sexual pleasure (reaching orgasm) becomes a central part of the woman's gender role, and in her marital role as the wife. It becomes also a marker of personal decision (for example, the woman deciding to have a child from 'that man' marks it with orgasm in intercourse; while deciding not to want a child to be conceived would be marked by no 'heat in the blood'). For the man, the woman's sexual experience (enjoyment) becomes a necessary goal – not for the sake of the woman, but for the desire to have offspring.

The Dusun belief system includes the *necessity of continuing mixing of hot blood* for the successful advancement of pregnancy. The fetus is believed to grow on the basis of constant nourishment by the hot blood of the mother and the father. As a result, there would be a collective-cultural expectation for a married couple's intensification of pleasurable sexual intercourse during the wife's pregnancy.

Segregation of knowledge by social position

Knowledge about conception and pregnancy reveals the inadequacy of considering all members of the given society as 'sharing' a 'common knowledge base'. In fact, power within society is created through limited access to some aspects of cultural knowledge. The secrecy of native herbal medicines can be considered part of their healing power, and the local medicine man would not reveal it publicly. Some knowledge is based on gender roles, which specify persons' social positions. Telefolmin men's and women's knowledge about conception is a good example. It should not be expected that all members of a given society share the understanding of how conception takes place. Childbearing is already biologically set up as an unequal event – females can have offspring directly, but males only through the females. So already by this biological limit, the direct knowledge about birth is available only to the birth-giving females, and ruled out in principle in the case of males. In the biological world, males and females have adjusted to such asymmetry. It is only in the human case where issues like participation by the male in the process of giving birth to a child becomes set up. No self-respecting male chimpanzee comes up with the idea that he should be present when a female gives birth to (possibly) his offspring. Yet in the human case, males can go to great extremes trying to secure their rights of participation in this event.

Within human societies, the two genders separate the relevant knowledge about conception, pregnancy and childbirth. As a result, males need not have elaborate folk-knowledge about how conception takes place and how fetuses develop, while women can have many stories to tell on that subject matter. Hiding information is a way to control it, and through that regulate one's social status in the society.

The case of the Telefolmin society (from the Sepik Region, in Papua New Guinea) gives us an example of gender separation of the knowledge of conception. Jorgensen (1983) revealed an unsophisticated pattern of knowledge about conception among the men, and a differentiated one among the women. The men (who were reluctant to talk about the topic) reported the idea that babies were formed by the combination of sexual secretions ('penis water' – *et ok*; 'vagina fluid' – *nok kul*) during intercourse. Repeated acts of intercourse were deemed to be necessary for the woman to become pregnant – since the semen had to accumulate to build the fetus. Once pregant, the intercourse should stop, as its continuation could lead to development of twins, which was undesirable.

The women's version of conception and pregnancy included topics that were unmentionable for males – the role of the menstrual blood. On the basis of the common knowledge (of women) of the cessation of menstruation during pregnancy, a conclusion was reached that the unexpended menstrual blood builds up the baby's bones during the fetal period.

Food and procreation

Behind the relevance of the blood (transformed into semen for men, and sexual fluids by women) is the basic process of eating different foods, and the preparation of those foods. Different foods can make the blood ready to 'become hot', others would calm (cool) it down.

The act of eating is in many societies related with the act of sexual intercourse, and sexual relations. This carries over to the semantic fields of words in a given language. The Asante Twi (in Ghana, West Africa) use the same verb (*di*) for eating and sex. That verb has many other meanings of possession, taking, inheriting etc. (Clark, 1994, p. 345). The act of food preparation (rather than sexual relation, even if the two may overlap) among the Asante is a marker of close relations. A woman cooking food for a man, and bringing food to the man, is establishing an intimate relation with the man. The activity of 'cooking for' becomes equal to 'living with'. Furthermore, it is usually exchange of foods that is utilized in regulation of social relationships in many societies.

The Xingu (Amazonian Indian tribes) indicate a direct connection between food, sexual prowess and conception (Gregor, 1985). Manioc flour is a staple crop for preparing food and drink. It is simultaneously a symbol of sexual power. The manioc flour (and other foods based on it) is produced by women (see Figure 8.1). The consumption of foods produced by women is understood to lead to the build-up of the sexual power of the men. Gregor's success in getting the Mehinaku (Xingu) villagers to try to draw the insides of a man, produced results that show the connection from the throat to the 'semen holder' (*yaki nain*) made directly (see Figure 8.2A). Men are aware that the female-produced foods – especially manioc products – generate sexual power and general health. The centrality of women's role is evident here – women prepare the powerful food, men consume it, and return the (processed) food to women in the form of their semen in intercourse.

However, the intercourse *by itself* is not believed to lead to conception. The 'baby holder' (*yamakunain*, the Mehinaku reference to the

FIGURE 8.1 *A Mehinaku woman preparing manioc flour (from Gregor, 1985, p. 83, reprinted by permission from University of Chicago Press)*

uterus) is ordinarily considered closed. If a woman wants it to 'become open', she eats roots that resemble men's or women's genitals, thus indicating not only the desire to open the 'baby holder' (become pregnant) but also what gender of child is desired by her (Gregor, 1985, p. 88). It is only after the woman's decision to have a child that the pregnancy is believed to happen.

There are two folk theories about conception among the Mehinaku villagers. First, fetal development is believed to depend upon semen accumulation. The uterus 'snatches' the semen and the creation of the baby begins. On the basis of semen accumulation, the fetal body becomes formed: head first, then the rest of the body. This first folk account is an example of *humoral explanation* of conception and fetal development. Different liquids (humours) become mixed and transformed in the process.

Secondly, the Mehinaku villagers adhere to a supernatural account of conception and fetal development. There exists a belief that a tiny woman – 'Grandmother Spirit' (*Yumeweketu* or *Atsikuma*) – lives just outside of the womb (see Figure 8.2*B*). The role of the 'Grandmother Spirit' is to mould and shape the incoming semen, so as to create the baby from it. She is also considered

to play a role in making the pregnancy proceed smoothly, and to pre-tell the mother (in her dreams) about the baby's future gender. Thus, the humoral and supernatural belief systems about conception and pregnancy are mutually supportive of each other in explaining the different outcomes.

This mutual support creates an explanatory complex that is both in line with common sense observations and with constructed supernatural explanations. The important moment in this complex is the transition from one to the other – women (that is, *real persons*) make foods (manioc products) which are *believed to* turn into sexual fluids. The latter get real persons (women and men) into sexual intercourse. Yet it is the *believed-in personified force* (spirit, in this case the ancestor's) that is seen as making the decision about whether the conception will take place, and the fetus be created. The everyday life (observationally verifiable) parts of this explanatory complex lend legitimacy to the supernatural one, and the latter makes the former meaningful. In some cases, the role of the supernatural component of the explanatory complex is most prominent, as in the case of the Bellonese.

Conception and the role of ancestors: Bellona islanders

As procreation is a way to continue human clan lineages, it is thus not merely a matter pertaining to the mother (of the baby to be) and the father. It is this embedding in the lineage that is usually integrated with the process of conception. As was seen above, conception is usually explained through some 'liquids mixing' and supernatural processes. The latter entail both immediate supernatural agents (such as the Mehinaku 'Grandmother Spirit' projected into the immediate neighbourhood of the uterus), and the mediated relating to deities.

The case of Bellona islanders (a small atoll among the Solomon Islands, half-way between Papua New Guinea and New Caledonia) is a good example of the latter (mediated) supernatural agent-making. The population of the island is small (428 inhabitants in 1938, when the island first encountered Christianity through missionaries). Through the efforts of Danish anthropologist Torben Monberg (1975, 1991) the indigenous system of the pre-1938 period of the Bellona Island is documented.

The dominant form of social organization among the Bellonese was patrilineal descent at different structural levels – those of clan and group. Marriages were patrilocal: the new wife joins her husband in the latter's natal household. Hence the extended family – in the Bellonese case extended so as to include deceased relatives – was

A Interior of a man

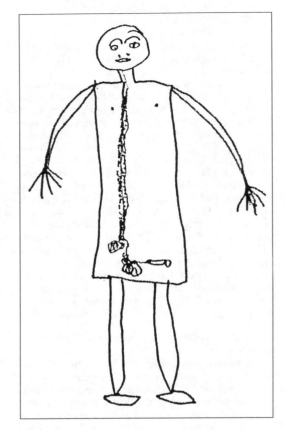

B Depiction of gestation

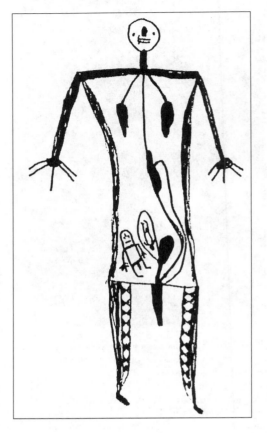

Explanation of A
A tube leads from the throat through the spine [dotted lines] to the organ called 'semen holder', which turns feminine foods (manioc-based) into semen

Explanation of B
Grandmother Spirit acts upon the baby in the womb. The substance of the fetus is semen, supplied through repeated sexual intercourse. The mother's consumption of manioc foods is carried to the breasts (where it becomes milk)

FIGURE 8.2 *Mehinaku drawings of the interior of a human being (from Gregor, 1985, p. 87 and 89, reprinted by permission from University of Chicago Press)*

the location for all childbearing. The Bellonese believed that the crucial role in producing off-spring was in the hands of deities, who could be approached most easily by the deceased relatives. Hence the practice of turning to the spirits of the patrilineal ancestors (at their gravesites) to ask for their assistance in persuading the deities to make the wife pregnant. The husband would enter into such communication with the ancestors – yet it is clear that success in this need not be guaranteed (Monberg, 1991, Chapter 10). The ancestors may succeed, or not – and for different reasons. First, they may be insufficiently close to the deities,

and hence ineffective. Secondly, they may be dissatisfied with the applicants – because of something they do (that is, think that they do).

The latter dissatisfaction can act as an omnipresent social control agent (the watchful eye of the ancestors). The belief in the critical role of the ancestors and deities in 'sending the child' to the wife of the living relative was supported by everyday observations. If a naive observer were to study conception through the use of correlational techniques – correlating frequency of copulation with acts of conception – the relationship might be less than clear. The same was true for everyday observers of life on Bellona; intercourse happens as a natural part of daily activities, yet it is only sometimes that a pregnancy results from it. Thus, the cultural construction of the notion that the woman becomes pregnant because of her husband's ancestors and deities 'send the child' with the common life uncertainties.

Unusual outcomes of pregnancy – miscarriages, twins etc. – were all explained as expressions of the 'ancestors' will'. By insisting on the absolute role of the patrilineal descent in the process of getting and being pregnant, the collective-cultural belief system created its own power base. Such explanation can never be proven false, and it has embedded in itself possibilities to explain each and every event that can happen.

Consider the question of why a child looks like his or her mother. The Bellonese had a simple answer – this occurs because there is an affiliation with the mother's father – and his patrilineage. How can unmarried women (rare as they would be) have children? Again, her ancestors on her father's side are to be thanked (or blamed). Can a married woman who has extra-marital affairs be impregnated by a man other than her husband? No, since it is not the male partner in sexual intercourse, but her husband's ancestors who cause the conception.

Summary: the generic explanatory complex of conception

The examples above are only a brief glimpse into the comparative-cultural materials on explanation of conception. Is there any common universal model that caters for all of the variation between societies? In Figure 8.3, an attempt is made to elaborate such a model.

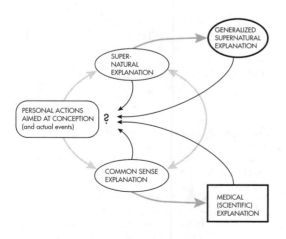

FIGURE 8.3 *A model of generic cultural explanation of conception*

The coordination between different parts of the generic cultural explanatory system depicted in Figure 8.3 can be seen as universal, rather than limited to the specific issue of conception. It is realistic to find the presence of some notion of the supernatural world in all human societies (see Steadman et al., 1996). It may appear at moments of personal stress, hence the supernatural component of the story is present even in cases where explainers claim to be fully 'scientifically rational'. The meaning-making process of the person moves constantly in the circle from actual experiences (for example, becoming, or not – yet – becoming pregnant, ill etc.) and common sense explanations in parallel with supernatural explanations. From the latter it can proceed to higher-level explanations being brought into the explanation – either on the side of generalized supernatural explanations, or through a turn to scientific knowledge. In the process of formal education (see Chapter 12), some of these parts of the system can be selectively blocked or eliminated: thus, for instance, Western schooling will result in the supernatural explanations for the given issue being blocked. A formally educated Bellonese islander of the present day may fully deny the participation of the ancestors' spirits in persuading the gods to make his wife pregnant. Instead, he may search for scientific knowledge to find out what may be wrong. Yet he may retain the relevance of generalized supernatural explanation as an unverifiable 'final explainer' of the issue: medical science explains how in reality the sperm fertilizes the ovum, but when and how that may happen is still 'heavenly will'.

The crucial integration ground of the different explanatory notions in Figure 8.3 is the domain indicated by '**?**'. Different explanations enter into mutually divisive (conflictual) or combinatorial relations precisely here – next to the next life event of the person which needs to be explained as it is happening. A number of different explanations are possible here:

1 The *either/or relation*. The supernatural and the common sense explanations can be in competition with each other. If one is perceived as appropriate at the time, the other is rejected (and vice versa). The ultimate result of this competition is the suppression of the other – either the supernatural explanations suppress the medical ones, or vice versa. This is the case where the rationality of the medical science replaces the cultural constructions of human beings.

2 The *and relation*. Both explanatory systems support each other – the supernatural explanations can specify further the operation of common sense ones (for example, cases where

sexual intercourse is accepted as necessary for conception, yet ancestors' desires would count as sufficient for it).

3 The *'pecking order' relation*. The two kinds of explanations can be set up in an order – either beginning with supernatural ones, and ending with the scientific ones (in case of no pregnancy, the woman first turns to the ancestors, but as a last resort to Western medical science); or vice versa (for example, the woman first tries out all medical means to get pregnant, but at a certain moment adds religious prayers to the complex of the treatment). This relation is widespread in Western medical practices in case of treating terminal illness – when all medical means fail, the psychological coping moves into the realm of supernatural constructions.

The functioning of this generic explanatory system becomes particularly evident in the case of events that are prolonged in time, and do not happen as expected immediately. Continuing illnesses (see Keck, 1993 for an example of co-ordination of indigenous and scientific treatments in New Guinea) are one such example, the failure to conceive another.

When conception fails: cultural treatment of infertility

In every society, women are under collective-cultural pressure to participate in the production of offspring. It is only in the case of contemporary industrialized and urbanized societies – and especially as a result of formal education – that the possibility of deciding not to have children has become gradually available. Yet even in these societies it is veiled in ambivalence, both at the level of collective-cultural suggestions, and in the personal-cultural constructions by individual women themselves of their life course.

In most societies, the failure to conceive is a major personal and social crisis. The crisis is centred on the woman (who does not conceive), rather than the male (who actually can be the reason of the failure). It evokes efforts to help the woman to conceive, yet if these efforts fail (or are perceived by others to fail because of the woman's own counteraction), it leads to social stigmatization. Barren women in most societies are viewed as potentially dangerous: they can be assumed to be 'witches'; their looking at other women's children may be deemed to carry 'the evil eye'. Thus, there is a major social price attached to barrenness in all societies.

Under such pressure, looking to supernatural support systems for the purposes of avoiding infertility – or overcoming the increasing danger of appearing barren – women turn to appropriate cultural mediating sources. For example, consider the case of the Aowin (in South-West Ghana: Ebin, 1982). The Aowin are matrilineal in descent. The local king appoints female spirit mediums and empowers them with symbols of spiritual relevance. Appropriately to the matrilinearity of descent, Aowin women (similarly to women in many other West African ethnic groups) are in a powerful role in the society. Their power is closely connected with fertility – not only of themselves (in the form of childbearing), but also of the land they cultivate. It is the fertility in general that is aimed at in the cultural co-construction of the lives of women and men. Childbearing is one part of such fertility.

Aowin women are assumed to have special mystical powers that allow them to bear children. Yet, like any power, if not adequately used, it can become dangerous. In the Aowin case, misused reproductive power is believed to turn the woman into a witch. Guidance as to how to contain the power is given to girls in their adolescent initiation ritual. The focus of the guidance is to direct the reproductive powers towards procreation within the social role system of the society.

In case of impending infertility (that is, women going to consult the spirit medium after not conceiving for a period of time, beyond the expected), witchcraft explanations are the most natural resorts. According to Aowin belief, witches are barren women who go naked through the night, sometimes flying upside down. The witch eats not with her mouth but with her anus, meeting her friends at night in the tall trees (Ebin, 1982, p. 148). Barren women are believed to 'eat children' (instead of bearing them). Here the reversal of the role is evident:

FERTILE WOMAN → BARREN WOMAN
{WITCH}

=

ORDINARY ROLE (giving birth) → REVERSE
(eating babies)

The power of the woman is believed to be reversely directed – instead of supporting her matrilineal kin, she attacks it. The social world is set up so as to do its utmost to prevent such reversals from happening, yet when they do happen, these are seen as legitimate counter-norm examples and are treated accordingly.

What constitutes such attacks? Any kind of friction within the given social system – quarrels with neighbours or co-wives, jealousy, envy, disrespect to elders – can become linked with the witchcraft estimations. A woman's anxiety

FIGURE 8.4 *An Aowin woman makes offerings to the river god and asks him to grant her a child (from Ebin, 1982, p. 153, reprinted by permission from Academic Press)*

Cultural models of childbearing age of women

The collective-cultural suggestions for childbearing are strictly organized along the age dimension, although in many societies other than ours the precise age of a person is less relevant than the age measured by way of passing sets of life cycle rituals. Yet we can chart out, along the scale of age, how and when women are exposed to different social expectations of childbearing (Figure 8.5).

Two (fictive) societies are represented in Figure 8.5. Society A is one with relatively late (in relation to the biological beginning of possible childbearing) positive promotion of conception, and negative pressure against conception during the teenage years. This may resemble the case in our contemporary United States, where 'teenage pregnancy' is constantly narratively constructed as a 'problem', and where focus on prolonged education delays women's childbearing in their life course age. At the same time, Society A is quite permissive at the prime childbearing age (20s and 30s), accepting negative orientations towards conception, and allowing women to decide to stay childless (for example, the minimum limit of the 'social push' does not reach the 'neutral pressure line'). By the time of the biological end of childbearing possibilities, the 'social push' minimum and maximum return to 0.

about not conceiving a child (that is, her personal-cultural fear of barrenness) is turned into a collective-cultural mechanism of regulation of social life. The woman (who is consulting an Aowin spirit medium – who is another woman) may be told by the medium that she does not conceive because of a spell cast by some other person (witch). Or she may be told that she is a witch herself, and therefore is not conceiving. As a remedy, the woman may go through a purification ritual (see Figure 8.4), and her social relationships in her own home compound are analysed by the spirit medium.

Women turning to deities to grant them children is a cultural practice all over the world. In secularized modern conditions, it is the powers of contemporary medicine to which infertile women now turn. The success of this recourse obviously depends on the biological and technological sides of the procedures. However, psychologically the phenomena of handling the escape from infertility remain the same in modern days as these were in the Aowin case.

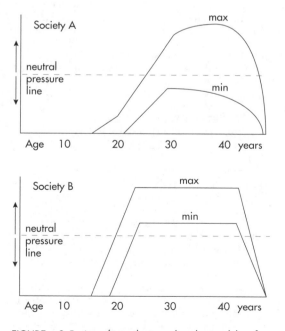

FIGURE 8.5 *Age-dependent cultural models for acceptability of conception*

Society B presents a very different picture. Acceptability and social push towards conception here begins quickly after menarche, and becomes prescriptively uniformly high in the major child-bearing decades. The minimum of the 'push' is above the line of neutrality. In Society B women would have to fight with their social environments – and with their own internalized personal cultures – if they of their own will want to live their lives not bearing children. They will have to deviate from the social norm, set by the collective-cultural model.

The end of the pressures towards conception comes here more abruptly. It can be marked by the woman's change of the status into becoming a grandmother (in many societies, that indicates the end of culturally acceptable childbearing). Society B is more likely to include coordinated social regulation through life cycle rituals – from an adolescent rite of passage (which legitimizes adult sexual status and may lead to marriage), to requirement for the marriage (at the threat of divorce) to have children, followed by the social construction of the success of the woman's life course accomplishments with each new birth.

The hypothetical cultural models depicted in Figure 8.5 make it possible to discover guaranteed misunderstandings in communication between Society A and Society B. When A looks at B, the 'problem' of 'teenage pregnancy' is easily detected. This is the case when a Euro-American cultural model is used to evaluate Afro-American teenage pregnancy patterns in the United States. When B looks at A, the women can be viewed as 'deprived of their accomplishment' because of the delay in their main task (childbearing) and because of the lack of consistency in the guidance towards conception.

CONSTRUCTION OF MEANINGS OF HUMAN DEVELOPMENT DURING PREGNANCY

In conjunction with the discovery of the biological state of being pregnant, the persons most involved with the pregnancy (the woman, her female kinfolk, the husband) become involved in the construction of the meaning of the developing baby. The child enters into the culturally constructed world long before actually being born – through the meaningful constructions set forth to make sense of fetal development. The contemporary heated controversy in the United States about 'when does life begin' (from which the socio-moral fights about acceptability or rejection of abortion at will emerges) is merely one domain of such meaning construction process. The more important feature (than practical decisions) is the explanation of the beginnings of the psychological life of the child, and its connections with the world of parents, and ancestors at large.

The universal cultural meaning that is used in any society to mark the cultural beginning of the person as person is the attribution of the status of 'soul' (in its many, language-specific, versions, which include the notion of 'baby' in the United States) to be the identity of the offspring. The specific age of the offspring – counted from conception – can vary. The 'soul' concept may be assigned to the embryo, fetus, newborn, infant when it begins to walk, or to the child when he or she can perform concrete tasks.

Among the tribes in the Altai mountain region (of Turkic language background), it is believed that the soul of the person (which is simultaneously his/her life power) – qut – is sent to the baby by the Mother-Creator. It lives in the mother's belly in the form of a 'red worm' (gysyl qurt). The semantic field of qut also includes the notion of happiness, success. The latter can be extended to relevant objects – qut also is a meaning applicable to amulets for the protection of cattle (Baskakov and Yaimova, 1997, pp. 10–11).

Collective-cultural constructions of the inherent essence ('soul' and its approximate equivalents in different languages) has corollaries in the efforts to diagnose the state of the fetus, its gender, and to predict its future. The development of every child, from conception onwards, is filled with uncertainties. Thus it is not surprising that expectant (and later, newly become) parents should be interested in some predictions for the future, so as to reduce the uncertainties. Much of such effort takes place in the symbolic domain.

Prediction of the child's sex has been relevant in many societies. As was shown above, that prediction is linked with the preference for one or the other sex. The Bellonese would turn to their ancestors to ask for a male child to be sent, so as to continue the patriline. Depending upon the socioeconomic organization of a society, one or the other gender may carry a societal preference. Thus, in most patrilineal descent based societies, it is the male gender that is desired; while in matrilineal cases the preference can be reversed. The socioeconomic activities of the society may lead to specific preferences. For example, the Kanjar (nomadic people in Pakistan – see Berland, 1982) prefer the birth of girls to that of boys.

Symbolic means of predicting the sex of the child can take many forms. Some of those include the use of symbolic objects. Thus, a British middle-class woman reiterates: 'My mother-in-law told me about . . . putting your wedding ring . . . on a chain or piece of string, and if it turns to the left [while held, on the string, over the abdomen of the pregnant woman] it's a boy and if it turns to the right it's a girl' (Homans, 1982, p. 248). The immediate linking of this super-natural testing procedure with the symbolic nature of the marital status (not *any* ring but the woman's wedding ring needs to be used) is notable here. During pregnancy, the woman is not only culturally guided towards having the child, but also towards her continuing social role in the framework of the given kinship network.

CULTURAL REGULATION OF WOMEN'S CONDUCT DURING PREGNANCY

While the fetus is developing – biologically – in the womb, the womb-owner is being culturally guided towards her new role in her collective-cultural world. Regulation of women's conduct during their pregnancies entails, in parallel, new ways of constraining their actions, thinking and feeling, as well as providing them with a new, powerful symbolic role, which is exemplified by the alteration of other restrictions. The full texture of the altered constraints guides the woman towards her new role as a mother.

Human actions are the best targets for social regulations, since they can be publicly visible. The same is true for speech. As was indicated in Chapter 7, many communicative messages are made public by selective silences, or through implicit allusions. Often this is the case about issues that are believed to be too dangerous for direct address (that is, linked with potential action of malevolent deities, or actions that may simply 'bring bad luck').

Cultural marking of being pregnant: personal and collective

It is most likely the woman who becomes pregnant who discovers the fact first. She will then establish some form of reference to this, her new status. It can be immediately publicly displayed, and shared with a special celebration. Alternatively, it can be downplayed. For instance, among the Baganda, women do not refer to their pregnancy directly. There is no word for fetus in their language, and very little social talk about development of the baby during pregnancy. When a woman publicly announces she is preg-nant she uses terminology far removed from the actual realm of expecting a child – such as 'I am not normal', 'some disorder has caught me' or even 'syphilis has caught me' (Kilbride and Kilbride, 1990, p. 104). It is remarkable that the illness concept (syphilis) is used as a masking reference to the state of being pregnant.

Within the personal-cultural domain, the woman can either downplay the presentation of her pregnancy (as in the example above), accept it in a matter-of-fact fashion, or create a personally important affective symbolic event out of this presentation. This may entail verbal communi-cation, or merely become indicated by special kinds of pregnancy clothes the woman makes (or buys) and begins wearing. All public presen-tations of one's pregnant status are simultane-ously self-presentations to the woman herself. They operate as semiotic self-guiding devices.

The collective-cultural meaning system may set up specific ritualistic practices to explicitly recog-nize a woman's pregnancy. In Japan, the tradition included the pregnancy sash (*iwata-obi* or *hara-obi*). This is a white cotton sash 4 metres in length, which usually was acquired from a temple, with luck-bringing inscriptions written on it by a monk (or, in modern cases, sometimes by an obstetrician – see Figure 8.6). The sash was to be worn by the pregnant woman at around 5 months into pregnancy (which was the time by which the pregnancy was considered established). It is a cultural marker of the solidity of the pregnancy, and prepares the woman for childbirth. The sash is worn tied around the abdomen, so as to 'prevent the stomach from chilling', to 'feel good', to keep the fetus from 'growing too large' (Ohnuki-Tierney, 1984, pp. 182–184). It consti-tutes a kind of symbolic corset that supports the pregnant woman on her approach to childbirth.

Restrictions on the pregnant woman's actions during pregnancy

The world of pregnant women is filled with culturally created restrictions. These may vary immensely from one society to another, and change dramatically over the history of the given society. When looked upon from our vantage

FIGURE 8.6 *An obstetrician in a contemporary Japanese hospital has written a red character of celebration and good luck on the pregnancy sash of his patient. (from Ohnuki-Tierney, 1984, p. 182, reprinted by permission from Cambridge University Press and Emiko Ohnuki-Tierney)*

point, across culture and with the habit of trusting the mythology of contemporary medicine, these action restrictions may strike us with their illogicality.

For example, consider the data from Sierra Leone (Table 8.1). Here we can see how specific activities have become linked with premonition for physical or symbolic problems at childbirth. It is important to remember that the data in this table come from an anthropologist's investigation of the leading (more knowledgeable) informants from among a women's secret society. In this sense, the data are not representative for the society as a whole, as different women in the same society have differential knowledge of this list of restrictions. We here have an exaggerated (or concentrated) picture that need not apply to each case. However, some subset of these restrictions will be in place.

There is a general picture. Certain physical antecedents are believed to be linked with physical consequences (abortion, premature labour, umbilical cord problems, difficult birth positions). Yet the role of supernatural agents is also embedded in the texture of these restrictions. This is particularly the case with erotic dreams of the woman, which may concern sexual relations with men other than the husband. The valuable and desired outcome – the uncomplicated birth of a healthy child – is used by the collective-cultural restrictions system to constrain the woman's intra-psychological (personal-cultural) world.

There are meaningful themes embedded in the table. First, the woman is expected to alter some aspects of her everyday household work (for example, lifting heavy loads, fishing, or washing heavy clothes). Secondly, the woman's sexual relations are re-organized. Sexual relations with

TABLE 8.1 *Collective-culturally defined threats to pregnancy and childbirth among the Mende and Sherbro in Sierra Leone*

Description of Activity	Explanation of negative effects
Taking purgative herbs (for example, *Morinda geminata*)	A laxative that can lead to abortion
Lifting heavy loads / Fishing for a long time with a hand net / Washing heavy clothes such as cotton blankets	Cause abortion or premature labour
Not moving during pregnancy	Causes uterus to become inert
Frequent intercourse (especially with a man other than husband)	Causes abortion, ante-partum haemorrhage, premature labour, or difficult birth
Erotic dreams / Dreams of intercourse with another man resembling her husband	Witchcraft
Dreams of another man different from her husband	Spirits of the wild
Wearing brassière or wrapping dressing cloth around the neck (rather than waist)	Causes the umbilical cord to wrap around the baby's neck
Standing at crossroads	Causes transverse lie presentation
Using pit latrine	Causes buttocks presentation
Lying on an easy chair or hammock / Intruding noisily in other people's affairs	Causes face presentation
Walking at night without a knife tied in the dressing cloth for protection	Causes fooling breach of an abnormal baby
Bathing or defecating outdoors at night	Will be seen by spirits of the wild and result in an abnormal baby
Standing in a doorway	Results in obstructed labour
Setting out on a journey with a head load and returning to collect a forgotten item	Leads to difficult labour

Source: C.P. MacCormack (1982) 'Health, fertility and birth in Moyamba District, Sierra Leone', in C.P. MacCormack (ed.), *Ethnography of Fertility and Birth*. (London: Academic Press). p. 136

other men are supposed to be diminished, both in practice and even in her dreams. Finally, we can see a case of analogical transfer of the notion of the *woman's* wearing anything around her neck, to the *baby's* wrapping of the umbilical cord around its neck.

Among the Baganda (in Uganda, see Kilbride and Kilbride, 1990, p. 104) it was believed that a pregnant woman could not sit on the same mat on which a man had sat, nor use the same cup or dish that he had used. When walking in the forest, the woman had to push away the grass along her path with a stick so as to chase off evil spirits.

In general – *redundant control mechanisms are set in motion to regulate pregnant women's conduct.* Similarly to the issue of conception, carrying the fetus until delivery is a valued cultural goal, reaching which is made to be conditional upon particular ways of acting, linked with the actions of supernatural agents. Spirits who 'see' the woman 'defecating outdoors at night' (see Table 8.1) are believed to make the baby abnormal. A concrete act (of biological necessity) is linked with the invisible, believed-in actions of powerful 'social others', who may cause an unwanted outcome. Given such redundancy, any everyday life action can be linked with any problem of childbirth, through the intermediate causal attribution to the 'bad will' of the spirits. The physical (real) events are linked with the person's wilful action (or refraining from it) through the construction of the supernatural agents. In a way, the more extraordinary the specific action restrictions on pregnant women are, the more plausible can be the suggested supernatural explanation.

SOCIAL CONTEXTS OF FOOD-RELATED ISSUES IN PREGNANCY

As was described above, food is more basic than most other issues of human lives (such as, sex) in the cultural regulation of human conduct. Hence it is not surprising that in relevant life course symbolic transformation rituals – such as marking birth, adulthood, marriage and death – food is constantly present in the ritual context.

Food and eating as cultural construction sites
Food-related actions are a constant focus of human collective-cultural attention, as the very process of getting food, processing food and providing food to the hungry or not-so-hungry people (for example, Western restrictions along the lines of 'weight-watching') is inherently one of cultural regulation of personal cultural worlds. It may be said that with every bite of food a human being eats, culture is being transformed from the collective-cultural to the personal-

cultural domain. What we eat (for example, being carnivorous or vegetarian; in the case of the former, eating chicken but not rat), how we eat (with hands or food-transport utensils), where we eat (home, or public place), and with whom we eat (immediate family, or social group) are all occasions for co-construction of personal cultures. Among the Kel Ewey Tuaregs in Niger, the act of eating can have social importance in terms of 'the evoking of good thoughts on the tasting of good foods' (*santi* – see Rasmussen, 1996, p. 66). Such comments – brief semiotic markers – indicate the psychological functions of eating occasions. Drinking 'to your health' (of liquids that often are not so healthy) in our society indicates a similar canalization occasion.

Furthermore, the collective-cultural identities of whole ethnic groupings can be organized through some foods, which become symbolic markers. Thus, the central role of rice in Japan (Ohnuki-Tierney, 1993) has been analysed in detail. Similarly, the cuisines in France, Italy, Germany (for example, the playing-out of German regional identities on the basis of different kinds of breads) can be viewed as creating food-based collective identity vehicles. This can happen also around the issue of drink – from Russian vodka to German beer to American coke. All in all, food intake is the basic nutritional process that is central for our biological survival. Furthermore, it constitutes the connection point of the organism-produced bodily fluids with substances taken in from outside, which play a role in the production of such bodily fluids. Collective-culturally it becomes transferred into a symbolic context, with functions different from its nutritional base.

Pregnancy and eating activities

When a woman enters pregnancy, her culinary habits change, both through biological reasons (development of craving for certain foods, and aversion for others) and by way of collective-cultural reorganization of her diet (social suggestions to eat some foods, and refrain from eating others). Furthermore, the cultural side can interpenetrate with the biological side – a woman may begin to crave (= unexplained biological urge) some foods that have a particular cultural role in the life of a given society (that is, the cultural domain). The changes in food-related actions during pregnancy are thus an intricate area for cultural-psychological analysis.

Food cravings and aversions during pregnancy
In general, about 30 to 70 per cent of pregnant women are expected to have some craving or

aversion. *Food cravings* are spontaneous irresist-ible urges to eat some particular foods. Pregnant women most often crave for fruits and fruit drinks, pickles, sweet foods such as ice cream or jam, vegetables, nuts and meat. In some cases, pregnant women are known to develop cravings for objects which are not considered edible in the collective-cultural system of meanings. These may include dirt, clay, plaster, coal, charcoal, ashes, or sand; or among living creatures, lizards, frogs, spiders, flies etc. She might even display cannibalistic cravings. Our modern technological productivity increases the list of craving objects – to include soap, toothpaste, chalk, ground cement and pencil erasers. In the psychiatric meaning system, such 'out of the ordinary' cravings have the name of *pregnancy pica*. Yet giving unusual cravings a fancy name does not explain their origin, which remains unknown in the complexity of the human biological organism.

Food aversions entail intense, emotional and physiological dislike of some foods, their smell, or taste. Pregnant women often become aversive to foods they usually eat or cook (see the Sinhalese case of aversion to rice, below), or even to those they had liked previously. These aversions disappear after the pregnancy is over.

Collective-cultural meaning systems accom-modate to the potential pregnancy cravings and aversions of foods. Provision can be made by the immediate social environment of the pregnant woman to satisfy at least some of the cravings. Prohibitions against not satisfying such cravings may build links with undesirable outcomes of pregnancy. For instance, in rural Ireland there exists a belief that if cravings are not satisfied, the child will be born with the tongue 'hanging out'. Yet the collective-cultural regulatory system (encoded in myths and folk stories) sets limits upon such granting of power to pregnant women who crave foods. Thus, on the Dingle peninsula in Ireland, the story of a pregnant wife and her husband taking a walk has been re-told:

> The woman suddenly craved a piece of her husband's flesh. Reluctantly, he obliged her. They walked a bit further and she asked for a second bite. Again the husband gave in to the bizarre craving. When the woman asked for a third bite, however, the husband pushed her over the cliffs into Dingle Bay. When she was washed ashore, 3 infants were found in her womb. (Scheper-Hughes, 1982, p. 275)

As all folk stories are creative reconstructions of reality, they provide the collective-cultural communication system (which used to be that of story-telling, or gossip) with symbolic material for creating moral messages. The limits of the satisfaction of cravings are clearly set up. The story recognizes the theme of cannibalistic crav-ings (which in real life milder forms can exist in women's feelings towards the husband, or her baby – exemplified by the joking use of notions of 'wanting to eat up' the other).

Collective-cultural regulation of food cravings in pregnancy needs to deal with extreme and somewhat exotic forms like cannibalistic cravings. It can take also the rather mundane form of transforming a usually non-edible substance into a food for pregnant women (but not for others – anybody eating it while not-pregnant will be looked upon with denigration). For example, Baganda women (in Uganda – Kilbride and Kilbride, 1990, pp. 105–106) frequently crave for eating clay, which has become a collective-culturally approved 'food' for pregnant women. It marks the special situation of pregnancy, yet at the same time becomes a substance for admin-istering herbal medicines (which are mixed with clay and eaten with it). The clay also operates as a means of preservation of the medicinal herbs.

Prescriptions for diet in pregnancy

In any collective-cultural system of meanings there exists notions of recommended, tolerated and undesirable foods for pregnant women. The woman's diet is culturally regulated.

We can include substances such as male sperm and tobacco as belonging to the category of foods. The former belongs to foods because of the close connection between sexual intercourse and food intake in collective-cultural meaning systems (as described above). Tobacco is a food (as well as a poison) in the belief systems of many societies (in South American indigenous folklore for example – see Lévi-Strauss, 1983, pp. 59 and 66). In fact, all substances that human societies use as foods can include ambiguity as to their status (for example, no longer sufficiently fresh food becomes poison-ous, and the freshness of a food is not easy to determine). Our contemporary glancing at the labels of supermarket-mediated foods, being consoled by the symbolic value of labels such as 'fat = 0%' or 'this . . . is 99% fat-free' indicates the supernatural nature of the efforts to find 'good' food through symbolic reassurances (which are forcefully provided by institutions, through authoritative statements on product labels).

Similar reassurances exist in the regulation of the diets of pregnant women in any society. The restrictions of sexual intercourse (or its inten-sification) after becoming pregnant (as described above) are thus part of the dietary reorganization of the pregnant woman's personal-cultural world. The cultural mechanism of such reorganization was clear above: if the fetus is believed to need the *nutrition* from the father through his semen in order to grow, the goal of getting the child is the constrainer of actions during pregnancy. Similarly, different foods that can be eaten during pregnancy are symbolically linked with one or another outcome of the pregnancy. Thus, the Dusun (on Borneo, Indonesia) believe that eating jungle jackfruit leads the 'baby to become a thief', eating the meat of the *red* deer is believed to cause uterine *bleeding* during pregnancy (notice the analogical thinking applied here). Drinking rice wine is linked with possible miscarriage, while chicken broth guarantees that the woman's blood 'stays soft' and continues to promote the normal growth of the child (Williams, 1969, pp. 36 ff).

Each society (at each historical period) creates its own list of suggested and stigmatized foods for pregnant women. Yet the cultural-psychological mechanism of such regulation is the same. *Particular foods become linked with beliefs about particular harms or benefits in the physiological, psychological and social symbolic presentations to the pregnant woman.* She cannot escape the suggestion complex – as she is herself in transition, filled with uncertainties – and she selectively appropriates some of the suggested practices and internalizes in her own ways the meanings used to substantiate the appropriated practices. As a result, a personal-cultural redundant control is established: the pregnant woman acts towards foods in socially suggested ways (which can be observed by others, as the action is publicly visible), and supports such action by her own internalized personal-cultural meaning system. The latter may include her own personal will. For instance, statements like 'I *like to* eat X because *it is good for my baby*') indicate the merging of the personal-cultural will indications ('I like/want/decide X') with generalized social suggestion which obviously is rooted in the collective-cultural domain ('*it is* good/bad for Y' can be constructed on the basis of external social suggestions, as there is no other basis to judge the reality of *this* given food to have *that* effect on *this* fetus).

Culturally regulated food habits in pregnancy and the reorganization of women's social roles

Much more than just the well-being of the fetus during pregnancy is at stake in the food-related interaction of the pregnant woman with her family members. Pregnancy is a temporary stage in the woman's move on in her own life course. The latter is itself collective-culturally canalized, as it involves a change in the social role of the woman with every pregnancy (and with her offsprings' childbearing, which may symbolically end her own, propelling the woman into the role of a grandmother).

Construction of signs – and especially symbols – is the crucial capacity of human beings.

Gananath Obeyesekere (1985) has analysed the symbolic reconstruction of pregnancy food cravings (*dola-duka* or 'desire-suffering') in Sri Lanka in the late 1950s and in 1961 as well as 1966. His comparison of two Sinhalese villages reveals how intricately pregnant women's food cravings reorganize their social roles.

The first case The village of Laggala was at the time of the study relatively remote from direct Buddhist influences. There was no Buddhist temple in the village, and Buddhist ceremonies were rare. In the Laggala context, the relationships between men and women were different from other areas in Sri Lanka: instead of mutual courtesy, the public inter-sex hostility was pronounced. Wife-beating by men, and verbal abuse of husbands by wives in retaliation, were common. Inter-gender distrust was also evident in men's swearing at women.

Such a social environment, filled with male verbal domination and distrust of male–female relationships created a context where women's gender roles were prime ways of changing the current status. During pregnancy, the husband – no matter what his relations with the wife may be – is collective-culturally expected to assist in the running of the household. Under ordinary circumstances, running of the household is fully under the control of the woman.

During pregnancy, women in Laggala were observed to symbolically reject their ordinary role by way of aversion to foods they usually cook. Thus, the smell and taste of the everyday staple food – rice – may become aversive during pregnancy:

> Rice is strongly associated with the social role of women. It is the staple Sinhala food; the woman helps her husband in the fields to make it grow and to reap it. Long hours are spent in drying it in the sun and arduously pounding it in a primitive mortar. The wife cooks rice once or twice a day and *if by chance it is not properly cooked*, or *if she fails to cook it at the right time*, she is invariably *abused and sometimes beaten*. The pots and pans have to be washed and cleaned. No wonder that the women reject rice and cannot stand the smell of rice being cooked. By contrast, *they like cold rice and rice in picnic bags*, which have different symbolical association. (Obeyesekere, 1985, pp. 646–647; added emphasis)

In addition to the aversion to the regular (daily) rice, Laggala pregnant women *craved some foods that they in their ordinary lives were not allowed to eat*. Among those are foods liked by children (sweets, cookies and sour things), foods used exclusively during festivals and visits to kinsmen (these foods mark explicitly the woman's exit from the everyday life roles – as a visitor, she is not cooking herself), and expensive foods (such as grapes).

Some foods are considered to be 'male food' – cigars and cigarettes, alcohol, foods that are linked with phallic symbols in the Sinhalese society. Laggala women were reported to crave for these, as well as for foods that by the prevailing cultural beliefs were dangerous to the baby. For example, pineapples are considered to damage the fetus. Yet Laggala women craved for pineapple, and these cravings had to be satisfied.

According to Obeyesekere (1985), the whole system of gender roles undergoes temporary reversal in Laggala during the wife's pregnancy. For example, as Laggala men are ordinarily dominant over women in the home life, they become subdominant during the wife's pregnancy. A husband who might have previously been beating the wife for not cooking rice by an expected time might now accept her refusal to cook any rice while she is pregnant. Furthermore, he might undertake long trips to buy expensive foods for her in the local town. Or he may have to provide the craving wife with male 'foods' – cigarettes.

Of course this role reversal is temporary; once the pregnancy ends, the roles reverse to a familar state. In this respect, pregnancy can be viewed as filled with moments of carnivalization (in terms of Bakhtin, see Chapter 3), which is a mechanism for temporary regulation of tension in social systems.

The second case   The village of Maedagama (in south Sri Lanka) was under strong Buddhist religious influence. There were several temples in the vicinity. Individuals – both men and women – had integrated the Buddhist notions of status and shame into their personal cultures. Men treated women with formal respect and courtesy. The gender roles were well-defined, and the rules of sexual conduct and standards of modesty were deeply internalized. Premarital sex and adultery were rare. Unlike the women in Laggala, Maedagama women performed important economic activities outside of the home, earning cash at the local tea and rubber plantations.

The reported food cravings of the Maedagama women during pregnancy reflected the cultural and economic differences between the two villages. There was no inter-gender conflict – and the *dola-duka* in Maedagama did not include foods or substances that could be interpreted as expressing male envy. Yet women in Maedagama (like in Laggala) craved for culturally 'harmful' foods, and foods that are linked with special life events. Yet, given the different regular eating patterns in the two villages, the function of the foods is different:

In Laggala the typical food taken by persons visiting kinsmen is *impulkiribat* (sweet rice); in Maedagama this item is almost never taken but they take 'curd and treacle' instead. 'Curd and treacle' all over the Southern Province of Sri Lanka is *par excellence* the 'visiting food.' Idiomatically, love or friendship between two persons is said to be like 'curd and treacle.' It is one of the most cathected and over-determined symbols in Maedagama associated with visits to kinsmen, love ('the need for attention and solicitude'), and for some with a nostalgia for their childhood. Maedagama women had no desire for the *batmula* (picnic rice) which Laggala women associated with pilgrimages and outdoor fun and festivity. Maedagama women carry *batmula* regularly to their men working in the rice fields. (Obeyesekere, 1985, p. 658)

An important part of life for the people in Maedagama was the framework of pilgrimages. These usually involve group tours by bus, and overnight stays in hotels. Eating 'out' during these pilgrimages is a special eating experience for Maedagama women. The particular foods consumed during such trips – but usually not at home – become objects of pregnancy cravings for women from Maedagama:

These foods are typically string hoppers (a noodle-like food), *pittu*, and hoppers (*appa*), all served in hotels and collectively known as *kade appa* ('shop hoppers'). Maedagama housewives make those occasionally themselves but the convention is to buy them from the 'shop.' To put it in Western terms, it is as if the woman wants to be taken out for dinner. The latter notion is simply non-existent in this society, but its closest approximation is the pilgrimage where women 'eat out.' Hotel foods at *dola-duka* recreate this experience. (Obeyesekere, 1985, p. 659)

This 'gender politics of food' involved in pregnancy cravings indicates the personal-cultural organization of at least some of the food cravings. Despite the difference in inter-gender relations between Laggala and Maedagama contexts – which makes a difference in the extent of role reversals during pregnancy – there is a basic unity between the two examples. Pregnant women from both communities use the contrast between ordinary and non-ordinary (yet recurrent) life experiences (indicated by special foods) as the cultural meaning on which the very personal uncontrollable urges for specific foods are based. The women in Laggala crave for sweet 'picnic' rice (which for them is linked with non-ordinary life events). The very same kind of rice for women from Maedagama belongs to the realm of ordinary foods. Yet their non-ordinary foods ('shop hoppers' from times of pilgrimages) likewise become the targets of pregnancy cravings.

Summary: what do cravings and aversions reveal for cultural psychology?

Here we see the counter-transposition of cultural construction from the conscious to the sub-conscious level. Somehow (nobody knows how) cultural meaning systems guide the direction of the craving. The personal culture proliferates through the sub-conscious field of basic personal feelings, transcending the rational and discursive levels of functioning. The person's 'gut feelings' become culturally regulated.

Similar phenomena can be observed in adjacent areas of human eating conduct – recognition by persons of having (by mistake) eaten something culturally non-edible. Thus, cases where one is told, after enjoying the meat at a dinner, that the meat is of that of your host's favourite cat, who was sacrificed for the honour of having you over for the meal, may result in vomiting out the (just previously) much-praised food. If the host, instead, says that the meat is of one of his sheep, freshly killed to honour the guest, the glorification story about the meal may continue even in the guest's memory. The only difference between the basic feelings about the food is in their cultural meaning, not in the specific sensations experienced while eating it. A similar issue arises around the 'raw' versus 'cooked' differentiation of the foods, where the same uncooked food object (for example, fish – different personal-cultural approaches to *sushi*) can be strictly rejected or accepted at the level of basic bodily feelings.

It is at the level of such basic vague but extremely explosive bodily feelings ('gut feelings') that the cultural nature of human psychology is ultimately demonstrated. It is a result of personal-cultural construction of the self. The collective-cultural world certainly is oriented towards channelling personal cultures into such a synthesis of the sub-conscious in cultural terms (see Chapter 12 on the goals of Quaranic pedagogy; and Chapter 13 on adolescents' identity). Yet nobody else but the given person can actually arrive at such a synthesis. The ultimate success of culture is in the self-construction by the person of their basic bodily feelings on the basis of co-constructed meanings.

CULTURAL ORGANIZATION OF THE LOSS OF PREGNANCY

Miscarriage (unintentional loss of the pregnancy) is a crisis event that needs cultural explanation and restitution. The system of a supernatural and common sense explanatory complex described above for conception, operates in the case of personally unexpected and undesired loss.

Within the personal-cultural system, a miscarriage can lead to dramatic personal upsets, including psychosomatic illness. Setting the miscarried fetus up in the cultural framework of loss of the person can entail funeral rituals for the aborted fetus. In Japan, memorial services for the aborted fetuses – *mizuko no kuyo* – have been part of such cultural reconciliation practices (Ohnuki-Tierney, 1984, pp. 78–79). Such rituals are held primarily by women who have themselves had miscarriages or terminations, and the ceremonies can make use of different objects in setting up public, symbolic places for the lost fetus.

First, one can purchase a tomb for the fetus. The tomb consists of a stone carved in the figure of a buddha in charge of children (*jizo*), wearing a red bib, and with flowers on each side (see Figure 8.7). The posthumously given name is written on the tomb. If a woman cannot afford a tomb, she can get the posthumous name written down on a tablet by the priest. The tablet is placed in the ancestral alcove of the family, and the deceased thus becomes a member of the network of ancestors to whom respect is being paid.

Another cultural way, recently implemented, to overcome the feelings related to miscarriage is to employ traditional wooden boards (*ema*) that are used to turn to deities for many reasons (such as asking for a cure from illness, or for success in passing university entrance examinations). The tablet includes a letter of wishes, which in the case of miscarriage may include wishes for the fetus to 'sleep peacefully,' and represents a begging for forgiveness by the mother. The issue of whether the fetus is a person (or just a biological organism growing to be born) is embedded in the human cultural construction of one's relations with ancestors, deities and the world of these others who are no longer with us.

Of course miscarriages can be interpreted in the collective-cultural framework as actions by malevolent spirits. In that case, some part of the local social system constructs a ritualistic solution to eliminate such influences. Since childbirth issues are in most societies a domain for women's expertise and dominance (the male obstetrician is a relatively recent historical construction), it is up to the women to act. This is similar to the case of culturally prescribed infanticide (see Chapter 9), where the fear of the extraordinary results of childbirth led to women's actions of elimination of such outcomes.

In an example of the Buu society (in Kenya), Irvine (1976) described a collective 'body-pinching' ritual that was indicated for women who had failed to give birth to a living child. In such a ritual (organized by women only), a group of women would 'punish' the aborting

FIGURE 8.7 *An advertisement display of tombstones for miscarried fetuses in Japan (from Ohnuki-Tierney, 1984, p. 79, reprinted by permission from Cambridge University Press and Emiko Ohnuki-Tierney)*

or miscarrying woman by way of pinching her body flesh (except breasts), in the context of a ritual dance. The 'target' woman's body is thus devastated by other women's nails, and she is forced to ask her husband for forgiveness for failing to produce live children. This form of ritualistic punishment is not different from corporal punishments used in medieval Europe, except for the executioners here being women, and the tools being their nails. Psychological effects are often produced collective-culturally in a context where physical harm is done, while framing it through meaning construction of cultural relevance. Buu women who had mis-carried were reported to accept their 'target' role in the ritual without efforts to escape.

Without doubt, such body-invasive procedures serve as cultural tools to mark the negative value the event has had in the collective-cultural domain. Similarly, cases of modern obstetricians conducting requested abortions without anes-thesia ('so that the women would feel the pain') is a cultural meaning construction of a collective-cultural kind, carried into the surgery room through the personal cultures of the obstetrician. The negotiation of meaning of the status of the fetus – is it a 'baby' or a 'fetus' (see Danet, 1980) – in the contemporary United States shows how semiotic mediation is the key divider between the fostering and elimination actions.

The social fights around the issue of abortion concentrate in the United States around the *control over* the woman's rights to decide upon *her own* childbearing as part of the personal culture, and as part of her adult life course. These fights – often with casualties (such as the people who are killed at bombings of abortion clinics) are ways to re-negotiate some issues of power in the given society. The issue of a woman's personal-cultural complexity in handling her own pregnancy is reduced to ideologically polarized social posi-tions of for or against abortion on demand, in the given (US) society. Thus it is an example of goals-oriented efforts by the collective-cultural domain to gain control over the personal-cultural sphere of all persons (who are expected to take a *personal* stand on that socio-moral issue), whether they are pregnant, women, or anybody else. The persons here are used as vehicles for the social negotiation of power in the given society. It is another example – similar to social guidance of women through activities and diet restrictions during pregnancy – where a personally salient issue is utilized for social functions.

The personal-cultural domain of deciding to have a baby, or deciding to abort, goes far beyond the simplified taking of stances between the 'right to live' versus 'right to decide'. It involves necessary ambiguity for the woman – each of the decisions has a profound impact on the woman's personal culture for the rest of her life, and that impact cannot be pre-determined. In most societies, this ambiguity is reduced by the strong collective-cultural promotion of the value of having children for all involved – the woman herself (as the fact of bearing children is set up as a condition for securing and improving her social position, and guarantees old-age security), the father of the children (and his patriline), the whole community, and so on (not to forget nation states at times glorifying mothers for their bearing children 'for the fatherland', which usually means getting more fighters for their military needs). This promotion, when internalized by women in their personal ways, disambiguates the decision whether to abort or not abort by eliminating the decision. This does not mean that the immediately accepted non-abortion trajectory is never reversed: it can be postponed to the time when the results of the pregnancy are clear. The same women who unquestioningly maintained their pregnancies may, under some conditions (defined by collective-cultural meanings), themselves get rid of the newborn babies. As will be seen (in Chapter 9), the conditions for post-partum infanticide are similar – in the need to overcome ambiguities – to those around the abortion decisions.

Yet, collective-cultural suggestions (for the 'unconditional' value of the children for a woman) cannot succeed as given. The personal-cultural reconstruction of such suggestions necessarily results in a variety of ways women relate to their pregnancies. Thus, in any society – independent of the extent of the collective-cultural pressures for the value of children – there would be some women who would prefer not to continue their pregnancies (at least the given ones, at the time). This results in the complexity of cases where the personally desired (yet in an ambivalent way) abortion becomes socially presentable *as if it were* spontaneous. The woman may elect to act in ways that could induce abortion, yet she cannot be blamed (including here, by herself) for doing that. Once the miscarriage has taken place, she may be appropriately unhappy for not getting the child. This ambivalence of a personal kind can be hidden behind the veil of collective-cultural acceptance of the high value of children.

FACING THE BIRTH

The whole period of pregnancy entails the cultural orientation towards the birth of the child. There can be elaborate preparation of the environment the baby is about to 'move into' – in our Western societies this takes the form of decorating the baby's bedroom, preparing clothes

for the baby, getting into discussions about what name to give to the baby, and in general being preoccupied by the anticipated event. These examples already indicate the cultural assumption of the independent existence of the baby, once born. The focus is on what the baby would need to have (own clothes, room etc.), rather than what the role of the baby is for the integrated kinship network (see Chapter 9).

Preparations for childbirth need not be limited to anticipating the baby; in fact, these preparations are for the whole event as such. Decisions about where the child should be born, and how the baby would enter into the social world, are made before the birth takes place. Such decisions are grossly overdetermined by the collective-cultural meaning system.

Childbirth settings

Childbirth can certainly take place in any setting where it happens, yet the appropriateness of the setting is collective-culturally defined. The general picture of different places is provided in Figure 8.8. The basic distinction of collective-cultural meaning systems on which the place of childbirth decision is made is the distinction between the socially textured (village, community, home) and cultural-but-untextured (or 'natural', external to the human-made contexts) settings. Both opposites here are collective-culturally constructed. Obviously, the meaning of 'own home' (be it personal dwelling, community, village, town, country) entails a superimposition

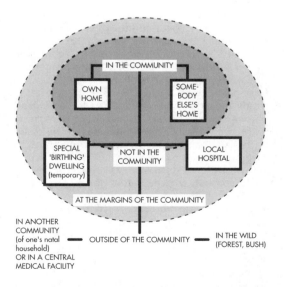

FIGURE 8.8 *Cultural organization of places for childbirth*

of generalized meaning (of identity – 'our') on a particular structured life setting. Yet the same applies to its opposite: anything outside of the 'our' place is set up as a meaningful construction.

Consider a rural context where a village is situated in the middle of a forest (or jungle). The villagers would see the forest surrounding their human-made space as filled with the 'other' world – a world of dangers, spirits, deities, wild animals etc. The forest can be seen as a place for the dwelling of powerful 'others', who simultaneously are dangerous and potentially helpful. To appease them, and to avoid potentially dangerous events taking place within the village, different activities can be prescribed to take place beyond the boundaries of the village.

This leads to the emergence of marginal territory around the community – culturally organized space which still is not part of the community, yet is used for specific functions. Many activities – childbirth (see the Kwaio example below), extra-marital love affairs (Gregor, 1985), women's seclusion during menstruation, loci of natural resources (for example, water wells, washing places in a river or creek, gardens and fields cultivated by the villagers) – may take place in this space at the margins of the community. Finally, the 'wild' context (further beyond the margins of the community) may be places visited for specific reasons (hunting and gathering trips).

There are many possibilities for locating the place for childbirth in this three-part classification of cultural space. These depend upon the particular meaningful linking of the event of childbirth with the larger meaning system of the collective culture.

Let us start from the assumption that the most appropriate place for childbirth is the woman's own home. This can be viewed to be so on egocentric (for example, the woman feeling best in her ordinary environment) or sociocentric (for example, the birth of the new child is an important family affair which should be catered for by the closest people, and not let 'outsiders' participate in it) grounds. Yet such argumentation is threatened by different linkages of the event with a wider meaning system. In our modern case, it entails the culturally constructed expert status of the medical system controlling childbirth. For instance, the notion of *need for medical help* at delivery can either lead to an outsider (midwife) being allowed in to the childbirth context at home (as is the tradition in different European contexts, such as Holland), or would force the family expecting the child to accept the social rule for childbirth happening in hospital (as in the United States), and under the control of a socially (educationally) legitimized expert (the doctor).

The same 'exodus' of the childbirth events from home to another place can be observed in the history of pre-industrial societies. This is based on the linkage of childbirth events with the intervention of possibly malevolent spirits. Often cases of unsuccessful childbirth (stillbirth) are explained by way of the effects of malevolent spirits, whose actions are believed to contaminate the place where the event takes place. In this case, it becomes obligatory to set up the place for childbirth outside of the community – either at the margins of the community, yet under social support of some community members (women); or totally in the wild. Ritualization of the childbirth event by the community (as in the Kwaio case) gives preference to the margin of the community; lack of such ritualization would privilege the contexts totally outside of the community.

Proof of such linkages with spirit beliefs (on the one hand) and collective ritualization (on the other) comes from cases where, if the birth happens to take place in the home when it should not, the house (home) where it happened has to be destroyed. This cultural relevance of demolishing the childbirth dwelling can occur also in case of a specially constructed 'childbirth hut'. A local (community) hospital is a culturally marginal place for childbirth – even if it may (architecturally) be located 'in' the village, it is meaningwise a 'foreign territory' (of outside-educated medical persons and their gadgets), and is hence functionally a place on the margin. The village hospital is a permanent birthing hut controlled socially by outsiders.

Of course, childbirth can be planned to take place completely out of the given community. The pregnant woman may migrate back to her natal household and give birth there (as well as stay there for some time after delivery). Or the birth can take place in some central medical facility which has no connections with the community. In that respect, for the parturient woman the 'central hospital' is a modern equivalent of a forest or bush – with the distinction that in the former there are other (unknown) human beings at times taking interest (and helping) with her progress in labour (and delivery), segregating the new mother from her offspring after the birth, and forcing her to leave the place after some administratively set time period.

Participation in the events: labour and delivery

Childbirth issues are usually the realm of women's knowledge, with men allowed into that only selectively and in ambivalent ways. Two basic kinds of persons can be viewed as potentially present at labour and delivery – specialists (midwife, obstetrician) or kinship group members. Of the latter, differentiation can be made by gender (for example, female kin-group members allowed, men not) or by age status (for example, children before puberty not allowed).

The absolutely given minimal condition of childbirth is that of the woman by herself, without anybody present. The woman may be expected to leave the public grounds (for example, village), go into the 'world outside' (forest, bush), give birth there (alone), and return to her ordinary role in the village, with the newborn baby simply added to her immediate set of everyday tasks. Surely such a minimal condition would be counterproductive from the standpoint of both the collective-cultural goal orientations of the social world surrounding the woman, and (through her internalization of her needs) her own personal-cultural world. Thus, in the very varied – across societies and across history of the same society – forms of social organization of childbirth are examples of inserting cultural objectives into the relevant transition phase for the parturient woman, and (of course) guarantees of the immediate cultural embeddedness of the newborn. Human childbirth, in contrast with the birth of the offspring in animal species, is a *culturally ritualized* event. The event is organized so as to include symbolic elements in the flow of actions that are necessary for the arrival of the baby.

The Kwaio sequence of childbirth events

The Kwaio (who live on the Malaita Island, one of the Solomon Islands in the Pacific) have a highly ritualized childbirth sequence, described by Roger Keesing (1982) in the context of his analysis of Kwaio religion. In the Kwaio society, the male and female realms of everyday life and collective-culturally relevant knowledge are strictly separated. This separation is marked by prohibitions against entering the knowledge and practice domain of the opposite gender.

Hence it is not surprising that Kwaio childbirth is a strictly women's affair. The childbirth related actions begin with the permanent place of female domain – the 'menstrual hut'. Women go to live in such a hut during their menstrual periods, following the seclusion rule. For the purposes of childbirth, a special 'birthing hut' is erected in the vicinity of the 'menstrual hut' – by the woman who is going to have the baby, and her assistant. The hut has two parts, one for the parturient (and the baby) and the other for the assistant. The sequence of entering into labour, the delivery itself and the return of the mother and the newborn into the village includes gradual separation of the parturient from the community (and the community from her), followed by similar step-by-step re-introduction (see Figure 8.9).

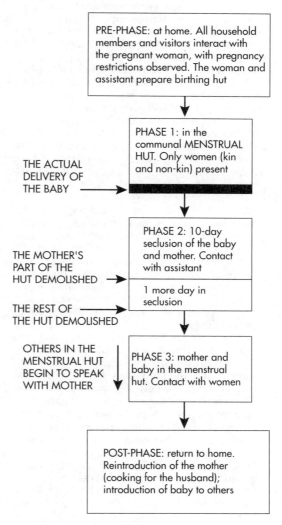

FIGURE 8.9 *The sequence of childbirth among the Kwaio (Solomon Islands)*

The pregnant woman at home during pregnancy is surrounded by all household members (female and male), and is regulated by the Kwaio pregnancy taboos and prescriptions (the pre-phase in Figure 8.9). When entering into labour, she is moved to the menstrual hut (which serves as the base for giving birth), surrounded only by women (kin and non-kin) – phase 1. This social support ends when the baby is born: the mother and baby will move into their part of the childbirth hut (and the assistant moves into her part of the hut) – phase 2. Nobody else is allowed to interact with the new mother for ten days (only the attendant can have limited contact). Yet the attendant is not allowed to enter the mother's part of the hut, and objects from any part of the outside world (even from the menstrual hut) are not allowed into the mother's part of the hut. The afterbirth is buried in the mother's part of the childbirth hut, and her bed is located on the place of that burial. The mother and the attendant cannot eat from the same tray.

The post-partum seclusion period of the Kwaio includes the maximum separation of the mother with her newborn. After ten days, the reverse process begins, and the mother and the baby re-enter the social world. This proceeds in a sequence of steps (see phases 2 and 3 in Figure 8.9):

1 The mother washes herself and the baby. The attendant shaves the mother's head, the mother gives the baby to the attendant to hold while she herself destroys her part of the childbirth hut. It is important that a pile of stones is placed on the place where the afterbirth is buried, so that the foraging pigs cannot dig it up. After the mother's part of the hut is destroyed, she and the attendant share the latter's (still remaining) part of the hut for one night.
2 The next morning, the mother and the attendant dismantle the remaining part of the childbirth hut. The attendant leads the mother and the baby back to the menstrual hut, scattering wood shavings on the way. These wood shavings have been prepared by a male priest (the only participation by anybody remotely male in these proceedings). The mother and the baby remain in the menstrual hut for five days, but she is not allowed to talk with anybody. That restriction becomes gradually lifted over the five days.
3 On the sixth day, the mother and the baby leave the menstrual hut – led by the attendant (who again scatters the wood shavings on the way) – to the house of the baby's father in the village. There the mother stays, in the company of the baby's father, cooking for him from the first day of re-entrance into the home. The other household members gradually join the new parents and the baby (the post-phase).

As a result of this ritual, the mother and baby are introduced into the regular village community only 17–18 days after the baby is born. The period before (and after) delivery is filled with solitary and female-assisted activities, fitting the gender segregation in the Kwaio society. Notice that there is no talk about 'father's participation' or 'family support' here. It is the women who – due to their status of gender – are helping others in childbirth (and prepare themselves for childbirth through participant observation).

Childbirth in the context of Western Java (Indonesia)

The case of childbirth in an Indonesian village (fully described in Wessing, 1978, pp. 127–130) provides a good example of the cultural organization of childbirth that takes place in the parturient's home. The woman stays through her pregnancy at home, and is guided through the pregnancy through monthly rituals. When the onset of labour is detected, the midwife is invited to the house. If the birth pains begin in the day-time, no special precautions for inviting the midwife to the site are taken. However, if the labour starts at night, a man with a torch would go to summon the midwife (the torch, aside from lighting the way, is believed to scare off evil spirits, especially that of *kuntianak*).[2] The protection against the evil spirits is of central relevance: for example, the believed-in possibility that the *kuntianak* may enter into the midwife herself is counter-acted by the midwife going to the house of the parturient under the escort of the man who summoned her (rather than alone). When she arrives, her first attention is not given to the woman in labour, but to warding off the *kuntianak*. A knife or another sharp object is placed near the expectant mother (prior to it, she would have worn some sharp object on her body, over the final months of the pregnancy). A number of plants are set up near the woman with a similar purpose.

The parturient woman is placed on the floor *with head upstream* relative to the local river. It is assumed that the baby will be born more easily if it follows the flow of the water. All doors, windows etc. are opened in the house. Everyone around loosens their clothing; belts and bras are taken off. Anything in the birthing environment that might symbolize tightness or constriction is altered in the direction of looseness. The woman is undressed, and covered only with a cloth. Various women from the neighbourhood – who come and go – are present, keeping her company as the labour progresses. The woman is never left alone. The children of the household are present all of the time (the only limit on them is that they need to be relatively quiet).

As is evident, the Indonesian case demonstrates how the childbirth can be a publicly open event (women of the neighbourhood coming and going; children being present), while through the whole sequence of action the primary symbolic concern is with the mother's survival. In some sense, the only figure who is excluded from the public childbirth in the woman's home is the feared *kuntianak*.

The process of delivery was described by Wessing as proceeding in a way where necessary actions of the birth and symbolic complements were intertwined. When the delivery got under way,

> . . . the midwife took some water in her mouth and spat it into the mother's vagina. She rubbed the mother's stomach with coconut oil and *barangsang* (a stimulant). Neighbor women now arrived and stayed. Every woman who came in stroked the mother's hair and encouraged her. The mother was given some warm water to drink and was told to keep repeating the proclamation of faith.
>
> Every time she tried to push the baby out someone would blow on the top of her head. This was done mostly by neighbor women, but her husband also participated. When it became apparent that she was going to have a difficult time, Pak Hadji, the grave guardian . . . was sent for. He came and sat behind her head to the left. He said a prayer and blew on the mother's head. The woman's husband was told to sit behind her head to the right side and lean over her. Later he stepped over her body, between her legs, and walked away. This was to encourage the baby to follow its father. (Wessing, 1978, p. 128)

The participation of the neighbours in the delivery process is a remarkable contrast to the example of the Kwaio childbirth sequence (above). The worry about potential dangers to the parturient entails the summoning (when complications emerged) of the 'grave guardian' to ward off the dangerous spirits. The cultural construction of the childbirth process entails strong reliance upon analogical reasoning – the woman is positioned so as to align the birth process with the direction of the water flow in the river; the husband 'walks away' in a symbolic effort to get the baby to follow him.

Once the baby was born, the cultural action focus moved from the mother to the newborn:

> the midwife whispered the proclamation of faith in his [the baby's] ear, along with admonitions to respect his elders and the *adat* (custom). While she rubbed the umbilical cord on his face she told him not to talk unnecessarily, while touching his mouth; while touching his eyes, not to see things that are not meant for his eyes; while touching his ear, not to hear things not meant for his ears. (Wessing, 1978, p. 129)

The role of the afterbirth in the symbolic organization of childbirth can be made into a relevant issue. In the West Javan case, the gender of the baby was linked with the actions around the afterbirth. If the baby was a boy, the afterbirth could be buried behind the house, or, alternatively, thrown into the river (so that the boy would travel and gain experience). Furthermore, his placenta could also be buried near a rice field (so as to expect him to be a good rice farmer). In

the case of girls, the afterbirth was always buried near the house (so that she would stay close to home). However, it could be buried in the yard (so that she would be bright-eyed and intelligent).

The Indonesian example gives us further evidence about the collective-cultural appropriation of the personal – biological, psychological and social – life course transition (childbirth) for the promotion of a relevant system of meaning. In different phases of childbirth, the mother or the baby attain the primary focus – yet in both cases the focus entails future-oriented meaningful actions on behalf of the participants in the event. The same cultural agenda exists in the midst of modern medicalized hospital childbirths, albeit in ways hidden behind the medical expert discourse.

Ritual nature of modern hospital childbirth

The sequence of events in the medical setting includes ritualizations which may be different from those of the Kwaio or the Javanese, yet proceed through a similar process of seclusion of the parturient, followed by social re-integration.

By insisting that childbirth take place in a hospital (rather than at home), the socio-institutional power of the medical institution (and the obstetrician) is socially marked. The history of perinatal medicine indicates an intense fight – from the seventeenth century onwards – on behalf of the male medical specialists to take over the traditionally female domain of delivering babies. A modern remnant of such history is the friction that at times surfaces in the relations of male obstetricians and female midwives. The friction is built – aside from issues of social power in a hospital context – on the issue of childbirth belonging to the culturally 'female' domain of human life activities, into which males are not expected to penetrate (except for special circumstances). The folk models of male <> female gender relations of a given society set the meanings background against which the issue of male childbirth helpers is viewed.

Yet the gender issue, translated into that of the male/female power relation (as in modern societies), only masks the social issue of negotiation of power between individual persons (who are involved in a given act, that is, giving of birth) and social institutions (such as hospitals as part of a medical establishment). In the context of contemporary hospitalized childbirth in the US medical system, the opposition between person's independent actions and social control of those actions is expressed in the form of ritualization of the whole process of childbirth.

Until the 1970s, the US medical system maintained control over the isolation of the parturient woman once she arrived in the hospital. The issue of letting close family members – husband, other children etc. – be present during the period of labour was a topic of negotiation in the 1960s and 1970s in the pertinent medical and psychological discourses. The psychological side of this dispute pertained to the importance of emotional support by close persons during the childbirth. Yet marital relations can be complex, involving cases where the participating husband (or other children) themselves may need to cope with the uncertainties and strain involved in the labour process.

As a result of the disputes of the early 1970s, the US medical system began to accept the presence of select 'significant others' of the woman during childbirth. Yet their presence was limited to some times, while at others the woman is exclusively under the control of the medical personnel. The contemporary 'standard procedure for normal birth' in US hospitals – recognizing the possibility of variation across hospitals – has been described in the following way:

> Upon entering the hospital, the laboring *woman is taken in a wheelchair* to a 'prep' room. There she is separated from her partner, *her clothes are removed*, she is asked *to put on a hospital gown*, her *pubic hair is shaved*, a vaginal exam is performed, and she is given an enema. She is then reunited with her partner, if he chooses to be present, and *put to bed*. Her access to food is limited or prohibited, and an intravenous needle is inserted in her hand or arm. Some type of analgesia is administered. A pitocin drip may be started through the IV. The external fetal monitor is attached to the woman by means of a large belt strapped around her waist to monitor the strength of her contractions and the baby's heartbeat. The internal monitor may also be attached through electrodes inserted into the baby's scalp, prior to which the amniotic sac, or membranes, must be ruptured. Periodic vaginal exams are performed at least once every two hours. (Davis-Floyd, 1992, pp. 73–74; added emphasis)

The emphasized parts of this description point to the symbolic ritualization moments embedded within the medical procedure. The first moment of takeover of control comes when the woman is asked to sit in a wheelchair – indicating the symbolic status of a person who needs to be 'taken care of' by the personnel. Note that the woman had been active on her own – walking and driving (or being driven) into the hospital. Childbirth is a normal biological event which would take place even if there were no hospitals – the human species would certainly long be extinct if all women entering into childbirth necessarily needed the help of wheelchairs. The function of this ritualistic moment is to assert the *dominant-but-caregiving* nature of the hospital. When seen through the eyes of women who are targets of such assertion, this entrance moment to the hospital can look different:

> I can remember just almost being in tears by the way they would wheel you in. I would come to the delivery or into the hospital on top of this, breathing, you know, all in control. And they slap you in this wheelchair! It made me suddenly feel like maybe I wasn't in control anymore. (Suzanne Sampson)

> The maternity room sent somebody down with a wheelchair. I didn't have any need for a wheelchair so we piled all the luggage up in the wheelchair and wheeled it up to the floor. (Patricia Hellman) (both quoted in Davis-Floyd, 1992, p. 77)

The personal-cultural reconstructions of the institutional procedures vary. Some women may indeed need the wheelchair, others would not need it but treat the symbolic role of the procedure along the lines suggested by the hospital. Whatever the specific way of looking at the wheelchair may be, the social re-organization of roles has taken place. In the 'standard procedure', the wheelchair marks the boundary of the 'world out there' (where the woman needs to be self-sufficient) and 'our hospital world' (where the woman is to be a 'patient' who is the object of the set procedures).

In all social institutions, efforts to fix the social roles of the persons in them take the form of some kind of use of objects of uniform. This is most clearly the case in the realm of clothing ('male' versus 'female' kinds of clothes as society's expected 'gender uniforms'; military uniforms; uniforms for patients, nurses and doctors in medical settings; 'business suits' as uniforms for people working in corporations; 'school uniforms' for schoolchildren). Thus, it is not surprising that the symbolic transformation of the parturient woman into a 'patient' entails a uniform – a hospital gown. The latter is supposed to be hygienic (entailing the institutional assumption that the woman's own clothing is not). In combination with the ritualistic act of body modification – shaving of the pubic hair[3] – it completes the boundary making between the woman's own personal world.

The hospital 'standard procedure' includes the placement of the woman onto a bed for the purposes of labour. This (supine) position is appropriate for control over the progress of labour by the medical personnel. In contrast with the hospital settings, there exist many body positions that are suggested to women to go through labour and delivery. In societies where childbirth has not yet moved to be under the control of medical institutions women are invariably encouraged to assume *a vertical* body position and move around during labour. Here the help of gravity in childbirth is utilized. In contrast, in hospitals women have been encouraged (sometimes even forced) to lie down, and not to move around. Undoubtedly a ward filled with women each labouring in their own beds would allow for easy overview of the whole situation by nurses and doctors, whereas labouring women running around in the ward and hospital corridors would constitute a moment of anarchy in a hierarchically ordered social system. The same result – the birth of the baby – takes place after the vertical/moving or horizontal/confined patterns of labour; the multilinearity of trajectories here reflects the convenience of the social control system.

An extension of the issue of social control over childbirth in modern medical settings is the introduction of new technologies. While these technologies undoubtedly improve the knowledge base for early diagnostics during pregnancy (for example, early knowledge of congenital malformations), they simultaneously serve the social function of semiotic marking of the power role of the medical personnel in the childbirth context. Use of new technologies requires specific expertise, which cannot be present among laypersons.

However, new technologies also lead to new uncertainties. The question of safety of these (now mostly concentrated on the fetus and baby, given the practical elimination of maternal mortality in contemporary hospital childbirth). These concerns for safety become similar in their semiotic organization as the traditional worries about the intervention – both positive and negative – by spirits. Technology is not merely a set of instruments used for medical tasks, but it acquires the value of semiotic mediation tools.

Utilization of cultural mediating tools
The psychological side of the woman entering into labour is necessarily that of stress and strain (if not pain, see above). Hence her own constructed set of semiotic mediating devices can be of specific relevance in her actions. Of course, the personal-cultural devices of coping are not visible unless the woman externalizes those.

Sheila Kitzinger (1982, p. 196) has described a case from a Christian religious sect in Jamaica, where the religious practices of trance carry over into the maternity wards. The congregational joint activities – with body movements, rhythmic chanting and trance – set the stage for facing childbirth. Women go to the childbirth hospital with their bibles, and spend the labour period on the ward in body rocking similar to their usual frame of religious ecstasy. In the pushing to

deliver the baby they may shout '*Gwan dahn Saviour! Gwan down Lord!*', thus explicating their religious practice and imagery in the process of childbirth. Here the woman is not 'holding herself back' or trying to hide her emotions, rather the opposite. Yet the emotions are closely linked with the semiotic organizer – religious imagery.

Semiotic reconstruction of 'pain'
Different systems of social suggestions oriented towards making childbirth painless have attempted to provide women with practical (gymnastics, massage etc.) and semiotic tools (suggesting what she would feel in the process). Their effort is similar to what the Jamaican revivalist sect succeeds in – creating a holistic psychological organizing network for childbirth. Yet, as these systems cannot rely upon full identification with their meanings, their success is necessarily limited to some cases, while other cases demonstrate their failure. This follows directly from the co-constructionist nature of the cultural transfer processes.

In many societies, cultural construction of desired meanings of childbirth have emphasized the desire for 'painless childbirth'. The usual construction (proliferated through laypersons' discourse) is: CHILDBIRTH IS PAINFUL → SOMETHING MUST BE DONE to make it painless (or at least less painful). Many personal cultural systems would accept this construction, but not all. For example, Lebra (1984, p. 168) shows that in Japan some women would themselves resist medical doctors' efforts to reduce the pain in childbirth, remarking 'painless delivery [by anesthesia] is certainly easier, *but lacks that much of value*'[4] (a 49-year-old Japanese mother of two). Here the personal-cultural construction acquires a different presentational force: CHILDBIRTH IS PAINFUL → that makes it VALUABLE personally, therefore → NOTHING MUST BE DONE to alleviate the pain. As is often the case, cultural ritualization of events makes use of the difficult (painful, strainful, fatiguing) activities of persons who are to go through it to get into a new culturally defined state. This applies both to collective-cultural rituals (see Chapter 13 on the stress, strain and pain encoded in traditional adolescent rites of passage), as well as personal-cultural ones. The lives of many people who devote themselves to religions and pass through rituals involve self-selection of different forms of mutilation of the body (self-flagellation by monks and nuns in medieval Christian monasteries and convents; hanging from hooks in the context of religious rituals in Sri Lanka – Obeyesekere, 1981). A person can construct a painful experience for themselves as a part of a personal ritual – of turning into a mother, for instance.

Social intervention efforts: 'painless childbirth' techniques

It is the social institutions that have attempted to intervene in the complex desires of women facing childbirth by promising different kinds of certainty for the occasion. The goals of the social institutions that suggest implementation of such techniques are as multi-faceted as those of modern drug companies fighting at the forefront of the war against disease by developing ever-new and powerful drugs (with ever-new side effects, and unpredictable interactions with other drugs). In both cases, the medical system is involved in the promotion of their social role in the given society.

The promise of painless childbirth in the 1950s in the Soviet Union is a good example of *how efforts to redefine meanings of childbirth pain* were undertaken for the gain of the medical and social system. The method – designed by Velvovsky and his colleagues (see English translation, Velvovsky et al., 1960) – entailed numerous regular 'pregnancy exercises' not unknown in any medical practice (such as information about anatomy and physiology of pregnancy, self-massaging techniques, gymnastic exercises, breathing drills etc.). In conjunction with these *prescribed actions* (compare that with prescriptions for action in pregnancy, see above), there were goal-directed efforts to persuade the women to look at their future (that is, at present unknown) experiences at the time of labour and delivery not in terms of the meaning complex of *'pain'*, but that of *'strain'*.

Velvovsky's system belonged to the realm of social organization of medicine. He tried to create a social network around pregnant women – of relatives, midwives, nurses, obstetricians – who would redundantly control the women's construction of their expectations in terms of 'strain' rather than 'pain'. The system also utilized the social representation (widely popular in the Soviet Union in the 1950s, as well as before) that there was a certain magical power in both 'Soviet medicine' and the 'Soviet people' themselves. The power of the latter, being assisted by the former, was rhetorically claimed to eradicate childbirth pain from human lives in the same way as the communist social system was to win over all others in social life. Of course, both claims proved to be utopian – yet it was an appropriate time of uncertainty (pregnancy) at which such constructs could be introduced. A number of aspects (except the social utopia) of the Velvovsky system were introduced by Fernand Lamaze in France in his efforts to prepare women for childbirth.

Childbearing extended psychologically beyond the woman

There is a certain Western cultural bias to look at the cultural processes about childbearing with the central focus on the woman. The act of childbearing is situated within some form of kinship group setting, and other persons participate in that transition in different ways. Obviously, the husband can play a central role (for example, asking his ancestors to arrange a child, as was the case with the Bellonese; or providing relevant food to the mother-to-be). The whole act of childbirth – including hospital birth in our contemporary world – is set up as a collective ritual occasion, with selective participation of different persons and institutions. The question of social role transformation during a woman's pregnancy touches upon the lives of all those surrounding her.

The couvade as described in psychiatry

The psychology of husbands of pregnant women has been demonstrated to take peculiar forms. Husbands often experience the same symptoms of pregnancy that their wives go through at the time ('morning sickness', toothache of no specifiable physical reason, abdominal pain, food cravings or aversions). This phenomenon has been documented separately in two domains of knowledge.

First, it has been documented by psychiatrists (who call it the *couvade syndrome*, from the French word *couver*, to brood, or hatch – Trethowan and Conlon, 1965). They have described cases in which husbands of pregnant women suddenly developed symptoms which lasted throughout the pregnancy, disappearing when the child was born. For example, Enoch, Trethowan and Barker (1967, pp. 59–60) describe a case of a 38-year-old Englishman who had suffered at each of his wife's six pregnancies. At the first (when he was 27) he suffered from morning sickness (while his wife did not report that symptom). On the day of the child's birth he was seized at work by severe stomachache, at the same time when the actual birth took place. During his wife's second pregnancy (he was 29 then), he again suffered from morning sickness. A year later he suffered from chest and stomach pain three months prior to his third child's birth. A year later his wife was pregnant again, and the husband suffered morning sickness, as well as abdominal pain precisely at the time of her giving birth. The fifth pregnancy was the easiest for him – only a few days of morning sickness.

During his wife's sixth pregnancy the husband began to interact with the psychiatrists. During this pregnancy he suffered from quite severe morning sickness, starting at about the second month of pregnancy, and from toothache. During the second trimester he suffered from abdominal pain, which returned three weeks before the expected childbirth. Then the man invented a ritualistic activity which was described in the following way:

> Without being able to give any good reason for doing so he obtained an incubator and put some bantam's eggs down. He gave these earnest attention even to the point of assisting in the birth of some chicks by easing the tough egg membrane open with tweezers. As soon as he did this his abdominal pain completely disappeared, and although he became extremely anxious and totally anorexic, on the day of the birth he suffered no pain. (Enoch et al., 1967, p. 60)

The invention of a personal ritual of assisting in hatching of the birds links this case with the collective-cultural prescriptions for husbands in many societies to act out aspects of pregnancy or childbirth (see below). Note that this was a symptomatic reliever of the problems – the overall anxiety pattern concerning childbirth still stayed. Psychiatric symptomatology of *couvade* has been demonstrated in countries where (obviously) psychiatrists are widespread and important, and (less obviously) where male affective domains are expected to be confined to the male personality world, and where men have been kept out of childbirth issues through their social role expectations. For instance, in England *couvade* is estimated to be present in around 20 per cent of husbands. Some males do not (or will not) accept such collective-cultural conditions, and one way of breaking out of these conditions is psychosomatization. Female pregnancy symptoms provide an easy guiding model for it.

The couvade as an anthropological phenomenon
A second disciplinary context where *couvade* has been described is cultural anthropology. Anthropologists have documented socially prescribed displays of symptoms of pregnancy and childbirth among husbands in many societies. It is possible to talk of *pre-pregnancy*, *pregnancy*, *childbirth* and *post-partum* versions of the *couvade*.

The pre-pregnancy version of the *couvade* has been described in Estonian folklore. In the case of the Võru area, it was believed in the eighteenth to nineteenth centuries that the woman could alleviate her future childbirth pain by a ritualistic possession of the husband on their wedding night:

> On the wedding evening she serves him plenty of beer seasoned with wild rosemary . . . , so that he may fall into a deep sleep. While he lies in this narcotic slumber, the woman must creep between his legs without his perceiving it (for if he wakes up, the good success is lost), and in that way the poor man gets his share of the future travail-pains. (Kreutzwald, 1854: cited via Oinas, 1993, p. 339)

The symbolic linkage of the husband's role with the diminishing of future childbirth pain is remarkable in its forward-oriented thinking (which surfaces in the Estonian mentality also in other forms). The woman takes the active sexual role in order to symbolically secure her chances for painless childbirth.

The pregnancy version of the *couvade* entails the emergence of pregnancy symptoms in the husband (as described above). A description of the changes in the husband is narrated in the case of the Hopi (a North American Indian tribe) in the following terms (by a woman):

> When one gets pregnant again, one's husband then also a little suffers *couvade* sickness in correlation with his wife. He is curiously enough like this: even if he has work to do he becomes too lazy to do anything. But he is not like that for a very long time; immediately as one . . . gets big with child he again goes back as he was. As he recovers like that, then again anything which he feels like doing, he does. (Voeglin, 1960, p. 493)

This Hopi version seems to reflect upon the husband's emotional co-relating with the beginning of his wife's pregnancy. This first reaction to pregnancy may not be so simple in other societies. Collective-cultural prescription of pregnancy taboos (described for women, above) can also be put upon the husbands. Here the unity of the parents is crucial – *both* the would-be mother and the would-be father of the baby are subjected to such restrictions. For example, among the Pilaga (South American Indian tribe) the husband of the pregnant woman is not allowed to eat armadillo meat (to prevent breech presentation at birth), and is restricted from carrying out a number of normal activities (playing hockey, riding a horse, cleaning a pipe, handling a weapon or cutting instrument (Métraux, 1949, p. 370)). This is culturally meaningful as there exists a belief in a powerful bond between father and the unborn child. Such power has to be handled carefully – hence the reglementation of the father's actions.

The childbirth version of the *couvade* can take any form of imitation by the husband of the events of birth. In an earlier description of the customs of South American Indians, Yves d'Evreux (in 1864) claimed:

He [the husband] lies-in instead of his wife who works as usual; then all the women of the village come to see and visit him in his bed, consoling him for the trouble and pain he had in producing his child; he is treated as if he were sick and very tired without leaving his bed. (Métraux, 1949, p. 369)

The husband's ritualistic imitation of childbirth events may entail other aspects of gender-role exchange. In his classic depiction of *couvade*, Frazer (1910) emphasizes how a male friend in New Guinea (rather than the father) plays out childbirth activities in the context of the men's clubhouse (surrounded and comforted by other men). He imitates pain and agony any time he hears the woman (in the distance) shouting in the pain of childbirth.

The ritualistic action within *couvade* can include cross-dressing. In Southern India, it has been described that as soon as childbirth pangs of the woman begin, the husband immediately takes some of the woman's clothes, puts them on, puts her kind of mark on his forehead and retires into a dark room (Dawson, 1929, pp. 20–21). A reverse use of objects of clothing during childbirth has been described in many contexts – some articles of the husband's clothing are taken into the wife's childbirth context to alleviate pain or to ease the delivery.

The post-partum version of the *couvade* entails restrictions on the father's conduct after the child is born – often in contrast with the absence of such restrictions on the mother. The mother, after childbirth, may return to her daily activities, while the father may be in seclusion for a while (Coelho, 1949). The most extensive post-partum *couvade* rituals have been described for the Garifuna (Black Caribs living in Honduras – Chernela, 1991) where the father may abstain from streneous activities in the first two or three years of the child's life.

The Mehinaku (a Xingu tribe in the Amazon basin – Gregor, 1985) do not practise the *couvade* during the pregnancy and childbirth, but after the child has been born. As soon as the child (especially the first) is born, the father of the child is assumed to resemble the mother. The taboos and restrictions of the mother are generalized to him. The father becomes secluded, refrains from sexual intercourse, and avoids those foods that the mother has to avoid in her post-partum experiences (fish). The mother can leave the seclusion once her post-partum bleeding ends, but the father's post-partum taboos continue. His seclusion continues until the infant assumes the status of a child (which means a move from 'lies around, gurgles, crawls on the ground and does not talk' to 'walks and talks' – Gregor, 1985, p. 195).

Couvade as 'sympathetic magic'

Descriptions of males imitating pregnancy and childbirth have been viewed as a form of *sympathetic magic* (Bronislaw Malinowski's term). It can also be labelled *pseudo-maternal couvade* – since it entails external enactment of features of pregnancy and childbirth. The husband's intra-personal feelings are not known – at least to anthropologists who describe what they can observe, and do not share psychologists' obsession of penetrating the intra-psychological domains of their informants.

However, as can be seen from the variety of specific versions of the pseudo-maternal *couvade* above, the practice of 'sympathy' with the woman is embedded in a context of collective action to deal with the symbolic powers of the spirit worlds. The husband's simulation of pregnancy, childbirth or post-partum symptoms of the wife can be directed not towards her (that is, there need not be 'sympathy' with the wife), but towards the believed-in world of powerful spirits. The phenomena of the ritualistic *couvade* are not esoteric at all, when viewed from this angle.

SUMMARY

Development of adults and the emerging offspring through the period of pregnancy is neither only a biological nor a personal affair. As getting pregnant, being pregnant and giving birth constitute a period of life course transformation, personal and collective cultures are intensely intermingled in this transition process. The whole process is coordinated socially – with the goal orientations of the society embedded in these coordination efforts. Through such coordination, social institutions protect their own status quo while coping with the desired yet potentially uncontrollable biological proliferation of their own species. Most profoundly such fear for the 'spoiling of society' has been evident in the social invention of eugenic selection of human species – the regulation of childbearing on the basis of the 'generic purity' of the parents. The history of eugenics remains beyond the scope of this book, yet it demonstrates at the level of societies what in this chapter was demonstrated at the level of individual childbirth cases. The social system maintains control over the relevant bifurcation points of development – conception, childbirth – in ways that maintain the psychological transformation of the persons within socially accepted limits. Moving pregnant women through pregnancy into childbirth is turned into a process of socially constrained evolution – and not a revolution!

In Chapter 9 the story of the social canalization of all co-developing persons (the infant and all of his/her functional kinship network) continues. Here, however, the contributions of the behaviour of the offspring force further cultural adaptations to come into being. The variability of culturally organized individual life trajectories grows as the newborn, through infancy, moves towards guaranteed survival, and towards a peripheral observer's position in the social life of the adults.

NOTES

1 Which has happened in human cultural history repeatedly: the 'Salem witch-hunt' of 1692 (see Trask, 1992) in North America, or Stalinist purges of the 1930s in the Soviet Union are but a few examples.

2 *Kuntianak* is the spirit of a woman who died in childbirth. This spirit is dangerous especially to women giving birth – as a result of that spirit, the woman may have birth difficulties, and in case of dying, would turn into a *kuntianak* herself (Wessing, 1978, p. 105).

3 In a similar vein, in many armies new recruits to military service have their heads shaved as a way of turning them into uniform (and uniformed) homogeneous role-bearers.

4 She explained about natural delivery: 'Only by tasting (*ajiwau*) it you come to understand the truth. You will understand precisely how *you* were born and what your mother was up to.'

REVIEW QUESTIONS FOR CHAPTER 8

1 Explain the notion of norms and counter-norms.

2 Describe different forms of cultural regulation of sexuality.

3 Explain the Dusun belief in pregnancy as resulting from the 'mixing of hot bloods'.

4 How are foods symbolically related to becoming pregnant?

5 Explain how everyday life phenomena and beliefs in supernatural forces work together in lay explanations of becoming pregnant – in the case of Bellona Islanders, as well as of our own.

6 Explain the *generic explanatory complex* of conception.

7 How are the social roles of childless women constructed in traditional societies?

8 Explain the cultural regulation of women's childbearing age.

9 Why is prediction of the baby's gender symbolically significant during pregnancy?

10 Explain different tactics (and their reasons) of a person's public announcement of pregnancy.

11 Explain the cultural rationale in the introduction of limits on conduct and eating for pregnant women.

12 How is eating a 'cultural construction site'?

13 Describe food cravings and aversions of pregnancy.

14 How are food cravings used to regulate social roles? Explain the differences between the two Sri Lankan villages described by Obeyesekere.

15 Explain the psychological ways of dealing with loss of pregnancy.

16 Explain the different locations where childbirth can take place.

17 How is human childbirth a ritualized act?

18 Describe the Kwaio childbirth sequence. Describe the distribution of psychological support provision at each stage.

19 Describe the role of 'social others' in Javanese childbirth.

20 Describe ritualization of childbirth in US maternity hospitals.

21 How is pain culturally constructed (around childbirth)?

22 Explain the notion of *couvade* in psychiatry.

23 Explain the notion of *couvade* as an anthropological phenomenon (ritual of 'sympathetic magic').

9

NEWBORN AND INFANT DEVELOPMENT: THE CULTURAL-ECOLOGICAL NICHE AND ITS SOCIAL FUNCTIONS

The arrival of the newborn in the physical world shared with his or her kinship group does not automatically equate with the arrival in the socio-cultural world. That latter arrival can be denied on collective-cultural grounds (as in the case of socially accepted or prescribed infanticide), or delayed until the child proves itself to be viable. The 'cultural birth' of the baby may take place either before actual delivery (as in the case of people who believe that babies are babies from conception onwards), or even years after the child has been around, as an infant, toddler or small child.

All this sociocultural organization of the child's entrance into the social world is set up by adults. Although these adults are usually the baby's parents, this is not an absolute rule. Another relative can be assigned the crucial role in determining the future of the child. Further-more, the whole environmental context of the newborn and infant is set up culturally as a structured setting.

The cultural-ecological niche

The *cultural-ecological niche* is a notion introduced by Charles Super and Sarah Harkness (1982) as a concept for analysis of the structured nature of the child's immediate settings. It refers to a struc-tured environmental context in which the physical conditions for life and culturally constructed meaning systems are intricately related. The crucial feature of the cultural-ecological niche is precisely this relatedness of the physical and cultural sides of a given life world:

> The niche that an infant is born into and subsequently modifies, is structured both initially and in its adap-tive constraints by the culture, that is, the *economic activities, social and family structure, physical ecology*, and the *value and belief system* of the caretakers. The points of pressure and flexibility in mutual adap-tation will be patterned by the niche as well as by the infant. (Super and Harkness, 1982, pp. 48–49; added emphasis)

The children are not 'very special' – although child psychologists may fiercely disagree with this point. They are just one part of the culturally important process of inter-generational contin-uity. *Children are valued as part of moving towards the future of the parents*, rather than for their inherent nature as children. In this respect, children are but a small – yet culturally highlighted – part of the temporal matrix of the development of the whole kinship network.

This cultural highlighting by the adults can take various forms. First, it can *distinguish* some aspect of ordinary child development and turn it into a noticeable realm. For example, in our (Western) societies, the transition of infants to the state of walking independently is distinguished in its social value from many other developmental transitions that take place in infancy (the cutting of teeth, for instance).

Secondly, the cultural highlighting can *exag-gerate* the symbolic importance of some distin-guished developmental phenomena. The focus on the 'crucial role' of child's attachment type (secure versus insecure), in relation to the mother, has been a focus of intensive social construction in Western societies since the 1940s. Here a certain phenomenon is not only noted, but is turned into a symbolic central issue for *all* of development.

Thirdly, the cultural highlighting may use *negative stigmatization* of some aspects of devel-opment – or other societies' handling of those. This will be seen in Anglo-American perception of infant swaddling practices, or the disputes around what kind of milk – mother's, other woman's, or cow's – should be fed to infants.

Fourthly, cultural highlighting may entail *purposeful silence* about some issue of development. In Western societies, dominated by the cultural-historical constructed fears about masturbation, children's investigation of their genitals, and play with them, is purposefully 'hushed up'. The adults may refer to it by silent convention about not letting 'such things' become prominent in the child's conduct.

The cultural-ecological niche is set up by persons who are involved in social activities. When a woman becomes pregnant, her particular social location (married or unmarried, already mother of other children), her work role (housewife or working in the fields, or in a factory), her environment (lives and works on home grounds or migrates daily to workplace), immediately set up the cultural-ecological niche for the baby (who is not yet born). It narrows down possibilities for the baby's life in specific ways. For example, a mother who is married, is waiting for her first child, lives on the home compound, has people who take care of her household work, and lives through pregnancy, presents the baby with a different niche at the birth than one who is having the baby out of wedlock, works in a factory, and has no social support network. Or an African mother who carries her baby in a sling on her back during the whole day, while participating in agricultural work, is very different from an African mother in the same society, but living in an urban middle-class household.

As can be seen, parents' economic activities are linked with the ways in which the infant is taken care of in a given society (and historical time). If the mother needs to return to out-of-home economic activities soon after the baby's birth, the baby is either weaned early, or carried with the mother. If the mother is not involved in such activities, the baby may be kept nursing for a longer time.

The cultural-ecological niche is built on collective-cultural meaning systems. As such, it is the general constructed meaning of the given kind of baby born to the given parents that becomes interpreted in the collective culture. This interpretation can lead to different outcomes – the history of cultural meaning-making of the birth is variable, to say the least.

COLLECTIVE-CULTURAL ORGANIZATION OF THE FATE OF NEWBORNS

Children are desired in general, but that does not mean that each and every actually born child is immediately accepted. Instead, the collective-cultural system pre-emptively sets up interpretive systems that allow for both directions of development – acceptance of the baby, or its rejection. The latter option becomes linked with unusual conditions – physical malformations at birth, birth of twins, and so on. The newborn is carefully watched for 'ill omens' of a supernatural or health kind. Already in ancient Babylon, different collective-cultural shared knowledge in the form of 'birth omens' was linked with detection of potential status of the newborn as a 'monster' (Jastrow, 1914). Birth of abnormal children ('monsters') was treated as the ill will of the deities, and was to be avoided. Infanticide under conditions of detecting a 'monster' was culturally prescribed, so as to protect the whole community from potential supernatural dangers.

In a similar vein, the evaluation system of newborns' physical strength for survival was put into practice in societies where warfare had a major role in adult lives (such as in Ancient Sparta). Redundant control over the fate of the newborn involves both the interpretation of the offspring's physical state, and its meaning in the context of the society. In this vein, children born with clearly visible handicaps (physical conditions) became viewed as efforts by some malevolent spirit to damage the livelihood of the whole community, and as a result such a child could have been killed.[1]

Dealing with twin birth: an unusual, yet normal event

A good example of unusual conditions of birth is that of twins. Twin births occur relatively rarely, producing physically normal babies (rather than newborns of clear physical handicaps) and thus are an intermediate case between the ordinary (single birth) and the extraordinary (multiple birth). In the history of human societies, multiple births have been regularly linked with the actions of spirits, ancestors, deities, or other extra-parental constructed agent.

The fate of twins has usually followed a simple interpretation rule: *if their birth is considered to be the work of malevolent agents, they may be killed*; but *if the interpretation indicates the action of benevolent spirits, they may not only be preserved but become specifically marked* out so as to be socially honoured. It is the case of twin births that indicates most clearly the unity of opposite life (and death) course trajectories prescribed collective-culturally for human offspring.

In the history of the Zulus (in South Africa), the fear of twins was widespread (Webster, 1942, p. 62). If twin birth occurred, both twins were killed immediately, and the whole event was covered with secrecy. A mother who bore twins was considered tainted, and such mothers were killed themselves if they bore twins a second time. The efforts of the British colonizers to fight such practices were slow to have any effect – the belief in the linkage of twin birth with that of malevolent spirits was more powerful than any external administrative power.

Historical transformation of practices: reversal of the role of twins among the Yoruba

The practice of twin infanticide in the history of human societies leads to understanding of how human meaning construction can move from one extreme position to the other. Not only can the practice of twin infanticide be stopped by cultural transformation, but it can move to its opposite – into the form of public honouring of the twins in the given society.

The history of the treatment of twins among the Yoruba (in Nigeria) is noteworthy (Chappel, 1974). An earlier (prior to nineteenth century) practice of twin infanticide became reversed in the nineteenth century and turned into its opposite over the following century. Yet at the level of personal cultures, negative feelings about twin birth may remain – depending upon whether the particular adults accept the symbolic explanation of the meaning of twins.

The canonical version of the Yoruba twins-honouring cult can be described as a story of interpreted outcomes:

> The birth of twins is a predestined event which is to be regarded as a lucky omen. Since *twins are a special gift from God* (*Olorun*) they must be treated with special care for they are, as it were, embryonic *orisha* (sacred beings). *If they are made to feel welcome the parents will derive material benefit from them, if not they will cause their parents, and any person who offends them*, suffering. Twins are *vengeful and demanding* and must be constantly placated. Extra care must be taken when one or both of the twins leave this world for it is then that they become 'real' *orisha*. (Chappel, 1974, p. 259; added emphasis)

The emphasized parts in this description allow us to recreate a story of reconstruction of the twin infanticide practice into that of twin honouring. In the latter, the fear of the unusual (which twin birth is) remains. Only instead of elimination of that feared unusual (by infanticide), the meaning system leads the adults to honour them, with the anxiety that if they were to 'leave this world' they would be more dangerous than when kept alive (that is, it is believed that twins would not die, but become spirits). The Yoruba belief system requires that even in the case of death of one of

the twins in childhood, the mother must replace him or her by a wooden image[2] which must be carried about, washed and dressed as if it were the deceased (departed) twin (Webster, 1942, p. 66).

The Yoruba myth of the twin honouring practices provides further narrative evidence for the unity of the opposites of killing and honouring twins. In 1964, Chief Ajanaku (of Lagos, Nigeria) told the following story:

> In older times twins were forbidden and anybody having them had to kill them before it came to the notice of the oba [local ruler]. Isokun, near Porto Novo, in Dahomey, was the first place where twins were allowed to stay, and this was because Isokun was not, at that time, part of the kingdom of Oyo. When those twins were born *the parents did not know whether to kill them or let them live because they were not in their own country* and it was not the custom in those parts to kill twins as in Oyo. So they consulted the *Ifa* oracle. *Ifa* said that they should keep the twins, but they would *have to dance around the town with them every five days*. This they did and everyone *took pity on them and gave them gifts*. In the course of time they became so wealthy that people began to say it was the twins who made them rich. This story eventually reached the ears of the *Alafin* at Oyo. He was convinced by what he heard that *these twins were lucky children*, so he said it was alright for the parents to keep them and not kill them as was the custom. (Chappel, 1974, p. 252; added emphasis)

Without questioning the reality of this story, a number of reflections in it are important to consider. The innovation is reported to have started on the *initiative of the parents* who lived outside of their native land (the Kingdom of Oyo, where collective-cultural rules prescribed infanticide), and who had access to an alternative collective-cultural rule system (of not killing the twins, in Dahomey). The parents turned to a diviner, who *suggested a public ritual* (dancing) that would replace the killing. The public nature of the ritual led to gifts to the twins from outsiders, which was believed to legitimate the 'lucky status' of the twins (and to prove that no harm came from them). The transformed practice was imported into the Oyo Kingdom, and set up in the collective culture *as an available alternative* to infanticide. Instead of a strict rule of killing the twins, now the parents could act in either way – kill them, or honour them as 'lucky children'. Yet in both cases the treatment was based on the fear of the potential power of twins – either when kept in the community and honoured (to appease the power), or forced to leave the community (by killing them).

Introduction of the infant into the social system

The social introduction includes both real human beings, and their imaginary 'co-players' whose supernatural powers can be feared. In Korea, there exists a traditional belief in the goddess of childbirth (*Samshin*). She is believed to rule the house from the beginning of the birth to some not strictly set time (varying from 7 to 100 days) thereafter (Sich, 1988, p. 498). The connection between the new baby, its mother and *Samshin* is made by the mother-in-law. The mother-in-law is the 'representative' of *Samshin* in the household, thus taking into her hands the power over all activities that take place in relation to the baby. This includes an attitude of humility, service (support to the mother, and cleaning of the house, doing household chores) and dedication to her daughters-in-law. For her, the healthy grandson is the most desired result of inter-generational continuity, and the mother-in-law does her utmost to attain her ideal.

The survival of the baby in the post-partum period is not guaranteed, so there are elaborate restrictions upon events at home after the birth. No one (except the household members) is expected to enter the house in the first few days after birth. This is linked with the belief that a stranger's entrance into the house may cause harm – by preventing the mother's milk from flowing. Mother-in-law prepares sacrifices to *Samshin* to guarantee the mother's flow of milk. Only after the nutritional success is guaranteed will the mother and baby be ready for public contacts.

The Sumbwa child display ritual

Social introduction of the newborn to the social world includes their introduction to the father, to their grandparents and to other relatives. The 'coming out of the house' ceremony among the Sumbwa (in Tanzania) includes a secret ritual of the household members, who are introduced to the child (and the child to them) through a ritual that binds the adults together symbolically in the service of the child's future.

In this ritual (*ituga*, described by Cory, 1961), first different paraphernalia of ancestor worship (calabashes, spear, any object that was used by the ancestors) are put in front of the house, when the baby is about 2 weeks old. The father of the child has not yet seen the child. In the evening of that day, the master of ceremonies (*Mbughere*) invites the parents, the child and all the grandparents to a secret location in the bush. In that location, ten small figurines are set up for the ceremony. Let us look carefully into the ceremony around the most important of those – the figurine of wisdom (*masala*):

> This figure is about three feet high. The mother steps in front of the Masala and kneels down, putting both hands on its shoulders. The father kneels behind it and puts his hands round its waist. Both close their eyes. The *Mbughere* joins them and exclaims:
> '*Liuba*, *Kongwa* and *Ngasa* [three superior spirits] help the child grow. They came, the parents, in order to get knowledge. They see now for the first time *masala*, the great, who is greater than all others. They will see later the nine lesser ones. Here you both see the origin of our clan, and our child will grow up healthy, for all you have seen today *masala* the secret of our clan.'
> He takes the child out of the arms of its grandmother and holds it over the head of *masala*. With a razor he scratches slightly the big toe of the baby's left foot so that a drop of blood falls on the head of the figure. He says:
> '*Child*, you have become a human being. You have been in the body of your mother, where nobody has seen you. Become a child who quickly learns to walk. Your house is where *masala* is. If there is no truth ask your father and the others. They will testify it, just as I have told you. Your father, like you to-day, once put his foot on *masala*'s head.'
> Father and mother get up, the grandparents disappear into the bush. The Master makes a little cut near the pubic bone of the mother and smears some clay from the figure on it. With his finger, to which thus adheres some blood and clay mixed together, he makes a small circle between the eyes of the baby. He does the same with the husband, with whose blood mixed with clay he makes a circle between the eyes of *masala*. After this the parents sit down, the mother in front of the figure, the father behind it. The Master orders them to take hold of each other's genitals by passing their hands between the legs of the figure. (Cory, 1961, p. 69)

A number of specific features of the description of this ritual are important for understanding its semiotic function. The ritual links the parents (and grandparents) through the baby with the spirit world of the ancestors. The use of blood – the baby's, and that of the mother and the father – is a moment of unification (with the wisdom world of the ancestors, represented by clay). The figure is in the centre of the actions – and continues to be so. The master of ceremonies emphasizes that the blood of the child comes from the mother, while the father 'gave his blood to *masala*' who is the origin of the clan. The parents are then instructed to lie down in front of *masala*, and are questioned as to feelings of fear or shame at the time of the birth (in case of the mother) and generation (the father). If both parents confirm they conceived the child and gave birth to it without shame and fear, the master requires a repetition of sexual intercourse as part of the ritual:

> The man executes a coitus between his wife's thighs. The Master sitting nearby pulls him away at the moment of ejaculation. Should the husband fail on account of circumstances the Master would proceed with the ceremonies, using dust from the ground instead of the sperm. The sperm which has dropped to the ground is mixed by the Master with clay from the figure of *masala* and the Master makes two lines with the mixture from front to back of the baby's head. If the baby is a girl, the vaginal fluid is used. The Master says 'Accept the power of generation from your father (mother).' (Cory, 1961, p. 70)

The use of sexual fluids in this ceremony parallels that of blood, described above. The unity of sexual fluids and blood is further exemplified here, and the baby is guided towards his or her gender-appropriate role in future reproductive life. Subsequently, the father is given a social demand of not cohabiting with the wife while she is feeding the baby (that is, instruction for post-partum sexual taboo), all centred on the well-being of the baby. At the end of the ceremony the master of ceremonies destroys the figure of *masala*. The ceremonies for the other nine figures are held on subsequent days, each having their particular future-guiding role.

MAKING THE BABY SAFE: CARE AND SYMBOLIC PREVENTION

The fate of the newborn is threatened by different dangers. Some are biological realities – various diseases have claimed many lives of the young. Others are constructed as cultural explanations. The latter become linked with the former, creating a meaning complex where biological events support cultural interpretations, and vice versa. In the words of Ana (a Puerto Rican woman in Santo Domingo), to keep children healthy meant to keep them clean, away from dirty water and away from the direct gaze of jealous people (Whiteford, 1997, pp. 214–215).

The realities of childbearing over centuries have included high newborn and infant mortality rates. Even though people in human social history were not epidemiologists interested in popula-tional rates of survival – but rather human beings hoping for the survival of *this* newborn child – the fact of being a newborn and infant as a dangerous period in development was a clearly recognized life fact. It gave rise to a large variety of efforts to protect newborns (and their kinship groups) against the culturally constructed dangers.

Protection against dangerous encounters with the world has been primarily symbolic, becom-ing verified through real-world happenings. The baby's death becomes explained through supernatural attributions, rather than through biological causes. Similarly, efforts to prevent such death are first and foremost in the realm of semiotic actions.

Symbolic dangers and symbolic immunization

The general most widespread danger to the newborn and infant is the possibility of coming under the influence of somebody else's 'evil eye'. The most obvious way to protect the child from such a danger is not to display the baby publicly. Yet this is not practical in many cases, so alter-native prevention strategies need to be devised. These operate in parallel with modern medicine's immunization – only at the symbolic level. By performing a symbolic act – of wearing an anti-'evil eye' amulet, or performing a protective ritual with the child, the baby is considered to be out of danger. Furthermore, the location in the home where the newborn and infant are kept may acquire symbolic protection devices. Thus, in Punjabi society (in India), the newborn child's cot is symbolically protected by tying an iron lock to it (Bajwa, 1991, p. 61). This lock is assumed both to threaten away evil spirits, and to protect the baby against death.

Some of the protective rituals include texts of incantations. Here is an Ancient Babylonian incantation against the evil eye:

> The evil eye has secretly entered and flies around.
> O, swooping-down *suskallum* net. O, ensnaring *huharum* net.
> She passed the door of the babies, and created rash among the babies.
> She passed the door of the women in childbed and strangled their babies.
> She entered the storage room and broke the seal.
> She dispersed the secluded fireplace and turned the locked house into ruins.
> She destroyed the *isertum*, and the god of the house is gone
> Hit her on the cheek, make her turn backward!
> Fill her eyes with salt, fill her mouth with ashes!
> May the god of the house return.
> (Van der Toorn, 1996, p. 122)

The 'evil eye' beliefs entail the unity of opposites: while on most occasions, eye contact with
other human beings is a benevolent social act,
at times (by some select kinds of persons – like
barren women) it can become viewed as dangerous. The 'evil eye' can be cast upon children
– intentionally or unintentionally – by other
pesons. Thus, cultural semiotic processes undertaken by active agents (persons who interpret
everyday life events) relate the behavioural phenomenon (that is, eye contact) with the cultural
meaning system (of benevolent, or malevolent
connotations). In other terms – the pro- or anti-
social nature of any episode of eye contact is
not a pre-given objective fact, but a result of a
co-constructionist interpretive process.

Treatment of 'evil eye' contagion
In a way, the fear of 'evil eye' in the history of
human societies is the psychological equivalent
of infectious diseases. As we can believe that we
got our 'flu from shaking hands with a sneezing
politician, or from contact with the saliva of our
boy- or girlfriend in the amorous occidental body-
fluid sharing otherwise known as 'kissing',people
in many societies (and in our own, in the past)
have treated the eye-gaze of some specifiable
agent as the cause for the baby's fussing, illness,
or death. As such, protective (preventive) efforts
are undertaken – protecting the baby against
the 'evil eye' can be seen as an act of *symbolic
vaccination*. Of course, as in the case of medical
vaccination, the 'infection' can still occur, despite
all protective efforts, in which case it needs to be
'cured' after the fact. Yet the notion of pro-active
prevention is of central importance.

When potential contagion by the 'evil eye' is
diagnosed, the collective-cultural system moves
into administering appropriate symbolic remedies. In Rajastan (India) the treatment of the 'evil
eye' includes seven red chilis and some salt
circled over the head of the sick child before these
are thrown into the hearth. Or, alternatively, a
sickle dipped into a plate of oil is drawn over the
baby's abdomen (Lambert, 1997, p. 261). The Kel
Ewey Tuareg (in Niger, see Rasmussen, 1996,
p. 71) use amulets consisting of a date and leather,
sewn into the hair of the baby. The use of staple
foods of symbolic power (chilis, dates) in the
prevention efforts indicates another intertwining
of the symbolic realms of food and that of well-
being.

Complexity of the meanings of 'evil eye' phenomena

In general, belief in the 'evil eye' is widespread
across cultural time and space (Maloney, 1976).

On the one hand, it is linked with the behavioural
act of looking at others (that is, a 'special way of
looking' amounts to 'eyeing' and bringing harm).
On the other hand, the notion of the 'evil eye' is
linked with a myriad of beliefs in other persons'
malevolent intentions, which need not include
any eye contact. The complex emotion of envy is
said to be linked with the looking (the Latin term
invidere from which Italian *invidia*, Spanish *envidia*
are derived; Kearney, 1976, p. 185).

'Evil eye' is thus a complex of social actions
linked with emotions of the bearer, that can
become dangerous to other persons, and to the
community at large. In different societies one can
find varied versions of differentiation in the 'evil
eye' beliefs, all of which have direct bearing upon
treatment of persons in social interaction, and
upon their status within the local community.
For example, in the little Southern Italian town
known as Locorotondo (Galt, 1991), two forms of
'evil eye' (*malocchio*) could be seen to function
– fascination (*affascene*) and envy (*mmvidie*):

> Of the two forms of evil eye, *affascene* is the lesser.
> Signaled by headache, it can be lifted through the use
> of an oil-and-water oracle and cure in conjunction
> with an incantation. Anyone who learns them may
> use the phrases and the oracle, but one is allowed to
> teach them to no more than three people during
> a lifetime on pain of losing one's curing ability.
> Amulets are ineffective against this form of evil
> eye. *Affascene* has its source in an unexpressed
> envy or admiration of others, and there are certain
> individuals – those whose eyebrows connect over
> their noses and who are said to have *occhi d'affascene*
> (fascinating eyes) – whose envy is most likely to strike
> in this form . . .
>
> *Mmvidie*, or envy, on the other hand, can be
> serious, and its symptoms tend to manifest them-
> selves in downturns of luck or in runs of ill health.
> Unlike *affascene*, *mmvidie* cannot be lifted; it just has to
> run its course. But, again unlike *affascene*, *mmvidie* can
> be warded off by various forms of amulet, either
> worn on the person or attached to animals or objects
> that must be protected. (Galt, 1991, pp. 740–741)

In neither case of the evil eye is it believed in
Locorotondo that the person inflicting harm does
so knowingly. In both cases, the folk belief system
includes a number of protective action strategies
that can be applied both before (amulets to protect
children, animals, or buildings against *mmvidie*
for example) and after a suspicious event of
social interaction has taken place (such as a person
who openly admires another and may make a
gesture of the horns with both hands and exclaim
'God protect!'). The specific practices of symbolic
protection against the 'evil eye' may vary across
societies, taking seemingly esoteric forms which

are still meaningful from the standpoint of the particular collective culture (see Maloney, 1976).

Culturally constructed paradoxes of the 'evil eye' become particularly interesting when we find versions of it in the case of closest interpersonal attachment contexts. Thus, Unni Wikan's description of the beliefs in an Omani town in the early 1970s reveals a special case of 'evil eye' – 'lover's eye' (*'en ilmuhibb*), which is considered to be even more powerful than the 'evil eye' of envious outsiders:

> In contrast to the ordinary evil eye, this is not a special power with which only some persons are endowed. Every person is prone to it, toward relatives, if their love is strong enough. Consequently the mother is the most dangerous source, followed by other close relatives. According to Sohari belief, the effect is caused quite inadvertently, indeed very much against the agent's will. All a loving mother need to do is look at her child and think of him as the most wonderful child of the world. Instantly the child may fall sick. (Wikan, 1982, p. 242)

Thus we are forced to confront the inherent complexity of the (at first glance) pro-social act of looking at a child – even the closest person to the child can be believed to cause harm, *if the act of looking occurs in a specific meaningful context*.

Constructing the baby in interaction with others: 'dangerous mouths'

As the examples of 'evil eye' phenomena demonstrate, the social construction of the newborn is a process of constrained coordination of perspectives between different adults, relating with the baby.

The social rules for *talking about* the newborn indicate the collective-cultural directions of setting up the newborn in the context of the given society. In the contemporary world of secular, medicalized childbirths, the visitors to the mother of the newborn are most likely (a) eager to have a look at the baby, and (b) be obliged to tell the mother how nice her baby is (even, if in reality, the newborn does not look very aesthetic by any criteria), and possibly (c) begin to comment upon the borrowing of some features of the baby's face as 'coming right from' the mother or the father. The mother may complement such rule-governed communication, by expecting it to happen, and by initiating any of the topics herself (for example, 'Do you want to see my baby?'; 'The baby is so beautiful!'; 'She has got my nose'). Such a collective-cultural baby-adoration ritual is historically possible in collective-cultural conditions where the newborn can be expected to survive beyond doubt (thanks to modern medical care) and where (in conjunction) the beliefs in supernatural 'fragility' of the baby have disappeared. Such conditions need not apply in other societies. In the following description of how American friends visited their Thai friend – mother of a newborn – after the birth in a hospital in Thailand gives us a good glimpse of an event that commences at the intersection of vastly different collective-cultural rules of talking about newborns:

> We recently visited a Thai friend who had just given birth to a bouncing baby boy in an upcountry hospital . . . The luck and fortune of a baby is very fragile. We came close to mishandling that fragile package and causing some cultural breakage. With an enthusiastic lack of caution, we waxed eloquent praise on the beauty of the baby only to be stopped in mid-sentence by the mother's stern expression and admonishing raised hand. She remarked disdainfully that her son was, alas, ugly and 'black as a Cambodian.' We started to protest and again extolled the merits of the baby, but a warning glance from a Thai nurse followed us out of the room and enlightened us as to why the seemingly not so proud mother had been so disparaging about her baby. We were told that one must avoid praise and compliments or the spirits will be attracted to such a wondrous creature and being jealous will steal the baby for their own. Thus, the mother, in fooling the spirits, was as insulting as possible. (Klausner and Klausner, n.d., pp. 110–111)

This episode can be seen as continuous with the 'evil eye' beliefs, only here it is the 'dangerous mouths' of the well-meaning friends that need to be avoided. Communication about the newborn is actually communication between the symbolic agents within the current power hierarchy. Such communication is strategic, rather than merely an exchange of information, or of intersubjectivity. Human talking about babies (and children at large) is goals-oriented. In the example given, we saw two goal orientations in direct clash. The American orientation was that of semiotic construction of a one-sided positive image of the baby, and of the beauty of motherhood. As such, it purposefully de-focused from the realities of the appearance of the baby (who indeed could look ugly), and of the uncertainties of feeling of the new mother. In contrast, the Thai goal orientation was that of concealing the baby from the spirits – by way of strategic denigration of the baby's characteristics. The two orientations were working towards establishment of *their* prescriptions for the semiotic demand settings (refer back to Chapter 7, especially to Figure 7.2). The two goal orientations capitalized upon the opposite parts of the field of real phenomena (for example, the same person can be nice at some time and beastly at others), *by actively eliminating the respective opposite from consideration*. Such unipolar construction of semiotic demand settings is characteristic of collective cultures' construction of the socially desired images. Out of the psychological reality of opposite characteristics being mutually interwoven and inseparable (and at times in ambivalent relations with each other), collective-cultural canalization creates unipolar order by eliminating the opposites, or subordinating them. The result is the propagation of ontological identities:

'the baby *is*
[UGLY or BEAUTIFUL]'
or
'the motherhood *is*
[SACRED or SATISFYING or BORING or SLAVERY]'

All the options (and many more) in the parentheses are possible, yet all of the possible statements are ontological – they posit that something *is* something else. It is precisely the possibility of the individual-psychological dynamics that may embrace both (all) sides of the phenomenon in a relativistic or ambivalent manner that leads the collective-cultural propaganda agents to work hard at turning *dialogical* reflection upon the phenomena into a *monological encantation* of the socially desired value statements. This is particularly pertinent in the negotiation of the sociocultural nature of the baby after childbirth, when the features of the baby become available to the mother, the father, and others.

British pediatrician Aidan Macfarlane has recorded some of the conversations between the mother, the father and the medical specialist (nurse, midwife, doctor) present immediately after childbirth (Macfarlane, 1977). The interaction between the new mother and the father of the baby (in the British context of the 1970s) reveals how immediately the meaning of the baby becomes the task of semiotic construction:

[The baby girl was born, the midwife takes care of her, shows the baby to the parents]

(1) *Mother*: Oh, *lovely*, oh, *lovely*. Oh [a cough]
(2) *Father*: Wow, there she is! Didn't take very long to come out, did you?
(3) *Mother*: Oh, that was *nice*.
(4) *Midwife*: *Very nice.*
(5) *Mother*: Oh, that was *very nice* [A hiccough] That was the sherry last night.
(6) *Midwife*: There, look.
(7) *Father*: Ah, oh, was it?
(8) *Mother*: Hello. [Father laughs]

(9) *Mother*: Oh, dear, what a lot of noise.
(10) *Midwife*: Well, if that was the sherry, you must have had a lot of sherry last night.
(11) *Father*: Yes
(12) *Mother*: Oh.
(13) *Midwife*: Two little bits under the arms there [referring to the baby].
(14) *Father*: No vernix.
(15) *Mother*: Oh, *how nice.*
(16) *Father*: What *a funny-colored beast.*
(17) *Mother*: It is *not a funny colour*. It is *nice*.
(18) *Father*: What a big one, isn't it?
(19) *Midwife* [laughs]: Are you *satisfied?*
(20) *Father*: I'm very satisfied.

. . . [baby given to mother]

(21) *Mother*: Oh, hello. Hello. Oh, *you* are *nice*. That's a lot of noise *for a little girl*. That's right – you've opened your eyes. That's *lovely*.
(22) *Father*: Oh, well, that's *a nice normal beast*, isn't it. Hello.
(23) *Mother*: Oh, that's *good*, that's *very good*. That's a *very good* and *nice* noise.
(24) *Father*: Miaouw.
(25) *Mother*: No, *not miaouw, that's the other sort.*
(26) *Father*: That's *nice.*
(27) *Mother*: Oh *you* are *nice*. What *a nice beast*. Oh [a hiccough] Oh [a hiccough]
(Macfarlane, 1977, pp. 44–47; added emphasis)

This dialogue (which is at times a trialogue – with the midwife joining in) reveals the immediacy of personal-cultural construction. The newly 'hatched' mother immediately begins to create exaggerated positive evaluation of the newborn girl (superlatives of 'nice', 'lovely' 'good' are flowing all over the otherwise messy delivery room context). The father at first maintains a secondary role in this construction, and (playfully) suggests the notion of 'funny coloured beast' to refer to the baby (line 16). The mother moves quickly to redirect the father from the 'funny coloured' notion (line 17) by marking the colour of the baby as 'nice'. Once the baby is given to the mother, she immediately turns her into her direct interaction partner (by referring to her as 'you' – line 21). She also introduces the first gender-linked evaluative comparison (about noise – same line). The father continues his construction of the baby as 'normal beast' (line 22), moving into playful assignment of the role of a cat to the baby (line 24), which is immediately counter-acted by mother (line 25). What we see subsequently is the father's acceptance of the attribution of evaluation ('nice' – line 26) and the mother's takeover of the father's playful 'beast' reference (line 27).

This undoubtedly unique playful interaction example illustrates the general process of construction of the meaning of the baby as the childbirth has taken place. The process is guided by the collective-cultural direction – *in what ways is it appropriate to present the baby to one another in social discourse*? In different societies, that direction can vary: in some (as the Thai case), the baby should not be presented in positive terminology (and better not presented in talk at all). In others – like the British example (and its numerous Anglo-American or Anglo-Australian etc. counterparts) – the construction of the baby's individual agency and positive social presentation begins at birth (if not earlier).[3]

It is instructive also to note the categorical nature of the meanings that were constructed in this episode. The function of social discourse around the newborn and infant carries the constructive function of an assault of (ideological) positional monologicality (for instance, the insistence of the 'nice', 'good', 'lovely' nature of the 'little beast') upon the free-floating and potentially uncontrollable dialogicality (where the father was observed to assign a pet role to the baby; which was suppressed by the mother). While cultural meaning-making processes are dialogical, they are often oriented towards turning their resulting meaning into a monological form. We can call this process *dialogical monologization* of human construction of meaning.

The psychological role of dialogical monologization.

I am inventing the notion of dialogical monologization to capture the goal-oriented nature of most (but not all) dialogical processes. The process itself is made possible by the co-presence of different sides of the meaning that is being constructed (for example, A and NON-A; or opposing voices in terms of Mikhail Bakhtin – see Chapter 3). Yet the process can move towards an outcome that establishes one of the opposites as dominating over the other (for example, A over NON-A; or one voice becoming dominant over another).

Sometimes the sub-dominant opposite becomes suppressed, and locally eliminated (let us call it *dialogical execution*). While the dialogical process entails tension between the opposites, the result of the process – after dialogical execution of the opposite – no longer includes any tension. The *result* of the dialogical process can be monological itself (refer back to Chapter 1 on process versus outcome distinction).

In general terms, thus, it can be posited:

DIALOGICAL
PROCESS: A <<in tension with>> NON-A

GOAL STATE: {dominance of either}
MEANS: sub-domination, execution
RESULT: A (or NON-A) dominance
              (tension becomes eliminated)

Of course, the monological result can (and does) enter into some other phase of dialogical oppositions, and so on – the monologicality of the result may be a temporary state. Yet here is an important general principle (of overcoming tensions in meaning construction): *human meaning construction strives towards overcoming of uncertainty inherent in dialogicality, in favour of monologicality of relatively fixed meanings*. This is part of the general adaptational nature of the human psychological system – it allows for constant adaptation to ever-changing conditions, striving towards (but never reaching) a state of equilibrium. Thus, *naming* becomes a vehicle for construction of relative equilibrium. Human beings are eager to name (and categorize) anything that is uncertain – and by that, gain control over the uncertainty.[4]

The role of human semiotic systems as producing constructed certainty out of uncertainty was recognized already by Henri Bergson in his *Creative Evolution* (Bergson, 1907/1911). For Bergson, human language was the main tool for stabilizing (psychologically) the otherwise ever-changing, never-recurring, flow of experiencing the immediate relations with the world.

In human development, it is the naming of the person that creates the specific power of monological personal identity. Yet the issue of naming of the baby is a part of this wider process of creating symbolic power – the baby is usually named for the sake (and within the system) of the collective cultural world.

Establishing the identity of the infant: naming practices

Giving a name to the baby is similar in function to the provision of a protective amulet to him or her – to defend the baby against symbolic dangers, as well as to establish his/her special role in the given society. This linkage can explain the variability not only in the practices of giving the baby a name, but also of those of making the given name usable within restricted social practices. Oftentimes, the name of the person becomes secret (that is, the given name is known by the bearer, and some of the closer kin, but is not to be used in public address). For social referencing, additional ('public') names are often invented. So the person may bear a secret (unused) name *and* a public one. For example, the Kayapo (in Brazil) have clear rules of mentioning a kin group member's name in public. Thus, the very ordinary-looking question 'what is your name?' is unacceptable in interaction with people from other societies (Bamberger, 1974). Furthermore, in some cases there are recurrent re-naming occasions as the person moves through their life course.

The role of different adults in the naming process varies widely from society to society – being, as a rule, a far cry from the Western practice of the mother and the father negotiating the name for their baby. The naming may take place quite late – once it is clear that the infant is going to survive beyond the first year. For example, among the Bororo (in Mato Grosso, Brazil) the naming process takes place only when it is detected that the baby is 'hardened' enough (usually some 5–6 months after birth). It is only through the naming ceremony that the child becomes 'socially born' and recognized (Fabian, 1992, p. 66). The child's midwife (*imarugo*) and the mother's brother (*iedaga*) preside over the naming ceremony. They become relevant persons (perhaps similar to Western 'godparents') for the whole of the life course of the named baby. The *imarugo* has a special power role in this. She,

. . . who at its birth held the power of life and death over it [the baby] (deformed babies *or those whose parents have had dreams of ill omen* prior to the birth are traditionally not allowed to live, the responsibility of action in such cases falling upon the midwife) now introduces the child to its new social life. (Fabian, 1992, p. 66; added emphasis)

The social power role in respect of the newborn includes both opposites – killing and honouring – depending upon the cultural conditions. Interestingly, here these conditions include parents' dreaming. Furthermore, the Bororo naming ceremony entails gender-linked body modification – the lower lips of boys are pierced during this ceremony, creating a hole from where male ornaments can be suspended.

'Automatic' naming practices

The Asante (in Ghana) are known for their naming of babies by automatic assignment, based on the particular weekday on which the baby is born. The automatic nature of the practice is built upon the belief that each week-day is governed by a specific type of soul, who enters the babies born on that day. Thus, the naming of the babies is actually elucidation of the spirits who have entered into the particular bodies, on the respective days. The Asante *personal* identity is therefore set up collective-culturally as their *identity of linkages with spirits*. Table 9.1 lists the first names of boys and girls born on each of the weekdays.

TABLE 9.1 *Asante (Ghana) child-naming practices*

Day of the week	Boy's name	Girl's name
Sunday	Kwasi	Akosua
Monday	Kwadwo	Adwoa
Tuesday	Kwabena	Abenaa
Wednesday	Kwaku	Akua
Thursday	Yaw	Yaa
Friday	Kofi	Afua
Saturday	Kwame	Amma

Source: Jahoda, 1954, p. 193

It can be seen that many of the Ghanaian leaders bear names that also specify their birthday. Thus, the current Secretary-General of the United Nations, Kofi Annan, can be known – from his first name – to have been born on a Friday, while the first leader of independent Ghana, Kwame Nkrumah, was a 'Saturday's child'.

The spirits who enter the children born on a particular day bring with them the child's soul (*kra*) that will govern the child all through his or her lifetime. Each day-spirit brings a different *kra*. In the collective-cultural belief system, Kwadwo (the boy of Monday) is believed to be quiet, retiring and peaceful. In contrast, the 'Wednesday's boy' – Kwaku – is expected to be quick-tempered and aggressive. These expectations may be the basis for self-fulfilling prophecies of collective construction of the social roles of different children. Gustav Jahoda's (1954) analysis indicates that the juvenile court records in Kumasi (the capital of the Asante region) included a higher proportion of young men named Kwaku than other names. During the Second World War, Adolf Hitler was named 'Kwaku Hitler' in the social discourse of the Asante.

Yet not all boys named Kwaku become troublemakers. As is obvious, the bi-directional culture transmission model presumes that social suggestion of a particular direction (or expectation) is followed by some, counter-acted by others, and neutralized by most. Naming is merely a canalization device for a particular direction in the potential development of a person, who actively creates his or her future, often contrary to the canalizing messages.

Name negotiated with the baby

On the Indonesian island of Bonerate (described by Bruch, 1990, pp. 24–25), the finding of the name for the infant is an intricate process of establishing relations. First the baby is given a *temporary name*. The named infant approaches humanity – while still remaining fragile. If 'insulted', he or she may decide not to live any more. It is assumed that if the name does not suit the baby (because of taboos that only the infant knows, but the parents do not), the baby will try to communicate this to the parents. The infant's cry is in most instances regarded as a cry for food – yet in some cases it can become interpreted as dissatisfaction with the proposed name. Especially the cry of the baby who has been well fed can be said to indicate name dissatisfaction. When the parents feel the temporary name does not satisfy the baby, they try another name. Once the infant indicates happiness with a name (through smiling and babbling), the name becomes fixed. The period of trial for the permanent name on Bonerate may last as long as five months. If, after the name is turned into a permanent one, the baby still shows signs of discomfort, then these signs become attributed to other causes, and not to the name selection. The collective-cultural meaning system defines both the 'open period' of name negotiation, and its closure.

Name negotiated within the kinship network

The following baby-naming case from Bihar, India (from the Munda society – Mundri, 1956) illustrates a case where an elaborate intra-kin group renegotiation of the naming of the baby took place. The case (which happened in 1953) involved the birth of a son to a village schoolmaster (Juni) and his wife (Dubki).

Seven days after the baby was born – and when the remnants of the umbilical cord fell off – the purification ceremony was organized. It involved the whole family as well as selected members of the community. The issue of naming the child became relevant in this social context – the villagers' first opportunity for social access to the new baby and his family. The newborn's paternal grandmother took the leading role in this stage of naming the child, suggesting the name of an ancestor in the family – Monor. In public, all participants agreed with the grandmother's argumentation ('his name is being forgotten in our family, it is necessary that we should give the newborn this name'). The boy's father (Juni) was not ready to accept this decision, yet waited until the following morning to circumvent the dominance of the grandmother – Juni's own mother – the previous day. She had bypassed the ritualistic method of selecting a name (*Tupi Nam*). In the morning, Juni appealed to his father (the newborn's paternal grandfather) with the demand that the ritualistic name-giving should proceed. The grandfather agreed, and the villagers were summoned to participate in the ceremony. The arbitration of the *Tupi Nam* ceremony moved from the kin group to that of the village community:

[the villagers] flocked together in front of the house of Juni who kept ready cold water in a brass pot (water brought from the surface spring . . . by Juni's mother on the same morning), a stem of *dubla* grass with one blade (brought by himself) and some sun-dried rice in a green *sal-leaf*. The assembly of the elderly persons then requested Nondo, one of the senior male members of the village, to perform the *Tupi Nam* ceremony. He agreed to do so, and after washing his face, hands and feet ceremonially with cold water sat down, facing the east, near the aforesaid materials arranged for this purpose. He first prayed to Singbonga to help him in selecting a suitable name for the baby and placed the stem of the *dubla* grass in the water kept in a brass pot. This grass all along remained floating on the surface of the water. Nondo further said, 'O Singbonga, I am dropping a rice grain in the pot in the name of Monor; let it and the dubla grass join one another, if of course, the proposed name is suitable for the new-born.' He dropped the rice grain which sank down into the bottom of the water and never floated up to contact the grass. Nondo raised his head and said, 'All of you can see that the rice grain and the *dubla* grass did not meet. This means that Singbonga is not pleased with this name. So let us discard it and choose another.' He then uttered the names of following persons one by one:

Sura (Juni's father's father)
Laka (Juni's wife's father's elder brother)
Bando (Juni's wife's elder brother)
Jado (Juni's father)
Nondo (one of the senior members of the village)
Jitray Deonra (Juni's father's elder brother's son)

But the *dubla* grass and the rice did not join one another. At last Nondo dropped a rice grain in the name of Jura (Juni's mother's younger brother). Now instead of sinking down like the previous rice grains, it began to float on the water and ultimately reached and touched the *dubla* grass like a lover embracing his sweetheart after a long interval of parting. All saw this scene with their eyes and Nondo declared gladly that the new-born would henceforth be known as Jura and not Monor. (Mundri, 1956, pp. 70–71)

A number of features of this description are worth further comment. Most obviously, the dominance fight between Juni and his mother set the stage for the community-mediated enactment of the ceremony. Yet for that, Juni and his father created a coalition, using the collective-cultural need for the ceremony as the core of overpowering the all too active grandmother.

In a general vein, however, the ritual entailed important semiotic construction moments. All the names tried out in the equivalent of a 'coin-tossing' procedure (that is, the floating together of the grass and the rice) were from the realm of the kinship group (except Nondo's own). Given the majority of the kinship names, the probabilistic procedure made it very unlikely that the baby would be named after anybody other than someone from the kinship group. The procedure thus *united certainty and uncertainty* – the latter was in the foreground of the technique, with the background carefully secured. Through a probabilistic technique it was clear that the name choice would remain among the collective-culturally acceptable ones.

Secondly, the ceremony indicates how the kinship group and village community negotiate a social issue. The dominance of the paternal grandmother was overcome by widening the whole procedure – yet letting it test the grandmother's suggestion first. As her suggested name failed the test, she had to accept the collective verdict. The collective nature of the decision-making took precedence over any individual initiative. No single person could determine the child's name. Likewise, the kinship group could not become divided over the issue of naming the baby. The collective power of the village community subordinated that of the kinship group, allowing the probabilistic procedure to be acceptable, yet with the guarantee that name continuity of the kinship group is a given. The process of child-naming described here mimics the structure of other relevant decision-making processes in the given society. If the functional social unit which gives the name to the baby is the mother, she does it. If it is the couple (mother and father), they do it, negotiating with each other, or turning to the wider group for arbitration. It can be the whole kinship group which negotiates its own symbolic continuity as well as interpersonal power relations in this naming decision (as was the case in the example). To solve the problem, the decision was produced one level up (communally).

Naming of the baby introducing naming changes of others
The naming of the baby is a change not only for the baby, but also for the people around the baby. Often they become re-named themselves, usually through ways that mark the relationship with the baby. In Korea, the child can be named in family discourse (for example, the child's name is Sunja). Together with this naming, the other members of the household begin to refer to one another by indicating their relation to the baby: the mother becomes addressed as 'Sunja mother', the father as 'Sunja father', the mother-in-law as 'Sunja grandmother', and the father-in-law as 'Sunja grandfather' (Sich, 1988, p. 499). The developing

child – through having been given a name – thus becomes a semiotic mediating device for the whole kinship network, marking the kinship roles in it and creating group cohesion.

Cultural construction of identity by body-related actions

The adults surrounding the newborn and the infant are culturally constructing the baby as a person not only through direct social interaction. The baby's physical environment becomes culturally organized in ways that are expected to guide the development of the baby in expected meaningful directions. The central point of these efforts is the baby's body. It is relative to the body that these guidance efforts are put to work.

Dressing the baby
The prominent case of cultural meanings inserted into the environment of newborns and infants is the gender-specific colour coding of the babies' clothing. It is appropriate for those societies which (at the level of ideology) propagate gender *equality* that in practical actions the parents of babies set up the stage for gender-differences (and *inequality*, built upon it). This fits well with the heterogeneity of the collective culture, and the unity of opposites within the same whole (see Simmel's ideas, in Chapter 4). The differentiation of the babies' gender by the colour of clothes (pink for girls, blue for boys) has been profound in Anglo-Saxon cultural history.

With the changes in the collective-cultural domain of contemporary societies, an interesting asymmetric condition emerges. The cultural rule boundaries of the gender-coding of clothes are modified for girls, but remain solidly in place for boys. This can be easily tested by way of considering the 'cross-colour' dressing possibility – would a parent (assuming the parent is eager to break down gender role barriers) equally easily dress her baby girl in blue, and her baby boy in pink, baby clothes?

The gender-specific function of clothing continues as the infancy proceeds. On US beaches in the summertime, one can observe female toddlers wearing two-piece bikinis, which accentuates the cultural necessity to guide towards covering of the breasts in public some dozen years before the issue of cultural organization of heterosexuality becomes directly relevant.

Transfer of the holding of the baby
In social contexts where different adults participate (and where the baby is present), the issue

of who holds the baby is of crucial importance for understanding the collective-cultural code system, as well as the dynamics of making (or breaking) the interpersonal relations of the adults. In our (occidental, urbanized and affluent) situations, the 'ownership' of the baby by the mother can be marked by the mother keeping her baby on her lap, and other adults merely being able to see the baby from some appropriate distance. As a special favour, the mother may temporarily give the baby to hold to a trusted friend, but most likely both of them transfer the baby back to the mother. The mother may – in the middle of group interaction – turn to the baby and isolate herself with the baby into a dyadic interaction routine. The other participants are likely not to be offended by such rude abandonment of the group interaction – the cultural value of the baby 'belonging to' the mother (and vice versa) becomes culturally marked that way.

Yet babies can belong to the mother without being culturally possessed – without the need for public demonstration of the 'ownership'. After all, the only concrete kinship tie that is verifiable and fortified is the mother–child tie. The mother is the mother of this baby, that role is unquestionable (even by role definition in cases of adoption), and does not require constant verification. Instead, the baby can become a participating object in the maintenance of social relations. For example, among the Baganda (in Uganda) the rules of public polite conduct require that the infant be passed to any adult visitor to hold, and that the infant becomes the object of adults' conversation (Kilbride and Kilbride, 1974). The infant becomes thus exposed to many adults, both kin and non-kin, without entering into interaction of any face-to-face kind. The adults who are given the baby to hold continue mostly to interact with other adults (thus, the baby is not considered an 'equal partner' in social communication, yet the baby is acknowledged as a person in his or her own – baby's – right).

FEEDING IN INFANCY AS A CULTURAL CONSTRUCTION

Cultural construction of infant feeding has many facets: what kinds of foods are appropriate, who should (or should not) feed the baby, what are the expectations for the baby's growth, etc. Feeding the baby is of central importance for survival – and hence a prime target for collective-cultural regulation of the conduct of not only the feeders themselves (mothers, wet nurses, etc.), but also of the 'social others' who may, by design or by happenstance, witness the act of feeding.

Private/public tension in the case of breast-feeding

As long as female breasts are culturally constructed to be sexual symbols (to be covered by the veil of privacy), the nutritional activity of breast-feeding is necessarily embedded within the opposition PUBLIC <> PRIVATE that governs any aspects of gender-related bodily exposure *as if* it is linked with issues of sexuality.

Culturally constructed privacy around breast-feeding is not merely the result of Western societies living under the belief systems of Christianity. It can occur under very many different circumstances. In the Sambia society in New Guinea, feeding is a concept spread from regular foods to transfer of all bodily liquids – semen of men and milk of women (which are considered gender-specific equivalents). The Sambia society includes secret same-gender 'symbolic feeding' practices for men growing through adolescence (see Chapter 13), which are transformed into cultural prescription for strict heterosexuality in conjunction with marriage. In line with the feeding notion of semen exchange – and a culturally constructed fear of semen depletion – it is not surprising that the breast-feeding of the baby by mothers is equated with the man feeding the wife with his semen. With this collective-culturally constructed background in mind, the following excerpt from an interview is neither surprising, nor exotic. In it, we observe an American anthropologist – Gilbert Herdt (H) – and Weivu (W) – a Sambia married man with two children – talking about men seeing women while breast-feeding:

H: Is it taboo to look at them while they're breast-feeding?
W: [Repeats the teachings:] You can't look at the mother feeding the baby and can't sit around with the mother and the baby. Instead, *you must stay with the men in the men's house.*
H: Yea, that [breaking post-partum taboo] no good.
W: If you watched the baby with its mouth holding on to the nipple of the breast, I'd think of my wife's mouth doing the same to my penis. If you think like that [voice speeds up] you won't let her be. You'll want to screw her. Then *you'll ruin your child.* (Herdt and Stoller, 1990, p. 138; added emphasis)

The crucial semiotic mediator here is the notion of *ruining one's child* (by breaking the post-partum taboo on sexual intercourse). The maintenance of the taboo here is organized by prescriptions for men to be in places where women cannot be present (men's house), or *not looking* at a breast-feeding woman (if she is in sight) to avoid the potential linking of the sucking by the baby with the practice of wife–husband *fellatio* (which is a normal and valued sexual practice in Sambia marriages – in line with the feeding-construct – Herdt and Stoller, 1990). Since sexual relations during the time the wife breast-feeds the baby are culturally prohibited, the observation of breast-feeding endangers the maintenance of this prohibition.

Biological and cultural organization of breast-feeding

The feeding process is undoubtedly the very first systematic experience in terms of time-regulated cultural activity in which the newborn partici-pates. Its nature and time-dependency is set up by the physiological organization of the sucking system.

The *anatomical conditions* that make the mother's breast-feeding and the baby's milk in-take possible entail the specific form of the nipple, and the matching functional action by the baby's mouth (see Figure 9.1).

The breast is anatomically suited for the feeding of babies. Its curvilinear form culminates in the nipple. At the time of lactation, the milk flow from the nipple requires the operation of a mechanical system which includes *positive pressure* and *suction* components. The positive pressure component maintains the holding (by the sucking system) of the nipple, while the suction component provides for the active extraction of the milk.

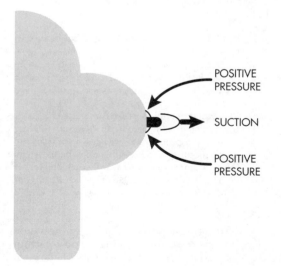

POSITIVE
PRESSURE

SUCTION

POSITIVE
PRESSURE

FIGURE 9.1 *The complementarity between the milk dispenser (the breast) and the sucking mechanisms of the offspring*

The milk delivery device (breast + nipple) and the milk extraction mechanism (the baby's mouth and its coordination of the two sucking components) is an anatomical prerequisite for granting the survival of the offspring. If the milk delivery system fails (in the case of the breast), it can be substituted by prosthetic devices (such as the 'baby-bottle' – but see a variety of breast substitute milk containers in the history of infant feeding, in Fildes, 1986). If – on the side of the offspring – the milk extraction system fails, the offspring's survival is in question; while the survival of the unproductive parent is not. The sucking system of the newborn baby is thus redundantly prepared for the different conditions of the milk delivery system that could be encountered. The sucking system is open for adaptation – it is not surprising that it is precisely the sucking system that has been open for different ways of instrumental conditioning (Bruner, 1969).

The *physiological system* that makes the process of breast-feeding functional entails unconditional reflexes on the side of both the baby and the mother. The newborn comes to the world with the ready *rooting reflex* (turning the head in the direction of a tactile stimulus that touches the corner of the mouth), as well as with the *sucking reflex* (sucking upon an oblong object inserted into the mouth. The sucking reflex consists of two coordinated components – the *mouthing* of the nipple (that is, the 'positive pressure' component – the baby puts pressure on the sucked-upon object from all sides, with the lips), and the *suctioning* of the liquid out of the nipple (sucking 'proper', or the 'negative pressure component'). The counterpart on the side of the lactating mother is the *let-down reflex* – the beginning of lactation from the breasts when stimulated by a key stimulus (in this case the baby's cry). In this sense, already anatomically and physiologically the mother–baby system of mutual adaptation guarantees the provision of food in infancy. The infant's cry (a distant stimulus) or bodily irritation reflected by the mother's tactile senses, leads to efforts to feed the baby.

It is important to note that complex physio-logical conditional reflexes can be worked out on the basis of the mother–baby feeding system. Newborns' sucking has been demonstrated to be flexible as an indicator of basic distinctions the baby can make about visual stimuli (Bruner, 1969; DeCasper and Fifer, 1980). The breast-feeding system can lead to generalized forms of conduct that can acquire relevance for baby–adult interaction outside of the interaction itself. Thus, a generalized anticipatory 'associative *reflex to the baby's position*' is an example of a complex form of conduct:

. . . the child, who has reached age 3–4 weeks and is being put by the mother underneath the breast into the specific feeding position, begins to perform rhythmic sucking movements 'in vain,' that is, already before any stimulus is touching the mouth.

. . . The sucking movements would continue for a short time, usually after 5–10 seconds the child begins to cry (if the breast is not given to him). (Denisova and Figurin, 1929, p. 81)

Such position reflex is a complex form of conduct, open to the mother's meaning-making in the process of feeding. The child's crying, at the delay of getting the breast, can easily become interpreted in terms of 'my baby doesn't like me' (should the mother construct such interpretation), and reacted to in terms of anxieties of the mother. This can lead to further negatively flavoured conduct by the baby, as an escalating process.

On the side of the breast-feeding woman, the biological reaction of the breasts to the infant cry (and the let-down reflex) can be complemented by personal feelings of desire to feed the baby. The physiological and the psychological sides of breast-feeding are closely intertwined. The feeling involved is closely tied to the sensuality of the person.

Process structure of breast-feeding

By *process structure* I refer to various forms of coordination of the actions of the feeder and the offspring during the actual feeding. It involves a look at different versions of turn-taking between mother and baby. The anatomical and physiological conditions that were described above are prerequisites for the process of feeding.

Different kinds of coordination of actions are shown in Figure 9.2. The infant's sucking movements can be of different duration (indicated by the different width of the bars in Figure 9.2), and can be grouped together into time-units ('bouts'). Dependent upon the infant's state of hunger, the breast-feeding may be characterized by bouts of longer or shorter duration. Thus, in the beginning phase of the feeding episode, the baby may be sucking almost constantly; as satiation takes hold, the bouts may shorten, and finally turn into episodic single-suck activity.

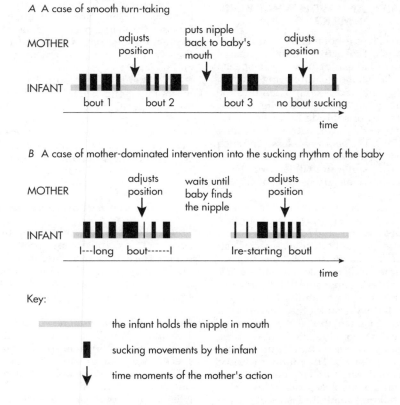

FIGURE 9.2 *Different versions of mother–baby breast-feeding action coordination (the* process structure *of breast-feeding episodes)*

The contrast depicted in Figure 9.2 is between two conditions of mother's complementary action that creates the *dyadic structure of the breast-feeding* process. In Figure 9.2*A*, the mother's timing of the adjustments of the infant's position, or other actions (such as interacting with the baby) are carefully timed to occur at times when the sucking itself is not taking place (Kaye, 1977). The action flows of the two partners – who are obviously unequal partners in this process (the baby needs food and needs the partner to provide it; the mother can set up the feeding condition in many ways) – are here mutually coordinated. The two 'dance smoothly' in the mutuality of giving (the nipple) and taking (the milk from it). In contrast, Figure 9.2*B* depicts a scenario in which the mother – for whatever reasons – does not adjust the timing of her actions to the sucking rhythm of the infant. Instead, she intervenes in the course of an ongoing 'long bout', then does not help the baby to get the nipple (once it has been lost by the baby), then intervenes again during the new bout.

THE 'GREAT MILK WAR': WHO SHOULD FEED THE BABY, AND WITH WHAT KIND OF MILK?

The milk fed to babies is not merely a nutritional substance, but one of collective-culturally created symbolic value. One can at times hear speech about some social habit or feature being taken in 'with mother's milk'. For example, among the Kel Ewey Tuaregs (in Niger), it is believed that the spiritual forces of solitude (*goumanten*) are transferred from mother to the baby with the milk (Rasmussen, 1995). The people possessed by such spirits are those 'who can't sit still and be with other people'. They suffer from illnesses of 'heart and soul'. Special rituals are used to overcome such spirit possession.

In the biological sense, the mother's milk is considered to be the most appropriate nutrition source for babies (Nichols and Nichols, 1981), yet in terms of *satisficing* milk of other species can be sufficiently adequate for the feeding of babies. The human milk may contain substances that protect babies against intestinal parasites (Gillin et al., 1983). The possibility that human infants can be fed with milk other than that of humans widens the adaptational capacity of the offspring – creating possible alternatives if the main (*the* most appropriate) food source is not available, for any reason. The number of such reasons is potentially large, and includes issues of socio-moral re-negotiation of social roles. Thus, thinking (and talking) about the issues of breast-feeding in the social and medical sciences has confounded moralistic and nutritional features.

How moralistic advice works: strategic maximization and discounting of satisficing

When persons or social institutions attempt to force (or persuade) others to follow their desires or policies, the possible 'relaxed' recognition that the same outcome can be achieved by multiple ways (that is, the principle of multilinearity and equifinality) becomes purposefully eliminated from social discourse. Thus, in order to get the 'social others' to accept a suggested scenario for 'the right way' of thinking (or acting), the enforcer/persuader of that 'right way' de-focuses from the possibility that more than one course of action (thinking) is sufficient. *The principle of satisficing becomes sacrificed in societal moralistic discourse for the sake of focus on maximization.* The latter becomes linked with the ideological goals of the moralizer – along the lines of creating the notion that, while there may be different ways of possible actions (or ways of thinking), among them there exists *the* 'best one' (= maximization) which is also *the 'right one'* in the sense of moral value. The moralistic social suggestion fuses the rational and the value-imbued sides of human conduct, letting the latter guide the former in the background. Moralistic social discourse is the opponent of any notion of doubt – yet it is precisely human capacity to doubt the adequacy of previous suggestions, rules and interpretations that is at the beginning of any new psychological and social development.

It is therefore not surprising that human reasoning about socially relevant matters easily takes the position that there should be 'right' and 'wrong' ways of living. Parents are appropriate targets for moralistic interventions, as they are vulnerable to social suggestions in their role of coping with the uncertainties around the survival and development of their infants.

The cultural meaning of milk

Milk is a substance produced by the biological body, yet immediately interpreted in the social realm. The lay interpretations do not produce many grand surprises in these interpretations. Yet the interpretations are crucial for the cultural canalization of the whole feeding process.

Mother's milk as transformed blood

The mother's milk is often presented as transformed blood. Such a construction leads to specific ways of treating the issue of feeding babies. It creates cultural – both personal and collective – distinctions that make issues of whether the baby should be fed the mother's milk or another woman's (a 'wet nurse's' for example), or whether the milk of animals (cows, goats) is appropriate as food for infants. The history of the ideologies about how to feed infants, which is documented for European societies in the sixteenth to nineteenth centuries, can be called the Great Milk War. Different social institutions, as well as persons, were involved in fierce rhetorical fights about what kind of milk, delivered by whom and from which kind of container (e.g., breast, bottle), would be appropriate for feeding babies. The issue was cultural, rather than nutritional.

The role of meaning extensions in cultural construction

The construction of the meaning extension *milk = blood* is an example of human semiotic regulation of social issues based on bodily substances. This link parallels others of a similar kind – between the father's semen and mother's sexual fluids in the course of conception and pregnancy (see Chapter 8). On the basis of how the extension is constructed, concrete action decisions about feeding the baby (and worries about feeding the baby) follow.

Of course, it is a collectively established fact that milk of a parent is relevant for the offspring among the mammals. The very basic act of feeding of the offspring (observable in cattle-herding societies in the case of animals) provides ample evidence about the different scenarios of the role of milk. The milk supply from the mother may be plentiful (or not), the offspring may suckle adequately (or fail to take in sufficient milk). At some time the parent stops giving milk to the offspring, who may still try to get it.

Yet the human cultural construction goes beyond the basics of mammal feeding practices. It inserts into these practices specific meanings, which are to regulate the process of feeding. For example, in Punjabi society the mother's breasts needed to be purified – by ritual washing of the breasts before breast-feeding began – so as to guarantee the symbolic value of the milk she would feed her baby (Bajwa, 1991, p. 57). This practice was also used in their cattle-herding practices – the udders of the cows were to be washed before they were allowed to feed their calves. Still the cultural construction is of human origin – it is the humans who have invented the ritual of the purification of the milk source (be it a woman's breast or cow's udders), not the cows!

The scheme of cultural construction of decisions about milk-feeding is simple:

WHOSE MILK IS APPROPRIATE FOR
FEEDING HUMAN BABIES?
(1) *exclusively* human milk
(2) *primarily* human milk

IF (1) then → *MOTHER'S* MILK or *OTHER'S*
MILK
IF (2) then → which other species can provide
adequate milk for babies?
(e.g., cows, goats, *but not* pigs, dogs, horses, etc.)

If the issue of whose milk is most appropriately fed to babies were merely one of nutrition, solutions to the problem of feeding would be simple. If the nutritional benefits of human milk are to be more important than any available animal milk source (cow, goat), then any lactating woman can be summoned to feed the baby. Precisely that happens among the Toraja (a society on the Sulawesi Island in Indonesia). The newborn baby is fed by another woman (than mother), without qualms, as explained by an informant:

> If one has just given birth, usually the fluid [breast milk] isn't flowing yet. [And so] someone else breast-feeds [the child] at first. Someone else is called, someone who had a child two or three months previously. (Hollan and Wellenkamp, 1996, p. 127)

The focus of cultural attention here is on the need to get the newborn adequately fed. This goal is reflected in the wet-nursing practices in Europe and North America: the very practical needs of the mother of the newborn (for example, the mother falling ill, losing her milk etc.) created a necessity for back-up feeding options (see Golden, 1996). No moralistic story-telling could happen when the baby was crying to be fed, and the mother – for whatever reasons – could not feed it. Another lactating woman was an appropriate substitute.

However, the social discourse about the activity of breast-feeding has been the playground for cultural dominance games about women's roles as mothers. That has largely happened in occidental societies – especially in those social classes that maintain their economic power.

Keeping women in the role of mothers

The primary function of the eighteenth and nineteenth centuries European social discourse about 'mother's milk' was to keep the women in their role as mothers. The discourse was specifically that of the affluent social classes – in which case the role of the woman included many other potential activities than being a mother and worker (as would be the case of lower-class women in rural areas of France, England, or of the United States). By suggesting to the women in affluent families that *they* breast-feed their own infants – rather than using milk of another lactating woman (a wet nurse) or of an animal – the women's concerns and activities would be constrained to the realm of children in the domestic sphere. The latter was presented in terms of its importance to the children, as well as fortified by its moral value (of a good woman and mother image). The threat of the opposite – a 'bad' mother who is involved in social gatherings, gossiping with her female friends, dancing at parties, going to theatres, and having illicit affairs with male friends – was the alternative social role for the woman, which was made the target for social eradication.[5]

For example, an eighteenth century English medical doctor was adamant about the moral downfall of society:

> It is grievously to be lamented, that so many *Mothers*, not only of high rank, but even of the common Sort, can with so much Inhumanity, and more than brutish Cruelty, desert their tender Offspring, and expose them to so many Dangers of mercenary Nurses, who are greedy only of the profuse Rewards bestowed on them at the Christening, and flight the small weekly Income that follows; and so being weary of the present Employment, perform it negligently, while they are looking out for a new Prey. But let us take a Survey of the Advantages that prompt Mothers so commonly to sacrifice their beloved Offspring. They are the more free Enjoyment of Diversions; the greater Niceness of adorning their Persons; the Opportunity of receiving impertinent Visits, and returning those insipid Favours; the more frequent Attendance of the Theatre, or the spending of the greatest Part of the Night on their beloved cards. These are the important Reasons, for which *Mothers* frequently banish their newborn *Infants* from their Sight, and rashly deliver them up into very doubtful Hands, whithersoever Fortune or Fate, either good or bad, happens to lead them. But these nice Ladies afterwards suffer deserved Punishments, for the Love of their Children, if they happen to survive, is more cool towards them, but warm and affectionate towards the Nurse who took them up, and performed the Duties of a real Mother. (Harris, 1742, pp. 18–19)

Texts like these were meant to create insecurity in the women, and guide them towards assuming the '*duties* of *real* mothers' themselves (instead of delegating those to servants). The promise of punishment – of the children preferring in their affection the nurses to the mothers – is similar to the theme of attachment issues discussed in English society after the popular adoption of John Bowlby's attachment theory (see Chapters 10 and 13). The cultural model of motherhood served as the semiotic organizer of women's socio-moral roles. It can be seen as a general rule – at any time a social institution of any society sets itself a goal of modifying women's conduct, that effort becomes translated into social suggestions – promotions and prohibitions – of issues in the

women's everyday lives that are relevant for themselves, and their social roles as women and childbearers. Efforts of social control take place in the realms of personal-cultural importance. These realms are also filled with uncertainties – be these about the future, or present, or feelings about the past. In this respect, the European fight for affluent mothers' own care of their babies is functionally analogous to the creation of many pregnancy taboos (as was described in Chapter 8).

Like most of moral crusades, the efforts to keep affluent women confined to their full motherhood could only be partially successful. The use of feeding alternatives became widespread in Europe, as well as in North America. Aside from liberating the woman from the regular dependency on the baby's feeding, the use of a wet nurse paved the way for the return of the mother to her role of wife to her husband. It was suspected (as reflected in the American discourse about wet-nursing – see Golden, 1996) that on many occasions the initiators of wet-nursing were the husbands of the new mothers, who desired to return to regular co-habitation with their lawfully wedded wife.[6] The belief in the benefit of human milk for babies – in contrast to cow's milk – created the special social role of the wet nurse.

The wet nurse

Affluent mothers could decide to have their infants fed by women other than themselves. The women who assumed – or sought out – such a role became *wet nurses*. The crucial aspect of wet nurses was that they necessarily *were lower in their social class status* than the mothers. In the most widespread cases, the wet nurses were of peasant social background (working for mothers of merchant or higher classes). As such, they would become servants. For instance, a peasant wet nurse would be brought in from the village to live with the master's family in town, feed the infant, and continue as a servant in the household after the baby was weaned (become a 'dry nurse' or caregiver). The entrance into servitude need not have entailed explicit monetary payments for the work, but – as was customary – the servants would have job security and the granting of economic well-being as members of the master's household.

A similar relative distinction applied to the servitude of wet nurses in royal households. Here the wet nurse had to be a servant to the royal family – which meant an aristocratic status of the 'lady wet nurse' (Fildes, 1986, p. 158). While the relative social position of a wet nurse had to be lower than that of the mother of the baby to be nursed, it could not be the lowest in the social system of the given country. Wet nurses, by and large, came from the poor – *but not the poorest* – social strata. This selectivity is understandable, if one considers the complexity of decisions, and the psychological ambivalence present in these decisions.

Biological prerequisites and their social evaluation

The wet nurse was a woman who could feed the baby – for which her milk production was crucial. This could be granted only if the wet nurse had, or had recently had, a child of her own. The latter scenario entailed her own infant's death (while her capacity to feed continued). While infant death was not a rare event in eighteenth and nineteenth century Europe, it certainly was an ambiguous event in the case of social construction of the appropriateness of a woman as a wet nurse. The reasons for the death of her own child could indicate carelessness in her caregiving – a feature which was as difficult to determine then as figuring it out for our present-day nannies and babysitters. If the woman's baby was alive, the question of whether the woman would have enough milk became crucial. The danger of the wet nurse not having enough milk for two babies led to the question of competition between the babies for the limited resource. The moral character of the potential wet nurses was carefully scrutinized – the candidates needed character reference letters from trustable previous employment sources.

Furthermore, the quality of the milk of the wet nurse was a crucial object for social evaluation. The milk was to have 'a sweet pleasant taste', rather than be salty, sour, bitter, or strange in any ways. Experts were not shy in giving advice how to taste the milk of a prospective wet nurse in 'the right way', as the following suggestion (from 1746 in England) indicates:

> . . . you must [first] cleanse your mouth well with water, get some of the milk upon a plate, and take several mouthfuls, a little of it not being sufficient to make a right judgment. (Fildes, 1986, p. 175)

Surely milk tasting of this kind and the expert wine tasting in our times look rather similar. The social role of the testing of course was different – the uncertainty of giving one's child the less-than-good milk of another woman was a serious peril, potentially leading to the loss of the baby.

The physical complexion of the wet nurse had to fit a stereotype of a woman to whom the 'fragile baby' could be trusted for feeding. The breasts of the nurse were to be 'a good medium size', full, and – obviously – containing plenty of milk. If the breasts were 'too big' it was found that these are difficult for the infant to suck, which may lead to hurting the gums, and might lead to development of a 'crooked nose' from being constantly pressed to one side. In contrast, breasts evaluated as 'too small' were considered as too difficult for the baby to suck, as these may hurt the jaws (Fildes, 1986, p. 171). The 'track record' of the reproductive success of the woman was likewise important – ideally, the wet nurse should have had two or three living children of her own, prior to being qualified for the new role.

There was also a belief (in the sixteenth and seventeenth centuries) that the sex of the wet nurse's own child would affect her milk. If her own child were a girl, and she wet-nursed a boy, it was believed that the boy could become effeminate while sharing the milk of the girl's mother (Fildes, 1986, p. 176). The employment of a newly pregnant woman as a wet nurse was not recommended – unless the wet nurse was impregnated by her own husband. The latter characteristic elaborates the moral social suggestions of the time.

Psychological characteristics of the wet nurse

Beyond the basics of feeding capacity, wet nurses were complex psychological targets of their employers' ambivalence around the issue of hiring somebody else to feed the child. There was a clear desire to find wet nurses who would resemble the mother. On balance, wet nurses of socially stigmatized general characteristics (such as red hair) were not considered appropriate – because of the assumed 'difficult character' of red-haired women.

A very central question about wet-nursing was the 'dangers of the night' – the wet nurse's potential to suffocate the baby by 'overlaying' of the baby (who slept in the same bed). Hence, drunkenness of wet nurses could be viewed as dangerous in two ways – the woman might provide unwholesome milk, and not be 'watchful in the night'. To protect the infant in the night, special objects of furniture (see Figure 9.3) were created. The *arcutio* is an ingenious cultural tool. It is both an infant protection device (see *d* and *e*, in Figure 9.3) and a support device for breast-feeding (see *c* in Figure 9.3). It represents the ambivalence concerning the conduct of wet nurses in their sleep: they need to feed the baby swiftly, and at the same time do it in ways that diminish the possibilities of the baby being suffocated by the nurse's body.

Socioeconomic characteristics of the profession

Wet-nursing was one of the quintessential service professions. It succeeded because of its economic

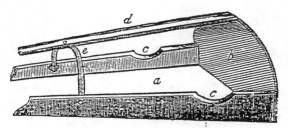

The drawing is from the year 1731. The *arcutio*, with the child in it, can be put on the bed under the bedclothes, without danger of smothering the baby. The construction, about 1 metre long, involved the following parts:
(a) The place where the child lies
(b) The headboard
(c) The hollows for the nurse's breasts
(d) A wooden bar for the nurse to lean on while suckling the baby
(e) A small iron arch to support the bar (d)

FIGURE 9.3 *A special device to protect the infant from being suffocated by the wet nurse at night – the* arcutio *from Florence (from Fildes, 1986, p. 197, reprinted by permission)*

incentives for women in the societies which practised it. The income earned through wet-nursing was equal or better to that available to the women in other professions (and with a lighter workload: women earning a similar amount through agricultural labour would have more demanding work tasks than wet nurses). In France, the prevalence of wet nursing in different rural areas was coordinated with economic fluctuations (based on better or worse harvests) – the regions that had poor harvests at certain times had higher proportions of women turning to wet-nursing in those years.

The 'live-in' nurse and the 'baby farmer'

The two types of wet nurse differed by way of the parents' supervision of their activities. Nurses who were brought into the household (in urban or rural areas) became servants in the household. This made possible constant supervision of the wet nurse's work by the baby's mother. The infant who was transferred to the care of a wet nurse did not thus separate from the actual mother. Instead, the social contacts now involved two significant female figures – the wet nurse (for immediate care) and the mother (who was at the head of the household).

Live-in wet nurses were vastly popular in European history. For example, out of about 90,000 inhabitants of Hamburg (Germany) at the end of the eighteenth century, around 5000 were wet nurses. As one anti-nursing weekly complained in 1724, wet nurses were kept in almost all homes in Hamburg, and they enjoyed such great consideration and wages that other servants were envious (Lindemann, 1981).

In contrast, the socioecological niche for the infant in the case of '*baby-farming*' entailed prolonged separation of the infant from the parents. The infant was taken out of the natal household to the home of the wet nurse. This usually entailed migration from the city to the villages. Such migration was necessitated by the general perception of the dangers of the town environment which was widely held at the time. Towns were the prime locations for proliferation of various disease epidemics in the Middle Ages and later; the countryside was thought to entail less dangers of this kind.

Thus, active migration of infants from their natal families in towns to the homes of wet nurses in the countryside was a recognized way of doing one's best for the babies' survival. As a vehicle of social regulation of this movement, the well-regulated (that is, *bureaucratic*) French society instituted a system that monopolized control over such activities. For over a century, from 1769 to 1876, the city of Paris had a working Bureau of Wet Nurses. Its role was to facilitate the finding of suitable 'baby farmers' (wet nurses) for urban families. During the time the Bureau existed, approximately one-quarter of all infants born in Paris were sent to the countryside to 'baby farmers'.

Evidence does not suggest that infants who were 'baby farmed' did in fact survive significantly better than those in Paris. The annual mortality rates of 'baby farmed' infants varied from 21 per cent to 29.5 per cent (Sussmann, 1977, p. 639). No comparable figures are available for families in Paris, but the mortality rate from child hospices in Paris itself were comparable, ranging from 23.9 per cent to 28.9 per cent (for the period 1815–1825 – Fuchs, 1984, p. 143). Probably the felt need for sending one's infant to the rural 'baby farmer' was built on the mythology of the merchant classes idealizing the quality of life of rural gentry. For the peasant women who worked as 'baby farmers', this activity provided improved sources of income.

Wet-nursing was a widespread practice until the early twentieth century, when different technological and historical factors brought it to its end. The development of refrigeration technologies allowed for delayed usability of milk. Now, about a hundred years later, most women have internalized the notion of the special nature of 'their baby'. Competitiveness with other women, and maintenance of personal property, have diminished the chances that one lactating woman might feed another woman's baby. Furthermore, the survival of infants is usually guaranteed by means other than fresh country air and the breast of a good-natured country woman with an ample milk supply.

INFANT CARE AS A CULTURALLY ORGANIZED PROCESS

Time cycles

Culturally speaking, the alternation of day and night is significant with regard to different feelings of danger and opportunity that have been constructed around the diurnal fluctuation. Thus, night-time is often assumed to be linked with the activities of spirits, dangers (of the darkness) etc. The transformation of night into day (and day into night) has been one of the major changes in the physical world around which cultural myths have been constructed. In the Christian meaning system, daytime has been associated with the world of God (*civitas Dei*), while the night belonged to that of diabolical forces (*civitas Diaboli*). This is a non-developmental (ontological) binary opposition. When viewed as a time-dependent cycle, the day/night (and its analogues in the seasons: summer/winter; spring/autumn) indicate passage of living organisms from death to life (and vice versa). The night precedes the creation – it 'gives birth' to the day (Brzozowska-Krajka, 1998, p. 38). Furthermore, the night is the locus for conception (in many societies, sexual activities are limited to evening or morning darkness), as well as of dangers to the well-being (death). In human cultural mythologies, night is by far better differentiated conceptually than the day. Even in the English language, this variability is encoded in the co-existence of the positive and negative connotations of events at night ('dreams' versus 'nightmares'), while the sub-mental activities during the day are less differentiated, and opposed to the state of activity (for example, there exist 'daydreams' but no 'daymares', and the former are set up in opposition with actions: a person who is acting is not 'daydreaming').

Psychologically, the night-time activities of adults are usually memorable because the dreams (or their negatively flavoured counterparts, nightmares) can be reported for that period of non-conscious life. Psychology has made use of the notion of dreams, making the assumption that through dream analysis it is possible to peep into the person's unconscious. Doing so in clinical practice constitutes a culturally created story about how one can access that part of the human psyche which is not directly accessible. Despite

the principal unverifiability of such access, the interest in human unconscious as revealed via dreams abounds in occidental societies.

It is also possible to find explicit construction of dreaming as instrumental efforts towards semiotic regulation of social and personal lives. The Mekeo society (in Papua New Guinea, Central Province) are documented to use dreaming in predicting future success (or failure), as well as a means to make major decisions for the waking life (Stephen, 1982).

The Mekeo interpret the events of the dream as the direct experience of the person's soul which is freed from the body during the night. In dreams, the dreamer can directly communicate with the spirits, and hence remembering and (wake-time) analysis of the meaning of the dreams is of crucial psychological relevance. They constitute a further cultural construction site – material from the dreams becomes the basis for further meaning construction during the wakefulness. Differently from the occidental (psychoanalytic) focus on dreams revealing what is *not allowed* to be dealt with during wakefulness, the Mekeo dreaming is the basis for the daytime activities. Dreaming is often prepared for by specific rituals. The magician who wishes to communicate with dead relatives through a dream prepares himself before going to sleep. He needs to take some relic of the dead relative (a finger bone, hair removed from the corpse before burial and kept for ritual purposes) and burn a piece of specially treated bark cloth near the relics, while reciting a spell to evoke the spirit. He then falls asleep – hoping that during the night the spirit will come and give him the desired advice (Stephen, 1982, p. 110).

Dreams of the Mekeo are used for multiple ends – gardeners want to determine which gardens and when to plant, hunters want good luck in their hunt, a young man may wish to seduce or marry a young woman etc. Whatever actually happens in the dream can be creatively combined during the waking time so as to arrive at the desired goal. The dreaming process is symbolically powerful as it allows the living persons to secure the support of the spirit world.

For early infant development night-time is constructed as a period of uncertainties, and of potential dangers. The active control by the adults over their own lives is lessened at night, and their control over the life of the offspring has the same characteristic.

Night-time activity

Certainly many events happen at night-time, but an ordinary and expected activity for the night in any society is that of rest – sleep. This obviously applies to the already socialized members of a given society, but not yet to newborns and infants. The patterns of newborn and infant sleep have different day/night cyclicity – with the result that the baby may be awake some of the night-time and asleep during the daytime.

The day/night cycle – corroborated by changes in light – is the basic cyclical marker of human life activities. This diurnal rhythm is different for newborns', children's and adults' life activities. First of all, young babies sleep at different times of both day and night. This creates the situation where babies are active at night (as described above), and asleep during the day. The overall picture of the amount of sleep within each 24 hour cycle by humans at different age levels is one of a slow reduction of the prevalence of sleep during childhood (see Table 9.2). Newborns sleep for 16 hours out of 24, and half of their sleep is light sleep. Light sleep is characterized by rapid eye movements (visible behind the closed eyelids for external observers). It is assumed that basic psychological activity of processing relevant experiences takes place during the REM sleep, which is also the period when human beings dream.

TABLE 9.2 *The extent of sleep (per 24 hour cycle) over the human life span*

Age	Hours of sleep in a 24 hour cycle	Percentage of REM sleep
1–15 days	16	50
3–5 months	14	40
6–23 months	13	30
2–3 years	12	25
3–5 years	11	20
5–9 years	10	18.5
10–13 years	9.5	18.5
14–18 years	8.5	20
19–30 years	8	22
33–45 years	7	18.9
50–70 years	7	15
70–85 years	6	13.8

Source: H.P. Roffwarg, J.N. Muzio and W.C. Dement (1966) 'Ontogenetic development of the human sleep–dream cycle', *Science*, 152: 608

Cultural organization of night-time for babies
The care given to the newborn and infant during the night-time obviously includes feeding, and may include efforts to calm the baby when necessary. The *location of the baby's place of sleeping* in the home environment is crucial for the organization of these caregiving actions. The most easily expected arrangement is that the baby

will sleep together with the mother (on her sleeping place – a cot, futon, mattress, bed). In this arrangement, there is immediate access for feeding, and the need to calm down the active baby can include total body contact with the mother (who herself is asleep, or half-so). An alternative sleeping arrangement is that of the baby having its own sleeping place (cradle or crib) in the same area as the mother's (with direct auditory contact at night, plus visual contact during the lighted times). Here, obviously, the care given during the night requires the mother to wake up and move to the baby (or the reverse transport), and the benefits of constant bodily contact are absent. Finally, as is widespread in the middle classes of European, North American and other societies, the baby may be assigned to its own private bedroom. This often sets up a grand ambivalence for parents, who on the one hand want to know that the baby is fine, but on the other hand want to keep their own privacy by distancing themselves from the baby. Oftentimes one can find two-way intercom systems in Western homes between the baby's bedroom and that of the parents. Once noises of distress are heard by the parents in the night, the mother (or the father) gets extra night-time exercise by rushing into the baby's bedroom and providing the care.

Infant sleeping places are made meaningful by different decoration. Thus, parents who are involved in decorating their baby's bedroom in specific ways (for example, colouring of walls, presence of toy animals, posters with smiling faces etc.) are setting the stage for cultural facilitation of the child's experiencing of the fixed-features space. The child's bed can be of a construction that reflects the collective-cultural beliefs about the ways and means through which the infant survives, and can be treated. The contrast that brings this out in the open is that between a cradle and a crib in the history of childrearing in the United States.

A cradle is a bed that is set up on a base that can be put into motion and provide the baby with rocking stimulation. A crib is a bed that does not afford such rocking motion. In the United States, cradles were used widely up to the end of the nineteenth century. From around the 1890s onwards, the medical social institutions began a campaign against the practices of rocking babies to sleep – and consequently against the adaptation of the baby's bed to such rocking (which was the cradle). The campaign against cradles was actually a social control effort over the character of the parents – it was assumed that parents' 'over-indulging' of infants by close contact and body-rocking was a sign of non-puritan ideology. Thus, the paediatrician L. Emmett Holt was described as a grand warrior against the cradle. In his view,

> The crib should be one that does not rock *in order that* this unnecessary and *vicious practice* may not be carried out. (Zahorsky, 1934, p. 664; added emphasis)

Obviously, the accusation of 'viciousness' of the provision of tactile/vestibular stimulation to infants was a message to the adults, calling forth their expected internalized feelings of 'doing things right' and being fearful about 'spoiling the baby'. Whenever social institutions target parents for the purposes of gaining control over their handling of the children, the general pseudo-concept of 'spoiling' becomes utilized in many ways.

The infant's sleeping place can also be constructed as a cultural tool for the benefit (rather than 'spoiling') of the infant. In the Ket society (in Siberia), two kinds of cradles have been used – temporary, and permanent. The permanent cradles (made out of cedar pine wood) were the primary places in which infants were kept from birth until about 2 years of age. If the child survived the hazards of the first year, the permanent cradle acquired the meaning of 'lucky cradle' and was preserved to house the next baby. A lucky cradle could not be abandoned – it could be given to relatives (whose children may be ill) in the hope that by putting the child in the cradle, the child might be cured (Alekseenko, 1988, pp. 18–19).

The activities of the night-time also include *adults' activities oriented towards changing the child's activation level* (from awake – including distressed – to asleep). Holding the baby, and rocking the baby to sleep is a universal invention that combines vestibular and tactile stimuli in this effort. Infant crying is a biologically aversive stimulus for adults, and needs to be avoided. It can be seen as potentially dangerous. Many of the oral incantations oriented towards crying babies give evidence of such collective cultural construction.

Crying is not only an aversive stimulus for adults, but – by way of breaking the silence at night – can be constructed as culturally dangerous. In an Old Babylonian lullaby dated back to the period 1950–1530 BC, the infant's crying is presented as potentially undermining the peace of the house in the supernatural sense. The reference to *kusarikkum* is to the 'god of the house' – a benevolent house-spirit:

> Little one, who dwelt in the house of darkness – well, you are outside now, have seen the light of the sun.
> Why are you crying, why are you yelling?
> Why didn't you cry in there?

> You have roused the god of the house, the *kusarikkum* has woken up:
> 'Who roused me? Who startled me?'
> The little one has roused you, the little one has startled you!
> 'As onto drinkers of wine, as onto tipplers. May sleep fall on him!'

> (Farber, 1990, p. 141)

The provision of wine (to babies – and to their parents – in order to make all sleep well at night) has also been a long-honoured tradition. Again, the occidental medically fortified (yet moralistically based) social representation of wine being an alcoholic beverage – which thus could be linked to 'poison' in the opposition FOOD < > NON-FOOD (POISON) – guides the perceptual discomfort of many persons who become aware of this practice. This discomfort would be absent in cases of the cultural construction of the fermented grape drink as regular food. The same substance (wine) is reconstructed in other ways in Christian religious rituals.

Aside from being asleep, it is *becoming asleep* and *waking up* that are regular psycho-physiological processes which are culturally regulated. Of course, in the case of exhaustion, a person would need no special ways to mediate the transition process. Yet human cultural life creates many cases where falling asleep or waking up are assisted by special action strategies (for example, leaving a baby with a security object, or an adult with a TV switched on), or even special chemical substances (drugs).

The process of going to sleep (and waking up) depends upon the designated location for the baby's sleeping. The infant may be set to sleep in a variety of locations, beginning with the most immediate (baby and mother sleeping together in full tactile contact). The next step of distancing entails the baby sleeping next to the mother, in the immediate (night-time reachable) distance and on the same sleeping surface.[7] The potential dangers of such closeness have been recognized (see Figure 9.3 above).

Once a different sleeping surface is utilized (for example, the child is put to sleep in a separate bed, a crib), the availability of tactile contact at night immediately diminishes. This sets up a night-time baby-care routine which involves a trip by the adult to the bed-site of the baby, at the least, for feeding or/and soothing purposes. This trip may be relatively short (if the bed-site is in the same architectural enclosure, or room, as that of the parents). It can be longer if the child is set to sleep in a different room. In affluent social classes one can observe a tendency to distance the baby to his or her 'own' bedroom, under the legitimization of children's 'need for their own' space. This arrangement creates the necessity for various 'baby-monitoring' systems (intercom), which accentuate the parents' ambivalence about closeness to and distance from the baby.

Different societies provide children of different ages with very varied sleeping arrangements. In Table 9.3 one can compare the sleeping environments of 3–4-month-olds in Japan and the United States. As is clear from the table, there is a major difference between the two countries. In Japan, sleeping is an activity where the infant is kept close to other family members at night, and is rarely set to sleep in a separate room. In the United States, the majority of infants are set to sleep alone in a separate room. However, as the United States is not a homogeneous society, one can detect different co-sleeping patterns within it: samples of US black and Hispanic parents have been found to be closer to the world's usual case (of co-sleeping between parents and children) than the white racial samples (Medoff and Schaefer, 1993).

The special case of the white US Americans which deviates from the ordinary and expected state of affairs in other societies sets up the socioemotional developmental niche of the babies

in a way that immediately reflects the characteristic of *enforced* distancing. As was clear above (Chapter 3), distancing is the core of human development. Yet its particular form of social negotiation in parent–offspring relations can be very variable. In the case of the day/night cycle, the practice – which is at first a mere spatial arrangement for sleeping (of setting the infant in a separate room) – can become a phenomenon of early exposure of the infant to strictness of night-time distancing. This is possibly in contrast with the experience of daytime equally strict non-distancing. This issue starts in infancy and continues in different forms (see Chapter 11) in early childhood. It is precisely at the time of cultural construction of 'horrors of the dark' (by the adults) that the infants (and later – children) are made to face such horrors by being set to sleep in their own rooms. The change from wakefulness to sleep (and back) may be the first recurrent experience where the infant encounters the paradoxical relation between being close and being distant in relation to the same person. From this point of view, the cultural regulation of how the infant moves from wakefulness to sleep (and back) becomes of crucial relevance.

TABLE 9.3 *Infants' sleeping arrangements at age 3–4 months in Japan and the United States*

Room and bed location of infant during the night	American Shand, 1981 Frequency	%	Japanese Shand, 1981 Frequency	%	Caudill and Plath, 1966 Frequency	%
Separate room, alone (always own bed)	71	83.6	13	28.3	3	4.1
Other person's room (with grandparent or sibling)	—	—	—	—	5	6.8
Parents' room (always own bed)	7	8.2	15	32.6	34	46.6
Parents' room (always own futon[a])	—	—	—	—	24	32.9
Sometimes parents' room and bed	7	8.2	3	6.5	—	—
Always in parents' bed	—	—	15	32.6	7	9.6
Total	85	100.0	46	100.0	73	100.0

[a] A futon is a Japanese quilt that is spread on the floor at night for sleeping. Since futons are placed next to each other, the infants' closeness to their parents during the night is comparable to sleeping in the parents' bed.

Sources: W. Caudill and D.W. Plath (1966) 'Who sleeps by whom? Parent–child involvement in urban Japanese families', *Psychiatry*, 29: 360; N. Shand (1981) 'The reciprocal impact of breast-feeding and culture form on maternal behavior and infant development', *Journal of Biological Science*, 13: 9.

Into sleep . . . and out of it: a culturally guided process

The alteration of sleep/wakefulness states is a natural physiological process, with its own organismic rhythms. The cultural regulation of the process sets up conditions for its occurrence in the human case. The basic physiological process prevails – for instance, a sleepy person would fall asleep no matter where, and irrespective of all the efforts by well-meaning 'social others' to keep him or her awake. Yet, the efforts to make oneself fall asleep (or get the infant to fall asleep) under the intermediate state of tiredness can pose a major problem for interaction.

How would a parent solve the problem? There are two 'boundary scenarios' – both in cases of the infant sleeping outside of tactile contact (and many versions in between the two):

(a) the parent puts the infant down in a crib, and leaves. The infant will have to get to sleep on his or her own, without direct adult involvement;
(b) the parent lets the baby fall asleep on his or her lap (or body in general), and subsequently puts the infant down.

In an example of scenario (b), a Japanese mother may let the infant fall asleep in her arms, then put the baby down. The latter effort can fail (the baby may return to an awake state), in which case the procedure may be repeated. Tactile contact is important. A US mother may put the baby down, look at it, and then leave.

Cultural organization of the waking of infants depends upon the kind of feeding schedule that is accepted. The infant can be woken up to be fed (while probably remaining half-asleep while feeding). The adults' construction of time becomes available to babies through the regularity of the routines (or lack of it). Our waking up is often surrounded by one (or more!) alarm clocks. The latter may be set up in locations (for example, across the room from one's bed) that do not allow easy half-asleep actions to switch them off and stop them disturbing our morning sleep.

Dynamics of the daytime

Over the course of the day, human activities are further organized around physiological needs. Food intake is certainly one of the major domains of cultural construction: what kind of foods are consumed, when (over the daytime hours), in whose company, and prepared by whom. This represents a case of cultural canalization of human activities. Daytime sleeping – having naps (for babies and for adults, for example a *siesta* in the afternoon) – is an example of cultural regulation of the daytime.

Together with the approach of evening and night, specific routines can be developed for the transition. These can be in the service of institutional goals (see the case of joint watching of the sunset in a Krishnamurti boarding-school, discussed in Chapter 12). Likewise, these activities can be oriented towards control over the activity levels of the young children.

Soothing the baby

Soothing a person is a task similar to that of guiding the infant to fall asleep – only in the case of soothing the task is to guide the other from a state of high or extreme activation towards a state of intermediate activation (see Figure 9.4). Notably, there is no cultural organization of getting an infant who is awake to be hyper-agitated (babies cry anyway), and the task of reducing the current activation state is a preoccupation more central than that of enhancing it.

The universal (to all higher species of primates, including human beings) means of soothing down an agitated other (of equal or sub-dominant rank) is tactile contact. It takes the form of huddling, embracing, caressing, tight whole-body holding, grooming, and many other versions of body-to-body contact.[8] In the case of human infancy, most of the soothing takes place through tactile contact, combined with vestibular (rocking the baby) and (at times) vocal stimulation (for example, singing a lullaby). These actions are episodic – they are triggered by the undesired activation state of the infant. A crying infant emits sounds that are aversive already at the level of the infant's own perception, thus calling forth efforts to regulate its state. As long as the cry is perceived as a sign for some internal discomfort of the baby (as in the beginning of infancy), the parent (or any other caregiver) is likely to soothe the baby without question. However, if the baby's cry is suspected of having become an instrumental means for the baby to control the actions of the adult (usually by the second half of the first year

BEHAVIOURAL CHARACTERISTICS

STATE	Eyes	Respiration	Body movement	Vocalizations
1. Deep sleep	Closed	Regular	Absent	Absent
2. Light sleep	Closed	Irregular	Can be present	Absent
3. Awake	Open	Regular	Can be present	Absent or quiet
4. Agitated	Open	Irregular	Present	Present (whining)
5. Crying	Open	Irregular	Present (jerky)	Present (screaming)

FIGURE 9.4 *Infant physiological activation states and the directions of their culturally purposeful regulation*

of life), a strategic form of counter-action may develop. The adult may try to 'diagnose' whether the given cry of the infant is 'real' or an 'effort to manipulate', and act accordingly. Even as the infant's cry differentiates in its acoustic form over the first year of life, there is no full distinction between 'help' and 'control' cries, which would lead the caregiver to superimpose his or her meanings of the particular cries upon the given situation.

The provision of the soothing/comforting efforts by the caregiver(s) is situated in the context of the *regular positioning of the baby* in relation to the caregiver. The infant can be in different locations in the course of the day (as it can be in different locations at night, as mentioned above):

> on the caregiver's body – in constant tactile contact and experiencing the caregiver's body movements through the vestibular stimulation those movements produce;
> in some mobile carrying device which makes it possible to keep the infant at a seeing/hearing distance, but which eliminates the immediate tactile/vestibular input of the caregiver to the infant;
> in some location outside of the control of the mother (but looked after by some other caregiver, who either assumes full responsibility for the care, or brings the infant to the mother when necessary) (for example, older siblings)

Keeping the baby constantly on the mother's body is the basic evolutionarily emerged standard for higher primates and human beings. As a result of development of cultural artefacts – slings (for carrying the infant on one's back, or in the front), cradle-boards, perambulators and car-seats – human beings have acquired the flexibility of keeping the infant away from their own (or others') body, at physical yet controllable locations.

Tactile contact in mother–infant daily lives

There exist extreme differences between societies in the total amount of tactile contact provided to infants. The so-called 'traditional societies' provide babies with overwhelming tactile experience, while the urbanized, industrialized societies set up infant care situations with reduced mother–infant tactile contact (see Figure 9.5). The contrast between the Anglo-American and !Kung hunter–gatherer societies (in Namibia) depicted in the figure is profound (Konner, 1978). The overall extent of the !Kung infants' tactile contact with their mothers is, by age 1.5 *years*, close to being the same as Anglo-American infants experience at birth (that is, at the time of maximum

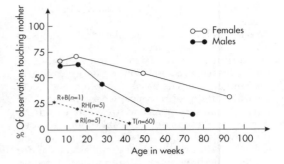

Straight lines = !Kung infants. Dotted lines = American and English infants from the studies by Rheingold (RH, home-reared; RI, institution reared), Tulkin (T) and Richards and Bernal (R+B)

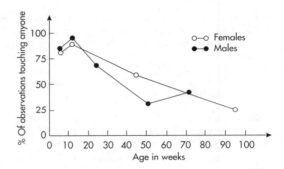

FIGURE 9.5 *Different conditions for mother–infant relations in the domain of general amounts of tactile contact (from Konner, 1978, by permission of Harvard University Press)*

tactile contact). The cultural organization of the newborn and infancy period in the Anglo-American world reflects the general suppression of tactile contact in the adult world.

Two strategies of mother–infant relation: distal and proximal

The two societies depicted in Figure 9.5 represent two possible strategies of organizing the parent–child relation. The *distal strategy* (here represented by the Anglo-American tactile contact pattern) entails keeping physical distance between the parent and the infant, and developing their relations through channels of visual, acoustic and objects-based communication. The distal strategy includes the necessity for constant regulation of the mother–infant distance: for times of necessary caregiving (feeding, cleaning), the mother and baby need to come to close contact, which can then be reduced. For example, if the mother breast-feeds the infant, the infant needs to arrive in close tactile contact with the mother. If the feeding is organized by a schedule (determined by the parent), the infant is brought to the contact at times controlled by the mother. Feeding 'on demand' (that is, when the baby indicates the desire to be fed) would require ample possibilities for reduction of the mother–infant distance under this strategy.

The *proximal strategy* is exemplified by the !Kung. The infants are constantly – starting from near 75 per cent of the whole time at the beginning of infancy, and remaining so for 25 per cent of time (boys) and 50 per cent (girls) – in tactile contact with the mother. Breast-feeding takes place when the baby indicates motor agitation ('on demand'). The proximal strategy is closely linked to the confounding of vestibular stimulation of the infant: when the mother carries the infant on her body, each and every movement of the mother's body constitutes a vestibular experience for the infant. Thus, the rhythmic stimulation of moving around, performing everyday tasks of a repetitive kind (such as pounding millet, a major task of an everyday kind in many African rural areas), singing and dancing, are all entering the infant's experience through the tactile/vestibular sensory channel. In the case of the proximal strategy, the child is a full participant in the sociocultural activities of the adults at the *sub*-semiotic level. This is a level where the construction of meanings – signs – has not yet emerged, yet all of the experiential field of the baby is already culturally organized.

Cultural organization of adult–infant interaction

Since the 1970s, it has been customary in developmental psychology to concentrate on mother–infant (and later father–infant) interaction as an important aspect of human social development. This interest reflects the limited sociocultural background of psychology, and brings out the ideological background of the research questions that are asked. As was obvious earlier in this book (see Chapter 6), the development of infants is embedded in a complex social network of a multi-aged kinship group, part of which inhabits the given household. If that, more general, basis were to be considered, the research focus on mother–infant (or father–infant) interaction would more appropriately be framed as a mother–father–infant triadic interaction. Or – remembering the extended/joint family contexts – the question might be grandmother–grandfather–mother–father–infant interaction in an extended family group. The empirical research tradition of parent–infant dyadic interaction is based on the European and North American

social expectations (for the mother's primary and exclusive role in the life of the infant; see also Chapter 10 on attachment theory making the same assumption). It is easy to see – throughout the coverage in the present book – that such narrowing of the mother's role to be the exclusive caregiver is a limited view. Yet it has dominated the past three decades of research in infant psychology.

Two models of interaction
Models of adult–adult interaction – of direct face-to-face kind – have been carried over to adult–infant interaction as cultural norms. Emphasis on specific features of such interaction – eye contact, turn-taking etc. – has been there in the conceptualization of mother–infant interaction. Such interaction is assumed to take place as a *goal in itself*: the goal of mother–infant interaction is to enjoy – both mother and infant – that interaction itself.

This constitutes a gross over-generalization of a local (Western affluent middle-class) collective-cultural construction to the status of a universal desired norm. Such over-generalization is symptomatic of the ease with which European and North American historical particulars of collective-cultural construction are – by way of social power and persuasion – proliferated to other societies. Probably there is no better special case to show the sociohistorical relativity of such generalizations as the case of mother–infant eye contact. As was shown above (in the section dealing with 'evil eye'), the mother's gaze at the baby can be considered potentially dangerous, not to mention intensive gaze by others. Looking at the baby in a frontal (face-to-face) position can be viewed as culturally dangerous at most, or at least an irrelevant waste of time with the baby (or even an asocial act of keeping the baby's attention only to the mother).

In different social settings the mother–infant dyadic exclusivity is violated even in the European/American middle-class environments. When the infant is brought to participate in a small group context, there may be collectively shared visual regard towards the baby (and from the baby to all persons present). The baby – situated on the mother's lap – may face the others (rather than the mother), which certainly provides for social experience. This kind of 'facing outwards' positioning of the baby was described to dominate in mother–infant interaction on the Marquesas Islands (Martini and Kirkpatrick, 1981). This placement indicates that the mother–infant interaction is embedded in a multi-person group setting, and that the exclusivity of the mother–infant dyadic relation is but one of the many versions of the relationship.

The major functional model of mother–infant interaction is that of the *interaction being a means to achieve specific goals*. Since the infant is helpless in many everyday tasks – due to slow motor development – there is a strict need for somebody else to assist in performing relevant tasks (of feeding, cleaning etc.). The infant's development is mediated by goal-oriented actions of other persons who interact with the baby. Many tasks in everyday life can be accomplished only through engaging the infant in interaction, and using that engagement to arrive at a goal. For example, getting the child dressed is a concrete everyday task that is possible only through interaction. Table 9.4 gives an empirical example of an episode of a mother dressing a 9-month-old infant into a shirt. The mother's strategic action (carrying the tube with her, offering it to the baby at decisive moments) indicates how problem-solving is embedded in the mother–infant interaction. Surely enjoyment of the interaction is not excluded from the picture, but it is secondary to the primary need to get the baby dressed.

TABLE 9.4 *Getting dressed: mother–infant interaction as a means to an end*

Child has been undressed in the bathroom, during which time he has shown interest in a tube of cream. Mother has removed it in order to give him a bath

Mother: Asks the child to get out of the bathtub to be dried.

Child: Climbs out.

Mother: Covers child with a towel and carries him over to another room. She takes the tube with her.

Both: Engage in social/verbal play.

Mother: Puts child on the back on the bed and starts to dry him.

Child: Complains.

Mother: Hands the tube to child.

Child: Takes it and plays with it while mother dries and dresses him.

BOTH: Are engaged in playful interaction.

Mother: Takes shirt and pulls it over child's head.

Child: Takes tube in both hands.

Mother: Takes child's first arm.

Child: Changes tube to second hand.

Mother: Pulls first arm into sleeve.

Child: Takes tube in both hands again.

Mother: Takes second arm.

Child: Changes tube to first hand.

Mother: Pulls second arm into sleeve.

Source: Kindermann and Valsiner, 1989, p. 33

Cultural highlighting of developmental transitions in infancy

Infant development entails a number of behavioural transitions, which may (but need not) become marked semiotically as symbolic indicators of the baby's meaningful relations with the social (as well as supernatural) worlds. In the folklore of infant care in the occidental medical world, 'milestones' such as the baby 'turning over' (from supine to prone position) independently, smiling to the caregiver, holding objects by the hands, creeping/crawling, walking independently, being wary of strangers, sleeping through the night (without waking up the caregivers) are all conceptualized as semiotic markers of one ('normal') or another ('problematic') kind of development. The construction of 'the norm' of infant development is a secular version of the meanings attached to different features of the baby's development in the supernatural worldviews of different societies in the history of culture.

Cultural construction of the relevance of teething: symbolic danger of supernormality

The appearance of the first teeth is obviously an important milestone for the development of the child's body. It has immediate implications for the feeding process (possibility of biting foods). Yet its symbolic relevance is not constructed culturally in all societies. Without doubt, the cutting of teeth is known, but the linkage of this with the supernatural world is not necessarily emphasized. Yet there are examples of the desire for lower teeth cutting first, encoded in cultural rituals of introducing the newborn to the society.[9]

The Kaguru (in Tanzania, East Africa) parents stimulate the lower gums of the infant – even sometimes cut the lower gums of the infant – in an effort to let the first teeth 'cut through' there (observations from 1957 to 1958, reported in Beidelman, 1963, pp. 54–56). This is based on the collective-cultural belief that a baby whose upper teeth develop before the lower ones is a 'supernormal' baby (*chigego*), who hinders the lives of the people around him or her. The *chigego* is believed to be extraordinarily clever, strong and vigorous – due to linkages with the spirit world. Such characteristics, as the *chigego* grows bigger, are believed to decrease the vitality and vigour of the child's kinship group. It was believed that *chigego* attracts misfortunes that do not hurt him or her, but which would harm others around. Thus, the dangers of bearing a *chigego* are culturally substantial. Before a Kaguru woman bears a child, special beads are worn as amulets against the child turning out to be *chigego*. At the time of teething – when the positive expectations of the lower teeth appearing first are fulfilled – the happy parents tie a bead necklace (*ihumbwaji*) around the neck of the baby to show their pleasure at the normality of the infant (and to communicate the fact of the child being non-*chigego* to anybody who encounters the baby).

The Kaguru fear of super-normality is directly tied to the belief in the collective good. An individual who grows strong at the expense of the others acquires an ambivalent status, and measures are taken to prevent such outcome from happening. Contrast this with the widespread belief in the United States in the positive features of having a 'super-normal' baby – one that *is ahead of its peers* (or age-set norms) in his or her motor development. This kind of super-normality is socially valued, and actively promoted by parents through various kinds of support tools for such development. Yet, a *hyper-supernormal* baby under these circumstances – one who is a 'little adult' in some aspect – may be disliked as a 'monster'.

Locomotion during infancy: cultural regulation of beginning to walk

In our society, we take it for granted that early achievement of independent locomotion (walking independently) is a sign of 'healthy' development. Parents can be observed to stimulate their babies' efforts to creep around, stand up, and make their first step as early as possible. Numerous prosthetic devices – such as 'baby walkers' – are utilized to arrive at the resemblance of the baby 'walking' *as early as possible*,[10] and to 'help' the child to begin walking. For all intents and purposes, such acceleration efforts should be detrimental precisely from the viewpoint of the parents (that is, a walking baby is also a falling baby – at times – and a baby who quickly gains access to the environment one level up from the pre-walking state forces parents to be 'on guard' about explorations of more objects in the child's vicinity). Nevertheless, the social competitiveness projected onto the infants, and the symbolic value of the baby 'standing on her or his own feet' may create a 'cultural blindness' to such inconveniences.

The tendency towards promoting early achievement of independent walking is certainly not universal in human societies. In fact, it can be precisely the reverse – *delay* in infants' walking independently can be made into a desirable feature. This has been documented for the Tuva ethnic group in Siberia, to the north of Mongolia (Diakonova, 1988, p. 157). The Tuva believed that the person's length of life is proportional to the time it takes the baby from the moment of birth to the beginning of independent walking. And as long life is of desirable value, the Tuva would prefer a baby to start walking independently later, rather than earlier.

And, last but not least, in many societies the time of infants' beginning to walk independently is culturally not marked at all. It is certainly noticed when it happens (just as we notice infants' teething) but, differently from the Kaguru, it is not turned into a cultural dramatized event but lacks symbolic relevance. Children just begin to walk, and that's it – no big deal!

Lay beliefs in infant motor restrictions

Social sciences have been vulnerable to the social representations in popular beliefs that link limitations on infant motility (through swaddling, or keeping infants on cradle-boards) through analogic reasoning with adult personality characteristics. Thus, a widespread discussion of the adequacy of the 'swaddling hypothesis' (Benedict, 1949; Gorer and Rickman, 1962) is an example of social sciences operating with analogic reasoning in ways similar to magical thinking.

The 'swaddling hypothesis' entailed that in societies where infants' movements are *physically* restricted, persons become *psychologically* restricted (subservient to authority). The popularity of the hypothesis flourished in the early years of the Cold War, as it allowed easy explanation for how the Russians so passively accepted the totalitarian nature of Stalin. The observation that newborns and infants in Russian childcare practices were swaddled led to the linking of infancy and adulthood. This hypothesis was based on a uni-directional notion of culture transfer.

Historically, swaddling infants and carrying them on cradle-boards was an option for baby care in a number of North American Indian societies. In Figure 9.6 an example of a Navaho cradle-board is depicted. The cradle-board (called *aweetsáal*, 'baby diaper') consists of three parts. First there is a back-board (covering the back area of about 23 by 90 cm), secondly there is the footboard (23 × 8 cm), which is attached to the main board by hinges, and finally, there is a hoop arching over the face area of the infant on the board. The infants were put on the cradle-board by first putting some bedding material on the back-board. This was covered by a blanket, and the infant was placed on the blanket. The blanket was then turned to cover the baby's body in full, leaving the hands and feet immobile (Chisholm, 1983, pp. 73–74).

The normative nature of human lay conceptualization of motor restrictions is reflected in hypotheses set forth by child psychologists who have expected those infants with substantial cradle-board experience to be *delayed* in the time they begin to walk independently. Both the parameter selected – developmental milestone

FIGURE 9.6 *The use of the cradle-board in a Navaho family (from Kluckhohn, 1974, p. 94)*

in walking independently – and the direction of the hypothesis (that movement-restricted infants are 'delayed') indicate the embeddedness of psychologists within their lay collective culture, and their intuitive assumption of a normative position. The existing empirical evidence (see Table 9.5) fails to detect differences between samples of infants with and without cradle-board experience in the age of beginning to walk independently.

Notice in Table 9.5 the wide range of reported ages of independent walking under all conditions (8–25 months). This variability indicates that average-based norms of independent walking are basically useless as indicators of children's development. There are further concerns about the precision with which such a supposed normative 'milestone' is located on the age scale of development: would Hopi and Navaho parents be as worried about week-to-week measurement of progress in their infants' motor development as could be expected from US white middle-class parents?

Physiological explanation of the lack of effects

The failure to find the expected 'developmental delay' in cradle-boarded and swaddled infants' development is no mystery. The development of muscle strength in biological organisms can take place in two ways – demonstrating multilinearity and equifinality – by *isotonic* and *isometric*

physical exercise. The isotonic strategy involves active movement of the limbs and development of the muscles through the movement at full extent. Although this may be the main notion of 'exercising muscles' that our lay minds may easily imagine, it is not the only one. Muscle strength is also developed through isometric exercising – pressing against a static obstacle, with increasing effort. The cradle-board is a device that limits the baby's mechanism of build-up of muscle strength to isometric exercising; the baby who is swaddled and on a cradle-board can develop muscle strength *precisely because* the body movements are restricted (Hudson, 1966).

Equifinality in the process of locomotory development

Another example of how child psychologists have overlooked variability and multilinearity of development is the perception of the progression from stationary to locomotory stage. Since 1900 (Trettien, 1900) it has been clear that there exist at least two trajectories in the infant's arrival at the stage of independent walking:

TRAJECTORY 1 :
no locomotion → **creeping/crawling** →
independent walking

TRAJECTORY 2:
no locomotion → **sitting/shuffling** →
independent walking

TABLE 9.5 *Summary of the existing evidence of the effects of cradle-board use on infant locomotion*

Study (culture)	Samples	Time on cradle-board	Index of development	
Dennis and Dennis, 1940 (Hopi)	63 infants had been on board; 42 had not	Mean duration of board use was 9 months (usually from first day); range 4–14 mth	Independent walking age (IWA)	
			Board users Mean = 14.98 mth S.D. 2.62 mth Range: 10–25 mth	*Non-users* 15.05 mth 2.24 mth 9–25 mth
Harriman and Lukosius, 1982 (Hopi)	48 infants had been on board; 133 had not	Mean = 3.9 mth S.D. = 2.1 mth Range: 0.5–12.0 mth	IWA	
			Board users Mean = 12.54 mth Range: 8–24 mth	*Non-users* 12.4 mth 7.5–24 mth
Chisholm, 1983 (Navaho)	21 infants had been on board	Mean = 10.28 mth Range: 1–21 mth Hours per day, by age: 0–3 mth: 15–18 3–6 mth: 12–15 6–9 mth: 9–12 9–12 mth: 6–9	Effects of board placement on mother–infant interaction: 1. Board enhances proximity 2. When off board, more intense bouts of interaction	

Sources: Chisholm, 1983, pp. 76–7, 173–4; Dennis and Dennis, 1940, pp. 79, 81; Harriman and Lukosius, 1982, p. 82

In cases of infants with physical handicaps (see Largo et al., 1985) different scenarios (rolling, bridging, snake-like movements) can be observed in the phase that is normatively (and indeed about 85 per cent of infants *do* go through Trajectory 1) viewed as the 'creeping/crawling phase'. Psychologists have attempted to develop a general (and normative) model of the development of locomotion by considering the trajectory that fits the majority into the normative and universally general picture of human development. This inductively based generalization is a nondevelopmental description of development – in fact, a faulty one.

Locomotion in the third dimension: climbing

Climbing is creeping, crawling or shuffling in the third dimension of the landscape. The terrain enforces a form of locomotion that entails close contact of the trunk with the surface. Thus, while infants 'climb' on horizontal surfaces while creeping and crawling on the floor, adult mountain climbers 'creep and crawl' along the vertical surfaces.

The evolutionary history of *Homo sapiens* provides ample evidence about the gradual disappearance of highly developed skills of moving in the third dimension. Many primate species move around by 'swinging' from one treetop to another (*brachiation*) – a skill that in human cases can be found developed (against the odds of imperfect anatomy of human beings) in circus artistes, gymnasts and pole vaulters.

The sensorimotor world of infants (in the second half-year of life) and toddlers includes possibilities to move around in three-dimensional space. Climbing is a natural extension of pulling oneself up with support, and from there follows the navigation of the two-dimensional surface (floor), or – if the object of support is of an appropriate kind – efforts of locomotion in the third dimension. Thus, the child is faced with a physical environment that affords both kinds of locomotion. It is the cultural construction of that physical structure by the child's caregivers that sets up the differentiated demand structure for the child's locomoting efforts. Thus, the infant (and toddler) in the context of a US middle-class family may be encouraged to walk, and climb some appropriate objects (for example, stairs, sofas), but not others (window sills etc.). The child's climbing can be enhanced by setting up specific microcontexts (see Valsiner and Mackie, 1985). Within these contexts (for example, guided climbing *up* the stairs), specific motor patterns are exercises which can be transferred – by the child – to other objects (or the reverse action of the same, for example, the child turning around and beginning to climb *down* the stairs, head first). Cultural canalization of children's motor actions is based on a network of general collective-cultural meanings, in which concerns about potential bodily injuries and transgressions of the socially constituted meaningful order are combined in remarkable complexes. Yet – in line with the bi-directional culture transfer model – the infants and children in general constantly re-negotiate the boundaries of that symbolic order.

THE OTHER PART OF LIFE: PSYCHOLOGY OF INFANT DEATH

Collective-cultural preparation of the parents and other kinship group members involves simultaneous construction of semiotic mediating devices for different possible outcomes of the life course. While the priority is with the guidance of the life course of the surviving and developing baby, at the same time the semiotic means for handling the death of the baby are being prepared. This duplicity is a realistic psychological pre-adaptation to different possible and probable outcomes. Throughout most of the history of human societies children have been born in the common knowledge that non-survival of the baby through infancy was probable. Hence, while attempting to do everything to help the baby develop through the hazardous first year of life, a system of collective-cultural mediation is set in place should the baby not be so lucky.

A number of means can be devised to be prepared for such an occasion. First, there is the delay (waiting period) before constructing the baby as a cultural human being (as was described above). Such delay – continuation of 'non-person' status of the baby through the most risky parts of infancy – would reduce the necessity to personal-culturally deal with the death of the baby, should it occur.

Likewise, different constructions of the 'other world' (of ancestors, or of hell and heaven) allow for production of mediation means for coping with the undesired but frequent event of child's death in infancy. The death of the baby can be presented (to the mother herself, and to others) as a return to the 'world of ancestors' (from where the baby has been viewed as if coming, in the first place), or to heaven (in cases of Christian religious conversion). The biological finality of the death of the baby (or of any person) is countered by the personal-cultural construction of the eternity of the survival of the 'departed other' into another place.

Among people in Teotlixco (in the south of Mexico), the bananaquit bird was believed to be the 'bird of the heart' into which the soul (*yolia*) was believed to turn after death, to fly away. The souls of the deceased infants were believed to fly away and gather at the 'nursemaid tree' which provided them with milk to survive (see Figure 9.7). Milk was said to be dropping from the leaves of the 'nursemaid tree', keeping the (deceased) infants' 'life spirit' alive in that other place. The deceased infants were considered to be extremely important for the living human world, as it was assumed that the deceased would one day repopulate the world.

FIGURE 9.7 *Dead infants sucking from the 'nursemaid tree' – an Italian copy of an early colonial Central Mexican document (from Furst, 1995, p. 26, reprinted by permission)*

The mothers of the deceased infants, meanwhile, can continue to count them as their own. This was the feature that surprised American anthropologist Nancy Scheper-Hughes in her stay in a poor village in the North-East region of Brazil. When asking a mother a seemingly simple and straightforward question – 'How many children do you have?' – she received an answer that would not make Western scientific fertility statisticians very happy: 'I have two here, and another two in heaven.' Yet such a way of counting fits very well the collective-cultural conditions in which the continuity (rather than division) between the world of the living and that of the dead is emphasized. The mothers who report *their* children in Heaven are telling the truth – of their having had these children. Only at the given time the children are seen as migrants in a land of no (direct) return. Yet the role of having these children remains to be of importance in the mothers' personal cultures.

Emotions at the death of a child

The collective-cultural guidance for the living at the time of the death of a child can be of two kinds. It either guides those losing the other person towards intense expression of their feelings (hence elaborate social support for crying relatives, built into funeral ceremonies), or guides them towards distancing from the event by way of resignation, meditation and self-control. Thus, the opposites of *cultural amplification* and *cultural attenuation* of feelings are equally possible ways of coping with the loss. Based on her Brazilian experience, Scheper-Hughes (1992, ch. 9) indicates the centrality of resignation (*conformação*) as the generic concept organizing poor Brazilian women's coping with the death of their children. This has parallel in the Balinese handling of feelings at the time of others' death (Wikan, 1990).

The Brazilian case is particularly important because, years later, the very same mothers (who had met their child's death with resignation) can re-tell the story of their death with much emotional amplification. Within the same personal culture, the operations of amplification and attenuation of feelings can be set up to work on different occasions – even referring to the same life event. In the collective-cultural domain, the co-presence of both suggestions for amplification and attenuation makes it possible to modulate persons' distancing of themselves relative to their life events (see Chapter 4). The opposites enable each other: the basic feeling of sadness (*tristeza*) is the basis for its opposite (*alegria* – romantic happiness) expressing itself in some life events. The latter can be collective-culturally prescribed, such as carnivals. The unity of the opposites may become an over-generalized feeling field that underlies all of human personal-cultural existence. *Saudade* is the bitter-sweet longing for something or somebody, beyond the pragmatic possibilities of acting to attain the desired object. It corresponds to the German feelings of longing for another place (*Fernweh*) and longing for home (*Heimweh*) (see Boesch, 1998, pp. 59–76) in the generality of the feeling and instrumentality being blocked within that field (refer back to Chapter 4 on general field-like phenomena and their study).

A case of cultural amplification of the feelings at death is well described by Catherine Lutz (1988) on the Ifaluk atoll in Micronesia, in the Pacific. The Ifaluk life is organized by the general feeling-notion of *fago* – a complex uniting compassion, love and sadness. At the time of the death and all through the funeral rituals, the collective-cultural canalization system of the Ifaluk guides persons to 'cry big' (rather than subdue one's feelings). Lutz experienced a 24-hour illness and death of a 5-year-old boy:

> At the moment of death, a great wailing went up. The dead boy's biological mother, seated on the floor mats near him, rose up to her knees as if she had been stabbed and pounded her fist violently against her chest. The adoptive mother, a woman of about sixty (and the boy's father's sister), began to scream and throw herself about on the ground. Others rushed forward to restrain both of them from hurting themselves, and the biological mother was soon sitting in stiff shock. The house filled with crying, from low moaning to loud wrenching and mucus-filled screaming to wailingly sung poem-laments, and continued without pause through the night. Both men and women spent tears in what seemed to me equal measure. It is customary that people take turns coming forward (or rather being invited forward by the closest relatives) to cry in the immediate circle around the body. A careful choreography of grief generally requires that those who are 'crying big' (or loudly and deeply) do so closer rather than further from the body, and those who are not crying move back from it. (Lutz, 1988, p. 126)

The instantaneous choreographing of the 'crying big' at the boy's death indicates the immediate cultural readiness to dramatize the feelings at the event. Death for the Ifaluk is not disappearance, but 'dying away' from the living, 'toward the spirit world' (Lutz, 1988, p. 128). Thus, the crying is the expression of sadness at departure, the shock of the departure, and concern for the persons who stay behind, rather than for the deceased *per se*. The function of the amplification of feelings at death is precisely a semiotic vehicle for the cryers to eliminate thoughts about the deceased from their minds. The grieving family members – such as mother and father of the deceased child – are thus encouraged not to think of the deceased, and express their *fago* for the living who are needy, instead. The rationale is twofold: their thinking of the deceased may interfere with their lives (for example, undermine care of the living children), and may 'make them ill' themselves. Yet during the immediate post-mortem period and through the funeral rituals, these very same family members are the ones who, by themselves, aided by collective-cultural guidance, are the primary 'big cryers'.

The time-pattern of the amplification and attenuation of feelings about death are almost completely opposite in the accounts of North-Eastern Brazil (Scheper-Hughes, 1992) and the Ifaluk (Lutz, 1988). The former lived through the immediate death of the child with resignation, but at later times would dramatize the event in re-telling the story. The latter dramatized the event as it occurred, and later did not return to it mentally. In both cases, it was the genetic dramatism that was utilized in a time-distributed manner in the collective-cultural and personal-cultural regulation of grief (see also Chapter 4 on the general centrality of genetic dramatism in human culture).

Infant burials: fossilized dramatisms

We have already seen in Chapter 8 how in Japanese society at the present time tombstones for aborted fetuses have become used as cultural markers of memory and forgetting. In societies where the death of the baby or young child is supported (for the living) by ritualization of the grief, burials constitute a crucial semiotic mediation context. The specific belief systems guide the execution of such rituals. For example, the photograph in Figure 9.8 was taken (by Sebastiaõ Salgado) in Ceará, North-Eastern Brazil, where it is believed that the deceased child's eyes should be kept open so that it can see better when going to heaven. This is in direct contrast with many cultural practices (likening death to sleep), where it is required that the eyes of the deceased be closed.

FIGURE 9.8 *A deceased child in the coffin – from Ceará, Brazil (photograph by Sebastiaõ Salgado, 1997, p. 69, reprinted by permission)*

GENERAL SUMMARY: CULTURALLY EXPLAINED INFANCY

The contents of this chapter lead to one general conclusion – what happens after the birth around the developing infant, and what is usually called 'care *for* the infant', is simultaneously a 'care *for the others*'. These 'others' are anybody who actually surrounds the newborn and infant (immediate members of the kinship network), as well as the wider public in the given social unit (hamlet, village, town, city etc.). Cultural construction of all social roles goes on in parallel – the newborn becomes a (gendered) child, the woman becomes mother; the man, the father; the parents of the parents become grandparents etc., etc. (aunts, uncles, neighbours of a family with the baby, wet nurses, bureaucrats who select wet nurses, etc.).

All these cultural construction processes are *over-determined by meaning*, both at the collective-cultural and personal-cultural levels. These meanings are organized into flexible complexes of a hierarchically ordered (but not strictly determined) kind. Thus, from one meaning-supported action (for example, infanticide) it is possible to move to its opposite (honouring infant twins). This is made possible by the unity of opposites that characterizes cultural meanings (Josephs et al., 1999). Yet, under different sociohistorical circumstances some of that flexibility of meaning construction is purposefully stopped. Then we can observe moralistic social guidance of the conduct of infants, their parents and others around them. In the next chapter, the cultural construction that involves a direction towards attaining inflexibility (which fails) in early childhood will be examined. As will be clear, such efforts do – and need to – fail. This is largely due to the active curiosity of the children who go 'beyond' their immediately present social contexts.

NOTES

1 In the history of human societies, we can see a tendency towards replacing infanticide under conditions described here, by creating rituals of purification for the baby, so as to get rid of the assumed effects of malevolent spirits. Similarly, the act of infanticide in the past of human history cannot be interpreted through the lens of our contemporary socio-moral perspectives.

2 The role of wooden figurines as replacements of the lost human beings, or as 'special spirit persons' important in human lives, is widespread in West Africa. It is the basis for creating wooden sculptures (which, by way of inter-societal commercial exchange relations, have by now became classified as 'African art' objects – beyond their original role as personal 'spiritual companions' (see Vogel, 1997)).

3 With modern technology – ultrasound-based

video tapes of fetal movements – the information about the visual image of the fetus is made technically available to the would-be parents. This can lead to the cultural construction process of the nature of the baby beginning before the baby is actually born.

4 This power of naming has its interesting history in medieval discourse about the dangers of demons. The belief that if one can name one's enemy, one establishes control over him, was widespread in the medieval world. For example, it was believed that by mere naming of the demon one can domesticate him (or her; Brzozowska-Krajka, 1998, p. 61). This magical belief may carry over to modern psychiatric and clinical-psychological discourse, where much emphasis is placed on arriving at the correct diagnosis of a disease.

5 The use of alternative feeding sources – wet nurses, or milk from animal sources – was certainly socially legitimate in the case of medical necessities, such as the mother not having sufficient milk.

6 In British North America (later the United States and Canada), as in many other traditional societies, the post-partum period of breast-feeding was linked with abstinence from regular sexual relations until the mother weaned the baby.

7 These surfaces vary as to their elevation from the rest of the surface. The minimum elevation is that of the main surface (floor, ground).

The notion of 'bed' entails a special surface elevated beyond the ground surface, to different heights. Sleeping surfaces can also lack contact with the ground, as these can be set up hanging downwards from support sources (hammocks, cradles for babies). The latter cases entail protection from ground-moving possible intruders (such as domestic animals), but limit the sleepers' possibilities for movement.

8 In higher primates – for instance in bonobos (*Pan paniscus*) – reduction of tension is mediated by various forms of sexual encounters (see Kano, 1992).

9 In the case of Sumbwa (north-western Tanzania) rituals of introducing the baby (described above), one of the birth figurines-based future developmental scenarios is dedicated to teething – wanting the lower teeth cut first (Cory, 1961, p. 72). The parents are instructed to give an amulet to the child if the cutting of the appropriate teeth is delayed.

10 It is interesting to note that 'baby walkers' are actually devices that support the infants' *leaping*, rather than walking *per se*. The infant in a walker is supported in the upright position, while the movement is generated by the push-off by the hindlimbs, with safe landing (if it is safe – the overturning of walkers has been shown to be a cause of accidents) guaranteed in the upright position.

REVIEW QUESTIONS FOR CHAPTER 9

1 Explain the notion of *cultural-ecological niche*.

2 Explain the notion of cultural highlighting, and describe its different forms.

3 Explain different ways in which twin births have been dealt with, in different societies.

4 Analyse the history of the reversal of twin infanticide among the Yoruba.

5 Explain the psychological processes involved in the Sumbwa child display ritual.

6 What is 'symbolic immunization'?

7 Explain the two forms of 'evil eye' – *affascene* and *mmvidie* – in the Southern Italian community of Locorotondo. How do these two forms socially regulate human conduct?

8 Explain why the young Thai mother refused the praise of her baby, given by the American friends.

9 In which ways are the cultural meaning of a baby constructed at the introduction of the newborn to the parents?

10 Explain the notion of *dialogical monologization*

11 Explain the functions of infants' naming practices for the baby, and for the adults.

12 Describe the 'self-fulfilling prophecy' of Asante naming practices.

13 How can the naming of a baby become an issue for the whole kinship group?

14 Explain the private/public tension inherent in breast-feeding.

15 Describe the biological bases for successful breast-feeding.

16 Explain the process structure of breast-feeding.

17 How do social institutions shift between satisficing and maximizing strategies in their suggestions to parents about relevant issues of childcare?

18 Explain the connections of the meanings of BLOOD and MILK, and the implications of such connections for human psychological processes.

19 How are women's social roles regulated through social highlighting of the assumed needs of the babies?

20 Under what social and economic conditions could wet-nursing emerge?

21 Explain the criteria used for evaluation of wet nurses, and of their milk.

22 Explain the psychological differences between a family employing a 'live-in' wet nurse, versus sending their infant to a 'baby farmer'.

23 What is the psychological role of the Teotlixco 'nursemaid tree'?

24 Explain the psychological mechanisms of coping with the death of an infant.

25 In what sense are infant burials 'fossilized dramatisms'?

26 Explain the role of dreaming among the Mekeo.

27 Describe human general sleeping patterns over the life course.

28 How is infants' place of sleeping culturally regulated?

29 Explain the tactics of adults in altering infants' activation states.

30 Analyse 'going-to-bed' as a culturally constructed setting.

31 Analyse the functions of tactile and vestibular stimulation in adult–infant interaction.

32 Explain two models of mother–infant interaction.

33 Explain the psychological functions of Kaguru parents' promotion of the cutting of infants' teeth.

34 Explain the cultural relativity of beginning to walk.

35 Explain the role of motor restraint in human development.

36 Explain equifinality in infant locomotory development.

37 Analyse infants' climbing as a trigger for cultural regulation of conduct.

PART FOUR

EARLY CHILDHOOD DEVELOPMENT

Once the child has survived the most vulnerable first year of life, the collective-cultural system slowly guides him or her in the direction of a gender-appropriate self-development trajectory. Aside from the usually assumed two trajectories – male and female – there are numerous intermediate versions of gendered self-constructions at the personal-cultural level of parents. This multiplicity is reduced by the collective-cultural two-part (male < >female) or three-part (male < > uncertain < >female) classifications. The social world of adults is oriented towards guidance of individuals into the two (or three) channels of self-development. The individuals nevertheless create their own personal developmental trajectory, precisely with the help of the propensity towards *persistent imitation* (see Baldwin, in Chapter 3). It is through the capacity of play in early childhood, and constructive fantasy later on, that individuals create their unique developmental life courses.

The study of early childhood entails an encounter with the notion of attachment, and with different constructions of how human emotional ties with others may guide individuals' psychological well-being over lifetime. The construction of attachment *theories* is itself an example of cultural construction, which is based upon the reality of attachment *phenomena*. Similarly to the parent framework of attachment theories (psychoanalysis), the question of adequacy of these theories is tested in their application to persons beyond the boundaries of the given (Euro-American) society, beyond the dominant (middle) social class.

Early childhood is rich in so to say 'silent' cultural-psychological phenomena. Much of the personal reconstruction of the collective culture proceeds through observational learning and peripheral social participation. This makes it a very difficult target for scientific investigation. Also, early childhood generally lacks the social institutional structure that begins to canalize human development later (formal schooling). Yet the playful, chattering and observant young child is an active co-constructor of human culture.

THE SECOND YEAR OF LIFE, AND BEYOND

The cultural expectations for children's motor development are reflected in the age period description of children. In psychology, such age periodizations are often linked with either levels of motor development (in early childhood), or with socio-institutional embeddedness of the children (for example, 'kindergarteners', 'pre-schoolers', '3rd graders').

Children in their second year of life are often referred to as 'toddlers'. That term is unabashedly English-language centred: no equivalents exist in other major languages. A 'toddler' is a little human being who toddles around, still exercising the skills of bipedal walking. In the third year of life, when walking becomes well-established and exploration of language use becomes a major proccupation, we do not have a simple analogous term ('babbler' stage is obviously past, maybe the 'verbal enquirer' or 'inquisitor' labels could fit that age). It is also a result of cultural construction that such a distinction between the second and the third year is made at all – in many societies, there is no necessity to differentiate age periods with such precision. The basic distinction is that of children under approximately 6–7 years of age, and those older. Yet all distinctions of this kind remain arbitrary.

CULTURAL ORGANIZATION OF WEANING

Similarly to the issues of beginning (and continuing) breast-feeding (see Chapter 9), the ending of the breast-feeding of a particular child is a phenomenon of potentially high psychological ambiguity, and one which is a likely target for collective-cultural canalization. Of course, the period of lactation has its own biological course in the case of the mother, creating the upper physiological boundary for the age of weaning. Cultural construction operates within these biological limits – the time (age of the child)

of finishing the practice of breast-feeding can be lowered considerably below the time length of biological possibility. In fact, the decision not to breast-feed *at all* can be viewed as the lowest level of time of weaning – weaning at the time of possible beginning of nursing.

Different societies around the world demonstrate varied ages of children for the time of weaning, mostly concentrating around 2 years of age (for example, in Indonesia 90 per cent of children are nursed until age 2 years – Niehof, 1998, p. 239). Yet the range of child's age within which breast feeding can be encountered is wide – from 0 (refusal to breast feed) to 5–7 years. The latter certainly is not an age at which the *breast*-feeding has any nutritional role for the child. Instead, it may indicate mutually pleasurable moments in the psychological relationship of the mother and the child through the sensuality of the mouth-to-breast encounter. This means that prolonged child–mother's breast contact in ontogeny can occur in societies where mother–child sharing of sensual experiences is not suppressed or repressed.

There are other reasons to limit the time of breast-feeding. First (and foremost) is the decision of the woman to become pregnant again. As breast milk has been often culturally constructed as a version of transformed blood, a cultural need for stopping the feeding of the child when the mother becomes pregnant follows. The mother's blood production system while pregnant needs to 'build up' the new baby, and continued breast-feeding of the previous child 'drains' her resources. This may become expressed in folk beliefs of avoiding competition between the siblings – one at the breast, the other in the womb. For example, if a Moroccan Berber breast-feeding woman becomes pregnant again, she has to wean the child. The nursing child is seen as 'stealing food' from the fetus (as in the Berber belief the breast milk is called 'white blood': Teitelbaum, 1981), and the fetus is seen as 'fighting back' by contaminating the mother's milk (after all, the fetus is still intimately 'inside' of the mother – and in contact with her blood flow). Here sibling rivalry is a two-fold process: both the child and the fetus are rivals to each other, and act against each other. In order to break this rivalry, the mother needs to separate the nutrition sources for the two – the child is moved to solid foods (and others' milk, such as goat's or cow's), while the developing fetus monopolizes the mother's 'blood resources' for its development.

The Berber cultural system of explanation creates a self-fulfilling prophecy. The weaned child usually suffers from diarrhoea caused by the herbs given to him or her to act against the harm of sibling rivalry *from the fetus*, which is carried to the child with the mother's milk. These signs are interpreted as proof of the 'effects' the fetus has had on the child – and thus purification (by the very same herbs) is necessary.

In contrast with the usual folk ideas about weaning in European and North American societies, which emphasize the potential danger of weaning experiences for the child's relations with the mother, the Berber parents are not worried about the effects of weaning on mother–child relations (as such relations are unquestionably granted by the social roles of the mother and the child). They are concerned about the potential ill-effects of any rivalry between siblings that can occur through the sharing of the mother's blood resource.

Other reasons for finishing breast-feeding can concentrate on the mother's activities. Surely her daytime subsistence activities can make it complicated to carry the child (especially a child beyond infancy) to her workplace (if that is at a distance from home). This carrying task can be delegated to the main caregivers – siblings – yet it implies breast-feeding by schedule (for which the transport of the child can be pre-planned) rather than 'on demand' (which requires constant closeness of the mother and the child).

An example of how these considerations enter into the cultural construction of weaning is visible in the comparison of weaning among the Ganda (in Uganda; Ainsworth, 1967, pp. 406–407) and the United States. In the US case – which can be characterized by on-schedule breast-feeding and mother–child separation at night – weaning may begin from the elimination of the *night-time* feeding periods from the feeding schedule. Both the child and the mother (in their separate rooms) begin to sleep through the night, without the mother feeding the child. Yet the daytime breast-feeding continues (in case of mothers who stay at home with the children). If the mother works outside of the home, and wants to return to her work life as soon as possible, early achievement of

total weaning (or as was described in Chapter 9 – hiring of a wet nurse) are the remaining options.

In contrast, the Ganda begin the weaning of children *by dropping the daytime feeding*. This is warranted because of the mother's subsistence activities – she may need to be absent from the child during long periods of work in the gardens outside of the village. Yet as the mother and child continue to sleep together, breast feeding continues at night-times. Eventually it becomes reduced also at night. The Ganda recognize that the process of weaning is not much to the liking of the children (and attempt to make it as easy as possible), yet there is no cultural meaning of 'potential harming' of the child attached to the issue.

CULTURAL CONSTRUCTION OF TOILET-TRAINING

The opposite alimentation process to feeding is elimination – excretion of various products of the body into the environment. Human cultural history has created special places, restrictions to access to these places (for example, separation of toilets for men and women), special rituals of treatment of human excretory products (in contrast with similar results of animal bodily processes – use of the excretions of domestic animals, but not of humans, as fertilizers).

The products of human elimination are usually culturally constructed as 'dirty', and distanced from the body with remarkable speed.[1] In ontogeny, the establishment of physiological control over the muscular system that controls elimination processes is one of the developmental tasks. Its precise location on the ontogenetic age scale is a result of a collective-cultural construction process. Similarly with the developmental course of nursing (above), the development of self-control over elimination is a physiological growth process in which the collective-cultural construction processes intervene in different ways (and at different times). Such intervention is not necessary – the biological body establishes the control mechanisms in the course of childhood anyway, and the physiological control mechanisms remain in place until old age.

Over the history of human societies, different cultural constructions exist for handling elimination control in childhood ('toilet-training' as it is known colloquially). In US society over the past century, the cultural construction of 'toilet-training' has been channelled to the recipient parents through the activities of 'medical experts'. That expert advice has varied remarkably from one decade to another. The notion of 'readiness for toilet-training' is a cultural meaning (usually phrased in terms of physiological discourse – '*neurologically* ready/unready' at age X) which operates upon the parents' actions in relation to 'toilet-training'. The expert advice could introduce specific elimination-enhancing practices – through parents' worries and actions – very early (for example see Bartlett, 1932, p. 232 on how to train infants from 1 month onwards for regular daily defecation – 'bowel movement'). The period of the 1920s and 1930s in the United States was the high time for strict 'training regimes' for infants and children. Before that time (1890s–1900s) and after (1940s to present) the focus on 'strict disciplining' of children was less prominently promoted in US society (see Stendler, 1950). Such dynamic shifts within a society's history are general characteristics of cultural dynamics. The discourse in US cultural history fluctuates between 'nature'-based ('toilet-training should start when the child is biologically ready') and 'nurture'-based (children should be *trained* as soon as possible by their socially responsible parents). It is not surprising that the flip-flopping

NATURE < *OR* > NURTURE
|
exclusive

social representation which has hindered developmental sciences in the past (see Chapter 3) stands also behind the historical fluctuations in cultural regulation of children's elimination. 'Being ready' in contrast to 'need to be trained' are cliches indicating the functioning of such representation. In contrast, the replacement of the 'exclusive OR' by 'inclusive OR' (= and) in that representation overcomes the schism. This was the focus for Lev Vygotsky's notion of zone of proximal development (which was described in Chapter 3), and is put into practice in the case of Digo toilet-training (see below).

Cultural history enters into the regulation of children's 'toilet-relations' also through modification of technological aspects of everyday lives. One of the practical rationales for early 'toilet-training' in the US context could be the extent to which dirty *non*-disposable diapers had in the past to be hand-washed by the mother. The technological advances of diapers (with the move to disposables) as well as laundry technologies (washing machines) have facilitated a more relaxed attitude towards the timing of elimination control in contemporary European and American societies (and in middle classes anywhere). Yet at the level of basic human perception the need to distance oneself from the elimination products of human bodies remains in place: no parent can deny that the smell of a 'dirty diaper' is something not easily enjoyable – especially if it is the parent who needs to change the diaper.

In a number of African societies, efforts to put in place cultural control mechanisms for infants' elimination have been located at early periods of ontogeny. Thus, Mary Ainsworth was astonished in the 1950s in Uganda that Ganda parents begin their efforts at infants' elimination regulation at the age of 2–4 months (Ainsworth, 1967, p. 77). What was absent from these efforts – on the part of the parents – was any trace of anxiety, guilt or struggle. Young infants were guided towards collective-cultural cleanliness standards of the Ganda from an early age and yet they were not expected to succeed quickly, and their failures were not failures of the 'trainers' (parents). Rather, the cultural set-up for elimination was canalization rather than 'training'.

Digo (an ethnic group living in coastal areas of Kenya and Tanzania, belonging to the Bantu language group) practices of guiding infants towards control over their elimination practices have demonstrated the possibility of early success (DeVries and DeVries, 1977). By age 4–5 months the infant is expected to urinate only in a culturally set body position. There is a practical need for such early achievement: the ground of Digo huts, with mud floors, acquires a strong smell if urine becomes mixed with the dust. The Digo first goals are to get infants to urinate 'outside of the house' and 'not in bed'. This requires cooperation of the infant and the caregiver.

A careful look at Digo 'toilet-training' practices demonstrates that a combination of basic physiological mechanisms – those of classical and instrumental conditioning, and behavioural modelling – is embedded in the process of urination control promotion. At 2–3 weeks of the infant's age, the caregiver begins to set the baby's body in an appropriate position. The caregiver sits with her feet stretched out in front. The baby is set up sitting on the caregiver's feet, facing away from the caregiver, while his body is supported by the caregiver. The latter emits a low-voiced noise ('*shuus*') that serves as the potential conditional stimulus (CS) for the urination to begin. Repetition of this situation (day and night) creates the specific cultural niche (see Chapter 9) for voiding. The child is expected to pick up the linkage of '*shuus*' with the appropriate setting sound and urinate when this sound is heard. Once urination occurs, the infant is *rewarded by feeding* (breast feeding), within the scheme of instrumental conditioning.

Digo promotion of defecation ('bowel movement') includes a different setting. The caregiver again sits on the floor, legs spread. The infant is put to sit on her feet facing her. The caregiver's feet create the edges of a 'human potty' for the infant, whose upper body is being supported by the caregiver. No vocalizations accompany this procedure. Once successful, the infant is again rewarded by breast feeding (DeVries and DeVries, 1977, p. 173).

The Digo practices constitute a cultural use of the basic reflex principles of *associative reflexes* (of Vladimir Bekhterev: Bechterew, 1932). The structured context entails a clear creation of a *special positional context* for urination and defecation. These two contexts are set up so as to differ from other contexts of being close to the caregiver's body, and to be differentiated from each other (in one case the infant faces outwards, in the other, towards the caregiver). The infant's body in both contexts is supported by tactile means in the precise elimination position. The possibility of early establishment of *positional associative reflexes* (Denisova and Figurin, 1929) is known from laboratory studies – the Digo set these up in everyday practice. The vocal conditional stimulus for urination begins to function in the context set up in its structure (body positions) and tactile support. Giving a reward for success only adds to the procedure.

Without doubt, adults' intervention into the physiological functions of children can be seen as 'an act of violence' – statements like 'How cruel it is to get little babies toilet-trained *before they are ready*' can occur readily. Yet all claims about children's 'readiness for something' are social representations that are culturally constructed and then guide adults' expectations and actions in respect to child development. The crucial role of the affective bonding between the child and the major caregiver is another notable social representation utilized widely in both the scientific and socio-moral organization of adults' actions upon children.

CULTURAL REFLECTIONS UPON AFFECT: PHENOMENA, THEORY AND PRACTICE IN THE ATTACHMENT PERSPECTIVE

The concept of attachment has found its place in contemporary child psychology. It is one of the very few obligatory terms that all US undergraduates need to know in order to be considered educated in psychology (at the baccalaureate level). The popularity of the attachment issues is a result of European and American social histories in the period after the Second World War (Eyer, 1992; Morgan, 1975). The focus on attachment grew out of the confounding of psychoanalytic ideas, experiences of human beings during the war and its sequel, and the social institutional focus on the effects of 'maternal deprivation'.

John Bowlby's attachment theory

The originator of the attachment theory was the English psychoanalyst John Bowlby (1907–1990). The theory was created by him slowly over his life course, especially from late 1930s to the late1970s. Its starting point was Bowlby's psychoanalytic professional background and his belief in the role of social environments – especially the role of the mother – in human development. This belief was not his invention; the ideological focus on the centrality of the mother in child development was widespread in Bowlby's own formative social environment (Britain of the 1920s and 1930s; see Van Dijken et al., 1998).

Bowlby saw the role of the mother as central in creating the child's social environment, especially in the first three years of the child's life. This role was assumed to be inadequate in observed cases of childhood delinquency (especially stealing; Bowlby, 1944; see also Chapter 14). Yet in the background was Bowlby's moralistic social philosophy that was oriented towards promoting harmony in society through 'correct' ways of creating family environments for children in their first years of life. This notion was cultivated by Bowlby in the context of work in the Child Guidance Centre in London – an institution set up in England on the basis of US example (see Van der Veer, 1999).

Beliefs are strong. In his explanation of the role of psychology in a democratic society, Bowlby stated:

Feelings of love and valuation for the adults tending him (normally the physiological mother and father) develop spontaneously in the infant from about six months of age onwards, but their degree will vary with the proximity and attitude of the parents. Broadly speaking, one is only fond of people with whom one is, or has been, in close daily contact. 'What the eye doth not see, the heart doth not long for.' Parents who are not often seen by the child are not loved in the way that those who deal with him daily are. (Bowlby, 1946, p. 66)

This expressed notion of centrality of daily contact of the child and caregiver could legitimize any form of caregiving – *as long as there exists a caregiver* (mother, wet nurse, older sibling etc.) *in the young child's immediate social environment*, the development of the child's affective relations with others would be sufficient. Evidence from the history of wet-nursing, 'baby farming' and other examples of child migration between households would prove Bowlby's point correct. Yet this was not what Bowlby's socio-moralistic stand entailed: he promoted the notion of the relevance of the *child's own mother* for the development of the affective life of the child. In this respect, Bowlby continued within the domain of social discourse in British society that had been fighting the employment of wet nurses. In Bowlby's (twentieth century) case, however, based on his psychoanalytic position, it was no longer the survival of the children but their emotional well-being that was made into the criterion of social desirability.

Normative sequence of the formation of the bond
Bowlby (1952, p. 53) saw the attachment bond emerging in a regular ontogenetic sequence. In line with his psychoanalytic assumptions, he saw the first six months of the infant's life as crucial for the establishment of the attachment bond. In any case, by the end of the first year of life the bond was assumed to be established. This first phase was followed by about two years of the time (the second and third year of the child's life) when the child *was supposed to 'need the mother as an ever-present companion'*. Finally, after the third year of life the child is assumed to be able to maintain the attachment relation with the mother without the latter constantly being present. Yet this third phase was seen as emerging only slowly – according to Bowlby, in the fourth and fifth year of life such a relationship 'can only be maintained in favourable circumstances and for a few days or weeks at a time'. After the seventh or eighth year, the relationship 'can be maintained, though not without strain, for a period of a year or more'.

Bowlby's own social context (similarly to Freud before him) guided him to accept the relatively slow timetable of separation from the parents that characterizes the Anglo-Saxon (and generally European) life courses for children in the conditions of the twentieth century. The practices of wet nursing and 'baby farming' (see Chapter 9) in the history of the very same European societies indicates that either Bowlby's charting of the life course for attachment are historically specific adaptations (that is, act as disproof of the generality of Bowlby's normative narrative), or can be compensated for through establishing attachment bonds with more than one person (mother and wet nurse) at the same time. The latter option – flexible organization of attachment ties – is a more likely candidate for reconciling Bowlby's ideas with historical evidence. Bowlby's assumed unilinear model of human development is proved incorrect. Even if for many mother–child ties his suggested timetable fits their individual particulars of a relationship, the generalization of these cases to a normative model for all cases is unwarranted.

Bowlby's sociopolitical agenda was behind this suggested generalization. If one follows his suggested unilinear course of stages in full, all

mothers should stay at home in an immediate caregiving role for their children for the latter's first three years of life. Assuming possible pregnancies in the latter years, it would lead to the proliferation of the moral slogan 'a woman's place is at home with her children'. This slogan is effective for the social purposes of keeping women out of work roles in contemporary post-industrial societies. *Bowlby's normative model was meant to canalize the development of adults (women) in their mid-life period*, through eliciting their personal-cultural commitments to their children.

Attachment bond formation as a relation (in contrast to a trait)

Bowlby adopted a systemic view of attachment. His systemic model developed over time, under the influence of different psychological perspectives that became popular. His starting point was psychoanalysis – and this remained the cornerstone of his model throughout its development. In the 1940s he built his social ideals around the work of Kurt Lewin (see Bowlby, 1946). Yet the Lewinian field-theoretic linkage later disappeared from his thought, as other perspectives became more prominent.

In Europe after the Second World War social negotiations over how different societies could be reconstructed after the devastation of war gave rise to questions of how to deal with children who were orphaned or homeless. The World Health Organization summoned John Bowlby to assemble a report on the available evidence on the role of mothers in child development. It is through that WHO report (Bowlby, 1952) that the notions of attachment theory gained their wider social status.

The WHO report is both a review and an ideological document. It was built on the premise of the mother's central relevance in childcare. Its sociopolitical function is indicated by the fact that WHO guided researchers to look at 'children who were homeless *in their native country*' (Bowlby, 1952, p. 6), excluding explicitly the children of wartime refugees. The theme of women's social roles was at stake: during the war, women had taken over men's roles in industry, while the men were fighting, dying and becoming invalids. The lucky men who survived the war and were demobilized went back home to no immediately available jobs. In that context, the WHO report included themes similar to the efforts in the eighteenth century to guide women's feelings in the 'mother's milk' issue:

The mothering of a child is not something which can be arranged by roster; it is a live human relationship which alters the characters of both partners. The provision of a proper diet calls for more than calories and vitamins: *we need to enjoy our food if it is to do us good*. In the same way the provision of mothering cannot be considered in terms of hours per day but *only in terms of enjoyment of each other's company which mother and child obtain*.

Such enjoyment and *close identification of feeling is only possible for either party if the relationship is continuous* . . . It should be remembered . . . that continuity is necessary for the growth of a mother. Just as the *baby needs to feel that he belongs to his mother*, the *mother needs to believe that she belongs to her child* and it is only when she has the satisfaction of this feeling that it is easy to devote herself to him. The provision of constant attention day and night, seven days a week and 365 in the year, is possible *only for a woman who derives profound satisfaction from seeing her child grow* from babyhood, through the many phases of childhood, to become an independent man or woman, and *knows that it is her care which has made this possible*. (Bowlby, 1952, p. 67; added emphasis)

The only appropriate career for women is here proved to be that of mothering – being a mother *who devotedly owns* her child.

By his own account, from 1951 onwards Bowlby integrated the notions of ethological theory into his psychoanalytic scheme. He was particularly interested in the observation of mother–infant bonding in non-human primates in their real life environments. This also indicated a major change in the empirical strategies of attachment research – while psychoanalytic traditions rely upon *post factum* reconstruction of the developmental course, the focus of ethology on direct observation led to the focus on mother–infant relations as those take place in the present.

Observations of phenomena of bonding

Observations of human emotional bonding were brought to the fore at a time of major world crisis – a war. The Second World War resulted in the devastation of human creations, both places and people. The roots of observations on the attachment phenomenon were in psychoanalysts' attention to children's relations with their parents when threatened by wartime separation (Freud and Burlingham, 1943), followed by similar separation later in other settings (hospitals).

After the Second World War, the behavioural sciences began accepting the discipline of ethology. Ethology – the science of behaviour in its natural contexts – was an innovation that mid-twentieth century biology and psychology was ready to entertain. The work by Konrad Lorenz and Nico Tinbergen on behavioural patterns of ducks and seagulls led empirical researchers to document appropriate human phenomena. The phenomena of child–adult bonding were prominent in that effort. Behaviourally, the phenomena of attachment surface in situations when there are external threats to the bonds.

A regular psycho-traumatic case (analysed in the Tavistock Clinic in London, Bowlby's home base) in which the attachment phenomena are displayed in their fullness is the hospitalization of young children. Here the physical reasons for hospitalization are interspersed with the act of the parents in leaving the sick child in the hospital (which was the practice in UK in the 1950s). Most young children – under 4 years of age – react initially with fretting when separated from their parents on admission to hospital. This is followed by adjustment to the conditions – yet traces of the traumatic separation can be visible behind this façade. James Robertson (1970), while making a film on young children in hospital, described a child (Laura) who was taken to hospital (for the purposes of hernia repair) for 8 days at age 2 years 5 months:

DAY 1: At the reception to the hospital, Laura is friendly and unafraid. When the nurse takes her away, undresses her and gives a bath, Laura calls for her mother. Yet her self-control returns to her. She is put into a cot and starts crying when the nurse takes her body temperature. When the mother comes to say good-bye, Laura

> . . . begins sobbing, then her face becomes set and solemn and apprehensive . . . Mother leaves for her consolation a piece of blanket she has had since infancy and which she calls her 'baby' . . . Throughout her stay in the hospital this 'blanket baby' and her teddy bear make a link with home and are clung to when she is sad or frightened. (Robertson, 1970, p. 22)

DAY 2: Laura woke up very early, spent much time quietly in her cot. Occasionally she asked for her mother. When being filmed,

> . . . she is quiet, but her expression is strained and sad and very different from that of the friendly and cheerful little girl who had been admitted twenty-four hours earlier. . . . She has difficulty in responding to the nurse who comes to play with her, pushes away the toy that is offered, and swallows hard as if controlling herself. Her eyes have narrowed, and her mouth droops. Then the friendly contact with the nurse again causes her feelings to break through and she cries for a short time for her mummy. (Robertson, 1970, p. 23)

Later, during her parents' visit, Laura declared 'I want to go home' and is distressed that her mother does not take her into her arms (which was not possible due to her stitches). When the parents left, Laura looked subdued.

DAY 3: In the morning, Laura was seen quietly clutching her teddy bear and 'blanket baby', not crying or demanding attention. Then, when a nurse comes to play with her, Laura is at first withdrawn, then

> . . . the contact with a friendly person again causes her suppressed feelings to break through and she cries bitterly for her mummy. When the nurse leaves, her usual control reasserts itself. But when the nurse returns shortly afterwards we see the same cycle of withdrawal, breakdown into bitter crying, and gradual recovery of composure after the nurse has left. The camera shows her frown and bite a trembling lip in the effort not to cry, and her eyelids flutter before her eyes. Twenty minutes later her face is still, and she sits quietly looking out at the ward. (Robertson, 1970, p. 24)

When her mother comes to visit in the afternoon, Laura makes no attempt to get to her at first, but warms up in about 15 minutes. The distancing from her mother is repeatedly observed during visits on DAYS 4–7.

DAY 8: Laura was released from the hospital. Her mother came and approached Laura:

> 'I've come to take you home.' Laura does not react immediately. She watches cautiously and un-smilingly as if unwilling to make the commitment of trusting her mother's words after these many disappointments. Only when her outdoor shoes are produced does she seem convinced of her mother's reliability. She comes to life, dresses eagerly, and insists on collecting every one of her personal possessions to take home. (Robertson, 1970, p. 26)

The sequence of adaptation to hospital of this selected case was used by Robertson as proof of the need to liberalize hospital routines to make them more fitting with children's emotional needs. It played an important socio-moral role in the British medical system. At the same time, the phenomena described provide evidence of a child's bonding with the mother as a process of progressive adaptation to the concrete circumstances (hospital). The attachment relationship becomes modified through the life experience in the hospital. The process of adaptation is characterized by continuous self- and other-control efforts.

Adding control systems theory to the attachment model

By the 1960s, Bowlby became fascinated by the then popular *control systems theory*. That theory emphasized the need for homeostatic control over dynamic processes. This fitted with Bowlby's previous notion of the attachment bond becoming the *set goal* for child–mother relations. Once established, that set goal was to be maintained homeostatically. Bowlby assumed that any deviation from the state of affairs in the bond would have to be returned to the previous established emotional equilibrium.

Detachment of the Attachment Concept: From Bowlby Towards a Strange Situation

Bowlby's psychoanalytic background set the stage for looking at attachment relations through the prism of the attached person's feelings. Thus, in Bowlby's own words,

> No form of behaviour is accompanied by stronger feeling than is attachment behaviour. The figures towards whom it is directed are loved and their advent is greeted with joy.
>
> So long as a child is in the unchallenged presence of a principal attachment-figure, or within easy reach, he feels secure. A threat of loss creates anxiety, and actual loss sorrow; both, moreover, are likely to arouse anger. (Bowlby, 1969, p. 209)

The feelings resulting from the attachment behaviour are personal – and hence it becomes possible to see attachment as an intra-personal phenomenon. Yet the focus on feelings can be maintained within a framework of systemic causality (and depicted through the intra-psychological reference frame). Yet that reference frame has not been maintained in the empirical work on attachment. Instead, attachment as a *dynamic relationship* has been turned into a construct of *categorical property* that is assumed to belong to a person (child, mother) and determine his/her conduct.

If attachment is assumed to be a property of the person (a trait, rather than a relationship between persons), it becomes similar to any other personality characteristic. Psychology has usually transformed concepts that originally refer to relationships, to depict assumed static properties of the individual. This is often accomplished by typologies – a particular generally labelled property becomes viewed as occurring in different classes (categories).

The conceptual history of attachment has proceeded in this way. First, there was the complexity of child–parent relationships depicted in psychoanalytic case accounts (for example, Bowlby's case descriptions of juvenile thieves – Bowlby, 1944). The complexity of cases becomes covered by the label 'attachment', which is an appropriate generic label for the complexity of phenomena. The label now begins to operate as a static descriptor of dynamic phenomena.

The translation of a dynamic relationship into a static property in psychologists' thinking usually leads to the attribution of causal properties to the assumed static entity. The model of causality that is assumed is of a direct linear kind (see Chapter 5). Thus, a static quality which was abstracted out of the complex process is turned into a singular causal agent which is seen to 'predict' some future outcome (see Figure 10.1).

The crucial moment in the transformation of research projects is the shift of the frame of reference. It usually takes place without much reflection on the part of the researchers, who are both motivated to ask the research questions in ways considered 'socially correct' by their peers and are aided by the conceptual lack of distinctions between generic and individual-specific language use (Valsiner, 1986). The notion of 'prediction of the future' emerges as a result of the reference frame shift, in line with societal concerns about the future of children.[2]

Attachment diagnostics: the Strange Situation

Since the early 1970s the study of attachment has become standardized – in method as well as in general ideas (Ainsworth and Wittig, 1969). It has lost the open-ended development that was characterized by Bowlby's gradual 'layering' of different theoretical traditions upon the original psychoanalytic basis. The concept of attachment has been overtaken by the practice

A GENERIC PROCESS

DYNAMIC PHENOMENA

↓

CREATION OF A CONCEPT THAT REFLECTS THE DYNAMICITY OF THE PHENOMENA

↓

SHIFT OF THE FRAME OF REFERENCE

↓

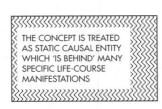

THE CONCEPT IS TREATED AS STATIC CAUSAL ENTITY WHICH 'IS BEHIND' MANY SPECIFIC LIFE-COURSE MANIFESTATIONS

B THE HISTORY OF THE ATTACHMENT CONCEPT USE

Child's relating to the parents (privileging the mother) is detected as a complex, inherently ambiguous, dynamic relationship.

↓

Bowlby's introduction of the ATTACHMENT concept as a general label to denote the DYNAMIC and MUTUAL nature of mother–child relations. As the child was seen as the one developing to become an adult through the attachment bond, the primary focus was given to the child.

↓

↓

ATTACHMENT is specified as 'being of' different TYPES (A, B, C for the child). The TYPES – once established in the first year of life – are assumed to 'be behind' the child's psychological manifestations over the life course. It follows that accurate detection of 'the types' for children allows for future prediction.

FIGURE 10.1 *Translation of relationship-based and dynamic theoretical notions into static linear causal entities in psychology's construction of knowledge (using the attachment concept as an example)*

of measurement of inter-individual differences. This indicates a shift in the frame of reference. While the original (Bowlby's) use of the attachment concept was set within the individual-ecological reference frame (since the relationship of the child – person – with the attachment object – the environment – was focused upon), the move to the measurement of 'attachment types' is set within the inter-individual reference frame (see Chapter 5).

The major originator in the latter change was Mary Ainsworth. She played the crucial role in the creation of the Strange Situation as a context in which to trigger the phenomena of the child's attachment to the caregiver.

The Strange Situation (SS) consists of a sequence of short episodes of enactment of real-life events. A child is necessarily at times left alone, or in the company of an unfamiliar, or semi-familiar, person. Without doubt such alterations of the social context relate to the child's established emotional relations with others. Thus, the departure of the mother can indeed trigger some anxiety (which can – but need not necessarily – be of the intensity of a 'fear of loss'). The presence of a stranger in the situation may amplify it – or not. The stranger, after all, makes efforts to relate with the child (see Episode 3 in Table 10.1), and can become a target of exploration, similarly to the toys present in the SS (see Figure 10.2).

The presence of toys around the child's chair is a part of the SS setting that is meant to create a tension between the attachment orientation and the exploration orientation. Exploration is important for the general uses to which the attachment concept is put – as the attachment is viewed as a 'secure base' for exploration, there need to be objects triggering the latter in the situation.

The *phenomenological strength* of the SS is in its closeness to the reality of everyday life. Of course, the exact mapping of the SS sequence onto everyday life can be limited. Such short time periods of separation (3 minutes) in fully public settings where the 'unfamiliar person' is a total stranger may possibly exist in doctors' waiting rooms perhaps (for example, where the mother leaves the child for a very brief period, in the company of strangers).

The *psychological uses* of the phenomenologic-ally strong SS concentrate on the following three moments (which are particularly scrutinized in

TABLE 10.1 *Summary of the episodes of the Strange Situation*

Number of Episode	Persons present	Duration	Brief description of action
1	Mother, baby, and observer	30 s	Observer introduces mother and baby to experimental room, then leaves
2	Mother and baby	3 min	Mother is non-participant while baby explores; if necessary, play is stimulated after 2 minutes
3	Stranger, mother and baby	3 min	Stranger enters. First minute: stranger silent. Second minute: stranger converses with mother. Third minute: stranger approaches baby. After 3 minutes mother leaves unobtrusively
4	Stranger and baby	3 min or less[a]	First separation episode. Stranger's behaviour is geared to that of baby
5	Mother and baby	3 min or more[b]	First reunion episode. Mother greets and/or comforts baby, then tries to settle him again in play. Mother then leaves, saying 'bye-bye'
6	Baby alone	3 min or less[a]	Second separation episode
7	Stranger and baby	3 min or less[a]	Continuation of second separation. Stranger enters and gears her behaviour to that of baby
8	Mother and baby	3 min	Second reunion episode. Mother enters, greets baby, then picks him up. Meanwhile stranger leaves unobtrusively

[a] Episode is curtailed if the baby is unduly distressed.
[b] Episode is prolonged if more time is required for the baby to become re-involved in play.

Source: Ainsworth et al., 1978 p. 37

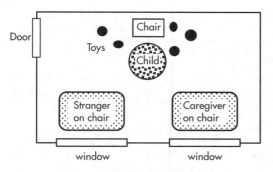

FIGURE 10.2 *A schematic depiction of the Strange Situation*

the case of mother–child departure – Episode 4 – and re-union – Episodes 5 and 8):

1 How is the mother used as the basis for exploration of the setting?
2 What is the child's response to the mother's leaving the room?
3 What is the child's acting towards the mother like at the mother's return?

The analysis of the child's specific behaviour at these junctions leads the psychologist to determine *the child's attachment type* (A, B, or C). Each of these major types is further divided into sub-types.

Types of child's attachment

The three general attachment types are further divided into *secure* (type B) and *insecure* (types A and C) categories. Thus, every child is attached to some attachment figure, yet the quality of that attachment may vary between secure and insecure kinds.

The secure kind of attachment In the terminology of attachment research, this is given the label 'type B'. In order to be detected to have this type of attachment, the child needs to

1 Use the mother as the secure base for exploration.
2 Seek the mother's comfort without hesitation when encountering frustrating circumstances.
3 Respond to the mother's return by approaching her with a positive emotional expression.

In sum, the child of 'type B' demonstrates a kind of self-regulation of affect that allows him or her to recognize the mother – in terms of pleasing her – while being involved in their own business of exploring the world.

The insecure kind of attachment This kind of attachment occurs in two types – A and C.

'Type A' (*avoidant* attachment): in order to be classified into this category, a child in SS has to act in the following ways:

1 Ignore the mother at her returns.
2 Not use the mother as the base for exploration.

Undoubtedly the child's avoidance of the mother is not well appreciated by the mother herself, who expects her child to pay attention to her, and use her (yet not too excessively) as the secure base for exploration.

Type C (*anxiously-ambivalent* or *anxiously-resistant*) attachment: here the child can earn such a label by showing the following pattern:

1 The child is distressed at the mother's departure.
2 At the mother's return, the child shows ambivalence towards the mother. This is expressed by interspersing the approach tendency (the child goes to the mother) with avoidance of the same mother (for example, when the mother tries to pick the child up, the child protests against it and pulls himself free).
3 When using the mother for exploration, the child is irritable and simultaneously tries to get free from the mother's guidance and clings to her.

Collective-cultural meanings of sociality and attachment diagnosis

It should be clear from the descriptions of the attachment categories that the diagnostic system is built up on the European-kind middle social class system of meanings (see LeVine and Miller, 1990). The mother (or her substitute caregiver) – rather than a social group (for example, mother, aunt and grandmother together) – is assumed to be in control over the child. The child is assumed to display *relative* independence – exploring the environment when the adults expect that to happen (for example, at the time of adult's departure) – and yet display social courtesy towards the adult (at the mother's returns). The latter dynamic is a prime target for cultural construction. Of course the success of such construction in the second year of life is still limited, yet tendencies towards it can be found. Obviously these apply to cases of collective-cultural prohibition for children against ignoring the social events of their immediate surroundings. In a number of studies in Japan (e.g. Miyake et al., 1985; Takahashi, 1985), it has been difficult to find 12–23-month-old children who would display the type A (avoidant) kind of attachment. A collective-cultural explanation of such failure can be given through reference to early construction of the social norm that *an adult person should not be blatantly ignored (avoided) by the child*. Of course, this cultural expectation need not be already in place in the social life of any Japanese child in their second year. However, there is the complementary side in the cultural organization of the adult's conduct: *adults are expected to provide close tactile contact immediately*. Hence there is no chance for the children to establish an 'avoidant' pattern – as was noted by Takahashi (1990, p. 28), in the Strange Situation most Japanese mothers rushed to pick up their infants before the infants exhibited any cue that they wanted (or did not want) to be picked up. Similar issues come up in cultural contexts pertaining to the other 'insecure' attachment category (C): the complex of child care in communally oriented societies can lead to its higher frequency. Yet frequencies explain nothing, and the issue of process of attachment must be considered (Sagi, 1990).

The issue of attachment is thus two-fold: on the one hand, there are powerful phenomena of human bonding; on the other, a moralistic theoretical perspective (which superimposes on women the exclusive role of motherhood) paired with a traditional non-developmental method of 'diagnosis' of a constructed characteristic. The question of attachment has been reconstructed to fit the conceptual realm of contemporary psychology. A sacrifice of relevant aspects of the phenomena is a necessary casualty in such reconstruction.

Psychology may do as it pleases (itself), but the attachment phenomena remain of central relevance for understanding human beings. In addition to the attachment bonds of the child to the primary caregiver (which are no doubt important), the establishment of parallel bonds with multiple members of the functional kinship network of different age levels is of importance. Such bonds are facilitated by the regular presence of very many different persons in the social world of a developing child.

SOCIAL ENVIRONMENT IN EARLY CHILDHOOD: GETTING SIBLING CARE, AND GIVING IT

As a general rule all over the world, the primary organizers of the social environments of young children (except for feeding) are older siblings, rather than the parents (Weisner and Gallimore, 1977). The exclusive role of the mother in early childcare (which was normatively prescribed by Bowlby, see above) is a cultural-historical artefact of a number of sociological factors: nuclearization of the households, lower reproductive success of

women, social politics of keeping work out of the home – and women out of work. The focus on exclusive 'maternal responsibility' for early childhood is a cultural construct of an ideological nature.

The birth of a new sibling establishes a situation where the older sibling(s) are necessary participants in the growth of the family. How such participation works would differ according to the set-up of the local collective-cultural system within the family. For example, a first child who has successfully monopolized the attention of the mother since birth, may display frustration when being 'displaced' by the new offspring (refer back to the issue of 'sibling rivalry' in the case of weaning). Yet *competition* with the new child is but one of the possible courses of development for the older sibling. Under adults' guidance – exemplified by integration of the older siblings into the caregiving tasks – the older sibling can internalize the role of the caregiver, and act in that role in ways that are *cooperative* with the new child, and with the whole family network. Of course, there is also the possibility of *neutral segregation* of the older siblings from caregiving to the younger. This takes place when the mother does not accept anybody else in the caregiving role.

In most of the world's societies, sibling caregiving is organized by a *hierarchical delegation* of the caregiver's role to older siblings by the mother. In the context of extended (or joint) family, there are usually many older siblings available for caregiving roles. Their hierarchical relationship is usually determined by their age. The older children are assigned to mind their younger siblings; the younger ones, still younger siblings, etc. The one higher in the hierarchy has the role of regulating the younger caregiver's actions with the target of the caregiving. If a 12-year-old and a 6-year-old are providing care of a 3-year-old, the 12-year-old supervises the 6-year-old's efforts. The mother of all three may remain in the background, supervising all of them *if it is needed*, but otherwise trusting the functioning of the multi-aged children's group (see Ochs, 1982).

The use of such delegated childcare roles within the pyramid of age/experience of the different caregivers is of high adaptive value both for the recipient of the care, as well as for the caregivers. Such a delegated network of childcare guarantees *functional substitutionability* of the caregivers should circumstances require it. This is particularly important in cases of societies where survival of the whole kinship group depends upon coordinated subsistence efforts of all members – old and young. Older children can be needed (episodically) in economic activities and then the care for the youngest siblings can be delegated to the next less-old siblings. Or, at other times, their work is not needed and then the older children may resume their leadership role of overseeing less-old siblings in the caregiving to the youngest ones. The caregiving network can flexibly expand and constrict itself, depending upon the basic survival needs of the whole kinship group. In simple terms – for a mother who has delegated the childcare role to older siblings, 'finding a babysitter' when needed is no problem.

Furthermore, the 'babysitters' thus found are experienced ones (as they have been 'trained on the job') who know the child to be cared for. Sibling caregiving is perhaps the first activity in which young children begin to contribute to the economic well-being of the whole family. This experience provides them with 'hands-on' experience with *guided participation* (see Rogoff, 1990; also Budwig, 1998).

The older siblings who take care of younger ones are not 'working' – in the sense of the culturally constructed exclusive opposition of WORK <> PLAY. In the sibling caregiving activity, the *task* of caregiving is part of the *joint play* of the multi-aged children's group. It is the play activity that dominates the world of youngsters.

DEVELOPMENT OF PLAY

Play is a curious construct. It is seemingly simple: we have no difficulty making statements like 'children play' and 'adults work'. Yet the meaning of the concept remains unspecified – other than through the age construct ('play is what children do' versus 'work is what adults do'). Efforts to define play have largely remained confusing, for example:

> Play [is] . . . exercise of any one function of mind and body in a way usually covered by such expressions as 'play is for its own sake,' 'play is not serious,' 'play involves make-believe,' 'play is an indulgence and is contrasted with work'. (Baldwin, 1902, p. 303)

Such non-specificity is characteristic of circular definitions. *Play cannot be defined in contrast with work*; it needs to be explained differently. Two basic explanations existed for play in the nineteenth century – it was viewed as the using up of surplus energy (Herbert Spencer) or as an inherent, native impulse of organisms (Karl Groos). In both cases, the specificity of play becomes reduced to general constructs (energy, or 'inherent tendency').

Situating Play

The core of play – of any animal or human of any age – is *persistent imitation* (see Baldwin's explanation of it, and his example of his daughters' play, in Chapter 3). The playing organism creates ever-new forms of behaviour, and operates upon the environment in ways that transcend the immediate demands of that environment. This is a necessary pre-adaptive process, given the uncertainty of the organisms' environments. Yet such process in and by itself is not play. Rather, play can be seen as a transformation of the future-oriented pre-adaptation to uncertainty into *constructed make-believe certainty and action upon it*. In this sense, a child in play rises above their current level of psychological development (paraphrasing Lev Vygotsky, see Chapter 3). Play entails goal construction in the realm of the possible (but not actual), and actions towards these goals *as if* the goal were real. This entails turning objects into animals or humans:

> A girl of 3 lavished her affection on a rude wooden foot stool. It was set on end, its legs were arms and feet, and it was dressed, named stooly, nursed when sick, taken to bed and table, taught to read and write, fed, and various parts of the body imagined. A scratch on the joint was a sore. A child of 2 did the same with an old red slipper; another with a bottle with cork head, eyes, necklace. (Ellis and Hall, 1896, p. 134)

This seemingly extreme example is not different from the construction of 'teddy-bears' and 'security blankets' (in children) or Rolex watches (in adults) as relevant psychological tools for human self-construction. Objects are treated in human actions not as these are, but as these are psychologically made up to be – the use of objects by humans occurs in terms of 'as-if' (*als ob* in German – Vaihinger, 1911/1920).

The notion of action in the 'as-if' domain has been of interest to thinkers throughout the twentieth century (for example, from Vaihinger to the contemporary 'theories of mind' empirical research tradition). The contrast between 'what really is' and 'what is in the sense of *as if*' (real/ virtual reality) is a non-developmental contrast. The developmental contrast is different (see Figure 10. 3).

The non-developmental look at 'as-if' treats X as if it were Y – substitutes the real reality with its virtual counterpart. As it is time-free, it does not lead to further construction of the real reality. It can just restore it in its previous form – by elimination of the as-if-Y and return to X.

FIGURE 10.3 *Static (non-developmental) versus dynamic (developmental) account of the 'as-if' (from Josephs, 1998, p. 184)*

In the developmental framework, the 'as-if' is treated as a particular contrast of what is (X1) with its oppositional counterpart (non-X1), treating the latter as *a possible next step in development* ('as-could-be non-X1'). As the result of the tension of X1 < > NON-X1 (the real at the time with its 'as-could-be' counterpart), novel reality comes into being (X2).

Construction of roles and counter-roles

An example of how such movement into the making of new reality takes place comes from Zilma Oliveira's study of the emergence of social *roles* and *counter-roles* in the interaction of young children in the peer group. According to Oliveira, each construction of a new form of conduct (role) entails the emergence of a complementary opposite (counter-role). The latter may be distributed between children in a peer group. For instance, a boy may assume the role of a father in play with a masculine object (belt), and immediately girls in the playgroup begin to refer to him as 'daddy' (Oliveira and Valsiner, 1997). The assumption by one child – through action with an object – of a role is reciprocated by the parallel construction of the counterparts (see also Chapter 3 on G.H. Mead). In general terms,

> As roles emerge in interpersonal experience, their main characteristic is an intersubjective polarity – even when alone the individuals' behavior presupposes a partner. For that reason, the actions of each partner in a dyad, triad, and so on, constitute role/counter-role pairs, confronted with the roles (and its implicit counter-roles) assumed by the partner(s). This role-playing process creates tensions and resolutions that continuously resignify the context, the objects, the roles to be enacted, and the participants themselves. Human interactions can thus be conceived as a process of confrontation and coordination of the roles played by the participants. (Oliveira and Rossetti-Ferreira, 1996, pp. 182–183)

It is through episodic construction of social roles in play that children's social role linking ('identity') becomes established.

Example: differentiation of gender roles in peer interaction The episodes that follow demonstrate how boys and girls in a peer group of 3–4-year-olds create gender role distinctions. The complementarity of male and female roles in human lives leads to constant negotiations about 'this gender'-linked objects (in opposition to objects not viewed as belonging to 'that gender'). The 'as-could-be' notion is played out in the emergence of future-oriented threats ('You'll turn into a woman'):

> In his group's playroom, Fabio (46 months of age) examines an empty plastic bottle of shampoo. Vanessa (37 months of age) tells him with a threatening posture and intonation: '*Vai virar mulher!*' (You'll turn into a woman!). Then she asks him, '*Dá o shampoo?*' (Give me the shampoo?). Fabio replies, loud and briskly, '*Não!*' (No). Vanessa manipulates some objects for a while and once again asks him, in a humble posture: '*Dá o shampoozinho?*' (Give me the little shampoo?). Fabio asks her, '*O quê?*' (What?) and continues to play with the empty bottle of shampoo. Vanessa, with her right hand very extended towards him, firmly demands, '*Dá o shampoo?*' (Give me the shampoo?). Fabio replies, '*Não vou dar não!*' (No, I won't give it!) and places the empty bottle inside a big toy car. After staring at Fabio for some seconds, Vanessa takes some other objects to play with. (Oliveira, 1998, p. 108)

This negotiation about the bottle entails the little girl's threatening tactic through which she attempted to get the boy to release the object. Three months later, in the same playgroup, Vanessa continued her use of the constructed gender-role threat in conjunction with negotiation of the possession of objects:

> Four children inspect some empty bottles of shampoo, deodorant, creams, among other objects such as a wooden bus, a doll, some handbags, a hat, and so on. Daniel (38 months of age) offers an empty shampoo bottle to Vanessa (40 months) saying '*Tó!*' (Take it!). Fernando (38 months), passing by, takes the bottle from Daniel's hand. Vanessa chases Fernando and, pointing to him, says, "*É minha! É p'a mim! Ele deu pá mim!*' (It's mine! It's for me! He gave it to me!), and adds, pointing to him as a menace, '*Vai virar mulher!*' (You'll turn into a woman!). Fernando keeps the bottle with him and plays with it, is observed by Vanessa, who after some seconds, goes to play with other toys. (Oliveira, 1998, p. 108)

Vanessa's crusade of threatening the boys with gender transformation illustrates the embeddedness of cultural construction of social roles in the context of a here-and-now emerging personal objective. The girl sets herself the goal of getting a bottle from the boys – and as a means to that end, makes use of the threat of the boys' loss of masculinity.

This small example indicates the *episodic* nature of gender-role construction. The generic social construct – role of 'man' or 'woman' – becomes negotiated in the middle of regular everyday happenings in children's peer groups. A threat – *'You'll turn into a woman'* – is used in peer interaction for the purposes of reaching immediate objectives. At the same time, the notion is turned into a publicly available communicative message that can be related with by anybody (boy or girl) present in the given situation. The incident passes quickly – yet it leaves 'traces' if picked up by the children present. It constitutes an example of how guided participation (see Chapter 11) works.

The distinctions made semiotically in children's peer group interaction have complementary structure in the personal cultures of adults. As is demonstrated by MacKain (1987), negotiation of the gender-role boundaries in relation to specific, episodic encounters within the mother–child–object world triad involve similar guidance. MacKain has described the case of a family with three children (5-year-old Dan, 7-year-old Lyle, and 3.5-year-old Amy) in which the mother had always believed that her children should be exposed to all types of experiences, with no distinction indicated between 'boy's kind' and 'girl's kind'. She encouraged her older son's play with dolls (however, after a temporary fascination with a cabbage-patch doll, Lyle abandoned it). Lyle's younger brother Dan was playing with dolls at first, but then abandoned these in favour of 'action figures' The boys were not allowed to play 'aggressive' sports (American football) and were re-directed by parents towards ballet and soccer. Yet, the mother herself reported being 'taken to the limits':

> Watching her [the mother] play with Amy, the 3.5-year-old [the mother was painting Amy's fingernails], Dan asked his mother to paint his fingernails too. "I could only bring myself to paint two [nails]. I knew it was ridiculous, but it just bothered me." (MacKain, 1987, p. 120)

The mother's self-report on her inability to act and her feelings about her own self-inability, indicate the semiotic marking of gender role differentiation in the mind of the adult. It demonstrates the inherent paradoxical nature of personal-cultural construction of gender (or any other) roles. A woman sets herself a goal of overcoming traditional gender-role distinctions for her children, promotes that, but cannot live up to her stated ideology when it comes to a specific issue of body decoration (fingernail painting) that is (in US society, until now) strictly considered to be a female gender-marker. Painted fingernails are publicly visible. She even attempts to overcome the boundary (painting two fingernails of her son), but then fails to do any more. She gets angry at herself because of the discrepancy between her inability to act and her stated ideological goal.

Re-enactment of adult social relations in children's play

Children's persistent imitation entails active reconstruction of their surrounding social world. The children play in the realm of *'as-if-could-be'*. Their observational experience of adults' everyday life activities provides a rich basis for their imaginative reconstructions. The themes for play are borrowed from everyday life, yet the ways in which play proceeds are constructive.

Playing house in Taleland Meyer Fortes (1970) described children's play among the Tallensi ethnic group (in Ghana). Playing house is led by a multi-aged group of girls. In the play (which is recognized by the children as such), the girls play the roles of co-wives involved in everyday activities – cooking, food delivery etc. In this play,

> Every feature of the real process is mimicked, but with the most ingenious imaginative adaptations. A pair of flattish stones or a boulder and a large pebble serve as 'grindstones.' For pots, dishes, calabashes, and ladles various things are used – old sherds chipped into roughly circular pieces . . . fragments of old calabashes . . . Pebbles make a fire-place, a thin piece of millet-stalk is the stirring-stick, some dried grass the firewood. Sometime a real fire is lit, but usually it is merely imagined. *Real grain is never used in such play – it is too valuable to waste thus, as the children themselves would be the first to insist.* (Fortes, 1970, pp. 65–66; added emphasis)

The unity of the play and its real-life counterpart activity is here observable in the children's conscious non-use of actual (valuable) materials (real grain). It indicates how in children's play the value of real-life activities is being culturally constructed.

Playing marriage among Brazilian Indians The Mehinaku children play games of marriage – and of jealousy. Such games take place outside of the village:

> The marriage game begins as a child's version of the wedding ritual. An uncle takes his nephew's hammock and ties it a few feet over the hammock of the bride-to-be. All the children participating in the game pretend to be married in this way, although without scrupulous attention to the rules of incest

avoidance and preferential cross-cousin marriage. The husbands then go hunting and fishing, returning from their trip with leaves that are said to be fish and monkey. The wives cook the 'food' and distribute it to the men. The game now has several variations. In one, the husbands and wives pair off and go to hidden areas around the village to engage in casual sex play . . . In another variation of the marriage game, called 'Jealousy' (*ukitsapi*), the boys and girls take lovers while their spouses are away. When the cuckolded partner returns from a fishing trip, he discovers his wife and his friend together in the same hammock. In a fury he pretends to beat his wife while his friend runs off. (Gregor, 1977, p. 113)

The social organization of adult mundane life activities surely cannot escape children as participant observers. It becomes translated into constructive play – which in its own right serves as an object of curiosity for adults.

Adults' interpretation of children's play

As children's play takes on a great variety of constructed novel forms, it is constantly testing the limits of collective-culturally established social norms. It is the adult world that is challenged by children's play, not the children themselves. Hence making sense of children's activities can become[3] a major meaning-making task for adults.

There are many ways in which the world of adults can present 'the other' to themselves (and to the others). The history of anthropology is filled with the rhetoric fights of anthropologists against the viewing of 'the other' by early discoverers, traders and colonial administrators as 'savages', 'primitives' and (at times) 'childlike persons'. Most of such designations have always carried an evaluative (negative) connotation. The possible exception is that of the use of the child as a social representation of 'the other' – here the representation includes a tie to the representer (a child eventually becomes an adult, just like the one who calls 'the other' a child).

What if 'the other' – described *as* a child – actually is a child? Here the whole array of adult rhetoric constructions comes in to play. 'Child' can imply an immature organism (which develops towards maturity). This creates an implicit *progressive scenario* for making sense of the child's current actions. Thus, a statement 'the child plays' can entail the connotation 'thus he develops'. Or a locally dismissive statement 'X is just child's play' may entail the connotation 'but she will grow out of it and become serious'. Possibly the definitional difficulties psychologists

encounter while defining play are remnants of the function of the notion of 'play' as used in everyday lay discourse. Statements such as 'it is just play, it is not serious' are rhetorical devices for adults to distance the children as 'social others' into a subordinate (yet promising for the future) social category.

Alternatively, the child can be presented in the framework of a *regressive narrative* scenario – the newborn is at the ultimate level of inherent goodness (or – innocence) which is threatened, fought, and finally reduced (or eliminated) in the course of the child's becoming a usual ('sinful') adult. A version of this scenario can be seen in societies where 'spoiling the children' at different age periods is made into an issue. Another version of the same is the construction of the child needing the help of adults in order not to follow the course of inherent moral downfall or potential hurt (for example, the notion that adolescent girls' heterosexual relations must be supervised by adults; or that young children must not operate with sharp objects). Regressive scenarios also may entail a belief in the superhuman powers of the young child.

The power of the young: the Ijaw case of Nigeria
According to the Ijaw (Leis, 1982), children under 5 years of age have a special connection with the female creator spirit *Wonyinghi*. This connection gradually weakens over early childhood. As a result of this belief (of the adults), the cultural niche of the young child is very different from that of most other societies. The adults are likely to interpret specific aspects of the child's actions as if those are evidence for the child's contact with the spirit world.

For instance, the child's pretend play becomes immediately interpreted as an act of contact with the spirits. A child – playing alone – may be observed distributing play food to imaginary playmates, and interacting with them. When adults ask the child with whom she is talking, the child might answer 'My friends, the other children'. There are no other children around, but the adult – on the basis of the belief that the child has supernatural powers – assumes that the child is interacting with the invisible representatives of the spirit world. The child's play is here not dismissed as 'pretend play', but interpreted as serious social encounter.

In the Ijaw collective system of meanings, such construction of the cultural power of young children is as ambivalent in its sociopsychological functions. This ambivalence is similar to the issue of treatment of twins (see Chapter 8). On the one hand, adults treat the young power-holders with respect. If an Ijaw woman wants to get pregnant, she may want to stay close to a living child and appease him, hoping that the child's 'special relation' with the spirit world would bring about the desired result. On the other hand, a miscarriage of a pregnancy can be blamed on the living child (his power, used in conjunction with sibling rivalry, getting the spirits to 'take back' the unborn child). Then the child – because of the assumed power – becomes the scapegoat for a mishap that takes place in the adult's world.

Collective construction of unreality

The coordination of collective action and its personal-cultural reconstructions can lead to the creation of unreality. Unreality is a necessary result of decision-making based on social consensus.

The case of a retarded 'genius' Pollner and McDonald-Wikler (1985) provided a description of a case of a child (5-year-old Mary) who was found by clinical psychologists to be intellectually at the level of a 2-year-old. Mary's family refused to accept the diagnosis, and took Mary to an in-patient psychiatric facility to establish *their version* of constructed interpretation of the child by the medical system as the authoritative statement about the girl.

The family's version of Mary's psychological status differed markedly from that established by clinical psychologists. The family claimed that Mary was very intelligent, and had managed to 'fool' all the clinical psychologists who had diagnosed her as 'mentally retarded'. According to them, Mary simply refused to behave in public in the same sophisticated ways in which she had been acting at home. They wanted this difference in Mary's behaviour to be identified and treated, so as to restore the image of Mary as a highly intelligent child in public. The claim by clinical psychologists that Mary was retarded was actively rejected by the parents, who took Mary from one psychological office to another to insist upon their version of the story, finally arriving at a psychiatrist's office.

The family members (mother, father, 12-year-old brother, 18-year-old half-sister) had created their collective delusion about Mary on the basis of supporting one another's interpretations of Mary's conduct – each of which was created in the same general direction of considering Mary very intelligent. The general mechanism of construction of shared unreality is simple. From a shared (consensual) orientation, each of the members of the social group observes some special aspect of the target phenomenon. This observation is interpreted in the shared direction, and communicated to the other members of the group. The latter accept the interpretation (on the grounds of shared orientation) because of the (supposedly) observational evidence of the communicator. 'Empirical evidence' is *assumed* (and declared) to guarantee objectivity – yet it merely supports the shared ideological orientation of the group members.

This kind of 'orientational framing' by Mary's family members led to interpretational activity not different from the Ijaw cases (described above). When Mary was (at home) observed to play, her conduct in the game became interpreted in ways confirming the ethos:

> once the game of "catch" [a ball] was inaugurated as a definition of "what we are now doing," a variety of game-relevant dimensions for understanding and describing Mary's behavior came into effect. She could be seen as either "catching the ball," "not catching the ball," "dropping the ball," "throwing well," and so forth. The game provided a vocabulary for describing activities that occurred while the frame was in effect. Even activities that seemed to fall outside the frame were describable: Mary's nonresponsiveness might be formulated as "not playing" or "playing very poorly." Framed within the structure of an activity and described with the activity-specific terminology, Mary's behaviors were endowed with an aura of significance and responsiveness. . . . Mary's passivity was reformulated into game-relevant terms. (Pollner and McDonald-Wikler, 1985, p. 244)

Human language use is *omniscopous* (Aphek and Tobin, 1990) – language use leads to covering all possible interpretations that are equally plausible. The statement that is made 'A is X' can be qualified 'but under certain circumstances A can also be non-X'. If X and non-X cover the whole field of possibilities, the qualified statement is necessarily true. If parents say 'Mary is so clever that sometimes she can leave an impression that she is retarded' they guarantee their presentation of Mary as always clever – when showing the cleverness, and when 'pretending' to be the opposite.

The use of interpretation of the other's intentions fills that side of omniscopic language use which otherwise cannot be explained. Thus, if a child catches a ball well, this is interpreted as superior achievement. If the child fails to catch the ball, an interpretation can be 'she is so smart so as to avoid the ball'. In both cases – whether the child catches the ball or not – the notion of the child's superior deliberate efforts becomes reified by interpretation. Success is interpreted as evidence of competence; failure as deliberate – and strategically 'smart' – avoidance of unwanted or unnecessary activities.

Human societies thrive on collectively created delusions which are not much different from the one in Mary's case. Consensual decision-making in any social setting is vulnerable to the creation of shared social 'group norms' (Sherif, 1936) and the use of those as the basis for consensual delusions about specific issues. In the realm of political discourse, the actions of social groups in terms of their being 'rebels' or 'freedom-fighters' is the meaning-base for elaborated collective constructions of interpretations of specific actions. The rich history of 'witch-hunting' in European and North American history provides many specific examples for collectively created delusions (Breslaw, 1997). Interpretation of human action entails construction of signs that are made immune to falsification efforts.

Two models of interpretation of play as sign

In the domain of psychology (and related disciplines), interpretation of children's play has been proved as important as was the case with the Ijaw. Only in the case of contemporary psychology, children are not feared for their supernatural powers. Instead, they are presented as objects for guidance, treatment, or (last but not least) labelling. Children's ways of being – and play is of foremost importance here – are of sign value to adult interpreters, psychologists and non-psychologists alike.

It is a longstanding tradition in Western cultural history to consider children innocent beings. Following from that social representation, children's play is often viewed as the *expression* of some true state of affairs that has taken place with children. If a child plays out an aggressive episode in relation to another child (or a doll), the adult who observes the encounter from the perspective of 'children are innocent' would easily assume a uni-directional culture transfer model (see Chapter 2). The result is a 'diagnosis' – that the child's play gives evidence about some event that has happened to the child themself. If 'child abuse' is a topic widely accepted as the primary danger for children, the interpretation of aggression in child's play, then the child may easily become suspected of 'having been physically abused' (because aggression is expressed in his or her conduct).

The *expression model of interpretation* of child's play is widespread in psychological efforts at diagnosis of childhood problems. It can be adequate only if the notion of the play as a 'mirror image' of some previous experiences is believed in. As was evident in the beginning chapters of this book, this belief has been widespread. The Ijaw example described above is one collective-cultural construction of that model.

Yet the belief in the expressive nature of children's play is just a belief, nothing more. An alternative belief – that children constantly produce new forms of conduct which, even if these are based on the child's previous experience, are not direct reflections of the past experiences – would lead to a different interpretation of children's play. This is the *construction model of interpretation* of child's play.

The construction model entails a focus on the here-and-now constructive nature of child's play. Using this model as the vantage point, the adult cannot say anything about whether the child's observed act of aggression represents *any* specific life event in the child's past. It may – or it need not. There may be partial uses of previous experiences in the current construction of child's play. Or there can be uses of the opposite phenomena to those that were actually present in the child's past. For example, a child who displays in play brutality towards a cat may do that on the basis of a loving family environment where cruelty to any animals (or humans) was eliminated by ways of ordinary conduct of family members. In opposition to the 'hyper-sweet' treatment of cats, the child can invent in play the opposite kind of 'treatment' of those sweet animals, and play it out.

It is obvious that an adult – from an expressional vantage point – would completely misinterpret this kind of cruel behaviour of the child. Hence, if the construction model is accepted by the interpreting adult, any diagnostic statement about the child is at least very complicated, or impossible. Yet the construction model allows for another realm of application: use of play as a device for therapeutic intervention. Here the constructive nature of play is used to guide the child towards future life events. This happens in children's play outside of any therapeutic framework: the examples above show how children create their own versions of action through persistently acting along the lines of adult models.

SUMMARY: FROM PLAY TO AUTONOMY

Development through action leads to the establishment of hierarchical complexity of personal-cultural systems. It is within these systems that semiotic regulators that guarantee autonomy of the person – signs that govern volition – come into existence. These belong to the realm of higher psychological functions. Human development is oriented towards achievement of personal uniqueness – guaranteed by autonomy – through the establishment and use of cultural mediating means. In Chapter 11, the emergence of cultural self-regulation in early childhood is described.

NOTES

1 In an interesting reversal of this general practice, one can consider the uses of human urine in different folk-medical practices – either as a curing liquid administered to the exterior of the body, or for intake.

2 In the case of looking at children's futures, psychologists often emphasize that prediction is a crucial feature of science (referring to the role of prediction in experimental studies). However, the latter prediction is not that of a future of a person, but of an outcome of an experiment, given the experimenter's narrowing down of the context and manipulation of specific parameters. Prediction of this kind is not applicable in studies of life course. Thus talk about prediction of future life course has little to do with scientific precision, but much with the cultural predicament of fortune-telling (see Aphek and Tobin, 1990).

3 Such preoccupation with making sense of children's play is not always the case: in societies where children are not viewed as of notable relevance (of social power), or where adults' belief systems do not include the neurotic tendencies that the adults must do their best for the children, the issue can be of little cultural relevance. There, children just grow until they reach an age when they begin to make sense.

REVIEW QUESTIONS FOR CHAPTER 10

1 Discuss the social origins of the terminology of age periodization.

2 How is the end of breast-feeding in ontogeny culturally organized?

3 Describe the ways in which children's eliminatory functions are culturally organized (or 'trained').

4 Explain the physiological bases of the success of early 'toilet-training' (on the example of the practices of the Digo).

5 Explain Bowlby's basic assumptions in his attachment theory.

6 Contrast the view of attachment as a *dynamic relationship* with that of *person's characteristic*.

7 Describe the Strange Situation and explain its rationale.

8 Explain the three attachment 'types': A, B, C.

9 Describe the social organization of child caregiving around the world.

10 What is play?

11 Explain the notions of being 'as-if' and being 'as-could-be'.

12 Describe the emergence of roles and counter-roles in children's play.

13 How can gender role differentiation be supported by children's play?

14 Explain the cultural constraining of gender roles, and their development.

15 Explain how manufactured toys can be inferior to natural objects in the support of children's development.

16 Explain two scenarios of play – progressive and regressive.

17 How is children's play interpreted as indicating their supernatural powers by the Ijaw?

18 How can a social group create an illusion of the development of the child?

19 Explain the differences between *expressive* and *constructive* views on play.

SELF-REGULATION AND PARTICIPATION IN EARLY CHILDHOOD

Early childhood is a period of slow emergence of children's autonomy. It could be said that such autonomy becomes established in the middle of the myriad of everyday activities in the first six life-years. Some of these activities are the same as those of adults and older siblings. Others are peculiar to the given age level and cognitive capacities.

Development of psychological autonomy entails the emergence of goal-oriented flexible actions, and of self-motivation. The will – or intentionality – is the ultimate psychological characteristic of human beings that distinguishes them from biological species. Cultural psychology therefore needs to make sense of human intentionality, as it is made possible through the creation of cultural implements. Intentionality develops relatively slowly over the childhood years, and reaches its adult state by post-adolescence.

Intentionality – or will – is not a case of 'absolute freedom' of acting 'as one pleases'. Rather, it involves flexible self-regulation that entails setting goal orientations; constructing short- and long-term goals, re-setting those when deemed necessary, and deciding how (if at all) to act in specific situations. Intentionality becomes possible through intra-psychological reconstruction of the social structure of the demand settings within the collective-cultural field. The emerging distinction between lower (involuntary) and higher (voluntary) psychological functions is a crucial step in the development of autonomy.

EMERGENCE OF HIGHER PSYCHOLOGICAL FUNCTIONS: THE ROLE OF SPEECH IN THE TEXTURE OF ACTIVITY

Higher psychological functions are *volitional* – the person establishes control over their psychological functions – remembering, feeling, thinking, acting, 'at one's own will'. This entails development of personal autonomy, possibilities of setting goals (and reaching those) and re-setting goals (abandoning old goals and setting new ones).

The development of higher psychological functions entails semiotic mediation. In early childhood it is possible to observe the establishment of the regulatory role of signs over the lower psychological functions. This is particularly important in the third year of life, in the context of speech-based regulation of actions.

Lev Vygotsky's model of 'mutually intersecting lines' of speech and cognitive development

Different mental processes – feeling, thinking, acting, remembering – emerge in parallel with semiotic functions. Vygotsky emphasized the *parallel* and *temporarily mutually integrated* notion of these functions (see Figure 11.1). Here we can see how the emerging speaking activity (communication line in the second and third year of life) becomes temporarily integrated with the line of cognitive functions. Both of these have, prior to the period of integration of the two, developed in parallel: the child's vocal production has moved from cooing to babbling to the use of words (within the speech line); while the domain of the child's actions with objects prior to the third year of life has had a logic of its own (Langer, 1980, 1986). The two lines have been developing in parallel in the psychological system of the child – even if in the realm of the child's social interaction in infancy and toddlerhood settings occur that guide the child towards their integration (Lyra and Winegar, 1997). In interaction, the cognitive and speech lines can be unified long before they become united in the child's own psychological structure.

Once the speaking activity line penetrates into the cognitive line (and vice versa), the child can be

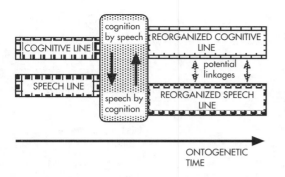

FIGURE 11.1 *Relationships between two parallel developmental lines (cognition and speech) (after Vygotsky)*

observed acting within both. Third-year children are noted for their readiness to be speaking while acting. The cognitive line becomes organized by speaking, and the speech line becomes guided by the cognitive side. Later, by the fourth to fifth year, the unity of the two lines is reduced. Yet the result remains: the cognitive line is now organized by internalized speech functions, while the speech functions become based on cognitive processes. The two lines become ontogenetically relatively autonomous – yet ready to become integrated again when necessary. At moments of cognitive difficulty, a person begins to speak aloud, even if there is no interaction partner available, nor a necessity for such speech.

The emergence of self-control functions of speech
The speaking child is simultaneously a self-regulating child. Alexander Luria (1969), in his focus on the constructive role of inhibitory processes, emphasized the emergence of self-regulatory functions of speech. A 2-year-old child can be observed making his first efforts to regulate his own conduct by way of emerging signs of speech. For example, a child is about to approach a potted plant in the home. Of course, the adults have stopped the child numerous times in the middle of the effort to take some soil from the pot and put it into his mouth. Now the child is alone – and reaches out for the soil. Yet the child says aloud 'No!', and stops the already started action. The 'no' has been brought from the realm of *inter*-action (with others) into that of *intra*-action: the child on his own initiative uses speech to regulate his own action.

From this preliminary example of autonomous self-regulation by signs in a 2-year-old we can extrapolate to the whole process of child development being a process of internalization – personal-cultural construction of signs – as a means to the end of self-regulation and self-control. Yet such personal construction is canalized by the

structured discursive environments that exist in the immediate social world of the young child. Such environments vary widely across societies.

DISCURSIVE ENVIRONMENTS AND THEIR USES IN ONTOGENY

The general concept of *respect* is a semiotic organizer of children's verbal communication with adults in most human societies. It is often the case in historical accounts of child development in European societies that the young child was not expected to initiate interaction with an adult, and be submissive if an adult addresses him or her. The contemporary adoration of active interventions by young children in adult interaction that we can observe in middle-class contexts is surely a new historical invention.

In the Columbian *mestizo* community (see Reichel-Dolmatoff and Reichel-Dolmatoff, 1961), respectful conduct of children towards adults is expected to occur in early childhood. At 2 years of age, the child is expected to show respect to adults by sitting quietly, not passing in front of the adult, or looking into the adult's face while speaking to him or her. If viewed within the framework of European or North American type of social interaction rules, such conduct (absence of eye-contact) would be immediately viewed as impolite or abnormal (for example, autistic). Yet in another society what is viewed as aberration in one becomes a crucial value in another. A child is not expected to express verbal gratitude for favours – to say 'please' or 'thank you' in the *mestizo* community would amount to expressing the person's inferiority. Adults do not use these terms either. At the same time, children's obedience to adults is constantly being exercised.

Young children develop under the conditions of collective-culturally regulated *speech environments*. For example, at some time around the child's second birthday, North American middle-class parents may become watchful of what aspects of their speech (foul language use, swearing, etc.) they try to keep out of their child's auditory environment. Yet they fail in such restriction efforts – at most the child can be exposed to both the language uses and the efforts by the users to 'hush up' some of the expressions in the child's vicinity.

In different societies – and social classes – it is possible to observe a great variety of socially appropriate access forms to adults' and older siblings' speech. Vocabulary that is usable in different situations of interaction, ranging from harmony to conflict, entails not only specific limits upon *what* can be said in what context, but also *who can say what to whom* (in the kinship group setting). The rules for speaking vary greatly from one society to another, often crossing incest rules that are strictly practised in the given society (Thomson, 1935).

The developing child overhears the speech of others, and through persistent imitation of the overheard forms, develops their own versions. Often the social conventions of language use entail codes of normalized language use which turn the extraordinary into the ordinary.

The Qalandar case

The Qalandar are peripatetic nomads, who travel around from village to village in Pakistan (Berland, 1982). According to one of Joseph Berland's Qalandar informants, 'our children first use [language] to abuse, then learn to talk' (Berland, 1982, p. 111). Berland observed no language use restrictions in Qalandar daily speech in the use of themes that would be shocking for North American middle-class contexts (sex, sexual organs, urine, faeces etc.). As British or American English-speakers can be proud of the implicitness of their expressions encoded into language, and politeness of interaction, the Qalandar take pride in creating new forms of explicit verbal abuse of others. Some examples from Qalandar speech are given in Table 11.1.

The children can overhear different kinds of speech, and these create their basis for their own navigation of the sea of interpersonal relations. Speaking also includes being silent – refraining from speaking is as important a cultural means of communication than is speaking. This has been demonstrated in the case of the Apache American Indians (Basso, 1970), who expect children to keep up respectful silence while interacting with others (especially adults). Apache children who have been away to school for long periods are scrutinized particularly for whether they have acquired the 'White American's useless habit' of talking 'too much' at school. This is similar to precisely these White Americans' insistence that children – in order to be polite – enter actively into conversations with others, and act as if they are on equal footing with the others in their communicative position.

Communication and meta-communication

Meta-communication is communication about communication:

Parallel: **Message Y (about Message X)**

| | | | | |

Communicative: **Message X**

The notion of meta-communication entails a focus on messages that *guide the direction of interpretation* of communicative messages. Such interpretation has two sides:

TABLE 11.1 *Examples of the socially accepted speech environment of the Qalandar*

Dyad	Abuse
Young son to father, to get or distract attention	My penis is in your mother's vagina!
Young daughter to father, when being scolded	Stop barking . . . go put your head in your mother's vagina!
Sister to brother, expressing anger or affection	You have a face like a monkey!
Sister to sister, expressing anger	Your face is like a big vagina with lice in it!
Elder sister to younger, unmarried sister, expressing anger	Stop barking or I will tear your vagina open and enter into it!
Mother to daughter, expressing displeasure	You are made of faeces!
Husband to wife, expressing anger about requests or demands	Your face is like a big vagina!
Husband to nagging wife	Stop barking and go fuck a dog!
Wife to husband, expressing anger	Go and fuck your sister (or mother)!
Father to daughter, to stop annoying him	Put your finger in your vagina!

Source: Berland, 1982, pp. 111–112

1 the direction of interpretation of the message itself;
2 the direction of interpretation of the intention of the communicator (relation with the recipient)

Thus, a communicative message 'This is *beautiful*!', when accompanied by a laugh, can be interpreted as 'You and I jointly understand that it is stupid to consider this beautiful'. The primary message is guided by the meta-communicative message to be interpreted in terms opposite to its primary contents ('beautiful' = NOT BEAUTIFUL), with the noting of commonality of the interpretation direction ('You and I agree that beautiful = NOT BEAUTIFUL').

The same example can provide further complexity if the accompanying laugh is perceived by the recipient as 'sarcastic'. In this case, the communicator is assumed to suggest to the recipient that he or she is subordinated in terms of inferiority of understanding.

In early childhood, communicative and meta-communicative functions develop together (Fogel and Branco, 1997). This is particularly relevant in situations of transition between activities. Negotiations of such transition can involve complex strategic uses of language.

Strategies of interaction with young children

The adults are the power holders who guide children's development through specific inter-action strategies. The most obvious of those strategies – commanding, requesting, limiting – require no elaboration. Through speaking with young children, adults set up settings for specific cultural objectives. The most widespread frame-work for such setting is adults' *teasing* of the children.

The structure of teasing
Teasing is an interactional framework that requires an established close relationship between the teaser and the teased. Parents all over the world – except for those societies (or families) where teasing can interfere with persons' self-values and social relations – use teasing as a means of communication with young children.

Teasing entails a structure of social suggestions which could be characterized by the following scheme:

* **Background state**: both the Teaser and the Teased assume that they share a particular value X. For instance, a mother and her adolescent daughter may share the *positive* value of feeling 'sexy' in their body presentation to others.
* **Specific communicative act**: The Teaser makes a statement to the Teased that suggests that the latter is in some way different from the value X – either displaying *the opposite of X*, or by insisting on the *exaggerated form of X*. Thus, in the example, the mother may say to her daughter '*What a sex-bomb you will be in this outfit!*' (positive X); or '*You can't apply to join the convent wearing this!*' (negative X).
* **Reception of the act**: The Teased recognizes the meta-communicative context of the act, and does not interpret it in serious terms. To continue the example – the daughter may answer (jokingly) '*Oh, I am afraid of those men's eyes on me*' (playfully denying the positive X, thus accentuating it); or just laugh and comment '*Oh, Mum!*'

Teasing is a seemingly non-serious way of making a point. The actual issues communicated

via teasing can indeed be occasional jokes, or they can become serious efforts at social guidance of the children. Note that the interactive episode of teasing is completely dependent upon the *background state* of assumed basic intersubjectivity. The same example given above would have a very different course if there were uncertainties in that intersubjectivity. If the value of X for the mother is negative, but for her daughter positive (and both know that difference), then instead of light teasing of the same encounter we would see an example of mother–daughter conflict.

Promotion of values through suggestions to the opposite
There are cases in parent–child interaction where the socialization process explores the dynamics of intersubjectivity. This dynamics in real life entails constant transformation of mutual under-standing between human beings into mis-understanding, and from there into new forms of understanding. *The status of assumed inter-subjectivity is always uncertain*, since the positions of participants in a relationship can be inherently ambivalent, or change over time.

One version of teasing is that of purposeful commanding of the child to act in a specific direction, while expecting the child to refuse to do so and act in the opposite direction. Jean Briggs (1979; see also Briggs, 1970) observed how an Inuit mother dealt with a food-sharing issue in the case of her 3-year-old daughter. Another child – a 4-year-old elder daughter – was outside of the tent, while the mother created a setting where the 3-year-old's establishment of values was both tested and promoted:

> *Mother*: [hands a candy to the 3-year-old daughter and says in exaggeratedly happy-excited-secret-persuasive voice] Eat it quickly and don't tell your sister, because it is the last one!
> *Three-year-old*: [breaks the candy into two pieces, eats one and takes the other outdoors to her sister]
> *Mother*: [says to the audience, with a pleased, and perhaps amused, smile] She never keeps things to herself; she always shares. (Briggs, 1979, p. 396)

In another example, Briggs described a middle-aged aunt talking to a 4-year-old niece who had just returned to the camp after a visit to her mother:

> *Aunt*: What a beautiful new shirt you have [voice of intense, excited delight]
> *Niece*: [smiles happily]
> *Aunt*: [in persuasive tone] Why don't you die so I can have it?
> *Niece*: [looks at aunt with blank face]
> *Aunt*: Don't you want to die?

Niece: [raises eyebrows in affirmative gesture – meaning that she does not want to die]

Aunt: Don't you want to die? Do die [persuasive voice]. Then I can have the shirt [reaches out towards the shirt with exaggerated clutching gesture, fingers clawed and tensed]

Niece: [looks at aunt with blank face]

Aunt: [changing the subject] Did you see your new baby brother?

Niece: [beams happily and raises eyebrows affirmatively]

Aunt: Do you love him?

Niece: [raises brows, smiling]

Aunt: Did you carry him on your back?

Niece: [raises brows and smiles happily]

Aunt: Do you love him?

Niece: [raises brows, smiling]

Aunt: [in exaggeratedly disgusted voice] You *love* him?! Why don't you tip him out of your parka and kill him? [confidential, persuasive voice; jerks her own shoulders forward to demonstrate the appropriate technique]

Niece: [looks at aunt with blank face]

(Briggs, 1979, p. 394)

The second example is basically an adult's dramatic construction of suggestions that are beyond the realm of desired actions in the collective-cultural belief system. The child is participating in this routine in a predominantly non-verbal way, yet is the target of the dramatized suggestions.

Briggs's examples indicate the complexity of communicative messages that exist in adult–child interaction. One of the partners can explicitly suggest something – yet hoping that the other does precisely the opposite. The voice dramatization (that is, the mother speaking to the child in a 'happy-excited-secret-persuasive voice') may be considered as a meta-communicative signal that specifies how the main message should be interpreted.

The social nature of children's speech

Children of 3–4 years of age are observed in child psychology to be involved in 'collective monologues' – different children in a peer group talking simultaneously, without specifying a recipient of their speech efforts. This phenomenon has been a target of a dispute between supposed sociocentric (Vygotsky) and person-centered (Piaget) analysis of children's speech development. Different forms of *children's conversations* emerge in the early childhood years, beginning from what Piaget labelled 'collective monologues', and moving step-by-step towards full conversations.

The *first level* (Stage I) of development of conversation entails – strictly speaking – no conversation as such, but can be labelled *collective monologue*. The child speaks herself, with no addressee specified, or confirmed. Such monologues entail the speaker's non-provision of interaction time for the other:

Den – a girl (4 years 5 months) is talking volubly as she works. Bea (5 years 10 months) comes into the room [wearing a sweater]. Den: '*You've got a sweater on, I haven't, Mummy said it wasn't cold.*' Den goes on working. Bea does not answer. (Piaget, 1959, p. 57)

Here the speaking child (Den) made no adjustment for Bea even to have a chance to answer her question. If this situation occurs in a group of children, one can observe speaking of this kind in parallel.

The *second level* (Stage II) of development of conversation entails *collaboration between children through shared activity*. These conversations may include either mutual agreement, or disagreement – yet in both cases these are exemplified in (or around) some definite actions (and not abstract thought). It can happen at this stage that some memory is evoked, but it is not made into an object of investigation by the speaking child. In Piaget's observation:

The children are busy with their drawings, and each one tells the story which his drawing illustrates. Yet at the same time they are talking about the same subject and pay attention to each other:

Lev (5 years 11 months): It begins with Goldylocks. I am writing the story of the three bears. The daddy bear is dead. Only the daddy was too ill.

Gen (5 years 11 months): I used to live at Salève. I lived in a little house and you had to take the funicular railway to go and buy things.

Geo (6 years): I can't do the bear.

Li (6 years 10 months): That's not Goldylocks.

Lev: I haven't got curls.

(Piaget, 1959, p. 58)

The children are speaking taking turns, yet they are not responding to one another. Gen's statement about his life is out of the context of the ongoing drawing task (which is otherwise the theme shared by the group activity).

The *third level* (Stage III) entails *collaboration on the themes of mental processes* that are not connected with the activity of the moment. Children converse in efforts to find an explanation. This can happen in a cooperative effort. In Piaget's observations, two children are searching together for the explanation . . . [of] the absence of their teacher . . .

> Mad (7 years 6 months): Oh, the slow-coach!
> Lev (6 years): She doesn't know it's late – Well, I know what she is. – And I know where she is. – She is ill. – She isn't ill since she isn't here. (Piaget, 1959, p. 64)

Similar structures occur also in quarrels:

> Ez (6 years 5 months): Ah! I've never had that.
> Pie (6 years 5 months): You've always had it to play with – That's for A. – Well, I've never had it to play with. (Piaget, 1959, p. 66)

The third level includes indication of the interweaving of the conversational positions of children with one another. Children's communicative patterns are built upon the *mental I-centredness* of the children. Such centredness of the self is a necessary starting point in any conversation (of adults, similarly to children), since the only perceptual-motor anchor point in communication is the person (Bühler, 1934/1990).

Yet the children's 'egocentric speech' is not free from actual acceptance of another person (or persons) as addressees. Piaget noticed a difference between the conditions where the 'social others' around were of different kinds. If a child is in the middle of a group of other children, these monologues are broken by questions of various kinds, rather than being a narrative comment upon ongoing acitivity. The latter may be the case in speaking when around adults. In the following example of a child's monologue which takes place in a social context (with an adult around). Hans (at age 3 years and 1 month) speaks while building a construction:

> . . . my making a house for the Chinese, 'm making a house, a very big house. I've made a house for the Chinese.
> Up high, the bedrooms. On the top I put the roof, the ceiling.
> Now the beds. I put the beds, a bed like that for the Chinese, a bed for the Chinese. The beds on top of one another.
> There. The Chinese sleep up there, near God. They are asleep. I have put them just there, near God.
> There is God [he puts a block in place].
> Here he has head, his little head.
> Look [he speaks to himself]: God is up there, on the roof. (Piaget, 1959, p. 242)

In the child's act of speaking, *the addressee is not specified*. The adults (who observe the child's speaking) are likely to interpret this lack of specification as if it were absence of the addressee.

The strict model of communication (if there is somebody who says something, it must be directly said to somebody else) is a limited view on human communication, even on the adults' side. It is often the case that one parent says something out aloud – which may be addressed to another parent, and/or to the child. Or a parent may say something to the other parent with the goal of the child overhearing it. Much of adults' speaking in interaction is similar to children's monologues.

Ego-centrism in Piaget's conceptualization

Piaget's notion of children's *ego-centrism* entailed *lack of differentiation between another and the ego*. It did not amount to the child 'being egocentric' in the sense of lay use of the term. Rather, the child (whose ego was seen as currently un-differentiated from the other) was precisely in the middle of a social context:

> The child loves to know that he is near his mother. He feels that he is close to her in each of his acts and thoughts. What he says does not seem to him to be addressed to himself but as *enveloped with the feeling of a presence*, so that to speak to himself or to speak to his mother appear to him to be one and the same thing. *His activity is thus bathed in an atmosphere of communion* or syntonization, one might even speak of the 'the life of union' to use the terms of mysticism . . . But, on the other hand . . . The child does not ask questions and expects no answer, neither does he attempt to give any information to his mother who is present. He does not ask himself whether she is listening or not. He *speaks for himself just as an adult does when he speaks within himself*. (Piaget, 1959, p. 243; added emphasis)

Piaget's realistic description of the child's situation – being *in-between* social unity and personal autonomy – captures the phenomenon well. Piaget refers to egocentric speech as *verbal incontinence* (Piaget, 1959, p. 38). The child cannot (and would not) regulate his speech – even if it is clear that there are other people around. The child in his egocentric speech cannot regulate the flow of speaking. That flow is the ground for imitation (in Baldwin's sense of persistent imitation).

Children's speech, however, is not merely an activity of speaking, but it is part of a given context of activities. Many of the child's activities remain within the realm of her individual play, or play with other children. Under some circumstances, however, that act of speaking acquires specific negotiation functions. Interactions around bed-time are a good example of recurrent culturally constructed settings.

'Going to sleep': from physiological state change to culturally constructed negotiations

Human regular transitions from daytime to night-time activities are an appropriate example of how physical, physiological, collective-cultural and personal-cultural sides of a regular transition *can become* integrated. The obvious night/day difference in physical conditions has led to rich collective-cultural mythology construction of what happens during the night in contrast to the day. The night is both construed as DANGEROUS (for example, all kinds of witches, evil spirits etc. fly around at night) as well as THRILLING (night is filled with adventures, it is an erotic and intimate time period). Different societies have created different meanings relating to the night – yet all of those indicate that there is something psychologically relevant in the night-time (Chamberlain, 1908). The psychological constructions about relevance of night-time come in the distinction of the realms of 'dreams' and 'nightmares'. The latter have been recognized in human cultural history for their immediate physiological 'effects': the Latin term for 'nightmare' – *incubus* – connotes the oppressive feeling in the chest. In the knowledge base of child psychology, there are similarly many indications of children's sleep disturbances, and difficulties of regulation of going to sleep and waking up (Nagera, 1966).

On the physiological side, human bodies' movement from daytime activities to night rest is one of physiological transition (as described in Chapter 9). This transition – be it in infancy, childhood, or adulthood – can proceed without any cultural focusing. In other terms – human beings just fall asleep (when tired) and wake up – there is no ritualization of such physiological transitions.

As is the case with cultural-psychological issues, under some social and psychological cultural needs such ritualization of sleep/wakefulness transitions can become constructed socially. It is in these cases that we can observe the concerns about children's 'getting to bed on time' or waking up on time. Different cultural tools – medicines for getting ourselves to sleep, and alarm clocks to wake us up have been devised solely for these culturally constructed needs.

Young children's cleverness in interaction rituals at bedtimes – trying to avoid going to sleep when the parents try to get them to bed – is widely known in folklore about children. Yet it is rarely seriously studied (an exception is Nelson, 1989). The following example of negotiation of bedtime comes from a Swedish example of children in kindergarten playing a scene of difficulty in going to sleep. The work of Swedish educator Gunilla Lindqvist (1995) in the area of aesthetics of children's play has led to children's dramatizations of various scenes (and theatre performances) as major activities of the children. The following was a dramatization of the theme of loneliness from a book by a Swedish author (Kaj Beckman's *Lisen Can't Sleep*):

> Carina speaks up: It is now evening, and Lisen is about to go to bed. She has had a wash, brushed her teeth and gone to the toilet. Her mother has been helping her. 'Lisen!' Carina calls, and the children can hear two voices from the corridor. It is Lisen, played by Kristina, in a nightie and with her hair in a ponytail, and her mother, played by Majlis.
>
> 'I'm not tired,' Lisen says. 'Do I have to go to bed although I'm not tired?'
>
> 'You must get to bed now. You need to sleep,' her mother replies in a firm voice.
>
> 'I want some water, I'm so thirsty,' Lisen pleads. 'I need to go to the toilet,' she continues.
>
> 'You have just been to the toilet, and brushed your teeth. Now I will get into the kitchen and do the washing up, and you'll be quiet and try to go to sleep.'
>
> 'I need to go to the toilet,' Lisen complains. She is now lying on her bed.
>
> The children laugh and look at one another. The older girls look both embarrassed and delighted at the same time.
>
> 'Mommy! I can't sleep, I want my doll,' says Lisen.
>
> 'Then you'll have to fetch your doll,' her mother answers from the kitchen.
>
> 'Shall I go and get it myself?' Lisen asks, surprised. She gets up and walks over to a chair where the doll is lying. Then she places the doll on the pillow.
>
> 'Good night,' says Lisen to the children. Everyone giggles.
>
> 'Mummy! Dolly and I can't sleep without Teddy.'
>
> 'Then go and fetch Teddy,' her mother says calmly.
>
> 'Do you know where Teddy is?' Lisen asks the children.
>
> 'If you can't find Teddy, you will have to take another toy,' her mother says from the kitchen.
>
> Lisen gets out of bed one more time and fetches Teddy.
>
> 'Mummy! Dolly and I and Teddy can't sleep without my lamb. Couldn't you fetch that?' Lisen asks imploringly.
>
> 'OK, I will give you your lamb, but then you have to go to sleep,' her mother says with determination.
>
> 'Mummy, I can't sleep without my lion.'
>
> 'You will have to get your lion yourself.'
>
> 'You can sleep there,' Lisen says 'Good night! Good night!' All the children roar with laughter.
>
> 'My bed is so crowded. There's me and my doll and my teddy and none of us can sleep – not without the ball,' Lisen continues.

'Well, that will really make it so crowded that you won't be able to sleep at all,' her mother replies and comes from the kitchen.

'But what about my cat?' Lisen goes on and on.

'Is it like this when you go to bed?' Lisen turns to one of the children.

'No,' they all answer, confidently. 'Take Pippi,' one of the children suggests.

'I can't sleep without Pippi, can I get her as well?' The children have encouraged Lisen. 'And can I have her monkey as well? And another doll?'

'Where can I go then?' Lisen mumbles to herself and gets into the bottom of the bed. Everybody laughs at her.

'Mummy! I can't sleep because the monkey and the cat and the lion and the lamb and I can't all fit in. It's too crowded.'

Lisen's mother comes into her room and moves the cuddly toys.

'If I close my eyes, I see scary things,' Lisen explains. 'Then I need all the animals with me.'

'But it is too crowded,' says Lisen's mother. 'Don't you want me to remove some of the animals?'

'Maybe I only want the cat,' Lisen says hesitantly.

'Do you want me to remove the other ones?' Lisen's mother asks one more time.

'If you want to, you can have my dog,' says Emil and hugs the dog tightly.

'Good night,' Lisen says and puts her head on her pillow.

(Lindqvist, 1995, pp. 88–89)

Here we see the dramatization of an episode which in itself becomes a trigger for genetic dramatisms (see Chapter 4) emerging from the children's joint actions. The children resonate with the going-to-bed negotiation displayed (by child actors) in their enacting of the scene. Furthermore, the audience joins in with suggestions. Young children have created for their own personal cultures ritualistic schemes for the event of going to bed. Such schemes are recognizable by other children, and can be complemented by them, when encountered in the social domain.

The inter-personal dramatisms at bedtime turn later – by adolescence – into internalized versions of ritualized actions necessary to get oneself asleep. A look at a rather extreme case, which nevertheless shows rather ordinary features, of a 12.5-year-old girl treated (psychoanalytically) for 'sleep disturbance' gives us an insight into a complex version of ritualization of the preparation for sleeping:

J.M . . . had among other symptoms numerous rituals and compulsive actions that she was forced [by herself] to perform at bedtime before she was able to settle down to sleep. Thus, for example, the window curtains had to be arranged to have a fold in the middle. She had to make sure that the arm of the chair did not touch the table and was separated from it by a space of one inch; the tablecloth had to be placed exactly in the middle of the bed; the books had to be arranged in a certain manner; other objects had to be placed in such a way that they would not fall to the floor during the evening making noises that would frighten and waken her. Similarly, two clocks in her room had to be kept at a certain distance from each other so that they would not make too much noise during the night and wake her, a preoccupation that was accompanied by an intense fear that one of the clocks might stop altogether, in which case she felt it would be impossible for her to sleep for weeks. (Nagera, 1966, p. 432)

Despite obviously extreme versions of the ritualization, the case indicates how a standardized sequence of events in the person's immediate environment becomes *regulated by the person themself* with the goal of buffering the going-to-sleep transition. Adolescence and adulthood entail many ritualizations of such kind. The rituals of adults in setting up series of alarm clocks at different distances from the bed so as to get up 'on time' in the morning can give us complex constructions of no less obsessiveness.

Between the virtual and the real: constructing understanding

Children's understanding of the world develops constantly at the intersection of experiencing the real and experiencing others' reflections upon the real. The young child can observe the father pouring himself a drink when alone and denying having drunk anything when the mother asks him about the suspicious odours emanating from him. The goal-oriented nature of human conduct guarantees that the child is constantly bombarded with conflicting information about the real and the virtual.

Contemporary cognitive child psychology has utilized the richness of the 'what is' and 'what seems to be' in a domain of experimental studies of children of different ages – labelled 'theories of mind' research (see Perner, 1991). The focus in that research has been to reveal the complexities of children's knowing and telling (to others) about some discrepancy between the real and the apparent.

Cultural psychology utilizes 'theories of mind' research as an example of the *outcomes* of some underlying child–environment interaction processes. This cognitive research tradition has not revealed the processes by which children's distinction-making of the real and the apparent proceeds ontogenetically. It follows from all of the goal-oriented nature of human conduct that the child assembles his or her own integrative perspective on the real versus virtual contrast. This can happen under the guidance of adults, in special settings that encourage contemplative reflection upon the world. David and Rosa Katz (1927) have been the pioneers of studying children's understanding of the world through the dialogues the children carry out with adults.

'Confession talks' The Katzes entered into dialogue with their children (boys, Theodor 6 years 9 months and Julius 5 years and 3 months at the time of the study), at bedtime. The children were found to be in 'contemplative mode' in bed, before sleep. The function of such in-bed talks was not to get them to sleep, but to reflect upon the events of the day (compare this function with the role of the 'sunset ceremony' in the Krishna-

murti school, see Chapter 13). This event is guided by the parents (who know, from other sources, about what the children did, or were likely to do, during the day). The children can be observed to employ various tactics of bringing their side of the day's events into the interaction setting. The different persons in relation to whom the possible 'misdeeds' of the children could be examined remain constant from one evening to another (grandmother, grandfather, maid, father), so the 'confession talks' have continuity of the personages involved, over time.

Let us consider one of the reported 'confession talks' analytically (the transcript is reported from Katz, 1928, pp. 338–339, commentaries are added). It included the mother (M) together with the older son Theodor (T) and younger son Julius (J, also referred to as 'Baby'):

Interaction	Commentary
M: Did you do anything wrong? Did you strike anyone?	
J: You must ask 'Did you strike Grandmother?'	J insists upon M's assuming of the regular turn-taking (game) nature of the encounter.
M: Did you strike Grandmother?	On this day, this topic of hitting adults seems to be of positive self-presentation value to J – knowing that he had not hit anybody, it gives him the possibility to deny any hitting anybody as this was true
J: No.	
M: Did you strike Aunt Olga?	
J: No.	
M: Did you strike Papa?	
J: No.	
M: Did you eat everything on your plate?	
J: Yes.	
M: Were you disobedient?	
J: Yes.	
M: What did you do then?	
J: I ran away from Aunt Olga.	
M: On the street?	
J: No, in the room. I wanted to get a pillow but Aunt Olga would not let me.	
M: Perhaps you went to an open window?	M suggests a transgression which J accepts; M then tests J's reflexive understanding turning the occasion into a guidance task for future safe conduct. She gets J to repeat the reason why it is unsafe, then suggests action blocking by the child
J: Yes, I was there.	
M: Should you go to the open window?	
J: No	
M: Why should not one go to the open window?	
J: Because you might fall out.	
M: Don't do it again, Julius. Did you do anything else wrong today?	
J: Yes, I cried.	
M: Why did you cry?	
J: I wanted to come to you.	
M: Did you do anything good today? Perhaps you handed Grandmother a chair?	M here overlooks the event and moves to positive deeds. She suggests to J an example of a positive action – but J neutralizes his agency in it
J: There was a chair and Grandmother sat down on it.	
M: Perhaps you picked up Grandmother's handkerchief for her?	
J: No, Theodor did that.	

M: Did you clean up the playroom?

J: Yes.

M: Did you put the chairs away?

J: Yes.

T: Mamma, I struck everybody today and I bit the baby.

M: Why did you strike at them?

T: They would not let me come to you from the playroom.

M: Why did you bite the baby?

T: Well, Mamma, you know he changed the locomotive and the cars around, and you know that won't do. The car is shorter and the locomotive is longer.

M: Well, is that so bad that you had to bite him?

T: No. You must always explain it. You must have a school

M: How do you come to think that?

T: Yes, you must always say, 'Theodor, don't bite!'
Mamma, I also pinched Baby's fingers in the drawer.

M: What, today?

T: No, at another time

M: Did you do it on purpose?

T: Baby held his finger in the drawer and then I closed it quickly.

M: Perhaps you were at an open window?

T: Yes.

M: Do you dare to do this?

T: No.

M: You know you must always watch out so Baby will not go to the open window. You know you are the older brother.
You straightened up your things?

T: Yes.

T joins the trialogue by bursting out his transgressions of the day. M proceeds to analyse the circumstances under which the events happened

M suggests a re-evaluation of the problem. T immediately reports the previously known action regulators
M proceeds to get T to externalize the specific self-regulatory utterance that has been suggested to T
T changes the topic, by volunteering another event
M is surprised, her knowledge does not include this
M introduces the 'on purpose' versus occasionally contrast, but does not proceed, letting T describe the event. Instead, she queries into the scenario of open window danger

M re-emphasizes T's role as *responsible* older brother. Then moves back to T

This little example of interaction demonstrates how – from the viewpoint of cultural construction of meanings of real-life events – the issue of 'truth' (of happenings), concealment of the reality and its future-oriented reconstruction, are all mutually intertwined. The adult converses with the children not merely about what happened during the day, but uses every moment of the reported events (transgressions) to insert some generic suggestive messages about the meaning-fulness of the events. Thus, the mother uses reports of the children being close to an open window (which, in the context of German city-apartment living, is of great danger) to create a meaningful context *for future avoidance* of similar situations, and for semiotic self-regulation devices (what the child should *say to themself* when appearing in such settings). She also 'weighs' different transgressions by introducing the notion 'on purpose' (yet not pursuing that enquiry). The reality of events that happened becomes turned into future-oriented handling of

similar events that might happen. The adult guides the children towards their own active externalization of their semiotic devices that are meant to be used when, in the future, similar situations might be encountered.

The developmental orientation in cultural psychology concentrates on how children create their new understanding in their everyday life contexts. The differentiation of the true and appearing distinction in ontogeny is crucial for children's development. Thanks to it, children can become sophisticated participants in everyday activities – autonomous persons who can act in participation of some activity, while being psychologically capable of distancing themselves from it.

CHILDREN AS PARTICIPANTS IN SITUATED ACTIVITY CONTEXTS

The notion of *participation* has been used in differ-ent ways in the social sciences of the twentieth century. The notion itself is that of a relationship between an agent (who participates) and object state (of participating). The agent is not expected to participate in the object in any intentional sense. Rather, there are many ways of participating, ranging from mere sharing of joint experience to active efforts to take part in some object activity.

Lucien Levy-Bruhl used the notion of participation to emphasize the inherent unity of the human cultural mind and its relation with the (super)natural world.

The law of participation

Participation was a concept brought into the early twentieth century by Levy-Bruhl (1985, p. 76), in conjunction with explanation of the uses of collective representations in human thinking. In what was then called 'primitive thinking', different objects could form relations with persons in the context of 'collective representations'. The 'primitive thought' seemed to contradict the axiom of identity used in classical logic – if something is X then it can't simultaneously be something else (Y). Yet in the case of 'primitive mentality', such consideration was widespread. The Bororo (South American) Indians would tell the visiting explorers (the German Karl von den Steinen, on whose travel stories Levy-Bruhl relied) that *they were red parrots (arara)* simultaneously with being humans. The European mentality could not tolerate such frivolous thinking (and hence classified it as 'primitive'), as for European ab-original logic if one is a person, one cannot be a parrot; and if one is a parrot, one cannot be a person.

Levy-Bruhl attempted to use the notion of participation to denote the unbounded fusion between the person and the surrounding environment. The 'primitive mentality' was characterized as 'participating' in the world in which the person belongs – the natural environment was attributed to be animated by 'souls', which in their turn would be fused with the being of humans. From that perspective, the Bororo thought about being humans and *araras* is similar to any thinking about fusion of the person with a constructed entity (for example, social roles: a person may consider themself to be simultaneously a person and a student). The participations can become so engrained as not to be visible for the person (who participates) nor for others (who can observe the person). The collective representations (on which participation is based) become internalized, and inherent in the conduct of a person. In this way, participation becomes a phenomenon of personal feeling which does not require symbolic fortification by rituals:

The Arunta who feels that he *is* both himself and the ancestor . . . knows nothing of ancestor-worship. The Bororo does not make the parrots, which are Bororo, the objects of a religious cult. It is only in aggregates of a more advanced type that we find an ancestor-worship, a cult of heros, gods, sacred animals etc. The ideas which we call really religious are thus a kind of differentiated product resulting from a prior form of mental activity. The participation or communion first realized by mystic symbiosis and by practices which affirmed it is obtained later by union with the object of the worship and belief called religious, with the ancestor, the god. (Levy-Bruhl, 1985, p. 368)

In contemporary cultural psychology, the use of the concept of participation entails *syncretic linkage* of persons' actions with the context of activity. The emphasis on the syncretic nature of persons' embeddedness in their social contexts stems from the efforts to make sense of the social nature of human personal psychological functions. Human beings are social – the social world of their upbringing participates in the personal psychological organization in the same way as 'forest spirits' would participate in the 'primitive mentality'. Likewise, the person participates in social activities, is fused with those, and *becomes* that activity.[1] Syncretic thinking in theory-building has similar consequences as in lay life – it explains complexity by superimposing upon it an all-encompassing generic term.

Barbara Rogoff's notion of 'guided participation'
Aside from the obvious theoretical difficulties with the use of syncretic notions, the basic fact of human development is that of the embeddedness of the developing person within the field of everyday life events organized by their meanings. Barbara Rogoff (1990, 1997) has emphasized the complexity of such embeddedness – not only is the developing person immersed in their cultural life-space, but he or she is guided towards some future objectives by other persons who organize that life space. Furthermore, that guidance can be episodic, implicit and engaging the developing person's own strivings.

Much of cultural development of persons is implicit, as it requires no directed teaching. Children simply are around their older siblings and adults, observing them, imitating them persistently, attempting to join in their activities. Sometimes they are let into these activities, at other times not. Later they may be given the responsibility for some of the sub-tasks which are necessary for the whole activity. Finally, the whole activity is delegated to their full responsibility. All in all, children's participation in adult activities is selectively guided. A schematic representation of that unity of participation and

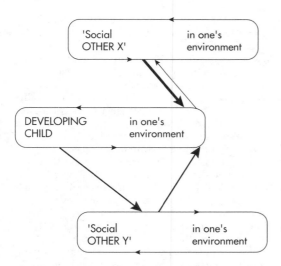

FIGURE 11.2 *Mutually guided participation as support and hindrance (after Rogoff)*

guidance is given in Figure 11.2. The developing child is intricately interwoven with his or her environment – there is no boundary between the child and the world.[2] The flow of the participatory activity is circular (as indicated by the arrows on the cyclical depiction of the oval for the child).

Simultaneously with the child's participation in his or her world, the 'social others' (two of them are depicted in the Figure 11.2, X and Y) participate in their worlds. As the worlds are mutually united, their participations begin to guide that of the child (and vice versa – the child's participation guides that of these others). In Figure 11.2 this is indicated by way of arrows from one person's participatory cycle into the other's cycles. In the case of 'social other Y', that guidance is depicted as mutually similarly directed with that of the child – the arrows from the child to Y, and from Y to the child, are in the same direction. In real-life terms, Y may support some ongoing activity of the child, thus promoting its further development.

The story for 'social other X', as depicted in Figure 11.2, is different – here the participation of the child is hindered by X (the arrows from X to the child are in the opposite direction). Here the issue of guided participation (of the child) takes a new form – the child's participation in his or her own world is blocked by the direction of X's participation in X's own world. In real-life terms, this is the case of an adult's intervention into a child's ongoing activities, attempting to slow them down, or guide the child to their extinction. Guided participation is always a complex of coordination of multiple personal participations of possibly very different goal orientations.

Social roles, power, participation and guidance

As indicated above, guided participation entails the unity of *directive guidance* (towards one activity and/or objective) and *eliminative direction* (keeping the developing person at a distance, or completely unaware of some possible objective or activity). All these guidance tactics are put into practice within interaction between persons who act within their social roles. Hungarian social psychologist Peter Bodor (1998) has emphasized the role of *guided* participation as being *guarded* participation. Social power relations between persons who interact with the developing child turn the guidance of the child into the guarding of the development. Some domains of knowledge are carefully kept away from the young child. Others are delayed in access (for example, the knowledge of the 'secret flutes' in Sambia society in New Guinea – Herdt, 1987; and see Chapter 13). Human development – all through the life span – is organized by *socially guarded participation*. Individual persons participate in their worlds (as depicted in Figure 11.2, above).

The social power structure of any society – exemplified through the power differences between social role expectations – leads to the inevitable variability of the knowledge bases of individual persons. The issue of access to skills and knowledge becomes organized through social institutions. It is important for social institutions to *promote the development of ignorance and competence* in the case of children *at the same time*. Ignorance is a valuable sociological characteristic in any society (see Moore and Tumin, 1949), since it creates the background upon which different forms of socially constructed competence are made detectable.

Creation and maintenance of ignorance – of some persons relative to others, or of some of a person's in-capabilities relative to his/her capabilities – is central for maintaining social power differentials. In the 'modern' (or 'post-modern') societies, fragmentation of knowledge (and technological skills) by making some persons 'experts' and others 'consumers' (of the presumed expertise) guarantees the economic relations between the 'haves' and 'have nots'. In the sociohistorical move of societies from 'producers' towards 'consumers' the differential ignorance is a phenomenon that necessarily increases. In the realm of human development, this direction is visible in the decrease of acceptance of the 'folk wisdom' about how to bear and bring up children (that is, the 'grandmother's wisdom' made available to younger generations by real-life participation by the younger generations in joint activities). At the same time, the role of 'experts' (in childbearing and child-rearing) becomes increasingly emphasized.

Contemporary American middle-class parents are guided towards ignorance by first having blocked their contact with childrearing (no experience of young children in taking care of their younger siblings). Secondly, their trust in their 'natural ways' of dealing with children is undermined by the *promotion of the need to turn to experts* for any kind of problems. This creates a profitable role for the experts – their re-presentation of common sense ('grandmother's') wisdom acquires the additional value of being valid *because of* their expert status. This social construction process is well-known in the realm of mass communication under the notion of *status conferral* (Lazarsfeld and Merton, 1948, p. 101). Status conferral is a process of creating a status through some – positive or negative – singling out of a target from the background. In the case of positive status conferral, we can look at the means by which the mass media single out some person, viewpoint, or social institution, and provide that singled-out target with an arena for public attention (television time, newspaper space etc.). In parallel to this act, it is suggested to the public that the target has special expertise (as otherwise he or she would not be singled out). Hence the mere appearance of a person on a TV screen creates the 'symbolic capital' of expertise. Note here the similarity of the processes of 'social construction of unreality' (see Chapter 10).

The negative version of status conferral takes the form of accepting actions by somebody upon others on the basis of these actions themselves. Thus, an arrest of a political opponent by the police can be used by bystanders as proof of the guilty state of the arrested (for example, 'police would not arrest the innocent'). Both the positive and negative forms of status conferral lead to the differentiation of power roles in society. The celebrities and the criminals are socially constructed in their roles by the same mechanisms.[3]

The guarded participation of young children's activities entails informal status conferral with respect to those in control of the children's development – parents, teachers, etc. By rejecting the young child's curiosity-born initiative to help the mother give care to the infant sibling, the mother guards the boundaries of her own exclusive control status as the mother. She maintains her 'expert' role in relation to her children (rather than allows the older sibling to develop into that role), even if she herself subordinates her 'expertise' to that of childrearing 'experts' by way of reading books on the topic 'how to be a parent' and consulting with child psychologists. Ignorance here is supported by assuming a hierarchical 'expertise' access (PSYCHOLOGIST

| | > MOTHER | | > YOUNG CHILD), where the sign | | > indicates dominance of one's expertise over the other (>) while access by the other to the assumed 'expertise' is carefully blocked. Teenage girls who become pregnant are assumed to be not ready for motherhood, and in need of expert evaluation and support. They are forced into the role of 'consumer' of 'expertise' precisely because they dare to move towards competence in an area to which (because of their age) they are not considered to have legitimate social access.

In social contexts where such 'expert' versus 'consumer' differentiation has not occurred, there is no difficulty for the older generations in letting younger generations participate in relevant tasks of everyday life. Instead of 'protecting' children from real-world encounters (and thus reifying themselves as the agents 'in control'), parents of children may support (and even require) from children participation in the real-world activities of the whole family. The account by a Nigerian parent about the value of children, reported as an epigraph to Chapter 12 of the present book (see p. 248), reflects that perspective. When one looks at children's participation in social contexts of differentially distributed power of social role relations, children are usually at the lower levels of the social power hierarchy. As such, they are appreciated for what they can do for their immediate family – rather than what their family can do for them.[4]

SUMMARY

Early childhood entails a myriad of contexts where guarded participation by children in the activities of adults and older siblings plays an important part in the internalization and externalization processes. The latter create the dynamic link between the collective and personal cultures. Our knowledge about cultural-psychological phenomena in early childhood is fully dependent upon the externalization by children of some results of their internalization processes.

Young children can be observed to be moving towards self-regulatory cultural processes (intra-mental psychological autonomy) precisely due to their modulated participation in the socio-cultural contexts. Such participation maintains the unique personal nature of the child (and of the participating adults). Autonomy for all interdependent persons is an important objective. In early childhood, it develops relatively slowly. In mid-childhood and adolescence that process of autonomization is guarded by the confines of formal structures of children's education, ranging from kindergartens to colleges.

NOTES

1 In a similar vein, contemporary social sciences seriously entertain the possibility that persons become 'texts', 'discourse' etc.

2 Rogoff follows the traditions of John Dewey (1896) in overcoming the 'dualism' between person and environment through positing a speedy flow of mutuality – in Dewey's terms, *coordination*.

3 This is particularly remarkable in cases where criminals become celebrities – a convicted killer who writes memoirs is turned into a literary expert.

4 Interestingly, a similar suggestion exists in the cultural history of the United States, in this case relating adult citizens with their national identity object – the country. The oft-quoted slogan expressed by John F. Kennedy 'ask yourself what you can do for your country, not what your country can do for you' clearly states the assumed hierarchy of social power.

REVIEW QUESTIONS FOR CHAPTER 11

1 Explain the difference between higher and lower psychological functions.

2 How would Vygotsky's notion of parallel and mutually linked lines (of cognitive and speech development) relate with the notion of multilinearity of development?

3 How are children expected to interact with people older than they?

4 Explain the psychological functioning of the discourse environments in the case of the Qalandar.

5 Explain the notions of communication and meta-communication.

6 How does teasing work?

7 How can values be promoted through suggestions to the opposite?

8 Explain Piaget's views on the move from collective monologue to shared activity, and from there to shared mental processes.

9 Explain Piaget's notion of ego-centrism.

10 Analyse the culturally constructed nature of 'going to sleep' routines.

11 Analyse the process of 'confession talks'. How are values socially suggested through such conversations?

12 Explain Levy-Bruhl's *law of participation*.

13 Describe Barbara Rogoff's notion of guided participation.

14 What can Peter Bodor's focus on guarded participation add to Rogoff's guided participation?

15 Explain the role of ignorance in social organization of human development.

PART FIVE

ENTERING THE WORLD OF ACTIVITIES – CULTURALLY RULED

Human ontogeny is remarkably slow – in comparison with any other species. It is also relatively well buffered against temporary guidance by environmental features in non-correctable directions. The developing human being is both open and resistant to re-directions – already at the biological level.

Cultural direction of activities is central to middle childhood and adolescence. There are numerous possibilities for collective-cultural direction of children's experiences. Middle childhood is a crucial period for working out specific relationships that developing children are establishing with the life contexts of the adults. These relations can vary on the basis of adults' symbolic construction of limits for children's entrance into their worlds. Different aspects of everyday life may be kept out of children's perceptual access and participation (for example, sexual activities of adults), while others may have been selectively promoted for the children to observe and participate in. In any society, children's entrance into the adult world of activities is differentially limited – in parallel, some activities are accepted, others promoted, and yet others ruled out from the child's world.

In adolescence, the construction of personal autonomy continues. However, it also becomes a target for collective-cultural intervention of various kinds. The transition of children into adults is a period of need for social role guidance – from the vantage point of the social institutions within which these roles become established. This role guidance takes place through initiation rituals, including formal schooling.

In a way, formal schooling can be viewed as a time-extended initiation ritual. Instead of a some days, or weeks, or months' long seclusion during which the initiates are taught skills and know-how that are not immediately known in the community, the formal schooling kind of initiation takes years – increasingly more years – and removes children from direct entrance into the economic system. This is a concomitant to children's stopping being economic assets to their families, to becoming economic liabilities. As a result, a special period of transition into adulthood – adolescence – becomes a focus for youngsters' finding their ways into the uncertainties of adulthood.

12

PERSONAL PARTICIPATION AND ITS SOCIO-INSTITUTIONAL GUIDANCE

Part of the joy of having children is to be able to send them on errands. What I look for in my own children is that they should be able to work. When a child can carry things like a gourd of palm wine with appropriate care, bring a day's supply of yams for the family or a day's support of firewood from the farm, then the child is old enough.

(A Yoruba parent's reflection; from Adeokun, 1983, p. 135)

How are distinctions made of children of different levels of psychological development? The usual categorization in occidental child psychology uses the age – denoted by birthday – to create age sets of 2-year-olds, 3-year-olds etc. Or, the age set construction makes use of the formal schooling framework – age becomes denoted by the school grade (for example, 'first-graders', '5th graders' etc.).

Why this desperation for creating same-age sets, or cohorts? In children's home environments, there is no sharp distinction between early and middle childhood in human development – the children just move from a state of relatively unstructured sets of activities to others. As they can be assigned new roles in the catering for everyday subsistence activities, children become integrated into the world of the whole kinship group *as co-producers* of the necessary resources for living. In the home life, it is the child's capability to perform special tasks – bring objects from other places, mind younger children, going to the shop or market to buy needed things. The home environment – even if it celebrates children's birthdays – evaluates children by their functional capacities. It is the socio-institutional world that sets up book-keeping about age cohorts, and makes the belonging to those age sets conditional for different access areas in social life. So, for example, the establishment of a 'legal

drinking age', or 'drivers' licence age' (21 and 16 respectively in the United States; 18 and 17 in the UK) are acts of societal regulation of age set access to different activities. The International Labour Organization sets the minimum age for legal working at 15 years. This creates a situation of labelling the activities of children under 15 in terminology other than work, while for the children who actually work from a much earlier age these social conventions can be but limiting factors.

CHILDREN'S ENTRANCE INTO ADULT ACTIVITIES: HETEROGENEITY OF ACCESS

A collective-cultural system of guiding children's entrance into the adult world is inherently heterogeneous – inherent owing to the multiplicity of needs of adults in getting children of different competence levels integrated into multi-age family groups. Some of the domains of adults' activities are purposefully promoted for the children – so that they may develop their autonomous actions (and need less of their caregivers' attention) in those domains. Other activity areas are available only for children's observation – but are not expected to be mastered soon. Finally, there are areas of 'secret adult activities' that are kept away from the children at all cost.

The whole field of children's activities is thus differentiated (see Figure 12.1). In Figure 12.1, three trajectories of individual children's development are depicted (TR-1, TR-2 and TR-3). These three individual trajectories are depicted in a field of three adult activities (A, B and C). These three activities differ in the ways in which the children are allowed to gain access to the activity. In case of activity A, children in early childhood are given access to part of the activity, which is subsequently fully blocked from them. The

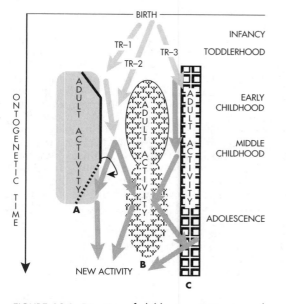

FIGURE 12.1 *Direction of children's activities towards participation in the social world*

boundary becomes semi-permeable by adolescence, and the children are encouraged to join in. In contrast, activity B – which is not allowed in early childhood – becomes unbounded (but not explicitly encouraged) as the children move towards adolescence. Finally, activity C is constantly open to the developing children to be involved in it.

The issue of integration of children into some activities of adults – while keeping them out of others – is crucial in the case of the economic livelihood of the household as a whole. Some joint activities are important to the sense of children's helping parents in their economic activities. Others take over functions (such as minding younger siblings) which allow parents to work on other economic tasks. Children can migrate to other households to help there (see Chapter 7). They can also work for hire outside home themselves, as the use of child labour in various production contexts has shown.

The introduction of laws that regulate children's participation in the economic system ('child labour laws') in the early twentieth century in most of Europe and North America has created a situation where the children's economic obligations to their parents have become backgrounded in our view of the family. The latter direction – turning children from being a family's economic (productive) assets into liabilities – is widespread in our industrialized world where work tasks

require long-term preparation of the labour force. Children are expected to become producers after their schooling. Their contribution to the family livelihood is limited in childhood years, when they are directed towards segregated activities (play).

In sum, children enter into the field of adult activities slowly, with preparatory periods, and are kept away from some adult activities. The whole patterning of the field is organized around the needs of the whole kinship network. Children become co-producers (with adults) in the creation of resources.

From play to co-production of economic resources: the Tallensi case

The specific functions that are delegated to children vary by society, social strata, needs of the tasks, and social representations of children's capabilities ('readiness for X') and fit into the role. The long phase of peripheral participation prior to entrance into the co-production of resources guarantees that there is sufficient background readiness for entering the new field of activities.

An example of the slow entrance of children into relevant co-production of resources comes from the experience of children in Taleland (in Ghana). As Meyer Fortes (1970) has described, Tallensi boys and girls are guided towards practical participation in kin-group productivity in their gender-specific ways. The boys are guided towards becoming cattle herders, and girls become involved in household management tasks. All these activities are built upon the ongoing play activities.

The play of 3–6-year-old Tallensi boys and girls is not strictly differentiated by way of gender-specific co-production tasks. Both boys and girls can be observed playing 'house' as well as 'cattle-herding'. Both can be assigned duties of looking after younger siblings when such needs exist. However, adults let the children begin to play around the agricultural activities of adults – girls who are approaching 5–6 years of age begin to carry small water pots, while boys are summoned to assist adults to scare birds off the fields of crops. Both boys and girls would be around at harvesting parties.

In the 6–9-year age range, Tallensi children's participation in kinship co-productive activities is set in place. Boys help men in house-building by carrying the necessary materials. They begin to go out together with older cattle-herding boys (older siblings). In their play, the preparation for future independent cattle-herding tasks becomes established. Girls in the same age range are actively involved in water-collecting and carrying, and help in cooking and food preparation. They gather wild edible herbs in the forest. Their play continues to reflect their housekeeping roles.

In the age range of 9–12 years, boys become fully responsible for cattle herding, and in tending agricultural crops. They establish their own farming practices, by growing ground-nuts in small plots. They participate in observational learning of complex adult male skills. At the same time, the boys' play acquires new features – they begin to make clay models, and play ritual events. In this period, the girls in this age range are entrusted with all major household tasks. Furthermore, they can begin to assist in public duties – as West African markets are women-dominated economic contexts, young girls begin to sell and buy merchandise similarly to adult women. Their previous 'housekeeping play' gradually fades out (as it is taken over by the real participation in housekeeping). By around 12 years of age, the boys' and girls' participation in adult economic activities has become gender-separated.

The important point emanating from this look at Tallensi children's play is the coordination of play and participation. The direction in which gender-specific participation proceeds is prepared and supported by previous and concurrent play. Children's play need not even be specifically directed towards production, yet it becomes transformed in that direction by the children themselves. Children observe the activities of adults, and even if their play is not guided by adults towards these activities, become involved in them themselves (see Chapter 11).

FORMAL AND INFORMAL EDUCATION

The distinction between informal and formal education is often made (Greenfield and Lave, 1982) in terms of directly opposing features of the two. Five contrasts (given in Table 12.1) are relevant. The process of formalization of education – its move from informal, everyday contexts to an institutional one – includes the *creation of physical and symbolic distance* between the two domains of experience (home and school). As we saw above (Chapter 8), a similar issue was at stake in the social institutionalization of the locations for childbirth. The question of locus of the event (education, childbirth) is a question of social control over its process as well as product.

Secondly, the formalization of education entails the *creating of the role of persons who are considered competent to teach*. Some social institution certifies who can (or cannot) teach children in the given formal schooling setting, and how these role-bearers should act in relation to the rest of the social world. The roles of teachers become institutionally defined – even if the person performing the role of teacher may be simultaneously a parent (and the parent's child may be in the same school). Also, at the level of formalized educational settings in early childhood – called 'preschools' or 'kindergartens' – the social role differentiation of the adult (as teacher and as caregiver) is not yet well established.

Thirdly, the move from informal to formalized educational contexts introduces a differentiation of 'expert' versus 'novice'. While in informal education settings there exists the differential

TABLE 12.1 *Basic contrasts between informal and formal education*

Function	Informal education	Formal education
1 Where does it take place	Within ongoing life in the course of everyday activities	Special place created locations (dwellings or designated places)
2 Who teaches?	Anybody in the immediate social environment	Specially identified (and certified by the controlling institution) persons
3 Who learns?	Everybody – both the more and the less experienced participants in the context	The persons (child, adult) who are given the social role of 'pupil' or 'student'
4 What is mastered?	Anything in the realm of socially shared knowledge, as it is needed by the local social unit	Knowledge and skills defined by the given curriculum, which is sanctioned by the social institution in control
5 How does it relate with the local context	Continuous with local history – in fact it makes that history	Discontinuous with the local traditions (except for as much as is inevitable); oriented towards breaking and changing it (for religious or political purposes)

knowledge and mastery of the participants (for example, adult specialists of some practices know those better than children who are apprentices), there is no strict build-up and maintenance of social role boundaries. Formalization introduces such differences between the asymmetric power roles.

Fourthly (and fifthly), the kind of knowledge that is mastered in informal and formal educational settings differs. In the informal settings, the learners move to master the socially shared local know-how and skills. The formal education framework introduces an institutionally promoted kind of knowledge which is not immediately available in the local community (and which may even be in opposition to what is acquired through informal education).

INFORMAL EDUCATION SETTINGS: UNCONTROLLED, YET RULE-GOVERNED

Any everyday life context in which a child encounters some new experience is a setting for informal education. Children themselves create their informal education by their curiosity. The 'social others' set up their rule-based expectations, yet the children themselves pick up that structure in their play. Their play turns into games. Games differ from play by way of explicit organization by social rules. It is possible to view games as play in which invented rules have been made to become fixed and consensually accepted.

Children's games have been of interest to psychologists, educators and researchers of folklore – yet mostly from a perspective of description of their form, rather than their psychological socializing functions. As is often the case, researchers have tried to create a classification system of different forms of games. One of those, created by Brian Sutton-Smith (see Lancy, 1984, p. 296), includes distinguishing of the games by way of levels of role-relations complexity within the game. Seven levels are distinguished in that system on the basis *of differentiation of roles and actions*:

- **Level 1**: Here belong games that involve *simple role-reversals* between players. Thus, in the 'hide-and-seek' game the roles of who hides and who seeks the hiders are reversed after each turn.
- **Level 2**: Games of role-reversals and action-reversals (for example, 'Release').
- **Level 3**: Games with a competitive emphasis that include internal coordination (for example, 'Dodge-ball' and 'Mark').
- **Level 4**: Competitive games that include external coordination (for example, marbles).

- **Level 5**: Games that involve sub-group differentiation that is external to the players. This includes games of role differentiation into players, coaches, referees, spectators.
- **Level 6**: Games in which sub-group differentiation is internal to the team of players; the role of players is differentiated (for example, baseball).
- **Level 7**: Games between teams in which sub-group differentiation inside the team is linked with competition between teams (for example, football).

Furthermore, games can be analysed by way of the *means/goals differentiation*. The goal may be limited to the activities within the game – so the goal of the game is to play the game. In other terms, there is no means/ends differentiation involved. The game is played in order to play it. For example, European football (soccer) on Polynesian islands is at times played to end in a draw (rather than one team winning over the other). This is a different story from the case where the same soccer game is played for the sake of winning a trophy (World Cup) – here the game is the means through which a goal external to the game itself is being sought. A particular national soccer team may move through a year-long sequence of matches on its way to the general goal of winning the World Cup. Each game in that sequence is being played by the same rules, and oriented at winning over the opponent. Yet the main objective in playing is an aspiration far away in future time.

Games and schooling

Games created within schooling are similar to the footballers' seeking the World Cup. When viewed through the lens of children's development of role-organized games, the activities in preschools (kindergartens) and schools can be viewed as canalizers of children's games towards new rule-based activities. Activities in a school are a new kind of game – one where the school creates the rules.

Special occasions created in institutions Any institutional ritual creates a stage for social canalization of games. Different seasonal and life course rituals – new year celebrations, examinations, birthday parties – all create episodes of social role direction. Each of the rituals in and by itself is not expected to have 'an effect' on the developing person, but their collective nature and seasonal recurrence are guiding the developing child in a particular, collective-culturally valued, direction.

As an example, let us analyse a birthday party in an Israeli kindergarten (described in detail in

Weil, 1986). It has a number of specific action moves that specifically guide the birthday child and all other participants towards collectively relevant values.

The birthday party begins with the parents and the child coming to the kindergarten by a pre-arranged time. They are greeted by the teacher. Other children are waiting, seated around three sides of the classroom. On the fourth side is a table with flowers, candles, presents and a birthday cake (baked by the child's mother). The birthday child is seated at the head of the table on a decorated chair, with their parents next to them. The teacher sits on the opposite side, among the children. Then,

> The teacher instructs the birthday child to place upon his head the garland of flowers lying before him on the table. He is told to light the candles (either inserted into the cake or arranged like flowers in a pot of earth or sand), which signify his age, and a mandatory additional candle representing 'the next year'; the birthday child lights the candles with the aid of his mother. (Weil, 1986, p. 330)

The group then sings different versions of 'happy birthday' songs, clapping as they sing. The teacher leads every move of the group – changing the song, noting when it is appropriate to dance, and when to finish the activity. She instructs the birthday child to invite his mother to dance (to the tune 'My dear mother', emphasizing filial love), then father, then grandparents (if they are present), then his friends.

After the dance, all children return to their seats, and the teacher leads the 'story-telling' phase of the ritual. The child's parents are asked to tell a story about a special event or a 'good deed' in the life of the child. The story usually is about some exemplary behaviour of the child – at home or in a public place. The parents' story is followed by blessings and good wishes, orchestrated by the teacher and given to the birthday child by the other children. The children raise hands to want to give the blessing, the teacher coordinates their sequence. Standard birthday blessings include 'may you be healthy', 'may you be big and strong', 'may you do well in your studies' etc. After the children have finished their blessings, the parents are given the opportunity to give theirs. Then representatives from the kindergarten present the child with gifts (for example, an album of pictures drawn by each classmate, and a present).

After the gift-transfers, the birthday chair is placed in the centre of the room and the birthday child sits on it. The adults and other children surround the chair, and raise it into the air as many times as is the child's age, plus a final toss

'for the next year'. After that, the participants go back to their seats, the birthday child blows out the candles, cuts the birthday cake and serves it to the other children. The parents leave. The ceremony is over. *At the end of the kindergarten day*, the birthday child gives each child a little bag with small presents (sweets, chewing gum etc.).

This description of a birthday party in an Israeli kindergarten indicates the complex structural unification of the personal-cultural and collective-cultural sides of an orchestrated game. The adults – especially the teacher – are in control of co-ordinating the sequence of action. The birthday child is given a special prominent role, yet it is defined in relation to his peers, parents and the kindergarten setting in general. Each participant adds to the unity of the child with the social group: gift exchanges, dancing and singing, blessings, food exchanges – all work towards the creation of a social event the importance of which is social promotion of general values through specific events.

The contents of the wishes given to the birthday child indicate the parallel promotion of the child's different social roles. In the case of the birthday party described above, seven of the values were emphasized in parallel (Weil, 1986, p. 335):

- **The good child**: This was communicated to the birthday child through desires for his behaving well, listening to parents. This value can be presented as linked with biblical command-ments ('honour your father and your mother'), and it can be presented as 'God-given law' (in directly religious kindergartens) or as mere honour (*kavod*) in non-religious kindergartens.
- **The good peer**: Messages praising the birthday child's getting along well with peers – in the form of *hevreman* (a person who is sociable and easy-going).
- **The good friend**: Praise for the birthday child's good choice of friends; loyalty to friends. This is exemplified by the act of sharing – the good friend shares their possessions (see also the sharing of the candies at the end of the birthday-day in the kindergarten).
- **The good pupil**: This involves being well disciplined in class and doing well in one's studies. Kindergarten children are not supposed to interrupt their teacher, and to participate in the assigned activities.
- **The good Israeli**: The suggestion is there that the birthday child (and vicariously other participants) should become good citizens of the country. In the kindergarten, such wishes are encoded into messages such as 'may you become a good soldier'.
- **The good Jew**: This relates to the build-up of religious identity (rather than loyalty to the

country) – the child should become a person who follows the commandments (*mitzvoh*).

- **The good person**: Here the focus is on a general humanistic attitude to life.

Each of these value orientations can be present within a particular ritual context together, or separately. They can be made to 'speak through the other' (see Bakhtin's notion of one 'voice' 'speaking through another' – ventriloculion). Thus, being a **good Jew** can lead to being a **good Israeli** through being a **good pupil**.

Promotion of identity chaining

This unification of the different values is central for creating a redundant system of control over those aspects of personal-cultural development which are most important for the given social institution to keep under control.

'Personal identity' is an ideologically valued way of potentially bonding the person to a social system – the identity is most usually linked with a social role that is simultaneously an organizer of the personal culture (for example, 'I am a good pupil') and part of the socio-institutional definition of the role. A 'pupil' is a child in a specific social role, with all the expectations put by the institution upon that role – in the activity contexts of a preschool or school. The chain of identity promotion continues, if it is socially suggested that by being a 'good pupil' the given child is at the same time a 'good citizen' in general.

Identity chaining takes the general form of a syncretic move from one social role to another, each of which is ill-defined, and the person is assuming each of these roles simultaneously:

I am X – and – **I am also Y** – and – **I am also Z**

In a syncretic system like this, promotion by a social institution constitutes an act of canalization of developing persons towards syncretic feeling and thinking. Thus, an example of syncretic phenomena in the personal world are dreams – where boundaries disappear. In a dream, it is possible that the same person may at once be an uncle and a brother (Werner, 1948, p. 53), whereas in real life this is an impossibility. While developmental perspectives upon human development have emphasized the gradual overcoming of syncretic thinking in cognitive ontogeny, the different social institutions selectively operate in the reverse direction. In some domains of knowledge, the developing person is guided towards increasing differentiation and hierarchical integration, while simultaneously (the

same person) is guided towards maintaining syncretic developmental states, or developing into those from a differentiated perspective.

The example from the kindergarten birthday party illustrates this well. Instead of a focus on differentiation of MYSELF from MY ROLE ('pupil', 'citizen' etc.), the collective-cultural guidance is oriented precisely towards elimination of such distinctions. Yet in the activities on cognitive-developmental (school-learning) tasks, the same children may be socially guided towards elimination of their syncretic reasoning in favour of a formal-logical one. The opposite state of syncretism is discreteness. The *human socialization system is simultaneously oriented towards promotion of discrete organizational forms in some domains of experience, and syncretic forms in others.*

As human beings belong simultaneously to different social groups – in which they assume different roles – there is a possibility for social institutions to guide the chaining of different roles in accordance with a pre-determined social hierarchy of such roles. Chaining of such roles hierarchically could be seen as the first step towards *identity fusion* – the subordinate identities are fused into the hierarchically superior ones. They are not lost in the process, they merely become subordinate parts of a larger whole (see Figure 12.2).

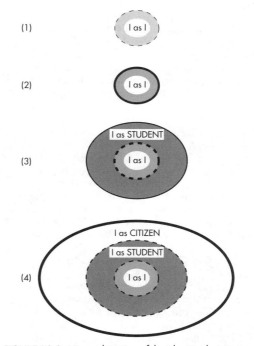

FIGURE 12.2 *Hierarchization of the identity chaining and fusing process*

AND HUMAN DEVELOPMENT

In Figure 12.2, the process of promotion of identity fusion is depicted in a general form. The emerging personal identity (I as I) of a child emerges in a home context, and consolidates (change from (1) to (2) in Figure 12.2). As the child enters a social institution – preschool or school – the new identity notion (I as STUDENT) enters into the child's life by way of taking the role of the student in the institution. The institution suggests to the child that the ' I as STUDENT' is superior to 'I as I', and includes the latter. The boundary of the latter in the context of 'I as STUDENT' becomes permeable (Figure 12.2 {3}). At the next step (step {4}) a still further hierarchically superior identity suggestion 'I as CITIZEN' emerges in the child's life, and is promoted to subsume the other two. Again, the boundaries of 'I as I' and 'I as STUDENT' become permeable, so the institutions that attempt to capture the child's identity *as citizen* can operate through the subsumed identities as *student* and as *I*.

The permeability of the boundaries indicates the syncretic nature of this identity fusion suggestion. It is a powerful social control mechanism for any social institution, since it opens the possibility for linking personal-cultural functions with those of social control. Consider the following statements – moralistic insinuations – which operate across the permeable boundaries depicted in Figure 12.2:

(a) Aren't *you* ashamed of *your* [action x]? *As a good student, you* should be ashamed!'
(b) 'Don't *you feel bad* that you are not eager to volunteer for military service? *As a good citizen*, one must be ready to defend our country. And *you were such a good student* in high school!'

The emphasized parts of these insinuation messages indicate the linkages between the assumed hierarchy of fused identities. In (a), the insinuator suggests to the person that his or her 'I am I' system, as being incorporated into the 'I as student' system, should get the person *by themself* to feel appropriately ashamed. In (b), the insinuation on the theme 'I as CITIZEN' is worked through the 'I as STUDENT', with the aim of getting the core personal 'I as I' feel – again by the person's own initiative – in a socially prescribed way.

The effectiveness of such identity fusing efforts is demonstrated in human lives repeatedly: every sacrifice of a young human life for a political cause can in principle bear with it a personal-cultural and collective-cultural construction of martyrdom, and the positive evaluation of the loss for the cause (for example, Sande, 1992). Cemeteries

filled with tombstones for soldiers killed for their motherland, or for the sake of revolution and progress, are symbols that fortify this identity fusion for those who were lucky to stay alive, and who may have only remote knowledge of the reasons for one or another war in the past. The identity fusion mechanisms are often used for political goals in the case of summoning the energies of adolescents for social or military action (see Chapter 13).

At times, the specific hierarchy can be the target of social suggestions. John F. Kennedy's often quoted maxim 'don't ask yourself what your country can do for you, ask yourself what you can do for your country' is a moralistic suggestion to maintain the hierarchy of the identity chaining and fusing process as described in Figure 12.2, in contrast to an opposite hierarchical scheme (where all institutional roles are subordinated to 'I as I'). The social order maintains the field of social role hierarchies in a state that fits itself, and then uses these hierarchies to attempt to guide, change and capture the developing personal cultures of persons who act within their socially structured environments.

Parallel promotion of syncretic and discrete sides of the personal culture

Every social system promotes two sides – syncretism and discreteness – in human personal cultures. It is noteworthy that the distinction between differentiation-promoting and syncretism-promoting experience domains proceeds roughly by the division of human psychological functions into 'cognitive' and 'affective'. It can be seen that in the industrialized societies (with emphasis on formal schooling, and progress in science and technology) the cognitive functions of children are persistently guided towards overcoming their undifferentiated (syncretic) state, towards the heights of the rigour of rationality. Yet, at the same time, the guidance of the affective domain – especially that side of it which entails potential controllability by a social institution – can demonstrate promotion of syncretic organizational forms (see Figure 12.3 below). Here we can observe gradual ontogenetic separation of the differentiation and syncretic forms, with temporary possibilities for their interpenetration (unification). Periods of such unification are themselves parts of social guidance of the differentiation of the two lines – they are temporary, limited by socially created boundaries, and – therefore – not dangerous for the canalization process. Thus, adolescents in many societies are allowed 'periods of culturally allowed heterosensual experimentation' (see Chapter 13 on

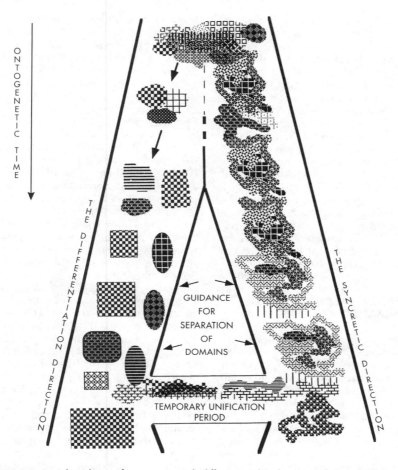

FIGURE 12.3 *Social guidance of persons towards differentiated and syncretic forms of self-organization*

Gikuyu practices of *ngweko*), even outside of any immediate supervision by the elders. Yet these periods work precisely for the social order that provides for the temporary and only indirectly controlled moments of 'regression' from the established order. In Bakhtin's terms, such periods of temporary unification are cases of carnivals. In a similar vein, on some occasions, such unification of the syncretic and the discrete is socially demanded (rather than merely socially allowed). This entails examples of children's enforced participation in religious rituals (for example, obligatory prayer in a schooling institution), or collective organization of ritualistic trance in many societies. These episodes of unification of the syncretic and the discrete are genetic dramatisms (as described in Chapter 3).

It is interesting that the necessary result of the process described in Figure 12.3 is the heterogeneity of the human personal culture. This fits well with the post-modern reflections upon the 'local nature of knowing' and fragmentation of human experiences. Yet this seems not to be anything new – the 'real person' in any society where formal schooling and industry are emphasized is expected to be rational in their professional activities, while being fully irrationally bonded to his or her identity objects – family, community, country and religious institution. The difference between the so-called 'primitive' and 'non-primitive' societies – to use the terms widely accepted by early twentieth century anthropology – is in how the boundaries between differentiation-promotion and syncretism-promotion are drawn on the map of everyday experiences in different settings.

Promotion of syncretic relations with the environment is often accomplished through symbolic marking of concrete environmental contexts. Children's environments are usually saturated with value-laden non-verbal signs. These range from objects and designs set up by parents in the child's immediate environment (bedroom designs, for example), to children's participation (with adults) in the activities in public settings which entail such symbols. Different kinds of religious symbols usually surround human beings – young and old – in their collective-cultural environments. Interestingly, these symbols are integrated into the personal-cultural systems of children with remarkable persistence over their childhood. The pervasiveness of these symbols is the hope of the social world to guide the child towards internally constructing an analogue to the external suggestions. The crucial point is keeping the developing child within the field that is saturated by such guiding signs. A formal schooling system is the setting where the task of keeping the child within the field is efficiently accomplished.

THE SOCIAL DEMAND SETTING OF FORMAL SCHOOLING

Formal schooling is a major intervention into the lives of children in their regular, everyday life contexts. It separates the children from their immediate contexts, while providing them with knowledge that would not be available in their local communities. Provision of such knowledge is not a socially neutral, or benevolent, act. Knowledge from outside involves somebody else's – the knowledge provider's – goal-oriented efforts to change the local ways of living and understanding the world. By providing outsiders' knowledge, the schools operate in the service of social powers that attempt to change the local ways (Watson-Gegeo and Gegeo, 1992).

The introduction of formal education is an act of purposeful social distancing of children from their background collective-cultural contexts. Formal schooling is oriented towards the children's establishment of their personal-cultural identities – in terms of values, loyalties and ways of thinking and feeling – in accordance with the expectations of social units larger than the children's family, kin group, or local community. This distinction is often semiotically marked, by setting up clear boundaries between the school territory and that of the outside world.

Symbolic marking of the territory and functions of schools in different societies

Schools are regularly 'foreign elements' in their local community settings. The distance between the school and the local context is created in ways that *both separate and unify the two places at the same time*. This is similar to the semiotic marking of other boundaries – those of the home and the street (see Hirschon, 1981) etc. By semiotic marking of the boundary of the school, the separation is given meaning that unifies the two sides.

Flagpoles   Let us consider the spatial lay-out of high schools in the United States. It is very often the case that the front side of the main building of the school is marked by two or three flagpoles (with flags on them) of unequal height. In case of a three-flagpole arrangement, the tallest of the poles is for the US Federal flag, the next highest for the flag of the given state, and the lowest – the flag of the school. There are a number of psychologically relevant moments in this boundary marking. First, *the dominance hierarchy of the social institutions* that the school represents (the United States > the state > the school itself) is encoded into the relative length of the flagpoles. Yet, that dominance hierarchy need not reflect the full set of actual relations. The Federal Government need not actually create the rules – or at least many of the rules – governing how local schools operate. For example, there is no centralized censorship of school libraries in the United States, while local (community-level) censorship, with elimination of representative classic books from school libraries because of their 'moral' or 'ideological' contents, has been documented. Thus, the actual symbolic display of the dominance hierarchy through the flagpoles may be a misrepresentation of the actual relations between the three social institutions. Yet that is not the crucial point: it is the local community (through its members) that is marked as different from the school, *yet united with it*, through the flags. While the markers separate ('push away to some distance') the local community, they simultaneously mark that community as a part of another social unit. The local school is subsumed under the larger social units (the state, the United States). Thus, the role of the flags and flagpoles is to create a distance that at the same time is unifying the 'outsider' (the community) and the 'insider' (the school).

The next important moment is the use of the front entrance area of the school for this symbolic display. The front/back distinction in the case of schools is similar to that of homes: the front is the direction from where outsiders are assumed to approach the institution, whereas the day-to-day running of the school may entail uses of side entrances, with the front door possibly never used (except for special public events).

Thirdly, the internal spatial structure of access within the school illustrates its role as a micro-society. The inhabitants of that society are (mainly) of two social strata – the teachers and the students. Each of them may inhabit different territorial parts of the school: the teachers may be secluded in the 'teachers' lounge' (or 'staff room') to where access by students may be limited. It is often the case that a student must ask for special permission to enter the teachers' territory during a break, so as to contact a particular teacher.

'Visas' to the bathroom In addition to the teacher/students symbolic segregation, the social control by the school over students' activities can take specific forms of symbolic capital construction. The physiological needs for elimination can capture students at any time – including in the middle of classroom activities. That would entail a temporary exist from the classroom field (which is under the teacher's control). Yet the satisfaction of elimination needs – going to the bathroom – is a biological necessity. Only the students know their needs (and can also easily pretend to have those), yet the teacher (who has no way of knowing) is the immediate social authority to allow for a trip to the lavatory, or not.

Yet, in an effort to socially regulate the informal teacher–student 'bathroom visit negotiation' processes, in a number of US schools one can find institutionalized 'bathroom passes' – special forms of 'exit visitors visas' from the classroom that indicate that the given student has the teacher's permission to go to the bathroom during the lessons. On the side of school organization, such 'bathroom passes' in US schools of course guarantee 'law and order' outside of classrooms during lesson times. Another school official, meeting a child in the corridor, can immediately verify the 'legality' of the child's current presence outside of the classroom. Yet, at the same time, the institutional introduction of such a passport system creates the psychological opposition between the power-holders (teachers) and the class of subordinates. As a result, the students and teachers become mutually opposite and distrustful 'social classes' within the school.

Similarities with indigenous formal school systems Aside from the tradition of European-type education, there are numerous other inventions of formal schooling contexts that create similar special locations for the school. Many of such 'formal schooling' contexts are extensions of rituals of adolescent introduction to the realm of secret knowledge of the given society. The West African 'bush school' (which is the quasi-public part of the secret society – *poro* – activities) is a good example (Fulton, 1972; Watkins, 1943).

The 'bush school' is closely related to the adolescent initiation processes. In the case of the Vai (in Liberia), the 'bush school' was set up in a special location in a forest. That location was never to be used for other purposes. All the constructed dwellings for a given session of the 'bush school' are burned at the end of the session. Each district (sub-chiefdom) has its own 'bush school', which in its organization can be likened to a military training camp[1] or a strict boarding school, in which

> Once boys have entered the forest, they are at no time allowed to return to the towns until their training is complete; nor under any circumstances are female visitors tolerated. No one except members of the society is permitted entrance to the area. If uninitiated persons approach it, they must make their presence known so that none of its secrets will be exposed. If a man trespasses, he will be initiated, while a woman under such circumstances will be killed. (Watkins, 1943, p. 668)

The hyper-secrecy of the initiation school is a way to build the symbolic value of the new skills, and to create group unity. The boys are taught a variety of skills characteristic of the adult male repertoire in the 'bush school'. They move from child roles into those of responsible adults. In this respect, the West African 'bush school' is similar to European-type boarding schools that were brought into the locations of colonized countries in order to change the children into the mores of the governing social institution (see Ellis, 1996 on a story of an American Indian boarding school).

Social engineering: homogenization and standardization

Formal education in any society promotes standardization and homogenization of the psychological functions involved – thinking, knowing and feeling – for groups or populations of persons. Such efforts are based on ideologies – formal schooling is an inevitably ideological enterprise. Different ideologies, of course, can be oriented towards different goals, hence issues of education within a given society are easily targets for public political disputes. At times this leads to institutional censorship of the contents of education – of textbook contents (see Delfattore, 1992). Any focus on 'political correctness' is an act of social censorship: the 'correctness' notion implies the personal following of the suggested 'right' ways of expression.

Furthermore, the semiotic texture – the social demand setting – of formal schooling frameworks bears the marks of the school's ideological background (religious or secular). It is the organization, often implicit, of the activities of children at school that carries the function of such ideological orientation. Oftentimes the main knowledge-providing orientation of schooling is not different in schools of different backgrounds (for example, the mathematics or physics studied at school may be similar), but how these basic curricular parts are taught, how the children are evaluated, and in what kinds of semiotically encoded activity settings such teaching/learning takes place would vary from one kind of school to another. The primary curriculum (of knowledge) may be the same, while the secondary curriculum (direction of social identification processes) would be different.

The crucial feature of any educational system is that persons who participate in it are necessarily always participating in some other, more central to them, system of experience – that of their own lives. The locus of any educational effort is persons' personal cultures, which (as was pointed out above), are not *directly* changeable by any external social suggestions. Hence we see in the context of formal education, efforts of attempting to find access ways into the internalization/ externalization processes of the students. All activities in the context of the school can be viewed as exercises *of directed internalization*. This goes hand in hand with *guided externalization* – the students are at different times required to bring out to the 'public sphere' (dominated by the teacher, but also possibly accessible to other students) their understanding (constructed internally) of some aspect of knowledge.

School as a cultivation place
In any society where formal schooling exists, it is an institutionalized version of intervention into the ordinary collective-cultural organization of human development. In terms of the opposition NATURAL < > CULTURAL (see Chapter 4, Figure 4.1), formal schooling belongs to the realm of *cultivation* (while informal education would belong to the natural kind of human cultural development). The image of cultivation of crops is quite adequate, since in the context of formal schooling the focus is on cohorts of learners (rather than particular individual ones). The cohorts can be defined on the basis of various index characteristics: by age set (for example, selecting children of particular age into a particular grade); by gender (different schools for girls and boys); by social class background (accepting only children from some social classes into the particular schools); or by way of expected outcomes of the schooling (for example, the distinction of the *Gymnasium* as the German secondary school preparing students for university versus the *Realschule* that would guide the student towards more practical professions). The

specific ways in which in a given country (and historical time) these criteria are used for creating a relatively homogenized set of students indicates the goals of the social institutions that govern formal education. Sociopolitical changes in a country usually lead to changes in the system of formal education.

HOMOGENIZATION OF CHILDREN'S CONDUCT AND BEING IN THE SCHOOL CONTEXT

Homogenization of the targets of formal education by age is by far the most widespread of the formal schooling practices. It is built upon basic cognitive development. Questions about 'are children age X ready for school?' are questions about age set construction. Restrictions upon acceptance of younger-aged children into school 'too early', and efforts to gain control over children of a particular age to go to school, indicate the social construction of a relatively homogeneous age set. It is the process of selection of targets for educational intervention. Given the public nature of the intervention, the homogenized base for it is necessary. Once taken into the context of formal schooling, the children are subjected to recurrent activity routines which further create the cohesion of the age set (grade). The social world of a school is filled by a sequence of semiotically created action rituals, as well as by different unifying objects (school uniforms, uniform contents of children's pencil boxes, textbooks etc.).

Classroom conduct as an example of homogenization

The context of a classroom is not merely an enclosed space in a school compound. Rather, it is a symbolic space the function of which is to keep the children 'within the field' of the prescribed activities. Within that field, the teacher can organize the structure of children's activities in many different ways. Which of those ways are used in a given context is a compromise between the specific educational task and the ideological social guidance functions of the particular society's educational setting. Let us contrast two situated activity contexts – a strict teacher-determined activity setting (in a Moroccan public school), and an 'open classroom' in a Canadian middle-class environment.

An example from a Moroccan public school The Moroccan system of formal education is in itself variable, including classroom settings of Koranic schools as well as public school classrooms arranged after French models.

The Koranic school follows the educational philosophies of Islam, while the public school system propagates the social position of the Moroccan government. In both kinds of classrooms the central and authoritarian role of the teacher is encoded into the conduct routines within the classroom. For example,

> The French writing lesson. The teacher calls for the chalkboards . . . Teacher says, 'Ready.' Everyone is sitting up at his desk with chalkboard in left hand and a piece of chalk in the right. Right hands are poised. The teacher reads aloud a sentence from her notebook. Unexpectedly no one moves, right hands still remain poised. The teacher slaps the desk with a ruler. The children at once bend over their slates, working slowly and painstakingly with their chalk. Several minutes later the teacher slams the ruler again. All slates go straight up in the air at arm's length, facing forward in the fashion of a placard parade. The teacher marches up and down the aisles, saying 'Wrong, correct, correct . . .' She slams her ruler for the third time and the boards are lowered, erased, and chalk poised for the next sentence. (Miller, 1977, p. 146)

This example of the structure of classroom conduct is maximally teacher-centred. The children are trained in unison within strictly determined time 'chunks' for a given task (writing a dictated sentence). One can look at such conduct structures from different perspectives. An ideologist for 'free education' may find this kind of 'drill' to be suppressive of 'children's creativity'. Proponents of basic education may emphasize that the teacher's activities in this dictation exercise are most adequately used. Yet both of these interpretations overlook the specific task-kind dependency of the given example. There are moments in classroom contexts where the maximum control role belongs to the teacher. In the same school, there can be other settings where the teacher's role is left to the background.

The example from a Canadian middle-class third grade classroom

This seems to provide, at first approach, a very different picture:

> A bright, well-equipped third-grade classroom. Miss Simms explains that today they will begin work on their Christmas pictures. They will draw with crayons . . .
>
> She explains the task. They will do, altogether, two Christmas pictures each, one today in crayon, one next week in paint. One picture will be on the religious side of Christmas, such as the manger scene,

the wise men, or the like . . . the other on Santa Claus . . . or something on the non-religious side . . .

> 'Now, you have two choices,' she declares. 'You can do either the manger picture or the Santa Claus picture this week – as you like. Then you will do the other one next week.' (Smollett, 1975, p. 221)

What the teacher accomplishes in this set-up of classroom tasks goes beyond mere organization of the specific drawing tasks. She creates a focus on choice by the children by themselves – on a task field that is strictly pre-determined as to what will be accomplished by the end (two pictures, one religious, the other not; one in crayon, the other in paint). While the task-field is fully determined, the ways of how to cover the whole field are left to individual children to 'fill in'.

The choice given to the children is not different from the lack of choice we saw above in the case of the Moroccan classroom – at the level of specific accomplishments. The children are only given, in the Canadian case, the *illusory feeling of 'their own' choice* of how to reach the goals. This fits the general social expectations for the consumer role in society. Persons put into consumer roles are expected to make choices between ready-made options, be these political candidates or brands of jeans in a shop, and to have worked out their clearly specified personal opinions – evaluative statements about the object of the opinion. In contrast, the consumer is guided away from questions about how the different choices have been made by their constructors, and *how one might create a new, not yet existing* option. That latter direction would characterize the producer role orientation, which in any society is carefully guarded by the social institutions that control the production of novelty in those areas of sociopolitical and economic life that allows for some, but not all, individual innovations to proceed.

Children, of course, challenge the efforts to guide their activities into the realm of mere choice-makers. In the Moroccan classroom, these challenges were eliminated from the picture. In that respect, that setting was freed from any counter-action possibility by the children (similarly to the 'multiple choice testing' frameworks elsewhere, see below). In Miss Simms's classroom, however, negotiation of boundaries of the task field is evident:

> Several children begin to put questions to Miss Simms, exploring the boundaries of their choices. 'Can we do it in pencil?' asks Tom. 'No, do it in crayon,' says Miss Simms, 'It must be in crayon.' Little Brenda whispers to another child: '. . . hard to do manger in paint; . . . try it in crayon first.' 'Miss Simms,' asks Brenda, 'can I make both pictures of the

manger?' 'No,' says Miss Simms, 'you have a choice – one subject for one picture, one for the other.' 'Can both pictures be in crayon?' asks a boy. 'No.' Brenda tries again: 'Miss Simms, can I make both pictures of the manger if I put Santa Claus in both of them?' Miss Simms walks to another part of the room without responding. (Smollett, 1975, p. 222)

The boundary negotiations of the task field are handled by Miss Simms not differently from the Moroccan teacher described above, only with the difference that the children have the opportunity to construct their challenges (which are invariably denied).

General similarities and differences between examples Thus, in a general sense, we could characterize the two conduct demand settings in a very straightforward way:

The Moroccan teacher:
TASK GIVEN ⎯⎯⎯⎯⎯⎯▶ OUTCOME
FROM
CHILDREN

Miss Simms:
TASK → CHALLENGES → CHALLENGES → OUTCOME
GIVEN   ALLOWED   DENIED   FROM
                                   CHILDREN

The middle ground in Miss Simms' interaction with children – allowing challenges to the task field boundary and denying the challenges firmly – prepares the children for efforts to negotiate with authorities while accepting the negative outcomes for such negotiations. This fits with the needs of social institutions where *both* the active efforts by individuals and their institutional selection of their innovations are concurrently emphasized. This is a preparatory ground for children's participation in democracy, where all citizens are given their chances to express their opinions, while the ones towards whom these opinions are voiced have equal opportunities not to listen. The Moroccan example operates differently – even a minute deviation from the fulfilment of the task would be observable as a 'great rebellion'.

Teachers' actions guiding children towards their future development

The comparison of the conduct structures in the two classrooms brings us to the most general question regarding teachers' roles: how, and through which techniques, can they guide children's development? The examples given above indicate the tactics of maintaining a social status quo – either in terms of strict rule-following, or as

rule-following choosers between given options in the consumerist environment. These two directions are certainly not all that teachers' tactics of promotion entail. While keeping children within the field of educational impact, the teacher's particular communicative actions relating to the task are parts of the zone of proximal development (Vygotsky's concept, see Chapter 3).

Three different tactics of the teacher's promotional effort are described in Figure 12.4. In any specific classroom task, some means (M1, M2, M3 . . .) can be utilized to achieve different ends (R1, R2, R3 . . .). Three tactics of the teacher are shown in Figure 12.4.

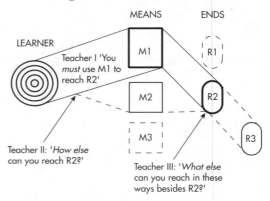

FIGURE 12.4 *Tactics of promotion of boundary maintenance and transcendence in teaching/learning settings*

The tactic (observed in the example of Miss Simms, above) that organizes the attainment of the task without promoting either alternative means to an end, or extension of mastered means to new ends, is that of Teacher I. This tactic does not work within the 'zone of proximal development' – it merely organizes the ways in which the given task is accomplished. In the example of the Canadian classroom of Miss Simms, it was the children's boundary negotiation efforts that were moving the drawing activity towards their own 'zone of proximal development', basically against resistance from the teacher.

Any tactic, be it introduced by teacher or learner, that promotes further development of the person needs to work towards the transfer of the here-and-now established means to new tasks. This is depicted by Teacher II in Figure 12.4, suggestion for the learner to look for alternative means to the same end, as well as by Teacher III, who suggests to the learner to extend the given solution to new tasks. Through such suggestions, the teacher prepares the learner for open-ended search for new ways and new solutions.

The teacher's suggestions to the learner are not mere benevolent acts of guidance, but rather complicated social acts. The same teacher can encode in the same suggestion to the learner a different *affective atmosphere* of the encounter. Thus, let us consider two different affective atmospheres for Teacher III in Figure 12.4:

> Benevolent Teacher III: 'What else can you reach in these ways besides R2?' ('Having solved this problem, of course you can solve others.')
>
> Malevolent Teacher III: 'What else can you reach in these ways besides R2?' ('Well, you succeeded in this, but surely you can't do it on others.')

The difference between the 'hidden agendas' of these two teachers is embedded in the meta-communicative channel in teacher–student interaction. In the context of the classroom, the teachers create a general atmosphere of the social group.

The social roles of 'rote learning'

The question of drill – at times considered as 'rote learning' of educational materials – is closely connected with the social organization of formal education systems. At the same time, it is indispensable for specific learning tasks. Materials that need to be mastered well, but for which there is limited or no previous knowledge base to support other tactics of mastery, become objects for rote learning. Within the same school, and same discipline, rote learning can co-exist with other modes of learning in ways that mutually support one another.

Rote learning is often accepted within the school setting when ideological value socialization is a desired goal. Thus, in the context of Islamic education, the following example illustrates the functions of rote learning contexts:

> A Muslim should be able to read the Qua'ran [Koran] even without being able to understand the words, *because the ability to read the Qua'ran itself has been used to evoke in people a response to the teachings of Islam* which sociologically has been very valuable. Beyond this most of these people will hardly go, *but provided they learn in their childhood to respond to the music of Arabic consonants and vowels*, and to the rhythms of the Qua'ran, *they will continue throughout their lives to have an emotional attachment to it*. (Husain and Ashraf, quoted in Wagner, 1983, pp. 185–186; added emphasis)

In a general sense, any educational activity is framed to put the learner into a specific sequence of teaching/learning action. These actions always carry a double function: direct knowledge or skill acquisition on the one hand, and indirect preparation of the person to the socially expected ways of feeling, thinking and acting on the other. The total activity structure of school classrooms gives a microscopic picture of the whole of the society for which the school stands.

Adjustments to homogenization: relations between different rule systems

A child brought into the school context is set up within a field from which there is no exit. All formal schooling systems keep the students within the field of educational activities – on the school territory, within a classroom, and often within a particular seat. Constraining of children's freedom of movement in the school context is similar to the phenomenon of infant swaddling (or cradle-board use, see Chapter 9). The function of such restraint is to maintain the children's activities within a range in which different educational efforts – both curricular and extra-curricular – can be inserted into the children's activity structure.

Given this function of the school, children who come from family backgrounds that are different would be faced with the need to coordinate different rule systems. By definition of its informal education focus, any home environment is different from a school environment. The contrast is especially profound if the collective-cultural background of the home is different from that of the school.

Discrepancy between the home and school rule structures

A case description of North American (Canadian) Cree Indian children's experiences between home and school may provide an illustration here (Sindell, 1974). Before Cree children enter school, they have few limits upon their actions in their home environments. They can explore their natural surroundings, there are no demarcated boundaries beyond which the children must not proceed. Of course, the children's lives depend upon the economic activities of their elders. Thus, the Cree hunting groups are small, and hence the number of children in a particular hunting group varies. A child may thus be the only one in a given group, or have very few peers. Adults are involved in their activities, rather than being involved in 'wasting' their attention on children. As a result, a Cree child in his or her home environment may spend much or all of the winter without playmates, and plays alone. Anything the child can reach is an adequate object for play. Of course, parents guard the child's contact with dangerous objects – they would divert the child's attention away from the object, or remove the object, *but without reprimanding the child*. Two- or 3-year-old children of the Cree have been observed to play with axes. The children have no fixed 'bedtime' – they fall asleep when tired. In general, the only limits adults put on children are related to immediate environmental dangers.

When Cree children, after having experienced this matter-of-fact free exploratory world at home, enter school (of the boarding school kind), they encounter not only many restrictions, but a multitude of *meaningless* (from their vantage point) restrictions upon their conduct. The school regime is oriented to control the conduct of many children within the same spatial confines. The children are required to eat three times a day at specified hours. They must wake up and go to sleep at collectively set, uniform times. They have to learn a number of arbitrary rules: for example, they may not be allowed to use the front side stairway of the school building. They are not allowed to leave the territory of the school, demarcated by the boundary of the school yard. When they are allowed to move outside of that boundary, an adult is required to accompany them.

Almost all of the child's needs require assistance from others in the school context. The child must depend upon the 'counsellor' of the group in which he lives for clean clothes, soap, toothpaste, and even toilet paper when it runs out. He must line up to get these resources at times of the counsellor's convenience (the first words of English that Cree children are reported as learning are 'line up!': Sindell, 1974, p. 336).

These everyday routine differences between Cree homes and Anglo-Canadian schools are combined with different main goal orientations proliferated in the two settings. For the Cree home conditions, lack of competition is a value taken for granted in the kin-group context. In the school, this is countered by guidance of children towards competition with other children on school tasks. This contrast has other concomitant features. Inhibiting overt aggression is valued among the Cree, who maintain positive affective ties with other kinship group members despite inter-individual differences (and mutual misunderstandings). This is crucial for coordination of group activities in a hunting–trapping group. Aggression for the Cree *includes not only fighting* but also direct contradicting of anybody else's requests, refusing others' direct request, and raising one's voice in conversations. These forms of conduct are unacceptable for any respectable person – and become stigmatized in the case

of drunkards. Yet, at the same time, laughing at other people's mistakes is not considered aggressive. This all does not mean that aggression does not exist among the Cree. There are accepted means of channelling it – through gossip, teasing and threat of witchcraft.

When a Cree child enters an Anglo-Canadian boarding school, the rule system of the setting expects almost the opposite from them than is usual at home. Open aggression displays are accepted, and different versions of re-channelled aggression (gossip) are actively discouraged. Television and observation of white Canadian children's conduct is a constant role model image for openly aggressive conduct. Furthermore, the children can be exposed to the behaviour of teachers which, from the Cree point of view, would qualify as that of persons who have lost their self-respect ('drunken behaviour'): tired and overburdened by duties, the teachers in the school may yell at the children, speak to them sternly, and even hit them.

Yet the fact of being kept within a confined environment, and the directed educational input into the Cree children in the boarding school, leads to effects:

> After one year of school parents report that their children 'only want to play' and are not interested in performing their chores. Thus, children have already begun to reject their parents' definitions of proper behavior. This kind of intergenerational conflict increases dramatically with each year of school experience. It is exacerbated because the children are in school all winter and thus, fail to learn the technical skills related to hunting and trapping as they mature. This has serious implications for identity conflicts in adolescence since the children are unable to fulfill their parents' expectations (Sindell, 1974, p. 339)

The Cree example leads to an emphasis about formal schooling as a vehicle of colonization by one social institutional power of another (indigenous) social system. Introduction of formal schooling in any context is an act that forces the previously existing, collective-cultural system, to adjust itself to the value orientations and conduct patterns of the social power that introduces the school.

Yet the history of introduction of formal schooling has historical results beyond the children. Parents of the children can accept the role of the school to take their children's development in directions that transcend the local social contexts.

Constructed mutual role expectations between home and school conditions

Human beings create both harmony and disharmony in their lives. The latter, when becoming functional in the social and psychological domains, turns into a new kind of harmony – harmony through disharmony. The externally introduced formal schooling framework can become part of the needs of the local community – yet a part relative to which there is constant ambivalence. On the one hand, the formal school brings in knowledge for children that could open ways for new forms of subsistence. On the other hand, the very same school distances the children from their traditional roles, and produces insufficiency in the basic skills (see the case of Cree Indian children not developing adequate survival skills due to boarding school).

Harry Wolcott (1967) took the role of a teacher in a Kwakiutl school in Canada. He encountered a divisive orientation on behalf of the local community in his efforts to become closer. Instead, the local community members expected the teacher to be a distant and all-knowing person:

> The teacher is expected to be 'smart' about the teaching and writing – that domain is left almost exclusively to him. Teachers are also perceived as a sort of repository of facts: 'Ask him, he's the teacher.' When the teacher does not have the answer surprise is usually registered. This expectation contrasts with the behavior of villagers, most of whom show little interest in commanding facts and minimize any evidence of controlling information, especially to an outsider. A frequently heard response to any inquiry is, 'I just wouldn't know.' (Wolcott, 1967, p. 81)

The opposition between school and community leads to the establishment of appropriate complementary role expectations. The teacher is an 'enemy' – from the outside world, who yet must know what the insiders do not. The teacher is expected to be a stern disciplinarian (when needed), and maintain their distance from children and villagers.

Collaboration between home and school conditions

Even if the formal schooling system is meant to break the informal schooling background of the home conditions, it can do so in ways that entail cooperation of the parents with the goals of the institution.

Continuities and discontinuities between home and school in the social demand settings have usually been seen as two opposing categories. Yet for the actual persons who develop, the contexts of home, school and other (for example, life activities that take place outside of home and out of school – in the streets, playgrounds, forests, others' homes, workplace) are personally coordinated. The person moves constantly between these various settings, and coordinates the experiences of each with one another.

The case of Japanese institutionalization of the formal education system entails a social requirement for and promotion of close cooperation between the parents and the teachers. This coordination begins early – already at the nursery school level. Nursery schools are not parts of the system of compulsory education in Japan. This means that these institutions – for 3–6-year-old children – are mostly private and outside of governmental control. The *yochien* is a nursery where the primary focus is 'becoming a Japanese' (Allison, 1991). Aside from an elaborate rule structure for the children in the nursery, there is a specific form of communication between the nursery and home established through a crucial cultural object – the lunch-box (*ōbentō*). The mother prepares the lunch-box for the child, and the child eats it (while in nursery). Yet the co-ordination of the parents and the teachers takes place through the expectations for the contents of the lunch-box: it is expected that the mother will prepare Japanese food in quantities presumed correct for a young child, and the child will consume it in full, every day (Allison, 1991). Rice in the Japanese meaning system is of direct value as an identity object – it is an indicator of wealth as well as of participation in a cultural group (Ohnuki-Tierney, 1993).

The mother's personal culture becomes institutionally bound through the making of the lunch-box for the child. Her conduct as mother is evaluated (by the nursery teachers) by her success in making the lunch-box. More importantly, she herself begins to evaluate her success through the child's *ōbentō*. Later, as the child moves on to school, the mother's assistance in the child's preparedness for the school tasks becomes another self-identity object for the mother. It is the objects that the Japanese child carries from home to school – and which are made publicly observable *by their obligatory social display nature* – that become targets of coordination of the public and private domains.[2]

The success of Japanese school education in guaranteeing good results in students' achievement in different sciences is well documented (Stevenson et al., 1986). It has also been shown to give rise to stress internally (Inagaki, 1986). The success story of Japanese education can be seen in its *institutional appropriation of the family*, turning it into a part of the formal education system. The parents – mothers – become additional teachers in the home conditions. They supervise children's homework, learn the expected knowledge together with their children (Lebra, 1984). They internalize their educational supporter/helper role (which was previously represented by the lunch-box preparation in preschool times). The parents organize additional after school activities for their children. The unification of the educational efforts of the home and of the school is of course guided by the school, but complemented by the mother's own self-value being made publicly visible by the child's performance in school.

Cognitive and social functions of formal deductive reasoning skills

The development of cognitive (mental) functions has two facets: that of knowledge creation (epistemological function) and that of mediating specific functions of social control. There exist three kinds of forms of logical inference – inductive, deductive and abductive (see Chapter 5). In the formal schooling contexts, these three are differentially promoted. The obedience orientation of any social institution would privilege the promotion of deductive reasoning. For different reality-related schooling tasks, the use of inductive reasoning may be emphasized. Yet the inductive reasoning is the privileged domain of the informal education system.

The main finding from comparisons of formally schooled and not-schooled persons in the realm of solving reasoning tasks is the mastery of automatization of the reliance on the recognized form of the task and the assumption of the deductive reasoning scheme at an instant (see Luria, 1976). For example, the following syllogism is given to a person:

MAJOR PREMISS: In the Far North, where there is snow, all bears are white.
MINOR PREMISS: Novaya Zemlya is in the Far North and there is always snow there.
QUESTION: What color are the bears there?

The benefit of formal education makes it possible to recognize this task immediately as a deductive reasoning task that has to be solved by simple application of rules. By following the rule – if ALL X are P and A is X, it follows that A is P. Yet unschooled subjects have found it impossible to accept the scheme trained in school. In Luria's expedition to Central Asia in the early 1930s, a 37-year-old illiterate Abdulrakhim from a remote Kashgar village responded to the presentation by assuming a strictly inductive orientation towards the task:

Abdulrakhim: There are different sorts of bears.
[the syllogism is repeated]
Abdulrakhim: I don't know; I have seen a black bear,

I have never seen any others . . . Each locality has its own animals; if it's white, they'll be white; if it is yellow, they will be yellow.
Experimenter: But what kinds of bears are there in Novaya Zemlya?
Abdulrakhim: We always speak only of what we see; we don't talk about what we haven't seen.
Experimenter: But what do my words imply? [the syllogism is repeated]
Abdulrakhim: Well, it's like this: our tsar isn't like yours, and yours isn't like ours. Your words can be answered by someone who was there, and if a person wasn't there he can't say anything on the basis of your words.
Experimenter: But on the basis of my words – In the North, where there is always snow, the bears are white – can you gather what kind of bears there are in Novaya Zemlya?
Abdulrakhim: If a man was sixty or eighty and had seen a white bear and had told about it, he could be believed, but I've never seen one and hence I can't say. That's my last word. Those who saw can tell, and those who didn't see can't say anything. (Luria, 1976, pp. 108–109)

The issue of refusal to assume a deductive reasoning scheme here indicates the major domain where the 'effects of formal schooling' can be found – in getting the schooled subjects automatically to recognize and assume a particular position in relation to a given task. Compare this with two scenarios of simple asking for directions in our everyday life. The first two steps of the two scenarios are the same:

1 *Asker*: How can one get from here to Park Avenue?
2 *Respondent*: Turn left to Downing, continue over the hill, and at the traffic light you are on Park.

The two scenarios differ in step 3:

3(A) *Asker*: *Right!* You know it correctly.
3(B) *Asker*: Thank you for your help.

The difference between 3(A) and 3(B) is in the communication (feedback) about the definition of the encounter. 3(A) indicates that the asker knew the answer, and was testing the respondent's knowledge. Answer 3(B) indicates that the asker did not know the answer, and now knows it. The counter-action to 3(A) is likely to be discomfort or anger ('so you were testing me – while I tried to help you'); to 3(B), feeling good.

Cultural construction of evaluation

An important aspect of formal schooling is the *formal evaluation* of the achievements of the students. Evaluation deals with the outcomes of the formal education – yet it is part of the process of channelling students through the formal system of schooling (for example, grade to grade transitions, directing students into different 'streams' of education – academic versus vocational – and, finally, rituals of finishing the participation in the given school system).

The formal European kind of schooling has been built upon the tradition of religious (monastery) schools, from which different kinds of secular schooling frameworks branched off. The evaluation systems of our present day bear resemblance to the ones used in the context of medieval times, or at the Protestant Reformation in Europe (in the sixteenth century).

The tactics of 'catechisms'

Catechisms were teaching/learning methods that emerged in Europe in the sixteenth century, as a result of the Protestant Reformation drive to make religious texts accessible to the lay public (Ozment, 1983). These were teaching devices that moved away – in a small step – from the then dominant 'rote learning'. The teacher (and author) of the catechism would *widen the field of possibilities* implied by the material, yet at the same time the control over the 'right answer' is rigorously maintained by the teacher. An example from Herbert Palmer's *An Endeavour of Making the Principles of Christian Religion . . . plaine and easie* (published in England in 1640) includes a sequence of questions given to the learner:

(1) QUESTION: What is a man's greatest business in this world? Is it to follow the world, and live as he list?
(2) ANSWER: No.
(3) QUESTION: Or is it to glorifie God, and save his own soule?
(4) ANSWER: Yes.
(5) QUESTION: So what is man's greatest business in this world?
(6) ANSWER: A man's greatest business in this world is to glorifie God and save his own soule. (Sommerville, 1983, p. 391)

There are a number of features of the activity. First, the catechism forces the learner to turn a potentially rigidly given desired suggestion – given here as line (6) – into a target of elaborate work on its meaning. Instead of repeating line (6) many times to master it (that would amount to 'rote learning'), the learner here *is guided to a sequence of standard questions*. By forcing the reader to repeat these standard questions, the learner is made to act within the field of acceptable possibilities – yet under full control by the teacher.

Secondly, these standard questions entail a

display of directing attention to the opposite of the fixed 'right answer'. This happens as the starting statement – (line 1), and is given the adequate answer (line 2). Only after exposing the learner to the opposite of what is expected from the learner, and to the denial of that opposite, would the catechism move the mental processes of the learner to the 'right' question and its answer (lines 3 and 4).

Thirdly (in line 5), the catechism entails the guidance of the learner to construct their own answer – along the pre-determined 'right' pattern – to the question. By forcing the learner to do that on their own the illusion of personal agency is created. A 'rote learner' of line 6 merely follows the instructions to learn that line; a person who is asked the question in line 5, and reads its full answer in line 6 is involved in an act of participation of an active kind. Yet the content in both cases – 'rote learning' and 'learning through catechism' – remains the same. The catechism provides the full right answer (which has to be read, rather than created). The opposition between the 'right' and the 'wrong' answers is thus emphasized in the catechism, whereas it is not part of the 'rote learning'.

Modern catechisms: multiple choice tests

The principles of catechisms are put into contemporary practice in the case of multiple choice testing formats of evaluation, to which there exists a corresponding pattern of knowledge construction in the teaching/learning process. As evaluation methods, multiple choice tests emphasize the recognition memory for mutually exclusive facts. They do not press for synthesis of new knowledge and in the case of ambiguity about the nature of implied knowledge would force a rule-governed 'right' answer to the question.

An example of the multiple-choice test format where the knowledge is not in question is an arithmetic test:

How much is $2 + 4$?
Choices: 4 5 6 7 8

A person who has mastered addition can easily calculate the undoubtedly correct answer, and choose it from the given alternatives. The person can also guess – and happen to be 'right'. From the right or wrong answers, it is impossible to re-construct the ways in which the answer was generated. Guessing the answer rightly, and calculating it, are not separable here.

Consider another example, taken (purposefully) from a knowledge domain where all parts of the whole are equally important. Yet the question suggests otherwise:

What is the most important part of human body:
     Choices: brain heart liver lungs

There is no 'right' answer to this question, as all the organ systems that are mutually inter-dependent are equally necessary for the life of the human body. None of them can be eliminated. Hence, the question – about the '*most* important' part – is itself misplaced. A 'right' answer to this question can only be created by consensual argumentation, and maintained by the social power of the evaluator. Note that the testee is not given some choices among the multiple choice list: absent are the answers 'all of the 4' and 'the question cannot be answered'. Here is the similarity with the seventeenth-century catechism described above: the field of possible answers is constructed as finite, and all answer choices are assumed to be independent of one another. These assumptions may fit for some domains of knowledge, and would not be applicable to many others. Any systemic knowledge cannot be directly tested by multiple choice tests.

Yet the use of multiple choice tests in educa-tional settings is widespread. Aside from mere convenience (of computerization of the grading procedures), such use entails the maintenance of the decision power of the tester over the testees. At the same time, such testing practices – and learning to be tested through such practices – guarantee the elimination of students' orientation towards synthesis of new knowledge, or crea-tivity. This does not mean that students become uncreative thanks to the multiple choice tests (if we were to remember the bi-directional culture transfer model, such testing should trigger counter-action to it, which is creative in itself). It merely means that schools with a strong focus on the multiple choice kind of knowledge guide students' general ways of relating to the world to those of needing pre-given choices to make, rather than being ready for the construction of their own (once the choices are not pre-given).

THE 'HIDDEN' CURRICULUM IN SCHOOL CONTEXTS: IDENTITY CHAINING IN EDUCATIONAL PRACTICE

Similarly to the promotion of syncretic psycho-logical phenomena in preschools and kinder-gartens (see Figure 12.3), identity chaining mechanisms are in place at school. The secondary (or 'hidden') curriculum in formal schooling entails purposeful promotion of identification with the particular social institutions. Most usually – given that the school represents socially more than itself – the promoted indentifications involve fusion of the immediately present (that is, the school) with the 'generalized other' institution. Thus, a particular Catholic school – with all its rituals, uniforms, ways of acting – promotes students' identification not only with the school, but with the Catholic social system as it exists, and, ultimately, with the Catholic religious values in general. Any national identity ideology operates along similar lines. Social institutions attempt to unite personal cultures of individuals with an object figure of identity (be that the teacher, sports star, a Lenin or a Hitler) – with subsequent generalization of the attained identity relation to general ideas (of socialism, nazism, or becoming a Liverpool football club fan). This process of identity chaining – a particular relationship with one (or multiple) figures in real life – becomes fused with general symbolic teachings.

Example from a Krishnamurti school

The context of a school in India built around the lines of the religious teachings of Krishnamurti can serve as an example for how the differen-tiating and unifying aspects of a formal education setting are organized (Thapan, 1986).

In Rishi Valley school (in Andra Pradesh, India – described by Thapan, 1986), the education was modelled according to the organizational structure of British boarding schools, while the ideological content was that of the teachings of Krishnamurti. The latter was centred on the gen-eral social representation of 'internal revolution within the mind', through which improvement of society was assumed to take place.

Given these goals, the central objective of the Krishnamurti school is guidance of children towards meditation – yet meditation within the lines of thought *in accordance with the ideology*. This guidance was mediated by the key role of the teacher. The teacher was responsible for bringing about academic excellence and 'psychological freedom' of the children by becoming a close yet authoritative friend.

The double role of teacher – as a friendly person, yet an authority figure – is an example of putting into practice the closeness and distance between the leader and the student (see further the practices in Noyes's community – Chapter 6). Such double linkage allows for the crafting of various school-context experiences.

The Krishnamurti school has been described to include two kinds of daily rituals that would build up intra-school social differentiation to-gether with 'we-feeling' as members of the institution.

The morning assembly The morning assembly is a daily event. Lasting about 20 minutes, it includes all children and adults of the school, without age, gender, or seniority segregation (which is present in the regular classroom activities over the whole day). The event is supposed to build a 'we-feeling' at the beginning of the day. Students sing and chant (in accordance with Krishnamurti's teachings), since

> the purpose of the musical component of the assembly is to *develop in the pupils an interest in, and an appreciation of, the elements of music such as rhythm and tone and the correct method of chanting*. The teachers say that the meaning of the songs and chants is not important and therefore do not explain their thematic content to the pupils. (Thapan, 1986, p. 206; added emphasis)

Note the similarity of this socialization tactic – reliance on appreciation of the rhythm of music and chanting – to the declared goals of Koranic pedagogy (above). The orientation of the morning assembly is towards acting outwards – the whole school in unison.

Promotion of internal meditation: the sunset ceremony By the end of the school day, all children of the Krishnamurti school are instructed to go to a special location to watch the sunset together. This joint experience lasts about 20 minutes. Students and teachers sit on the ground, or on rocks, facing the hills behind which the sun is setting. A bell is rung at the appropriate moment to start the event. Some of the students sit with closed eyes and meditate, others gaze at the hills and the sun – all in complete silence (Thapan, 1986, p. 208)

The sunset-watching (*asthachal*) ceremony is an institutional context promoting children's acting inwards – towards their intra-psychological (personal-cultural) construction. The focus is to guide students: after the school day, which includes orientation to externalization, the children's activities are reversely oriented inwards. The use of the ritual by children indicated that the children in the school had integrated the activity of meditation into their personal cultures:

> The response of the pupils [ages 12–17] in the school indicates that about half of them considered their experience of *asthachal* in terms of the relaxation they derived from it using such terms as 'peace', 'calm', 'silence', and expressing their ability to sort out their problems and worries, to understand their thoughts and to quieten and rest their minds at the end of a long day. Some of them expressed their appreciation of nature in terms of the 'beautiful' sunset, the setting and the surroundings. Others mentioned the 'joy' and

'happiness' they experience in *asthachal*, though a few referred to it as a dull routine activity. Moreover, the setting itself acquires a sacred value for the pupils as it is only used for this ritual: it is literally sacred, i.e., set apart. In their spare time, many of them visit the '*asthachal* place' to be alone and quiet. The setting is therefore associated with their positive experience at *asthachal* which they seek to renew at other times. (Thapan, 1986, pp. 208–209)

This depiction of the gradual internalization of the '*asthachal* place' as a special, personally meaningful 'sacred place' indicates the success of the school's cultural canalization efforts. By setting up a regular performance ritual in a special place and at recurrent times, the road is open for individual participants' personal construction of their meaning of the place, and their experiences within the place. The personal-cultural constructions vary, ranging from reflecting upon the ceremony as 'dull routine activity' to versions of personal feelings of beauty, devotion, or sacredness. Yet all of the participants in the ceremony are guided towards meditation – similarly to the Canadian classroom of Miss Simms (above).

Social institutions often embed into their ritual performance contexts moments of silence – usually interspersed with demands for prescribed actions. Psychologically, such sequential organization of outwards-oriented actions, followed by inwards-oriented actions, guides the relations of the person with the symbolic environment. This is central in guidance of people towards their own construction of goals based on their intra-psychological construction of imagination. Personal fantasies need to be turned into binding personal goals for the fantasies to guide human development (see Oettingen, 1997). A ritualistic setting where meditation is interspersed with specifically prescribed actions is a device to guide the person in that direction.

Internalizing value orientations

The full texture of school contexts guides children towards their personal construction of value orientations. For sure, neither the school – nor the informal education at home – can determine the specific value orientations the children will create in their personal cultures, but it can give it a direction for construction. Consider the following conversation between a Dutch anthropologist and a child from India:

> *Sukhail* [8-year-old Muslim child from Kerala, India]: My father thinks that caning is the best way to have children obey.

Question: But you, do you agree that teachers need to use the cane?

Sukhail: If a child makes mistakes it has to be beaten. Remembering the pain, it will never repeat the same mistake again.

Question: Don't *you feel angry* when your parents and teachers beat you?

Sukhail: I do, *but not for long. I know that it is for my good*. (Nieuwenhuys, 1994, p. 54; added emphasis)

Here we can get a glimpse of the ways in which feeling about child punishment works culturally, in between personal-cultural internalization (of the notion that being beaten is 'for *my* good'; and the pattern of de-escalation of anger), and collective-cultural practices of physical punishment. The practice (of caning) is introduced in the context of a semiotic frame ('this is for *your* good'– as I say as your authority figure), the child develops their internalized understanding of parental and teacher roles (and relations to the child) on that basis. Even when the opposite to this pattern, for example, strong conviction of the caning being 'wrong' or 'useless', is developed (counter-actively), it is on the basis of the given orientation.

Promotion of inter-child competition and cooperation in classrooms

If schools are the field of work (on educational issues) where children are being prepared for assuming key social roles in the social world, then the issue of preparation of children for the rules of competition and cooperation is central. Competition is usually promoted by any competitive evaluation system – exams, differential feedback on performance in classroom contexts etc. A crucial moment in that promotion is the introduction of 'honour codes' against cheating – assisting one another during exams. In competitively organized settings, the assistance by one student of another is unthinkable. This would be just the reverse in the case of collectively-oriented classroom settings.

In the context of a Mexican secondary school (Levinson, 1998), the explicit goal orientation of the school system was to promote unity of otherwise varied ethnic backgrounds of students. Such unity was created symbolically by uniting all children into one group – *grupo escolar* – the unity of which was promoted by the teachers on every possible occasion:

In the classroom, teachers tended to foster identification with the grupo in a number of ways. Exhortations to maintain grupo solidarity constantly punctuated the teachers' discourse. Classroom

lessons easily slipped into moral discourses promoting grupo solidarity; basic or technical school knowledges became embedded in broader, directive statements about social conduct and responsibility. In a biology lesson . . . Mr Gonzalez turned a discussion of the human immune system, the dynamics of white blood cells uniting to attack infected red blood cells, into an illustration of the need for the grupo to stick together and discipline its own: 'Here in the grupo too, we must unite against those bad elements who would disrupt our healthy functioning and progress.' (Levinson, 1998, p. 273)

In contrast, there was rarely any effort to promote inter-group rivalry. The result of such group-promotion efforts was indeed the creation of group cohesiveness, and peer demands upon grupo members to act in unison. The domains in which such cohesion is tested may be precisely actions against the very teachers who promote group solidarity. In a curious way, teachers' success in promoting group unity can be turned against the teachers themselves.

Social institutions are therefore careful in promoting children's peer group unity – this happens in a clearly goals-oriented fashion. The Mexican case is one where the teachers suggest to students that they all – teachers and students together – are building up joint 'Mexican unity' (in opposition to the 'bad elements'). The guarantee of success of an educational system is precisely the build-up of the 'we-feeling'. In some cases (the Krishnamurti example, above) this can take place without setting up an external opposing force. However, it is a basic sociopsychological principle that one group's internal unity is built in opposition to a real or imaginary outgroup. The system of formal education is itself a social system constantly in need of internal cohesion. Thus, social discourse about education – its quality, its paradoxes, etc. – is part of the social negotiation of both in-group coherence and between-groups relations.

SUMMARY: FORMAL EDUCATION AS SYSTEMIC INTERVENTION

Education is a purposeful intervention into the development of young human beings. It is the epitome of 'cultivation' in the sense of Georg Simmel (see Chapter 3). As such, education is always some form of intervention – into the wider context of informal guidance of children towards adulthood. In some cases (for example, missionary schools in colonial countries) such intervention is directly meant to 'capture' and 'change the souls' of the young of the given society.

A statement describing the missionary fervour of a school district administrator in the United States (Oklahoma) at the end of the nineteenth century, illustrates the ideology of intervention in a rather dramatic way. Talking of educating American Indian children, the administrator suggested:

> If we propose [sic] to educate Indian children, let us educate them all. If we look to the schools as one of the chief factors of the great transformation, why not establish at once to embrace the entire body of available Indian youth? . . . If there could be gathered by the end of 1893 . . . nearly all of the Indian children and they be kept there for ten years, the work would be substantially accomplished; for . . . there would grow up a generation of English speaking Indians, accustomed to the ways of civilized life. . . . Forever after this [they will be] the . . . dominant force among them. (Ellis, 1996, p. 15)

Formal schooling is indeed a powerful weapon for social change. Yet it works through engaging of the activities of its participants. The goals of introduction of schools by social institutions can work for the joint benefit of the social power, and of the recipients of education. Thus, the proliferation of literacy in Europe in the sixteenth century – in conjunction with the Protestant Reformation – led to an increase of religious-ideological control over the minds of people who, at the same time, could apply their new skills to reading of texts of very different kinds. Or, in our contemporary times, provision of higher education guarantees its recipients better chances in vocations – and the employers a better-prepared workforce.

Introduction of formal education can work in some degree of coordination with its informal counterpart. Some aspects of the informal education penetrate into the contexts of formal schooling. The teachers, at times, integrate aspects of parental roles into their teachers' roles. In counter-role assignments, the parents of the children may try to define teachers' roles as distanced from theirs (see the examples given by Wolcott, above). The school as a place is inclusively separated from the community within which it resides.

In situations of intervening into developing human minds, the use of the syncretic psychological functions of those minds is the domain through which interventions can work. This has been recognized in practice by religious, educational and political institutions that have guided children towards openness to further interventions. That openness is created through identity chaining and fusing processes. These processes reach their maximum socialization and – at times – use in adolescence.

NOTES

1 In contemporary West Africa, the 'bush schools' for adolescent boys are at times used to recruit boys into military training for political purposes. Building military camps along the traditions of *poro*-based 'bush schools' entails inserting new meanings (political ideologies) into an old collective-cultural secret education form (see Peters and Richards, 1998, p. 189).

2 The case of the Japanese lunch-box is not different from other societies: in any society where children go from home to preschool or school, the mother's role becomes publicly evaluated through the kind of clothes the child is dressed in, the child's cleanliness etc. The lunch-box in Japan is a notable case of making a cultural home–school coordination object from food-related self-organization.

REVIEW QUESTIONS FOR CHAPTER 12

1 Discuss the homogenizing role of marking birthdays in human life.

2 Explain the process through which the child enters into the realm of adult activities.

3 Describe Tallensi children's gradual introduction into adult productive activities.

4 Explain the differences and mutual relations of informal and formal education.

5 How are structures of children's games usable by social institutions to promote their values?

6 Analyse the sequence of actions in an Israeli kindergarten birthday party. How are different values encoded into the action sequence?

7 Explain the notion of *identity chaining*.

8 What is *idenity fusion*?

9   How does formal schooling promote syncretic and discrete aspects of personal culture?

10 Describe the symbolic organization of school territory.

11 Explain the functions of West African 'bush school'.

12 How is children's conduct homogenized in the school context?

13 Explain how 'Quaranic pedagogy' works.

14 What is children's 'own choice' in educational settings?

15 How can the teacher promote rule-following or creativity on a school task?

16 Explain the value of 'rote learning'.

17 Describe children's adjustment to school (using the Cree example, or your own).

18 Explain parents–students–teacher role relations in a Kwakiutl school.

19 Explain the psychological issues of the Japanese lunch-box.

20 How do syllogisms work in human thinking? Why is syllogistic reasoning brought into thought through formal schooling?

21 Analyse the clash between inductive and deductive reasoning processes (using the Abdulrakhim data).

22 What is the function of formal evaluations in an education context?

23 Explain the structure and function of catechisms.

24 Explain the psychological nature of multiple-choice tests.

25 Explain the functions of the 'morning assembly' in the Krishnamurti school.

26 How is the sunset-watching ceremony in the Krishnamurti school an example of collective-cultural promotion of personal-cultural development?

27 What is necessary for external promotion of values to guarantee success within the personal culture?

28 How is inter-child cooperation and competition promoted within the classroom?

13

ADOLESCENCE: MOVING THROUGH INTO ADULTHOOD

In the progression from childhood into adulthood, the period of active biological growth spurt – puberty – indicates a developmental period that is for all intents and purposes a crucial arena for cultural organization. Social institutions of various kinds share the interest in guiding the developing children into their specific social roles of adulthood. The elders – the keepers of the (often) secret wisdom of the tribes – would expect the young adults to accept their leadership in expertise. The formal political institutions would attempt to guide adolescents into the roles of law-abiding citizens. If the latter entails participation in the political system through the form of participatory democracy, the children are guided towards acceptance of the role of solving problems through building social consensuses and acceptance of majority-based decisions. If the political institutions define the role of 'law-abiding citizen' as that of unconditional follower of the political regime, the role becomes defined quite to the contrary. The children are encouraged to enter adulthood focusing on establishing a family and following the rules – rather than trying to participate in the political system actively. Under some circumstances, the age groups of teenagers – previously kept in subservient and non-participatory roles – can be singled out from all other social groups, with suggestions for helping the given political power to change the current social status quo. Military institutions – fighting for any political goal – are eager to capture adolescents' creative energies and direct those towards their objectives. Different religious institutions attempt to capture adolescents' eagerness to create a just and meaningful world for themselves by guiding the young in the direction of their belief systems. Economic producers of various kinds try to capture the 'children's markets' for their products – especially in societies where children are segregated from the world of

work and guided towards leisure activities which require use of buyable resources.

Last – but not least – the parents of the adolescents, as well as their whole kinship group, do whatever they think is best to guide the adolescents towards promising economic roles for their adult lives. This may include 'push' for the children to move into secondary and post-secondary education (if that is believed to guarantee economically feasible vocational tracks in the given society), or to the opposite – getting children out of the perils of education, into the world of work.

Of course, the picture painted here of children's becoming adults may seem one-sided: the child who is growing into adulthood is presented as the target of the manifold interests of social others – persons and institutions. Yet the central role in dealing with all these suggestions is the developing teenager themself. Tortured by the biological changes of his or her growing body from inside, and with the myriad of new social suggestions emanating from outside, the developing teenager is driven to a complex coordination task of all these. Any decision by the teenager is made under uncertainty about the future. The teenagers – based on their established personal cultures – create their domains of lively curiosity in both the ways in which the world outside functions, and the ways in which they could relate to the world. Teenagers create their own goal-directed activities which can entail strong motivation for achieving goals (in academics, sport, drinking, or other areas). Their interests may emerge (and disappear) remarkably quickly. They create personal secrecy, yet are parts of their home worlds. There are many ways in which human decision-making under varied pressures (and uncertainty) can proceed. If the different 'inputs' are reasonably simply ordered, the psychological phenomena of teenagers need not become objects of social concern in the given society. Instead, the psychological phenomena – 'side-effects' of the decision-making – may pass as aspects of the particular teenager, rather than become 'issues of the age of puberty' in the social discourse. The psychological phenomena of the teenage years are reality of a psychological kind, yet a specifically designated age period of 'adolescence' is a result of the creation of a semiotic demand setting, by adults.

PSYCHOLOGY'S CONSTRUCTION OF ADOLESCENCE

The notion of 'adolescence' as a specifiable age period is of recent origin. Interestingly, gender differences were present in the invention of the concept of adolescence. The issues of male youth – their activities, orientation of juvenile activities and channelling those in socially acceptable directions – were the main concerns in the late nineteenth century United States. For girls, the issues of their social guidance were less demanding – as girls' socialization was successfully overcontrolled.

The origins of adolescence as a special age of 'storm and stress'

The notion of adolescence being a period of 'storm and stress' was brought into psychology by G. Stanley Hall (1904), based on the folk model that came into existence in European and North American societies in the second half of the nineteenth century. That highlighting of adolescence is a cultural-historical construction, so we can see how a cultural invention of the common sense of a society became the cornerstone of psychological research. The 'storm and stress' of adolescence was to be guided in directions that would fit with a society that required school discipline and obedience of young workers in factories.

First, the focus on adolescent conformity concentrated on the question of how one could capture control over adolescent boys' actions through inculcation of their 'school spirit' in secondary schools. It was believed that through homogenizing the roles of boys in schools – similarly to the military establishments – social control could be established. Secondly, loyalty was to be promoted through the suggestion of 'hero figures' for adulation and emulation. The role of team sports and of star athletes within the teams, or within boys' clubs, was singled out as a way to direct young boys' energies towards socially acceptable goals (Kett, 1977, p. 243).

Of course, the combination of conformistic hero figure identification would guarantee success of social control better than either of the two tactics

separately. The focus on control seemed to by-pass a number of issues of becoming an adult – those that mattered for the adolescents themselves.

Psychology with an adult face (and voice)

The psychology of adolescence that exists in our contemporary psychology textbooks is written from the socio-ideological position of adults, rather than from the viewpoint of adolescents themselves. As a result, the cultural models that have dominated occidental psychology since the beginning of the twentieth century have become the axiomatic basis for looking at adolescents. This entails pre-stigmatizing the object of investigation. Adolescents are often presumed to be 'troublesome', 'naive', 'idealistic' etc. Often the psychologists address issues of how to cope with adolescents, rather than how the adolescents could cope with their lives, and the adults. The aim here is to change the positioning of the researcher from that of a worried parent (who looks at the adolescents with a 'what is wrong?' attitude), to a sympathetic co-thinker with the adolescents. The orientation taken here is progressive: how can adolescents co-construct their selves under the pressures generated by the biological maturation on the one hand, and collective-cultural guidance on the other? Adolescents are in a situation where they need to creatively negotiate their developing personal cultural systems with both the biological and social worlds. Needless to add that this is a complex task, and that such a task requires complex solutions.

Whose 'crisis', then, is that of adolescence? As adolescence in contemporary psychology has become presented as a 'crisis period', the question of *whose crisis* it is needs to be asked. Undoubtedly passing through the speeded-up biological maturation period would challenge the person's personal-cultural structure, and in this sense there is a creative period of turmoil within the child's personal world. This can be documented independently of any recognition (or non-recognition) of such turmoils in the social discourse about adolescence (as a 'special transition period'). As was demonstrated at the beginning of this chapter, the social discourse *about* adolescence is a recent historical construction of the twentieth century. Yet phenomena of psychological turmoil around the age of puberty can be found at any historical period, and in any society. Bell (1985) showed how the periods of puberty of medieval young women (who later were canonized as saints by the Catholic Church) included intra-mental turmoils and confrontations with their parents. The originators of the 'Children's Crusade' in the thirteenth century acted against the prevailing social expectations of their parents (and their need of the teenagers as workers in the fields), and left their homes in large numbers to reach the goal of 'liberating Jerusalem'.

Yet those who become engaged in talking about adolescents as 'difficult', 'problematic' and 'conflictful' are not adolescents themselves, but their parents. It is a major developmental transition for the parents themselves to see their child turning into a young adult. This may be a particularly different 'crisis' for parents in those societies where the parents' control function over the children is turned into a special goal-oriented task. Any society where 'parenting' – discourse about *how to be* a good parent[1] – is emphasized is likely to accentuate the issue of 'crisis of adolescence' as that of *parents'* crisis of loss of control over the development of the child. Where issues of adults' control over the offspring are not turned into an arena of self-construction by the adults, but is, instead, a matter-of-fact aspect of everyday life, it is not expected that the transition from childhood to adulthood will become a topic for concern for the adults. That transition may be carefully culturally orchestrated (for example, through elaborate initiation rituals that socially channel the transition), yet it is not of consequences for the adults' own psychological systems. It is in the modern (and post-modern) industrialized societies that *adults' talking about* 'difficult teenagers' is an indication of *adults' crisis* within their own selves. This is visible if we consider adults' concerns about adolescents' actions: the usual adult talk about those actions is in terms of how (awful) these are from the perspective of 'society' (meaning the adults themselves, losing their parental control). The focus of inherent meaning of these actions for the adolescents themselves is unlikely to be present in adults' discourse. This is to be expected, as more than ten years in a parental role necessarily turns the personal cultures of the parents into relatively rigid systems of being in a parents' role.

BIOLOGICAL DEVELOPMENT AND ITS CULTURAL FRAMING

Biological development speeds up around adolescence. It creates a situation in which children very quickly turn into quasi-adults. The physical growth spurt of the adolescent involves quickening of the speed of height growth for girls around 11–12 years of age, and 13–15 years of age for boys. The change in height has immediate implications for the social relations within the peer group.

The main moment of change concerns sexual maturation which creates the social need for granting collective-culturally acceptable forms of conduct. This leads in different societies to the organization of different ritualistic events that mark the symbolic transition of children into adulthood (rites of passage). On the side of the personal cultures of the adolescents, the marked speeding up of biological maturation creates the stress of psychosocial adjustment to emerging sexual feelings. These feelings are first and foremost played out on the basis of boys' and girls' body-related conduct.

Girls' adaptation to sexual maturation

The age at which girls in different societies experience the beginning of their menstrual periods varies – depending upon rural versus urban living conditions, as well as upon the geographical region. Each aspect of growth of secondary sexual characteristics – growth of breasts, of the pubic hair – and, of course, the arrival of the first menstruation are of double psychological importance. First, these changes force the girls to relate to their own psychological organization through the observable (to them) bodily changes. Secondly, these changes enter as symbolic events into their relationships with others – peers, mothers, fathers, etc. The menarche does not immediately make a girl into a fully reproductive woman. Instead, for about a year the girl's reproductive system does not produce eggs. Consequently, the newly menstruating girl is functionally infertile, and becomes ready for childbearing only slowly.

Psychological concerns of young girls include specific reactions to breast growth (Rosenbaum, 1979). In Western societies over the last centuries, the girls' 'coming of age' in the sense of breast growth leads to the use of the special purely feminine clothing object – the bra (see also Chapter 7). When young girls enter into the habit of using bras, their goal-oriented actions of either publicly demonstrating their larger breast size, or attempting to flatten the growing breasts, become publicly visible. Rosenbaum's interviews with adolescent girls revealed a number of psychologically interesting self-reflections:

One girl was somewhat uncomfortable because her breasts were too large, stating 'My breasts are a little bit too large for my age (14), but I'll grow into them.' Bigger was generally – within some limits – seen as better. Bigger was better not so much for the self, but because of the value big breasts were perceived to have for the boys – 'I worry about if my breasts are appealing to boys.' Large breasts were sometimes ambivalently perceived: They were more voluptuous, sexier, but also 'more of a bother.' The first bra was a rite of passage – an event they remembered. Most of the girls preferred to wear a bra – feeling that it 'looked better.' They felt that going braless was at times more comfortable, but many regarded it as too 'loose' and sexy. (Rosenbaum, 1979, pp. 244–245)

The developing personal-cultural concerns about the breasts are surely a result of their collective-cultural designation as arenas for public regulation of female sexuality. The occidental symbolic role of the breasts as a marker of sexuality leads to collective-cultural regulation of the public visibility of the breasts, which begins (in the United States and a number of other societies) from the two-piece bikinis at a very early age. The young child is put into a 'pre-bra' (the top of bikini) long before the breasts ever grow in adolescence.

Yet the focus on breast growth as a crucial psychological preoccupation is not necessarily the arena for self development. In other societies, adolescent girls may emphasize other parts of the body as indicating their feminine characteristics. The Xingu (in Brazil) adolescents wear special knee-bands which emphasize the form of the calves (see Chapter 7).

Young girls' personal experiences with menstruation are important indicators of the results of the collective-cultural socialization of girls' selves and their female gender roles. In most societies, women are made into gatekeepers of the moral guardianship of heterosexual relations of girls. Many North American girls have reported negative or ambivalent feelings, when recollecting their emotional states during their first period (Pillmer et al., 1987: 16 per cent negative, 51 per cent ambivalent, 10 per cent neutral feelings). Similar data from rural India show that 62–77.5 per cent of the girls from different religious backgrounds admit to being frightened by menarche (Murthi, 1993, p. 52). These non-positive relations are linked with social and self-evaluative feelings of the girl, as is evident in the following personal account:

I was flat, and my legs were sticks, and the boys would say, 'Hey, Flatty,' and I'd burst into tears and run home and say to my mother 'Why me? Why do I have to go through all that mess?' I thought it was the worst thing in the world. What happened was that I didn't get my period till real late. I was 13 and all my friends had started, and I was thinking maybe it wasn't going to happen to me. Like there was something wrong with me and I was different. So when I got it I felt so great – until I had it a couple of

times and it really started paining me. But even now like sometimes I really suffer – have cramps and my face all broken out, and I'll feel so bad I can't get out of bed – but I'll feel sort of pride because I'm a woman and I can produce a child, and the pain I'm feeling makes me different from my brother . . . (Rothchild, 1979, p. 218)

Here we can observe culturally constructed ambivalence in the girl's feelings about her impending role as a woman. In most traditional societies such ambivalence has not been produced – as the move to the role of a childbearing woman is never questioned. Instead, one can find positive canalization of adolescent girls' move through initiation ritual into adulthood, and into early childbearing.

The cultural meanings of menstruation

The beginning of menstruation in girls marks their biological readiness for adulthood. It is on that transition that collective-cultural guidance for the conduct of women is built. This process involves taking different positions – which lead cultural anthropologists into complicated interpretive games.

The widespread story told about menstruation is its 'polluting' nature, which becomes interpreted as a reason for secluding girls and women during that period. The 'pollution' notion has been linked with 'uncleanliness'. The notion that the menstrual blood is 'dirty' has been well-grained in European laypersons' minds. It has powerfully entered into anthropology – the classic anthropologists (for example, Alfred Kroeber) were selectively picking up the male position of looking at women's menstruation. Kroeber's own field notes reveal that the complexity of the issue was even greater than is apparent in his publications on the topic (Buckley, 1982).

In Kroeber's field notes on Yurok American Indians in California (from 1902) the positive notion of menstruation is expressed. That positivity faced Buckley seven decades later: a menstruating Yurok woman is required to isolate herself because she is at the height of her powers (rather than 'unclean', she is viewed as powerful and in contact with the Yurok cosmological world). In that time, she should not waste her energy on mundane tasks, nor be involved with men. Instead, she should take time for concentrated meditation to 'find out the purpose of life'. The blood that flows serves to 'purify' the woman, preparing her for spiritual accomplishments (Buckley, 1982, p. 49). The 10-day menstrual period for women is a cultural suggestion (autosuggestion) time – a time for meditating about one's life course future in goal-directed ways, a female parallel for Yurok male 'sweathouse' culture work.

Guided body preparation

The body of the young teenager needs to be ready, physically and psychologically, for its new set of functions. Among the Baganda (in Uganda), the menstrual seclusion of girls has been linked with direct instruction by the father's sister (*ssenga*). Soon after the menstruation has become established, *ssenga* used to instruct the girl in manipulating her genitals:

> The custom consists of manipulating the labia minora to physically elongate it. Elongation narrows the vaginal entrance and keeps it 'warm and tight' . . . Ssenga teaches the girl specific utterances and techniques appropriate during intercourse. Traditionally, women are taught to not only desire sex but also to lead an active sex life. A woman is expected to reach orgasm several times before the man and to respond throughout intercourse with vigorous body movements. A man is evaluated by women according to the length of time coitus is maintained before his orgasm . . . A too-rapid male ejaculation is likely to evoke female anger. (Kilbride and Kilbride, 1990, p. 92)

The interesting point in Baganda is the explicit collective-cultural guidance of adolescents (boys and girls) towards the value of sexual intercourse by a female relative of the father's side. Different members of the kinship group play different roles in the social development system in any society. The communication channels about emerging sexual functions may be blocked in the parents–children line. Instead, topics of sexual conduct can become a theme for discussion within the same-sex peer group, or open for communication with some less central relative or acquaintance. Even in our Western societies, there may be topics on which an adolescent girl would not eagerly talk with her mother, but would find it possible to chat with the mother's sister (her aunt). Or an adolescent boy may turn to an uncle (rather than father) for advice.

Boys' handling of sexual maturation

The direction for boys' sexual maturation takes the form of spontaneous ejaculation of the seminal fluid, usually at night. This begins usually one year after the beginning of the growth of the penis. As in the case of early infertility in girls, the beginning of boys' sexual activity keeps them infertile.

On the personal-cultural side, boys' growing sexual functions lead to their symbolic construction of masculinity. Adolescent boys may

compare their penis sizes, or invent specific 'urinating contests'. Furthermore, 'masturbation contests' of pre-adolescent boys have been described (in pre-1930s Kenya, among the Gikuyu):

> Before initiation it is considered right and proper for boys to practice masturbation as a preparation for their future sexual activities. Sometimes two or more boys compete in this, to see which can show himself more active than the rest. This practice takes place outside the homestead, under a tree or bush, where the boys are not visible to their elders. It is considered an indecency to be seen doing it, except by boys of the same age grade. The practice is given up after the initiation ceremony, and anyone seen doing it after that would be looked upon as clinging to a babyish habit, and be laughed at, because owing to the free sex-play which is permitted among young people, there is now no need to indulge in it. (Kenyatta, 1965, pp. 155–156)

The example of Gikuyu youth's age-graded sexual activities is in great contrast with the European and North American repression of sexual functions (and social stigmatization of masturbation). The social representation of 'masturbatory insanity' has a history of at least 300 years in European societies (see Hare, 1962). The 'evil nature' of masturbation has been communicated to young boys (and girls) in numerous ways – using the developing interest in sexual functions of the adolescents as an arena for promotion of puritan morality (see Hall, 1992). This leads to a simple question: what are the actual psychological functions of social singling out some aspect of human development (such as emerging sexuality at puberty) for socio-moral discourse in a given society? In different societies, the emerging sexual capacities of adolescent boys (and girls) capture their personal attention and interest. Yet in some (for example, the Gikuyu case) that interest can turn into active exploration of these functions – even if in relative privacy ('masturbation contests'). In others – such as in Western Europe – these interests are turned into arenas of internalization of guilt about one's sexual role, and repressive tendencies within the person. In the Hindu joint family context, the heterosexual interests may be intertwined with the tasks of maintenance of secrecy in a socially mutually observable context.

The case of Naik

Naik (a middle-class young man in Allahabad, India), in reflecting back upon his pre-adolescence and personal-cultural construction of sexuality, reveals the complexity of feelings, interspersed with interactional events. Naik had at age 10 occasionally seen his older brother masturbating, and began doing it in privacy himself. The collective-cultural stigmatization of masturbation led Naik to carefully hide the practice. In his words, 'I knew that what I was doing was bad and dirty which I was not supposed to do and, if I persisted, others should not know of it' (Kakar and Chowdhry, 1970, p. 70). Yet Naik continued his practice, hiding it from others. Collective-cultural restrictions on the practice were counteracted in his private secrecy. The adolescent private secret world is of value for development precisely because of its secrecy. Naik remembered an episode when his activities were almost discovered:

> One day in the evening, at around seven-thirty, I was masturbating in the corner of the room, without putting on the light. All of a sudden my mother came into the room. She asked me why I had not put on the light. I felt caught and replied in a rather angry tone that I was just sitting, that's all! She said, 'Do not sit in the dark like this, you may develop some bad habits,' and left. I felt very embarrassed and knew at heart that my mother must have understood what I was doing in the dark. After that I never practiced it in a situation where I might be caught nor did my parents later ever talk to me about it. I felt very guilty that even my mother had come to know about it. (Kakar and Chowdhry, 1970, p. 70)

Notably, this episode reveals the power of communication through the unmentionables. The parents would not talk with the son about his habit. The son thought they knew (but did not refer to it implicitly). Naik subsequently entered into a few (for him embarrassing) efforts to establish sexual relations with girls, after which he turned towards accepting the notion of an arranged marriage for himself. The value of one's 'own' choice – in the case of interpersonally negotiable relations – is not a *via regia* for human autonomous functioning. Almost all aspects of adolescents' autonomy are negotiated within the social network of the family, kinship and wider society. Although biological sexual maturation is a central developmental event that sets the stage for adolescents' sexual concerns and later reproductive life, it is by no means central in the psychological realm of the adolescents. Sexuality is an episodic concern, while the issues of finding one's own way in life – especially in the context of transforming society, in the sense of work roles and ideological allegiances – is the main task.

ADOLESCENTS' ENTRANCE INTO THE ECONOMIC DOMAIN OF ADULT SOCIETY

What the notion of 'economic domain' entails depends upon the given society at the given time.

Furthermore, it depends upon the specific subsistence activities within which the developing child is embedded, how the integration into the world of productive activities takes place. The move from childhood into adulthood would differ remarkably in the case of hunter–gatherers, cattle-herders, weavers, crop farmers, industrial workers, intellectuals, peripatetic entertainers, bankers and politicians. That difference would further be emphasized by the differences in economic life conditions: the process would differ in case of famine or periods of plenty, economic depression or quick economic growth, and so on. The differentiation between monetary and 'natural' economic exchanges within the given society create different conditions for adolescents' integration into the world of economic relationships.

A critical example: 'babysitting' – working for hire versus being in one's social role

One of the first experiences of children in jointly necessary everyday tasks is giving care for younger children (see Chapter 10). All over the world, children of varied ages serve as primary caregivers to younger children, thus freeing the hands of the mothers for more important productive activities. This system operated as economically necessary where the mothers' work on other tasks was too important to give up for the sake of watching over children.

In contemporary industrialized societies, where children have become separated from the world of economic activities through formal schooling and laws against hiring children into many jobs, the issue of childminding has been turned from part of the child's role into a working role. 'Babysitting' becomes a job which older children – primarily adolescents – do for hire. This may include the adolescents' own parents paying their adolescents to take care of their younger siblings when parents are out of the home. The monetary relationships have selectively entered the family context, yet in ways that are incomplete (for example, the mother does not expect to be paid for *her* work on childcare of the same younger child, for which she 'hires' her own older child). This is possible if there is sufficient surplus in family income (there is funding for such local hiring), and if the parents set the goal for getting the youngster into a role of economic autonomy. The latter role is certainly of a limited kind (until the children's income becomes sufficient). This time is postponed by prolonged and increasingly expensive formal schooling.

A version of 'babysitting' that introduces distinction between family role and that of 'work-for-hire' is the case where the adolescent 'babysits' somebody else's child and receives payment for that, while the same activity within one's family context is done as part of one's older sibling's role. The same applies to other everyday-kind of jobs: housecleaning, lawn-mowing, washing cars and clothes etc. In this predicament, the adolescents earn their money outside of the family, even if they may be keeping the money to themselves, they are co-producers of their family's livelihood, rather than a consumer.

Contemporary adolescence in industrialized societies

It is around adolescence that the coordination of two sides of the relationships with the economic world – that of consumer and that of producer – start to be worked out. The need for things that reify the adolescents' self-construction necessities (clothes, music, body-painting devices) require that adolescents possess economic resources. Yet at the same time the adolescents are – in different societies differently – secluded from easy entrance into income-producing activities (by legal restrictions on age of hiring, in many countries). Of course in many societies, often those of the so-called 'traditional' kind, the latter issue never surfaces, since children are from an early age incorporated into the productive work meant to generate economic resources for the whole family.

Participation in formal education all over the world is a main activity setting that keeps adolescents away from entering the world of work. Once they 'drop out' of school, the world of work is there to be their life environment. This 'dropping out' can be temporary (adolescents working, at home or elsewhere, after school hours). For example, adolescent girls on Tonga enter into a regular set of household work duties every day after school, which leave them little time for school homework (Morton, 1996, pp. 142–143). The adult women integrate the girls into their household work in ways that take the whole family's needs as the starting point.

Seasonal (adolescents summoned by their families to help out with work overloads) 'dropouts' from schools are also a real possibility for regaining the economic power of the young. And, of course, there are cases of basic termination of formal education when the future chances outside school are either more appealing or realistic – or at least seem so.

What is work?

Working is not an easily definable phenomenon. It is clear when adolescents work for hire in factories or service contexts (McDonalds), but it is very unclear when the work entails activities that are carried out without pay, in the context of home, for money or for kinship obligations. If the whole family specializes in the production of a kind that requires special skills, the informal apprenticeship in these skills can lead to the adolescent's move ('drop') out of the formal education system into the economic production role that in the given context fits both family and economic stability. A 12-year-old girl from an Indian weaver's family from a small village near Madras, India, explained her life world:

> I have always worked with my family when I was on school vacation, but then all my friends did the same and we later reunited during the school year. But this time I know I'll never go back. My family needs me here. I don't envy my friends in school, because in a year or two they too will drop out. I have known all along that school was only for a few years, that I was going to be a weaver always. My family is very important to me. They need me and I need them, that way we can all take care of ourselves and our families. We won't have any savings, but we can be sure not to starve. I hear that in the city, even if I can work, they won't give me a job. In Chinnallipatti, we will always have work. Only we can weave and we are needed. (George, 1990, p. 145)

Here we see the clear set-up of a positive economic integration of the adolescent into the family production business. The functions of formal schooling in making the young people ready for entrance into new social roles are not applicable here – in fact, the girl knows there is no job after a secondary school certificate, while her background family production promises an adequate adult role.

STRUCTURE OF ADOLESCENT PERSONAL CULTURE

Viewed from cultural developmental psychology, adolescence is a central period for the establishment of an elaborate structure of personal culture. Since personal culture is constructed through constructive internalization and externalization (as described in Chapter 3), the claim of uniqueness of adolescents' personal worlds is normative. Adolescents necessarily construct their sociomoral worlds in ways that go beyond that of their parents – yet are based on the social input from the very same parents. The added secrecy of the personal worlds of adolescents may be a troubling issue for parents, but for the psychological development of the adolescents is a necessary part of development (see Simmel's treatment of secrecy, Chapter 3). A number of central themes can be charted out to characterize adolescents' personal culture.

The myth of 'peer pressure'

In adult discourse about adolescents, all the negative (from the adults' viewpoint) aspects of conduct are easily explained through reference to 'peer pressure'. This indicates a non-systemic intuitive model of adolescents in the minds of adults. It is a model of a competitive kind – the parents view themselves in opposition to the rival – the peer group. Yet the peer group has emerged historically through adults' segregation of children's social relations into age-set cohorts. The model overlooks the systemic complexity of psychological growth in adolescence, as would be evident from an interview response by a teenager from a US middle-class background:

> There's all this crap about being accepted into a group and struggling and making an effort to make friends and not being comfortable about your own self-worth as a human being. . . . [But] the idea of peer pressure is a lot of bunk. What I heard about peer pressure all the way through school is that someone is going to walk up to me and say "Here, drink this and you'll be cool." It wasn't like that at all. You go somewhere and everyone else would be doing it and you'd think, "Hey, everyone else is doing it and they seem to be having a good time – now why wouldn't you do this?" In that sense. The preparation of the powers that be, the lesson they tried to drill into me, they were completely off. They have no idea what we're up against.' (Lightfoot, 1997, p. 36)

This adolescent points to the simplicity of the model of adolescent personal culture that contrasts parents and peers as two independent groups of direct-causal agents (see Figure 13.1A). In contrast, a systemic causality model (Figure 13.1B) would bring psychology of adolescence closer to the reality of the relations that adolescents establish between themselves and others.

The 'naïve adult model' (Figure 13.1A) is essentially a regular direct linear causality notion of 'influences' from outside sources on the adolescent, who in this scheme is described as a passive reactor to different influences. In accordance with that model, if the 'peer pressure' is more intense than 'parent pressure', the adolescent – like a passive billiard ball – is 'pushed' in the direction indicated by the 'winning power source'. In a similar vein, this model can be the basis for adults to try to monopolize their own pressure on the adolescent (that is, by keeping their child away from 'negative peer influences'). Obviously that orientation is adult-centred and represents the parents' need to maintain control over the conduct of the adolescents.

The systemic model (Figure 13.1B) reflects the position of adolescents. In their creative turmoil – triggered by the biological 'growth spurt'

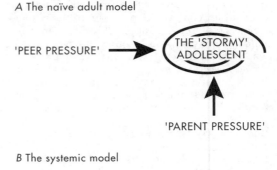

A The naïve adult model

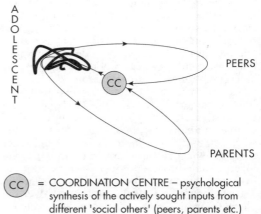

B The systemic model

CC = COORDINATION CENTRE – psychological synthesis of the actively sought inputs from different 'social others' (peers, parents etc.)

FIGURE 13.1 *Two constructions of adolescents' psychological life situation*

– they actively turn to different sources of social assistance, or of new experiences. They actively trigger feedback from these sources (peers, parents, anybody else), and coordinate the different perspectives they obtain by their active enquiry. On the basis of such coordination, they create their own personal-cultural systems that transcend *both* the parents' and peers' inputs. The adolescents actively explore both new action domains (creating adventures for themselves), utilize peer support[2] in these endeavours, and coordinate their actions with parental suggestions.[3]

The most crucial aspect of the systemic model depicted in Figure 13.1B is the 'Coordination Centre' (CC). It is at the intersection of actively triggered inputs from different sources that the synthesis of novel forms of adolescent personal culture takes place. In this process, the 'peer and parent influences' become the starting data for the adolescent person's own way of feeling and being. Given the relevance of personal secrecy for adolescent personal cultures, others need not obtain any access to the complexity of the coordination process.

Consider a description of a 'risky situation' by a 17-year-old girl:

I had about 15 people over when my parents were out of town for the weekend. That was really scary. *I was afraid I was going to get caught. It was so fun.* Parents make such a big deal out of leaving you at home and I guess my parents were scared I was going to have a party and trash the whole house. *But it is just kind of exciting to know that I can get away with it without them knowing.* But the house didn't get trashed and everyone was really responsible and *I felt kind of old being able to pull off something like that.* I invited only my closest friends and I told them that if there was going to be drinking that they are not going to drive and if they spend the night nothing [i.e., sex] happens. I made sure that the word didn't get out to anyone else and I made sure that there were only a few cars there. It was irresponsible to have it in the first place, but the way I handled it was responsible. (Lightfoot, 1997, p. 104; added emphasis)

This example shows how the adolescent girl uses input from parents ('parents make such a big deal out of leaving you at home and I guess my parents were scared I was going to have a party and trash the whole house') to create her own personal thrill-seeking situation. She reports testing the boundaries of what could be done in the area of phenomena labelled 'getting caught' – she avoids the latter by careful planning, yet gets the thrill from the possibility, which does not actualize. This strategy of self-construction is a version of general construction of possible scenarios in one's imagination – in this case, a scenario that became actualized in conduct. Human – adolescent or adult – imagination creates different scenarios of psychological tension, some of which are subsequently overcome, others maintained in a state of tension ('steady state') and still others tested out in real conduct. Among the latter, thrill-seeking is of importance. It provides the person with *autotelic* experience (Csikszentmihalyi, 1985),[4] as it leads to creation of scenarios of genetic dramatism. Such scenarios can involve images of real 'social others' (peers, parents) as well as imaginary ones. Many children or adolescents report making up imaginary friends or companions (Watkins, 1986). This kind of ideation is an example of constructing the interlocutor (in Figure 13.1B) who then enters into the process of personal culture construction as an active partner.

Adolescents' religious conversion phenomena are of similar kind. Here the imaginary companion created by the adolescent can be an image of a deity. The kind of deity invented can be canalized by the collective-cultural system – yet the result of construction is uniquely personal. For example, an adolescent from a Christian background may create her (or his) specific image of the Christian God – which may be seen as being different from the God worshipped by the parents. Likewise, all of so-called 'adolescent idealism' about justice in society, love between people etc. is an ideal construct of the nature of genetic dramatisms – 'idealistic' precisely because such constructs are meant to transcend the given here-and-now reality.

GUIDING ADOLESCENTS' MORAL CONCERNS: POSITIVE ORIENTATION TOWARDS SOCIETY

The personal-cultural 'adolescent idealism' is reflected in the content of many interactions that adolescents have with adults. Such interactions – about justice, fairness, beliefs and values – are the higher-level hierarchical integration basis for adolescents' personal cultures. It is in this function that efforts by the collective-cultural worlds of the adolescents guide the internalization process. In the history of the Jewish worldview, the inititiation of boys (at 13 years old) and girls (12 years old) emerged in the Middle Ages as the unity of personal religious study results with those of the Jewish community as a whole (Marcus, 1996). The bar mitzvah tradition in the Jewish socialization entails careful guided study of the sacred scripts, with discussions of their moral, social and emotional implications. In other religions, rituals of communion have carried similar roles.

Adolescents' construction of themselves can also take forms which are easily considered 'delinquent'. This follows already from the basic conditions for any thrill – it is a flirtation at the boundary of possibilities. Since many of such boundaries of possibilities are defined socially, it is the transgression of social norms that provides a ground for new thrills. Stealing is one of such activities in which adults' and adolescents' perspectives diverge.

The 'age for stealing': thrill-seeking at the boundary of property

Stealing is a label. It is a label attached to a category of acts of taking some object from some location to some other location, by some active agent. We take objects from one location to another all the time, yet we do not constantly 'steal' these objects. The whole issue of applicability of the label of stealing (or robbing) to an act of taking depends upon the meaning of *ownership* of the objects thus taken.

Can one steal from oneself? The simple answer is no. When I own an object and take it from one place to another it would be absurd to consider it my stealing of the object from myself. Yet if that object is a sculpture, previously displayed in the middle of a city, which I have bought legally (and hence my ownership of the sculpture now applies to the object located in the context of a publicly 'owned' environment, for example a city square), I can be accused of 'stealing the sculpture from the public' (as it had become part of the public environment previously to my buying it). Of course after the act of buying the sculpture I own it, and can remove it to some other location. Yet I can – at least metaphorically – be accused of stealing.

This example may be far-fetched, but conflicts between legal and moral 'ownerships' occur in the sociopolitical domain in less obvious ways. A company buys an old building in a city, planning to tear it down and replace it by a modern one. Yet the city power-holders stop it by reference to the historical building being listed as one that must be preserved. Zoning limitations on what an owner of a piece of land can build on their own property are an example of mixing of the boundaries of ownership (that is, the owner owns the land, but does not own the right to build anything they want on that land).

Transfer of ownership by socially legitimate acts
Social rule systems specify whether a particular act of taking an object – which belongs to somebody else – is stealing, or any of the legitimate object transfers. Obviously, *purchasing* an object from its owner is a legitimate socioeconomic act. Yet not all objects can be bought: buying another person (even with the person's own consent) would be considered an act of introducing *slavery*. Yet buying the performance of specific skills on a temporary basis – ordering a taxi, using a waitress to transport ordered food to one's restaurant table, or a woman to clean one's house, take care of children, or breast-feed them – is not an act of slavery but part of legitimate *service-for-hire*.

Similarly, *borrowing* (or *renting*) the object from the owner is a temporary but legitimate act of object transfer.[5] Asking another person – threatening by force – to give up one's possessions is not. Under ordinary circumstances, such act is considered *robbery* and considered legally outlawed. Yet, simultaneously, the sociopolitical system includes regular expropriation of some of the property of the owners by legal force – called *taxation* – which is *not* considered an act of robbery but the *duty* of the owners to give up the specified amount of owned resources to the superordinate political power unit. Yet, if the owners of property decide to give an extra amount of their resources

to some official in the power hierarchy, *that act of voluntary giving* is considered *bribery* and punished in accordance with legislation to fight something called 'corruption'. At the same time, owners of property are encouraged (and sometimes demanded) to make other kinds of voluntary contributions – to charitable organizations. These are neither bribery, nor robbery, nor an act of stealing.

This little exercise on different meanings that regulate the acts of transfer (temporary or permanent) of objects illustrates how the collective-cultural and personal-cultural systems of meaningful organization of everyday life worlds of human beings are structured by basic general (and ill-defined) meanings. This generality becomes very concrete if one situates it in a real-life activity context.

Boundaries between stealing and non-stealing
Consider two scenarios in a shop where specially valued objects – jeans – may be sold. An adolescent enters the store:

SCENARIO 1: The adolescent picks up a pair of jeans, goes to the specially designated store area to try them on.
SCENARIO 2: The adolescent picks up a pair of jeans, and goes out of the front door of the shop.

Both scenarios entail an act of taking the object (jeans) from one place to another, yet the physical boundary (of the door of the jeans store) is also the symbolic boundary between stealing and non-stealing. (Imagine Scenario 2 being followed up: the store security person goes after the adolescent, who is caught in his or her car, trying on the jeans taken from the shop, and who claims that he/she just took them to the car to try on!)

The situation with socioculturally set boundaries is an ample site for co-construction of psychological self-identity phenomena. This is what happens in case of regular adolescent thrill-seeking (Lightfoot, 1997). Among other thrills, shop-stealing ('shop-lifting') is one appropriately challenging task. That stealing can acquire psychological functions (rather than serve an economic need) is proved by phenomena of adolescents stealing an object (for example, jeans) which they have sufficient money to purchase – yet *the fact of stealing adds symbolic value* to the object which would not have been there otherwise.

Shop-stealing is largely a phenomenon of the teenage years, as evidence from Victoria (Australia) indicates (see Figure 13.2). The major peak is around 13–14 years of age.

Adolescent shop-stealing has been shown to include a number of functional sub-types

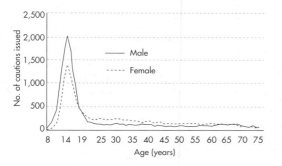

FIGURE 13.2 *Adolescence as a period of accentuated stealing efforts – data from Victoria, Australia (from Lawrence et.al., 1994 – reproduced by permission from Jeanette A. Lawrence)*

(Krasnovsky and Lane, 1998). These functions are experience of thrills, relations with peers, inherent desire for the products and performing a 'forbidden' act.

Three major social representations are used by laypersons to explain the fact of adolescent shop-stealing: 'greedy', 'needy' and 'troubled' (Lawrence and Hore, 1993). These representations are taken into account by the 'social others' of the stealers. As a phenomenon, stealing has led to *post factum* explanations of the developmental backgrounds of these 'needy' or 'troubled' youngsters.

In their ontogenetic history, child psychiatrists have tried to link at least some of the stealing tendencies to early social relations. It is in the prerequisites of stealing that John Bowlby's attachment perspective (see Chapter 10) found its origin.

Bowlby's ideology revisited: 'the rheumatic fever'?

Bowlby oriented his explanation towards the input from social environment as the precursor for stealing. His explanation was twofold. First, in the realm of public discourse of mental health, he suggested direct linear causality ('parental absence in early childhood' → 'psychopathology in adolescence'), rather than an explanation of systemic kind. However, his own empirical data include evidence in favour of the co-construction of stealing episodes in children and adolescents. Furthermore, when analysing his cases, Bowlby remained true to his psychoanalytic background and utilized models of systemic causality.

Bowlby's work was based on his analysis of cases of childhood and adolescent stealing, which he described as an analogue with contagious diseases:

theft, *like rheumatic fever*, is a disease of childhood and adolescence, and, as rheumatic fever, *attacks in later life* are frequently in the nature of recurrences. (Bowlby, 1944, p. 19; added emphasis)

Bowlby's explanation of the social context that leads to childhood and adolescent theft was, not surprisingly, phrased in terms of his attachment perspective (see Chapter 10), emphasizing the role of the mother in creating emotional conditions analogical to those of 'rheumatic fever'. The notion of the continuous and stable home surfaces in Bowlby's thinking as a basic assumption (see Chapter 5, and Figure 5.1):

in several cases sympathetic discussions with the mothers of the children revealed that their apparent love for their child was only one aspect of their feeling about him. Often an intense, though perhaps un-admitted, dislike and rejection of him also came to light. Furthermore very careful enquiries showed a *remarkable* proportion of children who, for one reason or another, had *not* lived securely in *one* home *all* their lives *but had spent long periods away from home*. (Bowlby, 1944, p. 20; added emphasis)

This is an example of Bowlby's participation in the public rhetoric about social policy of mental health. It is clear that Bowlby's interpretation represents his basis within the British collective-cultural organization of family in the mid-twentieth century. Even some 50 years later, ideological rhetoric about 'family values' proliferates in different societies.

Bowlby's summary data (presented in Table 13.1) tell a more complex story. Bowlby made much out of the difference between Grade IV thieves (14 cases out of 44) and controls (2 out of 44) in the column of 'prolonged separation', claiming that:

The foregoing statistical analysis has demonstrated that a prolonged separation of a child from his mother (or mother figure) in the early years commonly leads to his becoming a persistent thief and an Affectionless Character . . . (Bowlby, 1944, p. 121)

This statement is also within the realm of socio-political discourse, taking place at the popula-tional level. Yet it goes a step further: here we can see a classic misinterpretation of statistical evidence – a move from populational to generic-individual talk (see also Chapter 5).

Efforts to replicate Bowlby's sample-level finding (Naess, 1959) have not succeeded. The phenomenon of the child's separation from the mother at an early age can lead different children along multiple trajectories of their life courses (see Chapter 1 on multilinearity of development).

TABLE 13.1 *John Bowlby's data on children's and adolescents' theft*

| | | ETIOLOGICAL FACTORS | | | | |
Degree of stealing[a]	No. of cases	Possible genetic	Prolonged separations	Ambivalent mothers	Hatred by fathers	Recent traumatic event
Grade IV	23	8	14	9	3	1
Grade III	10	4	3	4	3	5
Grade II	8	5	—	5	—	4
Grade I	3	2	—	3	—	1
Total Grades I, II and III	21	11	3	12	3	10
Controls	44	19	2	32	7	11

[a] Grades of theft:
  Grade I: only one theft
  Grade II: a few thefts
  Grade III: irregular mild pilfering over a long period
  Grade IV: persistent and serious stealing, in most cases over a long period

Source: Bowlby, 1944, p. 120

In moving from one level to the other, Bowlby changed his model of causal explanation. At the populational level of discourse, his claim was set in terms of direct causality. This is the model of causality that is used in laypersons' discourse, and utilized in political rhetoric of any kind. Yet, as a psychoanalyst, Bowlby provided a systemic explanation of the phenomenon of stealing in childhood and adolescence that was directly psychoanalytic:

By stealing the child hopes for libidinal satisfaction, though in reality it proves ineffective, because the symbol of love has been mistaken for the real thing. From earliest days libidinal satisfaction is associated with obtaining possession of things. In infancy it is milk, in later years toys and sweets; and even in adult life a drink, a box of chocolates, a cigarette or a good meal are the bearers of kindly feelings from one person to another. Food and other objects thus become symbols of affection. *A child separated from his mother comes to crave both for her love and for its accompanying symbols in this craving*, if unsatisfied, later presents itself as stealing. The fact that most of these children stole food or money to buy food and that these thefts were often from their mothers, was clearly no accident. The food they *stole was no doubt felt to be* the equivalent of love from the mother whom they had lost, though *probably none was conscious of the fact*. (Bowlby, 1944, p. 121; added emphasis)

This explanation gives us an opportunity to elaborate the working of the mind of the researcher, along the lines of the 'two inductions'

of C. Lloyd Morgan (see Chapter 5, especially Figure 5.4). The fact of stealing exists in the loop of extrospective induction, yet the researcher's own introspective induction loop projects onto it the '*craving for love*' (which is assumed to be *not provided* by the mother), the '*feeling*' that objects *are equivalents for such love*, and proposition that the stealers would *have no conscious reflection upon it*. Extrospection provides the facts about the others' conduct, yet introspective projection by the researcher creates an explanatory system that would remain unchallenged because it is set up to be so.

A case of an 'affectionless character'
Bowlby emphasized the diagnosis of affectionless character among the different cases. Derrick O'C (age 11.5 years, reported stealing since age 8) was an example of such affectionless character – being separated from his foster mother at age 3 and living with a mother who never wanted him and disliked him (Bowlby, 1944, p. 45). Derrick had been charged by his father with stealing money from his overcoat pocket, and with stealing bicycles. His mother had claimed that Derrick

. . . pilfered on and off since he was eight, biscuits or pennies off the mantelpiece to buy sweets. He had only been known to steal one thing from school – a pen-knife – for which he had been caned. His parents always knew when he had stolen because he 'acts unnaturally'. It was this which led them to suspect him of taking the £3, which, they found subsequently, he had spent on fireworks, football matches, and sweets. (Bowlby, 1944, p. 45)

Derrick himself confessed the thefts, explaining these by reference to having been transferred to the care of a neighbour in the first three years of life. The mother had borne him at the beginning of her marriage, and seemed to 'have found him a burden' (as Bowlby described it):

> The mother continued to work and Derrick was parked out with the neighbour for his first three years. His mother visited him every two or three weeks but his principal attachment appears to have been to the foster-mother, whom he called 'Mummy Rosy'. When he was three years old, his mother became pregnant again, gave up work, and so had Derrick home. This was evidently a great shock to the boy, who had grown fond of his foster-mother and regretted leaving her. . . . A few months later Johnny was born and when Mrs. O'C. had recovered sufficiently to resume work both boys were sent to spend the day with another neighbour. When Derrick was sent to school he screamed a lot and was afraid to be left by his mother. However, he did well, was usually top of his class . . .
>
> The mother openly preferred Johnny because he was so much more responsive. She shouted at Derrick, was inclined to blame him for everything which disappeared and tried to shame him by saying 'If you weren't here we'd have had no troubles.' His father had often beaten him severely for the stealing and had kept him indoors. (Bowlby, 1944, p. 45)

Assuming that Bowlby's description of the case is sufficiently adequate, we can trace a complex system of mutual co-construction of a complicated relationship between the parents and Derrick, which may lead to the acts of stealing as one of its results. Stealing is not 'the problem' – some aspects of the family system in this case are. The case of the mother working – and child care delegated to others (see Chapter 7) is not unusual in any human society. Yet in the British social context of the late 1940s this wider human reality was not recognized, and the social demands for mothers' roles were moralistically promoted for women.

The case above is again heavily reliant on the adults' – parents, teachers and clinicians – views of Derrick's general development (and of the act of stealing within it). A careful analysis would reveal that Bowlby – as most mental health specialists would – created a double message about Derrick. First, the social circumstances surrounding his childhood were elaborated as causally leading to his stealing. Secondly, the outcome of his conduct was clinically diagnosed

(as affectionless character). Both social ideologies – built on the social representations of the role of the family – and the clinical outcome classification (psychiatric categorization of cases) were united in the explanation.

Constructing adolescent pathologies

The above excursion into Bowlby's analysis of adolescent thieves demonstrates the social power of psychiatrists' construction of a category of pathology, which can subsequently be linked with sociopolitical issues fought over in the given society at the given time. Contemporary psychology of adolescence (in the United States) may be similarly built on the basis of social concerns about aggressivity shown – at times through successful use of firearms – in social contexts. Similarly, the move of adolescent eating disorders into the centre stage of discussion of adolescence can be seen as a social construction of focus. In a society where adults have constructed their worries about 'right ways' of eating – allowing exercise clubs and diet food production to become lucrative industries – the issues of anorexia of adolescents often become focused upon. The practice of fasting for the sake of moral improvement has been utilized in most of the world's religions, in one or another form. Yet, when adolescents borrow from that time-honoured *social* control practices in their *personal* control efforts to gain symbolic capital (which thinness for girls has in occidental societies), it easily becomes a 'problem' – even a pathological one – associated with the 'special age' of adolescence. It is possible to trace how adults actively project their own psychological issues upon adolescents, and subsequently present the latter as 'being problematic'.

History of fasting
Our contemporary concerns about anorexic girls grow out of the long tradition in European-type societies of controlling one's soul through controlling the body. The cases of medieval nuns (later to become saints) where self-starvation was a major marker of religious devotion are now known (Bell, 1985). Fasting was a self-control domain that marked Christianity from the time of its emergence in third to fourth century Rome. Over the Middle Ages it became a socially regulated practice, and it is by the seventeenth century that fasting started to differentiate from being the single criterion of European Christian 'feminine piety':

> From the seventeenth-century on for many religiously inspired women excessive fasting (and

self-castigation in general) had lost its significance, as it was gradually superseded by tiredless charity, teaching, and care. Parallel to this evolution it is clear that from the early modern period on food abstinence did not occur any longer predominantly within a religious context. In the fifteenth and sixteenth centuries bewitchment and demonic possession became a popular interpretation of self-starvation. From the sixteenth century onwards, however, fasting became increasingly alienated from its traditionally religious background. Self-starvation became part of a rather pedestrian circuit where it gradually developed into a commercial spectacle. Particularly in the nineteenth century some exploited the admiration and astonishment which extended fasts still aroused, and made the 'hunger art' into a source of income. This no longer took place in cloisters or cells, but at fairs. Simultaneously self-induced starvation was annexed by the emerging medical sciences and labeled as pathological. (Vandereycken and van Deth, 1994, p. 31)

The secularized fasting became socially designated as pathological (as it undermined the goal of creating a 'healthy spirit' in one's body and mind). At the same time, the 'industry of beauty' in occidental societies was creating the desired image of thinness as a socially suggested goal (see also Chapter 7 on body forming). The two opposite rhetorical directions – 'thin is beautiful' and 'self-starvation is pathological' – have been in tension in occidental societies over the twentieth century. Adolescents both in the nineteenth (see Brumberg, 1988) and the twentieth centuries have been internalizing this tension into their personal cultures, where it can transform into excessive forms. The adults' equally internalized obsession with 'healthy eating' constitutes the background for adolescents' relation to their bodies through an anxious coordination of eating and non-eating (diets, self-starvation, induced vomiting etc.).

In the twentieth century, the focus on adolescent girls' anorexia has become widespread. The core of the syndrome is conscientious effort at weight loss, paralleled with self-control (in resistance to food-temptations), all leading to the emaciation of the body. Becoming thin becomes a personally set and obsessive, goal – yet the reaching of the goal does not liberate the person, but makes her increasingly self-punitive.

If the social suggestions for thinness are integrated constructively into the personal cultural world of the adolescent, the activity of achieving thinness and maintaining it can take complex forms. Anorexia in these cases can become a difficult pathological phenomenon, well out of control of anybody, including the adolescent herself.

A general issue involved in the striving for thinness is the meaning of feelings about one's own body. Thinness is in many ways a goal just opposite to the feminine ideal of sensuality and maternity, which over centuries has privileged healthy formedness of female bodies. This preference of course has been linked with a lower level of affluence of the preferers. The possibilities of constructing the value of thinness are prerogatives of the richer parts of the social order.

AUTO- AND HETEROSENSUALITY IN DEVELOPMENT

The person's body is always a cultural question. This is the case with an adolescent's relation to their own body, as well as relations between males and females. These issues enter the domain of personal-cultural ideations in full swing.

Construction of heterosexual experiences

The move out of childhood into adult life involves cultural guidance of heterosexual activities. In different societies such preparation takes a vast variety of forms, depending upon the collective-cultural meanings of sexuality (see Chapter 8), as well as upon the general organization of life course transitions. In societies where marriage takes place closely after menarche, girls are often allowed to enjoy their heterosexuality to the greatest extent – followed by marriage, with all of its constraints. Restrictions on adolescent heterosexuality can also be found where there are specific rules of property exchange in the given society (Schlegel and Barry, 1991, p. 131). It is both protection of transfer of property and treatment of adolescent girls as value linked with property, that leads to the restriction of heterosexuality.

However, the issue of regulation of young people's heterosexual experiences is the issue in different forms. Aside from the obvious – parental control – there have been various forms of societal organization of children's heterosexual experience. Most of these have utilized adolescents' heterosexual interests in the service of creating social group cohesion. The examples of the village dormitory, and the *ngweko* heterosensual petting arrangement indicate such appropriation. These two examples will illustrate a case where adolescents' heterosensual experiences are promoted – in one case under adult (*ghotul*), in the other case by peer (*ngweko*) guidance – to uphold a strict heterosexual social rule system. The third example – of the 'dating game' of US adolescents in this century – is an example of a cultural organization of heterosexual relationships that guides the participants towards elimination of sensuality (and simultaneous working-out of contractual character) of heterosexual encounters. The domain of growing interest in sexuality in adolescence is biologically guaranteed, and as such becomes an arena for different possible forms of culturally constructed regulation forms. Yet all of these forms lead the teenagers towards the same end – acceptance of the heterosexual role relationships within the adult social role expectations (of marital roles etc.).

The Muria *ghotul*

The 'Muria' is a general label used for various tribal ethnic groups in the Bastar State in Central India (Elwin, 1947), whose main subsistence activity is agricultural production. The *ghotul* is a village dormitory where children and adolescents of both sexes go for participation in social evening activities, and to sleep at night. All children of the community are expected to participate in the activities of the *ghotul*. These activities entail cultural guidance of adolescents' heterosexual experiences.

The symbolic meanings of the Muria *ghotul* were linked with a legendary figure, Lingo, to whom the origin of the village dormitory idea is traced. Lingo's personalized message to children – to learn the ways of communal life and work and satisfy one's sensual needs – has been utilized for organization of the *ghotul*.

There is another, adults-based, reason for the invention of the village dormitory. Namely, *it was considered sinful for parents to be involved in sexual intercourse in front of their children*. Thus the *ghotul* is an appropriate place that provides collective experiences for the children and privacy for their parents.

The traditional *ghotul* (in the first half of the twentieth century) took in children at about 6–7 years of age. The children would remain members of the *ghotul* until their marriage in late adolescence. All during the stay in the *ghotul*, both boys and girls were subjected to suggestions in favour of chastity. The children in the *ghotul* were subjected to '*ghotul* marriage' that lasted until their real marriage.

The *ghotul* supervisors (adults) set up social rules that de-emphasize the development of exclusive heterosexual bonds between boys and girls. No boy could treat any girl as 'his'. A boy and girl can sleep together for three nights, after which they have to change their sleeping partners. The goal of the *ghotul* is to enhance community cohesion – just the opposite of per-

sonalized relations. The participating children are expected to internalize the communal ideology, and turn it into their own personal convictions. Thus, a boy explained to the researcher:

> We change partners because we want everyone to be happy; if one boy and one girl are always together as if they were man and wife, then some would be happier than others; the best boys and the best girls would be the property of individuals instead of being the property of the *ghotul*, and the rest would be miserable. (Elwin, 1947, p. 344)

One can compare the *ghotul* context to other settings ('collective husband' in polyandrous marriages, see Chapter 6; Krishnamurti school, see Chapter 12) where young children's affective-sensual psychological functions are used to build joint group feelings. The goal for social canalization is strictly set at not allowing privileged partnerships to emerge. Since the heterosensual and heterosexual experiences are the prime areas where affective bonding is established, it is relevant to promote equal sharing of the experiences across persons.

The Gikuyu *ngweko* system and its historical change

The organization of the Gikuyu society (in Kenya) both in the past (the 1920s–1930s described by Kenyatta, 1965) and in the present (the 1980s described by Worthman and Whiting, 1987) provides a picture of how adolescents' heterosexual experiences are both permissive and restrictive at the same time.

The specific Gikuyu pattern of mutual fondling (*ngweko*) fitted the social organization of the Gikuyu society, which was age- and sex-cohort oriented. The social role of young girls was to strengthen the social fabric of the society organized around age cohorts of batchelor warriors. The primary unit of heterosexual relations was between age sets of young girls and young males, rather than between persons of the two genders. That created the specific context for the *ngweko* system, which involved the age period between adolescent initiation ritual and marriage (usually a range of four to six years).

Furthermore, the collective-cultural goal of organizing adolescents' heterosexual experiences required full maintenance of virginity by the time of marriage. Thus, on the one hand, the cultural system required heterosexual experimentation, while on the other it prohibited pre-marital sexual intercourse. This task was further complicated since the conduct of the age-sets was autonomous from any adult supervision. Often the age-sets visited each other in different villages, thus even creating geographical distance between the home grounds and play grounds.

A solution to this problem was guaranteed by setting up a redundantly controlled autonomous social context. First, the control over not becoming involved in sexual intercourse was distributed between both boys and girls, and shared within the given age-set. Furthermore, *ngweko* was presented symbolically as a sacred act, which involves both sharing of partners and sensual closeness. Jomo Kenyatta described the historical practice:

> The girls visit their boy-friends at a special hut, *thingira*, used as a rendezvous by young men and women. They bring with them their favourite food and drinks as a token of affection. These are shared among the age-group in the *thingira*, who eat their food collectively. No boy can eat or drink by himself what has been brought to him by his sweetheart; such act would be severely punished. In this way the boys who have no girl-friends are included in all entertainment, because the good-looking man of the age-group does not act for himself; his popularity is considered the popularity of the group as a whole, and his girl-friends are also regarded as friends of the members of the age group. So no matter how ugly a boy may be, his ugliness is compensated for by the more attractive members of his age group . . .
>
> Girls may visit the *thingira* at any time, day or night. After eating, while engaged in conversation with the boys, one of the boys turns the talk dramatically to the subject of *ngweko*. If there are more boys than girls, the girls are asked to select (*kuoha nyeki*) whom they want to have as their companions. The selection is done in the most liberal way. The language used is either in proverbs or indirectly as, for instance, the phrase '*Kuoha nyeki*' – to tie the grass – which is equivalent to 'Choose your partner.' In such a case it is not necessary for the girls to select their own intimate friends, as this would be considered selfish and unsociable. Of course, this does not mean that the girls do not sometimes have *ngweko* with those whom they are specially fond of, but generally they follow the rules of exchanging partners . . .
>
> After the partners have been arranged, one of the boys gets up, saying: '*Ndathie kwenogora*' (I am going to stretch myself). His girl partner follows him to the bed. The boy removes all of his clothing. The girl removes her upper garment . . . and retains her skirt . . . and her soft leather apron, *mwengo*, which she pulls back between her legs and tucks in together with the leather skirt, *mothuru*. The two V-shaped tails of her *mothuru* are pulled forward between her legs from behind and fastened to the waist, thus keeping *mwengo* in position and forming an effective protection of her private parts. In this position the lovers lie down together facing each other, with their legs interwoven to prevent any movement of their hips. They then begin to fondle each other, rubbing their breasts together, whilst at the same time they engage in love-making conversation until they gradually fall asleep. Sometimes the partners experience sexual relief, but this is not an essential feature of the *ngweko*.
>
> The chief concern in this relationship is the enjoyment of the warmth of the breast, *orugare wa nyondo*, and not the full experience of sexual intercourse. (Kenyatta, 1965, pp. 151–152)

This description indicates how the function of maintenance of age-group cohesion is the major task for the *ngweko* system. In the traditional Gikuyu society, the role of maidens was to strengthen the social fabric of the region

> . . . by entertaining the batchelor warriors, often those of their older brothers' age set, when they visited from neighboring hamlets. This ideally pan-territorial identification and social cohesion within the age sets was to be cemented by exogamous patrilocal marriages, with a shift in status to adult married woman marking the end of maidenhood stage. Maidens married at about age 19, while the warriors' first marriage occurred at around 26. (Worthmam and Whiting, 1987, pp. 149–150)

So *ngweko* was a cultural form that fulfilled a number of goals at the same time. First, it was an age-set group cohesion-building device. That cohesion is built through individuals' heterosensual experience – yet in ways that do not allow individuals to use the experience for the establishment of possessiveness of a specific other person. The social rule that prescribes food distribution within the group, and joint eating of the food, is a central symbolic aspect here (see also Chapter 8 about the role of food in interpersonal relations). Secondly, *ngweko* provided all participating individuals with guidance towards enjoyment of bodily pleasure – paired with strict self-control against sexual intercourse. Thirdly, it provided a transitory organization of bodily needs of young people for the period after leaving child status and before entering the full adult state (of marriage). Finally, it was meant to coordinate the balance between communities – as the visits by age sets of boys were to neighbouring villages.

African societies have undergone rapid changes in recent decades, since Kenyatta provided his account (which was his doctoral thesis in anthropology). Under growing breakdown of the traditional stable social structures in the rural areas, the Gikuyu *ngweko* system by now has basically disappeared (Worthman and Whiting, 1987). In line with such disappearance, childbearing out of marriage has grown. In 1940, no child in the Gikuyu society was born out of marriage. By the 1950s, 4.8 per cent were in that category, and by the 1960s the percentage had increased to 11.4 (Worthman and Whiting, 1987, p. 146). When Gikuyu adolescents were interviewed in 1983 about heterosexual relations, some of them were aware that such a practice existed, but none had been instructed by their elders in how to practise it. Heterosexual relations were reported by the adolescents as crucial for their selves in a way quite different from that of preserved virginity until marriage:

> Contraception is obtained by subterfuge, but young women fear that its use diminishes long-term fertility: sterility is much more negatively valued by both sexes than is premarital pregnancy, and has a strongly negative effect on a female's future. It is therefore an outcome more greatly to be feared than unwanted pregnancy. Males have little incentive to use contraception, and reported no use, but often *expressed the value of abstinence and self-constraint unless marriage was considered*. The two young men who were cited and fined more than twice in pregnancy cases during the recent study period were felt by other young men to be *unreliable 'bad lots' with unmanly lack of self-control*. (Worthman and Whiting, 1987, p. 161; added emphasis)

The particular cultural form of *ngweko* had disappeared, yet the basic values of male self-control remained in place. All cultural forms of regulation of heterosensuality are transitory constructions: they are sufficient for the whole structure of circumstances, but can become transformed when the circumstances change.

From 'courtship' to 'dating': adolescent heterosexual relations in the United States

Heterosexual relations in the United States in the second half of the twentieth century constitute a transformation of the earlier (nineteenth century) courtship system. The latter was closely supervised by parents, and involved visits to either the boy's or the girl's home.

In this century, the practices changed dramatically. A distinctive 'youth culture' emerged in US society. This entailed the differentiation of the realm of peer relations (or: horizontal, age set, social structure) from its inter-generational (vertical) background. This transition was channelled by the social institution of high school in the United States:

> By the early twentieth century, child labor laws forced many teen-aged children out of the workplace,

and compulsory education laws forced others into school. Even earlier, high school education had begun to replace low-level work experience, as the most important preparation for managerial positions in American businesses. (Spurlock and Magistro, 1998, p. 19)

The US 'high school' became thus a place for work – towards upwardly mobile social orientations – and teachers became the foremen (and forewomen) of the educational conveyor belts (see also Chapter 12).

Changes in the adolescents' lives in the United States were directly linked with macro-social processes of industrialization, urbanization and mechanization in the society. The enormous influx of immigrants in the 1890s, and the industrial development in cities, led the way to breaking of the person–parents–local community ties, and their replacement with identities of wider collectives, cities and social class segregation. The age set (of children at school, or in industry) establishes its own social norms and interactive practices. The separation of the latter from the control of the parents is made possible by city life, and by the adoption of the automobile.

This process was heavily veiled in the social discourse about morality. Thus, when working-class youth (in New York City) started to flock into dance halls in the early 1900s, 'public opinion' (which was then, as now, dominated by middle-class values and value carriers) entered into a rhetorical war against the proliferation of 'vice' (Peiss, 1986, pp. 97–114). Precisely at the time in US history as when traditionally over-regulated social norms of young women's conduct were breaking down (creating the 'dance hall culture' of the 1910s, and further liberation in the 1920s), the opposite forces in US society were attempting to construct a hyper-puritanistic moral ethos by illegalizing child labour, prostitution, and by attempting to 'save' the morals of the adolescents who led their lives without chaperones. Yet the gender relations of the parents continued at the peer level in the adolescent social worlds:

> Women enjoyed dancing for the physical pleasure of movement, its romantic and sensual connotations, and the freedom it allowed them. The commercial dance halls were public spaces they could attend without escorts, choose companions for the evening, and express a range of personal desires. Nevertheless, the greater freedom of expression women found in the dance halls occurred in a heterosexual context of imbalanced power and privileges. (Peiss, 1986, pp. 106–107)

The liberation of teenage and young adult heterosexual relations from the control of parents introduced a new form of control – by inter-group evaluation and intra-group competition. Young women came to compete for male attention in such public places, and the same socio-moral evaluative rules that the wider society carried entered into the world of adolescents. Even with parental control out of the way, the young re-introduced it at the level of the peer group. The role of the women in this re-introduction was crucial: their intra-group competition became paired with moralistic mutual evaluation (scape-goating, behind-the-back gossiping, coalition formation) and constituted a powerful social control system over the 'male urges'. Further-more, the unity of female 'being in control' was undermined by their intra-gender group com-petition. The focus on being 'together' (sisterhood idea) while actually being apart (rivalry) can be seen as creating the personal-cultural uncertainty which was (and is) used by any advice-givers for their profit. The cosmetics industry began to proliferate its help to women to create their self-dramatizations on a wide scale. Since the 1920s the faces and bodies of women in the United States have been targets of the cosmetics makers, with willing cooperation of the women them-selves (see Peiss, 1998). 'Making up' the face is reminiscent of body painting in any society, and bears resemblance to veiling. A made-up face can be viewed as a veiled face, where the veiling is either invisible or barely visible.[6]

The dating script

The dating system emerged in the 1920s in con-junction with the emergence of public activities in the community (village dances) and increasing mobility of the adolescents without dependency on the parents. Leisure became increasingly commercialized – hence the emergence of a new 'market' that would cater for the personal-cultural needs of the adolescents who brought their pri-vate relationships to specially prescribed public places (Modell, 1983). The automobile created a sphere of separation of the adolescents from the parents. This created a domain of activities that could not be directly supervised by adults.

In accordance with *the basic unity* of competitive and conformist social orientations in US society (see Mead, 1930), the dating system that emerged in the 1920s can be viewed as a micro-image of the wider society. Yet that society has persistently blocked the understanding of the unity of the opposites – competitive individualism and con-formist collectivism – from its self-representation. This collective-cultural 'blinder' has led to folk models that create everyday life in simple oppositions – the positive is always opposed to negative, the black to white, and progress to regress.

In case of US adolescent dating, there were a number of hidden assumptions guiding the construction of the dating system. First, there was the *rhetoric of gender*. The two genders were assumed to act in a specifically divergent manner in heterosexual relations. The males were assumed to possess aggressive, by-themselves uncontrol-lable, sexual urges. The only way to handle such urges would be the strict, controlling moral stance – 'true womanhood' – which was supposed to heroically withstand the uncontrollable sexual advances on behalf of the young men.

Secondly, there was the puritanical look at sensual (and sexual) pleasure as morally inappro-priate in itself. This basic cultural canalization has of course been present in the Anglo-Saxon tradition since the seventeenth century, and has been one of the cornerstone values of the establishment of British North American colonies (and later of the United States and Canada).

Thirdly, there was the economic orientation (costs/benefits analysis of interpersonal relations) that was widespread in the rapidly developing capitalist society. Particular heterosexual relations became 'measured for their value' in terms of the culturally constructed symbolic capital. The latter varied by social class: it was the case that the middle-class heterosexual relations of US adolescents were more rigorously overcontrolled by the 'marketplace orientation' of heterosexual relations. It became important for a man (or a woman) for the sake of their own personal-cultural construction of 'self-esteem' how the partner with whom they appeared in public looked in the eyes of the latter. The self-esteem of the young man or woman was thus put on the 'market of evaluation' on the basis of the characteristics of their displayed partners. The actual heterosensual (or sexual) activity was secondary to the social value-constructing function of the 'date'.

Thus, by the 1920s,

> Boys or young men asked for the company of a girl or young woman to some public amusement – dance, movie, party, or other social event. They went without adult supervision or interference. The male member of the couple paid and frequently in the 1920s provided transportation. After the main event, the couple often went out to eat and frequently would try to find some private place for necking. Whereas physical intimacy became an expected element of dating, the limits of sexual experience depended on the girl and to a large extent on her class. Middle-class women typically placed greater limits on their physical freedom with male partners than working-class women did. (Spurlock and Magistro, 1998, p. 26)

Thus, dating in the 1920s replaced courtship – and turned what was previously a 'marriage-making' process into a setting of leisure in heterosexual company where the pay-offs were in terms of temporary accumulation of social capital. Dating began to 'rule in' a number of strictly standardized hetero-erotic practices (kissing, petting), while retaining strict rules upon accessibility of sexual intercourse. In its puritanic ethos, American dating is as overcontrolling for actual sexual intercourse as the Gikuyu *ngweko* system was. Yet the *ngweko* system guided the participants towards enjoyment of the pleasure of heterosensuality, while the American dating system worked against the enjoyment of any pleasure. The specific heterosexual practices which became allowed became immediately symbolized – the 'departure kiss' a girl was expected to give her dating partner (if she decided to do so) was a symbolic friendly gesture. Likewise, the allowable tactile contact forms were quickly and easily turned into the lists of 'dos' and 'don'ts'. The male was always to take the initiative – and the female, in a complementary way, to regulate the terms of her acceptance of the initiatives. Instead of heterosexual intimate sharing, the collective-cultural orientation of the dating was towards turning it into a strategic game played between adolescents. The following excerpt from an interview with a US adolescent (in the 1960s) indicates the internalization of the 'game' nature of the activity:

> *Interviewer*: You see this [dating] as pretty much a game of strategy?
> *Adolescent*: Definitely! It's one of the most fun games around too. Because you never know what's going to happen . . . It's up to you. There are no rules, really. There might be a couple of rules that you take for granted, but basically . . .
> *Interviewer*: Like what [rules]?
> *Adolescent*: Well, not to do anything really nasty. Like go out with his best friend – break a date with him and go out with his best friend or something like that. Nothing really drastic, but aside from that there aren't too many rules, and *you've just always got to make sure that you're on top*, that you are winning because *if you're not winning you're losing and there's no tie*. So you always make sure you're winning. (Schwartz and Merten, 1967, p. 466; added emphasis)

The construction of dating as a competitive game eliminates the possibilities of developing collaborative relations between the partners. This example is perhaps an extreme case of a situation in which the collective-cultural moralistic orientation attains its goals through changing the nature of the setting – a heterosexual encounter

that is turned into a competition eliminates the pleasure of sexuality (which is culturally not desired) and substitutes it by the pleasure of winning (which is culturally desired).

The dating system of US adolescents, similarly to many other aspects of the interpersonal relations, moved to acquire the status of an informally understood script – or a contract. Goodchilds and Zellman asked their adolescent informants about female conduct patterns that would make it accepted that the male partner would be upset. These entailed a number of 'leading actions' towards sexual intercourse, which were not followed up:

> Two female behaviors stand out as inconsequential – responding to the male's kisses and lying down next to him. These are followed . . . by several relatively noncommittal behaviors – dating a man several times, allowing the man to 'touch and feel' her body, kissing the man first, and allowing the man to lie on top of her. A significantly more serious breach of contract is entailed if a woman 'touches the man below the waist'; worse yet would be to undress or allow herself to be undressed or to undress the man. The most reprehensible of the 11 behaviors in the eyes of the young people, male and female, is for the woman to change her mind – 'to say yes to sex and then say no'. Subjects of both genders shared this view that anger was justifiable when the female partner displayed certain behaviors but refused sex. (Goodchilds and Zellman, 1984, p. 237)

The emergence of legalistic contractual orientation in adolescents' heterosexual dating emerges here as a constructed form. Similarly to the Gikuyu *ngweko* system, the 'dating system' is under immediate peer control. Again similarly – yet in different directions – the 'dating system' leads the teenagers to re-construct the legalistic aspects of their adult society in their intimate relationships. As a result, the puritanical goal of distancing pleasurable feelings from the intimate encounters is achieved. The pleasure becomes subordinated to the meanings or morality and responsibility.

Social institutionalized temporary homo-eroticism: the Sambia case

The cultural guidance arena for adolescent sexual functions can also guide adolescents – interestingly enough, this is documented for males – towards homo-erotic practices, *which are subsequently to be reversed* into heterosexual ones. The case of the Sambia in New Guinea has been described by Gilbert Herdt (1980, 1982, 1987a, 1987b, 1990). The Sambia are a group in the

Eastern Highlands of New Guinea. Their not very numerous society (estimated population 2000 persons) is dispersed over a wide region. Men are hunters (and warriors), both women and men garden.

In terms of gender-role socialization, the Sambia assume qualitatively different trajectories for men and women. Gender groups are segregated from each other through boundaries constructed to gender-specific knowledge. The inter-gender social boundaries are internalized with the help of generic meanings, like 'shame'. For example, Sambia men would avoid mentioning of terms like menstrual blood or vagina as such mentioning is linked with promoting shame.

In line with that, social relations between the sexes are not only polarized but also hostile. For males, it means that boys are brought out from women's care and gradually initiated into the male secret world. *The primary identification of the boys is expected to be with other men* – loyalty to age set and respect for men older than they. This loyalty build-up is the cultural basis for the homo-erotic practices:

> Maleness is thought to depend on the *acquisition of semen* – the stuff of 'biological' maleness – for precipitating male anatomic traits *and* masculine behavioral capacities (e.g., prowess). Femaleness rests on the creation and circulation of blood, which is held, in turn, to stimulate the production of menstrual blood, the menarche, and final reproductive competence . . . In the native model . . . the femaleness is a natural development leading into feminine adulthood; maleness is not a naturally driven process but rather a personal achievement of which men wrest control through ritual initiations to ensure that boys attain adult masculine competence. (Herdt, 1982, p. 195; added emphasis)

The initiation rituals for boys include stages, at each of which the boy is brought into contact with the secret male knowledge, and guided to participate in male practices. For boys of Sambia, the notion of semen as a necessary food for growth leads to the acceptance of fellatio in the case of relations with older peers and adult males. It is an equivalent to mother's milk in its nutritional power – and hence has a central symbolic role in the male adolescent initiation. Similarly with the prevailing notion of semen as equivalent of blood (see Chapter 8, above), the Sambia boys acquire their masculine strength through the input of semen from their older age set peers and adults. All this takes place in the complete secrecy of the men's house, and is not to be discussed publicly.

The personal-cultural side of the introduction to semen intake by young boys is likely to be anxiety-ridden, especially as their pre-initiation life period does not provide them with any evidence of the practice. In Herdt's description of the self-report of one of the boys (Kambo), his worries about the first time were about not getting pregnant (indicating his lack of knowledge about pregnancy) and not receiving the urine in his mouth (Herdt, 1987b, pp. 280–281). These worries, however, were overridden by the meaning that the semen is 'just like mother's milk'. The instructions for the boy by peers and elders were coercive about the need for swallowing the semen, and linking it with the power of the milk.

Are the Sambia boys 'homosexual'? The case of Sambia male adolescence puts the easy labelling habit of European-type societies – which in our current time are dominated by journalistic sensationalism – to a critical test. The Sambia practice can be labelled 'homosexual' with remarkable ease. Yet it is not – the practice is embedded in a society where the preparation for manhood is (1) based on strictly male transfer of secret knowledge, and (2) the build-up of masculine power is assumed to go through semen intake. The latter is obviously available only from other males. The former – knowledge transfer – is age-set graded and hence needs to proceed from older age grades downward to younger ones. As the function of Sambia semen transfer is that of *symbolic nutrition* (rather than an example of same-gender sexual fixation), the phenomenon is probably closer to the patterns of 'wet nursing' (where non-parent females were hired to provide breast milk to the infants, for the sake of their health). Herdt's data indicate that early hetero-sexual *fellatio* is likewise presented to the young within the meaning system of nutrition (Herdt, 1987b, p. 178).

Once the Sambia adolescent boys become initiated into full manhood, the institutionalized fellatio disappears. The young males become married, and their sexual functions proceed fully within the realm of ordinary procreational hetero-sexual practices. Some exceptions – lack of success in making the transition to heterosexuality – have been reported to occur (Herdt, 1980). The Sambia meaningful concern about semen loss now becomes displaced into another secret male realm of adults – drinking tree-sap for the 'replacement' of semen lost to women in regular intercourse. Thus, the meaning of semen as a crucially powerful source of energy is retained in the self-system, but its collective-cultural role is transformed.

While creating a cross-gender separation at the internalized level, shame is clearly not regulating examples of homo-erotic and hetero-erotic contacts in the case of the practice of fellatio in male adult–adolescent–boy relations, as well as in boy–girl relations. The canalizing role of shame is overrun by the notion of 'food'. What for outsiders looks like a homo-erotic practice – *fellatio* – in the Sambia context is an act of gender-specific nutritional practice that cannot be accomplished in other ways.

RITUALS OF PASSAGE INTO ADULTHOOD

The notion of adolescent initiation rituals has been a popular topic in anthropology, leading to often exotic (and horror-filled) description of the customs of bringing adolescents into adulthood. In reality, most socially relevant transitions of human life course – birth, marriage, childbirth, death – are organized into one or another version of ritual. Coming 'of age' is as relevant an event: it is, for the adults, a kind of 'harvest festival' of children beginning their ripe adult life, filled with new demands. In some respects (see Chapter 12) all formal schooling can be seen as a (rather long) initiation ritual of children from their home backgrounds into the adulthood of participation in the particular kind of society.

Not every society has elaborate adolescent initiation rites (see Brown, 1963, for an overview). Those which do not, organize the transition in other ways – all transitions from childhood into adulthood are culturally organized. Thus, in US society a generic initiation rite is not present. Yet many of the specific rituals of attainment of specific cultural goals – drivers' licence tests, entrances into sororities or fraternities, and standardized test taking (SAT etc.) all are set up to have features resembling one or another side of adolescent initiation rites. In societies where initiation rituals have been elaborate – and in a literal sense blood-letting – they tend to become modified (such as in African societies). The system of initiation ceremonies is a dynamically changing set of action, feeling and reasoning tasks that adjusts itself to circumstances.

The traditional Gikuyu initiation ceremony

Jomo Kenyatta (1965) has described the Gikuyu initiation rites in the form they had in the 1930s. For both sexes, the ritual involved the physical operation of circumcision. The issue of (especially female) circumcision in African societies has received much attention worldwide yet the specific cultural context of the operation has not been carefully localized.

The sequence of the ritual
First, each of the children is prepared at home. About two weeks before the initiation the girl is

put on a special diet, which is believed to protect against loss of blood during the actual circumcision, as well as serve as a precaution against blood poisoning. The girl is assigned a female sponsor (*motiri*) who examines her and provides her with preparatory instructions for the ceremony. The *motiri* serves as an examiner – figuring out that the girl has had no sexual intercourse so far or indulged in masturbation. If the girl has broken these prohibitions (and confesses those to the *motiri*), the girl needs to undergo a special purification ritual.

Secondly, about three to four days before the ritual itself, the girl is taken to the homestead where the ceremony is to take place. There she meets all the other girls (and boys) who are scheduled to go through the initiation ceremony together. All of the youngsters are ceremonially adopted by the homestead as their children. What follows is a dancing ceremony that is considered to be an act of communion with the ancestral god (*morungu*), to protect the initiates. The dancing ceremony lasts the whole night. In the morning, the parents of all the children perform a ceremony of blessing. After that, the boys and girls return to their natal homes.

Thirdly, *the day before* the actual circumcision, the Gikuyu children participate in the Great Ceremonial Dance (*matuumo*). This involves body modification for girls – the *motiri* shaves one's girl-protégée's hair. The clothes are removed, and the girl is given a body massage. This is followed by a kin group ceremony of reunion with the ancestors. The *matuumo* dance begins at noon: it involves dancing around a decoration activity on an arch. Once that is accomplished (by the afternoon), the boys and girls are gender-segregated. The girls as a group move to a sacred tree, after which the boys are given the command to run to the tree (about a 2-mile run). The activities around the arrival at the tree are significant for the formation of the age set structure:

> The crowd which has already gathered around the tree await the arrival of the boys in order to judge the winner of the race. They shout and cheer merrily as the excited boys arrive, raising their wooden spears, ready to throw them over the sacred tree. The significance of this ceremonial racing is the fact that it determines the leader of that particular age group. The one who reaches the tree first and throws his wooden spear over the tree is elected there and then as the leader and the spokesman of the age-group for life. It is believed that such a one is chosen by the will of the ancestral spirits. . . . The girl who arrives at the sacred tree first is also regarded in the same way. She becomes the favourite, and all try to win her affection with the hope of marrying her. (Kenyatta, 1965, p. 135)

It is clear that both the age set group cohesion (through prolonged dances) and the within age-set differentiation (of leaders who would remain in that position for life) happens at this phase. All the events in the ritual as described are closely intertwined with the meaningful relations with the ancestors' spirits. At the end of the ceremony at the sacred tree, all youngsters give an oath to the tribe as a whole. This is an act of collective identity declaration. It includes a focus of keeping the tribal secrets from outsiders (including the not yet initiated members of the tribe).

Fourthly – and finally – the circumcision ceremony is performed. That happens on the next day after the loyalty oath. The procedure takes place in the early hours of the morning. First, the girl initiates are taken to a river, where

> They go up to the waist in the river, dipping themselves to the breast, holding up ceremonial leaves in their hands; then they begin shaking their wrists, dropping the leaves into the river as a sign of drowning their childhood behaviour and forgetting about it forever. The initiates spend about half an hour in the river, in order to numb their limbs and to prevent pain or loss of blood at the time of operation. The sponsors superintend to see that the initiates bathe in the correct manner, while the mothers, relatives and friends are present . . . , singing ritual and encouraging songs . . . (Kenyatta, 1965, p. 138)

After the bathing, the initiates are instructed to march to the homestead where the operation is to take place. Their path is not to be crossed by anybody (this is guaranteed by blowing a cere-monial horn, understood by others to keep out of the way). The initiates are instructed to hold their arms and hands in a special way – with both hands raised upwards, elbows bent, pressed against their ribs, with the fists closed and thumbs inserted between first and second fingers. This is a posture to signify that they will endure the operation firmly and fearlessly.

In the place of circumcision, the girls sit down in designated places. The sponsors sit behind them, holding their bodies. Only women are allowed on the premises – female circumcision is a strictly women's business. The girls recline, facing the sky, being embraced by their sponsors from behind. An old woman goes around, throwing cold water onto their genitals. The girls are supposed not to show any fear. Then a woman circumcision specialist emerges from the crowd, wearing special face-paint, and proceeds to cut the tip of the clitoris of each girl, with a special Gikuyu razor. Immediately the wound is treated by sprinkling some milk with herbs on the wound – to reduce the pain and check bleeding. Imme-diately the girl is covered with a new dress by the sponsor. As all the girls have been operated upon, the crowd begins to sing praise-songs for the girls who did not cry. The new initiates are then taken to a secluded hut for seclusion and recovery for six days.

The whole sequence of the initiation ritual illustrates the sequential nature of combining physical strain and stress features of the experi-ence with social support from different sources, and promotion of the social order into which the adolescents are initiated. Strictly speaking, the adolescents are initiated into an age set dominated course of adult development, with its internal organization (determined by the sacred tree ceremony). The function of the whole cere-mony is to guide the persons towards relevant linkages in the Gikuyu society – with the spirits of the ancestors (the dancing ceremony in phase 2), with the social role expectations (examination for sexual purity and – if necessary – purification, in the beginning). The passing of childhood is woven into the ritual in the bathing ceremony. The initiates are under external social suggestion to show fearless bravery all through the cere-mony, while specific techniques to guarantee it by themselves (note the way of holding hands before arrival in the circumcision place) and by the supportive 'social other' (the sponsor restraining the girl's body from behind). The actual circum-cision act is the culmination point of the whole ceremony. Excision of the tip of the clitoris becomes a bodily sign for the whole event – to be with the woman all of her life. As such, the collective-cultural ritual is being brought onto the woman's body – in a location of greatest significance for her feminine role.

The body-symbolic nature of circumcision may perhaps explain why the controversy in many African societies about female circumcision flares brightly, and why the practice is maintained against so many efforts by colonizers and health authorities to eradicate it. Symbols prevail as the functions they carry are supported by both personal and collective-cultural needs, which converge precisely in the case of painful pro-cedures. By endurance of pain as a symbolic activity, the personal-cultural system of a person gets a boost which cannot be available through activities that do not involve bodily sensations.[7]

ADOLESCENTS AS SOCIAL ACTORS: ROLE OF ADOLESCENTS IN SOCIAL INNOVATION

It is known already from the world of non-human primates that social innovation finds its roots in the activities of the young and the juvenile representatives of the species. In the case of

Japanese monkeys, it is the juveniles that begin new technological innovations in the monkey troops, such as washing grain out of sand (Kawai, 1963; Nishida, 1986). The case with humans is similar – it is the juvenile representatives of *Homo sapiens* who master the uses of the internet, crack computer codes and initiate solutions to the major problems of the world. These creative successes of adolescents entail many temptations for different social institutions to appropriate their creative activities by providing those with socially valued direction. Conversely, the socially undesirable directions become 'social problems'. An appropriate example of such differentiation is the question of *homicide* versus *suicide* committed by adolescents.

Two faces of homicide

Homicide can be of two kinds: anti-social and pro-social. The former are feared (and turned into the 'problem of adolescent aggressivity'). In contrast, cases of pro-social homicide by adolescents – in the context of recruitment of adolescents into military groups fighting for specific adults' political goals – goes without any such 'problem' construction (see Peters and Richards, 1998).

The reality of war is widespread around the world. Children in many parts of the world grow up with the realities of military takeovers of power, military robberies etc. Hence it is not surprising that they become easily recruited by military groups.

Interviews with youth involved in the military conflicts in Sierra Leone (Peters and Richards, 1998) provide evidence of the personal-cultural construction of wartime roles by adolescents. For example, a woman (20 years of age and with one child at the time of interview) who had volunteered to go into the army at age 16 provides a picture of ordinary-looking adaptation of herself (and her peers) to the wartime atrocities:

Q: What were you doing at the time you joined?
A: I was at secondary school in Freetown (Form 2).
Q: What made you join up?
A: I had a boyfriend who was a soldier, and I followed him from Freetown to Daru. I was attracted by the uniform. *Full combat looks smart.* I sent my mother a picture of me in full combat [gear] . . . That was the first she knew I had joined.
Q: Is the combat gear what makes girls want to fight?
A: Lots of young women followed the rebels . . . because they offered them items, and their regular men did nothing for them.
Q: Did you take part in fighting?
A: Yes.
Q: How did you prepare for battle?

A: I *just prayed* . . . I did not take any drugs . . .
Q: Did you kill rebels in battle?
A: Yes, plenty. Also, when soldiers came back to camp with rebel captives I would be ordered to 'wash' them.
Q: What was that?
A: To kill them.
Q: Why was that 'washing'? Did you spray bullets?
A: No, bullets are expensive. I would kill them one by one.
Q: Did you ever feel it was wrong to fight?
A: *I was defending my country.*
Q: Did you ever feel sorry for the dead rebels?
A: At first, when we advanced. And saw dead bodies, I would feel sorry, but we had to kill them. . . . They *would kill us first if they had the chance.* Rebels kill and split open the bellies of pregnant women. *Rebels rape any women soldiers* they catch . . . [Government] soldiers raped us sometimes in the forest, but they are more careful . . . The rebels, they all join in.
Q: Did you become pregnant at the war front?
A: I swallowed gunpowder as a contraceptive.
Q: Who showed it to you?
A: No one . . . I discovered it for myself. But I first took it to become brave for battle. If you take gunpowder before you sleep you will wake with red [fierce] eyes. (Peters and Richards, 1998, p. 191; added emphasis)

This rather revealing exposure of a young African woman's experiences in the local war is important in a number of ways. First, it indicates the personal-cultural reconstruction of the suggested positive meaning of the fighting (and killing) – 'I was defending my country'. Secondly, in parallel with that, we can observe acceptance of the fear of the enemy (who is supposed to rape any woman . . . while one's own soldiers rape women 'more carefully'). Thirdly, the girl's attachment to her boyfriend and the construction of the 'real smart' nature of herself in full military gear indicates how the attraction value can be promoted through power-possessive instruments (which military equipment is). As can be seen from the example, the move from ordinary adolescence to military actors in uniforms, and further to the role of socially sanctioned killing of the opponents, is well prepared by the social institutions that promote loyalties.

Similarly, suicide can be viewed as an anti-social act (of the person killing *oneself* for no *socially valued* reasons), or as a socially hailed act of political or religious martyrdom. The young student – Jan Palach – who set himself alight in 1968 in Prague, in protest against the Soviet military invasion of the then self-liberating Czechoslovakia, was an act of personal-cultural decision, yet along the lines of a clear social message. This is different from out-of-social context suicides.

Adolescent suicide

It is not only the fact that suicides happen during adolescence that is notable, but that they can happen in a sequence. News of 'chain suicides' usually shock the lay public, who cannot imagine why and how such young and promising people can leave their friends behind and just kill themselves.

The adolescents themselves may have a far less dramatic account of such events. The personal-cultural meaning systems can move towards creation of generic existential feelings – such as loneliness and feeling misunderstood. As general feeling fields (at times also considered as depression), such constructions can overwhelm the adolescent personal world. At the same time, the thrill-seeking orientation (described above) can be co-present. The unity of existential despair with trying out new ways of conduct can lead to self-destructive course of actions.

Events of suicide happen in adolescence, and are part of the personal-cultural life world, as the following example (from an interview about friendships in peer groups) shows. A 12th-grader (Peter = P) answered the interviewer's (I) questions in a rather matter-of-fact way:

I: Do you have a best friend?
P: No, I don't have a best friend any more.
I: Used to?
P: Yeah, but he's dead now. It was Jeff.
I: Sorry. Friends now?
P: Tommy, ah, I got a bunch of 'em up there. Wade, Benny, Sammy, ah, Kenny, Jay – that's about all I hang around.
I: Any others?
P: Pat? Well, he – he just committed suicide about a month ago. And then a week after that, another of my friends killed himself by 'OD-ing' [overdose of drugs]. First it was Jeff, and you remember Ned?
I: Sure.
P: He – he killed himself and then Pat and then Tim.
I: Why did Pat kill himself?
P: He was just depressed.
(Cairns and Cairns, 1994, pp. 202–203)

Peter's story (answering to the questions of the interviewer whom he has known from similar occasions over previous years) comes to resemble a matter-of-fact report about the network of friends who have passed away through suicide. The social network of friends reported by Peter comes to include the dead ones (notice his bringing in Pat after the interviewer's insistence upon more friends).

Who are friends?

The personal cultures of adolescents create distinctions of different kinds: 'friend' is a term basically definable only by a particular person from his or her vantage point. Hence, a look at friends needs to take the position of concrete adolescents.

A 14-year-old white US girl from a rural habitat commented:

> I think [a friend is] somebody that is loyal. Somebody that would *stay on your side no matter what* anybody – well, if somebody started a rumor and everyone believed it, somebody that wouldn't believe it. Or somebody that, if they knew you did it, they wouldn't say 'Aw, you did it' *just to be like everyone else*. (Konopka, 1967, p. 85; added emphasis)

This conceptualization of friendship indicates the anti-social nature of the notion itself. A friend is an *unconditional supporter* in case of either unjustified, or justified, moves of social group stigmatization of the individual. The reference to the role of rumours in such social stigmatization is recognition of the main channel through which adolescent girls' groups are involved in their power reorganization.

A 15-year-old black US girl from an urban environment commented:

> [A friend is] someone who . . . when you really need them, they will come. Someone who sticks close and is truthful and, y'know, *I won't really have to worry about them goin' out and tellin' your business* or something like that. (Konopka, 1976, p. 367; added emphasis)

Here the feature of not sharing between-friends' communicated information with outsiders is emphasized. The issue of adolescent friendship thus becomes the inter-personal buffer mechanism in relation to social group processes (that are regulated by social rules similar to those of the given society as a whole). Friendships are self-constructed interpersonal ties beyond kinship ties.

Friendships become particularly important for personal-cultural systems under social circumstances where the kinship social support network for some reason is not functioning as the support system for the given person, and that person is faced with wider social networks (that operate as a society). Friendships guarantee that the possible interventions by the social institutions (or groups) into personal-cultural domains that are not accepted by the person, can be neutralized, or counter-acted in adaptive ways.

ADOLESCENTS AND THE POLITICAL LIFE IN SOCIETY

The embeddedness of adolescents in different kinds of social groups is the framework through which they are brought into the adult political world. It entails all of their experiences – at school, in the home, in the public space. In the adolescents' ways of relating with the social world of the adults one can trace the changes (or lack of those) in the latter.

There is no reason for any person – young or old – to accept the political system of any country as if it is a positively valued given. Certainly political institutions of power – often through formal schooling – attempt to 'hook' the individuals to become loyal followers of whatever is covered by the notion of social participation. Yet, along the lines of the bi-directional culture transfer notion (see Chapter 4), it is to be expected that adolescents make up the ranks of both the most active followers of political ideologies, and the most active sceptics.

An example of the latter comes from Hungary in its post-communist build-up. An adolescent reflects upon his role in the political system:

> Neither I nor my family nor anyone of my acquaintances took part in political life earlier. I didn't like politics, and still I don't, because as a child I couldn't talk about it. I don't support a political programme of any kind. And I am so very uninterested in it that I haven't even thought about which party's programme I could accept. Actually none of them. They can only promise. (Attila, 17-year-old Hungarian adolescent; from Van Hoorn and Komlosi, 1997, p. 243)

Attila's non-participatory orientation would not surprise anybody who considers political systems by their particular impacts on everyday life. He noticed the multiplicity of novelties – some new opportunities (freedom to travel) occurring with new stresses (unemployment).

Attila's case certainly looks as if it is a 'failure' from the viewpoint of any political institution, as by default the non-participant in a democratic process does not work for the basic ideology of participatory democracy. Yet it is actually a success of adolescent autonomy in making sense of a world filled with different rhetorical presentations of social ideologies. It is the adolescent who – in his or her politically powerless position – has a chance to see through the paradoxical nature of social systems. Of course, those social systems do their utmost not to let the adolescents see that.

Socio-institutional strategies of using adolescents for political purposes

The political world of society is at times ready to use the youthful energies of adolescents. It is in these cases that the usual separation of children from the adult world (by keeping them at schools) becomes reversed. In fact, political systems in efforts to capture the minds of the youth have attempted to do the same as religious systems have done – provide the youngsters with meaningful goal-oriented recreational activities into which the ideological messages are inserted. Most of such messages are those of a social class or group distinction or evaluation kind ('we' versus 'they'). A particular distinction of that kind can be transferred through analogical reasoning to another. For example, the wave of anti-semitism in Germany in the early 1930s was based on social class distinctions (the working class versus the capitalists), which the Nazi propaganda transferred into accusations towards Jews (see Jahoda, 1998).

The case of the Nazi youth organization (Hitler Jugend, HJ) in the 1930s is a good example of opening up a pipeline for the youth to enter public life. The growth of that organization went hand in hand with Hitler's coming to power: in 1932 it had only 108,000 members, in 1933, 2.3 million, in 1936, 5.4 million (Michaud, 1997, p. 263). The ideology of HJ promoted Hitler's father role very strongly, emphasizing the requirement to the youth to 'belong to the fuhrer'. These social demands were combined with physical activities. (In June 1934 Saturdays in Germany were declared 'national youth days', on which all HJ members were excused from school to go marching.) In this way, HJ members were singled out as special young people, who were given authority to improve society by 'civic action'. The activity of marching (in a group) was appropriate for the ideological tasks – marching eliminates individual thought and emphasizes group feeling. It is a kind of a 'magical rite'. The Nazi power emphasized the need for physical fitness for the HJ, linked with the push to merge the body with the political loyalty ('your body belongs to the nation').

The female side involved summoning the reproductive functions of the youth to the service of the political regime. The need to keep up the 'arian birthrate' led to the social suggestions that 'real German women' should bear children 'for the fatherland'. The Nazi political effort to capture the idealistic energies of the young was paralleled by the Soviet system. The movement of 'young pioneers' and the 'young communist league' were set up to work for the Stalinist ideology. Independent of different kinds of political ideologies, the manner of social guidance of children, adolescents and young adults towards loyalty to any given political system is similar. As an example, let us consider the ways in which the 'cultural revolution' in China (in the 1960s) proceeded to channel adolescents' readiness to change the social system.

The case of 'Red Guards' in the Chinese 'Cultural Revolution'

In the Chinese context, educators from early stages of schooling tried to guide the children's peer group to converge in its goals with that of adults' political organization (that is, the Chinese Communist Party). In doing so, they made use of an ancient aspect of the Chinese tradition – examination of one's moral character in interaction with designated 'social others'. This was traditionally a teacher, but at the time of the 'Cultural Revolution' this was substituted by the peer group organized by the political appointee from the Party. The peer group regularly – weekly – went through group sessions of criticism and self-criticism, in which

> . . . the dozen or so small group members were supposed freely to exchange ideas, to bring up their own and others' particular problems, both political and personal in nature, to discuss each other's bad thoughts and backward performance, or praise each other for having performed good deeds. (Chan, 1985, p. 53)

The psychological function of such a group was to guide the processes of interpersonal evaluation toward using the content material that was ideologically accepted, so that the political-ideological content of all evaluations was omnipresent. In the context of coming up with self- or other-criticisms, the group members reiterated the same political ideas to one another. As a result of such immersion in such a situated activity context, the Red Guards came to use the politically correct ideas in their own reasoning and feeling. The cultural-psychological mechanism here is similar to the case of Koranic education (see Chapter 12), where children were explicitly guided to become bonded to the melodies of reciting the sacred text. *By setting up a repetitive activity in a social peer group context, and inserting into it specifically directed ideological and moral contents, the organizers of such settings can expect to guide the internalization/externalization of participants not only in the desired direction, but towards a result that surpasses the initial social suggestion.* When the personal autonomy of the participant is aligned with the ideological goals of a group,

the person begins to think and feel in the expected direction of their own free will. Chinese 'Red Guards' and US groups of Alcoholics Anonymous (AA) operate with the same general principles of activity-demanding guided participation (see Holland et al., 1998, Chapter 4).

A crucial practice for engaging the adolescents in the 'Cultural Revolution' was to introduce the evaluative contrast (*negative*) PAST < > (*positive*) PRESENT. Old people were brought to the groups of 'Red Guards' to 'recall bitterness of the past and sweetness of the present', to appeal to the feelings of the youngsters. Their storytelling of the present pleasure of living was immediately linked with the insertion of the role 'Chairman Mao' had played in it. Furthermore, strong suggestions that 'Chairman Mao' brings that happiness of the present to each member of the 'Red Guards' was likewise inserted. The small peer group context – the sharing of experiences with peers – added to the emotional atmosphere of the occasion. As one girl 'Red Guard' remembered (after leaving China and escaping to Hong Kong),

> All the students cried when they heard the stories. The atmosphere was that if you didn't, others might think you didn't have class consciousness. There was this type of suppressiveness . . . and it became a show. Those girls didn't have to wail so loud; they really went ooh . . . ooh . . . ooh; they might be moved but not to that extent. If they hadn't cried it actually would have meant they were genuine, but to cry like that was faked . . . But I was *really* moved. (Chan, 1985, p. 55)

Here is an example of a participant's account of a set-up situation suggesting to persons that they generate their genetic dramatisms as personal-cultural mechanisms of bonding with the political system. The girl reported that even as she herself was sceptical of the sincerity of the other girls' conduct, she herself was moved by the setting of 'sharing experiences'.

Here we have an example – similar to the 'sunset ceremony' in the Krishnamurti school (described in Chapter 12) of an *institutionalized internalization-guidance setting*. The political party sets up a 'sharing occasion' – between the old and the young – during which the conduct of the participants is scripted through their assumed role-performances. Some of the participants are genuinely moved by the occasion, others show off their façade 'class consciousness' in exaggerated forms. Some may even distance themselves from the event intra-psychologically, and just 'sit through' the occasion. Yet each and every participant experiences the given setting in some way – and already in this 'keeping of participants within the field' can be seen the potential power of political use of settings of this kind in guidance towards loyalty. Socially orchestrated affective sharing in a group context is a setting where the collective- and personal-cultural processes of development become intertwined.

'Learn from Lei Feng'

The use of small-group work for building ideological loyalties was added to in the 'Cultural Revolution' by the provision of positive role models. The 'Learn from Lei Feng' campaign started in 1963, and provided adolescents with a model that linked values of helping others with ideological loyalty to the teachings of Chairman Mao. Lei Feng was a young Chinese man who perished in an accident at the age of 22. Yet he had (supposedly) kept a diary in which he glorified the teachings of Chairman Mao. The diary also gave evidence of small, altruistic deeds that Lei Feng had done for others. For example, he would (anonymously) wash his classmates' clothes, or volunteer to perform menial tasks in the community. His diary, filled with descriptions of his little good deeds (and glorification of Chairman Mao), was published and made into a target for emulation by the young. It provided a basis for the desired ideological model of being a 'little cog' in a 'large machine'. The propagation of the model was by top-to-bottom hierarchical proliferation. The Chinese Young Communist League meetings were used to propagate the myth of Lei Feng:

> A campaign was launched in the schools and even the universities to emulate the type of anonymous mundane chores that Lei Feng had engaged in. Ironically . . . this exercise in humble chores-doing soon became subverted by the student contest to be upwardly mobile. In classrooms where students were competing to get into the league [the Young Communist League] and through that into a university, Lei Feng's type of good deeds provided concrete standards by which league members could appraise the political performance of would-be candidates. *The writing of diaries and the circulation of them for public criticism, above all to league members, became an important way to show activism*; so too did the secret washing and mending of classmates' clothes and sheets and the anonymous cleaning of windows and sweeping of floors. Teenage activists often became hard-pressed to think of new and ingenious ways to outdo each other. They vied to think of new types of *anonymous good deeds that classmates were likely to catch them doing*. (Chan, 1985, p. 64; added emphasis)

This description needs further commentary in two ways. First, the phenomenon of writing diaries and circulating these for public feedback is an adjustment of an accepted Chinese practice of keeping *two kinds* of diaries (Eberhard, 1982) – one for showing to an authority figure (teacher) for feedback about one's moral character, and the other for one's purely private use. The case of the Young Communist League members reading classmates' diaries (as the classmates circulated those) was an example of substitution of the authority figure in this task: no longer was it an adult (teacher), but a fellow student (in a political power role – of supporting, or not, the given diary writer at the admissions to the league). This demonstrates how the hierarchical power structure (elders controlling the young) was altered in the Chinese 'Cultural Revolution', where the politically loyal youngsters were directed to overthrow the power of their parents.

Secondly, the proliferation of Lei Feng type of 'anonymous deeds' for gaining the competitive edge in peer relations created the need for performing those deeds in such a way that the decisively relevant peers – members of the league – would 'accidentally' discover who is doing (or has done) those. Here the important task was to 'get caught' in ways that look unplanned and yet were carefully planned. The adolescents' sophistication of group-negotiation of unity and hierarchical differentiation were carefully appropriated by the political system. On the one hand, the political institutions provided the grounds for ingroup/outgroup differentiation ('we' – the members of the 'Red Guards' – against 'them' – the parents, remnants of the 'old ways' of living, or other peers not initiated into the 'politically progressive' movement). The youngsters were provided with the feeling of a 'special mission' in re-vamping Chinese society to further the progress of communism. At the same time, however, the political system made use of intra-group competition, by providing the criteria by which the character of each group member needed to be evaluated. The adolescents themselves would compete in 'being the best follower' of Chairman Mao (or by washing one's competitor's clothes so that others would know it, emulating Lei Feng).

What can one learn from the 'Learn from Lei Feng' campaign?

The principles used in this political engaging of adolescents are universal for any kind of mass communication process. The communicative message – the published diaries of Lei Feng and public references to it – were supplemented by local, small-group level activities that were meant to guide the adolescents to act in accordance with the model in their local peer group context. This combination of both mass- and group-communication means creates redundant control over persons' activities.

SUMMARY: ADOLESCENCE AS A SOCIAL DELAY

This chapter has indicated numerous culturally patterned psychological phenomena at the time of transition from childhood into adulthood. Yet as a specifiable period of human development, adolescence is a recent cultural construction. It has become accentuated due to the delayed entrance into social adulthood in most Western societies (see Figure 13.3).

Tension is created in the age range of the delay – between the developing children's goal-orientations towards being autonomous participants – together with people older than they – in the socioeconomic life, and the parents' generation setting up limits to slow down the children from reaching that goal. Both agents who set the boundaries are acting with uncertainty: children desire to be 'grown-ups' (but are uncertain how to be so); the parents are equally unsure about what their child's being 'grown-up' means under conditions of a changing society. A good test of this explanation can be found in those times and societies where adults and children shared the set of expected boundaries on children's conduct at puberty. Such sharing was the case in societies where elaborate adolescent initiation ceremonies were held. These ceremonies were uniting both the initiates and adults in joint defining of the social roles of the initiates. Secondly, such sharing would be the case in societies (or individual families) where economic needs make the parents' and adolescents' expectations similar. Under conditions where the parents need the children's active participation in economic work, and children share that need (that is, the social group

of family has a common goal), phenomena of 'adolescent crisis' can be absent.

In addition, the delay comes out of the pressures of different social suggestions that are oriented towards the teenagers. The social world first constructs the distanced world of adolescents by way of their suggestions – of the 'difficult period' – and then attributes to the young people, who indeed may accept such social construction, causality for the 'problems' the adolescents have. In other terms, the nice trick of explaining phenomena by their label is practised: the 'problems of adolescence' are caused by the special age period of adolescence, which is known by its troublesome nature. Once the time and age boundaries of the activities of adolescence are eliminated, the adolescents are viewed to 'have grown out' of that difficult period of 'storms and stresses'.

The examples about adolescents in societies other than European type demonstrate how the integration of youngsters into the economic and social worlds of adults can proceed without the 'storms and stresses' of adolescence as a conflict-ridden age period. Surely there are many other 'storms and stresses' in the lives of the whole families – economic hardships of the whole family, fears of robbery, military actions and diseases. Yet these hardships unify the family and lead to joint action towards common goals. The special age of adolescence becomes noticeable when such common goals no longer exist, and where the adults' goals and those of their offspring begin to differ. The issues of adolescence are issues of friction within age group relations, under conditions of heightened multilinearity of personal life courses.

NOTES

1   There is a psychological difference between questions *'how to be a parent?'* and *'how to bring up children?'*. The former indicates the self-centred role of the task of bringing up children – the (culturally defined) 'success' in it is part of the adults' self-identity processes, aside from including know-how about childrearing (which is the target of the latter question). It is not surprising that the verb 'parenting' is not translatable into other languages, and lacks complementary analogous terms: brothering, sistering, childing (see Valsiner et al., 1997).

2   The case of conformity to peer group here is only one of the many possible uses of the resources emanating from peers.

3   That coordination can take various forms: accepting parental suggestions, or rejecting them, or – most likely – ignoring or neutralizing those. These strategies of counter-action to

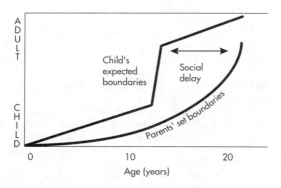

FIGURE 13.3 *Adolescence as an emergent phenomenon of social delay*

parental control efforts are crucial for adolescent development.

4 *Autotelic* activity is activity where the goal is in the activity itself – gaining the feeling of thrill from a situation where one could get caught, or could get into a dangerous situation, but did not, can lead to 'the flow experience'.

5 Our contemporary legal and moral disputes around *buying the services* of another woman to bear a child for otherwise childless married couples in Europe and North America is a good test case of the boundaries of the meanings involved here.

6 The social rules of 'make up' of faces indicate the inherent ambivalence of the social display

of this practice. The desirable version of 'make-up' is one where its result can be attributed to be the 'real face', i.e., an external observer cannot detect that the face had been cosmetically modulated. At the same time, social value distinctions are easily made if make-up is used in excess.

7 Compare this issue with the question of 'painless childbirth' (Chapter 8). Going through the experience of childbirth for many women is a symbolic experience of initiation into motherhood, and the childbirth experiences as personal stories – retold – become personal symbols that are used by them throughout their lives.

REVIEW QUESTIONS FOR CHAPTER 13

1 How is the *age period* of adolescence a cultural construction?

2 Whose crisis is the 'crisis of the adolescent'?

3 Describe major biological changes at puberty. How do these changes set the stage of cultural-psychological phenomena?

4 Describe girls' cultural adaptation to maturation.

5 Describe boys' cultural adaptation to maturation.

6 Explain the issues of 'danger' of pollution and 'social power' of separation, in case of cultural construction of menstruation.

7 Analyse the participatory and 'work-for-hire' scenarios for taking care of children ('babysitting') in adolescence.

8 Discuss the relations between working and schooling in adolescence.

9 In what sense is 'peer pressure' a myth?

10 How are parent and peer perspectives coordinated in the lives of adolescents?

11 Explain how stealing is a form of adolescent thrill-seeking.

12 Analyse the conceptual background of stealing, robbing, borrowing, voluntary giving and loaning. How are these notions relevant for the lives of adolescents?

13 Demonstrate how Bowlby constructed the idea of the home environment being a precursor for adolescent stealing.

14 Explain the cultural history of fasting.

15 Explain the relations of sensual, heterosensual, and heterosexual experiences in adolescence.

16 Describe the system of Muria *ghotul*. How did it promote heterosensuality and social group cohesion?

17 Explain the psychological organization of the Gikuyu *ngweko* system.

18 Describe the move from 'courtship' to 'dating' in US adolescents' personal worlds.

19 Why is dancing an activity targeted for possible collective-cultural guidance?

20 Describe the 'dating script' – as *you* know it.

21 Explain the Sambia male practices of 'semen feeding'.

22 What is the function of adolescent initiation ceremonies?

23 Describe the Gikuyu initiation ritual, and explain the psychological functions of its different parts.

24 Explain how adolescents' personal cultures are open to guidance by collective cultures.

25 Describe different models of adolescents' friendships.

26 Explain the functions of resistance to political participation in adolescence.

27 Analyse the ways in which the loyalty of Chinese 'Red Guards' was promoted during the 'Cultural Revolution'

28 Analyse the social suggestions in the 'Learn from Lei Feng' campaign.

29 In what sense is adolescence a 'social delay'?

EPILOGUE

CULTURE IN DEVELOPMENT WITHIN SEMIOTIC DEMAND SETTINGS

This book brought together themes from psychology and anthropology within the realm of cultural developmental psychology. Two lines of thought moved in parallel all through this coverage. First, there was the line of deductive construction of the arenas where one would expect semiotic mediation to be used to diminish the uncertainty of the development, and guide it towards desired goals.

But, then, who decides what those goals are? Who sets these goals? All through this book, the social institutions of various kinds were mentioned as the collective agents who determine their interests in the directing of human development. These institutions – governments, religious organizations, schools, political parties etc. – are all involved in the social processes of transformation (or no change) of the given society at the given time. That is a social process in which human beings are involved in all aspects of their lives (and death). They are conceived, and born, in the middle of social dramas. They grow up, and are schooled, in the middle of those. They join the negotiating powers at diplomatic tables or military battlefields, losing their lives or winning medals (or both). All of human social existence is set up in the multi-voiced field of sociopolitical, socioreligious and socioeconomic activities. Human beings are indeed 'political animals'.

This social background is relevant – but not determinative – of the issues of cultural psychology. It would be a crucial mistake to reduce all the psychological phenomena – which are semiotically mediated – to texts, narratives or discourses. The latter are constantly being produced, and reproduced, but not as givens, by passive 'users' or followers. The whole focus in cultural developmental psychology is on the active role of the developing person, who constructs new semiotically mediated knowledge (and regulates their own actions) in settings filled with different social demands. The latter are encoded through signs.

The semiotic demand setting is a structured context for a local activity which is guided by goal orientations that are built along lines that need not have anything in common with the local setting. On numerous occasions in this book, the preoccupations of adults about 'problems of children' – be these fetuses (alive or aborted), twins born (killed or honoured), infants clinging to their mothers (or to wet nurses), children going to work or to school, adolescents making love or making war – were playgrounds for regulating adults' own lives. Children are a salient part of these lives, and hence social negotiation of adults' social relations is most powerfully projected into the children and presented in terms of children's needs.

In sum, the issues richly covered in this book can be expressed by way of a few basic principles:

1 Human development entails continuous encountering of new experiences. Stability of the human psyche is constructed through discounting the novelty and recognizing the basic similarities of the new to the old.
2 Semiotic mediators – signs of any kind – are constructed as means to reduce the uncertainty of the permanent movement ahead in human personal living. This construction process is unique: the personal culture is the basis for moment-to-moment adaptation to the expectations of the immediate future. Personal cultures are based on the semiotic input from the environment and from the social suggestions of the other people.
3 Collective culture is a heterogeneous structure resulting from externalizations of personal cultures. It serves as a canalizing device for human conduct.

4 In the course of development, persons create – or appear in the middle of – various dramatic events (genetic dramatisms) which unify their cognitive, affective and volitional functions into key moments of construction of meanings.

5 Meanings that human beings create (through signs) are of various kinds, including closed and open field-type mediating devices. The latter are particularly powerful organizers of human feeling, thinking and acting, as their outer boundaries are non-fixed. These open-field meanings can be speedily overgeneralized to cover the person's relations to the whole world.

A major focus in this book has been on methodology. Cultural psychology needs a re-vamped notion of methodology, which unites theoretical and empirical work all in one inves-tigative effort. It is in that respect that the history of the cultural-historical direction in psychology – of Lev Vygotsky, Alexander Luria – as well as other sociogenetic traditions (of Georg Simmel, George Herbert Mead, or Mikhail Bakhtin) are of relevance. Psychology in general, and cultural psychology in particular, is a science that needs to build itself up with full knowledge of its own history. Proud ignorance – that glorified by the notion of present-day 'progress' – is a short-sighted solution to cultural psychology's pressing problems.

Last (but not least), this book has been a testimony to the universality in variability. Cultural-psychological phenomena may take an infinite variety of specific forms and yet operate on the basis of a limited number of basic principles. I hope that this book helps the reader to try to reconstruct such basic principles by looking behind the façade of variable local con-ditions. If this has been the case, the effort was not wasted. We all live in our uncertain personal worlds – yet by understanding that the world of others is similar in its basic organization, we may begin to appreciate humanity in its fullness.

REFERENCES

INTRODUCTION

Valsiner, J. (1987) *Culture and the Development of Children's Action*. Chichester: Wiley.

Valsiner, J. (1989) *Human Development and Culture*. Lexington, MA: D.C. Heath.

Valsiner, J. (1997) *Culture and the Development of Children's Action*, 2nd edn. New York: Wiley.

Valsiner, J. (1998) *The Guided Mind*. Cambridge, MA: Harvard University Press.

CHAPTER 1

Bergson, H. (1907/1945) *L'Evolution créatrice*. Geneva: Éditions Albert Skira.

Bourdieu, P. (1991) *Language and Symbolic Power*. Cambridge, MA: Harvard University Press.

Cortazar, J. (1967) 'Secret weapons', in J. Cortazar, *End of the Game and Other Stories*. New York: Harper & Row.

Engels, F. (1940) *Dialectics of Nature*. New York: International Publishers.

Hakfoort, C. (1992) 'Science deified: Wilhelm Ostwald's energeticist world-view and the history of scientism'. *Annals of Science*, 49, 525–544.

Herbst, D.P. (1995) 'What happens when we make a distinction: an elementary introduction to co-genetic logic', in T. Kindermann and J. Valsiner (eds), *Development of Person-Context Relations*. Hillsdale, NJ: Erlbaum. pp. 67–79.

Simon, H. (1957) *Models of Man*. New York: Wiley.

Zadeh, L. (1965) 'Fuzzy sets', *Information & Control*, 8, 338–353.

CHAPTER 2

Ash, M.G. (1995) *Gestalt Psychology in German Culture, 1890–1967*. Cambridge: Cambridge University Press.

Fischer, K.W. and Bidell, T.R. (1997) 'Dynamic development of psychological structures in action and thought', in W. Damon and R. Lerner (eds), *Handbook of Child Psychology*, 5th edn, vol. 1: *Theoretical Models of Human Development*. New York: Wiley. pp. 467–561.

Gottlieb, G. (1976) 'The roles of experience in the development of behavior and the nervous system', in G. Gottlieb (ed.), *Neural and Behavioral Specificity*. New York: Academic Press. pp. 25–54.

Gottlieb, G. (1992) *Individual Development and Evolution*. New York: Oxford University Press.

Gottlieb, G. (1997) *Synthesizing Nature–Nurture*. Mahwah, NJ: Erlbaum.

Siegler, R.S. (1996) *Emerging Minds: the Process of Change in Children's Thinking*. New York: Oxford University Press.

Valsiner, J. (1984) 'Two alternative epistemological frameworks in psychology: the typological and variational modes of thinking', *Journal of Mind and Behavior*, 5 (4): 449–470.

Valsiner, J. (1997) 'The development of the concept of development: historical and epistemological perspectives', in W. Damon and R. Lerner (eds), *Handbook of Child Psychology*, 5th edn, vol. 1: *Theoretical Models of Human Development*. New York: Wiley. pp. 189–232.

Van Geert, P. (1994a) 'Vygotskian dynamics of development', *Human Development*, 37: 346–365.

Van Geert, P. (1994b) *Dynamic Systems of Development: Change Between Complexity and Chaos*. Hemel Hempstead: Harvester–Wheatsheaf.

Von Baer, K.E. (1828) *Über Entwicklungsgeschichte der Thiere: Beobactung und reflexion*. Königsberg: Bornträger.

Werner, H. (1948) *Comparative Psychology of Mental Development*. New York: Follett Publishing Co.

Werner, H. (1957) 'The concept of development from a comparative and organismic point of view', in D.B. Harris (ed.), *The Concept of Development*. Minneapolis: University of Minnesota Press. pp. 125–147.

CHAPTER 3

Bakhtin, M.M. (1934/1975) 'Slovo v romane' [Discourse in the novel], in M. Bakhtin, *Voprosy literatury i estetiki*. Moscow: Khudozhestvennaya Literatura. pp. 73–232. (in English translation Bakhtin, 1981.)

Bakhtin, M. M. (1981) *The Dialogic Imagination*. Austin, TX: University of Texas Press.

Baldwin, J. M. (1894a) 'Imitation: a chapter in the natural history of consciousness', *Mind*, 3 (new series): 26–55.

Baldwin, J. M. (1894b) 'Personality-suggestion', *Psychological Review*, 1: 274–279.

Baldwin, J.M. (1895) *Mental Development in the Child and the Race*. New York: Macmillan.

Baldwin, J.M. (1898) 'On selective thinking', *Psychological Review*, 5 (1): 1–24.

Baldwin, J.M. (1906) *Thought and Things: A Study of the Development and Meaning of Thought, or Genetic Logic*, vol. 1: *Functional Logic, or Genetic Theory of Knowledge*. London: Swan Sonnenschein & Co.

Baldwin, J.M. (1908) 'Knowledge and imagination', *Psychological Review*, 15: 181–196.

Baldwin, J. M. (1911) *Thought and Things: a Study of the Development and Meaning of Thought, or Genetic Logic*. Vol 3. *Interest and Art Being Real Logic*. London: Swan Sonnenschein & Co.

Baldwin, J.M. (1915) *Genetic Theory of Reality*. New York: G.P. Putnam's Sons.

Baldwin, J.M. (1930) 'James Mark Baldwin', in C. Murchison (ed.), *A History of Psychology in Autobiography*, vol. 1: New York: Russell & Russell. pp. 1–30.

Konkin, S.S. and Konkina, L.S. (1993) *Mikhail Bakhtin (Stranitsy zizni I tvorchestva)*. Saransk: Mordovskoe kniznoe izdatel'stvo.

Mead, G.H. (1905) Review of D. Draghiscesco, *'De role de l'individu dans le determinisme social'* and D. Draghiscesco, *'Le probleme du determinisme, determinisme biologique and determinisme social'*, *Psychological Bulletin*, 5: 399–405.

Mead, G.H. (1912) 'The mechanism of social consciousness', *Journal of Philosophy*, 9: 401–406.

Mead, G.H. (1913) 'The social self', *Journal of Philosophy*, 10: 374–380.

Mead, G.H. (1925) 'The genesis of the self and social control', *International Journal of Ethics*, 35: 251–277.

Mead, G.H. (1930) 'The philosophies of Royce, James, and Dewey in their American setting', *International Journal of Ethics*, 40: 211–231.

Mead, G.H. (1932) *The Philosophy of the Present*. Chicago: Open Court.

Mead, G.H. (1934) *Mind, Self, and Society*. Chicago: University of Chicago Press.

Simmel, G. (1904) 'The sociology of conflict', *American Journal of Sociology*, 9: 491–525, 672–689, 798–811.

Simmel, G. (1906) 'The sociology of secrecy and of secret societies', *American Journal of Sociology*, 11 (4): 441–498.

Simmel, G. (1908) 'Von Wesen der Kultur', *Österreichische Rundschau*, 15: 36–42.

Simmel, G. (1910) 'How is society possible?' *American Journal of Sociology*, 16: 372–391.

Simmel, G. (1971) *On Individuality and Social Forms: Selected Writings*. Chicago: University of Chicago Press.

Simmel, G. (1984) 'Flirtation', in G. Simmel, *On Women, Sexuality, and Love*. New Haven, CT: Yale University Press.

Simmel, G. (1990) *The Philosophy of Money*, 2nd edn. London: Routledge.

Valsiner, J., and Van der Veer, R. (2000) *The Social Mind*. New York: Cambridge University Press.

Van der Veer, R. and Valsiner, J. (1991) *Understanding Vygotsky*. Oxford: Basil Blackwell.

Vygotsky, L.S. (1935) 'O pedologicheskom analize pedagogicheskogo protsessa', in L.S. Vygotsky, *Umstvennoie razvitie detei v protsesse obuchenia*. Moscow-Leningrad: Gosudarstvennoie Uchebno-pedagogicheskoie Izdatel'stvo. pp. 116–134 (text of a lecture delivered in 1933).

Vygotsky, L.S. (1960) *Razvitie vyshikh psikhicheskikh funktsii* [Development of higher psychical functions]. Moscow: Izd. Akademii Pedagogicheskikh Nauk.

Vygotsky, L.S. (1966) 'Igra i ee rol' v psikhicheskom razvitii rebenka', *Voprosy Psikhologii*, 12 (6): 62–76 (partial text of a lecture delivered in 1933).

Vygotsky, L.S. (1984) 'Problema vozrasta', in L.S. Vygotsky, *Sobranie sochinenii*, vol. 4: *Detskaia psikhologia*. Moscow: Pedagogika. pp. 244–268 (text of a lecture delivered in 1933).

CHAPTER 4

Bullough, E. (1912) '"Psychical distance" as a factor in art and an aesthetic principle', *Journal of Psychology*, 5. 2, 87–118.

Cirillo, L. and Kaplan, B. (1983) 'Figurative action from the perspective of genetic-dramatism', in S. Wapner and B. Kaplan (eds), *Toward a Holistic Developmental Psychology*. Hillsdale, NJ: Erlbaum. pp. 235–252

D'Andrade, R. (1984) 'Cultural meaning systems', in R.A. Shweder and R.A. LeVine (eds), *Culture Theory: Essays on Mind, Self and Emotion*. Cambridge: Cambridge University Press. pp. 88–119.

Festinger, L., Riecken, H. and Schachter, S. (1956) *When Prophecy Fails*. Minneapolis: University of Minnesota Press.

Freeman, J.M. (1981) 'A firewalking ceremony that failed', in G. R. Gupta (ed.), *The Social and Cultural Context of Medicine in India*. New Delhi: Vikas Publishing House. pp. 308–336.

Josephs, I. E., and Valsiner, J. (1998) 'How does auto-dialogue work? Miracles of meaning maintenance and circumvention strategies', *Social Psychology Quarterly*, 61, 1, 68–83.

Kaplan, B. (1983) 'Genetic-dramatism: old wine in new bottles', in S. Wapner and B. Kaplan (eds), *Toward a Holistic Developmental Psychology*. Hillsdale, NJ: Erlbaum. pp. 53–74.

Kroeber, A.L. (1948) *Anthropology*. New York: Harcourt & Brace.

Lévi-Strauss, C. (1983) *The Raw and the Cooked. Introduction to the Science of Mythology*, vol. 1. Chicago: University of Chicago Press.

Malinowski, B. (1944) *A Scientific Theory of Culture*.

Chapel Hill, NC: University of North Carolina Press.

Rogoff, B. (1990) *Apprenticeship in Thinking*. New York: Oxford University Press.

Shannon, C.E. and Weaver, W. (1949) *The Mathematical Theory of Communication*. Urbana, IL: University of Illinois Press.

Sherif, M. (1936) *The Psychology of Social Norms*. New York: Harper.

Sherif, M. (1937) 'An experimental approach to the study of attitudes', *Sociometry*, 1: 90–98.

Sigel, I. (1970) 'The distancing hypothesis', in M. Jones (ed.), *Effects of Early Experience*. Coral Gables, FL: University of Miami Press. pp. 99–118.

Sigel, I.E. (1993) 'The centrality of a distancing model for the development of representational competence', in R.R. Cocking and K.A. Renninger (eds), *The Development and Meaning of Psychological Distance*. Hillsdale, NJ: Erlbaum. pp. 141–158.

Sigel, I.E. (1998) 'Remembering Karl Bühler: discovering unanticipated resemblances with my distancing-representational model', *From Past to Future*, 1 (1): 1–15.

Strauss, C. (1992) 'Models and motives', in R. D'Andrade and C. Strauss (eds), *Human Motives and Cultural Models*. Cambridge: Cambridge University Press. pp. 1–20.

Van Geert, P. (1998) 'We almost had a great future behind us: the contribution of non-linear dynamics to developmental-science-in-the-making', *Developmental Science*, 1 (1): 143–159.

CHAPTER 5

Branco, A.U. and Valsiner, J. (1997) 'Changing methodologies: a co-constructivist study of goal orientations in social interactions', *Psychology and Developing Societies*, 9 (1): 35–64.

Buckley, T. (1982) 'Menstruation and the power of Yurok women: methods in cultural reconstruction', *American Ethnologist*, 9 (1): 47–60.

Bühler, K. (1907) Tatsachen und Probleme zu eine Psychologie der Denkvorgänge I, *Archiv für die gesamte Psychologie*, 9, 297–365.

Cairns, R.B., Elder, G. and Costello, E. (eds) (1996) *Developmental Science*. New York: Cambridge University Press.

Danziger, K. (1990) *Constructing the Subject*. Cambridge: Cambridge University Press.

Duncker, K. (1945) 'On problem-solving', *Psychological Monographs*, 58 (5): 1–112.

Gigerenzer, G., Swijtink, Z., Porter, T., Daston, L., Beatty, J. and Krüger, L. (1989) *The Empire of Chance*. Cambridge: Cambridge University Press.

Köhler, W. (1925) *The Mentality of Apes*. New York: Liveright.

Levina, R. (1968) 'Ideas of L. S. Vygotsky about the planning speech of the child', *Voprosy psikhologii*, 14: 105–115.

Lewin, K. (1927) 'Gesetz und Experiment in der Psychologie', *Symposion*, 1: 375–421.

Lewin, K. (1931) 'The conflict between Aristotelian and Galileian modes of thought in contemporary psychology', *Journal of General Psychology*, 5: 141–177.

Lewin, K. (1949) 'Cassirer's philosophy of science and the social sciences', in P.A. Schlipp (ed.), *The Philosophy of Ernst Cassirer*. Evanston, IL: The Library of Living Philosophers. pp. 271–288.

Morgan, C.L. (1894) *Introduction to Comparative Psychology*. London: Walter Scott.

Parker, I. (1998) 'Against postmodernism: psychology in cultural context', *Theory and Psychology*, 8 (5): 601–627.

Sander, F. (1927) 'Ueber Gestaltqualitäten', in *Proceedings and Papers of the 8th International Congress of Psychology, 1926*. Groningen: P. Noordhoff. pp. 183–189.

Siegler, R.S. and Crowley, K. (1991) 'The microgenetic method: a direct means for studying cognitive development', *American Psychologist*, 46: 6–6–620.

Simon, H. (1957) *Models of Man*. New York: Wiley.

Smedslund, J. (1995) 'Psychologic: common sense and the pseudoempirical', in J. A. Smith, R. Harré and L. van Langenhove (eds), *Rethinking Psychology*. London: Sage. pp. 196–206.

Stern, W. (1911) *Differentielle Psychologie*. Leipzig: J. A. Barth.

Valsiner, J. (1986) 'Between groups and individuals: psychologists' and laypersons' interpretations of correlational findings', in J. Valsiner (ed.), *The Individual Subject and Scientific Psychology*. New York: Plenum. pp. 113–152.

Vygotsky, L. S. and Luria, A. R. (1993) *Studies in the History of Behavior*. Hillsdale, NJ: Erlbaum. [Russian original from 1930].

Werner, H. (1927) 'Ueber Pysiognomische Wahrnehmungsweisen und Ihre experimentelle Prüfung', in *Proceedings and Papers of the 8th International Congress of Psychology, 1926*. Groningen: P. Noordhoff. pp. 443–446.

Werner, H. (1959) 'Significance of general experimental psychology for the understanding of abnormal behavior and its correction or prevention', in T. Dembo and G. Leviton (eds), *The Relationship between Rehabilitation and Psychology*. Worcester, MA: Clark University Press. pp. 62–74.

Wertheimer, M. (1945/1982) *Productive Thinking*. Chicago: University of Chicago Press.

CHAPTER 6

Aiyappan, A. (1937) 'Polyandry and sexual jealousy', *Man*, 37, No. 130.

Altman, I. and Ginat, J. (1996) *Polygamous Families in Contemporary Society*. New York: Cambridge University Press.

Berland, J.C. (1982) *No Five Fingers Are Alike*. Cambridge, MA: Harvard University Press.

Bradley, M. S. (1983) '"Hide and seek": children on the underground', *Utah Historical Quarterly*, 51: 133–153.

Brusco, E.E. (1995) *The Reformation of Machismo: Evangelical Conversion and Gender in Colombia*. Austin, TX: University of Texas Press.

Cannon, C.A. (1974) 'The awesome power of sex: the polemical campaign against Mormon polygamy', *Pacific Historical Review*, 43: 61–82.

Carden, M.L. (1971) *Oneida: Utopian Community to Modern Corporation*. New York: Harper.

Clignet, R. (1970) *Many Wives, Many Powers: Authority and Power in Polygynous Families*. Evanston, IL: Northwestern University Press.

Dredge, N.T. (1976) 'Victims of the conflict', in C.L. Bushman (ed.), *Mormon Sisters: Women in Early Utah*. Salt Lake City, UT: Olympus Publishing Co. pp. 133–155.

Drijvers, J.W. (1987) 'Virginity and asceticism in late Roman Western elites', in J. Blok and P. Mason (eds), *Sexual Asymmetry in Ancient Society*. Amsterdam: J. C. Gieben. pp. 241–273.

Elliott, D. (1993) *Spiritual Marriage: Sexual Abstinence in Medieval Wedlock*. Princeton, NJ: Princeton University Press.

Ferraro, G. (1976) 'Changing patterns of bridewealth among the Kikuyu of East Africa', in W. Arens (ed.), *A Century of Change in Eastern Africa*. The Hague: Mouton. pp. 101–113.

Foster, L. (1979) 'From frontier activism to neo-Victorian domesticity: Mormon women in the nineteenth and twentieth centuries', *Journal of Mormon History*, 6: 3–21.

Foster, L. (1984) *Religion and Sexuality: the Shakers, the Mormons, and the Oneida Community*. Urbana, IL: University of Illinois Press.

Gies, F. and Gies, J. (1987) *Marriage and the Family in the Middle Ages*. New York: Harper & Row.

Goldschmidt, W. (1976) *The Culture and Behavior of the Sebei*. Berkeley: University of California Press.

Goodson, S.S. (1976) 'Plural wives', in C.L. Bushman (ed.), *Mormon Sisters: Women in Early Utah*. Salt Lake City, UT: Olympus Publishing Co. pp. 89–111.

Gwaku, E.L.M. (1998) 'Widow inheritance among the Maragoli of Western Kenya', *Journal of Anthropological Research*, 54: 173–198.

Hall, L.A. (1992) 'Forbidden by God, despised by men: masturbation, medical warnings, moral panic, and manhood in Great Britain, 1850–1950', *Journal of the History of Sexuality*, 2 (3): 365–387.

Hardy, F. (1983) *Viraha-bhakti: the Early History of Krisna Devotion in South India*. Delhi: Oxford University Press.

Hare, E.H. (1962) 'Masturbatory insanity: the history of an idea', *Journal of Mental Science*, 108, No. 452: 2–25.

Hartley, W.G. (1983) 'Childhood in Gunnison, Utah', *Utah Historical Quarterly*, 51: 108–132.

Kilbride, P.L. and Kilbride, J.C. (1990) *Changing Family Life in East Africa: Women and Children at Risk*. University Park, PA: The Penn State University Press.

Kleiman, D.G. (1984) 'Implications of monogamy for infant social development in mammals', in M. Lewis (ed.), *Beyond the Dyad*. New York: Plenum. pp. 91–108.

Laqueur, T. (1990) *Making Sex: Body and Gender from the Greeks to Freud*. Cambridge, MA: Harvard University Press.

Levine, N.E. (1988) *The Dynamics of Polyandry*. Chicago: University of Chicago Press.

LeVine, S. and Pfeifer, G. (1982) 'Separation and individuation in an African society: the developmental tasks of the Gusii married women', *Psychiatry*, 44: 61–75.

Majumdar, D.N. (1954/55) 'Family and marriage in a polyandrous society', *Eastern Anthropologist*, 8: 85–110.

Majumdar, D.N. (1960) *Himalayan Polyandry*. Bombay: Asia Publishing House.

Maltz, D.N. (1978) 'The bride of Christ is filled with his spirit', in J. Hoch-Smith and A. Spring (eds), *Women in Ritual and Symbolic Roles*. New York: Plenum. pp. 27–44.

Menon, U. and Shweder, R.A. (1998) 'The return of the "white man's burden": the moral discourse of anthropology and the domestic life of Hindu women', in R.A. Shweder (ed.), *Welcome to Middle Age! (And other Cultural Fictions)*. Chicago: University of Chicago Press. pp. 139–187.

Mernissi, F. (1987) *Beyond the Veil*. Bloomington, IN: Indiana University Press.

Nieuwenhuys, O. (1994) *Children's Lifeworlds: Gender, Welfare and Labour in the Developing World*. London: Routledge.

Petrovski. A.V. (1984) 'The theory of activity mediation in interpersonal relations', in L.H. Strickland (ed.), *Directions in Soviet Social Psychology*. New York: Springer. pp. 99–112.

Prince Peter of Greece and Denmark (1963) *A Study of Polyandry*. The Hague: Mouton.

Raha, M. K. (1996) *Polyandry in the Global Context: Stasis and Transformation*. Presidential Address to 83rd Session on Anthropology and Archaeology, Indian Science Congress. Calcutta: Indian Science Congress Association.

Raina, J.L. (1988) *Structural and Functional Changes in the Joint Family System*. New Delhi: Concept Publishing House.

Riesman, P. (1977) *Freedom in Fulani Life*. Chicago: University of Chicago Press.

Rogoff, B. (1990) *Apprenticeship in Thinking*. New York: Oxford University Press.

Sheldon, C.H. (1976) 'Mormon haters', in C.L. Bushman (ed.), *Mormon Sisters: Women in Early Utah*. Salt Lake City, UT: Olympus Publishing Co. pp. 113–131.

Sherif, M., Harvey, O.J., White, B.J., Hood, W.R. and Sherif, C.W. (1961) *Intergroup Conflict and Cooperation: the Robbers Cave Experiment*. Norman, OK: The University Book Exchange.

Ssennyonga, J.W. (1997) 'Polygyny and resource allocation in the Lake Victoria Basin', in T.S. Weisner, C. Bradley and P.L. Kilbride (eds), *African Families and the Crisis of Social Change*. Westport, CT: Bergin & Garvey. pp. 268–282.

Stark, R. (1996) *The Rise of Christianity*. Princeton, NJ: Princeton University Press.

Stephens, W.N. (1963) *The Family in Cross-cultural Perspective*. New York: Holt, Rinehardt & Winston.

Stern, M. and Stern, A. (1981) *Sex in the Soviet Union*. London: W.H. Allen.

Uplaonkar, A.T. (1995) 'The emerging rural youth: a case study of their changing values towards marriage', *Indian Journal of Social Work*, 56 (4): 415–423.

Valsiner, J. (1996) 'Devadasi temple dancers and cultural construction of persons-in-society', in M.K. Raha (ed.), *Dimensions of Human Society and Culture*. New Delhi: Gyan Publishing House. pp. 443–476.

Valsiner, J. (1998) *The Guided Mind*. Cambridge, MA: Harvard University Press.

Van den Berghe, P.L. (1979) *Human Family Systems*. New York: Elsevier.

Welter, B. (1966) 'The cult of true womanhood: 1820–1860', *American Quarterly*, 18: 151–174.

Whittaker, D.J. (1984) 'Early Mormon polygamy defenses', *Journal of Mormon History*, 11: 43–63.

CHAPTER 7

Abbott, E. (1908) 'A study of early history of child labor in America', *American Journal of Sociology*, 14: 15–37.

Aptekar, L. (1988) *Street Children of Cali*. Durham, NC: Duke University Press.

Aptekar, L. and Stöcklin, D. (1997) 'Children in particularly difficult circumstances', in J. Berry, P.R. Dasen and T.S. Saraswathi (eds), *Handbook of Cross-Cultural Psychology*, vol. 2. *Basic Processes and Human Development*. Boston, MA: Allyn & Bacon. pp. 377–412.

Berland, J.C. (1982) *No Five Fingers Are Alike*. Cambridge, MA: Harvard University Press.

Borel, G. and Silva, M.L. (1987) *Garotos de rua*. Rio de Janeiro: Editora Cátedra.

Bronfenbrenner, U. (1979) *The Ecology of Human Development*. Cambridge, MA: Harvard University Press.

Castle, S.E. (1995) 'Child fostering and children's nutritional outcomes in rural Mali: the role of female status in directing child transfers', *Social Science & Medicine*, 40 (5): 679–693.

Coffin, J. (1996) *The Politics of Women's Work*. Princeton, NJ: Princeton University Press.

Cunnington, C.W. and Cunnington, P. (1992) *The History of Underclothes*. New York: Dover.

Gell, A. (1993) *Wrapping in Images: Tattooing in Polynesia*. Oxford: Clarendon Press.

Glynn, P. (1982) *Skin to Skin: Eroticism in Dress*. New York: Oxford University Press.

Gregor, T. (1977) *Mehinaku: the Drama of Daily Life in a Brazilian Indian Village*. Chicago: University of Chicago Press.

Gregor, T. (1985) *Anxious Pleasures: the Sexual Lives of an Amazonian People*. Chicago: University of Chicago Press.

Gurevitch, Z.D. (1990) 'The embrace: on the element of non-distance in human relations', *Sociological Quarterly*, 31 (2): 187–201.

Haiken, E. (1997) *Venus Envy: a History of Cosmetic Surgery*. Baltimore, MD: The Johns Hopkins University Press.

Herzfeld, M. (1992) *The Social Production of Indifference: Exploring the Symbolic Roots of Western Bureaucracy*. Chicago: University of Chicago Press.

Hobbs, J.J. (1989) *Bedouin Life in the Egyptian Wilderness*. Austin, TX: University of Texas Press.

Holmes-Eber, P. (1997) 'Migration, urbanization, and women's kin networks in Tunis', *Journal of Comparative Family Studies*, 28 (2): 54–72.

Isaac, B.L. and Conrad, S.R. (1982) 'Child fosterage among the Mende of Upper Bambara Chiefdom, Sierra Leone: rural-urban and occupational comparisons', *Ethnology*, 21: 243–258.

Kojima, H. (1996) 'Japanese childrearing advice in its cultural, social, and economic contexts', *International Journal of Behavioral Development*, 19 (2): 373–391.

Mernissi, F. (1987) *Beyond the Veil: Male–Female Dynamics in Modern Muslim Society*. Bloomington, IN: Indiana University Press.

Murphy, R.F. (1964) 'Social distance and the veil', *American Anthropologist*, 66: 1257–1274.

Nicolaisen, J. and Nicolaisen, I. (1997) *The Pastoral Tuareg*. Copenhagen: Rhodes.

Ogden, J.A. (1996) '"Producing" respect: the "proper woman" in postcolonial Kampala', in R. Werbner and T. Ranger (eds), *Postcolonial Identities in Africa*. London: Zed Books. pp. 165–192.

Ohnuki-Tierney, E. (1994) 'The power of absence: zero signifiers and their transgressions', *L'Homme*, 34 (2): 59–76.

Pandey, R. (1991) *Street Children in India: a Situational Analysis*. Allahabad: Chugh Publications.

Perrot, P. (1994) *Fashioning the Bourgeoisie: a History of Clothing in the Nineteenth Century*. Princeton, NJ: Princeton University Press.

Poddiakov, A.N. (1998) 'Learning, education and development with social counteraction and inhibition'. Paper presented at the 15th Biennial Convention of the International Society for the Study of Behavioural Development, Berne, July.

Rasmussen, S.J. (1991) 'Lack of prayer: ritual restrictions, social experience, and the anthropology of menstruation among the Tuareg', *American Ethnologist*, 18 (4): 751–769.

Reed, E.J. and Jones, R. (eds) (1982) *Reasons for Realism: Selected Essays of James J. Gibson*. Hillsdale, NJ: Erlbaum.

Rogoff, B. (1990) *Apprenticeship in Thinking*. New York: Oxford University Press.

Sampa, A. (1997) 'Street children of Lusaka', *Journal of Psychology in Africa*, 1 (2): 1–23.

Shi-xu (1995) 'Cultural perceptions: exploiting the unexpected of the other', *Culture & Psychology*, 1 (3): 315–342.

Solberg, A. (1997) 'Seeing children's work', in N. de Coninck-Smith, B. Sandin and E. Schrumpf (eds), *Industrious Children*. Odense: Odense University Press. pp. 186–209.

Van Enk, G.J. and De Vries, L. (1997) *The Korowai of Irian Jaya*. New York: Oxford University Press.

Vygotsky, L.S. (1935/1994) 'The problem of the environment', in R. van der Veer and J. Valsiner (eds), *The Vygotsky Reader*. Oxford: Basil Blackwell. pp. 338–354.

Wagner, A. (1997) *Adversaries of Dance: From the Puritans to the Present*. Urbana, IL: University of Illinois Press.

Wikan, U. (1982) *Behind the Veil in Arabia: Women in Oman*. Chicago: University of Chicago Press.

CHAPTER 8

Baskakov, N.A. and Yaimova, N.A. (1997) *Shamanskie misterii Gornogo Altaya* [The shamanistic mysteries of the Attai Mountains]. Gorno-Altaisk: Gorno-Altaiskii Institut Gumanitarnykh Issedovanii.

Berland, J.C. (1982) *No Five Fingers Are Alike*. Cambridge, MA: Harvard University Press.

Chernela, J.M. (1991) 'Symbolic inaction in rituals of gender and procreation among the Garifuna (Black Caribs) of Honduras', *Ethos*, 19 (1) 52–67.

Clark, G. (1994) *Onions are My Husband: Survival and Accumulation by West African Market Women*. Chicago: University of Chicago Press.

Coelho, R. (1949) 'The significance of the couvade among the Black Caribs', *Man*, 49: 51–53.

Danet, B. (1980) 'Baby or fetus? Language and the construction of reality in a manslaughter trial', *Semiotica*, 32: 3–4, 187–219.

Davis-Floyd, R.E. (1992) *Birth as an American Rite of Passage*. Berkeley, CA: University of California Press.

Dawson, W.E. (1929) *The Custom of Couvade*. Manchester: Manchester University Press.

Ebin, V. (1982) 'Interpretations of infertility: the Aowin people of South-West Ghana', in C.P. MacCormack (ed.), *Ethnography of Fertility and Birth*. London: Academic Press. pp. 141–159.

Enoch, M.D., Trethowan, WH. and Barker, J.C. (1967) *Some Uncommon Psychiatric Syndromes*. Bristol: John Wright & Sons.

Flandrin, J.-L. (1985) 'Sex in married life in the early Middle Ages: the Church's teaching and behavioural reality', in P. Ariès and A. Béjin (eds), *Western Sexuality*. Oxford: Blackwell. pp. 114–129.

Frazer, J.G. (1910) *Totemism and Exogamy*. London: Macmillan.

Gregor, T. (1977) *Mehinaku: the Drama of Daily Life in a Brazilian Indian Village*. Chicago: University of Chicago Press.

Gregor, T. (1985) *Anxious Pleasures: the Sexual Lives of an Amazonian People*. Chicago: University of Chicago Press.

Herdt, G. (1997) *Same Sex, Different Cultures: Gays and Lesbians Across Cultures*. Boulder, CO: Westview Press.

Homans, H. (1982) 'Pregnancy and birth as rites of passage for two groups of women in Britain', in C.P. MacCormack (ed.), *Ethnography of Fertility and Birth*. London: Academic Press. pp. 231–268.

Irvine, J. (1976) 'Changing patterns of social control in Buu society', in W. Arens (ed.), *A Century of Change in Eastern Africa*. The Hague: Mouton. pp. 215–228.

Jorgensen, D. (1983) 'Mirroring nature? Men's and women's models of conception in Telefolmin', *Mankind*, 14: 57–65.

Keck, V. (1993) 'Two ways of explaining reality: the sickness of a small boy of Papua New Guinea from anthropological and biomedical perspectives', *Oceania*, 63 (4): 294–312.

Keesing, R. (1982) *Kwaio Religion: the Living and the Dead in a Solomon Island Society*. New York: Columbia University Press.

Kersenboom, S.C. (1984) *Nityasumangali: Towards the Semiosis of the Devadasi Tradition of South India*. Utrecht (published Doctoral Dissertation, No. 52).

Kilbride, P.L. and Kilbride, J.C. (1990) *Changing Family Life in East Africa: Women and Children at Risk*. University Park, PA: The Penn State University Press.

Kilbride, P.L. and Kilbride, J.C. (1997) 'Stigma, role overload and contemporary Kenyan women', in T. Weisner, C. Bradley and P.L. Kilbride (eds), *African Families and the Crisis of Social Change*. Westport, CT: Bergin & Garvey. pp. 208–223.

Kitzinger, S. (1982) 'The social context of birth: some comparisons between childbirth in Jamaica and Britain', in C. P. MacCormack (ed.), *Ethnography of Fertility and Birth*. London: Academic Press. pp. 181–203.

Lebra, T.S. (1984) *Japanese Women: Constraint and Fulfillment*. Honolulu, HI: University of Hawaii Press.

Lévi-Strauss, C. (1983) *From Honey to Ashes. Introduction to a Science of Mythology*, vol. 2. Chicago: University of Chicago Press.

Menon, U. and Shweder, R.A. (1994) 'Kali's tongue: cultural psychology and the power of "shame" in Orissa', in S. Kitayama and H. Markus (eds), *Emotion and Culture*. Washington, DC: American Psychological Association. pp. 237–280.

Mernissi, F. (1987) *Beyond the Veil: Male-female Dynamics in Modern Muslim Society*. Bloomington, IN: Indiana University Press.

Métraux, A. (1949) 'The couvade', in J. H. Steward (ed.), *Handbook of South American Indians*, vol. 5. *The Comparative Ethnology of South American Indians*.

Washington, DC: US Government Printing Office. pp. 369–374.

Monberg, T. (1975) 'Fathers were not genitors', *Man*, 10: 34–40.

Monberg, T. (1991) *Bellona Island Beliefs and Rituals*. Honolulu: University of Hawaii Press.

Obeyesekere, G. (1981) *Medusa's Hair*. Chicago: University of Chicago Press.

Obeyesekere, G. (1985) 'Symbolic foods: pregnancy cravings and the envious female', *International Journal of Psychology*, 20: 637–662.

Ohnuki-Tierney, E. (1984) *Illness and Culture in Contemporary Japan*. Cambridge: Cambridge University Press.

Ohnuki-Tierney, E. (1993) *Rice as Self: Japanese Identities Through Time*. Princeton, NJ: Princeton University Press.

Oinas, F.J. (1993) 'Couvade in Estonia', *Slavic and East European Journal*, 37: 339–345.

Rasmussen, S.J. (1996) 'Matters of taste: food, eating, and reflections on "the body politic" in Tuareg society', *Journal of Anthropological Research*, 52: 61–83.

Scheper-Hughes, N. (1982) 'Virgin mothers: the impact of Irish Jansenism on childbearing and infant tending in Western Ireland', in M. Artschwanger Kay (ed.), *Anthropology of Human Birth*. Philadelphia, PA: F.A. Davis & Co. pp. 267–288.

Steadman, L.B., Palmer, C.T. and Tilley, C.F. (1996) 'The universality of ancestor worship', *Ethnology*, 35 (1): 63–76.

Trask, R.B. (1992) *'The Devil hath Been Raised': a Documentary History of the Salem Village Witchcraft Outbreak of March, 1692*. Danvers, MA: Yeoman Press.

Trethowan, W.H. and Conlon, M.F. (1965) 'The couvade syndrome', *British Journal of Psychiatry*, 111: 57–66.

Velvovsky, I., Platonov, K., Plotichev, V. and Shugom, E. (1960) *Painless Childbirth Through Psychoprophylaxis*. Moscow: Foreign Languages Publishing House.

Voeglin, C.F. (1960) 'Pregnancy couvade attested by term and text in Hopi', *American Anthropologist*, 62: 491–494.

Wessing, R. (1978) 'Cosmology and social behavior in a West Javenese settlement', *Papers in International Studies, Ohio University: Southeast Asia Series*, No. 47 (Athens, OH).

Williams, T.R. (1969) *A Borneo Childhood*. Oxford: Blackwell.

CHAPTER 9

Alekseenko, E.A. (1988) 'Child and childhood in the Ket culture', in I.S. Kon and Ch.M. Taksami (eds), *The Traditional Education of the Cultures of Siberia*. Leningrad: Nauka. pp. 9–37.

Bajwa, R.S. (1991) *Semiotics of the Birth Ceremonies in Punjab*. New Delhi: Bahri Publications.

Bamberger, J. (1974) 'Naming and the transmission of status in a central Brazilian society', *Ethnology*, 13: 363–378.

Beidelman, T.O. (1963) 'Kaguru omens', *Anthropological Quarterly*, 36: 43–59.

Benedict, R. (1949) 'Child rearing in certain European cultures', *American Journal of Orthopsychiatry*, 19: 342–350.

Bergson, H. (1907/1911) *Creative Evolution*. New York: Henry Holt & Co.

Boesch, E.E. (1998) *Sehnsucht: Von der Suche nach Glück und Sinn*. Berne: Hans Huber.

Bruch, H.B. (1990) *Growing Up Agreeably: Bonerate Childhood Observed*. Honolulu, HI: University of Hawaii Press.

Bruner, J.S. (1969) 'On the voluntary action and its hierarchical structure', in A. Koestler and J.R. Smythies (eds), *Beyond Reductionism*. London: Hutchinson. pp. 161–179.

Brzozowska-Krajka, A. (1998) *Polish Traditional Folklore: the Magic of Time*. Boulder, CO: East European Monographs.

Chappel, T.J.H. (1974) 'The Yoruba cult of twins in historical perspective', *Africa*, 44: 250–265.

Chisholm, J. (1983) *Navajo Infancy: an Ethological Study of Child Development*. New York: Aldine.

Cory, H. (1961) 'Sumbwa birth figurines', *Journal of the Royal Anthropological Institute*, 91: 67–76.

DeCasper, A. and Fifer, W. (1980) 'On human bonding: newborns prefer their mothers' voice', *Science*, 208: 1174–1176.

Denisova, M.D. and Figurin, N.L. (1929) 'On the question of early alimentary reflexes in infants', *Voprosy geneticheskoi refleksologii I pedologii mladenchestva*, 1: 81–86.

Dennis, W. and Dennis, M.G. (1940) 'The effect of cradling practices upon the onset of walking in Hopi children', *Journal of Genetic Psychology*, 56: 77–86.

Diakonova, V.P. (1988) 'Childhood in the traditional culture of Tuva and Telengites', in I.S. Kon and Ch.M. Taksami (eds), *The Traditional Education of the Cultures of Siberia*. Leningrad: Nauka. pp. 152–185.

Fabian, S.M. (1992) *Space-time of the Bororo of Brazil*. Gainesville, FL: University Press of Florida.

Farber, W. (1990) 'Magic at the cradle: Babylonian and Assyrian lullabies', *Anthropos*, 85: 139–148.

Fildes, V. (1986) *Breasts, Bottles and Babies: a History of Infant Feeding*. Edinburgh: Edinburgh University Press.

Fuchs, R. (1984) *Abandoned Children: Foundlings and Child Welfare in Nineteenth Century France*. Albany, NY: SUNY Press.

Furst, J.L. McKeever (1995) *The Natural History of the Soul in Ancient Mexico*. New Haven, CT: Yale University Press.

Galt, A.H. (1991) 'Magical misfortune in Locorotondo', *American Ethnologist*, 18 (4): 735–750.

Gillin, F.D., Reiner, D.S. and Wang, C.-S. (1983) 'Human milk kills parasitic intestinal protozoa', *Science*, 221: 1290–1291.

Golden, J.L. (1996) *A Social History of Wet Nursing in America: From Breast to Bottle*. New York: Cambridge University Press.

Gorer, G. and Rickman, J. (1962) *The People of Great Russia*. New York: Norton.

Harriman, A.E. and Lukosius, P.A. (1982) 'On why Wayne Dennis found Hopi infants retarded in age at onset of walking', *Perceptual & Motor Skills*, 55: 79–86.

Harris, W. (1742) *A Treatise of the Acute Diseases of Infants*. London: Thomas Astley.

Herdt, G. and Stoller, R.J. (1990) *Intimate Communications: Erotics and the Study of Culture*. New York: Columbia University Press.

Hollan, D.W. and Wellenkamp, J.C. (1996) *The Thread of Life: Toraja Reflections on the Life Cycle*. Honolulu, HI: University of Hawaii Press.

Hudson, C. (1966) 'Isometric advantages of the cradle board', *American Anthropologist*, 68: 470–474.

Jahoda, G. (1954) 'A note on Ashanti day names in relation to personality', *British Journal of Psychology*, 45: 192–195.

Jastrow, M. (1914) *Babylonian–Assyrian Birth-Omens*. Giessen: Alfred Töpelmann.

Josephs, I.E., Valsiner, J. and Surgan, S.E. (1999) 'The process of meaning construction: dissecting the flow of semiotic activity', in J. Brandtstädter and R. Lerner (eds), *Action and Development: Origins and Functions of Intentional Self-Development*. Thousand Oaks, CA: Sage.

Kano, T. (1992) *The Last Ape: Pygmy Chimpanzee Behavior and Ecology*. Stanford, CA: Stanford University Press.

Kaye, K. (1977) 'Toward the origin of dialogue', in H.R. Schaffer (ed.), *Studies in Mother–Infant Interaction*. London: Academic Press. pp. 89–117.

Kearney, M. (1976) 'A world-view explanation of the evil eye', in C. Maloney, (ed.), *The Evil Eye*. New York: Columbia University Press. pp. 175–192.

Kilbride, P.L., and Kilbride., J. E. (1974) 'Sociocultural factors and the early manifestation of sociability behavior among Baganda infants', *Ethos, 2*, 296–314.

Kindermann, T. and Valsiner, J. (1989) 'Strategies for empirical research in context-inclusive developmental psychology', in J. Valsiner (ed.), *Cultural Context and Child Development*. Toronto-Göttingen-Berne: C. J. Hogrefe and H. Huber. pp. 13–50.

Klausner, W. and Klausner, K. (n.d.) *Conflict or Communication*. Bangkok: Business Information & Research Co.

Kluckhohn, C. (1974) *The Navaho*. Cambridge, MA: Harvard University Press.

Konner, M. (1978) 'Maternal care, infant behaviour and development among the !Kung', in R.E. Lee and I. DeVore (eds), *Kalahari Hunters-Gatherers*. Cambridge, MA: Harvard University Press.

Lambert, H. (1997) 'Illness, inauspiciousness and modes of healing in Rajasthan', *Contributions to Indian Sociology*, 31 (2): 253–271.

Largo, R.H., Molinari, L., Weber, M,, Comenale Pinto, L., and Duc, G. (1985) 'Early development of

locomotion: significance of prematurity, cerebral palsy and sex', *Developmental Medicine & Child Neurology, 27*, 183–191.

Lindemann, M. (1981) 'Love for hire: the regulation of the wet-nursing business in eighteenth-century Hamburg', *Journal of Family History*, 6: 379–395.

Lutz, C.A. (1988) *Unnatural Emotions*. Chicago: University of Chicago Press.

Macfarlane, A. (1977) *The Psychology of Childbirth*. Cambridge, MA: Harvard University Press.

Maloney, C. (ed.) (1976) *The Evil Eye*. New York: Columbia University Press.

Martini, M., and Kirkpatrick, J. (1981) 'Early interactions in the Marquesas Islands', In T. M. Field, A. M. Sostek, P. Vietze and P. H. Leiderman (eds.), *Culture and Early Interaction* (pp. 189–213). Hillsdale, N.J.: Erlbaum.

Medoff, D. and Schaefer, C.E. (1993) 'Children sharing the parental bed: a review of the advantages and disadvantages of cosleeping', *Psychology, 30* (1): 1–9.

Mundri, L.S. (1956) 'A Munda birth', *Man in India*, 36: 56–72.

Nichols, B.L. and Nichols, V.N. (1981) 'Human milk: nutritional resource', In R.C. Tsang and B.L. Nichols (eds), *Nutrition and Child Health*. New York: A.R. Liss. pp. 109–146.

Osborn, A.J. (1996) 'Cattle, co-wives, children and calabashes: material context for symbol use among the Il Chamus of West-Central Kenya', *Journal of Anthropological Archaeology*, 15: 107–136.

Rasmussen, S. (1995) *Spirit Possession and Personhood Among the Kel Ewey Tuaregs*. Cambridge: Cambridge University Press.

Rasmussen, S. (1996) 'Matters of taste: food, eating, and reflections on "the politic" in Tuareg society', *Journal of Anthropological Research*, 52: 61–83.

Scheper-Hughes, N. (1992) *Death without Weeping: the Violence of Everyday Life in Brazil*. Berkeley, CA: University of California Press.

Sich, D. (1988) 'Childbearing in Korea', *Social Science and Medicine*, 27 (5): 497–504.

Stephen, M. (1982) '"Dreaming is another power!" The social significance of dreams among the Mekeo of Papua New Guinea', *Oceania*, 53 (2): 106–122.

Super, C.M. and Harkness, S. (1982) 'The infant's niche in rural Kenya and metropolitan America', In L.L. Adler (ed.) *Cross-cultural Research at Issue* (pp. 47–55). New York: Academic Press.

Sussmann, G.D. (1977) 'Parisian infants and Norman wet nurses in the early nineteenth century', *Journal of Interdisciplinary History*, 7 (4): 637–653.

Trettien, A. (1900) 'Creeping and walking', *American Journal of Psychology*, 12: 1–57.

Valsiner, J. and Mackie, C. (1985) 'Toddlers at home: canalization of children's climbing activity by culturally organized environment', in T. Gärling and J. Valsiner (eds), *Children within Environments: Towards a Psychology of Accident Prevention*. New York: Plenum. pp. 165–192.

Van der Toorn, K. (1996) *Family Religion in Babylonia, Syria and Israel*. Leiden: E.J. Brill.

Vogel, S.M. (1997) *Baoule: African Art Western Eyes*. New Haven, CT: Yale University Press.

Webster, H. (1942) *Taboo: a Sociological Study*. Stanford, CA: Stanford University Press.

Whiteford, L.M. (1997) 'The ethnoecology of dengue fever', *Medical Anthropology Quarterly*, 11 (2): 202–223.

Wikan, U. (1982) *Behind the Veil in Arabia: Women in Oman*. Chicago: University of Chicago Press.

Wikan, U. (1990) *Managing Turbulent Hearts: a Balinese Formula for Living*. Chicago: University of Chicago Press.

Zahorsky, J. (1934) 'The discard of the cradle', *Journal of Pediatrics*, 4: 660–667.

CHAPTER 10

Ainsworth, M.D.S. (1967) *Infancy in Uganda*. Baltimore, MD: Johns Hopkins University Press.

Ainsworth, M.D.S. and Wittig, B.A. (1969) 'Attachment and exploratory behavior of one-year-olds in strange situation', in B.M. Foss (ed.), *Determinants of Infant Behaviour*, vol. 4. London: Methuen.

Ainsworth, M.D.S., Blehar, M., Waters, E. and Wall, S. (1978) *Patterns of Attachment: a Psychological Study of the Strange Situation*. Hillsdale, NJ: Erlbaum.

Aphek, E. and Tobin, Y. (1990) *The Semiotics of Fortune-Telling*. Amsterdam: John Benjamins.

Baldwin, J.M. (ed.) (1902) *Dictionary of Philosophy and Psychology*. New York: Macmillan.

Bartlett, F.H. (1932) *The Care and Feeding of Infants*. New York: Farrar & Rinehardt.

Basso, K. (1970) '"To give up on words": silence in Western Apache culture', *Southwestern Journal of Anthropology*, 26: 213–230.

Bechterew, V. (1932) *General Principles of Human Reflexology*. New York: International Publishers,

Bowlby, J. (1944) 'Forty-four juvenile thieves: their characters and home-life', *International Journal of Psychoanalysis*, 25: 19–53 and 107–128.

Bowlby, J. (1946) 'Psychology and democracy', *The Political Quarterly*, 17: 61–76.

Bowlby, J. (1952) *Maternal Care and Mental Health*. Geneva: World Health Organization.

Bowlby, J. (1969) *Attachment and Loss*, vol. 1: *Attachment*. New York: Basic Books.

Breslaw, E.G. (1997) 'Tituba's confession: the multicultural dimensions of the 1692 Salem witch-hunt', *Ethnohistory*, 44 (3): 535–556.

Briggs, J.L. (1979) 'The creation of value in Canadian Inuit society', *International Social Science Journal*, 31: 393–403.

Budwig, N. (ed.) (1998) 'Special Issue on guided participation', *Clark Working Papers on Developmental Psychology*, 1, 1, 1–61.

Denisova, M.D. and Figurin, N.L. (1929) 'On the question of early alimentary reflexes in infants', *Voprosy geneticheskoiu refleksologii i pedologii mladenchestva*, 1: 81–86.

DeVries, M.W. and DeVries, M.R. (1977) 'Cultural relativity of toilet training readiness: a perspective from East Africa', *Pediatrics*, 60: 170–177.

Ellis, A.C. and Hall, G.S. (1896) 'A study of dolls', *Pedagogical Seminary*, 4: 129–175.

Eyer, D.F. (1992) *Mother-Infant Bonding: a Scientific Fiction*. New Haven, CT: Yale University Press.

Fortes, M. (1970) 'Social and psychological aspects of education in Taleland', in J. Middleton (ed.), *From Adult to Child: Studies in the Anthropology of Education*. New York: Natural History Press. pp. 14–74.

Freud, A. and Burlingham, D.T. (1943) *War and Children*. New York: Medical War Books.

Gregor, T. (1977) *Mehinaku: the Drama of Daily Life in a Brazilian Indian village*. Chicago, IL: University of Chicago Press.

Josephs, I.E. (1998) 'Constructing one's self in the city of the silent: dialogue, symbols, and the role of 'as-if' in development', *Human Development*, 41 (3): 180–195.

Leis, N. (1982) 'The not-so-supernatural power of Ijaw children', in S. Ottenberg (ed.), *African Religious Groups and Beliefs*. Meerut, India: Folklore Institute. pp. 151–169.

LeVine, R.A. and Miller, P.M. (1990) 'Commentary', *Human Development*, 33: 73–80.

Luria, A.R. (1969) 'Speech development and the formation of mental processes', in M. Cole and I. Maltzman (eds), *A Handbook of Contemporary Soviet Psychology*. New York: Basic Books. pp. 121–162.

MacKain, S.J. (1987) '"I know he's a boy because my tummy tells me": social and cognitive contributions to children's understanding of gender', Chapel Hill, NC: University of North Carolina (unpublished PhD dissertation).

Miyake, K., Chen, S.-J., and Campos, J.J. (1985) 'Infant temperament , mother's mode of interaction, and attachment in Japan', *Monographs of the Society for Research in Child Development*, 50: 276–297.

Morgan, P. (1975) *Child Care: Sense and Fable*. London: Temple Smith.

Niehof, A. (1998) 'The changing lives of Indonesian women: contained emancipation under pressure', *Bijdragen tot de Taal-, Land- en Volkenkunde*, 154 (II): 236–258.

Ochs, E. (1982) 'Talking to children in Western Samoa', *Language in Society*, 11: 77–104.

Oliveira, Z.M.R. (1998) 'Peer interactions and the appropriation of gender representations by young children', in M. Lyra and J. Valsiner (eds), *Child Development within Culturally Structured Environments*, vol. 4: *Construction of Psychological Processes in Interpersonal Communication*. Stamford, CT: Ablex Publishing Corporation. pp. 103–115.

Oliveira, Z.M.R. and Rossetti-Ferreira, M.C. (1996) 'Understanding the co-constructive nature of human development: role coordination in early peer interaction', in J. Valsiner and H.-G. Voss (eds), *The Structure of Learning Processes*. Norwood, NJ: Ablex Publishing Corporation. pp. 177–204.

Oliveira, Z.M.R. and Valsiner, J. (1997) 'Play and imagination: the psychological construction of novelty', in A. Fogel, M. Lyra and J. Valsiner (eds), *Dynamics and Indeterminism in Developmental and Social Processes*. Hillsdale, NJ: Erlbaum.

Pollner, M. and McDonald-Wikler, L. (1985) 'The social construction of unreality: a case study of a family's attribution of competence to a severely retarded child', *Family Process*, 24: 241–254.

Robertson, J. (1970) *Young Children in Hospital*, 2nd edn. London: Tavistock Publications.

Rogoff, B. (1990) *Apprenticeship in Thinking*. New York: Oxford University Press.

Sagi, A. (1990) 'Attachment theory and research from a cross-cultural perspective', *Human Development*, 33: 10–22.

Sherif, M. (1936) *The Psychology of Social Norms*. New York: Harper & Brothers.

Stendler, C.B. (1950) 'Sixty years of child training practices', *Journal of Pediatrics*, 36: 122–134.

Takahashi, K. (1985) 'Behavior changes in the Strange Situation procedure among young Japanese children between the 12th and 23rd month'. Paper presented at the meeting of the Society for Research on Child Development, Toronto.

Takahashi, K. (1990) 'Are the key assumptions of the "Strange Situation" procedure universal? A view from Japanese research', *Human Development*, 33: 23–30.

Teitelbaum, J.M. (1981) 'Primitive peoples and weaning: the role of weaning behaviour in preindustrial societies', in D.N. Walcher and N. Kretschmer (eds), *Food, Nutrition, and Evolution*. New York: Mason. pp. 83–95.

Vaihinger, H. (1911/1920) *Die Philosophie des als ob: System der theoretischen, praktischen und religiösen Fiktionen der Menschheit*, 4th edn. Leipzig: Felix Meiner.

Valsiner, J. (1986) 'Between groups and individuals: psychologists' and laypersons' interpretations of correlational findings', in J. Valsiner (ed.), *The Individual Subject and Scientific Psychology*. New York: Plenum. pp. 113–152.

Van der Veer, R. (1999) 'Soziale Konstruktion und Kultur: Die historische Wurzeln einer kultur-bezogenen Entwicklungspsychologie am Beispiel der Bindungstheorie', in I. E. Josephs and S. Hoppe-Graff (eds), *Entwicklung als soziale Konstruktion*. Berlin: Pabst.

Van Dijken, S., Van der Veer, R., Van Ijzendoorn, M.H. and Kuipers, H.-J. (1998) 'Bowlby before Bowlby: the sources of an intellectual departure in psychoanalysis and psychology', *Journal of the History of the Behavioral Sciences*, 34 (3): 247–269.

Weisner, T. and Gallimore, R. (1977) 'My brother's keeper: child and sibling caretaking', *Current Anthropology*, 18: 169–180.

CHAPTER 11

Basso, K. (1970) '"To give up on words": silence in Western Apache culture', *Southwestern Journal of Anthropology*, 26: 213–230.

Berland, J.C. (1982) *No Five Fingers Are Alike*. Cambridge, MA: Harvard University Press.

Bodor, P. (1998) 'Opening up Pandora's box: remarks on Barbara Rogoff's theory of human development', *Clark Working Papers on Developmental Psychology*, 1 (1): 39–45.

Briggs, J.L. (1970) *Never in Anger: Portrait of an Eskimo Family*. Cambridge, MA: Harvard University Press.

Briggs, J.L. (1979) 'The creation of value in Canadian Inuit society', *International Social Science Journal*, 31 (3): 393–403.

Bühler, K. (1934/1990) *Theory of language*. Amsterdam: John Benjamins.

Chamberlain, A.F. (1908) 'Notes on some aspects of the folk-psychology of night', *American Journal of Psychology*, 19: 18–42.

Dewey, J. (1896) 'The reflex arc concept in psychology', *Psychological Review*, 3, 3, 357–370.

Fogel, A. and Branco, A.U. (1997) 'Metacommunication as a source of indeterminism in relationship development', in A. Fogel, M. Lyra and J. Valsiner (eds), *Dynamics and Indeterminism in Developmental and Social Processes*. Mahwah, NJ: Erlbaum. pp. 65–92.

Herdt, G. (1987) *Sambia: Ritual and Gender in New Guinea*. New York: Holt, Rinehardt & Winston.

Katz, D. (1928) 'The development of conscience in the child as revealed by his talks with adults', in M.L. Reymert (ed.), *Feelings and Emotions: the Wittenberg Symposium*. Worcester, MA: Clark University Press. pp. 332–343.

Katz, D. and Katz, R. (1927) *Gespräche mit Kindern: Untersuchungen zur Sozialpsychologie und Pädagogik*. Berlin: Springer.

Langer, J. (1980) *The Origins of Logic: Six to Twelve Months*. New York : Academic Press.

Langer, J. (1986) *The Origins of Logic: 12–24 Months*. Orlando, FL: Academic Press.

Lazarsfeld, P.F. and Merton, R.K. (1948) 'Mass communication, popular taste and organized social action', in L. Bryson (ed.), *The Communication of Ideas*. New York: Harper & Brothers. pp. 95–118.

Levy-Bruhl, L. (1985) *How Natives Think*. Princeton: Princeton University Press.

Lindqvist, G. (1995) 'The aesthetics of play: a didactic study of play and culture in preschools', *Acta Universitatis Upsaliensis*, No. 62.

Luria, A. R. (1969) 'Speech development and the formation of mental processes', in M. Cole and I. Maltzman (eds), *A Handbook of Contemporary Soviet Psychology*. New York: Basic Books. pp. 121–162.

Lyra, M. and Winegar, LT. (1997) 'Processual dynamics of interaction through time: adult–child interactions and process of development', in A. Fogel, M. Lyra and J. Valsiner (ed.), *Dynamics and Indeterminism in*

Developmental and Social Processes. Mahwah, NJ: Erlbaum. pp. 93–110.

Moore, W.F. and Tumin, M.M. (1949) 'Some social functions of ignorance', *American Sociological Review*, 14, 787–795.

Nagera, H. (1966) 'Sleep and its disturbances approached developmentally', *The Psychoanalytic Study of the Child*, 21: 393–447.

Nelson, K. (1989) *Narratives from the Crib*. Cambridge, MA: Harvard University Press.

Perner, J. (1991) *Understanding the Representational Mind*. Cambridge, MA: MIT Press.

Piaget, J. (1959) *The Language and Thought of the Child*, 3rd edn. London: Routledge & Kegan Paul.

Reichel-Dolmatoff, G. and Reichel-Dolmatoff, A. (1961) *The People of Aritama*. London: Routledge & Kegan Paul.

Rogoff, B. (1990) *Apprenticeship in Thinking: Cognitive Development in Social Context*. NY: Oxford University Press.

Rogoff, B. (1997) 'Evaluating development in the process of participation: theory, methods, and practice building on each other', in E. Amsel and K.A. Renninger (eds), *Change and Development: Issues of Theory, Method, and Application*. Mahwah, NJ: Erlbaum. pp. 265–285.

Thomson, D. (1935) 'The joking relationship and organized obscenity in North Queensland', *American Anthropologist*, 37: 460–490.

CHAPTER 12

Adeokun, L.A. (1983) 'Marital sexuality and birth-spacing among the Yoruba', in C. Oppong (ed.), *Female and Male in West Africa*. London: Allen & Unwin. pp. 128–137.

Allison, A. (1991) 'Japanese mothers and *obentōs*: the lunch-box as ideological state apparatus', *Anthropological Quarterly*, 64 (4): 195–208.

Delfattore, J. (1992) *What Johnny Shouldn't Read: Textbook Censorship in America*. New Haven, CT: Yale University Press.

Ellis, C. (1996) *To Change Them Forever: Indian Education in the Rainy Mountain Boarding School, 1893–1920*. Norman, OK: University of Oklahoma Press.

Fortes, M. (1970) 'Social and psychological aspects of education in Taleland', in J. Middleton (ed.), *From Adult to Child: Studies in the Anthropology of Education*. New York: Natural History Press. pp. 14–74.

Fulton, R.M. (1972) 'The political structures and functions of Poro in Kpelle society', *American Anthropologist*, 74: 1218–1233.

Greenfield, P.M. and Lave, J. (1982) 'Cognitive aspects of informal education', in D. Wagner and H. Stevenson (eds), *Cultural Perspectives on Child Development*. San Francisco: W.H. Freeman.

Hirschon, R. (1981) 'Essential objects and the sacred: interior and exterior space in an urban Greek locality',

in S. Ardener (ed.), *Women and Space: Ground Rules and Social Maps*. London: Croom Helm. pp. 72–88.

Inagaki, T. (1986) 'School education: its history and contemporary status', in H. Stevenson, H. Azuma and K. Hakuta (ed), *Child Development and Education in Japan*. New York: W.H. Freeman. pp. 75–92.

Lancy, D.F. (1984) 'Play in anthropological perspective', in P. K. Smith (ed.), *Play in Animals and Humans*. Oxford: Blackwell. pp. 295–303.

Lebra, T.S. (1984) *Japanese Women: Constraint and Fulfillment*. Honolulu, HI: University of Hawaii Press.

Levinson, B. (1998) 'Student culture and the contradictions of equality at a Mexican secondary school', *Anthropology & Education Quarterly*, 29 (3): 267–296.

Luria, AR. (1976) *Cognitive Development*. Cambridge, MA: Harvard University Press.

Miller, G. D. (1977) 'Classroom 19: a study of behavior in a classroom of a Moroccan primary school', in L. C. Brown and N. Itzkowitz (eds.), *Psychological Dimensions in Near-Eastern Studies*. Princeton, N.J: Darwin Press.

Nieuwenhuys, O. (1994) *Children's Lifeworlds: Gender, Welfare and Labour in the Developing World*. London: Routledge

Oettingen, G. (1997) 'Culture and future thought', *Culture & Psychology*, 3 (3): 353–381.

Ohnuki-Tierney, E. (1993) *Rice as Self: Japanese Identities through Time*. Princeton, NJ: Princeton University Press.

Ozment, S. (1983) *When Fathers Ruled: Family Life in Reformation Europe*. Cambridge, MA: Harvard University Press.

Peters, K. and Richards, P. (1998) '"Why we fight": voices of youth combatants in Sierra Leone', *Africa*, 68 (2): 183–210.

Sande, H. (1992) 'Palestinian martyr widowhood – emotional needs in conflict with role expectations', *Social Science & Medicine*, 34 (6): 709–717.

Sindell, P.S. (1974) 'Some discontinuities in the enculturation of Mistassini Cree children', in G.D. Spindler (ed.), *Education and Cultural Process: Toward an Anthropology of Education*. New York: Holt, Rinehardt & Winston. pp. 333–341.

Smollett, E. (1975) 'Differential enculturation and social class in Canadian schools', in T. R. Williams (ed.), *Socialization and Communication in Primary Groups*. The Hague: Mouton. pp. 221–231.

Sommerville, C.J. (1983) 'The distinction between indoctrination and education in England, 1549–1719', *Journal of the History of Ideas*, 44: 387–406.

Stevenson, H. W., Lee, S-Y. and Stigler, J.W. (1986) 'Mathematics achievement of Chinese, Japanese, and American children', *Science*, 231: 693–699.

Thapan, M. (1986) 'Aspects of ritual in a school in South India', *Contributions to Indian Sociology*, 20: 199–219.

Wagner, D. (1983) 'Rediscovering "rote": some cognitive and pedagogical preliminaries', in S.H. Irvine and J.W. Berry (eds), *Human Assessment and Cultural Factors*. New York: Plenum. pp. 179–190.

Watkins, M.H. (1943) 'The West African "bush" school', *American Journal of Sociology*, 48: 666–675.

Watson-Gegeo, K.A. and Gegeo, D.W. (1992) 'Schooling, knowledge, and power: social transformation in the Solomon Islands', *Anthropology and Education Quarterly*, 23 (1): 10–29.

Weil, S. (1986) 'The language of ritual of socialization: birthday parties in a kindergarten context', *Man*, new series, 21: 129–141.

Werner, H. (1948) *Comparative Psychology of Mental Development*. New York: International University Press.

Wolcott, H. (1967) *A Kwakiutl Village and School*. New York: Holt, Rinehardt & Winston.

CHAPTER 13

Bell, R.M. (1985) *Holy Anorexia*. Chicago: University of Chicago Press.

Bowlby, J. (1944) 'Forty-four juvenile thieves: their characters and home-life', *International Journal of Psychoanalysis*, 25: 19–53 and 107–128.

Brown, J.K. (1963) 'A cross-cultural study of female initiation rites', *American Anthropologist*, 65: 837–853.

Brumberg, J.J. (1988) *Fasting Girls: the Emergence of Anorexia Nervosa as a Modern Disease*. Cambridge, MA: Harvard University Press.

Buckley, T. (1982) 'Menstruation and the power of Yurok women: methods in cultural reconstruction', *American Ethnologist*, 9 (1): 47–60.

Cairns, R.B. and Cairns, B. (1994) *Lifelines and Risks: Pathways of Youth in Our Time*. Cambridge: Cambridge University Press.

Chan, A. (1985) *Children of Mao*. Seattle, WA: University of Washington Press.

Csikszentmihalyi, M. (1985) 'Emergent motivation and the evolution of the self', in D. Keiber and M. Maehr (eds), *Motivation and Achievement*, vol. 4. Greenwich, CT: JAI Press. pp. 93–119.

Eberhard, W. (1982) *Life and Thought of Ordinary Chinese*. Taipei: The Orient Cultural Service.

Elwin, V. (1947) *The Muria and their Ghotul*. Calcutta: Oxford University Press.

George, I. (1990) *Child Labour and Child Work*. New Delhi: Ashish Publishing House

Goodchilds, J. D., and Zellman, G. L. (1984) Sexual signalling system and sexual aggression in adolescent relationships, in N. M. Malamuth and E. Donnerstein (eds.), *Pornography and Sexual Aggression*. Orlando, Fl.: Academic Press. pp. 233–243

Hall, G.S. (1904) *Adolescence*. New York: Appleton–Century–Crofts.

Hall, L.A. (1992) 'Forbidden by God, despised by man: masturbation, medical warnings, moral panic and manhood in Great Britain, 1850–1950', *Journal of the History of Sexuality*, 2 (3): 365–387.

Hare, E.H. (1962) 'Masturbatory insanity: the history of an idea', *Journal of Mental Science*, 108 (452): 1–25.

Herdt, G. (1980) 'Semen depletion and the sense of maleness', *Ethnopsychiatry*, 3: 79–116.

Herdt, G. (1982) 'Sambia nosebleeding rites and male proximity to women', *Ethos*, 10 (3): 189–231.

Herdt, G. (1987a) *Sambia: Ritual and Gender in New Guinea*. New York: Holt, Rinehardt & Winston.

Herdt, G. (1987b) *Guardians of the Flutes*, 2nd edn. New York: Columbia University Press.

Herdt, G. (1990) 'Secret societies and secret collectives', *Oceania*, 60: 360–381.

Holland, D., Skinner, D., Lachiotte, W. and Cain, C. (1998) *Identity and Agency in Cultural Worlds*. Cambridge, MA: Harvard University Press.

Jahoda, G. (1998) '"Ordinary Germans" before Hitler', *Journal of Interdisciplinary History*, 29 (1): 69–88.

Kakar, S. and Chowdhry, K. (1970) *Conflict and Choice: Indian Youth in a Changing Society*. Bombay: Somaiya Publications

Kawai, M. (1963) 'On the newly-acquired behaviors of the natural troop of Japanese monkeys on Koshima Island', *Primates*, 4 (1): 113–115.

Kenyatta, J. (1965) *Facing Mt Kenya*. New York: Vintage Books.

Kett, J. (1977) *Rites of Passage: Adolescence in America 1790 to Present*. New York: Basic Books.

Kilbride, P.L. and Kilbride, J.C. (1990) *Changing Family Life in East Africa*. University Park, PA: Penn State University Press.

Konopka, G. (1976) *Young Girls: a Portrait of Adolescence*. Englewood Cliffs, NJ: Prentice-Hall.

Krantz, C.A. (1994) *Affecting Performance: Meaning, Movement, and Experience in Okiek Women's Initiation*. Washington, DC: Smithsonian Institution Press.

Krasnovsky, T. and Lane, R.C. (1998) 'Shoplifting: review of the literature', *Aggression and Violent Behavior*, 3 (3): 219–235.

Lawrence, J.A. and Hore, P. (1993) 'Greedy, needy, or troubled? High school and university students' natural and induced views of shopstealers', *Australian and New Zealand Journal of Criminology*, 26: 59–71.

Lawrence, J.A., Hart, P. and Wearing, A. (1994) 'Archival analysis of cautions issued to shopstealing in Victoria, 1988 to 1991'. Technical Report Presented to Victoria Police Research Coordination Committee, March.

Lightfoot, C. (1997) *The Culture of Adolescent Risk-Taking*. New York : Guilford Press.

Marcus, I.G. (1996) *Rituals of Childhood: Jewish Acculturation in Medieval Europe*. New Haven, CT: Yale University Press.

Mead, G.H. (1930) 'The philosophies of Royce, James, and Dewey in their American setting', *International Journal of Ethics*, 40: 211–231.

Michaud, E. (1997) 'Soldiers of an idea: young people under the Third Reich', in G. Levi and J.-C. Schmitt (eds), *A History of Young People in the West*, vol. 2: *Stormy Evolution to Modern Times*. Cambridge, MA: Harvard University Press. pp. 257–280.

Modell, J. (1983) 'Dating becomes the way of American youth', in L.P. Moch and G.D. Stark (eds), *Essays on the Family and Historical Change*. College Station, TX: Texas A&M University Press. pp. 234–252.

Morton, H. (1996) *Becoming Tongan: an Ethnography of Childhood*. Honolulu, HI: University of Hawaii Press.

Murthi, M.S.R. (1993) *Sex Awareness among Rural Girls*. Delhi: B.R. Publishing Corporation.

Naess, S. (1959) 'Mother-child separation and delinquency', *British Journal of Delinquency*, 10: 22–35.

Nishida, T. (1986) 'Local tradition and cultural transmission', in B.B. Smuts, D.L. Cheney, R.M. Seyfarth, R.W. Wrangham and T.T. Struhsaker (eds), *Primate Societies*. Chicago: University of Chicago Press. pp. 462–474.

Peiss, K. (1986) *Cheap Amusements: Working Women and Leisure in Turn-of-the-Century New York*. Philadelphia, PA: Temple University Press.

Peiss, K. (1998) *Hope in a Jar: the Making of America's Beauty Culture*. New York: Holt.

Peters, K. and Richards, P. (1998) '"Why we fight": voices of youth combatants in Sierra Leone', *Africa*, 68 (2): 183–210.

Rosenbaum, M. (1979) 'The changing body image of the adolescent girl', in M. Sugar (ed.), *Female Adolescent Development*. New York: Brunner/ Mazel. pp. 234–252

Rothchild, E. (1979) 'Female power: lines to development of autonomy in adolescent girls', in M. Sugar (ed.), *Female Adolescent Development*. New York: Brunner/Mazel. pp. 274–295

Schlegel, A. and Barry III, H. (1991) *Adolescence: an Anthropological Inquiry*. New York: Free Press.

Schwartz, G. and Merten, D. (1967) 'The language of adolescence: an anthropological approach to the youth culture', *American Journal of Sociology*, 72: 453–468.

Spurlock, J.C. and Magistro, C.A. (1998) *New and Improved: the Transformation of American Women's Emotional Culture*. New York: New York University Press.

Valsiner, J., Branco, A. U., Melo Dantas, C. (1997) 'Co-construction of human development: heterogeneity within parental belief orientations', in J.. E. Grusec and L. Kuczynski (eds), *Handbook of Parenting and the Transmission of Values*. New York: Wiley. pp. 283–304

Vandereycken, W. and van Deth, R. (1994) *From Fasting Girls to Anorexic Girls: the History of Self-starvation*. New York: New York University Press.

Van Hoorn, J. and Komlosi, A. (1997) 'Adolescents' understanding of their social ecology: theoretical considerations', *Polish Quarterly of Developmental Psychology*, 3 (4): 237–244.

Watkins, M.M. (1986) *Invisible Guests: the Development of Imaginal Dialogues*. Hillsdale, NJ: Analytic Press.

Worthman, C.M. and Whiting, J.W.M. (1987) 'Social change in adolescent sexual behavior, mate selection, and premarital pregnancy rates in a Kikuyu community', *Ethos*, 15: 145–165.

INDEX